From *Tapas* to Modern Yoga

From *Tapas* to Modern Yoga

Sādhus' Understanding of Embodied Practices

Daniela Bevilacqua

equinox

SHEFFIELD UK BRISTOL CT

Published by Equinox Publishing Ltd

UK: Office 415, The Workstation, 15 Paternoster Row, Sheffield, South Yorkshire S1 2BX
USA: ISD, 70 Enterprise Drive, Bristol, CT 06010

www.equinoxpub.com

First published 2024

British Library Cataloguing-in-Publication Data
A catalogue record for this book is available from the British Library.

ISBN: 978 1 80050 440 0 (hardback)
978 1 80050 441 7 (hardback)
978 1 80050 442 4 (ePDF)
978 1 80050 503 2 (ePub)

Library of Congress Cataloging-in-Publishing Data
Names: Bevilacqua, Daniela, author.
Title: From Tapas to Modern Yoga : Sādhus' understanding of embodied practices / Daniela Bevilacqua.
Description: Bristol, CT : Equinox Publishing Ltd, 2024. | Includes bibliographical references and index. | Summary: "Extensively based on fieldwork material, From Tapas to Modern Yoga primarily analyses embodied practices of ascetics belonging to four religious orders historically associated with the practice of yoga and hatha yoga"-- Provided by publisher.
Identifiers: LCCN 2023046775 (print) | LCCN 2023046776 (ebook) | ISBN 9781800504400 (hardback) | ISBN 9781800504417 (paperback) | ISBN 9781800504424 (epdf) | ISBN 9781800505032 (epub)
Subjects: LCSH: Yoga--History. | Sadhus--India--History. | Tapas (Asceticism)--Hinduism.
Classification: LCC B132.Y6 B445 2024 (print) | LCC B132.Y6 (ebook) | DDC 294.5/436--dc23/eng/20231218
LC record available at https://lccn.loc.gov/2023046775
LC ebook record available at https://lccn.loc.gov/2023046776

Typeset by Witchwood Production House Ltd, Sheffield

To those who are no longer here

Contents

List of illustrations

Acknowledgements

My list of acknowledgements could be very long, as there are many people who made this work possible. First of all, I would like to thank James Mallison who gave me the opportunity to be part of his ERC-funded Haṭha Yoga Project,[1] even though he barely knew me at the beginning of the project. So, thank you for your trust Jim *bhāī*! A tremendous thank-you also goes to my colleagues Mark Singleton, Jason Birch and Jacqueline Hargreaves for their patience and answers to my many questions about yoga. When I started this research, my knowledge of yoga was rather average and the Haṭha Yoga Project team has always been very helpful and supportive. It has been a pleasure to walk this incredible yogic journey together.

My thanks also go to Véronique Bouillier, without whom none of my ethnographic research would have been possible: she will always be on my gratitude list.

Then, of course, a huge thanks goes to all the *sādhus* I have met over the years, people who have been so generous to give me some of their time. I feel grateful and lucky to have had the opportunity to learn from them, and in this book I have done my best to record their words. I have named most of them in Appendix 1.

I also thank all the scholars who, over the years, have answered my questions or shared interesting and useful conversations: Adrian Muñoz, Borayin Maitreya Larios, Seth Powell, Philip Deslippe, Christèle Barois, Dagmar Wujastyk, Dominic Wujastyk, Suzanne Newcombe, Patricia Sauthoff, Philipp Maas, Lucy May Costantini, Ruth Westoby, Karen

1 The research for this book was funded by the European Research Council (ERC) under the European Union's Horizon 2020 research and innovation programme (Grant Agreement No. 647963).

O'Brien-Kop, Elizabeth Demichelis, Joseph Alter, Ian Baker, Alex Watson, Patrick McCartney, Jerome Armstrong, Stuart Ray Sarbacker, Dominic Steavu, Dolly Yang, Federico Squarcini, Gianni Pellegrini, Pinuccia Caracchi, Ysé Tardan Masquelier, Carl Ernst, Gordon Djurdjevic, William Pinch, to name but a few who came to mind. I apologise to anyone I may have forgotten. Special thanks go to Lubomir Ondračka, an incredible scholar and an invaluable friend, who not only supported me over the years but also read this book carefully and gave me very important insights. Thank you Lubomir for the time we spent together analysing it: it was really priceless.

A big thanks also goes to the friends and people I met in the field, who shared their experiences and part of their journeys with me. I would also like to thank all the yoga practitioners and teachers I have met over the last years who appreciated my work and gave me a reason to finalise this book. I would also like to thank Equinox Publishing and in particular Sarah Lee and Val Hall for their support, human presence and for listening to my requests; to Mark Lee for the cover; and to Dean Bargh for his incredible editorial work on this book.

Last but not least, thank you to my beloved Alessio who has seen this research grow and experienced all its ups and downs, and to my family, papà Francesco, mamma Sabina, my sisters Mara and Alessia, thank you for always being there. You have been and will always be my main strength.

Note on transliteration

For the transliteration of titles of Sanskrit literary works and Sanskrit technical terms particularly related to yoga (e.g. *saṃnyāsa*, *āsana*, *kumbhaka*, *prāṇa*) I have chosen the standard IAST conventions for diacritics. I have maintained the Sanskrit transliteration to avoid confusion, with the exception of words refering to practices that will be mostly described for their contemporary use (e.g. *jap*, *vyāyām*) or which appear primarily in relation to the contemporary ascetic world (e.g. Nāth, *samāj*, *mahant*)—these will have a Hindi transliteration. In general, the use of Hindi is marked with an 'H.' in brackets. I often append to the names of *sādhus* the honorific 'jī' which is used in Hindi as a way of showing respect.

Terms that are common in English today, such as yoga, yogi, etc., will be written without diacritics, but the word 'yogi' will have diacritics and will be capitalised when referring to a specific individual of the Nāth *sampradāya* (e.g. Yogī Gorakhnāth), and will have diacritics when used to specify a yogic identity, e.g. *yogīrāj*. The same word, when used in different contexts, might be transliterated differently to emphasise a different role. For example, I will transliterate *āśrama* (S.) to describe the four brahmanical stages of life, while using *āśram* (H.) to denote the place where *sādhus* or pilgrims may live; I will write *darśan* to describe the vision of a deity to distinguish it from *darśana* as a philosophcal system; *rāja* yoga when describing a specific form of yoga found in textual sources, but *yogīrāj* to describe a specific ascetic figure, thus maintaining the Hindi pronunciation. The various types of yoga will simply be emphasised using italics: hence, *rāja* yoga, *haṭha* yoga, etc.

Place names will be generally transliterated without diacritical marks, unless they are religiously significant, or where diacritical marks are essential for disambiguation. Author names and well-known persons, including yoga-related gurus, from the modern period are generally written without diacritical marks, following their organisation's convention or the author's name used in their publications.

I have done my best to be consistent, even if this has sometimes led to mixing Sanskrit and Hindi, especially in the case of quoting *sādhus*' words, while maintaining the general transliteration (in Sanskrit) of yoga-related terms. It is an attempt (possibly with limited success) to avoid completely privileging the textual over the oral. I apologise for any annoyance that inconsistencies may cause the most scrupulous scholars.

Preface

I first encountered yoga in 2006 in Rishikesh. At that time, I was studying Hindi and wanted to practise some yoga as well. Once back in Italy, I tried to follow this practice, but I failed miserably. I resumed practising yoga in 2010 in Varanasi, while conducting field research for my PhD: I found *āsanas* practice rather boring, but my back and neck benefited greatly. Once back home, my yoga practice was put aside, as was my interest in yoga: that was until February 2015. Shortly before submitting my doctoral thesis, I was asked to participate in a research project (the Haṭha Yoga Project) to conduct ethnographic research among Indian ascetics (my field) to investigate their practice of yoga and *haṭha* yoga in particular. The proposal was intriguing because it allowed me to continue working in my field, and to thoroughly examine a practice that had repeatedly appeared in my life. After a few months of research, I realised that what I had occasionally practised did not correspond to my interlocutors' understanding of yoga.

This book does not aim to discredit modern yoga, nor to state what yoga is in general. Rather, it seeks to describe the embodied practices of a specific group of people—Indian *sādhus* belonging to traditional groups—being mindful of reporting their words rather than developing interpretations. The reader will find in Appendix 1 a list of the majority of *sādhus* with whom I spoke during my research. In order to avoid repetition in the book, the information on where and when I met them is collected there; when possible, a short biography is also provided.

Map of fieldwork locations

PESHAWAR
LAHORE
PAKISTAN
RISHIKESH
NEPAL
PASHUPATINATH
BHUTAN
KAMAKHYA
DELHI
GORAKHPUR
JAIPUR
KARACHI
PUSHKAR
ALLAHABAD
VARANASI
DHINODHAR
MONT ABU
UJJAIN
SANCHI
INDIA
KOLKATA
MODHERA
OMKARESHWAR
JUNAGADH
DABHOI
HYDERABAD
AJANTA
ELLORA
WARANGAL
PANHALE KHAJE
HYDERABAD
BADAMI
SRISAILAM
HAMPI
BALLIGAVI
SRINGERI
MANGALORE
TARAPITH
BIRNAGAR
KOLKATA
GANGASAGAR
JHARGRAM
GARH JUNGLE

Author's drawing

Introduction

In the ascetic context, yoga has to be understood as a *sādhanā* or as a part of a *sādhanā*, a religious discipline. Yoga has developed over the centuries in different religious contexts and with different aims, most of which focus on creating a connection or a reunion with a deity or a universal soul, but also on developing powers to be used for other people's well-being or, again, for spiritual betterment. To advance on the yoga path, the methods can vary and *haṭha* yoga is just one among many. But the understanding of *haṭha* yoga can differ among *sādhus*,[1] so even the techniques to which it refers can vary: not only physical techniques based on bodily movements and breathing, but also austerities and strict observances.

What, then, is yoga, and particularly *haṭha* yoga, among Indian *sādhus*? Who is a yogi and who is a *haṭhayogī*? Why do *sādhus* perform austerities (*tapasyā*)? What is the link between *tapasyā* and yoga, and especially *haṭha* yoga? How do *sādhus* learn physical techniques? Is modern yoga affecting the ascetic understanding and practice of yoga?

This book addresses these (and other) questions using a multidisciplinary approach in which a variety of historical sources are used as scaffold for ethnographic data. What struck me in talking to *sādhus* and reading the secondary literature on the history of *tapasyā* and yoga/*haṭha* yoga practices is the fact that, although some of them have disappeared from textual sources, they have been kept alive by practitioners. Furthermore, I realised

1 The word *sādhu* is derived from the root *sādh*, which means 'to reach one's goal', 'to make straight' (Monier-Monier 1899). The term indicates a good and virtuous person, which is why it is attributed to saints, sages and holy men. Its feminine form is *sādhvī*. Another general word to identify an ascetic is *bābā*, which literally means 'father', while *mātā*, 'mother', is used for a female ascetic.

that various 'labels' (e.g. *tapasyā*, *haṭha* yoga, yoga) have over the centuries accumulated layers of practices and meanings, even interchangeable ones, making it difficult to understand their history, but also that these labels in the ascetic context are of secondary importance to the practices themselves. Therefore, while introducing the history of these practices in its chapters, this book does not attempt to provide a definitive perspective of them, and this is for two main reasons. Firstly, we are still far from having a definitive understanding of them because much information is lacking, especially related to oral transmission; secondly, as Jacques Derrida made clear, it is impossible for an individual to master 'the empirical endeavour of either a subject or a finite richness' because 'there is too much, more than one can say' (Derrida 1978: 289).

Recalling a definition given by Joseph Alter, this book does not approach yoga as 'a seamless, timeless, ancient tradition' but rather as 'a complex amalgam of power principles that derive from different priorities and forms of practice' (Alter 2012: 411). That is why it does not look at yoga practitioners *tout court*, but rather focuses its attention on a specific category, that of Indian *sādhus*. Ascetics, yoga and *haṭha* yoga are presented not as ideals (there won't be a general 'Yoga' or an 'ideal yogi') but as realities reconstructed in part through historical evidence and textual sources and mostly through examples coming directly from ethnographic fields. This approach could be interpreted as a way to engage with ethnographic material following the ontological turn proposed by scholars like Morten Axel Pederson (2012): the 'turn' is mostly about how to get descriptions right, how to use data without depending on a fixed theoretical framework but rather by using original interpretations that come directly from the field.

Indeed, another of the purposes of this book is to present different portraits of Indian ascetics to overcome that still present exotic image that wants them isolated on a mountain, meditating. The Indian ascetic world is extremely complex and organised, and this explains why, to do this research, a selection had to be made. I focused my attention on sections of four traditional ascetic orders connected with *haṭha* yoga: Yogīs and *aughaḍ* from the Nāth *sampradāya*, *saṃnyāsīs* and *nāgās* from the Dasnāmī *sampradāya*, *tyāgīs* and *mahātyāgīs* from the Rāmānandī *sampradāya*, and Udāsīs from the Udāsī *akhāṛā*.[2] Through the ascetics of these orders, I intend to provide interpretations of yoga and *haṭha* yoga that have been somewhat neglected but may be helpful in reconstructing the development of these complex traditions.

2 Therefore, whenever I mention *sādhus* or ascetics, I refer exclusively to those belonging to these specific ascetic orders which will be described in Chapter 2.

Yoga Studies

Indological studies on the philosophy and theories of yoga began around the middle of the 19th century and—despite some scepticism about its practices (see Singleton 2010)—have produced a vast amount of literary works on what has been classified as Classical Yoga (see Maas's bibliography [2013]). In recent decades, our knowledge about the history of yoga has been further developed thanks to textual studies on tantric traditions (see for example the works of Hélène Brunner [1994] and Alexis Sanderson [2009]), and on *haṭha* yoga textual traditions (see for example Bouy 1994; Mallinson 2007a, 2007b; Birch 2011).[3]

Given the dissemination of yoga practices across the world, and the increasing number of people practising one of the several types of yoga, it was inevitable that scholars from various disciplines would have turned their attention towards these practices and their resulting communities. General introductory volumes on the history of yoga were produced in 2001 by Georg Feuerstein and Ken Wilber and in 2003 by David Carpenter and Ian Whicher. These scholarly interests could properly develop after Elizabeth De Michelis (2004) published her study on modern yoga and its various subcategories, which provided the general theoretical substratum needed for the development of Yoga Studies. Yoga has been evaluated both for its transnational aspect, since it is taught and practised at a global level, and for its transcultural aspect, since practices and theories are negotiated and adjusted according to various local contexts. In addition to these two aspects, many scholars have adopted a transdisciplinary approach. In 2005 Knut A. Jacobsen edited *Theory and Practice of Yoga*, to evaluate the flourishing of yoga in a variety of religious and philosophic contexts. In 2008, Gerald Larson and Ram Shankar Bhattacharya produced a comprehensive overview of the field: *Yoga: India's Philosophy of Meditation*, Volume 12 of the *Encyclopedia of Indian Philosophies*. In the same year, Mark Singleton and Jean Byrne edited *Yoga in the Modern World*, which presents yoga's contemporary manifestations through various perspectives. In 2010, Singleton then published his masterpiece—*The Yoga Body: The Origin of Modern Posture Practice*—in which he reconstructs the history of the origin of modern yoga taking into consideration archival evidence as well as the voices of the remaining protagonists of that era. In 2012, David G. White edited *Yoga in Practice*, which investigates the history of yoga through textual sources and provides an analysis of different religious traditions into the colonial and post-colonial periods. In 2014, Singleton and Ellen Goldberg edited *Gurus*

3 A more comprehensive bibliography on the topic will be provided in Chapter 4.

of Modern Yoga, which explores the role modern international gurus have had in building practices and discourses of modern transnational yoga in India and elsewhere. In recent years the amount of literature on the history of yoga (see for example Burchett 2019) and modern transnational yoga (see Newcombe 2019) has notably increased.

Nevertheless, when I started to work on yoga practices in present-day India, I was surprised to discover that scholars have rarely focused their attention on non-international Indian practitioners[4] and, especially, on non-international ascetic practitioners of yoga. Ethnographic descriptions of ascetics' yoga practices are to be found in a number of works on specific religious orders or on *sādhus*: see the works of John C. Oman (1903), George W. Briggs (1938), Robert L. Gross (1992), Sondra L. Hausner (2007), Véronique Bouillier (2008) and Matthew Clark (2006). Likewise, there are a small number of journal articles on the topic: see especially the articles by Ramdas Lamb (2005, 2012) and James Mallinson (2005, 2011b, 2012b, 2013c). While these sources provide hints about the yoga practice of ascetics, no study focusing entirely on this subject has ever been carried out before. This book, therefore, attempts to remedy this lack of information, or at least tries to offer a starting point for further research.

Framing the content

Before providing information about the ethnographic research that enabled the collection of information for this book, I think it is important to clarify a few issues so that this book can be properly positioned in the field of yoga literature, especially considering a possible comparison between its contents and works on modern yoga.

Tradition

In the world of modern yoga practitioners, there is often a search for the 'traditional' yoga. The word 'tradition' comes from the Latin verb *tradere*, which means 'to pass on', 'to hand over'. This does not indicate a product of the past passively received, rather a product developed by those living in the present from what has preceded them. Hence, considering that there are many 'presents' which follow one another over centuries, and exist at the same time in different geographic areas, it is clear that a tradition can be

4 Exceptions are the works of Joseph Alter (2008) and Raphael Voix (2008), which provide interesting information on the reinterpretation of yoga in contemporary India.

elaborated in very complex ways by those who transmit it. And this is very much the case with yoga in Indian traditions and present times.

For this reason, it could be useful to look in general at traditions as realities in constant evolution.[5] The changes that occur in a tradition often depend on a comparison with something new or different coming from outside or inside: the presence of new groups; the spread of new teachings or techniques; the appearance of outstanding individuals; the adoption of a tradition in another context with its subsequent reinterpretation; and so on. As a tradition does not necessarily evolve in the same way or at the same time in different geographical areas, this means that a tradition can present inner sub-traditions which should be analysed both in their individuality and as part of the wider tradition. As I have shown elsewhere (Bevilacqua 2018a), while investigating present traditions we should imagine a structure that goes from the most abstract idea of that tradition (e.g. yoga), to the actualisation of the idea in a more specific theoretical frame (e.g. *haṭha* yoga), to the different forms in which this can be actualised among a specific general group (e.g. *haṭha* yoga among ascetics), to a specific section of this group (e.g. *haṭha* yoga for Nāths or *tyāgīs*), and finally to a singular individual within a specific section (e.g. yoga for a specific *sādhu*).

For this reason, an unchanging, immutable yoga tradition simply cannot exist. Yogic traditions should be contextualised and their characteristics stressed along with the socio-political-religious environment in which they arose.

Religious and spiritual

In this book I will often use the words 'religious' and 'spiritual' as synonyms because ascetics were and are rooted in a religious milieu and so are their yogic practices. That is why references to God are often present in yoga textual sources and always in the words of ascetics.[6] In the past, as well as in the present, a yoga practice among ascetics without a theological context simply did not exist. For this reason, it is necessary to clarify what I mean when I talk about yoga as a spiritual practice.

---

5 The use of the term 'evolution' emphasises not only the gradualness with which a tradition can evolve (which of course can sometimes be accelerated as a result of internal and external stimuli) but also conveys the idea that a tradition (or part of it) changes in order to allow its preservation. See Bevilacqua 2018a.

6 In this book I use the word 'God' to refer usually to the *iṣṭa devatā* (preferred deity) of an ascetic, but also to the various references of divine inference in yogic practice, such as God's grace, Yoginīs or Ādi Guru, etc.

'Spirituality' is a difficult word to clarify because, as with all cultural ideas, the meanings associated with it change according to time and space. In modern times, spirituality became a blend of humanistic psychology, mystical and esoteric traditions, in which a subjective daily experience creates a new approach and understanding of the sacred, not connected with an organised religious institution. But if we consider spirituality in a more 'traditional' way, it was a process of re-formation the purpose of which was to 'reconnect the original shape of man, the image of God' (Waaijman 2002). *Spiritualitas,*[7] indeed, was the mystic side of religious traditions; it was an inner process that developed inside a person but which found its expression and possibility through a religious organisation. It was in the 1970s that the word completely detached itself from the official religious scene to enter different social arenas (Palmisano and Pannofino 2018).[8]

Hence, while in India yoga as a spiritual discipline was (and is often still) taught by gurus associated with religious groups or institutions, in a lay, transnational context it suggests more a modern idea of spiritual practice. If we want to understand yoga and *haṭha* yoga in their historical development and as lived by contemporary *sādhus*, we have to keep in mind this distinction. This is not to criticise the spiritual use of yoga among modern practitioners, rather the opposite: it is to point to the fact that we are going to deal with a specific approach towards yoga that cannot be compared to the practice of modern lay practitioners who are not part of religious organisations, since the two (the Hindu ascetic and the lay practitioner) start from different premises and may aim for different results.

Selecting Hinduism

In this book I will use the expression 'Hindu asceticism' simply to stress that I am not going to take into consideration forms of asceticism that are practised in other Indian religions such as Buddhism and Jainism. Furthermore, I will deal with a specific aspect of Hinduism that can be defined

---

7 *Spiritualitas* comes from *spiritus* ('breath', 'breath of life', hence 'life'), and it was the Latin word used to translate the Greek substantive *pneuma* ('spirit') and the adjective *pneumatikos* ('spiritual'). As we will see, *prāṇa* has a similar value in the Indian religions as vital breath and life force, and it is often connected with *ātman*, the self/soul of the individual.

8 For an interesting discussion on the link between esoteric/occultist approaches and the development of various forms of spirituality in the 19th century, and how they affected the intelligentsia of Bengal, led to the formulation of Neo-Vedānta and, by consequence, to influence modern yoga, see De Michelis 2004, especially the first three chapters.

as Modern Hindu Traditionalism.[9] The word 'Hinduism', indeed, can be considered as an umbrella term under which further categories are possible and it can be useful to clarify its different aspects.

De Michelis (2004: 37) proposes a useful classification (influenced by Halbfass 1990) in which Hinduism is divided into Classic Hinduism, Modern Hindu Traditionalism and Neo-Hinduism, thus making clear that various Hinduisms co-exist, each characterised by the influences it has received and assimilated, and the changes that it has subsequently undergone. The label 'Classic Hinduism' embraces all those religious traditions present in pre-18th-century India, i.e. before the advent of British colonial power and therefore before the promotion of forms of Westernisation. The British/Western 'imported culture' affected society and religions, leading to Neo-Hinduism and Modern Hindu Traditionalism.

Neo-Hinduism reinterprets textual sources perceived to be outmoded, providing new meanings that resulted from the encounter with the West, while bypassing the role of traditional schools and religious orders in favour of a unified Hindu religion (Sardella 2013: 235). As we will see in Chapter 7, many modern gurus who began to leave India at the end of the 19th century to preach in the West can be considered representatives of Neo-Hinduism.

Modern Hindu Traditionalism appears as a middle path between Classical and Neo-Hinduism. It rejects the Western aspects of Neo-Hindu thought and practice, representing itself as the contemporary development of older traditions. It supports the presence and the inner differences of the various religious groups (*sampradāyas*) as constituting a multifarious Hindu lore. Since the gurus and ascetics presented in this book belong to *sampradāyas* that can be defined as part of this Modern Hindu Traditionalism, they will be referred to as 'traditional' when being compared with modern gurus/*sādhus*.

Orality and embodiment

In this book I look at religions mostly as lived rather than as represented. Therefore, I won't focus my attention on religious narratives supplied by institutions (or by texts), but at the ways in which ordinary people (in this case ascetics) 'remember, share, enact, adapt, create and combine the "stories" out of which they live' (McGuire 2008: 111), hence how yoga/

9 There has been much discussion about the terms 'Hindu' and 'Hinduism', their origin and their use. Given the complexity of this topic, I suggest reading comprehensive works such as Llewellyn 2005.

haṭha yoga is lived in India by traditional ascetics. This means paying particular attention to orality, which is the *sādhus*' way of transmitting their teachings.

Scholars have often confined their attention to textual sources, probably because it was difficult to collect oral traditions, especially in the field of initiatory groups or, probably, because they were not interested in practices or ideas not acknowledged in texts. Whatever the reason, the result is a lack of critical examination of the traditions and interpretations orally transmitted by lineages that still exist today (Lorea 2018: 19).

In this book I provide a repertoire of emic perspectives to demonstrate the importance of hearing from living practitioners not only to understand yogic traditions but also to evaluate the role and use of texts in the development of these traditions. Orality has always had a particular importance in the Indian religious context—the Vedas, for example, have been transmitted orally despite the implementation of writing, because of the specific religious role of the oral transmission[10]—but it also had a clear social reason. Indeed, the majority of people could not participate in literate culture and, therefore, non-literate people had to commit the transmission of their texts not to paper but to memory (Smith 1990: 4). As we will see in Chapter 5, this consideration is still valid among contemporary ascetics, many of whom are non-literate or semi-literate.

Among *sādhus* orality also depends on the dynamics of transmission which are based on a direct relationship between a guru and a disciple. This relationship is vital in ascetic society and it is considered the main source of ascetics' knowledge: more important than books are one's guru's words and the words of all the gurus and knowledgeable *sādhus* an individual meets on the spiritual path.[11] The oral training involves different levels of memorisation and different kinds of 'texts': *sādhus* learn by heart the texts and mantras related to worship and specific rituals. Similarly, they learn esoteric knowledge also through riddles, used as a mnemonic device easier to remember than 'the dry, cumbrous philosophical terminology of

10 The necessity to use sacred speech correctly had the purpose of sustaining the *dharma*, therefore orality had a key role in the preservation of tradition (Larios 2017: 25).

11 This does not mean that books are not used by ascetics. I emphasise again that in this book I am focusing on specific ascetic sections and on specific ascetics who use embodied, physical practices—and who may read booklets with notes, or books on worship and prayers—rather than ascetics who live in monasteries and spend their time analysing and writing theological manuscripts in Sanskrit as part of their *sādhanā*.

the scholastic traditions' (Bharati 1965: 170). *Sādhus* also absorb lots of stories about their order, gurus, ancestors and their religious values and spiritual practices through different oral narrations which often have a less fixed nature.

These vibrant and differentiated possibilities of learning, consequently, make it difficult to say that yoga is an antisocial practice (Alter 2006: 764). This idea would be correct dealing with an ideal yoga and ideal yogis—already enlightened individuals—but not considering yoga as a *praxis*, a practice that needs time and instructions. The presence of a guru during the practice is often forgotten. It is true that the practice *per se*, i.e. the exact moment in which the individual is able to practise independently, is to be spent alone; however, before and after that, the individual is connected with his guru and other practitioners, as well as other gurus. We should not imagine yogis as isolated figures that start their practice by themselves (completely antisocial). Yoga is antisocial when performed 'proficiently', but its trainings and some of its practices do not occur in an antisocial context because the experience of the community's teaching is part of the *sādhanā*.

When it comes to physical practices, *sādhus*' learning does not need many words: even more than an oral transmission, a physical transmission is necessary because, rather than giving explanations, the guru shows a practice to his disciples and asks them to repeat it. The associated theories will eventually be embodied.

McGuire (2008: 188) used the label 'embodied practice' to refer to 'those ritual and expressive activities in which spiritual meanings and understanding are embedded in and accomplished through the body (e.g. bodily senses, postures, gestures, and movements)'. I consider this a useful label because it does not suggest a unique source for yoga practice and philosophy; rather it enables us to create associations with different philosophies. As we will see, yoga and *haṭha* yoga techniques are present in different religious and philosophical contexts, supported by different interpretations.

Given the concept of embodiment, a few words on the role and understanding of the body is required, although the topic will be properly developed in Chapter 5. There is no sense of duality between the mind and body in Hindu traditions because the mind, considered in its various components (*manas*, *buddhi*, *citta*, *ahaṃkāra*), is still related to a bodily, material dimension. A dichotomy is rather between the mind-body complex and the *ātman*, the self. This is a very important point which is crystal-clear when one talks with *sādhus*, although this dichotomy is not necessarily based on an opposition. The limits of the body is a fact acknowledged by *sādhus*, just as they understand that what constitutes the body can become an obstacle for the individual spiritual path. However, the body (in its entirety of body-mind) is also an instrument, especially in the practice of yoga and *haṭha* yoga. It is the container of the *ātman*,[12] a container that can be properly 'exploited' (just as the human birth),[13] and this exploitation finds its realisation mainly in two ways: by keeping the body healthy because the *sādhanā* requires it to be in good shape, or by exposing it to strenuous austerities. The material body is implicated in reaching the ultimate aim of the spiritual practice, but its role changes according to the stage of practice, moving across a wide range of activities (which also include behaviours, etc.) towards a refinement of action which eventually leads towards body and mind inaction. In these processes, there is no attachment to the body since its materiality implies its limitations. The practices of yoga (using the term 'yoga' in a broader way) have the purpose of disciplining, knowing and controlling the tool (the body-mind), but eventually this use of the body aims to overcome it: the embodiment aims for the disembodiment since the experience of yoga would happen on a different plane of reality, that of the Self, which is a transcendental plane.

Eventually, we have also to connect the term 'embodied practices' with yogic performance: as we will see in Chapters 3 and 5, *sādhus* can use their practices (austerities, *āsanas* or *kriyās*) as a form of performance and entertainment for the amusement of crowds and for economic gain.

Secrecy

Among ascetic groups teachings were usually, and still are, transmitted through initiation: they were revealed only if and when an adept was ready for them.[14] Even texts on *haṭha* yoga support this stand. For example, the *Haṭhapradīpikā* claims that the *sādhanā* must be kept secret: 'It becomes

---

12 Once in Kolkata, I went to a hospital to meet the guru of Jogī Bābā, one of my main interlocutors. He was in the hospital for dialysis, but despite this he was quite lively. When I asked him how he was, he replied that his *ātman* was in good shape and that only his body was in pain.

13 Several ascetics stressed the fact that being born in a human body is a 'golden chance' that should not be wasted because only human beings are able to pursue the path to salvation.

14 On the role of secrecy, see Urban 1998, 2003, 2010: 93–115; Padoux 2011: 113–114; Lorea 2018.

potent when kept secret but impotent when revealed.' (1.11).[15] Similar claims became a kind of topos in some forms of esoteric literature, to such an extent that to assert the secrecy of the teaching probably aimed at elevating the concealed thing itself (Lorea 2018: 14) in order to spread a doctrine and attract new adepts, especially wealthy patrons.

There are various levels of secrecy that can be concealed in textual sources and in the oral transmission. In both the cases the key to overcoming them is the same: to be in the presence of an expert, the guru, who knows how to properly interpret the content of a text, and in general knows the practices and can explain them to the disciple. However, receiving these explanations is not a given: different disciples, or disciples on different levels of *sādhanā*, receive different knowledge. In fact, only those who are qualified have the authority (*adhikāra*) to transmit or receive specific forms of knowledge. We will see in Chapter 5 that physical characteristics and age are also important variables in determining who can have access to full physical yoga training. In my conversations with *sādhus* the belief that teachings have to remain secret often arose, mainly because, they explain, lay people can completely misunderstand and misinterpret them. Instead, a student, before becoming a disciple, has to be tested by the guru who will then lead him/her towards the spiritual knowledge and path more appropriate to his/her nature.

Religious orders manage different forms of knowledge and deal with secrecy in different ways. Today, some traditions are more open to disclosing the secret teachings to avoid them being lost (see Baker 2019: 9) or to provide proper interpretation of teachings that were wrongly interpreted (see Lorea 2018: 19). If we look at the traditional Hindu ascetics' world, it seems that the attitude remains more conventional. *Sādhus* are keen to talk with those who are willing to learn (as they say, a *sādhu* answers questions and does not preach to those unwilling to listen), but there is a big difference between talking and teaching. An increasingly present vicious circle makes things even more complicated: it is difficult today to find real, good students, and it is equally difficult to find real, good gurus. This lack on both sides determines the decline and probable demise of some practices. However, this is not pushing gurus to instil at any cost their knowledge into their disciples: still the skills of the disciples are more important than the loss of the knowledge. It is better to lose a practice rather than to pass it into the wrong hands.

---

15 In this book I use the *Haṭhapradīpikā* online beta edition edited by James Mallinson, Jason Birch, Jürgen Hanneder and Mitsuyo Demoto-Hahn: http://hathapradipika.online.

In search of *sādhus*

Given the complexity of Indian religions, I initially looked at the historical development of the practices and of the religious orders, because yoga as a physical and religious discipline developed inside religious orders and was affected by their historical developments. Hence, I used a diachronic perspective considering secondary literature on ascetic orders and on the history of yoga to reconstruct the historical background necessary to understand the mobility of ideas and practices. A fundamental support was given by *haṭha* yoga's textual sources (especially the manuscripts collated and edited by the other members of the Haṭha Yoga Project), the contents of which were compared, when possible, with visual evidence from the past—especially with *āsana* sculptures in temples or other buildings (like walls or gates)—as well as ascetic contemporary practices collected through ethnography. Since ethnography represents the core of this work, below I will describe how I conducted my research, also considering problems and obstacles faced during these years.

Places, times and interlocutors

The ethnographic material I present in this book stems from four main rounds of fieldwork held in different regions of India from November 2015 to March 2019. During this period, I collected visual archaeological evidence but mostly ethnographic data. Since the ascetic society is composed of several orders and suborders, the only way to collect proper data, reaching as many ascetics as possible, was through prolonged field trips. I deem time, indeed, as one of the main tools to properly engage in the ascetic context, because only through time can one build proper relationships with *sādhus* (see below).

My first round of fieldwork ran from October 2015 to May 2016. It began in Varanasi, a city in which I had previously conducted research and I already knew some ascetic practitioners. Furthermore, in Varanasi were representatives of all the religious orders I intended to meet. I remained there for four months, before travelling south with Professor James Mallinson. Together we attended the proclamation of the *rāja yogī* of the Nāth *sampradāya* in Mangalore[16] and then visited important archaeological sites (among which were Hampi, Sringeri, Panhale Kaji and Dabhoi) where we

16 For a comprehensive description of the event, see Bouillier 2008.

looked for historical material and visual evidence of ascetic practice.[17] I then travelled to the Siṃhasth Melā (festival) in Ujjain, arriving one month before it began to talk with those ascetics who were already there arranging their camps, so I might move more easily among them once the festival started. Attending religious gatherings was fundamental for the research because it was during these festivals that I could search for practitioners: sometimes, outside their tents, *sādhu*s display billboards with photos of themselves doing *āsana*s or other practices. Sometimes, simply by talking about my ongoing research, I was directed to meet someone in specific who could help me.

My second round of fieldwork ran from the end of December 2016 to July 2017. During this period, I attended the Gaṅgā Sāgar Melā and spent some time in Kolkata and neighbouring areas (like Shantiniketan, Birnagar and Tarapith). After West Bengal, I again met Professor Mallinson and Dr Mark Singleton with the purpose of visiting other outstanding places such as Taranga Hill, Mount Abu, Dhinodhar and Junagadh. In March I travelled to Rishikesh, looking for traditional ascetics. In June 2017, I attended the Ambubācī festival in Kamakhya. Again, I arrived in the city a few weeks before the festival in order to get in touch with local ascetics who could facilitate introductions to the *sādhu*s due to arrive later.

The third round of fieldwork began in January 2018 and lasted until June 2018. Initially I was in West Bengal; again I attended the Gaṅgā Sāgar Melā in Kolkata, but mostly I visited a yogi living in Garh Jungle close to Shantiniketan, and another in Jhargram. I then moved to Uttar Pradesh where I spent some more time in Varanasi and Allahabad. I passed through Kolkata to continue my research in Orissa and in Nepal. I then went to Gorakhpur (Uttar Pradesh) specifically to attend the *yoga śivir* (H., camp) organised by Yogī Śivanāth, after which I returned to Kamakhya for the Ambubācī Melā.

The last round of fieldwork started in South India in December 2018 with visits to archaeological sites such as Shri Shailam, Ellora and Ajanta to continue searching for visual hints from past practitioners. The fieldwork then moved to Allahabad for the Ardh Kumbh Melā where I stayed from January 2019 until March 2019. In 2020, Professor Mallinson and I visited several Hindu pilgrimage centres in Pakistan (Hinglaj Mata, Lahore, etc.), concluding the data collection.

This description of my movements is just a summary, although further glimpses will be given in the chapters. Clearly, it is difficult to 'locate' the field: it was not a fieldwork that was focused on a specific place, and it was

---

17 The sculptures of the Mahudi Gate at Dabhoi were our main discovery in terms of archaeological finds. See Chapter 5, p. 198.

not a multi-sided fieldwork designed to examine the circulation of the practices in a wider time-space (Marcus 1995: 96). In fact, I followed the route of religious festivals and the mobility of *sādhus* necessarily influenced my own. Therefore, I would describe my fieldwork as being religiously sided because it occurred in different religious places, the 'religiosity' of those places being 'objective' or 'subjective' and 'permanent' or 'temporary', as dictated by the ascetics' movements. Places like Varanasi and Rishikesh are religious places with a traditional religious role, so I knew I could meet helpful *sādhus* there at any time. Other places, like Allahabad, Kolkata, Ujjain and Kamakhya are objectively religious but in a more temporary way, which means that at specific times (i.e. during a *melā*) a predictable number of *sādhus* are in town.[18] Those *āśrams* I visited because I was invited by *sādhus* can, on the other hand, be considered 'subjective', which means connected to a specific order—therefore personal—and temporary or permanent according to the history of the place in question.[19] I usually went to such places having already met the ascetic elsewhere and having been invited to visit him to continue our conversations.

I aimed to spend as much time as possible within each group, collecting qualitative data through direct and indirect interviews. As mentioned, I began the research in Varanasi visiting *sādhus* with whom I was already acquainted, but in most cases I had to build new relationships. This inevitably took place at *āśrams* and temples or at religious festivals. When I found a potential interlocutor at a festival, I would sit among people and wait until I was asked to introduce myself; in more private situations I directly introduced myself and my aims. Rarely did I interview anyone during the first encounter, since I preferred to get to know them better, and them to know me better, before doing so. Recorded interviews took place with those *sādhus* with whom I spent more time and who were at ease in front of the recorder; otherwise I opted for casual conversations. I found this latter approach very constructive, because it enabled different points of views,

18 This does not mean that there are no ascetic centres or *āśrams* belonging to the studied orders in these places, but rather that the number of ascetics ordinarily residing there is low, with the 'religious value' of these cities being activated only at specific times.

19 For example, in Orissa I went to meet a Nāth Yogī who is the *mahant* (H., abbot) of an *āśram* the history of which goes back at least a couple of centuries. Therefore, although isolated, this place is economically financed by past concessions, and, being known within the order, it is frequented by the Nāths who roam the area. Jogī Bābā, on the other hand, lives in an *āśram* in the jungle which he built himself and was accordingly very concerned about its future (see Bevilacqua 2018b).

questions and topics to emerge. Furthermore, a casual conversation usually comprises an exchange of information: just as I was interested in knowing about my interlocutors, so too were they curious about me. This approach led ascetics to speak freely with me, on their terms and on a wide range of topics. A key aim for me was to establish a friendly environment in which there was no perceived pressure to tell me something.

Because I decided to engage mostly with 'grassroots' *sādhus*, who were often uneducated, my conversations were predominantly in Hindi and I spoke English in only two cases. Although it was not always possible to completely understand those *sādhus* who did not have Hindi as their mother tongue or spoke in regional dialects, I chose to forgo having an interpreter since I did not want my interlocutors to feel uncomfortable about having their words translated into a language they did not understand. I mitigated the risk of misunderstanding by asking the same question to the same *sādhu* on different occasions or by asking for further explanation later. In those interviews that were recorded, the transcription cleared up any uncertainties. Furthermore, my choice to forgo an interpreter put the *sādhu* in a position to decide whether or not to talk to me—and to what extent. That meant that completing my set of questions could sometimes take days or even weeks. I did not follow a written questionnaire: I knew the kinds of questions and topics I wanted to talk about, and I tried to ensure they arose during the conversations. I might spend days without asking a single question simply because the timing was not right or the ascetic was too busy or too tired to talk to me, and I did not want to be a further source of stress. In some cases, making me wait was a kind of test to verify whether I was really interested in listening. I consider making time to listen and to wait to be two of the most important tools in ethically qualitative ethnographic fieldwork. From a qualitative point of view, the stronger the connection with the interlocutor, the more accurate and well articulated the answer can be. From an ethical point of view, I see the researcher as the one who is there to learn from the interlocutor—it is the researcher who needs the subjects—and the only way to prevent the process being one of 'stealing' from them is to build relationships and find a way of paying them back.

Paying back means trying to re-create a balance between the exchanges. Offering practical help can be one approach. In my case, I gave an appropriate *dakṣiṇā* (donation) to most of my informants according to the circumstances (which was more difficult in the case of Kumbh Melā where there were hundreds of ascetics). In those places in which I spent more time, I also bought food or necessary items for the temple or *āśram*, or helped by doing some cleaning. Moreover, my persistent presence in religious *melās* and my movement among different groups fostered awareness and support from the new *sādhus* to whom I was introduced by those I already knew. Sometimes the difficult conditions in which I had to work (for example, travelling by bicycle from one camp to another under the midday April sun or sitting for hours in a corner while various *sādhus* were performing their austerities) impressed the *sādhus* to the extent that they wanted to reward me somehow.

All these experiences facilitated conversations about yoga, *haṭha* yoga and *āsanas*, leading to *sādhus* assisting with my research by showing me postures, and in several cases allowing me to take photos or videos of them. A few *sādhus* were willing to teach me *āsanas* even without initiation and I was more than willing to participate in these classes. I was also fortunate to observe some collective and individual performances of *āsanas* during religious gatherings.

However, it was not always easy. Basically, ascetics reacted to my research in one of two distinct ways: positively or sceptically. The 'positive ascetics' appreciated the fact that foreigners are interested in Indian culture and are making efforts to understand key religious issues such as those of yoga and *haṭha* yoga. The 'sceptical ascetics' did not grasp why I would collect information from a variety of *sādhus* rather than practise and learn to understand yoga personally.[20] Such an attitude is understandable: yoga for ascetics is a spiritual discipline and has a specific spiritual meaning and purpose—it is a private path, and as such it should remain in the private sphere.[21] Because it is an individual, inner experience, *sādhus* claim that it cannot be described by words, nor can it be understood by someone who

20 Some among this category refused to talk to me; others, although sceptical, nevertheless chose to help me.

21 As Gustaaf Houtman argues in his study on Buddhism in Burma, the place in which fieldwork is conducted can have a significant bearing on the outcome. He compared his work on meditation in a monastery with that in a meditation centre: 'While in the monastery knowledge can be received in a social context and transmitted between people, in the meditation centre knowledge is not conceived in its "received" form but only as an experiential knowledge derived from lengthy private dedicated "work"' (Houtman 1990: 156). Those meditating in the centre would have neither the time nor the inclination to talk to the anthropologist, since social pleasantries are a distraction to meditation. Houtman admits that neither his personal experience nor his anthropological training had equipped him to address such an intrinsically antisocial activity.

is not on the path.[22] Yoga is a full-time commitment for those who follow its *sādhanā*.

However, since my research focused on physical yoga practices (e.g. *ṣaṭkarma*, *āsana*, *prāṇāyāma*, *mudrā*, *bandha*), and since *sādhus* do not have any particular restrictions about talking about these techniques, it was possible to collect data. These physical practices are textually understood or defined as *haṭha* yoga, but when I asked *sādhus* the simple question 'What is *haṭha* yoga?' the answers revealed several different meanings and also prompted discussions about key elements of yogic practice and yoga more generally, providing an emic understanding[23] of various labels and concepts.

In total, I was able to collect the words and ideas of about 109 *sādhus*: 26 Vaiṣṇava *tyāgīs*, 32 Nāth Yogīs, 47 Dasnāmī *saṃnyāsīs* and four Udāsīs. Among these, two interlocutors were from the Kabīr *panth* (H., sect); three were disciples of more modern *saṃnyāsīs*; while two belonged to tantric non-celibate sects. To these I should add the information given to me by five Indian yoga teachers trained by *sādhus*.

It is difficult to gauge the significance of these numbers without knowing how many ascetics in total there are in each order. It is also difficult to identify the social background of these individuals because, once one enters the *sādhu samāj* (H., *sādhu* society), one's previous life is left behind, and *sādhus* prefer not to talk about their past. However, this has not always been the case.[24] What I can say, therefore, is that among my interlocutors there were *sādhus* who were initiated during childhood and others who entered the ascetic path after having fulfilled their social duties, i.e. getting married

22 A very similar argument is given by Johanna Cook (2010: 20) when investigating meditation. She writes: 'the emphasis placed upon the experiential dimension of meditation makes it a particularly thorny challenge for anthropology: in many ways research about meditation is an attempt to "eff" the ineffable [. . .] some questions were met with responses such as "acknowledge" or meditate and you will know.' Houtman (1990: 156), too, declares that he had to work mostly with informants whom he describes as '"improvising" meditators' because they were open to talk about their experiences, while monks advised him to engage in three months' full-time meditation for 20 hours a day, without talking or writing, if he wished to obtain results.

23 In general, an emic understanding is one in which the approach and ideas of the interlocutor are reported, in contrast to an etic report, which provides a description of a phenomenon from a neutral and scientific viewpoint. In this case, the emic understanding concerned techniques that were directly experienced, practised or transmitted in a certain way.

24 See Appendix 2.

and having children. In Appendix 2 I provide a few hints about their stories, when they were openly shared, to bring their characters and individuality to life. It is there one can also find my descriptions of where and when I encountered each *sādhu*, so as to avoid repetitions in the book or interruptions when sharing words from several *sādhus* in the same section.

Among my informants there are only four women: one *tyāgī*, one *saṃnyāsinī* and two Nāths. Because of this, I mostly use male pronouns when describing the practices of *sādhus*, unless specific information was given by a female practitioner. As I will explain in Chapter 1, the ascetic world is indeed a male world, in which women are not always welcomed, especially when physically demanding practices are concerned. Therefore, one might wonder how I could undertake my research at all and whether my being a woman has affected my data collection.

My positionality

'Positionality' refers to the fact that all 'researchers are positioned by age, gender, race, class, nationality, institutional affiliation, historical-personal circumstances, and intellectual predisposition', and that, once they enter into a community, they introduce themselves to it and to the future interlocutors (Chiseri-Strater 1996: 115).

My position as researcher was clear because I wanted it to be clear. I consistently defined myself as a researcher and a student: someone who was not looking for a guru but rather collecting useful insights about yogic practices. I always clarified my intention of not wishing to be initiated and that I unfortunately held no particular faith.

In comparison with other studies among yoga practitioners,[25] my fieldwork has two fundamental differences: (1) the researcher is a woman in a male context, and (2) the difficulty of being a practitioner in an ascetic context. In many ethnographic works among practitioners, scholars have elected to participate in the practice they are studying. In these cases, many of the informants are women, as women represent the bulk of modern yoga practitioners today. In my case, over four rounds of fieldwork, from October 2015 to March 2019, which covered a variety of regions and religious

25 See for example the work of Joanna Cook (2010), who chose to become ordained and practise meditation in order to understand what it means to be a monk/nun and how monastic identity is formed through ascetic practice. The members of the monastery were aware that her ordination would be limited to one year, during which she would carry out her anthropological research. Another case is that of Ingrid Jordt (2007), who became a Buddhist nun for several years, focusing on *vipasyanā* as a diplomatic link between Burma and the rest of the world.

orders mostly in North India, only a very few of my interlocutors were female. The reality of the society of *sādhus* is very much a male one, in which gender roles are still strongly delineated and in which a female presence is limited. Female asceticism is culturally and traditionally discouraged, but there is also another key reason why ascetics prefer to limit female participation and that is *brahmacarya* (celibacy). It is therefore preferable to keep women at a distance or to maintain only limited contact with them. This is quite possible in India because it is unlikely that an unmarried woman will spend much time alone with *sādhus*. If this were to happen, however, certain behaviours must be maintained, and, thanks to my previous research among Vaiṣṇava ascetics, I was aware of this and knew how to behave in front of *sādhus* in order to be considered a respectable woman.[26] There were a couple of mitigating factors, however: the fact that I was a foreigner, a researcher, and my ability to speak Hindi, which taken together broke the barrier of distrust and suspicion. In a country in which the majority of women still live under the protection of their fathers and husbands, the fact that I was living far from my family, self-reliant, unmarried, childless and over thirty years of age piqued the curiosity of many *sādhus*. This situation was accepted and even seen as a sign of courage—something to notice and appreciate. My being a foreigner, therefore, enabled me to go and stay in places where Indian women are not usually allowed.[27]

Being a woman not only made it possible for me to contact and speak freely with Indian female ascetics, but it also served as a reminder for me to ask male ascetics questions about the role of women in yoga practice. Sometimes, young *sādhus* felt they could share their feelings or emotions with me just because I was a woman, on the assumption I could understand them better than their brethren. This points to an aspect of asceticism relevant to the present day: that of social media and external output, something not directly related to the topic of yoga or *haṭha* yoga but which, as we will see in Chapter 7, can influence it.

In some circumstances, though, being a woman was a limiting factor: I had to let go of some interesting interlocutors because they eventually tried to get me into bed. After a few noteworthy days of conversation, one old

26 See Bevilacqua 2018a.

27 Once, for example, I was in Varanasi and was with a *saṃnyāsī* of the Āvāhan *akhāṛā*, which has a place near Daśāśvamedh Ghāṭ. Without warning, the *mahant* invited me for breakfast; as I entered, I saw a board reading 'women are not allowed'. I asked the *mahant* whether I could actually go in; he simply looked at me and said 'don't worry, don't worry, it doesn't count'. Nevertheless, I never spent a night in an *akhāṛā*—something else that is prohibited to women.

ascetic tried to convince me that I would find the complete knowledge I was looking for with the help of some special tantric and sexual practices which he was willing to teach me. This brought my visits to his place to an end.

It is impossible to gauge whether being a male researcher would have led to more, or different, material being collected. I can say that the *sādhus* with whom I spoke at length were not embarrassed to talk about such topics as menstrual blood or the retention of semen. I sincerely believe that the quality of the data depends, as it usually does, on the relationship built with the individual subject. Field research is, after all, a human experience based on the 'social interaction of ethnographer and subject' (Berreman 1962: 11).

The most significant factor influencing my data collection was that I was never a practitioner among *sādhus*. The barrier to being a practitioner stems from the fact that *sādhus* only offer proper teaching to those who are initiated into their orders. If I had wanted an initiation, I would only have needed to choose which tradition I wanted it to be in, since *sādhus* today are more than willing to initiate foreigners; in fact, the idea of initiation occurred to some *sādhus* because of my spending time with them. Although some pretended in front of other *sādhus* or lay people that I was his or her *celī* (disciple), none ever pushed me to become initiated, and they always accepted my justifications: that it was not my goal and that I had to finish my research before giving serious thought to having a guru. My decision not to be initiated into a tradition was a practical one but mostly an ethical one. From a practical point of view, to be initiated into one specific order would have meant remaining close to the guru, at least during the religious festivals, limiting the time that could be spent with *sādhus* from other *sampradāyas*. Furthermore, when one becomes a disciple it is more complicated to have a dialogical exchange with the guru because one is not supposed to question his/her words. I did not avoid initiation to evade discipline, but rather, from an ethical point of view, because it was awkward for me to take initiation (with the requisite duties and the faith around which such duties revolve) only in order to obtain deeper information about practices.

The problem of revealing secret knowledge collected through ethnographic research is an old one. Urban (1998: 209) calls this the 'double bind of secrecy': if a researcher, having been initiated, acquires access to esoteric knowledge, how much of it can they share or publish? On this issue, I find myself on the same page as Edward Conze, who declares:

> esoteric knowledge can [. . .] under no circumstances be transmitted to an indiscriminate multitude. There are only two alternatives. Either the

> author has not been initiated [. . .] then what he says is not first-hand knowledge. Or he has been initiated. Then if he were to divulge the secrets [. . .] he has broken the trust placed in him and is morally so depraved that he is not worth listening to (Conze 1962: 271–272).

As already mentioned, this caveat does not obtain if the guru himself supports the sharing of esoteric knowledge with a wider audience.

As far my research is concerned, I did not consider it appropriate to acquire any esoteric knowledge that was not supposed to be shared with not-initiated readers.[28] This was an important ethical foundation for my fieldwork: my informants were always fully aware of my role and that my work was to be made public, and we were both aware that nothing secret was to be revealed.

Furthermore, when ascetics asked me if I used to practise yoga, they were not referring to *āsana*s; rather, as will be explained in Chapters 5 and 6, they were enquiring whether I used to meditate. While I can practise *āsana*s, I am certainly not a person who meditates or follows a *sādhanā*. If I were, the meeting with so many *sādhu*s would have likely benefited my personal practice; however, the information presented in this book would not have been any different.

The structure of this book

This book aims to offer an understanding of the complexity of Indian asceticism and the practices of yoga and *haṭha* yoga among Indian ascetics, while providing a historical and theoretical framework. The past and present intertwine to support each other in these chapters, encouraging inquiry and advancing hypotheses. This is an important point in light of the role of modern yoga and the fact that it necessarily influences the practice of traditional *sādhu*s. But to properly understand this 'pizza effect',[29] an overview of the starting point is needed, i.e. the ascetics' perspective. With no intention of offering a detailed investigation of all the different topics it

28 Some *sādhu*s told me that they were disclosing more than they should, but they justified themselves by pointing out that I was doing research and it could be useful for me.

29 In a 1970 article, Agehānanda Bharati created a model which he calls the 'pizza effect'. In Italy, pizza used to be looked down on as a poor man's food. But, having migrated to America and then returned to Italy, it became a highly respected dish. Notwithstanding its historical inaccuracy, the story serves as a meaningful metaphor for Hinduism: having been first exported to the West around the turn of the 20th century, the product that returned to India garnered widespread attention.

introduces, this book aims instead to present a broad view that can stimulate further investigation.

Chapter 1 provides a schematic introduction to Indian asceticism and to tantric and devotional religious settings: these would go on to strongly influence the development of Hindu renunciation, of yogic practices and, in general, religiosity in India. The important concepts of *sampradāya* (religious order) and *paramparā* (lineage) are then explained, as well as the role of patronage in developing ascetic orders. There is also a brief introduction to female asceticism and warrior ascetics. This general, historical introduction to Hindu asceticism paves the way for a deeper understanding of specific ascetic orders in Chapter 2.

Chapter 2 more specifically focuses on the ascetic society: it introduces the *sampradāyas* of Nāths, Dasnāmīs, Udāsīs and Rāmānandīs, the orders traditionally connected to the practice of *haṭha* yoga and yoga *sādhanā*. Here, ascetic orders are framed within their historical development as well as according to their present manifestation. The chapter goes on to explain how, despite addressing different deities and belonging to different orders with different rules, *sādhus* may show strong similarities with regard to the practices they follow. It concludes with an analysis of the *sādhu samāj*: why individuals enter it and its general organisation.

These two chapters on asceticism are fundamental in gaining an understanding of the environment in which theories and practices were created, shared, adopted and adapted by different groups.

Chapter 3 investigates the practice of *tapasyā* (austerity) and relates it to the development of the concept of yoga and *haṭha* yoga. Descriptions of past practices draws on sources ranging from Greek historians to Western Orientalists. Subsequently, I introduce *sādhus*' present practice of austerities with an explanation of why they perform them. Through these criss-crossed references between past and present a certain continuity among practices will be acknowledged, demonstrating the fluidity of the ascetic world and the fact that a single word can attract layers of meanings over the centuries, according to the needs of the times.

Chapter 4 addresses *haṭha* yoga. It starts by considering definitions found in Sanskrit textual sources, then demonstrates that vernacular sources have a different understanding of *haṭha* yoga, often associating it with *tapasyā*. This *haṭha–tapas* relationship will be also found among the various meanings that the label '*haṭha* yoga' evokes among contemporary *sādhus*. This raises questions about the purpose of *haṭha* yoga textual sources in Sanskrit and, moreover, about their intended audience.

Chapters 5 and 6 engage with the yoga *sādhanā*, considering also auxiliary topics. Chapter 5 begins by providing a general introduction to the yogic body, going on to focus on *yama*, *niyama*, *āsana*, *prāṇāyāma* and *pratyāhāra*. In addressing physical practices, particular attention is paid to *āsanas* and *kriyās* (actions) to purify the body, some *mudrās* (such as *vajrolī* and *khecarī*) and *bandhas*. The chapter investigates how *sādhus* learn these different practices, and the contexts in which they choose to demonstrate them, which serves to emphasise the importance of pilgrimages and religious festivals. The different roles and practices of breath control are described, leading ultimately to the retraction of the senses (*pratyāhāra*). These different practices are contextualised with material from textual sources. Chapter 6 continues the investigation of the yoga *sādhanā* by focusing on *dhāraṇā*, *dhyāna* and *samādhi*. Preceding that, however, it considers general issues, such as where the internal steps of yoga are to be practised, and the role of mantras and of cannabis, clarifying the latter's use among ascetics. In dealing with *dhyāna*, the practice of *jap* (H., repetition) is discussed, as is the awakening of *kuṇḍalinī*. This leads to the topic of *samādhi* and the role of *karma* in the quest for *mokṣa* (liberation). These two chapters, therefore, aim to divulge the ascetics' approach to yoga, which will underpin an understanding of their perspectives and approach to modern yoga, as discussed in Chapter 7.

Chapter 7 evaluates whether—and if so how—transnational yoga is influencing *sādhus*' practices. It discusses *sādhus* who learn about yoga in modern centres, studied for degrees or PhDs in yoga, as well as *sādhus* who simply attended 'Western yoga class' in order to be able to teach abroad—but who distinguish this yoga from the *yog* (Hindi pronunciation) taught by their guru. It also presents typologies of *sādhus* teaching (modern) yoga. The role of social media and the internet in influencing their practice and the way some *sādhus* talk about yoga will also be examined. Finally, it presents controversial yogic figures such as Bābā Rāmdev, and discusses the establishment of the International Day of Yoga.

In the Conclusion I briefly revisit the most important topics presented in this work: the ascetic society; the fluidity of labels and practices in the *sādhu samāj*; and yogic identities. Two appendices follow: in Appendix 1, I describe the religious festivals I attended; Appendix 2 provides information about my ascetic interlocutors and the places and times I encountered them.[30]

30 The reader will notice that in some cases I do not attribute a *sādhu*'s words to a specific *sādhu*. This is usually when those words are critical of another. I have done this to protect their privacy and avoid possible repercussions among the *sādhu samāj*.

1
Hindu Asceticism and Religious Movements

Asceticism is a very complex phenomenon within Indian religions, because it manifests in a plethora of orders, further subdivided into lineages, each of which developed and organised according to its geographical location. These are broadly grouped under the modern umbrella of the *sādhu samāj*, or society of *sādhus*—*sādhu* being a generic term for holy men, sages and seers (the vast majority of which are male). Given the enormous number of ascetic possibilities, this book focuses on a specific category: that of celibate ascetics, who develop detachment (*vairāgya*), through denial and discipline, in order to achieve spiritual goals. Detachment is not only from the body's desires, and its sensory involvement with the world, but from society itself. For this reason, this understanding of asceticism can be considered synonymous with renunciation, although what is renounced from the 'brahmanical' society depends on the theoretical background of the ascetic group in question. Celibacy (*brahmacarya*) is a particularly significant criterion here, because many of the earliest textual sources on yoga emphasise its importance in securing results, thereby demonstrating that the yoga *sādhanā* (discipline) initially developed and spread in an ascetic context before becoming popularised among householders.[1]

1 In India a distinction is made between a renouncer and *gṛhastha*, the latter term basically referring to householders, i.e. those with a family; the emphasis is on the fundamental difference between the two (ascetics who have no family and

This chapter provides a historical introduction to Indian asceticism, tracking its developments. It begins by presenting, first, the substratum from which, presumably, various ascetic streams sprang, and then its 'brahmanical' version. It follows with a brief introduction to some of the earliest Hindu 'theistic' groups, going on to focus on the two traditions that have most affected Indian religiosity—the tantric and the devotional—and which have dramatically influenced the rise of ascetic orders and the development of yogic practices. Ultimately, terms such as *sampradāya* and *paramparā* are explained, and the different roles and contexts in which *sādhus* operate are presented, with the aim of clarifying how the ascetic world was structured and how innovations were, and still are, introduced. Where possible, any hints of the presence and role of ascetic women will be identified.

In general, the chapter aims to introduce the various sources (brahmanical, tantric and devotional) from which Hindu ascetic orders have developed. It makes a point of emphasising the constant interaction between ascetics and lay people. Given the complexity of the topics and the wide time span covered, the chapter will be schematic in form. The experienced reader may therefore skip certain sections, while the general reader may find it useful to understand more fully the ascetic orders described in Chapter 2, and also to understand the basis behind the explanations given by ascetics when talking about embodied practices.

The sources of Hindu asceticism

A comprehensive understanding of how renouncer traditions originated in South Asia is difficult to grasp, because South Asian societies have experienced the effects of numerous cultural and political influxes, making the development of these societies harder to track (Olivelle 2008c: 13). The most highly approved theories are divided between those that claim that renunciant traditions represent a logical development of ideas present in Vedic sacrificial culture (see Heerstaman 1964) and those (supported by scholars such as Bronkhorst [1993] and Pande [1974]) which acknowledge that point, but also take on board a separate tradition that used meditative

---

householders who do have a family and therefore have to follow and respect brahmanical and social conventions and customs). As we will see in Chapter 4, it is likely that some *haṭha* yoga practices, on the other hand, arose in a non-celibate religious milieu and some of its more controversial practices were then interiorised or reinterpreted by celibate ascetics. Similar developments have been testified to among celibate groups regarding tantric practices and rituals.

practice and abstention from activities to seek liberation from rebirth—a goal not described in the early Vedas. What can be said with certainty is that renunciant traditions developed over the centuries alongside the development of theories and soteriological systems.

Vedic literature provides glimpses of different typologies of ascetics and hermits—*ṛṣi, muni, yati, vrātya*—sometimes describing features that continue to characterise asceticism in India today. *Ṛṣis* are presented as hermits in the forest, alone or in the company of their wives. In the *Ṛg Veda* (10.136), the *muni* is described as *keśin*,[2] the long-haired one who wears dirty soil-coloured rags, carries drugs which he shares with Rudra (a Vedic deity later identified as a terrifying form of Śiva) and is 'girdled with the wind' (*vātaraśana*), which is understood to mean that he can fly through the atmosphere (Olivelle 2008b: 149). The *vātaraśana muni/keśin* is also said to be *unmādita*, a term used to refer to behaviours in which the ascetic appears mad, frenzied, intoxicated or in a trance. Other interesting attributes are *ūrdhvamanthinam* and *ūrdhvaretā*, meaning, respectively, 'one who retains his sperm' and 'one who pulls up his sperm', likely indicating some kind of sexual control (*Ṛg Veda* 151).[3] The *vrātya* appears in the so-called *Vrātya Kāṇḍa*, the 15th book of the *Atharva Veda* in the Śaunaka version. He is said to be able to become Mahādeva (The Great God) and move in the four directions, and section 15.3 claims that 'he stood a year erect', evidence of the practice of extreme forms of asceticism.[4] The words used to denote asceticism were *tapas*, inner spiritual heat, and *śrama*, fatigue, effort and toil (see p. 101).

With the exception of the *ṛṣis*—who had the vision of the Vedas through their *tapas*—ascetics were probably not representatives of the standard Vedic religion, which was instead run by priests. The central religious practice of the Vedas was sacrifice, the purpose of which was to influence the deities, who controlled natural forces, into acting according to human wishes. The sacrificial rituals required the presence of qualified priests, who knew the necessary procedures and recitations. The ritual substances would be transported through the fire to the deity being invoked. Fire was thus central to Vedic ritual, representing a transformative link between the worldly and divine realms which could be activated through the powerful mantras of the Vedic Saṃhitās. Depending on the inclination of the gods, individuals were thought to reach a sort of heaven upon their deaths, or a dark realm lying beneath the earth. Over the centuries, as the ritual grew

---

2 For an analysis of this figure, see Werner 1989.

3 On the role of semen and retention of the semen, see Chapter 5, p. 193.

4 Cf. the *khaṛeśvarī* practice described on p. 133.

more complex, commentaries and philosophical texts were produced, such as the Brāhmaṇas, the Āraṇyakas and eventually the Upaniṣads, building the foundations of Brahmanism.

According to Bronkhorst (2007: 81–83), by 400 BCE, from this brahmanical culture, located in the northwest of the Indian subcontinent, a certain form of asceticism emerged. Since the execution of sacrifices could impose various restrictions on the sacrificer (such as fasting, sexual abstinence, limitations of speech, etc.), this may have led some brahmins to cultivate an ascetic lifestyle. Brahmanical ascetics would retreat to the forest, abandoning their possessions but keeping their fire offerings, and surviving on what the forest had to offer. Eventually, some would become the final offering of the sacrifice by voluntarily entering into the fire (Bronkhorst 2007: 84).

The practices of Vedic/brahmanical ascetics would be further developed in coming into contact with the cultural milieu that Bronkhorst (2007) calls Greater Magadha. Located east of the confluence of the Ganges and Yamuna rivers,[5] the region of Greater Magadha had a different culture from that of the Vedic and early post-Vedic periods, being based on belief in rebirth and karmic retribution. It was thought that all actions had consequences in this or in the next life, resulting in the continuous alternation of birth and death. It was in order to free the individual from this life–death cycle that various forms of asceticism developed. The ascetic culture of Greater Magadha is known mainly from Buddhist and Jain textual sources—developed around the middle of the 1st millennium BCE—which present various theories and methods to overcome rebirth and karmic retribution. The Jains based their soteriological methods on inactivity and painful austerities. Others began to question the true nature of the self,[6] or manifest a fatalistic attitude (the Ājīvikas). Buddhists, on the other hand, believed that the main cause of rebirth was desire and the intention behind actions and that, therefore, karmic retribution derived from them. Their method was based on the practice of various forms of meditation to create a state of

---

5 This was the area responsible for the second urbanisation of India and for the rise of political structures which eventually led to the creation of the Maurya Empire and its successors.

6 Bronkhorst argues that, although there is no single known movement that advanced such a position, there is sufficient evidence to believe that the idea that knowledge of the true nature of the self could lead to liberation is a product of the spiritual culture of the Greater Magadha. This method, however, is only weakly attested to in the Buddhist and Jain canons, while it is more strongly present in the early brahmanical texts (Bronkhorst 2007: 28).

mind capable of pacifying desire. These various ascetic groups would be identified as *śramaṇa* in brahmanical sources.

According to Bronkhorst, 'Hindu' asceticism arose from the contact and confrontation between brahmanical ascetic culture and the ascetic culture of Greater Magadha.[7] Since the *śramaṇa* groups were the politically supported ones in North India, over time brahmanical schools began to accept and absorb the ideas of rebirth and karmic retribution, which were not known in the Vedic tradition. This led to a search for an alternative 'use' of the Vedic religion. Some seekers of religious experience began to interiorise the Vedic sacrifice, transforming it into mental operations, overcoming the role of the priests.

It is in the Upaniṣads[8] in which the intersection of these new religious trends is visible. The Upaniṣads questioned the relationship between the soul (*ātman*) and the ultimate reality (*brahman*), and introduced the ideas of *karma*, rebirth and transmigration, as well as release from rebirth (*mokṣa* or *nirvāṇa*) as the goal of life. The individual was imagined as trapped in the *saṃsāra* (wheel of life) by the continuous alternation of birth and death, thus stuck in a state of suffering. Since the cause of rebirth was recognised in desire and ignorance, knowledge became the source of release. This knowledge had to be the result of the effective elimination of ignorance, but to obtain that it was first necessary to eradicate desire, and this could be realised through renunciation.

The need to detach oneself from the *saṃsāra* in order to attain such soteriological knowledge led to the advocacy of an ascetic lifestyle and a combination of methods based on ascetic and meditative practices.[9]

The renouncers of the time were called *parivrājaka*, *parivrājaṭa*, *pravrājaka* and *bhikṣu*, terms related to their status as wanderers and beggars (Olivelle 2008d: 132). There were ascetics who lived in hermitages in the forest, possibly with their wives (following the example of the *ṛṣi*);

---

7 Not all scholars support this position, and debate about the 'direction' of cultural influxes is still open and very much alive. For example, in May 2021, the University of Alberta organised a symposium to discuss Bronkhorst's hypothesis. Here, I use the Greater Magadha theory because the idea of the two sources for Hindu asceticism is very useful in understanding how different religious practices with different aims can co-exist in ascetic orders.

8 The Upaniṣads comprise a collection of texts of religious and philosophical nature, produced in India probably between c. 700/600 BCE and c. 200 CE. It is in the Upaniṣadic environment in which techniques such as breath control, withdrawal of the senses, meditation, concentration, contemplation, absorption and austerities (*tapas*) are taught for soteriological aims.

9 These methods will be presented in Chapter 3, p. 103.

others who were celibate, and among these some lived in the wilderness (following the example of the *muni/śramaṇa*); and others still, who lived near towns and villages where they begged alms (following the example of the *śramaṇa*). They distinguished themselves by dressing differently, 'practising' philosophy and investigating reality through different means (austerity, meditation, study, intoxication) and for different purposes, each interacting with 'society' in their own way. The *śramaṇas* might be not only Buddhists or Jains but representatives of all those groups (linked or not to the Vedic lore) whose practices differed from those of the 'brahmanical' ascetics.

The brahmanical perspective on renunciation

As the ideologies underlying ascetic life undermined many of the core values of Brahmanism—home, marriage, family and fire rituals—manuals of law and conduct such as the Dharmasūtras (likely dating back to the last centuries BCE) began to limit their impact by domesticating forms of asceticism into a brahmanical framework. They identified two main typologies of ascetics: those who lived in the forest (*vānaprastha* and *vaikhānasa*) following ascetic practices but maintaining the ritual fire with the aim of rebirth in heaven; and those who had no sacred fire (*parivrāja*) and sought liberation from rebirth through inaction or wisdom. According to Bronkhorst (1998: 13–20), the *parivrāja* is probably the forerunner of the *saṃnyāsī*. These two typologies were presented in the structure of the *āśramas*, four possible life choices that an individual could follow: as a celibate student (*brahmacarya*); as a householder—a married adult with a family (*gṛhastha*); as a forest hermit (*vānaprastha*); and as a complete renouncer (*saṃnyāsa*). Around the 1st century CE, it seems that *āśramas* were reinterpreted as codified life stages that a man of the first three *varṇas* had to follow (Olivelle 2008a: 34–36).[10] *Vānaprastha* and *saṃnyāsa* were converted into institutions for the man who, having fulfilled his life duties, could devote himself to austerities and meditation in preparation for his death. According to this perspective, those who had access to a brahmanical

10 A hymn in the *Ṛg Veda* (10.90) describes the sacrifice of the body of the Puruṣa (the primordial man) from which four *varṇas* (colours/groups) originated: brahmins, *kṣatriyas*, *vaiśyas* and *śūdras*. Brahmins were given the highest ceremonial rank, as they emerged from his head. As *kṣatriyas* were generated from his shoulders, they were assigned to the protection of other creatures, while *vaiśyas*, born from the thighs, were designated for trade and productive activities. *Śūdras*, rising from the feet of the Puruṣa, were appointed to service.

life could eventually renounce it, along with important symbols of brahmanical society: the sacrificial thread and the topknot which declare one's status and, more importantly, the fire ritual celebrations, which were interiorised. Eventually, the ritual of renunciation marked the social death of the individual and the complete interiorisation of the sacrifice.[11] In fact, the ritual of renunciation celebrated the social death of the individual and the complete interiorisation of the sacrifice.

This life-structure was a theological brahmanical idealisation that did not reflect the social and religious reality of the time. According to Olivelle, *saṃnyāsa* must have acquired its generic meaning of 'renunciation' around the 3rd to 4th centuries CE, when it became a technical term under which many and different lifestyles and institutions of asceticism coalesced, at least theoretically (Olivelle 2008d: 141).[12]

The Dharmasūtras and the Saṃnyāsa Upaniṣads[13] attempted to codify and regulate ascetics' conduct. These texts discussed the rules that different types of renouncers had to follow, including, for example, how to beg for food, where to sleep, what to wear and so on. In these texts, therefore, renouncers were classified according to their behaviours and activities rather than their religious affiliation or belief.[14] Moreover, they were identified by external features, still present today, such as a begging bowl (made of clay, wood or gourd); a staff; a water pot; a waistband; a loincloth;

---

11 Given the internalisation of the sacrifice, renunciation could become a further refinement of the ritual, itself able to produce powerful effects: renunciation, for instance, was believed to erase sins, to produce heavenly rewards for the renouncer's relatives and to dissolve the bonds of marriage (Olivelle 1992: 71).

12 For example, the *Mānavadharmaśāstra* (c. 2nd or 3rd century CE) uses *saṃnyāsa* only to indicate a specific type of ascetic and not renunciation in general, and the *Āruṇi Upaniṣad* (probably the oldest among the Saṃnyāsa Upaniṣads) uses different terms such as *yati, parivrājaka, bhikṣu, tyāgī* and *yogī*, but not *saṃnyāsī* (Olivelle 2008d: 140).

13 The Saṃnyāsa Upaniṣads are a collection of 20 texts written in Sanskrit which deals with the theme of *saṃnyāsa*, renunciation. This does not constitute an indigenous classification: it was Paul Deussen who first used (and created) the category of Saṃnyāsa Upaniṣads. The oldest group was probably written around the last centuries BCE, while the mos recent group dates to the medieval period. However, it is impossible to date them as the texts do not contain information about their authors or the date or place of composition (Olivelle 1992: 4–11).

14 It is interesting to note that this still happens today: an ascetic who has perfected a specific practice is known by the name of that practice. Therefore, Barfānī (snow) Bābā is the typical name for an ascetic famous for his mountain practice, while Monī Bābā is the name for the ascetic following a vow of silence.

etc. Renunciation was presented as a series of stages through which the individual gradually detached himself from the senses and materiality.

But who could become a renouncer? Textual sources are inconsistent in their answer: while some texts (such as the *Mānavadharmaśāstra*) declare the ascetic path possible only for male brahmin, others (such as the Saṃnyāsa Upaniṣads) allowed it to individuals of the first three *varṇas*, excluding *śūdras* and women. Female asceticism was often discouraged, as women were not considered suitable for Vedic knowledge:[15] they had to follow a specific *dharma* (*strīdharma*), which depended on their nature (*strīsvabhāva*) and was fully realised through marriage, domestic life and child-rearing.[16] But the actual situation was very complex, and socio-political circumstances often influenced the access of an individual to ascetic groups. For example, the *Mahābhārata* portrays ascetics of all castes and genders: in some passages, women are described as philosophers, hermits and renouncers, and *kṣatriyas*, *vaiśyas* and *śūdras* are said to have entered *saṃnyāsa* after receiving the king's permission.

However, upholding a brahmanical ideology, the *Mahābhārata* also wanted to limit the impact of renunciation by providing a reinterpretation of ascetic ideals, adapting them in a specifically brahmanical context for householders. This is evident in the *Bhagavadgītā*, which introduces a different path to liberation, based on *jñāna* yoga (the method of knowledge) and *karma* yoga (the method of action).[17] As is well known, the *Gītā* reports the dialogue between Kṛṣṇa and Prince Arjuna while they are on the battlefield. Arjuna does not want to fight Bhīṣma and questions whether

15 As Anant S. Altekar notes, in ancient times girls underwent the *upanayana* ceremony and were educated together with boys. Nevertheless, by 300 BCE women's education suffered an arrest probably caused by the new fashion of child marriage. This meant a 'serious handicap to advanced studies' for girls, as the age in which these studies were usually accomplished, that of 12 or 13, became the new marriageable age. Hence, the *upanayana* was first reduced to a formality to accomplish before marriage, and then dropped out altogether (Altekar 1962: 16). Ancient Upaniṣads, such as the *Bṛhadāraṇyaka Upaniṣad*, portrayed women as intellectuals and experts of religious matters. Altekar, reporting other examples, affirms that these female philosophers remained unmarried in order to pursue their spiritual goals (Altekar 1962: 12).

16 On the role of women in Hindu civilisation, see Altekar 1962; on roles and rituals for Hindu women, see Leslie 1992; and on the history of female asceticism, see Denton 2004.

17 Chapters 13–42 of the *Bhīṣmaparvan*, the sixth book of the *Mahābhārata*, constitute the 18 chapters of the *Gītā* (200 BCE–200 CE). It refers to the period of the *Mahābhārata* war in the Kurukshetra when Bhīṣma was Kauravas's general.

he should go into battle and kill his relatives for the sake of the kingdom, let himself be killed, or become a renouncer to avoid the negative effects of actions required by inherited social duties. These questions enable Kṛṣṇa to expound the concept of *karma* yoga whereby one performs actions regardless of their fruits, following the individual *dharma*.[18] According to this perspective, it is not necessary to abandon action (hence not even ritual actions) but rather the desire for its outcomes. For the *Gītā*, therefore, the true *saṃnyāsī* was not one who renounced his duties but one who renounced attachment to their fruits.

Early theistic ascetic movements

The first centuries CE represent a period of intense economic and cultural exchanges between different parts of the Eurasian continent. In India, Buddhism had enjoyed royal patronage for centuries due to the presence of foreign rule. As Vedic Brahmanism was marginalised, other forms of brahmanical rituals developed and new popular cults sprang up around deities who had previously played a secondary role. Textual sources, such as the epics and Purāṇas,[19] reveal that around the 4th century CE some ascetic movements began to acquire a more sectarian nature, focusing their worship on deities such as Viṣṇu, Śiva and the Goddess. In this section I introduce a few of these early theistic ascetic movements and then focus on the changes that tantric and *bhakti* movements brought to the Indian religious landscape, strongly influencing the development of religious orders and their relationship to society.

Śaiva ascetic groups

From the 4th century CE onwards, Śaiva religious movements,[20] i.e. those addressing their worship to the god Śiva, spread and developed further

18 On the *Bhagavadgītā*, see Maitra 2018; Malinar 2009. I will deal with this important text in Chapter 3, p. 104.

19 The Purāṇas are a body of Hindu religious texts initially transmitted orally and then in manuscript form, which date back to the first centuries CE but continue to the present day. In fact, the word *purāṇa* itself means 'old', 'ancient', 'primordial'. They combine old and new literary and mythological material to construct devotional poetics associated with the main Hindu deities, integrating various local traditions or cults into a broader pan-Indian Sanskrit tradition.

20 I follow Sanderson's (1988: 660) definition of Śaivism as 'a number of distinct but historically related systems comprising theology, ritual, observance and yoga,

under the *tāntrika* wave (see below), dominating the religious landscape of the Indian subcontinent.[21]

The god Rudra, depicted in Ṛgvedic hymns as 'clothed in an animal skin, brown, with a black belly and a red back' (Flood 2003: 204), became better known in Upaniṣadic literature as Śiva, the 'Auspicious One'. The *Śvetāśvatara Upaniṣad* already manifested a form of theism centred on this Rudra-Śiva, but it is in the Purāṇas that different Śaiva groups are mentioned.[22] These included the Pāśupatas, Kālamukhas and the Kāpālikas who can be considered followers of the so-called Atimārga (the Higher Path).[23] These early Śaiva groups were initiatory—to have access to the teachings and rituals, an individual had to be initiated by a guru, who was a fundamental part of the path to liberation.

The Pāśupatas are probably the oldest Śaiva group and can be considered the prototype for subsequent Śaiva orders because of the traits that would later identify them: sexual abstinence, nakedness, matted hair, a body smeared with ashes, sleeping on dirt or ashes, and living in cremation grounds.

Most of the information on the Pāśupatas comes from a few texts, notably the *Pāśupatasūtra* preserved within Kauṇḍinya's *Pañcārthabhāṣya* commentary, dated to the 4th–5th century CE, but the group probably existed even earlier. They were worshippers of Maheśvara and regarded themselves as the *paśu* (cattle) of their *pati* (Lord/God), also identified as Rudra (Acharya 2011: 458). They believed in prescribed rules based on a strict code of ethics, called *yamas* and *niyamas*, in which sexual continence, *ahiṃsā* (non-injury) and *tapas* (asceticism) were crucial to securing union (*yoga*) with the Lord. The Pāśupata ascetic aimed to end suffering by achieving yoga with God: the yogi was indeed the one who realised

---

which have been propagated in India as the teachings of the Hindu deity Śiva'.

21 Sanderson (2009: 252) calls this period the Śaiva Age, because Śaivism 'legitimated, empowered, or promoted key elements of the social, political and economic process that characterises the early mediaeval period', and, by increasing its appeal to royal patrons, became the group that dictated the religious trends to which other groups had to adjust.

22 Some of these Śaiva groups were mentioned in the works of later philosophers, although not always with clear distinctions: Śaṅkarācārya mentions Māheśvaras, i.e. followers of Maheśvara (the Great Lord, one of Śiva's epithets); Vācaspati Miśra (c. 850) divides the Māheśvaras into four groups—Śaivas, Pāśupatas, Kāpālikas and Kāruṇika-siddhāntis; Yamunācārya (c. 1050) lists Śaivas, Pāśupatas, Kāpālas and Kālamukhas, and his disciple Rāmānuja (c. 1017–1137) repeats this classification (Lorenzen 1978: 1).

23 See Sanderson 1988: 664–667.

his identity with Maheśvara, which implied that the practitioner himself became the master (Īśvara) (Hara 1999: 595). The *sādhaka*s (adepts) were only brahmins but could access the path whenever they wanted, receiving the teachings from a preceptor, the *ācārya*.

It is likely that, while some Pāśupatas followed a rigorous ascetic system, others served a lay Śaiva community, performing rituals in temples, including those dedicated to other deities (Bisschop 2010: 485). While the *sādhaka*s were those who performed the various stages of the Pāśupata's path to liberation, the *ācārya*s were probably those who engaged with the community of worshippers who believed in Pāśupata's teachings but could not commit to the ascetic lifestyle. By managing temple properties, they gained followers among the laity and the patronage of rulers. Pāśupatas probably spread across the Indian subcontinent in the period between the 4th and 8th centuries, but then came into competition with Siddhānta Śaivism, which led to their gradual disappearance (Acharya 2011). Rather than a complete demise it was, however, a transformation because Pāśupatas' teachings survived and were transmitted by other groups: the Kālamukhas and the Kāpālikas, which lasted until around the 13th century.

The name Kālamukha may refer to the fact that adepts used to mark their foreheads with a black streak, while their body was covered by ashes. The Kālamukha ascetics were likely part of a section of the Pāśupata group, and doxographic material from southern India refers to their practices of bathing in the ashes of cremated people, eating these ashes and worshipping Rudra with alcohol (Sanderson 1988: 666). They flourished from the 11th to the beginning of the 13th centuries and, during this time, they became custodians and managers of temples, also collecting donations for their own *maṭha*s (monasteries). This information is only recorded in epigraphs; textual sources have not survived. It seems that the Kālamukha doctrine did not conflict with the Vedas and that their monastic training included sources such as the *Lākula-siddhānta* and the *Pātañjalayogaśāstra*,[24] which may explain why they were labelled as *śivayogī*s (Lorenzen 1972: 105). Once again, we can suppose that there were different actors in the group: those who maintained a relationship with donors and those devoted to esoteric practices.

As suggested by Andrea Acri (2018: 1), likely the term Kāpālika 'could have referred, according to the context, to ascetics belonging to a distinct sect, to one of the related suborders within the Atimārga (such as the Somasiddhāntins, the Mahāvratins, etc.), or to Śakti- or

24 See p. 104.

Bhairava-worshipping tantric practitioners who shared with the Kāpālikas the *kāpālikavrata* and other antinomian observances'. Probably originating from southern India or the Deccan, Kāpālikas appear most frequently in sources from the 6th to 12th century CE. However, since their works have not been preserved, it is difficult to separate fictitious elements from their possible reality (Törzsök 2011: 355). *Kapāla* means skull and, in fact, the Kāpālika used to carry or handle skulls in their religious routine. They were also known as Mahāvratins[25] as they practised the 'Great Observance' (*mahāvrata*), which consisted of emulating Bhairava—the deity they worshipped and another fierce aspect of Śiva—who beheaded the god Brahmā. As penance for killing his fellow deity, Bhairava had to live outside society for 12 years carrying a skull as an alms bowl. Consequently, the typical portrait of the Kāpālikas depicts them eating from a skull bowl (presumed to be that of the person they sacrificed) and worshipping their god with a pot of wine. Their practices were considered transgressive by mainstream groups, as they were said to perform human sacrifices with offerings of human flesh, blood and marrow and to practise sexual rites to obtain supernatural powers (*siddhi*). Furthermore, at the conclusion of their *mahāvrata* ritual, they aimed to be possessed by Bhairava, becoming God himself, which was their notion of final liberation.[26] Kāpālikas appear to have died as a recognised group by about the 14th century, probably assimilated by other Śaiva tantric orders such as the Kanphaṭās (or Nāths) or the Aghorīs, whom they closely resemble—for example, in the use of skulls and inhabiting cremation grounds.

Vaiṣṇava ascetic groups

The 1st millennium also witnessed the development of other traditions devoted to Viṣṇu, the 'All Pervasive'. Viṣṇu was a minor deity in Vedic religion. In some Brāhmaṇas, he began to be likened to Nārāyaṇa, the Supreme God, but it is mainly in the Purāṇas that mythologies and cosmologies centred on him developed.

Sanderson (2009: 58–60) argues that, from the 4th to the 7th century, the royal preference for Vaiṣṇavism was limited to the Bhāgavata faith, promoted and adopted by the Gupta kings. What we know of the history of the Bhāgavata cult is very fragmentary. According to Colas (2018: 300), the term *bhāgavata* was a socially valued name or title, but as it has had different connotations it is still difficult to say whether it pertained to a

25 On the various meanings of the *mahāvrata* ritual, see Lorenzen 1978: 73–82.

26 On Kāpālika, see Sanderson 2006; Törzsök 2011, 2020.

single community that developed over the centuries. The Bhāgavata tradition was associated with aristocratic patrons and probably was present in some areas of Madhya Pradesh and Rajasthan. The earliest approximately datable documentation is from the 2nd–1st centuries BCE. As Colas (2018: 296) points out, the *Bhagavadgītā* probably belongs or was affiliated with it. Unfortunately, evidence on the Bhāgavata cult is scanty, as the group is only mentioned in doxographies from the 7th century onward, often as a synonym for Vaiṣṇava.

Starting around the 2nd century BCE, Sanskrit literature documents forms of asceticism and yoga associated with devotion to Nārāyaṇa promoted by the Vaikhānasa and, later, the Pāñcarātra traditions. In Vedic texts, *vaikhānasas* are seers and sages in the lineage of Vikhānasa and are similarly described in the *Nārāyaṇīyaparvan*, a section of the *Mahābhārata*. The *Baudhāyanadharmasūtra* (c. 2nd century BCE) describes them as hermits who live in the forest, eat roots and fruits, do austerities and light sacrificial fires (Colas 2012: 590). The *Vaikhānasasmārtasūtra* devotes special attention to hermits and ascetics, arguing that the renouncer stage is reserved only for brahmins (Colas 2003: 236). The text also describes the role of the conduct of different ascetics: there are wifeless hermits who follow the dietary habits of renouncers and also practise austerities (such as standing perpetually on one foot, or holding their arms aloft), while others live with their wives but completely renounce fire sacrifice, and some are ecstatic and only seek spiritual liberation (Colas 2012: 591). The *Sūtra* distinguishes three classes of yogis, depending on the object of meditation and approach to the deity (Colas 2003: 237). It is worth noting that the Vaikhānasa *Vimānārcanākalpa* (c. 10th century CE)[27] is the first text to describe a non-seated yoga posture: *mayūrāsana* (the peacock pose). However, this text belongs to the Vaikhānasa 'tantric' literature. Here ascetic practices are absent, which denotes a change in the target audience: householders, or Vedic students who were to enter the temple priesthood. Whereas for the *Vaikhānasasmārtasūtra* the aim of the practice was spiritual liberation, Vaikhānasa tantric literature also promoted enjoyment in this life and in the other worlds, as supported by tantric approaches (Colas 2012: 592).

27 By the 9th century CE, inscriptions demonstrate that the word *vaikhānasa* identified a Vedic school, a medieval community of temple priests and hermits (Colas 2012: 590). From the end of the 10th century, mentions of Vaikhānasas became more prominent in South Indian inscriptions and, by adapting and changing identity and activities over the centuries, they were able to survive until the present (Colas 2012: 604).

Tantric movements

Tantric traditions probably emerged during the Gupta dynasty (320–550 CE),[28] but their roots are still uncertain. The word *tantra* literally means 'loom, warp or weave' and might suggest the 'knitting' of various traditions and teachings. Tantra should therefore be understood as a literary genre, although not all tantric texts are called Tantra. The term *tāntrika*, in fact, defined groups of texts produced as early as the 5th century by Śaiva groups and later by Buddhist and Jain, Vaiṣṇava and Śākta groups. *Tāntrika* was used to indicate a form of revelation and approach to ultimate reality different from the *vaidika* (i.e. Vedic). These texts were considered 'revealed' by deities: the Śaiva scriptures derived from Śiva's teachings to his wife Devī; Vaiṣṇava and Śākta tantric traditions were revealed by Viṣṇu and the Goddess, respectively. The transmission of these divine and timeless expressions would have been facilitated by accomplished masters (Siddhas) between the 7th and 13th centuries, when most of the tantric scriptures came to light (Gray 2016). These texts, often obscure, dealt with a wide range of topics, but mostly described codes of conduct, practices and rituals. These aimed not only at *mokṣa*, but also at *bhoga* (enjoyment of the world) and powers (*siddhi*).

Tantric traditions did not develop in a coherent, linear fashion; they manifested great diversification among ritual ceremonies, meditation techniques and the worship of deities. However, they all shared the idea that release from *saṃsāra* was compatible with the pursuit of material benefits[29]

28 The earliest reference to tantric practices is found in a 423 CE stone tablet inscription from Gaṅgdhārm in western Mālwa district, which refers to a temple to the mother goddesses. As Hatley (2012) points out, unlike other Gupta-era inscriptions that present protective World Mothers, this inscription is exceptional as it refers to the Mothers 'who make the oceans tumultuous through powerful winds arising from *tantras*', and associates them with *ḍākinīs*, a label used to refer to *yoginīs* in tantric textual sources.

29 In this section I focus on Śaiva tantric paths, but Vaiṣṇava tantric groups also developed, the Pāñcarātra, for example, among them. The origin of this tradition dates back to the 5th or 6th centuries or possibly earlier. However, Pāñcarātra scriptures are difficult to date due to a lack of early commentaries or manuscripts (Rastelli 2011). Its followers dedicated their worship to Nārāyaṇa and aimed at liberation as well as worldly pleasure. Fundamental traits of Pāñcarātra rituals and their path to liberation were devotion and the grace of God, as well as the doctrine of Viṣṇu's four *vyūhas*, four successive emanations which were simultaneously part of his essential nature. This doctrine seems to have evolved alongside the concept of *avatāras*, the descents of Viṣṇu on Earth. The Pāñcarātra, with its complex doctrines, rituals and devotional approach, influenced several Southern thinkers who

and transcendent powers. The Path of Mantra (Mantramārga) and the Path of the Clans (Kaulamārga) can be seen as expressions of this idea. They differed from the Atimārga in their deliberate quest for *siddhi*, which were not 'simply' obtained but intentionally sought after. To acquire them, individuals had to receive an initiation (*dīkṣā*) and specific knowledge about mantras and their powers. Mantras were, in fact, the key to the practice: they gave the practitioner a new ritual status through initiation; they were the tools to be used during spiritual practice; they were the means of securing powers. Tantric mantras ranged from *bīja* (seed) mantra to long 'garland-like' formulae of 20 or more syllables (*mālāmantra*) which embodied the tantric deities but were indecipherable to outsiders.[30] Liberation became possible through the guru and the mantras received and was offered not only to male brahmins but to people of all *varṇa*s and both sexes. The emphasis on feminine power (*śakti*) is another significant difference from the Atimārga.

Tantric goals required the deification of one's body. To this end, various tools were used. These included mantras; *maṇḍala*s and *yantra*s (geometric symbolic patterns); *mudrā*s (bodily seals);[31] ritually inscribing the physical microcosm with external macrocosmic elements and assigning icons and sounds to specific locations (*nyāsa*); meditation (*dhyāna*); and ritual worship (*pūjā*). The body was recognised as an important tool to be harnessed in practices that could make it divine, potentially leading to immortality. This notion had a great influence on the development of *haṭha* yoga (see Chapters 4 and 5).

The Mantramārgic texts constitute a huge corpus of works that falls into two groups: the relatively homogeneous canon of the Śaiva Siddhānta tradition and the heterogeneous corpus of non-Siddhānta revelations (Sanderson 1988: 668). They were widespread throughout India in the second half of the 1st millennium CE but were later restricted to the South.[32]

---

would lead the development of devotional Vaiṣṇava groups, such as the Rāmānuja *sampradāya*, which paved the theoretical path for the *sādhus* of the Rāmānandī *sampradāya*.

30 As Dominic Goodall and Hanuraga Isaacson (2014: 124) have pointed out, initiation and mantras were also required for Vedic sacrifices and for the Atimārga; however, 'these elements have been reconfigured and, in some cases, reinterpreted: the spells of the Mantramārga are with five exceptions (the five *brahmamantras*) not Vedic, and initiation (*dīkṣā*) is no longer simply a necessary rite of entrance into a new religion [. . .] but has become instead a transformative rite'.

31 These bodily seals are different from haṭhayogic seals; see pp. 150f.

32 As mentioned by Flood (2003: 217), by the 11th century the Śaiva Siddhānta had faded in Kashmir but developed in Tamil Nadu, where it has existed to the present time.

In the Śaiva Siddhānta, the Vedas remain authoritative and their distinction between purity and impurity was followed, while the non-Siddhānta rejected it (Sanderson 1995: 17).

The Śaiva Siddhānta Tantras were probably composed no earlier than the 5th century CE. Through daily rituals the initiated individual removed the impurity covering his soul: by purifying the body through the imposition of mantras (*nyāsa*) and through inner and outer worship, a divine body was created. This path could lead to the grace of Śiva (*śaktipāta*) and, with initiation (*dīkṣā*) to liberation. Once liberated, the soul, instead of merging with Śiva, was to become equal to him, sharing his powers of omniscience and omnipotence but remaining distinct from him (Flood 2003: 210–211). This was the path for the *mumukṣu*, the individual who desired *mokṣa* (in this context, liberation at death). However, another path was possible: that of the *bubhukṣu*, who wanted to enjoy worldly powers (*bhoga*). Those who pursued this goal had to undergo additional rituals and were technically called *sādhakas*.

The Śaiva Siddhānta priests, who constituted the mainstream of tantric traditions, accumulated prestige by performing public rituals in temples, widely disseminating tantric theories and practices, and shaping the routine of religious centres. While Śaiva Siddhānta rituals could be public, non-Siddhānta traditions focused on private worship, addressing both male (primarily Bhairava) and female deities (Sanderson 1988: 668–671). Around the 6th and 7th centuries, aggressive female deities, known as Yoginīs, became the primary object of worship of some antinomian groups that performed violent and sexual rituals at the cremation ground. These rituals aimed to produce polluted substances derived from copulation, because the more polluted, extreme and transgressive the ritual and its performers, the more powerful its results were believed to be.[33] The initiate had to join one of the *kulas* (clan, family) associated with one of the Yoginīs or Mother Goddesses who, if properly propitiated, were supposed to confer *siddhi*.

A significant body of Śaiva literature concerning the Yoginīs and their clans developed in the Kaulamārga, well established by the 9th century. Here, initiation was realised through possession by the Goddess and the consumption of impure substances; sexual intercourse with a consecrated consort was part of private worship, while sanguinary sacrifices during collective orgiastic rites were celebrated by the initiates with low-caste women (Sanderson 2014: 58). Sex was 'aestheticised' and orgasm was emphasised not as a means of producing offerings, but rather as a 'means of access to a

33 The use of sex is not present in all tantric traditions, but in those groups that have a Kāpālika origin (Padoux 2002: 20–21).

blissful expansion of consciousness in which the deities of the Kula permeate and obliterate the ego of the worshipper' (Sanderson 1988: 680). The consumption of meat and alcohol was a way of intensifying the experience and, consequently, a way to 'gratify the goddesses of the senses' (Sanderson 1988: 680).[34]

There is strong evidence that groups of itinerant renunciates and lay practitioners met at pilgrimage sites for ritual gatherings, especially those sites today known as *śākta pīṭhas*.[35] It was probably during these gatherings that some of the specific features of *kula* practice developed. Some ascetic couples may have attracted the attention of householder couples who wanted to be initiated without losing their status, especially if they were wealthy and in leadership positions. This may have led to the development of rituals tuned for an audience of householders (Samuel 2008: 254).[36] The wealthy individuals who, in general, turned to tantric initiation in search of immortality and powers included social elites and royalty. The fierce character of non-Siddhānta scriptures likely rendered them particularly attractive to those eager to seek supernatural assistance against enemies and calamities (Sanderson 2014: 31).

---

34 There were four Kaula sub-traditions: the Eastern transmission (Pūrvāmnāya) focused on Śiva and goddesses such as Kuleśvara and Kuleśvarī from which developed the Trika tradition; the Northern transmission (Ūttarāmnāya) presenting the fierce goddess Guhyakālī from which the Krama tradition developed focused on the goddess Kālī; the Western transmission (Paścimāmnāya) centred on the goddess Kubjika; while the Southern transmission (Dakṣiṇāmnāya) focused on the beautiful goddess Tripurasundarī. These traditions were well established in Kashmir by the 9th century (see Sanderson 1988: 682–690).

35 There are different lists of these *śākta pīṭhas*, although it is not clear how this network of pilgrimage sites arose. Today they are associated with the myth of Dakṣa's sacrifice and the self-immolation of Satī: Satī, outraged by the insult her father Dakṣa directed at her husband Śiva, who was not invited to the celebration of a sacrifice, decided to kill herself. When Śiva discovered this, he sent Vīrabhadra to kill Dakṣa, while he picked up Satī's body and wandered into the mountains consumed with grief, causing the collapse of the world. Viṣṇu then struck Satī's body with his discus, causing it to scatter on the ground in pieces; the places where the pieces landed, supposedly maintaining her divine presence, became *śākta pīṭhas*. On the *śākta pīṭhas*, see Urban 2010: 31–51.

36 A contemporary practitioner told me that Kaula lineages still exist but are kept secret to avoid the spread of the practices. He clarified that, although the practices are taught to couples, a single individual can perform them if he is unable to find the right partner. The only difference is that they will be less effective and take longer to be successful.

However, during the 10th century, groups of celibate renouncers countered these transgressive elements, which thereby became internalised and domesticated into contemplative exercises. This led to the later distinction in the tantric traditions between a 'left-handed' path (*vāmācāra* or *vāmamārga*), characterised by antinomian practices that involved the actual use of polluted ingredients,[37] and a 'right-handed' path (*dakṣiṇācāra*) in which practices and 'ingredients' were internalised (Bharati 1965: 228). A range of Śaiva ascetic groups adopted theories and practices from this tantric background alongside yogic and haṭhayogic techniques, as we will explore.

The presence of these several paths linked to tantric groups, often including the management of temples, led to tantric concepts, rituals and institutions becoming a fundamental part of India's social, religious and political life from the 7th to the 13th centuries. To be properly sustained, these temples needed groups of devoted followers. In these Śaiva groups, devotion (*bhakti*) was expressed as the grace of God descending on a person—which was a prerequisite for initiation—but also as devotion to one's own guru who, by conducting the ritual procedures and the teachings necessary for the individual's spiritual growth, was the representative of God on Earth (Katsuyuki 2011: 116–125). These tantric expressions of *bhakti* were, in part, sustained by the growth of popular devotional traditions. The symbiotic relationship between tantric groups and *bhakti* is particularly evident in the observation that, although the number and the importance of tantric groups declined after the 13th century, their rituals and techniques endured in *bhakti* milieux (Burchett 2019).

Bhakti movements

The word *bhakti* is derived from the Sanskrit root *bhaj*, meaning 'to share in', 'to belong to' or 'to worship', and is usually understood to mean devotion.[38] A theistic structure of *bhakti* can be traced back as early as the *Bhagavadgītā*, which claims that by God's grace individuals can attain ultimate liberation and become one with the Supreme God (18.54–56). However, this devotion was supportive 'only' of the ultimate goal, namely soteriological knowledge (*jñāna*).

37 This would be the *pañca-makāra-sādhanā*, or the *sādhanā* of the five 'Ms': *mada* (wine), *matsya* (fish), *māṃsa* (meat), *mudrā* (parched kidney bean and other aphrodisiacs), and *maithuna* (ritualistic copulation).

38 See for example Hawley, Novetzke and Sharma 2019: 6.

Both the early Śaiva and Vaiṣṇava movements attributed an important role to devotion,[39] but the form of devotion that this section analyses is grounded in personal experience and the pursuit of mystical union with the highest God, to be developed through self-surrender and an emotional approach. Movements centred on this idea of *bhakti* flourished from the 7th century CE onwards, dramatically influencing Indian religiosity and playing a fundamental role in shaping many ascetic orders. Each of the main deities of Hinduism (Śiva, Viṣṇu and the various forms of the Goddess) had distinct devotional traditions, although the Vaiṣṇavas, in particular, emphasised this approach as the means and goal of the religious path. For this reason, we will focus here on Vaiṣṇava devotional groups.

The word *bhakti* encompasses a wide range of movements and groups, geographically differentiated (Chandra 2003: 286), whose common characteristic—and innovation—was to worship by creating a mutual and intense exchange of love between the devotee and the deity. This devotion had a soteriological value in itself. Devotional groups were very successful because their religious paths were often open to all social groups and their practices were simpler and less ritualistic than tantric ones.

In the South, the spread of a devotional approach was carried out by itinerant poet-saints known as Ālvārs,[40] who composed thousands of devotional hymns in local languages. The Ālvārs regarded Viṣṇu/Nārāyaṇa—along with Śrī (divine feminine manifestation)—as the *paratattva*, or Supreme Truth; they used *bhakti* and *prapatti* (surrender) as a means to achieve the supreme life goal (*mokṣa*), and they deemed service to God and godly men an important duty of a true Vaiṣṇava (Srinivasa 1994: 20). In their poems, the grace of God was endless and transcended the laws of *karma* and caste, which is why there were women and *śūdra*s among them.[41]

Southern *bhakti* transformed the senses into instruments for attaining knowledge of God and establishing a passionate loving relationship with Him. Devotional *pūjā* became an external action of the inner yoga process, expanding the emotional features of the *bhakti* yoga taught by the *Gītā*. Around 850 CE, for instance, the *Bhāgavata Purāṇa*, composed in the Tamil area, strongly broke with Vedic religious ceremonies, declaring participation in devotional worship free from any qualification of birth or status.

39 See for example Katsuyuki 2011: 116–125.

40 The Śaiva representatives of the devotional current in the South were the Nāyanār, 63 Tamil saints who lived between the 6th and 11th centuries (see Little 2018). On Śiva *bhakti*, see Pechilis 2019; Ben-Herut 2019.

41 On caste and gender, see Pauwels 2019.

This *purāṇa* became a key text for *bhakti* currents, as it proposed a form of *bhakti* yoga capable of leading the devotee to transcend his individual self and develop an ecstatic love for the Supreme Being (see Bryant 2017; Gupta and Valpey 2013). The text codifies the necessary practices: listening to the names and stories of God to purify the mind (*śravaṇa*); chanting or reciting the names of God (*kīrtana*)—a practice related to repetition (*japa*) of the names of God; remembering God by constantly focusing the mind on Him (*smaraṇa*); serving at the feet of God (*pādasevana*); celebrating *pūjā* at the statues of God (*arcana*) to develop love; praising or showing respect (*vandana*); approaching Viṣṇu as a servant (*dāsya*) or friend (*sakhya*); and removing self-centredness and dedicating all actions to God (*ātmanivedana*).

In the 9th century, Nāthamuni (823–951 CE) collected Ālvārs' songs and preached their devotional approach, combining it with Sanskrit Vaiṣṇava sources. After Nāthamuni, the transmission was continued by Yamunamuni, whose main disciple was Rāmānuja (traditionally, 1017–1137 CE). This lineage is recognised as the foundation of the Śrī Vaiṣṇava *sampradāya*, to which the history of the Rāmānandī *sampradāya* is strongly linked. With Rāmānuja, *bhakti* entered the Vedānta school[42] and established itself as a means of attaining *mokṣa*.[43] In fact, *bhakti* was recognised by Rāmānuja as the only means to liberation, since ultimate release could only be achieved through the grace of God.

From the South, *bhakti* spread to North India. The growth of *bhakti* in popular movements[44] was facilitated, on the one hand, by the defeat of the Rajput states by the Turks in the 12th century CE, which limited brahmanical religious hegemony and, on the other hand, by the internal political stability that followed under the Islamic sultanates.[45]

42 Vedānta, literally the 'end of Veda', is a philosophical current which developed around interpretations of three main textual sources: the Upaniṣads, the *Bhagavadgītā* and the *Brahmasūtra* (400–450 CE). Over the centuries, however, various schools of Vedānta arose—structured around commentaries on these texts—differing from each other on the basis of their ontologies, with regard to such issues as the nature of *brahman*, the relation between *ātman* and *brahman*, the nature and the means of attaining *mokṣa*, and the status of the phenomenal world.

43 On Rāmānūja's Viśiṣṭādvaita Vedānta, see p. 80.

44 I support here the concept of *bhakti* as a 'popular' movement in the sense given by Lorenzen (2004: 4): a movement in which most of the followers (though not necessarily their leaders) come from middle- and lower-class groups and not from the elite.

45 It should not be forgotten that the rooting of *bhakti* groups in the North was facilitated by the presence of Sufism. While the arrival of Turkish rule caused the

Expressed mostly in vernacular poems and manuscripts,[46] carried and recited by itinerant ascetics, travelling singers, and scholars, *bhakti* circulated in public settings shaping a 'distinctive *bhakti* sensibility' (Burchett 2019: 17). This sensibility manifested itself in a multiplicity of groups expressing distinct theological attitudes pertaining to the nature of God as an object of worship: those with a brahmanical background preferred a *bhakti* directed towards an anthropomorphic manifestation of the divine (*saguṇa*), supported by a ceremonial apparatus. Others preferred a *bhakti* not oriented towards a specific, qualified God; rather, they addressed its name, without further attributes (*nirguṇa*). The *nirguṇa* groups—many of them led by individuals who would be known as Sants—were numerically smaller than the *saguṇa* ones, although John S. Hawley (1995: 175) assumes that there was probably no strict *nirguṇa–saguṇa* division in the early *bhakti* period.

The different *bhakti* groups manifested distinct attitudes towards social conventions, although even those with a more liberal approach remained tied to the religious context and never gave rise to a social movement. While *nirguṇa bhakti* rejected caste hierarchy and all conventions based on caste distinctions, *saguṇa bhakti* upheld the value of the caste system and the role of brahmins. It advocated devotion to a personal living God and rituals of idol worship, indirectly encouraging and reconfirming the need for brahmins as a social class. In general, tantric and *bhakti* movements made women, and others, equal in the eyes of the deity, but this equality did not extend to the economic or social level. The *bhakti* ideology, containing both radical currents and conservative forces, created the delusion of religious equality, which in reality did not allow for the access of lower-caste people into the ritual arena (Champakalakshmi 2004: 70).

---

collapse of tantric groups, devotional movements found a close association with Sufism. A section on Sufism is beyond the scope of this book as it does not consider relations between *sādhus* and contemporary Sufis. However, it should be pointed out that Sufis found inspiration from the yogic practices of lineages such as those of the Nāths (Burchett 2019). On the history of Sufi groups in India, see Alvi 2012; Eaton 1978, 1993; Parveen 2014; on their relationships with other religious groups, see Asher and Talbot 2006; and with Nāths in particular, see Ernst 2003, 2016.

46 Novetzke has stressed the fundamental role that *bhakti* movements (in both North and South) had in the spread of vernacular/local languages: vernacularity absorbed 'the very character of regionality, causing vertical social relations to be embraced within the quotidian world where the elite and non-elite meet. In this way, vernacularisation implicitly espouses a political theology of everyday life—the idea that theological concepts, when transferred to the quotidian world, come to embody central questions about everyday social relations' (Novetzke 2019: 92).

From an ascetic point of view, devotional approaches stimulated the spread of various religious orders founded by renouncers who made devotion and renunciation central to their teachings. The *nirguṇa* gurus opened up the ascetic path to individuals belonging to all castes (even out-castes), while the *saguṇa* gurus, despite advocating a liberal approach to devotion, were more concerned with brahmanical purity rules and created some restrictions on initiation or asceticism. Despite these differences, in these groups *bhakti* became the goal of religious life and the means to achieve it: it led to the grace of God, which led to *mokṣa*. *Mokṣa* itself could mean complete liberation from the cycle of rebirth, as well as attaining one of the heavens of Viṣṇu/Kṛṣṇa in order to continue to be devoted to Him. Since not all *bhakti* orders followed the same *sādhanā* or identified God in the same way, ascetic paths were highly differentiated, increasing the ascetic possibilities an individual could undertake.

However, this does not mean that ascetic groups (brahmanical, tantric or devotional) were properly organised at the pan-Indian level. As we have seen, some monastic communities appear around the 7th–8th centuries, but it is likely that they were locally circumscribed. This is understandable if we consider the structure of asceticism as based on the transmission of teachings (*sampradāya*) from gurus to disciples, thus creating small groups structured around different lineages (*paramparā*) which could spread in different areas.

In the previous sections, we have been introduced to various religious landscapes in general terms, some representatives of Hindu asceticism having been mentioned. The following sections will outline the main elements and roles that shape the general structure of ascetic organisations. These will form a useful platform for the next chapter, in which we will move from the more general to focus on specific orders.

Sampradāya, *paramparā* and guru

The term *sampradāya* refers to 'received doctrines or teachings' and, in religious contexts, it came to designate a 'tradition' or 'religious system'.[47] It is likely that a *sampradāya* was initially a general set of theories, practices and rules proposed by a guru to his disciples. Later gurus could improve on it

47 Analysing the term *sampradāya*, Squarcini (2008: 46) stresses that the word *-dāya* in its first occurrence was linked to the transfer or partition of goods. Therefore, etymologically the word *sampradāya* refers to an act of transfer.

through their own practices and achievements and then pass it on to their own disciples.

These guru lineages were called *paramparā*, which more commonly means 'one after the other', indicating an uninterrupted sequence. The *paramparā* was thus a succession of gurus and disciples that created a spiritual chain through which a body of practices, theories and rules was transmitted. The various *paramparā*s could form specific subgroups within a *sampradāya*. This *sampradāyik-pāramparik* aspect of Hindu religions[48] was and still is very distinctive and meaningful because it allowed, and allows, constant innovation: the teachings could be redefined and revised by each successive generation of gurus. It is therefore clear that the transmission of a tradition did not remain static as the teachings were constantly updated.

Prior to the organisation of pan-Indian communities, Hindu asceticism was based on these *sampradāya*s and their various *paramparā*s, which may have differed (also according to their geographical location)[49] but were all centred on the figures of gurus and their teachings. In fact, it was only in the 16th–17th centuries that pan-Indian ascetic communities were established. The presence of various lineages within *sampradāyas* allowed the individual seeking a religious path the possibility of looking at the different opportunities present in the ascetic environment. Moreover, the absence of strict institutionalisation allowed learning from different gurus to cross the boundaries of a *sampradāya*.[50]

The term 'guru' denotes a person with a high level of expertise in a particular field. In this book, the term is used to refer to a spiritual teacher, someone who has soteriological expertise and can teach it to disciples bound to him through initiation. But the figure of the guru as teacher and spiritual master is also a product of time, although the evolution of one type of guru did not necessarily supplant the others. In the Vedic period, for a guru to be recognised as such, he had to 'belong to the right family, and to know the particular texts by heart' (Broo 2003: 74). He was a teacher, and his disciples were *brahmacārī*s (celibate students). His main function was (and still is among those who continue to follow this tradition) to transmit the Vedic canon. It is in the early Upaniṣads that the word 'guru' takes on the meaning of spiritual master (Torcinovich 2007). In tantric contexts, the

48 This label is used by Kasturi (2010: 123).

49 See for example Bevilacqua (2018a: 59–97) for the geographical developments of the Rāmānandī *sampradāya*.

50 However, as I have already mentioned, and as the next chapter is going to show, not everyone actually had access to the ascetic paths.

guru was associated with the deity and the initiate was expected to accept his instructions because he had knowledge of the magic mantras and rituals necessary to achieve the identification with God. In the 7th and 8th centuries CE, the guru lived in institutionalised monastic contexts and was worshipped by ascetic disciples as well as lay communities and kings (Sears 2014: 173–174). In *bhakti* currents, on the other hand, the guru was someone who, having attained the grace of God, could act as an intermediary for the disciple. Clearly, there were no strict guidelines or univocal approaches toward guruship.[51]

Settled *sādhus*, *maṭhas* and patronage

The economic support, land grants and respect that the gurus obtained from donors, especially from kings, determined the development of monastic institutions, so that there were not just wandering ascetics or those living at the margin of villages and cities in hermitages, but also individuals living in monasteries. Communities of Hindu ascetics became institutionalised toward the second half of the 1st millennium CE through the construction of *maṭhas* (monasteries).

Religious leaders managed *maṭhas* that were not only places of religious learning but also intellectual, administrative and educational centres, involved in charitable activities such as feeding pilgrims and the poor and establishing hospitals, thanks to the patronage of royal supporters (Clark 2006: 183, 185). Patronage could stem from conversion[52] or pragmatism. Donating land to religious leaders was a way of allowing them to develop economically and culturally, without posing a threat to the ruling power. This attitude was advocated by both Hindu and Muslim rulers and can be interpreted as the 'consent-to-rule' described by Mahesh Sharma. Sharma (2009: 15) argues that, when a political power has cultural or religious symbols that differ from those of the local population it seeks to control, it builds its consensus through the co-existence of disparate symbols in order to receive the approval of the local population. In the contexts we are considering, political rulers gave support to religious communities to gain societal recognition. We can infer that *sampradāyas* with a broader social appeal attracted the

51 As shown by Antonio Rigopoulos (2009: 229), a text such as the *Gurū Gītā*, which glorifies the guru-*tattva* (the principle of the guru) as the absolute *brahman*, the model of devotion and knowledge, was popular throughout India and was appropriated by Śaiva, Vaiṣṇava and Śākta groups.

52 See Moran 2013; Asher and Talbot 2006.

attention of rulers and their donations, to the extent that religious centres could have several patrons from different geographical areas. This created a mutual dependence between royal and religious authorities: the royals relied on the religious authorities to implement their agenda, while the religious authorities benefited from royal patronage to promote their positions. However, because of this mutual dependence, tensions between these two spheres of power were not uncommon (Stoker 2016: 20).[53]

It was through the charisma of gurus and the subsequent centres or monasteries they (or their successors) were able to establish that *sampradāya*s and *paramparā*s could be transmitted and then codified. Changes in the historical context, then, often pushed *sampradāya*s toward a more precise definition of their identity in comparison to other groups and communities. As we shall see in the next chapter, this favoured the systematisation of Hindu religious orders throughout northern India, leading to their institutionalisation in the 17th century. This was also promoted through a vast production of texts in regional languages and hagiographic works (Stoker 2016: 21).[54] These textual efforts were produced by ascetics settled in monasteries, the so-called *sthānadhārī sādhu*s. But, as already mentioned, within each group there were different typologies of *sādhus* to cover different roles in a centre and in the *sampradāya*. As not all individuals could follow the same religious practice, even pragmatic activities such as managing a place or working for the development of the order could become spiritual disciplines—likewise, writing texts in honour of the respective *sampradāya* or engaging in military actions.

Wandering ascetics and armies

It was not unusual for wandering *sādhu*s to organise themselves into armies, the structures of which are still present (see next chapter).[55] John

53 Although it is true that the presence in the North of the Sultanate affected the role of religious specialists, the governments of the Delhi Sultans were pragmatic and developed a cooperative relationship with Hindu groups. This approach was maintained and strengthened in the 16th century during the rise of the Mughal Empire and its consolidation under Akbar, who was able to overpower the various Sultanates and Rajput principalities scattered throughout northern India.

54 This was especially true with the advent of movable-type printing, which favoured vernacular presses and the spread of popular books. See Lutgendorf 1994: 77.

55 Unfortunately, this fascinating topic has not attracted much scholarship; see, however, the work of Farquhar 1925; Orr 1940; Cohn 1964; Lorenzen 1978; Bouillier 1993; Pinch 2006.

N. Farquhar (1925: 436–437) argues that fighting ascetics were depicted in the chronicles of Rajputana, described as naked and devoted to the god Bhairava. The earliest reference we have is Bāṇa's *Harṣacarita* (7th century CE),[56] in which two ascetics supporters of Bhairavācārya (probably a Kāpālika from Deccan) join the personal guard of King Pushpabhuti of Sthanisvara (i.e. Thanesar).[57] It is likely that some groups of Śaiva ascetics[58] were hired as soldiers and later started travelling in companies, influencing other groups to organise their own warriors. The label for these ascetics was *yogī*, which began to be used as an adjective to define ascetics characterised by nudity, matted hair and ashes to cover their body.

The landscapes of warrior ascetics developed as more actors appeared, probably influenced by the military culture of the early modern age (Pinch 2020: 159). Although *yogī*s as a group were still present, there were also *gosains*, *saṃnyāsī*s (to label Śaivas), *fakīr*s (for Sufis) and *bairāgīs/vairāgīs* (for Vaiṣṇavas). At times, they were also identified as *nāgā* (naked; S., *nagna*) because warrior ascetics tended to wear little or no clothing.

The first properly documented clash involving warrior ascetics is the Battle of Thanesar, a Śaiva shrine located north of Delhi. In 1567, a fight broke out between two groups of Hindu ascetics, witnessed, but also 'directed', by the emperor Akbar. An account in Persian (Nizam-ud-din Ahmad's *Tabaqāt-i-Akbarī*) claimed that it was *yogī*s against *saṃnyāsī*s, while another (Abu'l-Fazl's *Akbar-nāma*) stated it was *purī*s against *kurs*, two sections of the then fledgling Dasnāmī *sampradāya* (see p. 56). The *yogī/kur* group received the support of the emperor and succeeded in defeating the *purī*s.[59] This battle proves the presence of organised ascetic

56 The *Harṣacarita* demonstrates that Hindu ascetics used to fight well before the arrival of Muslims and that, therefore, the idea that Hindu ascetics organised themselves to face groups of Muslim warrior ascetics is a projection of contemporary communal friction and a reinterpretation of Indian history.

57 See also Pinch 2006: 59.

58 Lorenzen reports that in the earliest epigraphic source in which Kāpālikas are mentioned (dated to 960–974 CE) under the Western Ganga King Narasimha III, they appear to 'be either religious mercenaries or simply battlefield scavengers' (Lorenzen 1972: 25).

59 The identity of these two groups is unclear, and the textual and visual material is simply too scarce and not entirely reliable to lead us in one direction rather than another. There are two main positions among scholars. According to Pinch (2006: 33–44), the *kurs* were *jogis* belonging to branches of the future Nāth *sampradāya* which were then included in the Dasnāmī *sampradāya.* He argues that Thanesar was an important Nāth pilgrimage place, and the term *kur* would identify *gir* (Giri), because the two terms appear almost identical in Perso-Arabic script. These

warrior groups, which means that they had probably existed for some time. Nevertheless, it was from the 16th century onwards that these groups began to increase in numbers to such an extent that, by the late 17th century, ascetic soldiers were employed as part of the infantry and cavalry by various rulers, accumulating power and wealth. As Pinch (2006: 70–71) notes, while at the end of the 16th century these groups were small bands of between 300 and 600 men specialised in close-quarter combat, later ascetic captains were able to form groups of 20,000 men, with greater tactical specialisation and variety of weapons.[60]

But why was there such a large number of warrior groups? Lorenzen (1978: 67) suggests that, during uncertain political periods, temples and monasteries, which had become similar to fiefs—and their *mahant*s (abbots) similar to local landlords—may have looked for support and protection, and this facilitated the creation of loyal ascetic armies to protect them from robbery or persecution. Pinch (1996: 29) adds social causes: a loosening of social restrictions to stimulate recruitment; the influx of peasants and others of low or marginal status into monastic communities; and the recruitment of *śūdra*s, untouchables and women. Ecological[61] and political shifts may also have led to the sale or abandonment of children to local institutions or families of landed magnates, enabling military slavery (Pinch 2006: 81).

Can we interpret the life of an ascetic warrior as a religious path? If we follow the words of the poet Padmākar,[62] who describes the deeds of Anūp

---

would be the *yogī*s, who were numerically disadvantaged although, according to Abu'l-Fazl, they were the ones to whom the place belonged by inheritance, while the *purī*s had settled later. On the other hand, Mallinson (2012b) believes that the *kur* and *purī* were originally Vaiṣṇavas and suggests that they were later included in the Dasnāmī *sampradāya*. He supports this by considering a visual representation of the battle (a Mughal painting) in which several ascetics wearing Vaiṣṇava *tilaka* are depicted and by the fact that the Purī surname is found only in Vaiṣṇava names predating the 16th century.

60 There are several reports from European travellers—for example, the records by Pietro Della Valle (see Grey 1892), Gemelli Careri (see Ser 1949), Marco della Tomba (see Lorenzen 2010), Francis Buchanan (see Pinch 1996)—that describe these wandering bands of *yogī*s, depicting them with matted long hair, and carrying 'swords, spears, iron-tipped staves and iron-discs' (Pinch 2020: 160).

61 The years 1554–1704 saw four major famines which put great stress on agrarian regions and caused numerous periods of dislocation and food shortages (Pinch 2006: 80).

62 In the late 18th century, Padmākar wrote the *Himmatbahādurvirudāvalī*, a poem about the deeds of Anūp Giri and Umrao Giri, two of the most successful warlords of that century. See Pinch 2018.

Giri, one of the most successful *gosains* of the 18th century, it would seem so:

> There are two types of men in this world who go on to pierce the beautiful disc of the sun: those who have been following the path of yoga by birth and fight with calm indifference, and those whose passion is roused by the battle and fights to the death then and there (Pinch 2020: 163).

Echoing the *Gītā*, these verses illustrate the possibility of fighting with detachment, remaining indifferent in the chaos of the battle. Ascetics were, indeed, considered the perfect soldiers, accustomed to physical disciplines and trained in austerities and itinerancy.

The warrior ascetics were organised into regiments and armies. These regiments were identified as *akhāṛā*, a word that can refer to a monastery, but especially to the training ground where martial arts are customarily practised in India, emphasising the physical training to which *nāgās* are subjected.

Warrior ascetics were probably very common in 18th-century North India, with some groups acting as mercenary soldiers, or even bandits (Pinch 2020: 159). They were often internally fluid: Pinch reports that in the deposition of 'Govindgeer', captured in northern Bengal in 1794, it is claimed that in his army there were 'four hundred Mussulmaun Fakeers, one hundred Hindoo Sonassies, four hundred Seapoys, twenty Byragies and the rest are people of different descriptions' (Pinch 2020: 166).[63] These ascetics competed for control of the pilgrimage routes, which allowed them to invest in urban landownership, moneylending and trading in luxury goods in urban centres (Cohn 1964: 175–183). Economic interests often led to clashes for power in strategic places, especially between *gosains* and *vairāgīs*. A major battle at Haridwar in 1760 is remembered to this day. Ghurye (1953: 126) reports that, according to one account, 18,000 people died, while the *District Gazetteer* of Nashik claimed 'only' 1,800 died.[64] From that point, the territory of Haridwar fell under Śaiva control. The Vaiṣṇavas were only allowed to return when the British took control of the town.

---

63 Deposition enclosed in C.A. Bruce, Judicial Officer, Cooch Behar, to George H. Barlow, no. 7 of 19 September 1794 (dated 27 August 1794), present in the British Museum, Bengal Judicial Department Criminal Proceedings. See Pinch 2020: 166n30.

64 Farquhar (1925: 449) reports of a Sikh cavalry in 1796 being under an Udāsī leader, attacking various groups of armed ascetics at Haridwar and killing 500 of them. On the relationship between Sikhs and Udāsīs, see Chapter 2, p. 82f.

Warrior groups flourished in the 18th century, when the Mughal Empire was collapsing and the exploitation by the East India Company had begun. However, the East India Company and subsequently the British Raj was to constitute the main threat to the power and activities of warrior ascetics: these warriors claimed the right to collect taxes from the villages they passed through on their seasonal wanderings and therefore jeopardised the Company's sovereignty. Initially allying with powerful *gosain* commanders, the Company soon turned to criminalising armed ascetics and suppressing ascetic bands in Bengal and Bihar, choosing to support devotional and monastic ascetic groups instead.

The fact that *nāgā* groups survived amidst the East India Company's monopolisation of armies in the late 18th–19th centuries—and continue to be an important component of both Śaiva and Vaiṣṇava orders—suggests that their contribution to religious life was, and is, more social than militaristic, providing a means by which low-caste individuals can enter ascetic groups (Pinch 1996: 29).

Conclusion

In this chapter, I have summarised the origins and earliest examples of Hindu asceticism, and highlighted two very important religious movements: the tantric and the devotional. In fact, Hindu asceticism developed in response to existential questions, particularly about the 'individual soul' in a macrocosmic frame. The emergence of theories about human actions and the cyclical process that led to rebirth, meant that one way of attaining liberation from this cycle of suffering was to renounce social life and worldly activity. This path to *mokṣa* was mainly reserved for high-caste men and was based on a cognitive transformation that produced liberating insight. Tantric and devotional movements, relating to the deities through new approaches, introduced other goals and opened their paths to a wider variety of people who did not necessarily have to undertake a renunciatory path to follow a *sādhanā*.

I have also tried to show that asceticism can be considered from the point of view of the individual or from the point of view of its centres, where ascetics also had a duty to maintain relations with secular society and patrons. These paths co-existed and collaborated to enable the survival of a tradition and its subgroups. All roles were fundamental. The settled ascetics living in monasteries could be renowned preachers, writers or caretakers of lands and temples, building stable bridges with lay people. Wandering ascetics could help by spreading teachings, developing and combining practices, creating the aura of mystery and charisma essential to attract the attention of householders and royals who, later, were also attracted to them by their valour in warfare.

The ascetic and the secular worlds have always been in dialogue, which is why various religious currents (brahmanical, tantric, devotional) have often proposed a path to liberation for householders as well, whether it was the *karma* yoga of the *Gītā*, the tantric *dīkṣā*, or the grace of God in *bhakti* movements. Asceticism probably originated in groups of celibate renouncers, but it developed over the centuries alongside the development of soteriological theories, manifesting itself through multifarious trends. In the 15th century, therefore, the subcontinent witnessed the presence of multifarious ascetic groups: ascetics closer to an adherence to brahmanical instructions and goals, hermits, tantric *sādhaka*s, Śaiva and Vaiṣṇava devotional ascetics, Sants, Buddhists and Jains monks, and Sufis. Their practices and ideas were not siloed, however, and inaccessible to one another: *sampradāya*s were in continuous exchange with each other, even on a competitive basis, to meet the religious needs of an always changing socio-political environment.

2
The Ascetic Path of Traditional *Sampradāyas*

The *sādhu samāj*, the society of *sādhus*, is composed of numerous groups (*sampradāyas*) and their subgroups (connected to different *paramparās*), each of which follows specific rules and has its own attitude towards the lay society and the divine. Each is recognisable externally by symbolic elements that show sectarian affiliation: the clothes worn; the *tilaka* (mark) applied to the forehead; the *mālā* (necklace); the specific greeting used.

The *sādhu samāj* can be considered a parallel structure to lay society, in which new forms of hierarchies and relationships are built. Individuals are recognised according to the *sampradāya* in which they are initiated, the lineage to which they belong, and their guru. The bond with the guru defines the 'ascetic family' of the individual: the guru is a spiritual father and his fellow *sādhus* are considered 'uncles' (H., *kākā*) by the disciple, while all the disciples of a guru become 'brothers' (H., *guru-bhāī*). In addition to these 'family' relationships, in a *sampradāya* there are other hierarchies that are manifested through the different roles a *sādhu* plays within it. There are *sādhus* who occupy high positions, becoming representatives of the *sampradāya* at a national or regional level (such as the *jagadguru*, the *mahāmaṇḍaleśvara*, and the *maṇḍaleśvara*; see below); others, known as *mahant*, who own *āśrams* or who manage and represent locally various centres of the *sampradāya*, just as there are *sādhus* who live in monasteries and spend their lives doing their *sādhanā* and *sevā* (service), and others still who wander in itinerant groups. Power relations can be present not only within the order itself but also among different *sampradāyas*.

Despite this, the ascetic world has proved to be very fluid. This chapter, by focusing on four *sampradāyas*, will highlight their characteristics, show that they share a common symbolism and, as we shall see in the following chapters, the same set of practices and a very similar way of understanding them. They are the Dasnāmī, the Nāth, the Rāmānandī *sampradāyas* and the Udāsī *akhāṛā*. They represent an important section of Hindu asceticism although they are mostly widespread in the north of India. I have focused my attention on these orders because they are traditionally connected to the practice and development of *haṭha* yoga and yoga *sādhanā*. In fact, they can be considered the heirs of religious movements and approaches analysed in the previous chapter. However, their historical development is not clear: they have a very complex past and an equally complex present. Firstly, it is difficult to define when these orders were established and by whom, since their supposed founders are often deified and their historical realities lost under layers of interpolations and interpretations. They only began to organise themselves on a pan-Indian level from the 16th century onwards, and it was mainly around the 18th century that a process of identity creation was refined.

Secondly, they do not have linear, homogeneous histories because the different *paramparās* that constitute them have often evolved separately, affected by the location of their centres and the social, political and religious events that occurred over the centuries and contributed to the local development of practices and approaches. Therefore, while we identify *sādhus* according to their *sampradāya*, ascetics identify themselves primarily through the branch they belong to and their *paramparā*. This means, for example, a Vaiṣṇava Rāmānandī will identify first as a *tyāgī* (see below), and then as a Rāmānandī. This depends on the importance placed on the guru–disciple bond and the *paramparā* that establishes the new life of an individual in the ascetic society.

In this chapter, I describe the aforementioned *sampradāyas* through a diachronic and synchronic approach: through secondary sources I will briefly frame their history, while through my fieldwork data I will provide information on their current status. This approach will enable the reader to connect the various *sādhus* that appear in this book to their specific orders, providing representations of 'real' rather than 'ideal' *sādhus*, while broadening the general understanding of who an ascetic is. By taking into consideration *sādhus*' accounts, I will address general issues—such as the reasons behind the ascetic choice, and who can undertake the ascetic path—and describe the guru–disciple relationship.

The Dasnāmī *sampradāya*

Dressed in orange, a *rudrākṣa* rosary hanging from the neck, three horizontal lines on the forehead and a staff or a trident in hand: this is the typical portrait of a *saṃnyāsī*, and the image that most often comes to mind when imagining renouncers in India. As we saw in the previous chapter, the *saṃnyāsī* is *the* renouncer according to brahmanical texts on asceticism. Today, this tradition is represented by the Dasnāmī *sampradāya*, the largest Śaiva ascetic order in India.

Highly differentiated in its organisation and composition, today the *sampradāya* claims descent from Śaṅkara, the 8th-century philosopher of the Advaita Vedānta. According to a widespread tradition, Śaṅkara is said to have established four monasteries (*maṭhas*), based on the four directions: in the north, the Jyotir (Joshi) Maṭh located in the town of Badrinath (Uttaranchal); in the south, the Śṛngerī Maṭh in Sringeri (Karnataka); in the east, the Govardhana Maṭh in Puri (Orissa); and, in the west, the Sāradā Maṭh in Dwarka (Gujarat). He is also said to have united various groups of *saṃnyāsī*s under ten 'names' (which is why the *sampradāya* is called *das* 'ten', *nām* 'name'), most of which recall places: Giri represents the mountain or hills; Pārvat the snowy mountains; Sāgar the sea; Purī the town; Sarasvatī the institutions and teachers; Bhārtī all of India; Van the forest; Araṇya the grove; Tīrth the holy place; Āśram the place of refuge. These names are still used today by *saṃnyāsī*s to identify their 'family' within the *sampradāya*.

However, this entire tradition needs to be revisited, especially the figure of Śaṅkara. Several authors[1] have demonstrated that Śaṅkara was more likely a Vaiṣṇava, or had a Vaiṣṇava religious background informed by Pāñcarātra, rather than being a Śaiva. From the mid-14th century onwards Śaṅkara was probably envisioned as a Śaiva by the authors of his early hagiographies to meet the demands of Vijayanagar patrons.[2] However,

1 Neveel 1977; Alston 1980; Hacker 1995, Clark 2006.

2 Advaita Vedānta, indeed, gained political respectability and became prominent in Vijayanagar in the 14th century, thanks to Vidyārayana, a reputed author and mentor of the funders of the Vijayanagara Empire, who declared *pārampārik* link to Śaṅkara and to the temple complex of Śṛngerī (see Pinch 2006: 37). Note that the *saṃnyāsī* Manimaheś Bhārtī claimed that the Śṛngerī Maṭh was Vaiṣṇava before

the earliest hagiographies do not mention that Śaṅkara established four *maṭhas* nor that he founded a renunciate order. While Anantānanda Giri's *Śaṅkaravijaya* (dating from after the 14th century) claims that Śaṅkara had 12 disciples, the works that immediately follow state that he had four main disciples and that he only founded the *maṭhas* of Śṛngerī and Kāñcī. It is between the 16th and 17th centuries—when the *maṭhāmnāyas*, short Sanskrit texts attributed to Śaṅkara—were produced that we find the attribution to Śaṅkara of four disciples and the foundation of the four *maṭhas*. The *maṭhāmnāyas* proclaim the conquest (*digvijaya*) of the four quarters by Śaṅkara, his foundation of monasteries and also the foundation of an order of ascetics with ten lineages (Clark 2006: 225). It is in these texts that the ten Dasnāmī names are linked to the four *maṭhas*, outlining, perhaps for the first time, a Dasnāmī identity.

But what is the origin of these ten lineages? That is a difficult question to answer, due to the lack of textual sources and, often, the reinterpretation of the past through mythological perspectives or current values.[3] According to Pinch (2006: 38), this tenfold enumeration is related to the process of incorporation and institutionalisation that took place in northern India, when regional varieties of ascetic practices and styles evolved into a more cohesive and institutional form of monasticism. In fact, there are no references to the ten names before the 16th century. This is not to say that these lineages—some of which probably had no real connection with the Advaita Vedānta tradition—came into being at this time, but rather that they were brought together under a unified organisation (that of the four *maṭhas*) in this period. An early presentation of the ten names is found in the *Dabistān-e Mazāheb*, a Persian work probably composed around 1655, the author of which describes the religious groups in South Asia, including ten groups of *Sanyásis* (which are not called Dasnāmī):

> [. . .] Ban, A'ran, Tīrthah, A'shram, Kar, Parbatah, Sākar, Bhārthy, Perī and Sarsatī. They are frequently holy men, and abstain from eating flesh, and renounce all intercourse with women. They are said to follow the dictates of Datāteri, whom they also venerate as a deity, and say that he is an incarnation of Naráyan, and in the retaining of breath attained to such a degree that he is exempted from death [. . .] There are two classes of Sanyásis: the one, the *Dandaheri*, do not wear long hair, and are attached to the

becoming Śaiva, and because of this he believed that Vaiṣṇava *sampradāyas* were more ancient than the Śaiva ones.

3 To give a simple example, in 2017, I was told by a *nāgā saṃnyāsī* that Śaṅkarācārya was born before Christ (2,500 years ago) but that he also organised the ten orders to protect the Hindu Sanatana Dharma from Muslim invasions.

> precepts and regulations of the smriti or of the law: the second are the *Avadhùtas*; they are like the other class, they wear the zunar, and drink water mixed with ashes [. . .] they let their hair grow so that it becomes like ropes, and this they call juta; they do not bathe every day, and rub their head and body with ashes, which they call bhabùt [. . .] Some of this class of men of consideration and opulence, are escorted by files of elephants; they have carriages, fine apparel, courtiers, servants on foot and horseback (138–148).

Interestingly, the two classes described in the *Dabistān* are still present today. They represent the two possible paths to become a *saṃnyāsī*: the path of the *daṇḍī*s and that of the *nāgā*s (*avadhùta*s in the text) from the *akhāṛā*s.

*Daṇḍī*s are renunciates who carry a single staff (*daṇḍa*). They are all brahmins who have accomplished their social and domestic duties and retired in old age to pursue religious goals. However, a *brahmacārī* (celibate student), especially if attached to one of the four *maṭha*s, can become a *daṇḍī saṃnyāsī* without going through the householder stage: if he declares his decision to remain celibate for life, he can become a *naiṣṭhika* (eternal) *brahmacārī*. He will take one of the names Svarūp, Ānanda, Prakāś or Caitanya, which are related to the four main *maṭha*s, and continue his studies. After a training that usually goes from one Kumbh Melā to the next (lasting 12 years), he can then get the *saṃnyāsa dīkṣā*, taking a new surname (Āśram, Bhārtī, Sarasvatī or Tīrth)[4] just as *daṇḍī*s do.

The *saṃnyāsa dīkṣā* is the main Dasnāmī initiation, both for *daṇḍī*s and future *nāgā*s. During this initiation a *virajā homa* (rite of purification) is performed, through which the individual renounces his previous life, as well as brahmanical *saṃskāra*s (sacraments) and rituals. The topknot (*śikhā*) of hair is cut off and the sacred thread (*janeu*) is definitively removed. Then, the initiate performs his own funeral ritual to celebrate his death in the transient world, officially entering the Dasnāmī family.[5] It is through this ritual that the individual becomes a *saṃnyāsī*. Thereafter, the *daṇḍī* is given his new surname.

---

4 I thank Gianni Pellegrini for clarifying the path of the *brahmacārī*s and for pointing out that it is not uncommon that, after a period of apprenticeship, a *naiṣṭhika brahmacārī* may decide to enter a *sampradāya* that is not necessarily that of the Dasnāmī. I also thank him for his explanation of the *daṇḍī*s (personal correspondence, 20 May 2020).

5 I was told that *saṃnyāsī*s see all men as walking dead: the difference between a *saṃnyāsī* and others is that the *saṃnyāsī* decides to die to society before his body is dead, realising the impermanence of life.

*Daṇḍī*s follow the path of knowledge (*jñāna*), the study of the texts but also meditation. The highest stage of achievement is recognised by the title *paramahaṃsa* (supreme self), which identifies an individual who has attained the absence of *bheda* (distinction) and is capable of recognising the supreme principle in everything. There is, however, also a lineage called *paramahaṃsa*, which pertains only to persons from the three main *varṇa*s.

While the *daṇḍī*s follow the procedures of the Śaṅkara's *maṭha*s and are known as *śāstradharī*s, dwellers specialised in sacred doctrine, the *astradharī*s are those who specialise in weapons and are also known as *triśūldharī*s or 'trident users' or *nāgā* (naked) *sādhu*s. The latter belong to the *akhāṛā*s.[6]

In 2016, Ravīndra Giri, a *nāgā saṃnyāsī* from Varanasi, described these two paths in this way. He said

> There are two *sādhanā*s that we follow: in one people ask and we explain, we give knowledge, but if after explaining someone continues to misbehave, then the *daṇḍa* [staff] comes: we punish them [...] these two *sādhanā*s are *śāstra* and *astra*. If it is not understood with words, then with swords. And this is what the *nāgā saṃnyāsī*s do.

The *nāgā*s' military structure is, in fact, their distinguishing feature.

In the previous chapter we mentioned that *gosains* were Śaiva *saṃnyāsī*s who fought for the protection of their religious orders but also acted as mercenaries, traders and bankers, acquiring considerable wealth and influence. They were divided into *akhāṛā*s, of which, today, there are seven: the Mahā Nirvāṇī, the Aṭal, the Nirañjanī, the Ānanda, the Jūnā, the Āvāhan and the Agni.[7]

It is difficult to ascertain when these Śaiva military groups were established, since no records exist. A Hindi manuscript in the possession of the bards of the Nirvāṇī *akhāṛā*, found by J. Sarkar, potentially dates their foundation. Sarkar (1930: 83), however, acknowledges the limits of this

---

6 Dazey (1990: 303) suggests *nāgā*s were probably a separate Śaiva sect that converted to Advaita philosophy in the early medieval period, but he does not provide any evidence to support his claim (see also Clark 2006: 67).

7 It is interesting to note that, in British documents from 1882 concerning the organisation of the Magh Melā in Allahabad (*General Department North, Western Provinces and Oudh*, Proceedings Volume 1882 U.P. State Archives, Lucknow, p. 11), the Śaiva *akhāṛā*s listed as attending the holy baths are: '(1) Nirbani, (a Nanga Goshain), (2) Niranjani, with whom were associated the Junni'. Most likely this represented a major division because, at least today, the Ānanda *akhāṛā* is linked to the Nirañjanī *akhāṛā*; the Āvāhan and the Agni to the Jūnā; and the Aṭal to the Mahā Nirvāṇī.

source: it was no more than 50 years old at the time (although it may have been transmitted orally for much longer), and represented the tradition of only one *akhāṛā*, allowing the possibility that different bards from different *akhāṛās* sang different songs. He does nevertheless supply the given dates and suggests that a thousand years have been omitted from each. Such an adjustment, however, gives bizarre results. According to this calculation, the Nirañjanī *akhāṛā* was founded in 1903 CE, yet there is evidence of its presence in the Kumbh Melā of 1840. Clark (2006: 57–58) cites other sources, such as the Hindi newspaper *Āj* (14 January 2001), according to which the foundation dates of the *akhāṛās* range between 547 and 1149 CE.[8] Still, there is no evidence to support this dating.

Each *akhāṛā* is assigned a tutelary deity: the Jūnā has Dattātreya, although it is said to have previously had Bhairava; the Āvāhan *akhāṛā* has Siddha Gaṇeśa; the Nirañjanī has Kārtikeya (the son of Śiva and Pārvatī); the Ānanda has Sūrya; the Mahā Nirvāṇī has the sage Kapila; the Aṭal has Gaṇapati and the Agni has Gāyatrī. According to Ghurye (1953: 117–119), the *mahants* of the Mahā Nirvāṇī were prominent and famous ascetics, which is why the *nāgās* of the Mahā Nirvāṇī lead the procession for the holy bath during the Kumbh Melās and enter the water first.

There is a further subdivision into *maṛhis*, a vernacular form of the word *maṭha*. There are 52 *maṛhis* divided among the ten families: four *maṛhis* for the Bhārtī and the Van, 16 for the Purī and 27 for the Giri. These subdivisions are particularly useful in organising camps during the Kumbh Melā, suggestive of the military past of these groups, which are also notable for their hierarchical structure.

Although the Dasnāmī world is dominated by the Śaṅkarācāryas, the chiefs of the four *maṭhas* attributed to Śaṅkara,[9] the *akhāṛās* are structured differently and have appointments of their own: at the apex are the *ācārya*

8 More specifically, the Āvāhan in 547 CE, Aṭal in 647 CE, Nirvānī in 649 CE, Ānanda in 855 CE, Nirañjanī in 904 CE, Jūnā in 1060 CE and Agnī 1149 CE. These are closer to those proposed by Sarkar if the thousand-year adjustment is ignored.

9 Given the power associated with the figure of the Śaṅkarācārya, today there are several *maṭhas* claiming to have been established by the philosopher and, as a consequence, more people assuming the Śaṅkarācārya identity. However, there are currently four *official* Śaṅkarācāryas, three of which are: Śrī Niśalānada Sarasvatī for the Govardhana Maṭh, Śrī Bhārtī Tīrtha for the Śṛngerī Maṭh and Svāmī Sadānanda Sarasvatī for the Sāradā Maṭh. Since 1953 there has been a dispute about the succession of the Śaṅkarācārya seat for the Jyotir Maṭh. It would appear that Svāmī Avimukteśvarānanda Sarasvatī currently holds this position. It should be mentioned that the Kāñcī Maṭh also claims to have been funded by Śaṅkara. This is, however, a highly controversial site, the heads of which (first Jayendra

mahāmaṇḍaleśvaras, followed by *mahāmaṇḍaleśvaras*, *śrī mahants* and *mahants*. In all *akhāṛās* there is an administrative body called the *śrī pañca* or *pañcāyat*, the members of which (*śrī mahant*) are elected every six years and led by a *sabhāpati* (president). Below the *mahants* is a hierarchy of other elected officials: *thānāpatis* (property managers), *koṭvāls* (guards), *pujārīs* (who perform ritual worship), *kārbārīs* (assistants), *sacivs* (secretaries) and *koṭhārīs*/*bhaṇḍārīs* (who manage daily supplies). The *ācārya mahāmaṇḍaleśvara* does not always belong to the *akhāṛās*. According to Ghurye (1953: 123), *nāgās* used to entrust their 'spiritual' leadership to the *paramahaṃsas*, but their role was then taken by the *mahāmaṇḍaleśvaras*.[10] A *maṇḍaleśvara* or *mahāmaṇḍaleśvara* (someone whose disciple has become *maṇḍaleśvara*)[11] is a crucial presence during the initiation, as only he can perform the *saṃnyāsa dīkṣā*.

To become a *nāgā* the individual must undergo several initiations. The first is called *pañca guru saṃskāra* because the initiate acquires five gurus: one who will give the secret mantra for the *sādhanā*; one to give the *laṅgoṭī* (loincloth); one to give the *vibhūti* (ash); another the *mālā* (rosary); and the fifth a sacred thread.[12] This initiation complete, the individual is considered a *mahā puruṣa* (great person/self). After a period of apprenticeship (traditionally 12 years) the most committed will move on to the *virajā homa* initiation, described above. The individual will then be known as *saṃnyāsī* or *avadhūta* (someone who is beyond ego consciousness, duality and common worldly concerns). It is during the *virajā homa* that the two sections of the Dasnāmī *sampradāya* come together: both prospective *daṇḍīs* and prospective *nāgās* are initiated by the same *ācārya mahāmaṇḍaleśvara* during the Kumbh Melā (Clark 2006: 68).

If the *avadhūta* is deemed fit to become a *nāgā*, he must undergo another ritual, which starts by standing for 24 hours near the *akhāṛā* flag in the Kumbh Melā camp. Afterwards, the guru will pull the disciple's penis three

---

Sarasvatī and latterly Vijayendra Sarasvatī) have been the subjects of scandals and allegations.

10 According to Sarkar (1930: 92), from around 1800 CE the word *mahāmaṇḍaleśvara* replaced the title *paramahaṃsa*.

11 Ghurye (1953: 123) points out the intriguing etymology of the word, which means the lord of the *maṇḍala* (region), alluding to the previous politico-administrative value of the charge.

12 The bestowing of a sacred thread could derive from the fact that many prospective *mahā puruṣas* come from low castes, and will not have undertaken the *upanayana* ceremony. However, since entering *saṃnyāsa* entails renouncing brahmanical rules, this ascetic thread could represent a temporary access to Brahmanism that is discharged with the *virajā homa*.

times, in three directions, breaking the membrane under the skin, in a ceremony called *ṭāng toṛe*, or, literally, 'broken leg' (Clark 2006: 98). The individual is then considered fully initiated into the *akhāṛā*.

As mentioned in the previous chapter, *akhāṛās* have a long history of including individuals from a variety of social backgrounds, which is why, even today, most of them accept people of all *varṇas*, some are open to female ascetics and, since the late 1960s, also to foreigners.[13] The Jūnā is the *akhāṛā* with the largest number of female ascetics, and during religious gatherings it establishes a section called the *māī bāṛā* (H., mother's enclosure) where 'grassroots' *saṃnyāsinīs* gather, while influential *sādhvīs* may have their own camp. However, a number of women from the *māī bāṛā* have complained to me that they do not receive the same treatment as their male brothers and that they are on the lowest rung of the ascetic hierarchy.[14]

To complete the description of *saṃnyāsīs*' physical appearance with which we began this section: the necklace (*mālā*) they wear is made of *rudrākṣa* seeds (*Elaeocarpus ganitrus*); they may carry a staff (if they are *daṇḍīs*) or a *triśūla* (trident), and the *tilaka* that they apply on their forehead is made of horizontal lines (*tripuṇḍra*), to which red dots can be added—one in case of *daṇḍīs*, and up to five (three in the centre of the forehead and two at the side) for *nāgās*.[15] Traditionally, *nāgās* were naked or covered in *vibhūti*, but today they wear saffron-coloured clothes, especially when in public spaces. Dasnāmīs greet each other with 'Oṃ Namo Nārāyaṇ'.[16]

---

13 As told to me by Gianni Pellegrini (personal communication, 20 May 2020), in the past *mahants* were unwilling to offer complete initiation to foreigners who could obtain only the *mahā puruṣa* status. Today, things have changed for reasons that I have fully analysed elsewhere (Bevilacqua 2020).

14 Rarely, Indian female *saṃnyāsinīs* were, and are, able to occupy important positions. One such exception is Gītā Bhārtī, the first Indian woman to be elected as *mahāmaṇḍaleśvara* of the Nirvāṇī *akhāṛā* in 2001. This appointment makes her one of the spiritual leaders of the *akhāṛā*, bestowing the right to initiate males into the order. However, any attempt to promote a female *akhāṛā* has been quashed by the *akhāṛās* (see Bevilacqua 2017b; DeNapoli 2019). On female ascetics, see the end of this chapter, p. 92.

15 A *sādhu* from the Āvāhan *akhāṛā* explained these dots to me: the one on top represents 'Oṃ Namo Nārāyaṇ'; the lower one the *śakti*, the one in the middle the *mahā śakti*, and those on the side *mātā* and *pitā*, thus forming a kind of spiritual family.

16 It is a point of interest that this is a Vaiṣṇava greeting. As noted by Mallinson (2012b: 20), this is an 'ancient Vaiṣṇava *aṣṭākṣara* salutation taught in a wide range of Dharmaśāstra texts'. The use of this greeting is also seen by Mallinson as evidence that Vaiṣṇava lineages were absorbed into the Dasnāmī *sampradāya*.

From a theoretical point of view, *saṃnyāsīs* follow the Advaita Vedānta to seek spiritual liberation through the acquisition of *jñāna* (knowledge) of one's true identity—that is, the identity of *ātman* and *brahman*. The self (*ātman*) is considered equal to the highest metaphysical reality (*brahman*), transcending all forms of duality in the state of consciousness. Since the *brahman* is present in every human being and every life (*jivātman*), all living beings are considered spiritually interconnected. The reality is *brahman*, but the transient reality is *māyā* (appearance), which is always changing and spiritually misleading. Duality is caused by misunderstanding *māyā* as a spiritual reality. *Avidyā* (ignorance) is at the root of human suffering: the purpose of the individual is to achieve *jīvanmukti* (liberation during life) by realising the *ātman-brahman* identification through self-knowledge. This can occur through *anubhava* (immediate intuition), a direct awareness free from constructions. Since *brahman* is ever-present, knowledge of *brahman* does not require ritual actions, but the cultivation of virtues, mental disciplines and metaphysical knowledge. It follows that, for the Advaita Vedānta, the state of celibacy and renunciation are the fundamental conditions by which to pursue this path of learning to attain *mokṣa*.

Saṃnyāsīs, however, do not exclusively follow this path and, as we will see in the next chapters, *akhāṛās* provide several alternatives in which more psychophysical practices, such as yoga and *tapasyā*, are included. Furthermore, male and female ascetics of the *akhāṛās* follow a specific ceremony that takes place morning and evening and binds the ascetic to his/her guru: the disciple goes before the guru (or someone higher in the hierarchy if the guru is not present) and looking straight into his eyes he or she recites a specific mantra. The guru maintains this eye contact and recites the mantra in response. This is an important moment during which, I was told, an 'unspoken' transmission takes place and a special bond and trust is created in the order.

Since *saṃnyāsīs* celebrate their funerals during the initiation, they do not need to be purified by the fire of the funeral pyre; therefore, they are not cremated once they die: rather, their body is buried or simply left in a river.

To conduct my research among Dasnāmīs, I focused my attention mainly on *nāgā sādhus* because of their physical training and because it is among them one is most likely to find ascetics who perform yoga and austerities. I worked especially with *sādhus* from the Jūnā *akhāṛā* as it is the largest, with centres spread all over northern India, but I also had interlocutors from the Āvāhan, Aṭal and Nirañjanī *akhāṛās*.

The Nāth *sampradāya*

Historically known as Yogīs, the ascetics belonging to the Nāth *sampradāya* are traditionally associated with the practice of yoga. Therefore, I will pay particular attention to this group and its history, although, as always, it is difficult to reconstruct its past or origin because historical evidence is scant and the events and changes it underwent were very complex and remain unclear.

Traditionally said to have been established by Guru Gorakhnāth (see below), it is more likely that, initially, there was no unified, pan-Indian Nāth order,[17] but rather disparate lineages of yogis that followed different local traditions and were continued by descendants of Śaiva esoteric and tantric orders, namely Pāśupatas, Kāpālikas and Kaulas. Some lineages met and mingled with other traditions, such as that of the Siddhas, drawing on esoteric practices that used physical techniques (especially breath control) and alchemical manipulation (Bouillier 2008: 6).

Although the Sanskrit word *nātha* (lord, master; H., *nāth*) is commonly used today to refer to members of the *sampradāya*, the term is not found in pre-modern literature describing a specific group, and the followers of those lineages later known as Nāth *sampradāya* were simply referred to as 'Yogī' or 'Jogī'.

The legendary figures of the Nine Nāths, the deified and immortal teachers of the order, and the Eighty-four Siddhas are central to the history and cult of the *sampradāya*. The term *siddha* means 'perfected' and denotes semi-divine human beings renowned for their powers (*siddhis*) and antinomian behaviour that resulted from mastery of yoga, alchemy and other esoteric practices. Legends about Siddhas transcend sectarian boundaries and Siddhas with the same names are found in lists belonging to both the Kaula and Buddhist traditions—so much so that some scholars have hypothesised a Buddhist origin or strong Buddhist influences on the Nāths' ancestors.[18] As pointed out by Mallinson (2011b: 410), the features attributed to the Siddhas are also present in the Nāth *sampradāya* and the names of some Siddhas recur in the lists of the Nine Nāths, but these lists may

---

17 Vijay Sarde (2023: 21–36), using early vernacular sources in Marathi, demonstrates that 'an institutionalised form of the Nath Sampradaya had fully emerged in Maharashtra during the 12th and 13th century' and became predominant in Western India (Gujarat and Maharashtra).

18 For a summary of the scholars who have debated this issue, see Mallinson 2019: footnote 2; the author also presents an engaging discussion about the connection between Vajrayāna Buddhism and Nāthism in South India.

differ. The identity of the Nine Nāths is therefore not fixed, although there is a shared belief that the tradition originated with Ādināth, the 'Original Nāth' later identified as Śiva or one of his manifestations, who transmitted his teachings to Matsyendranāth.

According to one of the best-known legends about Matsyendranāth, he was able to hear Śiva expounding the doctrine of yoga to Pārvatī while he was in the belly of a fish and the divine couple was on the seashore.[19] Matsyendranāth transmitted it to Gorakhnāth, who developed it further with the practices of *haṭha* yoga. That said, it should be considered that Gorakhnāth likely lived in the 12th century and Matsyendra in the 9th. Mallinson (2011b: 412) suggests that Matsyendranāth lived in the Deccan (southern India) and was probably a follower of the Kaulamārga, specifically the Pūrvāmnāya (Eastern) and Paścimāmnāya (Western) lineages, since several texts associated with these traditions—involving sexual and antinomian practices—are attributed to him.[20]

The figure of Gorakhnāth (or Gorakṣa) is also very mysterious; scholars disagree on both the date and place of his birth.[21] The first reference to him dates back to the 13th century: he is mentioned in many *paramparās* related to tantric Śaiva schools and appears in an inscription found in the Kalleśvara temple, in the state of Mysore (Karnataka) (1279 CE). Later references come from Nepal, Maharashtra, Punjab, Rajasthan and Bengal.

There are numerous legends involving Gorakhnāth, Matsyendranāth and his various disciples (see Muñoz 2010: 55–109). This guru–disciple relationship is of particular interest because in several stories Gorakhnāth is depicted rescuing his guru 'from a brood of women among whom he was frolicking, oblivious of his Yogic condition' (Bouillier 2013: 159). This has been interpreted by some scholars as a metaphor to describe the shift from sexual tantric practices of the Kaula tradition to their sublimation into inner practices for celibate ascetics.[22] The fact that *Gorakṣaśataka* 101 claims: 'If we must have intercourse, it takes place in a mind dissolved in the void, not in the vagina', would demonstrate this intention (see Mallinson 2012a).

19 There are several legends about the origins and life of Matsyendranāth; see Muñoz 2010: 55–80.

20 See for example the *Matsyendra Saṃhitā*, analysed by Kiss (2021).

21 As summarised by Bouillier (2013), there are scholars like Mallik (1960), Dasgupta (1976) and White (1996) who suggest a Punjabi origin for Gorakhnāth; Briggs (1938) suggests he was from eastern Bengal while Mallinson (2011b) locates him in the Deccan.

22 See also Mallinson 2019: 272.

An account by Ibn Battuta testifies to the presence of Jogīs in Delhi and around Khajuraho in 1342 CE. However, the earliest references to Gorakṣa in northwestern India date back to 1480 CE (Mallinson 2011b: 412). At that time, the Jogīs' lineages of northern India did not refer to Gorakṣa but to another guru, Jālandharnāth.[23] Horstmann (2014) argues that Nāth Yogīs 'in the sense of ascetics paying allegiance to a genealogical line of Nāths with Śiva as the supreme Nāth' emerged in written sources from the 13th century onwards, but their identity remained fluid for a long time, overlapping with that of various other ascetic groups.

By the 16th century, vernacular sources attest to the existence of a Nāth community at an advanced stage of consolidation, consisting of often itinerant ascetic groups, competing for status and patronage with *saṃnyāsī*s, *bairāgī*s, and Sants. In this same period, Gorakṣa became the tutelary 'deity' of Yogī orders also in the Gangetic plain (Mallinson 2011b: 17). Gorakhnāth's fame and teachings seem to have overshadowed those of other Yogīs, and various texts on *haṭha* yoga—such as two of the earliest, the *Vivekamārtaṇḍa* and the *Gorakṣaśataka*—as well as a heterogeneous corpus of verses in vernacular languages, have been attributed to him. The link between the Nāth *sampradāya* and yoga/*haṭha* yoga seems unanimously accepted in the ascetic society, and this explains why its members were (and are) those traditionally known as Yogīs.

Since the techniques of *haṭha* yoga also aimed at obtaining superhuman powers (*siddhi*s) and control over natural phenomena, a multifarious body of stories and legends about the Yogīs developed, which also attracted the attention and support of kings (see Muñoz 2022). This is especially true in Nepal, where powerful Siddhas and Yogīs were (and are) revered as protectors of kingdoms.[24] Royal support, as well as the support of Muslim emperors, could turn Nāth Yogīs into landlords, powerful priests and political advisors. These roles have survived to the present day, adapting to new political scenarios.[25]

---

23 For example, the lineage of the Jogī kā Tilla monastery, today in the Pakistani Punjab and one of the most important monasteries until Partition, was traced back to Jālandharnāth, until the 17th century, after which point it became known instead as Gorakh kā Tilla (Mallinson 2011b). The Udāsī Bhole Bābā said to me that Matsyendra and Jālandhar were both born from the semen of Śiva which fell in the water: in the case of Matsyendra it was swollen by a fish; in the case of Jālandhar it simply went into the water. During fieldwork, it was interesting to note how some popular stories related to specific *sampradāya*s were well known even among others.

24 See for example Bouillier 1992, 1997; Zotter 2018, 2022.

25 See Bouillier 2008; Bevilacqua and Stuparich 2022.

The oldest form of organisation of the order divides it into 12 *panth*s (H., path), accounting for its other name Bārahpanthī (Twelve Paths). Mallinson (2016c) reports that a list of 12 Yogī *panth*s is to be found in the *Nujūm al-'ulūm*, an illustrated encyclopedia completed around 1570 CE and commissioned by the rulers of Bijapur. The aforementioned *Dabistān* also refers to the presence of a religious group of Yogeśvaras divided into 12 sects.

During our fieldwork trips, Professor James Mallinson and I visited the ancient caves of Panhale Kaji[26] (Maharashtra) and the gates of Dabhoi (Gujarat), dating back to around the 12th century, where we verified the presence of carvings of 12 Nāths, which suggests that this 12-*panth* schema may be much older (Mallinson 2016c).[27] The history of the *panth*s is complex: different lists, as well as different names and numbers of *panth*s appear, to the extent that the sub-sects exceed 12 in number. Therefore, rather than actual groups, these likely represent the names of schools (*paramparā*s) of individual gurus with their followers (Briggs 1938: 62). Briggs cites a tradition according to which there were initially 18 *panth*s of Śiva and 12 of Gorakhnāth. These two groups fought each other and as a result many *panth*s were destroyed: only 12 survived to form the order of the Gorakhnāthīs (Briggs 1938: 63). Groupings of 18 and 12, however, are still seen in the organisation of the *jamāt*, an Arabic word meaning 'group', 'community'. Indeed, Nāths can be both *sthānadhārī* (settled) and *ramtā* (itinerant). Those who wander are often associated with the *jamāt*. Today, there is a single *jamāt* consisting of a hundred or so Yogīs who continuously travel together following an itinerary based on Nāth places and festivities. The *jamāt* is run by two *mahant*s: one would represent the so-called *aṭhārah panth* (the path of 18) and the other the *bārah panth* (the path of 12).[28]

Today, Nāths are grouped under the Akhil Bhāratvaṛsīya Avadhūt Bheṣ Bārah Panth Yogī Mahāsabhā (Pan-Indian Association of the Yogi Renouncers of the Twelve Panth), an association established in 1932 by Yogī

---

26 Situated on the Konkan coast of Maharashtra, the site consists of a series of caves initially used by Buddhist monks and later occupied by Śaiva and Nāth ascetics (see Deshpande 1986). The reliefs showing the 12 Nāths date back to the 13th–14th centuries CE (see Mallinson 2019).

27 Īśnāth said that there is also a half-*panth*—that of the 'middle-sex'—by which he was referring to *hijṛā* (today also known as *kinnar*s). Considering that *hijṛās*/*kinnar*s often share the crematory grounds with Aghorīs and Nāths (see Bevilacqua 2022b), it would be interesting to further investigate the existence of this half-*panth*.

28 On the organisation and activities of the *jamāt*, see Bouillier 2008: 35–40.

Digvijaynāth, the *mahant* of the Gorakhpur monastery (Uttar Pradesh) with the aim of uniting all lineages and Yogīs under one authority.[29] Indeed, the Yogī Mahāsabhā has established the official list of the 12 *panths*,[30] linking each *panth* to a disciple of Gorakhnāth (Bouillier 2008: 32–35).

To become a Nāth, an individual must go through two initiations. The *sampradāya* was (and still is) open to everyone. Yogī Śivanāth, the *mahant* of an ancient Nāth *āśram* near Bhubaneswar (Orissa), stated that Nāths do not belong to the Hindu caste system (*varṇa*). They are '*pañcambar*, a term which is not in the *śāstra*, since it was said by Gorakhnāth', he said, meaning that they come from a fifth *varṇa*, the Rudra *varṇa*, and that they follow a fifth *āśrama* which is that of the *avadhūta*. This means, Yogī Śivanāth pointed out, that Nāths are actually beyond the constraint of the *varṇas* and the four *āśramas*, they do not follow the Vedic attitude (H., *ved bhāv*), they pay respect to all and have no restrictions in initiation.[31]

In the Nāth *sampradāya*, too, there are five gurus for the initiation, although two are the most important: the one who cuts the *coṭī*, the tuft of hair left at the top or back of the shaven head, and the *cīrā* guru—the guru who splits the ears—who is important for the second initiation. In the first initiation the disciple is shaved and given a *śelī*, a long black thread, twisted according to precise rules, to which a *rudrākṣa* seed is tied. Also tied to this is a flat ring made of metal, wood or bone and a small whistle or horn called *siṅgī*, which has been an attribute of Yogīs from at least the 10th century onwards.[32] The *siṅgī* is also called *nād* from the sound it produces (S., *nāda*), which is thought to be the sound of the *kuṇḍalinī* rising in the body of the Yogī. Usually, it is blown during morning and evening worship and before meals. Following this, the mantra-guru gives the disciple a new name and reveals to him the *panth* to which he will be affiliated. The disciple also receives the initiation of the ashes (*vibhūti*), which he will apply to his forehead while he also receives the initiation of the clothes. The adept is now called *aughaḍ* and must continue his ascetic training to verify if he is

29 For information about the Mahāsabhā charter and the features that describe the Nāth *sampradāya*, see Bouillier 2008: 25–32.

30 These are: Satyanāthī, Dharmanāthī, Rāmnāthī, Bairāg, Kapilāṇi, Āīpanthī, Naṭeśvarī, Gaṇġanāthī, Rāval, Pāvpanthī, Mannāthī and Pāgalpanthī.

31 As we will see in Chapter 7, this has opened the door to foreigners, especially those interested in yogic practices. See also Bevilacqua 2020b.

32 The earliest textual reference to the *siṅgī* is a description by Ibn Battuta, recorded in 1361 CE, but a statue of Matsyendranāth wearing an antelope-horn *siṅgī*, dated to the 10th century by the Government Museum of Mangalore, testifies to its earlier use (Mallinson 2019: 8n51). See also Bouillier 2008: 103.

suitable for the ascetic life. Traditionally, this stage lasts 12 years. The nature of an *aughaḍ* is not entirely clear and probably varies according to regions or 'countries'. According to some Nāths, since an *aughaḍ* is not complete, he can be either a *sādhu* or a *sāṃsārik* (H., worldly) person, because, if he does not want to pursue the ascetic life after training, he can go back and get married, leaving the *sampradāya*. Others claim an *aughaḍ* should be considered a prospective renouncer and cannot leave the *sampradāya*.[33]

There are *sādhus* who remain in the *aughaḍ* stage. This may happen for one of several reasons: there are lineages that do not include the earrings initiation (see below); there are *sādhus* who do not want the *kuṇḍal* because they are afraid of the ceremony; and there are *sādhus* whose guru has died before they could be declared ready for the second initiation. The latter are generally called *aughaḍ pīr*, with the word *pīr* coming from Urdu and meaning 'master', 'lord'. This is an interesting detail that highlights a typical Nāth feature: several Nāths declare themselves to be neither Hindu nor Muslim, and that Gorakhnāth had several Muslim disciples, including the famous Ratannāth, also known as Haji Ratannāth for having made a pilgrimage to Mecca.[34]

The second initiation is the one that gives Yogīs the name Kanphaṭā. This initiation consists of splitting both ears (H., *kan phaṭnā*) in order to insert the large round earrings (called in Hindi *kuṇḍal*, *darśan* or *mudrā*)[35] which, for centuries, have been symbols of this *sampradāya*.[36] The incision is made in the thick cartilage of the ear and is performed in private, just the guru and the disciple. This ceremony is called the sacrament of the incision

33 In all my experience I have never met a *sāṃsārik aughaḍ*.

34 On Ratannāth, see Bouillier and Khan 2009; Bouillier 2003, 2015.

35 The *mahant* of the Bartrihari *guphā* of Ujjain stated that the *kuṇḍal* proves that the Nāths received the teaching directly from Śiva: they are indeed the only group that wears earrings similar to those worn by the god.

36 Mallinson (2016c) has listed the 13 insignia commonly attributed to Yogīs in vernacular texts, namely the *Cāndāyan*, *Mirgāvatī*, *Madhumālatī* and *Padmāvat*: ash (*vibhūti/bhasma*), rosary (*japa-mālā*), staff/crutch (*daṇḍa/baisākhī*), skin/tiger-skin (*chālā/kesari-chālā/baghachālā*), bowl (*khappara*), earrings (*mundrā*), meditation crutch (*adhārī*), horn (*siṅgī*), patchwork cloth/cloak (*kanthā*, *cirakuṭā*), discus (*cakra*), wooden sandals (*pāṁvarī*), ascetic's viol (*kiṁgarī*), *rudrākṣa* seeds. Other additional insignias were: bag (*kothī*), thread (*śelī*), yoga-belt (*jogauṭā*), trident (*triśūla*), girdle (*mekhali/mekhala*), matted locks (*jaṭā*), puzzle (*dhandhārī*), water-pot (*udapāna*), loincloth (*kachauṭā*), parasol (*chātā*), red clothes (*bhesa kai rātā*). Many of these are common among ascetics.

(H., *cīrā kar cheḍnā saṃskār*) and was explained to me in detail by Yogī Śivanāth.[37]

A channel (*nāḍī*) inside the ear is cut (H., *cheḍnā*) to enable the ascetic to maintain his *brahmacarya* and, thus, the stability of his mind. But not all gurus can do it: only those who know Ayurveda and the *nāḍīs* system.[38] Those who make the cut use a specific knife and recite a specific mantra while cutting. After the cut is made, a small piece of *nīm* tree (*Azadirachta indica*) is inserted into the wound to prevent infection and the *sādhu* is isolated.[39] After nine days, *kuṇḍals* made of clay, washed with Ganges water, are inserted.[40] During these nine days, the *sādhu* is considered a *navanāth svarūp*, a form of the Nine Nāths, which is why people go to see him. For 41 days he stays indoors[41] and eats only *sudu halvā* (a sweet), ghee or *sūjī kā halvā* (another sweet). At the end, he goes out and exchanges his clay *kuṇḍal* for others made of gold, silver or stone.[42] Those who receive *kuṇḍals* are called *kuṇḍaldhārī* or *darśanī*: *kuṇḍals*, in fact, are given to those who have experienced the *ātman darśan*, the vision of the soul, i.e. self-realisation; thus they symbolise the *siddha* (perfected) Yogī. However, Yogī Śivanāth admits that anyone can attain them today.

After this initiation, the ascetic may add the title Yogī before his *sādhu* name. While an *aughaḍ* may go and ask for alms (*dakṣiṇā*) at a hundred houses (*soghārī*), a Yogī may go to only nine (*nogharī*). Yogī Śivanāth also said that a Nāth Yogī is identified by the *śelī* and the *siṅgī* as described above, the *jaṭā* or dreadlock, the *jholī* (a small bag), the clothing of Bhagvan (god),

37 The procedure can also differ slightly; see Briggs 1938: 32–33.

38 It is said that, if the cut is not properly done, the individual, even after years have passed, can develop physical problems and in some cases even die. On Ayurveda and its link with *sādhus*, see Chapter 7, p. 287ff.

39 Nāth jī whom I met in Kamakhya in 2017 said that some *sādhus* cover their ears all the time to avoid infections, and that, at the beginning, the cut is so painful that the new Yogī will have problems turning his head properly.

40 Nāth jī called these earrings *yog daṇḍa*. He said that they weigh 100 g, the necessary weight to enlarge the hole. The aim is to render the *kuṇḍal* perfected (*siddha*). Some Nāths, in order to make their *kuṇḍal siddha*, continue to wear clay earrings of different weight (80 g, then 50 g) for 12 years, following specific rules, such as not bathing in rivers, not removing flowers from trees, not blowing the *śaṅkh* (H., conch), in order to protect the earrings as they are quite fragile.

41 Nāth jī said that during this time the *sādhu* follows an *aghorī kriyā*, which means that for the entire time he won't bathe, wash his hands with soap or change his clothes.

42 Nāth jī claimed that the exchange of earrings has to happen secretly, with the head covered so nobody might see the Yogī.

the *kuṇḍal* in the ears and the ashes on the body.[43] 'Ādeś' is the greeting used by the Nāths, meaning '[please give me your] order' (Mallinson 2011b).[44]

Regarding female initiation, I was told that in India a woman can only be initiated by a female Nāth guru.[45] For this reason, there are not many female Nāths; however, those I met told me that once they join the order, there is no gender distinction and a woman and a man may sleep and stay in the same place, which is otherwise impossible in the *akhāṛā*s. This was later confirmed by their male brethren.

Nāths wear yellow-saffron robes like the Dasnāmīs, but those who follow or consider themselves on the path of the *avadhūta*, or who are *aughaḍ pīr*, may also wear black clothes. Īśnāth, an *aughaḍ pīr* living in Nepal, made this clear. He wears only black and, being part of the Āī *panth* which is considered to be the *panth* originated by a female disciple of Gorakhnāth (Āī could stand for Māi; see Briggs 1938: 67), he also applies the *kājal* on his left eye. Speaking of the colour black he said: 'This is a colour of my *sampradāya*. It is not my wish, it is because it was given to me by my guru. He was an *aughaḍ*. Black is for the *aughaḍ*.'

Like other ascetics, Yogīs often wear turbans of different shapes. Itinerant Nāth ascetics, mostly from the *jamāt*, cover their body with ash and are almost naked, especially during specific ceremonies.

Although they have wandering groups, today the *sampradāya* does not have an *akhāṛā* branch, which seems rather anomalous considering that there were armed ascetics in all the main *sampradāya*s. This is a controversial issue that could be closely linked to the organisation of the Nāth *sampradāya* between the 16th and 17th centuries (Mallinson 2011b). Both Pinch (2006) and Ghurye (1953) state that groups of warrior Yogīs were 'simply' assimilated by Dasnāmīs. Ghurye mentions some subgroups of the Jūnā *akhāṛā*, named Sūkhada and Gudada by H.H. Wilson (1976 [1861]: 148–149), and Sukhads and Ukhads by Grierson (1918: 866–867), who argues that they were 'all

43 Yogī Śivanāth pronounced this saying: '*śelī, siṅgī, sirjaṭā, jholī, Bhagvān bhes, kan kuṇḍal, bhasm se, Śiva Gorakh Ādeś*'.

44 According to Sarde (2023: 27), the word *ādesu* appears twice in the Marathi source *Līlācaritra*, in the description of Nāth Yogīs.

45 This is not true in Nepal, where several gurus 'run away' to have female disciples. But the reality is complex: as a Yogī from Haryana told me, if an average ascetic gives initiation to a woman, he will have to pay money to the *sampradāya*, he will have to give a *bhaṇḍārā* (feast) and a double *dakṣiṇā* (money offering). If he cannot afford this, then he is excluded from the *sampradāya*. However, the most powerful gurus can give initiation to women without any particular consequences. In other cases, the female disciple is simply hidden away to avoid criticism.

Śaiva mendicants, yogis, said to have been branches of Aughat or Oghar sect of yogis founded by Brahma Giri, a Gujarathi disciple of Gorakhnath'. Wilson says that the Gudadas wear earrings like the Kanphaṭā Jogīs or a wooden cylinder passed through the earlobe (in Ghurye 1953: 119–120). Another similar group is that of the Alakhiyā,[46] which today is considered part of the Dasnāmī, but, according to Ghurye (1953: 122), for 'observances and practices [. . .] were originally [. . .] Yogis or Nāthapanthi ascetics'.

If we consider again the miniature of the Battle of Thanesar (see p. 49), among the various warriors depicted there are some wearing the *siṅgī*. Although we cannot consider this visual representation proof of what actually happened there, we can nevertheless interpret it as a visual repertoire which the artist had of the ascetics who used to fight, among which there were Yogīs. Not only are some ascetics depicted wearing the *siṅgī*, but other items usually worn by Yogīs can be seen, such as the peculiar patchwork robes or the headband round the top of the head (see Losty 2016: 3). Lorenzen (1978: 46) adds to the discussion the fact that, before having Dattātreya as tutelary deity, the Jūnā *akhāṛā* was known as the Bhairava *akhāṛā*.[47] Pinch (2006: 40) considers the connection between Nāths and Dasnāmīs by looking at other interesting evidence: around 1300 in

46 Interestingly, these subsections no longer exist, with the exception of the Alakhiyā: there is in fact a moving *akhāṛā*, also known today as the Alakh Nirañjan, composed of individuals who gather during religious festivals, wearing tunics, hats with feathers and a rope around their waist. As Clark (2006: 66) argues, they are often married and have the special role of singing and playing the drum during *melās*, proceeding from one Dasnāmī *dhūnī* to another, collecting money and flour in a skull-shaped coconut container, also used among Nāths.

47 The link between Dattātreya and Gorakhnāth is an interesting one: the aforementioned *Dabistān* (vol. II, 139–140) tells of a contest of yogic power between Gorakhnāth and Dattātreya: '[. . .] Datáteri, for the sake of trial, smote Gorakhnath on the head, who took the appearance of iron. Datáteri told him: "Thou hast not done well, there is not striking iron". When Gorakhnath himself bade him to combat, Datáteri glided off from the body, in the same manner as water glides off, and reunited safely again. [. . .] Afterwards, Gorakhnath disappeared in the water; Datáteri, having found and recognised him in the shape of a frog, brought him forth. When Datáteri concealed himself in the water, Gorakhnath, in spite of all his searching, could not succeed in discovering him, because he was mixed with the water, and water cannot be distinguished from water'. Another story would be synthesised by the saying '*Dattā Gorakh ek māyā, bīc men aughaḍ samāyā*'. This refers to the picks present at Mount Girnar in Gujarat: among five picks, there is one of Gorakhnāth (the highest of all), one of Guru Dattātreya, and the middle 'is filled' (*samāyā*) with another called Aughaḍ Shikar, which would represent the in-between status of the *aughaḍ*. And in fact, at Girnar, Dattātreya, besides being

Ayodhya, a monastery demonstrated a shift 'from preceptors whose names ended in Nāth to preceptors whose names ended in Giri'. A similar change occurred in the lineage of *mahants* of a shrine at the Chunar fort. These shifts can be interpreted as an absorption or as one order ousting the other from its place, as Rāmānandīs did with the Nāths of Galta.[48]

Historical evidence of armies of Yogīs is provided by Ludovico di Varthema who, travelling in India between 1503 and 1508, met the 'king of the Jogis' who was married and had children, and many of the Yogīs with him were armed. However, there are also several accounts of travellers describing unarmed Yogīs, like that of Duarte Barbosa in 16th-century Delhi, and those describing celibate Yogīs, such as the records of Pietro Della Valle in Ahmedabad in 1620 (see Pinch 2006: 57, 62). Therefore, we can assume that there were probably individual Yogīs who fought, as well as some armies. However, some of these armed groups were absorbed by the Dasnāmīs, prompting other leaders (who might be the ancestors of today's *mahants* of the *jamāt*) to avoid any armed competition while maintaining their independence and security. This could also be a consequence of the reorganisation of the *sampradāya* on a pan-Indian scale, which started in the 16th century and lasted until the 19th. It was during this period that power was concentrated in monasteries located in the north, with the exception of the Kadri Maṭh in Mangalore (Karnataka).[49]

According to Mallinson (2016c), the establishment of a pan-Indian Nāth order was 'marked by the wearing of hooped earring through the cartilages of the ears rather than the lobes' which, to go by Mughal paintings, were not worn before the 18th century. However, Monika Horstmann, examining vernacular sources produced by other religious groups around the 15th–17th centuries, has shown that Yogīs and Yoginīs are repeatedly described wearing earrings after having their ears split.[50] Since split ears were at the time 'a stock motif in popular poetry' taken for granted at the beginning of the 16th century, this presupposes, according to Horstmann (2014), a long

connected with the Aghorīs, is linked to Western Nāthism and worship of the Devī (see Rigopoulos 1998: 98).

48 See Bevilacqua 2018a: 80–84.

49 On Kadri Maṭh, see Bouillier 2008: 57–147.

50 For example, in the *Padmāvat* (written by Jāyasī in 1540 CE), a Yoginī talks about herself saying 'I have split my ears and inserted *mudrās*' (601.6), which, according to Horstmann (2014), means that 'she does not wear the earrings in her lobes, but that she has split ears, that is, split cartilages' otherwise she would 'need not be expressly mentioned in a distinctly yogic context'. Furthermore, Sundardās (disciple of Dādū, 17th century) in his *sākhī* (anecdote) 16.23 describes Yogīs as *kana pharāi* which means 'by splitting one's ears'.

process that began much earlier. Mallinson (2016c) responded to this argument by saying that, in depictions of Nāth Yogīs from the Mughal era (and earlier) period, Yogīs wear hooped earrings in their earlobes so large that they would require the lobes to be cut off rather that the usual piercing.

According to Yogī Śivanāth, originally Nāths had earrings in their lobes like many others, but when Guru Gorakhnāth gave initiation to King Bhartṛhari, the latter asked him what was the difference between a Nāth and a snake charmer (H., *saperā*). Gorakhnāth then decided that the Nāths would be those with the ears cut in the middle. Yogī Rudra Nāth also placed the change at the time of Bhartṛhari, when his guru Jālandharnāth decided to create a distinction with the *aughaḍ*.[51]

It is very difficult to compare these sources (visual, textual, oral), but what can be deduced is the importance of these earrings and, I will add, the importance of maintaining the ears intact. From my conversations with Nāths, it emerged that, if the ear is completely fragmented (H., *khaṇḍit*; in this case, split in two), the Yogī must undergo *jīvit samādhi*[52] and, if he does not want to, he must 'go home'. We can assume that the presence of this rule prompted individuals to cut their ears in the thickest part, rather than the earlobe (because that would have been too risky). However, it is also possible that different lineages wore earrings in different ways and that eventually one custom took over. In general, I was told that, in order to become a Yogī, an individual cannot have a 'fragmented' body part. This rule may have been instituted to discourage Yogīs from fighting and may also explain the numerous groups of householder Nāths that exist.

As several studies have demonstrated,[53] householder or *gṛhastha* Yogīs are quite numerous throughout India. In the colonial census they were considered a caste the members of which acted as 'bards and musicians, priests of small temples dedicated to Bhairava or to the Devī, magicians (with powers over locusts or hail), and weavers' (Bouillier 2013). Is it possible that these *gṛhastha* Yogīs represent 'fallen' or *khaṇḍit* individuals, who then had to begin their own tradition? Or, instead, do they represent a legacy of married Yogīs present in the South and belonging to the Kaula groups mentioned in the previous chapter? According to Śyām Ānanda Nāth, a Kaula follower, the Nāth *sampradāya* has, in fact, two paths: one

51 It is not unusual that different Nāth interlocutors associate Bhartṛhari with different gurus. As Briggs (1938: 65) points out, in several traditions Bhartṛhari was initiated by Jālandharnāth but was also a disciple of Gorakhnāth.

52 *Jīvit samādhi* means a *samādhi* while still alive, but probably in this case would mean to leave the body (die) before its time.

53 See Gold 1999, 2002; Gold and Gold 1984; Freeman 2006.

for renouncers established by Gorakhnāth and one for householders established by Matsyendranāth.

From a religious point of view, Nāth Yogīs combine several approaches. They worship Ādi Śiva in his *nirguṇa* form, which is commonly associated with concepts of being without distinction, without form (*nirākāra*), permeating the body and the world. Because they follow Śiva *nirākāra*, the order does not worship a specific deity. Yogī Rudra Nāth said that it is very rare to find a Nāth in a temple in the morning doing *pūjā*, because Nāths do *pūjā* at their *dhūnī*/*dhūnā* (firepit). As owners of a *dhūnā* (*dhūnādharī*) they perform *pūjā* at Gorakhnāth and at their sacred *dhūnā*. A Nāth saying claims: 'There are many people, but only one *dhūnā*.'[54]

Nāths are especially associated with yogic powers and tantric practices to purify and transform the body in order to perfect it and, in doing so, overcome the process of rebirth and decay, achieve immortality, the vision (H., *darśan*) of this Śiva *nirākāra* and its realisation. During a conversation in the Gorakhnāth Maṭh in Varanasi, I was told that a Nāth Yogī is one who realises that 'the *tattva*s that he sees outside are also inside. That is why instead of searching for them outside, he will look for them inside.' For this reason, the Yogī is said not to seek union with God, but to become one.

Yogī Śivanāth stated that the Nāth *sampradāya* focused on four main issues: yoga, Tantra, Ayurveda and *rasāyana* (alchemy). Several Yogīs associated the Nāth tradition with the development of Ayurveda, some attributing this endeavour to Siddha Carpaṭnāth, others to Cauraṅgīnāth.[55] Today, however, the connection between the *sampradāya* and tantric practices is questioned: some Nāths prefer not to be called tantric, as they do not want to be associated with black magic.[56] During my fieldwork I only met *aughaḍ*s who claimed to follow tantric paths: for example, Rāmayi Nāth claimed to follow a Bhairava *sādhanā*, while Oṃ Nāth declared himself to be a follower of a left-hand tantric path devoted to Mahākālī and that, through his *paramparā*, he is related to the Aghorīs in that 'they eat some parts of the human body' (his guru used to eat pieces of brain, he said). In Pashupatinath, Īśnāth explained that Tantra is a *vidyā*, a science, which anyone can study with a tantric guru—usually a householder—and that therefore anyone can become a 'tantric'. A Nāth, he continued, can follow a tantric *sādhanā*, such as an *aghorī sādhanā* performed in the crematory ground, but only if he gets permission from his guru.

---

54 '*Dhūnā ek duniyā anek*'. On the role of *dhūnā*, see below, p. 88.

55 On the stories of these two Nāths/Siddhas, see White 1996: 125–126, 132, 160, 238–239, 261, 294–300; Muñoz 2010.

56 See Timalsina 2011.

However, the fact should not be ignored that there were (and are) Nāth ascetics who followed (and still follow) a more devotional attitude (see Horstmann 2021), and that devotion, along with yoga, is becoming an attractive tool to draw devotees and new forms of patronage (see Bouillier 2008: 277–281).

The Rāmānandī *sampradāya*

Recognisable by the vertical *tilaka* on their foreheads and their mostly white or brownish robes, the Rāmānandī *sādhus* form the largest Vaiṣṇava group of northern India.

The *sampradāya* is said to have been organised in the 15th century by Rāmānanda. However, almost nothing is known about him, and scholars are still uncertain about his place and date of birth, his lineage and therefore whether he really established a Rāmānandī *sampradāya*. These uncertainties are due to the fact that, although Rāmānanda is considered an iconic figure of medieval India, the lack of evidence has left some aspects of his life open to debate and, at the same time, has created a narrative vacuum that has been filled in different ways over the centuries. The narration of Rāmānanda's story has developed according to the specific historical context in which his hagiographies were written, reflecting the development of specific religious approaches in the *sampradāya*.[57]

According to one of the most shared traditions, Rāmānanda was a disciple of Rāmānuja, but decided to leave the order due to behavioural discord, establishing a new group in which devotionalism (*bhakti*) and a *sādhanā* based on the god Rām were accessible to all, regardless of gender, caste or religion. His teaching, based on *prapatti*, self-surrender to God as the sole refuge and focus of devotion, led Rāmānanda to attract disciples from different social strata (such as Ravidās, who was a *camār*, an untouchable), religions (such as Kabīr, who was a Muslim) and gender (such as Padmāvatī, a woman). Traditionally, 12 close disciples are attributed to Rāmānanda, whose names, nevertheless, vary according to the sources.[58]

Rāmānanda's liberal religious approach likely laid the groundwork for the development of various religious trends in the *sampradāya* that became increasingly differentiated from each other over the course of centuries. The order was probably influenced by Ramaite groups present in Varanasi and

57 See Bevilacqua 2018a: 18–56.

58 Today, the *sampradāya* follows the list proposed by Nābhādās in his *Bhaktamāl* (c. 1585 CE), which includes: Anantānanda, Sukhānanda, Surasurānanda, Narahariyānanda, Pīpā, Kabīr, Bhāvānanda, Senā, Dhanā, Raidās, Padmāvatī and Surasarī.

by the practices of Nāth Yogīs. Later, when it moved to Rajasthan, it also embraced the devotional trends prevalent there. This has resulted in the *sampradāya* today being composed of three main branches: that of *tyāgīs*, *nāgās* and *rasiks*.[59]

The word *tyāgī* is related to *tyāga*, which means 'abandoning', hence 'renunciation'. I have advanced the hypothesis that the *tyāgī* group emerged from Rāmānanda's interpretations of some popular yogic traditions present in the Varanasi area which later Rāmānandī gurus further developed into a distinct *sādhanā* (Bevilacqua 2018a: 74–79). *Tyāgīs* continue to practise ascetic techniques that are observed in early texts. For instance, the aforementioned *Vaikhānasasmārtasūtra* (c. 7th–8th centuries) describes practices of celibate hermits which are still typical of contemporary *tyāgīs*: sitting among five fires; remaining in a pool of water; sitting in *virāsana*; maintaining silence; inverting the body and standing on one foot; etc. (Mallinson 2012b: 12). These practices were later mixed with those of Śaiva and Nāth ascetics who lived in the northern and western parts of the subcontinent and who produced works on *haṭha* yoga. It is possible, in fact, that Kṛṣṇadās Payahārī—the alleged founder of the *tyāgī* branch who lived in Galta (Rajasthan)—and his disciple Kīlhdev, were influenced by Nāth Yogīs. As we shall see, *tyāgīs* may practice the yoga *sādhanā* and austerities to achieve self-control and overcome the senses, desires and ego in order to achieve the grace of God and his *darśan* (H., vision).

It is very difficult to reconstruct the history of this sub-tradition within the *sampradāya*,[60] as several factors led to a lack of documentation: the wandering lifestyle of these ascetics; their living in solitude or in small groups; and their low social status and lack of education, which may have contributed to the inability to document their history in writing. Currently, there are several subgroups, often gathered in brotherhoods (such as the *Terah bhāī*, or 'Thirteen Brothers'), which may join together to form larger groups called *khālsā*.[61] *Tyāgīs* are often organised into itinerant *jamāt*, but they may also own or run centres.

59 I have extensively analysed the history of the Rāmānandī *sampradāya* elsewhere; see Bevilacqua 2018a: 59–128.

60 For further information, see Bevilacqua 2018a; Gross 1992; van der Veer 1988; Lamb 2011; Burghart 1978.

61 Van der Veer (1988: 110) interprets the symbolic differences between these subgroups as marks of various historical circumstances: they may indicate a schism between members of a group which resulted in a parting of ways as well as organisational differences.

According to Ramdas Lamb (2012: 177), during the 19th century the suborder of the *mahātyāgī*s, characterised by stricter rules of behaviour and renunciation, arose from the *tyāgī* branch. In this regard, the *mahātyāgī* Śyām Dās said to me that in the past there were 13 *tyāgī* families and from these families ten *sādhus* decided to go to the Himalayas, naked, to practise extreme forms of *tapasyā*. For this reason, on their return, they were called *mahātyāgī*s. Today, however, he said, there are no major differences between the two groups, as their *sādhanā*s are very similar. Furthermore, *mahātyāgī*s were supposed to have a unique *pīr*, but with the development of several *khālsā*s this tradition is no longer followed.

It is likely that the *nāgā* component of the Rāmānandī *sampradāya* developed from the *tyāgī* section. We can assume that wandering *tyāgī*s started to learn some military techniques to protect themselves from the *nāgā*s belonging to other *sampradāya*s, or that some *tyāgī*s were influenced by the training of other *nāgā*s. The establishment of *jamāt*s would have contributed to the formation of small groups of trained ascetics who later decided to organise themselves into separate sections. Early evidence of the existence of militant Rāmānandī ascetics is found in an imperial order of Aurangzeb from 1692 or 1693 which authorised five Rāmānandī commanders to move freely throughout the Empire (Orr 1940: 87). Since Śaiva and Vaiṣṇava ascetics were involved in activities such as trading and banking, clashes between their *nāgā*s occurred,[62] particularly involving the Rāmānandīs, as many *vairāgī*s (see previous chapter, p. 49) were from this *sampradāya*.

According to Lorenzen (1978: 68), Rāmānandī ascetics organised themselves into more structured armies in the 18th century due to the political instability of the period, inter-sectarian conflicts and conflicts between political and religious groups.[63] Consequently, the Vaiṣṇava *sampradāya*s decided to institutionalise their *nāgā*s into three *anī*s,[64] the Nirmohī, the

---

62 Ghurye (1953: 177) quotes that 'one Bhairava Giri Gosāvi had vowed not to take his daily meals without killing at least one Vaishnava Bairāgi', and also explains that the enmity between the two divisions of ascetics was so great that frequent bloody fights occurred, especially on the occasion of Kumbh assemblage.

63 Horstmann (forthcoming) tells us that the first conference to consolidate the military organisation was held in Vrindavan in 1713.

64 According to Ghurye (1953: 179), *anī* is the short form of the Sanskrit word *anika*, meaning army. Nevertheless, they are today called *akhāṛā*s in general discourse, because they are part of the Akhāṛā Pariṣad, an organisation that assembles the heads of *nāgā* sections from different Hindu orders.

Nirvāṇī and the Digambar, organised into eight sub-units called *akhāṛās*. These *nāgā* groups still exist today.

The *rasik* branch differs from the others because it produced unique literary works which trace its evolution. The word *rasik* derives from *rasa* (juice), a term that in philosophy represents an aesthetic enjoyment able to create emotions (*bhāva*) in the beneficiary of the aesthetic moment. Therefore, *rasik* can be translated as 'emotional'. The *rasik* branch was influenced by the Kṛṣṇa worship of the Gauḍīya *sampradāya* and established a form of Sītā-Rām worship based strictly on emotions. Devotion to Rām was manifested by re-enacting the bond of a slave (*dāsya*) with his master; of parents with their son (*vātsalya*); of a person with a friend (*sakhya*), or of a lover with his beloved (*śṛṅgārī*). Among these groups, the most numerous—and probably representative of the branch before the influence of the Kṛṣṇa worship—is the *dās*(*ya*) section. However, many *dās* today do not directly identify themselves as *rasik* because, according to them, *rasik*s are those who adopt a feminine appearance to worship God. Examples of this tendency are the subgroups called *svasukhī* and *tatsukhī*, in which different roles are attributed to the *sakhī*s, the female companions of Sītā. In the *svasukhī* the devotee identifies as a *sakhī* who desires a *pati-patnī-bhāva* (husband–wife) relationship with Lord Rām and yearns for union with him. In the *tatsukhī śākhā*, the *sakhī* does not seek union with Rām and merely shares the happiness of the holy couple (Caracchi 1999: 173–174). *Rasik*s, who are often theological specialists because many come from high castes, are mostly *sthānādhārī*s and look after temples and devotees.

In general, to become a Rāmānandī, one goes through a *pañca saṃskāra* initiation.[65] Through it, the disciple receives a new name that ends according to the branch he belongs to[66] and a mantra, which is whispered into his ear by the guru, to be used for the *sādhanā*. Then the Vaiṣṇava *tilaka* (the *ūrdhvapuṇḍra*) is applied to the forehead, as well as the chest and abdomen, while a bow (on the left) and arrows (on the right), symbols of Rām, are usually drawn on the arms.[67] The Vaiṣṇava *tilaka* usually consists of two white vertical lines and a red one in the middle. The colour of the *tilaka*, its size and characteristics can vary considerably as they manifest

65 To become a *nāgā* an individual already has to be an ascetic. Furthermore, to become a 'complete' *nāgā* there is a long path characterised by four *śreṇī* (grades). Every *śreṇī* lasts for three years, so 12 years of training are necessary to become a *nāgā*.

66 Mostly we find the name Dās (slave) appended at the end, and especially in *rasik* groups, the name Śaraṇ (shelter) or Prāpaṇ (attainment).

67 More commonly, the *ūrdhvapuṇḍra* is drawn on the arms.

the various *paramparā*s present in the *sampradāya*. Sometimes a red dot may be included below the red line, or it may replace it, taking a form called *lāl Śrī*, which is said to symbolise Lakṣmī or Sītā. Sometimes the red line is replaced by a white dot, while in some lineages, the words 'Sītā Rām' are written on either side of the *tilaka*.[68] The *tilaka* is normally made from a paste prepared by rubbing a piece of sandalwood and adding water and clay to form a white or cream-coloured paste. However, sandalwood is not always necessary and clay can be used alone. Rāmānandīs also use a yellow-brown clay called *rāmrāj* and sometimes also mix orange and yellow colours. They all wear a *kaṇṭhī* which is the Vaiṣṇava *mālā* (rosary) made of *tulsī* (basil). Some *tyāgī*s also wear earrings made of *tulsī* which can be useful tools to put in the ears to isolate them during meditation.

To note, during the initiation novices are not completely shaved but keep the *śikhā* or *coṭī* (the topknot) and change the *janeu* (if they are wearing one) for another sacred thread made from *muñja* grass, prepared by other Rāmānandīs.[69] The *śikhā* and the new *janeu* symbolise the Rāmānandīs' vow to continue performing Vedic and brahmanical rituals. For this reason, when they die, not all Rāmānandī ascetics are buried (as in the case of *saṃnyāsī*s and Nāths) but they may be burnt to perform the last brahmanical ritual, the *agni saṃskāra*. Śaiva ascetics shave the topknot and remove the *janeu* during the initiation to symbolise the abandonment of the worldly order. Rāmānandīs, on the other hand, keep the *śikhā* and replace the *janeu* to show that they are not renouncing the (brahmanical) world but are detached from it (*virakta*): they do not 'die' from their previous life (as *saṃnyāsī*s do), they are 'simply' not attached to it. This different attitude depends on Rāmānandīs' theological background and religious aims, which is *bhakti* and the worship of God.

In the Vaiṣṇava ideology, knowledge alone cannot cause liberation, and action, particularly religious ritual action, should accompany the pursuit of knowledge. Rāmānandīs follow the Viśiṣṭādvaita Vedānta, so they

---

68 Entwistle (2003: 22) reports that some Rāmānandīs interpret the form of their *tilaka* as representing Rām and his brother Lakṣmaṇ standing on either side of Sītā, while the stroke at the base, which is called *siṅhāsana* (lion throne), represents Hanumān kneeling at their feet. During my fieldwork, some Rāmānandīs gave me this interpretation, while others told me the *tilaka* actually represents the footstep of Viṣṇu.

69 According to *tyāgī* Monī Bābā, the *muñja janeu* comes from Hanumān and should be self-made. A long process goes into producing it: the *sādhu* has to put the dry grass together, roll the strands and then weave them. It takes a lot of patience and time. But it is possible that some *sādhus* prepare it for others, as they do for the thread used to insert *tulsī* seeds into the *mālā*.

acknowledge the existence of *brahman* but as characterised by multiplicity, the *ātmans*. The *ātman* is recognised as eternally real but eternally distinct from God: individual souls retain their separate identity even after *mokṣa*. In the Viśiṣṭādvaita Vedānta, *bhakti* is the only means of liberation, since final release comes only through the Lord's grace. Therefore, Rāmānandīs' main purpose is not to attain *mokṣa*, but *bhakti* itself and the worship of God, because only God can provide *mokṣa*.

Despite their different approaches, Rāmānandīs share similar devotional practices: they worship Rām through *bhajan* and *kīrtan* (H., devotional songs) and *nām jap* (H., repetition of God's name). There are no strict boundaries between *saguṇa* and *nirguṇa sādhanās*, although on a more practical level many *sādhus* find the *nirguṇa* devotion easier because it does not require images of deities to be formally and properly worshipped twice a day (see Lamb 1994: 134). *Saguṇa* worship, in fact, requires time, possession of ritual items, a supply of offerings and the knowledge of various prayers that a wandering *sādhu* does not always possess.

The appearance of Rāmānandī ascetics depends on the branch they belong to. *Tyāgī*s mostly have matted hair (*jaṭā*) and beards. Rāmānandī *nāgā*s and *rasik*s may have long hair and beards, but *rasik* who hold high positions[70] may shave their heads and faces, arms and armpits. *Tyāgī*s and *nāgā*s may have similar clothing: they wear a *laṅgoṭī* (loincloth) and a cotton cloth draped around the body, or around the hips, like a *luṅgī* (a kind of apron), which is mostly unstitched. *Tyāgī*s can also be almost naked (they say to be naked '*maryādā se*', with dignity, following Rām's example)—which means that they always wear a loincloth made of different textiles (see the next chapter, p. 122)—whereas *nāgā*s are not supposed to be naked, probably to avoid being confused with *tyāgī*s. Usually, the colours worn are white, ivory and yellow, although during my fieldwork I have seen several Rāmānandīs, especially those in high positions, also wear ochre-coloured

---

70 Before the 20th century, it seems that Rāmānandīs had to rely on *ācārya*s from the Śrī *sampradāya* (Rāmānujīs). However, in the early 20th century, a group of radical Rāmānandī ascetics led by Svāmī Bhagavadācārya challenged the mainstream narration that claimed that Rāmānanda was part of Rāmānuja's *paramparā* to get rid of the Rāmānujī legacy and declare the independence of the Rāmānandīs from the Rāmānūjī (Śrī) *sampradāya*. Through several religious debates, the reformists were able to affirm their stand. The event had a further important development: the recognition of Rāmānanda as a *jagadguru* and the bestowing of the title of Jagadguru Rāmānandācārya in order to provide the *sampradāya* with a religious leader. However, over the last decade, the number of Jagadguru Rāmānandācāryas has increased. See Bevilacqua 2018a: 107–123.

robes.[71] *Rasiks* may wear white or orange robes draped around their body, as well as *luṅgīs* and *kurtās*. Rāmānandī *tyāgīs* and *nāgās* also carry a *kamaṇḍala*, or water-pot, a common accessory among wandering ascetics. Leaders may carry a *tridaṇḍa* enveloped in an orange cloth.[72]

Rāmānandīs greet each other with 'Jai Sītā Rām', or 'Jai Śrī Rām', or 'Sītā Rām': the reason why they are often referred to by other *sādhus* as Sītā Rām *bābās*.

A social characteristic shared by *tyāgīs* and *nāgās* is that neither have restrictive rules on novice recruitment and therefore anyone can enter these branches, even women. However, the reality is quite different from theory, and during my fieldwork I rarely encountered Rāmānandī women. It seems that Vaiṣṇava *tyāgīs* are stricter than Śaiva on the issue of female ascetics and have some opposition to *sādhvīs* (see below, p. 92).

In the course of my research, I worked mainly with Rāmānandī *tyāgīs*, a few *mahātyāgīs* and a few *nāgās*, because they are the ones connected with the practice of austerities and yoga.

The Udāsī *akhāṛā*

The Udāsī *akhāṛā* is a smaller order compared to the others mentioned, but it is truly fascinating because, although it has its roots in the Sikh tradition, it also presents features typical of Śaiva and Vaiṣṇava groups. Unfortunately, its history and current organisation requires further study.[73]

71 This tradition began with Svāmī Bhagavadācārya who became the first Jagadguru Rāmānandācārya and, going against tradition, decided to wear an ochre-coloured robe. It is likely that, from that time on, the Jagadguru started wearing this type of dress to distinguish himself from the common Rāmānandī ascetics (who wear white robes) and to resemble the appearance of the Śaṅkarācārya (see Ghurye 1953: 168).

72 The word *tridaṇḍa* (three staffs) is generally associated with Vaiṣṇava ascetics, and Rāmānuja is said to be the founder of a school of asceticism of *tridaṇḍīs*, i.e. of ascetics who carry three staffs (Gurye 1953: 54). According to Gurye (1953: 72), in the *Mānavadharmaśāstra* a *tridaṇḍī* 'is one who controlled his body, speech and mind with the help of intellect'.

73 Here, I mostly rely on the PhD work of Kiranjeet Sandhu (2011), who was supervised by an expert in Udāsī history, Singh Sulakhan (1982).

According to tradition, the Udāsī *akhāṛā* was founded in Punjab by Śrī Cand (1494–1629)[74] the eldest son of Guru Nanak (1469–1539).[75] The word *udāsī* denotes one who is indifferent or heedless of worldly attachments and, as reported by Sandhu (2011: 1), was used to refer to the missionary tours (*udāsiyān*) of Guru Nanak, who was said to have worn the robes of a renouncer during these journeys. Nanak's son, Śrī Cand, allegedly asked his father if he too could wear the *udāsī* garb, a request that was granted. However, his decision to keep the vow of celibacy and become a lifelong renouncer was not approved by Guru Nanak, who considered the practice of virtues in ordinary life more important than renunciation and austerities. According to John C. Oman (1903: 195), Śrī Cand was supposed to succeed Nanak but the guruship was passed on to Angad instead, which caused the former such disappointment that he 'threw ashes on his head and person, in token of his grief and abasement'. Another version of the story sees him performing austerities that were not in line with Guru Nanak's teachings. Similarly, his brother Lakhmī Cand allegedly created a group of non-celibates called Bedīs. Since neither of them adhered to the father's preaching, Nanak appointed Angad as his disciple and successor in 1539 (Sandhu 2011: 4). Śrī Cand is said to have opposed this nomination and then founded the Udāsī order.

As can be surmised from these stories, initially there was friction between the two groups, Sikhs and Udāsīs, with the Udāsīs being the dissidents. However, it seems that, 40 years after Guru Nanak's death, Śrī Cand made peace with Guru Rām Dās, Nanak's fourth successor (Sandhu 2011: 12). Śrī Cand's longevity also allowed him to meet the sixth Sikh guru, Har Govind (1595–1644) and adopt Har Govind's son Gurdittā so as to succeed him as abbot of the Udāsī order. In this way the two groups became closer (Oman 1903: 195). Bābā Gurdittā established four groups called *dhuans* (hearths) connected to four of his disciples who came to be known as the *ādi*-Udāsīs. In addition to these four *dhuans*, six *bakhśīś* (bounties) and various sub-*bakhśīś* were established (Sandhu 2011: 225). The purpose of the *bakhśīś* was to spread the teachings of Guru Nanak and Śrī Cand. *Sādhus* who belonged to these organisations travelled widely, establishing new centres. Udāsīs soon became custodians and priests of Sikh shrines, and were responsible for reading and expounding the writings of Nanak

74 Some sources claim that Śrī Cand died in 1643, at the age of 149.

75 Guru Nanak is considered the founder of Sikhism and its first guru. Many of his teachings have been collected in the *Guru Granth Sāhib*, the central religious scripture of Sikhism regarded as the eternal living Guru after a lineage of ten human gurus. On Sikhism, see McLeod 2007, 2004; Shackle and Mandair 2013.

and Govind Singh, collected in the *Ādi Granth* and *Das Pādśāh kā Granth* (Wilson 1976).

Due to their popularity, Udāsīs received support from the Mughals and Sikh rulers, in particular Mahārāja Ranjit Singh (1780–1839). The number of Udāsī establishments increased significantly in the early 19th century, although they were not organised under a main centre and several autonomous monasteries existed. It was during this period that they defined themselves as an *akhāṛā* to indicate that their religious ideology, beliefs and practices differed from those of Sikhs, despite their veneration for Guru Nanak and their recitation of the *Ādi Granth*. In fact, in 1779, the Pañcāyatī Baṛā Udāsī *akhāṛā* in Prayag was established by *mahant* Pritam Dās (1752–1831) to unite the Udāsī centres affiliated with the *dhuans*. In 1840, the Choṭā (or Nayā) Udāsī *akhāṛā* was founded by Santokh Dās.

Bhole Bābā, an Udāsī living in Rishikesh, told me how the Pañcāyatī Baṛā Udāsī *akhāṛā* was founded according to tradition. He connected Pritam Dās with Bankhandi Sahib/Bābā, an Udāsī who travelled from Punjab to Nepal to do *tapasyā*, and there due to his *sādhanā* he obtained the power of long life (therefore he would still be alive). Pritam Dās decided to go to Nepal and to do *tapasyā* to have the *darśan* of Bankhandi Bābā. On arriving, he began a 12-year practice, during which time he was fed by a child who brought him a glass of milk every day. The child was in reality Bankhandi Bābā. After 12 years, not realising that he had the *darśan* of the saint, Pritam Dās refused the child's milk and declared that he would begin another 12 years of *tapasyā* drinking nothing, not even milk. The child then told him to start walking in the direction of a smoke visible from the jungle, an instruction Pritam Dās obeyed. Once there, he recognised the boy, but in the body of Bankhandi Bābā, who enquired what he wanted. Pritam Dās asked for his blessing to create the Pañcāyatī *akhāṛā*. Bankhandi Bābā took some *vibhūti* from the *dhūnī*, wrapped it in a piece of cloth and gave it to him saying 'this is the *svarūp* of Bābā Śrī Cand' and from this he made four *mahants*, *pujārīs* and the *jamāts*. Pritam Dās left with them.

Although I could not find this story anywhere else, Sindhu (2011: 188) claims that 'Mahant Santokh Das and Pritam Das gathered a large number of *chelas*, popularly known as *Bankhandi Jamat*'.[76]

In 1881, Udāsīs were still the most powerful religious group among Sikhs and benefited from land concessions. However, under the British rulers they began to lose power and, in the first half of the 20th century,

76 Probably the Bankhandi mentioned by Bhole Bābā is the Udāsī who founded the sanctuary of Sadh Belo in Sindh in 1823 (see https://www.dawn.com/news/1413676, last accessed January 2021).

their losses were substantial (Sandhu 2011: 65). In those years, the status of Udāsīs was further compromised by the rise of the Singh Sabhas[77] and the Gurdwara Reform Movements (also called the Akālī Movement).[78] The Akālī Movement wanted to take back the Sikh shrines from Udāsī control, and as Udāsīs were unable to counter Akālīs' allegations they were eventually forced to leave the shrines (Sandhu 2011: 61). Udāsīs formally separated from the Sikhs through the Gurdwara Act of 1925.

Udāsīs preach the message of Guru Nanak and revere the *Guru Granth*, yet their religious identity is not Sikh. Their religious approach, philosophy, beliefs and practices can be found in the *Udāsī Bodh* written by Sant Rein in 1858. The work is a dialogue between Śrī Cand and Guru Nanak, in which Udāsī views on '*dukh* [sufferance], *pap* [sin], *pun* [merit], *karma, maya, gyān, bhakti, mukti, vairag, brahm, narak* [hell] and *swarg* [paradise], the five evils and the creation of the world' are presented (Singh 1983: 293).[79] It also contains the Udāsīs' belief in Hindu scriptures, in the *bhakti* and Sikh paths, as well as:

> their belief in the *Nathipanthi* and *Samnyasi* traditions of *dhunis*, and paying reverence to the ashes; their belief in the *nanga* tradition, wearing only a loincloth, and *jatan* on head, and their belief in the *paramahansa* tradition of wearing ochre-coloured full clothes, beside a *topi*, a *seli* and a *phul-mal*, rosary of flowers (Singh 1983: 293).

In this text, God appears in both *nirguṇa* and *saguṇa* form. Although Udāsīs show reverence for Sikh scriptures and in their main shrines they shield the *Ādi Granth*, they also believe in the Vedas, Purāṇas and Śāstras, and worship the *pañca devās*, five Hindu deities: Śiva, Viṣṇu, Durgā, Gaṇpati and Sūrya. Moreover, Udāsīs do not follow the Sikh doctrine of the unity of

---

77 The Singh Sabha Movement began in Punjab in the 1870s as a reaction against the proselytising activities of Christians, Muslims and Hindu reform movements. The movement aimed to 'propagate the true Sikh religion and restore Sikhism to its pristine glory; to write and distribute historical and religious books of Sikhs; and to propagate Gurmukhi Punjabi through magazines and media' (Barrier, Singh and Singh 2002: 225).

78 The Akālī Movement aimed to reform the Gurdwaras during the early 1920s. It was started by the political wing of the Singh Sabha, which was later known as Akālī Dal.

79 Much of the existing Udāsī literature was written after the 1920s and had the purpose of framing a specific Udāsī identity to confront the Akālīs. Therefore, since it was part of the battle for the control and management of Sikh shrines, it contains very little historical information on the life and mission of Bābā Śrī Cand (Sindhu 2011: 9).

the guruship, as they believe that an advanced Udāsī, who has received the grace of God, can be as valuable as a Sikh guru (Sindhu 2011: 123). *Bhakti* indeed plays a fundamental role in the Udāsīs' religious attitude, since, without devotion, knowledge of God is not possible and neither is *mokṣa*.

Today they are closer to Śaiva groups, with whom they share an Advaita Vedānta monistic approach. Another influence to note is that of the Nāths, who had long been active in Punjab and their presence also appears in Guru Nanak's compositions, in which Gorakhnāth is often his interlocutor (McLeod 1980: 68, 103). For this reason, Gorakhnāth enjoys particularly consideration by Udāsīs. In a conversation with Lakṣmaṇ Dās, an Udāsī from Varanasi, I was told this story:

> Our Śrī *ācārya*, Śrī Cand Bhagvān, was also a *yogīrāj*. We are very close to the Nāth because Śrī Cand Bhagvān was a form of Gorakhnāth [. . .] What happened . . . There was a *śāstrārtha* [philosophical debate] between Guru Nanak and Gorakhnāth. When such things happened, it was customary for the winner to become the guru, and the loser the disciple. Gorakhnāth was the *avatāra* of Śaṅkara, Nanak that of Viṣṇu. Nanak was following a correct code of conduct, because Viṣṇu takes all deities into account, so Gorakhnāth lost. Gorakhnāth said that he would support his *putr* [Nanak's son] with his reincarnation, which would be recognised by the earring in one ear. When Śrī Cand was born, he already had *jaṭā* and *vibhūti*. Thus it was recognised that he was the *avatāra* of Gorakhnāth. For this reason, we are Udāsīs and wear the *mudrā* in one ear.

Another similarity with Nāths (but also with Sikhs) is the acceptance of everyone into the *akhāṛā*, without concern for caste. Obviously, to enter one has to be accepted by a guru and go through the *dīkṣā*.

In the Udāsī initiation ceremony, the novice is supposed to drink the water in which the feet of five *mahant*s have been washed. At this point, a ceremony called *jhara akhāṛā* takes place, during which the individual leaves all his property to the *akhāṛā* and swears to follow its rules (Sandhu 2011: 105). If he is less than 18 years old, he is called *vastradhārī* (who wears clothes). During the initiation, the novitiate is given the *laṅgoṭī*, his body is covered with ash and the Udāsī *tilaka* is applied. This has a *tripuṇḍra* shape (but often the entire forehead is coloured) and a red dot in the middle. He is also given a *śelī* similar to that of Nāths, a *pagrī* (turban) and ochre-coloured clothes, although white, red and black can be also worn. Today, many also wear a necklace with the image of Śrī Cand and a *rudrākṣa mālā*. However, an important part of the Udāsīs' accessories is the single half-moon shaped earring called *mudrā*, worn in the lobe of the right ear, mentioned by Lakṣmaṇ Dās.

During the initiation, the disciple is shaved, receives the mantra, recites the Śrī Cand mantra and the *paramparā* of his guru, and then gets his new name. Sandhu (2011: 128) argues that the names of the Udāsīs generally end in Dās or Brahm, and if he is a *nāgā* in Dās or Saraṇ. She does not mention Muni, which is the name I generally found instead among Udāsīs along with Dās. In fact, as *tyāgī* Phalāhārī Bābā told me during the 2019 Kumbh Melā, Muni Udāsīs are similar to Dasnāmīs and Nāths, while Dās Udāsīs are closer to Vaiṣṇavas, and practise *tapasyā* in similar ways.[80]

To become a *nāgā*, an Udāsī undergoes a ceremony similar to that of *nāgā saṃnyāsīs*. The ceremony takes place during the Kumbh Melā and the individual, who is designated a *nirvāṇa* Udāsī, must apply ashes on his body for the entire time of the Kumbh Melā, living close to the *dhūnī* and continuing the practice of wearing *vibhūti* for at least three years.

Udāsīs also have their *jamāt*, consisting of four *mahants*, plus *koṭhārīs*, *bhaṇḍārīs*, *pujārīs*, and the *sādhus* who follow it. According to Bhole Bābā, even today a *jamāt* may consist of 40–50 people. The Baṛā Udāsī *akhāṛā* is today divided into four groups (called *pangats*) based on geographical locations, so when Udāsīs greet each other they define themselves according to their *pangat*, i.e. *dakṣiṇa* (southern), *uttara* (northern), etc.[81] The greeting used among Udāsīs is *māthā ṭeknā*, which means 'I bow with my head', as a symbol of obedience or prostration before another individual.

Symbols of asceticism and austerities

Although all ascetics practise austerities in some way (see p. 116f.), *sādhus* who follow yogic or austerity-based *sādhanās* and have an itinerant lifestyle share outward similarities that embody a specific symbolism. Wandering *sādhus* usually carry a water-pot (*kamaṇḍala*), wear a loincloth (*laṅgoṭī*), an ascetic bag (*jholī*), often made by the *sādhus* themselves, which contains secret pockets to conceal important and small objects, a waistband with a similar function to the *jholī*, and 'fire tongs' (*cimṭā*), which can be used for protection but mostly to handle the *dhūnī* (firepit). The use of the *dhūnī* among wandering *sādhus*, particularly *saṃnyāsīs*, is surprising

80 Unfortunately, I have met only one Udāsī woman—in Ujjain Siṃhasth Melā in 2016—and we were not able to talk properly. She had long *jaṭā*, which testified to her long-time presence on the renunciation path, and she was comfortable sitting around the *dhūnī* of her brethren smoking a *cilam* (see p. 243).

81 I would like to thank Thor Lindgren (Shakti Baba) for sharing this information with me (personal communication, 25 June 2020).

considering that brahmanical sources state that ascetics should abandon any sacred fires. The 12th–13th-century *Nāradaparivrājaka* (197) makes this point clearly: 'bathing, muttering prayers, divine worship, sacrifices, propitiatory rites, and rites such as the fire sacrifice do not apply to him' (Olivelle 2008e: 168). To go by this list, *sādhus* do many things that are not permitted, especially considering the attention they pay to morning personal cleaning activities, or daily routines centred on morning, midday and evening worship of their *iṣṭa devatā*. This 'inconsistency' may, on the one hand, confirm that brahmanical sources did not present a realistic portrayal of ascetic reality; on the other hand, it may signify a historical development that occurred over the centuries for practical reasons, perhaps under the influence of non-brahmanical ascetic groups. For example, returning to the use of the *dhūnī*, we might ponder whether it is a development of Vedic firepits or a practice adopted from other groups (like Sufis) for practical reasons, such as cooking and performing oblations.

The *dhūnī* is worshipped by all wandering *sādhus*, who consider it a sacred space, a formless guru to be worshipped and properly guarded (and for the *saṃnyāsīs* of the Jūnā *akhāṛā* it is the guru Dattātreya himself). It is to the *dhūnī* that the *sādhu* gives the first sip of his *chai*, or the first bite of his food, as is usually done for deities. Sometimes *sādhus*, especially those who follow an esoteric path, place special objects inside their *dhūnī*, such as bones or skulls, to make it more powerful. The *dhūnī*, in fact, confers powers but also absorbs the power of the *sādhu* who usually meditates near it. Doing *dhyāna* in front of the *dhūnī* brings results more quickly, while offering to the *dhūnī* is a form of meditation that may lead to the rising of *kuṇḍalinī*. Consequently, the *dhūnī* of famous and powerful *bābās* are preserved as memorial, like their *samādhi* (tombs), to bear witness to their presence in the world. The special respect for the *dhūnī* also lies in the fact that it is a source of *vibhūti*, which is often given to devotees as *prasāda* (consecrated food). The *dhūnī* thus symbolises the cremation grounds and physical death, but also the transition from the worldly to the sacred realm, the dissolution of the ego and the destruction of worldly attachments.[82]

There are three more elements that have traditionally characterised wandering ascetics: nakedness, *jaṭā* and *vibhūti*. These have been

82 The Nāth *dhūnī* is called *dhūnā* and, theoretically, it should be made only with *gobar* (H., cow dung) so as to have thinner ashes. When the *gobar* is old, the Nāth opens the *dhūnā* with a specific instrument, places the new *gobar* inside and covers it. The Nāth *dhūnā* is quite deep and is made with five different products, which are mixed. However, I have observed that the majority use wood logs, simply for convenience.

described by Gross (1992: 306) as 'cultural symbols' of asceticism that are multivocalic and multireferential. Nudity symbolises rebirth and transition although, as we have seen, not all *sādhus* remain completely naked. Nakedness also signifies absence of possessions, the rejection of physical comforts and detachment from the body. It also separates *sādhus* from the class and caste distinction manifested through clothing. *Jaṭā* (matted hair) denotes contempt for appearance, control of natural and physical forces, non-attachment to the ego, practice of *tapas* (austerity), yogic control and the rejection of conventional social rules.[83] Ash, called *vibhūti* or *bhasma*, symbolises disregard for the body and refers to death, cremation, sacrifice and the practice of austerities.

These specific traits of asceticism are all present in specific sections of the described *sampradāyas*. Similarities in external appearance often correspond to a similarity of practices. These similarities often stem from the fact that individuals can learn from various gurus even though they belong to different *sampradāyas*, which leads to a kind of homogeneity in practices among various groups. This demonstrates that the ascetic landscape was fluid and remains so even after the institutionalisation of various traditions. It also proves that the core of asceticism is still based on an individual quest and an individual path undertaken under the guidance of a guru.

Entering the ascetic world

Why does an individual decide to become a *sādhu* and how does he or she undertake a specific *sādhanā*? This topic is important because it brings the topic of asceticism into the realm of human agency. The examples provided here emphasise the different reasons behind such an important choice, avoiding the clichés often expressed in textual sources and highlighting the role of the guru.

In my time spent with *sādhus* I sometimes attempted to ask when and why they had decided to receive initiation and thus who they were beforehand. This last question did not always result in an answer: many respected the rule that, once initiated, one should not talk about the 'previous' life,

83 In general, we can observe different forms of ascetic symbolism in the hairstyle: shaved heads are for *sādhus* who follow the path of *jñāna* and are 'teachers'; normal or long hair is for *nāgā* and *rasik* Rāmānandīs, or in general *sādhus* who do not follow a specific form of austerities or are not part of specific tapasic groups. However, we should not forget that there are also bald *sādhus*. A new trend I have witnessed recently is the use of fake *jaṭā* worn mainly by bald *bābās* or by those who want to pretend they have been on the ascetic path for longer than is the case.

yet there were also *sādhus* who spoke openly about their past. On the other hand, although the 'when' was sometimes unclear, as many *sādhus* had no idea of the exact date or year of their initiation, the 'why' was often stated frankly.

Dissatisfaction with lay life and the insignificance of *sāṃsārik* (worldly) concerns were quite common answers. Garuḍ Dās, a Rāmānujī *tyāgī* whom I met in the Siṃhasth Melā, pointed out that a spiritual journey often begins because of the need to answer the question 'Who am I?'. Obviously, he said, renunciation becomes a way of answering this question, since the 'I' cannot be found in the body once one realises that the body is going to dissolve. Therefore, the practice begins with learning to detach.

As we have seen, the quest to understand this 'I' was present in the Upaniṣads and seems to continue to push people towards asceticism. The *saṃnyāsinī* Durgā Bhārtī pointed out that, when an individual truly wants to answer questions about the self and existence, and wants to find God, he or she must abandon the world so that *tyāga* and *vairāgya* can develop and, from these, the complete renunciation that will enable these questions to be answered. Durgā Bhārtī said:

> Our task as human beings is to understand the origin of things: that is, the five *tattvas* (elements). All animals have a purpose; what is the purpose of human beings? To seek. If the human being does not use this opportunity, then he is a *paśu*, just another animal, who does not understand that mine and yours do not exist, because everything is impermanent, and you cannot enjoy your money once you are dead. We are all dead.

Durgā Bhārtī's words emphasise that human life is considered a gift that must be exploited to achieve soteriological goals.

But the reasons for choosing an ascetic life may also depend on age and possibilities. There are *sādhus* who entered the ascetic world when they were children. In these cases, the reasons may be different: they may have done so to leave a difficult family situation; to leave school; to stay with *sādhus* who roam from village to village. A *mahātyāgī* told me that, as a kid, he thought *sādhus* were magicians and he wanted to become a magician himself, so he left home. But a son who decides to leave the family causes great pain, especially if he is the only son. Therefore, a guru often discourages young men from taking initiation. Moreover, since mothers and fathers are considered to be the first gurus of an individual, runaway children will still have to return home after 12 years to receive the blessing of their parents, otherwise they will not be able to fulfil their ascetic path.

There are also abandoned children who are rescued by *sādhus*, as well as children who are offered to a *sādhu*: a Nāth told me he was donated by his family to the *āśram* of a Nāth guru, because thanks to his power his mother was able to become pregnant but, in return, had to donate her first child. A child in the *sādhu samāj* is never alone and can count on the subsidiary family created around his guru.[84]

Nāth jī said that the true *sādhu* is the one who takes *dīkṣā* in childhood, before the mind is defiled and full obedience to the guru's words can be achieved. According to him, only one who is *sādhu* from childhood can bring the teachings of the guru to fulfilment. Nāth jī took *dīkṣā* in Haryana as a child and said that his guru often kicked him, an 'expedient' that seems to be a widely shared experience among *sādhus*. A *nāgā saṃnyāsī* also said that his guru gave him a lot of love but also many blows with the *cimṭā* and the *daṇḍa* (staff). But, according to him, even those were teachings because, somehow, he always understood something deeper from these acts by the guru.

It is true that those who have been *sādhus* from childhood and are particularly skilful in their ascetic path are highly respected in *sādhu* society. In fact, it is not age that generates respect, but the years spent as an ascetic that count. Indeed, many take initiation later in life.

In some cases, parental pressure is such that those who would like to devote themselves to an ascetic life have to wait until they meet social expectations, i.e. have children. For example, one of my main interlocutors, Jogī Bābā, told me that although he was mentally a *sādhu* from childhood—'since I was in the womb of my mother', he clarified—his family forced him to marry. He said:

> I gave them what they wanted, a daughter-in-law and a granddaughter, they made their peace with it and I left. The girl is also married, has a son and they live in the city. We have no ties, sometimes they come, but I do not care. When you become a *bābā*, then you have to put aside your previous relationships, the woman, the mother, the father. This is our *dharma*.

Another *sādhu* I met in Allahabad, told me that he decided to become a *saṃnyāsī* when he was nine years old. However, his family opposed his decision, especially his mother who was scared of being abandoned. She asked him to wait until she died. He started working, never married and eventually became an ascetic in 1988. Since then, he has never returned to his family village.

---

84 This does not mean that there are no dangers for children in the *sādhu samāj*. A *sādhu* who was initiated during his childhood told me that, although his guru took good care of him, when he started travelling he always carried a big *cimṭā* with him to protect himself from nasty *sādhus*.

There may be reasons other than spiritual ones for entering the ascetic path, especially in adulthood: there are young men who are afraid of the responsibilities and expectation of Hindu social life and marriage, so they prefer renunciation; there are people who are running away from difficult situations and prefer to 'disappear'; and people who see asceticism as a job and an easier way to 'put food on the table' or to have a shelter or make money. And, of course, there are elderly people who see a religious institution as the perfect refuge for their last years, especially considering that there is no adequate government assistance for the elderly in need.[85]

As we have mentioned in the previous chapter, embarking on the ascetic path was and still is more difficult for women than for men, because the ascetic choice challenges the brahmanical image of women that would have them dependent and submissive to a man. Therefore, as in the past, women continue to face several difficulties in fulfilling their religious quests.[86] One of the obstacles comes from the *sādhu samāj* itself. Since celibacy is fundamental in asceticism, women are seen as an impediment to men's spiritual realisation, and their presence as suspicious and unfavourable. Male ascetics may have different attitudes towards female ascetics. In my experience, I have found a greater closure towards female ascetics among Rāmānandī *tyāgīs* than among other groups: on asking about women in the Rāmānandī *sampradāya*, I have often been told that there are no female ascetics, at least not 'real ones'. There seems to be a lot of distrust towards gurus who have female disciples, especially if they are young. Somehow, the guru–*śiṣya* relationship is not taken seriously in the case of women and their practices are often ostracised. For this reason, female disciples are rarely taken to the major religious gatherings, especially if there is no special arrangement for their stay. Sometimes they only attend a few days or the most important day.

Some ascetics believe that women should follow their *dharma*, which is marriage and the caring of the family and children. Some believe that women have less *guṇas* (quality) than men, so they are not suitable for renunciation. However, others also admit that women who undertake the ascetic path out of desire are often more upright than men and can achieve spiritual results faster. Then there are those ascetics who accept the presence of women on the assumption that the *ātman* has no gender and therefore anyone can embark on the path of renunciation if they wish to abandon the

---

85 On the role of religious institutions and their replacement of government infrastructures, see for example Copeman and Ikegame 2012.

86 An exemplary case is represented by Rām Priya Dās, the only female ascetic I met to have been initiated in her childhood, and who had full training in yoga physical techniques. See Appendix 2, p. 354.

saṃsāra. Gurus who accept young female disciples often do that at their peril, as they must face social criticism and continually demonstrate the integrity of their choice.

The studies of Clémentin-Ojha (1998) and Denton (2004) have shown that the reasons behind a young woman becoming an ascetic are not always related to a religious calling—which remains, according to them, the main cause—but may be because of critical social or economic conditions. From Denton's work, among the female renouncers she has encountered:

> Few have entered the ascetic world out of an entirely free choice. [. . .] (i) most have been placed here by impoverished, high caste families unable to provide a dowry for them, (ii) some have been sent by relatives unable to feed and clothe an orphaned child, (iii) some have parents who simply desire an orthodox education and protection for them, (iv) a few appear to have either been rejected by their husbands [. . .] (v) some are unable to compete in the marriage market because of physical disability or unattractiveness, suspicions about mental or emotional capacity, or relatively advanced age (Denton 2004: 137–138).

Most of the female ascetics I met during my fieldwork matched this description: they were women of advanced age or widows who did not want to become a burden on the family; others embarked on the ascetic path as a last stage of their life: having fulfilled their social duties as women, they felt free to devote their lives to religious goals.[87] Many female devotees have expressed to me the desire to retire to an *āśram* following their guru as soon as they no longer have family duties to perform. In such cases, renunciation is accepted by male ascetics. Many also advocate asceticism for women after wrong marriages, or if they cannot marry. The *bhakti* path is the suggested practice for them.[88]

However, the decision to become an ascetic, for both men and women, is only a starting point which needs the presence of a guru to be fully

87 However, I have noticed that there are also some wealthy families who support and sustain, even financially, the rise of their daughters as religious figures who are then admitted into orders. Sometimes, if they have enough devotees to support them, they are allowed to have their own camps. Moreover, as Clémentin-Ojha (1985) noted, the presence of female gurus has increased in recent decades, but they are often transformed into a socially benign mother figure, devoid of sexual and potentially harmful connotations. Modern female gurus are not considered in this book for reasons explained in the Introduction.

88 On women learning the yoga *sādhanā*, see Chapter 5, p. 206.

accomplished. As Durgā Bhārtī says, 'only a guru can disclose the path. The guru gives the *sādhanā*, the mantra and *gyān*,[89] and then you have to practise it.'

The role of the guru

> 'Reading a book does not bring real knowledge, only the words of the guru and the individual experience can bring knowledge.'
>
> Garuḍ Dās

The decision to become a renouncer must be followed by the search for a guru, although many *sādhus* claim that it is the guru who enables the individual to find him. According to Garuḍ Dās, indeed, one cannot look for a guru because 'if you do not have knowledge, how can you recognise a true guru? The guru is the one who switches on the light and enables his disciple to see. But not all the people recognise the guru.' Therefore, he said, a guru reveals his identity only to those he chooses: if an individual lacks skills, the guru does not waste his time.

As Gianni Pellegrini explained to me, in the Indian context the relationship with the guru is fundamental, and is even more important than the order to which one belongs:

> It is a strong, intuitive bond that arises immediately from the sight between the two, the potential disciple and the potential guru. [. . .] It all depends on *Īśvara kripā* (the grace of God), the desire of God and his grace that will allow these two individuals to meet and produce in the heart of the disciple-to-be the desire to renounce the world.[90]

Where to find a guru or how to meet a guru depends on the circumstances. Sometimes he is an ascetic known to the family, or an ascetic who runs a temple or *āśram* near to the family's village, or he can be someone introduced by someone else, or met by chance. Whatever the circumstances, it is a life-changing encounter for two individuals, because being someone's guru is also a responsibility.[91] Often, the attraction to the guru or the 'guru-

---

89 *Gyān* is the Hindi for *jñāna*. I will use this Hindi form when reporting *sādhus*' words.

90 Personal communication, 20 May 2020.

91 For this reason, there are ascetics who do not want disciples at all. A Rāmānandī *sādhu* told me that he did not want disciples because the guru has to take care of them until they achieve their spiritual results. From his words, it seems that if the

to-be' captures the attention of a 'disciple-to-be', rather than the *sampradāya* of the guru. Therefore, it is not unlikely that an individual who was Śaiva by family might become Vaiṣṇava having been attracted to a Vaiṣṇava guru, because the guru–disciple bond matters more than religious affiliation.

However, every initiation has to be gained: previously, in almost all *sampradāyas*, there was a 12-year training period with the guru, during which the disciple had to 'serve' the guru, while the guru had to 'study' the disciple in order to work on his spiritual development in the most appropriate way for him.

With the initiation, the guru becomes the *param pitā*, the 'supreme father', who opens a new life to his spiritual child. As a *bābā* in the Gorakhnāth Maṭh in Varanasi told me: 'When you get *dīkṣā* from a guru, you learn to recognise even your own body as the representation of your guru, as belonging to him. In our Nāth *sampradāya* we say that one should not do what the guru does but what the guru tells.' This saying was repeated by other *sādhus* of different *sampradāyas*. Kamal Giri, a *saṃnyāsī* of the Jūnā *akhāṛā*, explained: 'You do not have to see what the guru does; you must grasp his words. If you catch his activities, you will follow them, but you will not learn anything.'

A young Rāmānujī *tyāgī*, Rām Avadhūt Dās, pointed out that 'A *mahātmā*[92] does not read any *śāstra*; he knows them through the guru-*paramparā*. Everyone can read a *śāstra* and a book, [. . .] but what is transmitted by the guru, that teaching is secret [H., *gupt*].' The transmission of the teachings takes place from guru to disciple and is mostly oral. Training, however, does not only consist of spending time with the guru, but also of travelling and attending religious gatherings. As Kamal Giri said:

> Travelling is also very necessary, because in the beginning the young *sādhu* has to look for *gyān* here and there: the more *sādhus* he encounters, the more different *anubhavas* [experiences] he can have. Moreover, he will have to face different situations, and it is through them that he will realise the presence of God. Otherwise, sitting at home or in the *āśram*, how could he? Sometimes hardships also bring *gyān*.

Travelling offers the opportunity to receive information and teachings, as *sādhus* learn by listening to stories, often told around the *dhūnī*, or by observing the practice of other *sādhus*. For this reason, one can also have more than one guru. In fact, an individual has one *dīkṣā* guru, the guru who

---

disciple does not reach his goal, then the guru will have to be reborn to continue teaching him. However, I am not sure if this is a widespread idea.

92 'Great soul'; this is the honorific applied to important and accomplished gurus.

gives initiation, but, if permitted by the *dīkṣā* guru, he may have several *śikṣā* gurus, those who provide further teachings. Īśnāth reported:

> I received many things from my guru jī, but it is not like one has only one guru. My guru gave me a couple of practices and I practised them, then I met other gurus, there were many, each of whom gave me something. Because this is our life, we sit with various gurus and *pīrs* and so we gain knowledge. You have *kākā* [uncle] gurus and you learn from them, from the family.

These *śikṣā* gurus may come from different *sampradāyas*: for example, Garuḍ Dās told me that, despite all the techniques he practised, he could not find inner peace. Therefore, he began to wander from the Himalayas to the jungle, spending time with various yogis suggested along the way. Then, in 2000, he met a *siddha* Yogī who taught him a specific *dhyāna sādhanā* which opened the *śakti-path* and enabled him to attain *paramātman*.[93]

The process of learning from gurus is, therefore, highly individual and depends on the gurus that a *sādhu* meets in the course of his life. However, it also depends on an individual's skills and opportunities. One of the guru's duties is, indeed, to study the nature of his disciples and then suggest to them the spiritual path best suited to their abilities. This means that the same guru will teach his disciples differently according to their potential. A true guru will evaluate how his disciple behaves, what his goal is and what his *bhāva* (nature) is, because 'everyone has to do his own *karma*: the guru will have to do his work and the disciple his own'.[94] To illustrate this, Garuḍ Dās told me that, while he was steered towards the yoga *sādhanā*, his guru-*bhāī* (brother of the guru) was instead directed towards a more devotional practice based on *bhajan* and *bhakti pūjā*. This means that, although yoga is considered in the wider world to be a discipline open to all, which today one can learn simply by watching tutorials on YouTube, in the ascetic world nothing is taken for granted: it is the guru who decides whether or not to give a teaching and on which religious path to direct his disciple. Obviously, not all gurus can teach the yoga *sādhanā*—only those who are acquainted with it. Therefore, it is possible to learn yoga not from the *dīkṣā* guru but from a *śikṣā* guru.[95] But, again, if the 'yoga-guru' does not think a disciple is suited, he will not teach him. In fact, according to *sādhus*, not all

---

93 See Chapter 6, p. 254f.

94 The words of Rāghavendra Dās, a young Rāmānandī *tyāgī*, initiated into the order when he was a child.

95 For example, *tyāgī* Rām Caraṇ Dās's guru was a *tapasvī* living in the jungle of Junagadh, Gujarat. It is only when Rām Caraṇ Dās moved to Ayodhya in 1960 that he learnt yoga from the temple *pujārī*.

individuals are suitable for yoga as a *sādhanā*, because not everybody has a mind that can be brought under control through yoga practices.

Conclusion

In this chapter we have seen that different *sampradāya*s require different initiations to enter the ascetic world; that approaches to brahmanical rituals and lay society may differ just as the religious goals underlying asceticism do: not only *mokṣa* but also *bhakti*; not only union with God but also becoming God or participating in his grace. We have seen that Dasnāmīs and Rāmānandīs are more related to the brahmanical world than the other *sampradāya*s mentioned. This is evidenced by the fact that, for them, the use of a thread to be worn as a *janeu* is still present: in the case of the *saṃnyāsī*s it must be received and then renounced during the second initiation, whereas for Vaiṣṇavas it becomes an ascetic *janeu*, symbolising their right to still celebrate brahmanical rituals.[96]

*Saṃnyāsī*s and *tyāgī*s seem to be the heirs of groups described in brahmanical Upaniṣads, and this association and the fact that they are the most numerous ascetic groups enable them to act at times—through the figures of Śaṅkarācāryas, the various Jagadgurus, and pan-Indian organisations (such as the Akhāṛā Pariṣad, the Dharma Sansad, etc.)—as representatives of a traditional religious power.

However, as we saw, *sampradāya*s are not static, and, although their roots can be anchored in a brahmanical soil, their developments and sections allowed them to be influenced by new religious trends, whether tantric or devotional. Indeed, the orders here presented can be interpreted as the heirs of the religious paths mentioned in the previous chapter: brahmanical asceticism, tantric asceticism and devotional asceticism, although each group presents differentiations and features that demonstrate the intermingling of these various forms of asceticism. These orders have often found ways to provide access to people of low castes and, consequently, to women, although female ascetics could (and can) rarely have access to high charges or positions.

The fluidity of the *sampradāya*s' structures, with their subgroups created to adapt new ideas to meet people's spiritual needs and pursuits, also

96 Speaking of the differences between *saṃnyāsī*s and Vaiṣṇavas, Dayānanda Purī pointed out that Vaiṣṇavas look more at the rules to be followed and pay attention to the purity of the body, whereas *saṃnyāsī*s think that the body can never be pure, because it is part of *māyā* and made by *māyā*.

led to the fluidity of teachings and practices. For this reason, the same practices can be performed and explained by different ascetics in a similar way. This has often allowed me to write general descriptions, jumping from the words of one *sādhu* to another, even if they were members of different *sampradāyas*. What differs, in fact, is not so much the practice or its interpretation but its role in the more general plan of individual *sādhanā* and its ultimate religious purpose, which can vary.

3 'Prācīn Yog': Tapasyā from Past to Present

Since ancient times, various strenuous techniques have been practised by ascetics in India, whether Buddhists, Jains, or belonging to the lineages and groups that would later form 'Hindu' *sampradāyas*. Some of the most strenuous techniques involved the production of *tapas*, a powerful inner heat. The development of ideas and practices (*tapasyā*) related to the word *tapas* led to it becoming synonymous with asceticism and to be applied in various ascetic contexts with reference to different activities and techniques. When yoga began to be theorised, a strong link was established between *tapas* and yoga, and the practices usually associated with *tapas* were understood as part of yoga. It is therefore not surprising that the *ūrdhvabāhu* Amar Bhārtī (see below) described *tapasyā* as 'the ancient yoga' (*prācīn yog* in Hindi).

The history of *tapas*, *tapasyā* and their interrelation with yoga and *haṭha* yoga is rich and complex. In this chapter, I will initially provide a brief historical overview of the ideas and practices associated with the term *tapas* within the history of Indian religions and asceticism, considering some of the current studies on the subject. This first section, therefore, seeks to demonstrate that, like the word 'yoga', *tapas* has taken on a wide range of meanings in different literary and religious contexts and has been associated with a number of practices. The second section will consider evidence from the past—from the earliest Vedic texts to the descriptions of travellers and Orientalists—that mention techniques identified as *tapas*, in order to reconstruct a certain continuity from past to present. These descriptions, in fact, will lead us to contemporary practitioners. The third section of this chapter presents the current practice of *tapasyā*s through ethnographic data. Considering the scarce number of detailed accounts about *tapasyā*s in the present, this section aims to provide a comprehensive overview of the subject, framing *tapasyā*s in three main etic categories—behavioural, annual and highly physically demanding—but also showing that other practices (such as *āsana*s or *sevā*) can be experienced as a form of austerity. At the end of this chapter, the reasons behind the practice of *tapasyā* will be explained and its socio-religious aspects will also be assessed.

The journey through the historical development of *tapas* and the ethnographic analysis will allow us to emphasise the deep connections with yoga and *haṭha* yoga and, at the same time, broaden our understanding of *tapasyā*. The wide range of ideas associated with *tapasyā* will prove that layers of meanings accumulated over the centuries often still co-exist.

Once upon a time there was *tap*

The word *tapas* derives from the Sanskrit root *tap*, which means 'to give out heat', 'to make hot' or 'to be hot', so the noun *tapas* can be understood as 'heat'. This heat develops through ascetic fervour and 'ascetic practice', i.e. *tapasyā*. *Tapasyā* refers more generally to austerities, but it also includes activities and practices produced through intense discipline which, in turn, generate further heat. In general, the *tapas* (ascetic fervour) required to perform *tapasyā* (ascetic practice) produces more *tapas* (inner heat).

In the Vedas, *tapas* was understood as natural heat associated with either the sun or fire. It was conceived as the power at the beginning of all great events, because it was creative and transformative and preceded the deities themselves. The *ṛṣi*s were engaged in *tapas* and were inspired (by it) during the compilation of the Vedas; Indra conquered heaven by *tapas*; Agni was produced by *tapas* and the Primal Being practised *tapas* before the creation of the world (Bhagat 1976: 18, 107, 115). In the *Ṛg Veda*, *tapas* was an important concept which referred to ascetic practice; being a *tapasvī*, someone who practises *tapas*, was a way of securing access to the gods. Indeed, hermits, kings, gods and *asura*s devoted themselves to *tapas* to compel the gods to grant their desires. Through *tapas* one could obtain incredible powers—such as reaching the highest point of the cosmos, possessing great strength, gaining wisdom hidden from others and the ability to defeat death (Olson 2015: 2)—as well as the sexual and fertilising energy needed to create rain, productive fields, or biological offspring (Kaelber 1989: 3–4). It should be noted, however, that *tapas* is something that could also be lost. In many stories, such loss is related to the discharge of semen, given the link between celibacy and the accumulation of *tapas*.[1] For this reason, deities, fearing the power accumulated by a *tapasvī*, will send *apsarās* (divine nymphs) to seduce him. Angry reactions against the *apsarās* (or others) will also cause the loss of *tapas*.

Vedic sources not only present several examples of *tapasyā*, but also shed light on the development of the word and associated practices. In the *Atharva Veda*, the celibate Vedic student, the *brahmacārī*, undergoes physical and mental disciplines (fasting, remaining isolated or silent, sleeping on the floor or not sleeping at all, and breath control) to acquire knowledge of *brahman*, the reason why later on *brahmacarya* began to be associated with celibacy (Bhagat 1976: 17). The *Śatapatha Brāhmaṇa* (3.4.3.2) equates the consecration ceremony for the Soma sacrifice with *tapas*, since it is associated with a set of practices (restraining from company, fasting, silence, etc.) used to produce the necessary heat (Galewicz 2020). In the context of the sacrifices elaborated in later Vedic literature, *tapas* is associated with *śrama* (concentrated effort) to indicate the means and the determination to achieve a particular goal.[2] In some sections of the *Ṛg Veda*, *tapas* was associated with pain and suffering, often produced through self-inflicted heat and pain (Bhagat 1976: 18, 107).

It was thought that austerity and self-imposed bodily mortifications (*tapasyā*) produced the inner fire capable of transforming the individual into a vessel of heated potency, elevating one above the human condition. Through this heated potency, *tapasvīs* could obtain not only powers but also their own purification.[3]

When new interpretations of sacrifice were introduced in the Āraṇyakas, shifting the focus from an external sacrifice to an internal or mental one,

1 As Wendy Doniger (1981: 40) has pointed out, Hindu mythology provides many examples of the role and value of the male seed, and specifically the ascetic's seed, which 'is fertile in itself'.

2 As we have seen in Chapter 1 (p. 26), *śrama* identifies a source of exertions which was associated with ascetic contexts outside the Vedic paradigm (*śramaṇa*; see Olivelle 1993: 11–16). According to Bodewitz (2007: 153), *śrama* represents those efforts that precede the sacrifice and which, along with *tapas* and *vratacaryā*, does not necessarily have direct ritualistic connotations.

3 Kaelber (1989: 55) makes a distinction between *tapas* as a means of ritual purification used by ascetics and *tapas* as penance for specific transgressions. The scholar shows that *Mānavadharmaśāstra* equates *tapas* and penance since *tapas* 'removes or destroys the guilt or evil incurred as a consequence of immoral acts' (11.102), while in 4.107 the text informs that man destroys his 'sins' by *tapas*, and in 5.109 the individual soul is cleansed by it.

tapas, along with celibacy and fasting, became a tool for purifying the body, enabling the practitioner to be indifferent to desire. It was in the philosophical milieu of the Upaniṣads, where the attention was on knowledge of *ātman* and its relations to *brahman*, that *tapas* became properly associated with ascetic activity, acquiring the meaning of asceticism in general. Entering the domain of asceticism as a way of life, *tapas* was practised by those who left society to concentrate on the liberation of the self, to stop the fluctuations of the mind or to clear accumulated karma. In fact, *tapas* became a tool for attaining knowledge and *mokṣa*, closely associated with yoga.

Tapas and yoga

The *Kaṭha Upaniṣad* (c. 3rd century BCE), continuing the philosophical speculations on the knowledge of the self and its identity with *brahman* begun in the early Upaniṣads, adopted a new term to indicate the method and goal to be followed by the practitioner-ascetic: yoga.[4] This method aimed to restrain the senses in order to restrain the mind, thereby producing a stillness in which the intellect was inactive, thus facilitating knowledge of *brahman* and *ātman*.[5] In this Upaniṣadic and yogic context, *tapas*, along with *brahmacarya*, faith, truth, etc., became one of the means of achieving that purification of the mind that leads to control of the sense organs (Crangle 1994: 107–108).[6] However, in the *Śvetāśvatara Upaniṣad tapas* is also associated with *dhyāna* (Crangle 1994: 107–108).

In the epics (*Mahābhārata*, *Rāmāyaṇa*) and Purāṇas, *tapas* continues to be associated with a plurality of situations. In the *Mahābhārata* the

---

4 I leave aside previous understanding or examples of yoga because, as pointed out by Mallinson and Singleton (2017: xii), although there are ascetic figures in the Vedic texts which suggest 'mystical ascetic tradition similar to those of later yogis', and some practices are mentioned 'which may be forerunners of later yogic techniques of posture and breath-retention [. . .] it is entirely speculative to claim [. . .] that the Vedic corpus provides any evidence of systematic yoga practice'.

5 'When the five senses, along with the mind, remain still and the intellect is not active, that is known as the highest path. They consider yoga to be a firm restraint of the senses. Then one becomes undistracted, for yoga is the arising and the passing away' (*Kaṭha Upaniṣad* 6.10–11, from Mallinson and Singleton 2017: 17).

6 Practices such as *āsanas* and *prāṇāyāmas* were often still referred to as *tapas* in later yogic contexts (see Mallinson and Singleton 2017: 92–94).

word *tapas* appears at least 3,000 times, and is a means or an instrument to achieve other ends (Hara 1979).[7]

Tapas and yoga appear in similar contexts in the epics: *tapasvī*s are called *yogī*s and their practice of *tapas* is frequently designated as yoga. According to Bhagat (1976: 205), in considering the *tapas*–yoga link, there are three groups of narratives in the epics: those that present old examples and teachings of *tapas* in which yoga does not appear; tales and teachings in which *tapas* and yoga are synonymous and directed to the achievement of physical and mental powers; and tales or passages in which an elaborated yoga philosophy is presented. For example, in the 12th book of the *Mahābhārata*, the *Śāntiparvan*, and more precisely its third subsection, the *Mokṣadharmaparvan*, behaviours and rules for attaining *mokṣa* are described, and here *tapas* is not only the power that permeates the three worlds (12.217.15) but also the practices of celibacy, non-violence and control of speech and mind that eventually lead to knowledge (12.217.16) (Olson 2015: 42).

In the epics, yoga and *tapas* are both recognised as methods for achieving spiritual and worldly goals through the manipulation of the powers they produce. In the *Mahābhārata*, the term *siddhi* (perfection, realisation, powers)[8] seems to denote supernatural abilities obtained through austerities and often by yogic means (Lamb 2012: 427). Since *tapas* was integrated into yogic practice, the powers resulting from it were assimilated too: in the Upaniṣads and epics, self-restraint, *tapas* and *vrata* (vow) are used to gain control over one's body and mind in order to obtain *mukti* (liberation) and *siddhis*. As Mallinson and Singleton (2017: xiv) have pointed out, texts of the period show that 'ascetics of all traditions engaged in austerities' and

7 In the *Mahābhārata*, for example, Kapila practised *tapas* for a hundred years to obtain a hundred sons; Muni Baladhi practised austerities to have an immortal son; and the king of Vidharbha did the same in order to have offspring. Arjuna through his penances obtained celestial weapons from Maheśvara, while Sunda and Upasunda, two *asura* brothers, obtained a boon from Brahmā by means of which they could be killed only by one another. Women are often depicted performing austerities to get a husband, the most famous example being that of Pārvatī fasting for a thousand years to acquire not only ascetic powers but also Śiva's favour. Ambā, in contrast, practised *tapas* to take vengeance on Bhīṣma, while Arundhatī did so to resolve a 12-year drought, and the daughter of the sage Kuṇigarga performed austerities to attain proficiency in yoga, so that she could assume any form she liked. See Bhagat 1976: 205; Brockington 2020: 83.

8 Bhagat (1976: 272) mentions the ability to know the intent of others, to acquire intuitive vision, discover things, knowing people's past, present and future.

that 'methods which might be differentiated as yoga and *tapas* were complementary parts of early ascetic practice'.

Within the Vedic and brahmanical tradition, however, there was also a certain opposition to extreme forms of *tapas* that led to their reinterpretation, as was the case with *saṃnyāsa*. In its 17th chapter, the *Bhagavadgītā* denounces the practices involving forms of asceticism that 'torture the elements in the body (17.5–6), and instead it presents three varieties of *tapas* according to the *guṇas* (*sattva*, *rajas* and *tamas*)[9] in support of a sattvic form of *tapas* (17.14–17). This consists of:

> 17.14 Worship of the gods, the twice-born, teachers, and wise men; purity, rectitude, celibacy and non-violence; these are called austerities of the body.
>
> 17.15 Words that do not cause distress, truthful, agreeable, and beneficial; and practice in the recitation of sacred texts; these are called austerities of speech.
>
> 17.16 Peace of mind, gentleness, silence, self-restraint, purity of being; these are called austerities of the mind.
>
> 17.17 This threefold austerity practiced with the highest faith by men who are not desirous of fruits and are steadfast, they regard as sattvic.[10]

These activities are qualified as sattvic 'heated discipline' when they are practised with the highest trust by those who are engaged in yoga and desire no reward for their actions (17.17). Therefore, the *Gītā* identifies *tapas* as the discipline that by purifying the body and mind suppresses instincts and impulses, advocating an ethical approach to every action.

A similar attitude can be found in the *Yogaśāstra* of Patañjali (around 400 CE). Patañjali proposed a yogic method based on an eightfold path to overcome the suffering created by ignorance, following a moral and ethical code of conduct and a discipline aimed at controlling the body and breath to gain control of the mind. This method was based on restraint (*yama*), observance (*niyama*), posture (*āsana*), breath control (*prāṇāyāma*), withdrawal from the senses (*pratyāhāra*), concentration (*dhāraṇā*), meditation (*dhyāna*), and a deeper, over-meditative state (*samādhi*). This yoga would

---

9 These can be considered the three qualities that form the material world (*prakṛti*). *Sattva* is good, illuminating, positive and constructive; *rajas* is active, chaotic, impulsive, potentially good or bad; and *tamas* is the quality of darkness, ignorance, destruction and lethargy.

10 Sargeant 2009 [1984]: 647–650.

lead to control of the fluctuation of the mind, i.e. *cittavṛttinirodhah*.[11] In the *Sūtra*, *tapas* is mentioned as part of *kriyā* yoga together with *svādhyāya* (self-study) and *īśvarapräṇidhāna* (devotion to God), and as part of *niyama*. Therefore, it is identified as a necessary preliminary activity of yoga practice. Patañjali's *tapas* is not understood as self-mortification or injury to the body, rather as a set of practices to tame bodily and mental habits, to prepare the individual for inner practices.

The use of intense forms of *tapasyā* has persisted, nevertheless, among various ascetic groups and lineages. Pāśupatas, for instance, were known for their *atitapas*, extreme asceticism (Acharya 2011; Bisschop 2020: 17), and the Kāpālikas and Kālamukhas placed particular emphasis on penances (see Lorenzen 1972: 32, 100). These practices were probably maintained through oral transmission rather than through textual sources.

In fact, textual sources on yoga and *haṭha* yoga omit references to *tapas* and *tapasyā tout court*. The *Haṭhapradīpikā*[12] criticises exertion (1.15) and warns (1.61) against *kāyakleśavidhi*, 'observances which harm the body'.[13] A vernacular source such as the *Gorakh Bānī* (Sayings of Gorakh)[14] offers a dual understanding of *tapas*. On the one hand, Gorakh, hypothetical author and founder of the Nāth *sampradāya*, seems against physical *tapas*:

> In wooden sandals, the foot slips, oh Avadhūt!
> Iron chains harm the body.
> Being naked, keeping silent, eating only milk:
> Yoga is not achieved in such a way (39).

On the other hand, in *sabadī* 253, he states that: 'Self-control is the essence of the yogi who does *jap* and *tapas*' (Djurdjevic and Singh 2019: 149). He was referring, in the first *sabadī*, to a *tapas* based on strenuous austerities which, by mortifying the body, could not be supported by an ascetic who

11 Through this method, the self of the yogi, who follows an ascetic lifestyle based on detachment (*vairāgya*) and meditative practices, remains in its true, undefiled essence and is thus not subject to suffering. As for Sāṃkhya, its goal is not to create a union: rather, a division between transient realities (*prakṛti*) and the *puruṣa* (consciousness). According to the *Yogaśāstra*, *mokṣa* is isolation (*kaivalya*), or absolute independence.

12 See p. 153.

13 I thank Professor James Mallinson for bringing this passage to my attention and for providing me with the translation of *kāyakleśavidhi* according to his most recent work as part of the 'Light on Haṭha Yoga' Project.

14 I consider here the translation of the *Gorakh Bānī* by Djurdjevic and Singh 2019.

considers the vigorous and healthy body a fundamental tool[15] and, in the second *sabadī*, to a *tapas* based on intense meditation that was accepted and practised.

However, as Jason Birch and Jacqueline Hargreaves (2023) suggest, it seems that, after an initial resistance to physical austerities, *haṭha* yoga textual sources from the 17th century onwards show a possible attempt to reintroduce forms of *tapasyās*, transforming them into *āsanas*.[16] Birch gives the example of *tapakār āsana*, described in the *Jogapradīpakā*, an inverted posture that requires the use of rope: 'the yogin places his right shoulder on a piece of hanging rope to launch himself into the inverted position. He then secures his body upside down by holding the rope with his feet' (Birch 2017). This practice was described in several sources as a form of *tapasyā* (see below, p. 138).

Tapasyā in practice: glimpses from the past

What were the austerities that were practised? Ranging from the hermits found in Vedic Saṃhitās and early literary sources, to accounts of *tapasvīs* provided by travellers and English employees, this section provides examples of *tapasyās* that will be useful in drawing comparisons with current practices. As we shall see, the array of activities listed as *tapas*/*tapasyā* are multifarious, reflecting the different contexts in which they spread and were adopted.

Although the nature of *tapas* itself is not described, the Vedic literature nevertheless offers a variety of practices. An early example is that of the *muni* (*Ṛg Veda* X.136.1–7), a term that not only identifies a hermit (cf. p. 26) but also abstinence from speech (Bhagat 1976: 108). The *Śatapatha Brāhmaṇa* (9.5.1.4) claims that 'the whole practice of *tapas* is when one abstains from food'. Fasting, in fact, is one of the oldest and most followed forms of *tapasyā*. A particular food-related austerity is when the individual drinks only milk, often hot milk: '[h]is food consists of the [hot] fast-milk only' (*Śatapatha Brāhmaṇa* 3.1.2.1), '[f]or tapas it is when [one] lives on

15 As we will see in detail in the next chapter, with the spread of texts on *haṭha* yoga the cultivation of the body became important because a healthy body was necessary to support the practice, and to acquire powers and possibly immortality.

16 Rather than actually emerging in the 17th century, it was at this time that these practices began to be acknowledged in textual sources. Iconographic evidence, for example the sculptures of *āsanas* in Dabhoi, reveals that strenuous postures were probably already present in the 13th century. On Dabhoi and postures, see Chapter 5, p. 198.

fast-milk only' (*Śatapatha Brāhmaṇa* 9.5.1.2). *Manu* (11.215) mentions the *taptakṛcchra* or 'hot penance', which consists of drinking hot liquid such as milk, water, clarified butter or inhaling hot air and fasting for prescribed periods (Kaelber 1989: 53, 58).

The importance of fasting in the ascetic context also appears in the Buddhist Pali Canon (see the *Majjhima Nikāya*), when Siddhartha, having abandoned his privileged life at court, adopts the life of an ascetic for six years, enduring intense self-mortification together with a group of hermits. During this time, he would undergo intensive fasting, reducing his body to that of a skeleton. Another strenuous practice to sustain his meditation was to hold his breath for such a long time that he felt violent pains in his body (Akira 1993: 25–26).[17]

The retention of breath was in fact considered a form of *tapas*: *Manu* (2.83; 6.70) argues that *prāṇāyāma* is the best or highest form of *tapas*, and the *Vasiṣṭhadharmaśāstra* (25.5) confirms this, explaining that through *prāṇāyāma* one generates *tapas* 'even to the ends of the hair and nails' (Kaelber 1989: 58).

The mental absorption of ascetics performing *tapas*, often related to the practice of yoga, has been frequently described in ways that convey their obstinacy. The brahmin Jājali stood as still as a piece of wood and was so absorbed in *tapas* that a pair of birds built their nest in his matted hair (*Mahābhārata* 12.262); Cyavana sat in *vīrāsana* and remained in the same spot, completely motionless, for such a long time that creepers covered his body and he eventually turned into an anthill, yet continued to practise *tapas* (*Mahābhārata* 3.122ff.) (Bhagat 1976: 207).

Greek sources also offer us historical glimpses of strenuous physical practices. Strabo, for example, describes the meeting of members of

17 While the Buddha is represented in the Canon as criticising the use of austerities as being not helpful for liberation (see Bronkhorst 1993: 1–3), Jain traditions have placed a special importance on *tapas* and mortification of the body. *Tapas* is divided into external and internal. External *tapas* includes austerities such as fasting, food almsgiving, mortification of the body through bodily postures and solitary living. Internal *tapas* refers to spiritual exercises that involve self-discipline, cleansing and purification of the mind through scripture reading, service to others, modesty, meditation, etc. (Bhagat 1976: 183). Pratibha Pragya (2020: 179) claims that 'almost all early records of *āsana* are based on ascetic *tapas* practices'; in fact, the 30th chapter of the *Uttarādhyayanasūtra* describes 12 types of austerities, and, under the label *kāyakleśa*, various postures, such as *vīrāsana* or *utkaṭāsana*, are described. See also Pragya 2020: 173 for references to the *Tattvārthasūtra*; and Wiley 2012: 145–194.

Alexander the Great's entourage with the gymnosophists in the 4th century BCE. There were:

> [...] fifteen men standing in different postures, sitting or lying down naked, who continued in these positions until the evening and then returned to the city. The most difficult thing to endure was the heat of the sun, which was so powerful that no one else could endure without pain to walk on the ground at mid-day with bare feet (Mallinson and Singleton 2017: 88).

We cannot call these postures *āsanas* as the term has not been used here. However, as we will see later in this chapter, some of these 'tapasic postures' were going to be considered *āsanas*, while maintaining their function of *tapasyā* in some ascetic contexts.

The *Rāmāyaṇa* also provides a good collection of different *tapasyās* practised by ascetics: holding the legs upwards and the head downwards; standing in the water; staying in the midst of five fires in summer; drenching oneself in the wet season; remaining in water in winter; eating once a month; abstaining from food and subsisting on air; standing on one leg with the arms raised; offering one's limbs to the fire; etc. (Bhagat 1976: 258). A similar list is presented in the *Śiva Purāṇa*, in its *Pārvatī Khaṇḍa* (chapter 22) of the *Rudra Saṃhitā*, in which Pārvatī's austerities are described. This narration is interesting because, as Menā, Pārvatī's mother, declares (22.23): 'For a woman to go to a penance-grove for the realisation of her desire is what we have never heard of before.'[18] In reality, there are several examples of women practising demanding austerities in Vedic literature and epics, but these were probably an exception at the time of the *Śiva Purāṇa* (c. 10th–11th centuries), as still perceived by contemporary *sādhus* (see below). The *Purāṇa* tells us that Pārvatī 'wore tree barks and fine girdle of Muñja grass (22.29); [...] eschewed necklace and wore the pure deer skin (22.30)' and:

> In the summer she kept a perpetually blazing fire all round and remaining within continued muttering the mantra (22.40). In the rainy season she continuously remained sitting on the bare ground on the rock and got herself drenched by the downpour of rain (22.41). During the winter, with great devotion she remained in water throughout. During snowfall and in the nights too she performed her penance observing fast (22.42). [...]
>
> The first year she spent in taking fruits, the second in taking leaves, in the course of her penance. She spent many years thus (22.47). Then Śivā,

18 I use J.L. Shastri's translation of the *Śiva Purāṇa* (1970).

> the daughter of Himavat, eschewed even the leaves. She did not take any food. She was engrossed in the performance of penance (22.48).
>
> Since she, the daughter of Himavat, eschewed leaves from her diet she was called Aparṇā by the gods (22.49).
>
> Then Pārvatī performed great penance standing on one leg and remembering Śiva, she continued muttering the five-syllabled mantra (22.50).
>
> Clad in barks of trees, wearing matted hair and eager in the meditation of Śiva, she surpassed even sages by her penance (22.51).

Many of these practices are also attested visually.[19] Depictions on buildings and in artwork demonstrate the importance of austerities, but also the conflation of yoga and *tapasyā*: ascetics were often represented as *tapasvīs*, but it is sometimes difficult to recognise whether they are performing a *tapasyā* or a yoga practice.[20] One of the most represented *tapasyās* is that of standing with raised arms. A very famous example of this is the sculpture of King Bhāgīratha[21] at Mamallapuram (7th century CE). In it, he is depicted emaciated and standing on one foot, with both arms up (*ūrdhvabāhu*), looking at the sun. In Patan, Gujarat, among the sculptures of the Rānī Kī Vāv ('The Queen's Stepwell', 11th century CE), *ūrdhvabāhus* are used as decorative motifs to fill in the spaces between the main deities (see Photo 1).

Fine arts provide countless examples of sages, yogis and *tapasvīs* portrayed in small gatherings or while performing austerities. Noteworthy are the *rāgamālās*, a collection of paintings depicting musical modes. Not only are yogis and *tapasvīs* represented here, but also female ascetics, sometimes while performing the *khaṛeśvarī* (standing) austerity.[22]

Medieval stories offer other interesting examples of *tapasyā*, such as that of Dharamnāth, a Nāth *yogī* considered to be both a disciple of Matsyendranāth and a member of the Satnāth lineage of Punjab. His *tapasyā* has been transmitted and practically maintained to this day (see p. 139). According to tradition, in Dhinodhar (Gujarat), Dharamnāth

---

19 Since it is impossible to introduce here in detail the rich material that visual sources can provide, the interested reader could refer to Chakravarty 1970; Dallapiccola and Verghese 1998; Sears 2013; Diamond 2013; Powell 2018, 2023.

20 See on this topic Powell 2023.

21 The identification of this king performing *tapas* is open to debate: some scholars claim him to be King Bhāgīratha who brought the Ganges to Earth, while others identify him with Arjuna (see Sears 2013).

22 While sometimes female ascetics might be depicted performing austerities, they are never represented performing *āsanas*, other than seated ones. I mention the topic of women and physical practices in Chapter 5 (p. 206).

Photo 1 *Ūrdhvabāhu*, detail from the Rānī Kī Vāv, Gujarat, 2017.

stood on his head for 12 years, with closed eyes, 'resting on a conical ball of hard stone' (or on a betel nut). Such was the *tapas* accumulated during those years that the first thing he saw, when he finally opened his eyes, was burnt by the fire: he eventually dried up the sea, leaving the present Rann of Kutch, a salt marsh in the Thar Desert (Briggs 1938: 117).[23]

Legends and stories like this abound in medieval literature,[24] especially in hagiographic works, although, again, it is very difficult to discern whether specific practices and their results should be considered *tapasyā*, yoga or *haṭha* yoga. For example, the *Rasik Prakāś Bhaktamāl* (1712 CE), describing the Rāmānandī Kīlhdev, relates that he was so absorbed in *haṭha* yoga that, when a royal procession passed by and someone, seeing him so motionless, drove a nail (*kīl*) into his head, he did not feel it and the nail even disappeared (Śrīvāstav 1957: 189). This story resembles the condition attained by ascetics practising meditative *tapasyā* previously mentioned, but here the same practice itself is described as *haṭha* yoga.

The practice of austerities did not go unnoticed by Persian scholars, nor by European travellers and merchants who enriched their tales and depictions of Indian places and people with images and descriptions of 'exotic' ascetics.

The author of the *Dabistān-e Mazāheb* (17th century, vol. II) talks about a certain 'Ganeś a-man', disciple of a *gosain*, who 'practised the restraining of the breath assiduously'. Once '[. . .] he restrained his breath so that his belly, filled with wind, extended beyond his knees' (vol. II, 145).[25] In Kiratpur he met another *saṃnyāsī*, 'Kalyan Bharati', who could hold his breath for two watches (i.e. six hours), while in 1638 in Kashmir he met a man supposedly able to hold his breath for nine hours. The author also states that there were *saṃnyāsīs* who stood on one leg for 12 years and were called '*Thávésar*', while those who maintained continuous silence were

23 This was not Dharamnāth's first penance. He arrived in Kutch, Gujarat, from Peshawar in about 1382, searching for a suitable place to perform *tapasyā*. While he was absorbed in his practice, his disciple Garībnāth was supposed to take care of him. However, since the inhabitants of the area did not support him, Garībnāth had to sell wood to provide his guru with food, while an old lady had to cook for them. When, 12 years later, Dharamnāth discovered the pain his disciple and the old lady went through, he cursed the people, and all the cities in the vicinity were swallowed by the earth. To atone for this wrathful impulse, Dharamnāth began his second *tapasyā* in Dhinodhar, although a portion of the hill split off because of the weight of his sins. This story was collected by Briggs (1938: 118) consulting *The Indian Antiquary*, vol. VII, 50.

24 For examples, see White 2009: 1–37; Burchett 2019: 181–194.

25 Excerpts from the *Dabistān* are taken from Shea and Troyer 1843.

called '*Máunínas*' (145–148). Later, he speaks of a class of ascetics ('dervishes') who practised *tapasyā* or 'devout austerity' and who 'by great and difficult penances, banish every illusion from them' and claim:

> to have the power to cause rain to fall or to cease; to attract whomever they like, and to render him obedient to their will; to give information of whatever is concealed, and to reveal the secrets of the hearts; to possess the knowledge of the good and the bad hidden in the minds; as well as that of the relations and history of the world; and upon the mirror of their hearts are reflected the lights of secrets [. . .] the splendor of the universe (239–240).

The accounts of European travellers also provide interesting descriptions of ascetics.[26] Jean-Baptiste Tavernier, in India between 1638 and 1643, described encounters with *sādhus* among whom were *ūrdhvabāhus*, *sādhus* with arms crossed behind their heads and long nails, and *khaṛeśvarīs*, standing ascetics (1679: vol. II, 419–423). François Bernier, who was in India between 1655 and 1668, provided specific information on ascetic groups (1709: vol. II, 97–168). For example, 'Jogis' were naked, covered in ashes, had long matted hair, usually sat under trees and engaged in painful austerities, with spindly arms and long, twisted nails due to their raised arms. He also described *khaṛeśvarīs* whose calves were so swollen that they looked like thighs, and ascetics who carried heavy chains similar to those used to tie elephants (1709: vol. II, 121). Bernier also noted how among the various 'species of yogin' there were those who 'spend hours in handstand position, or in a variety of other postures which are so difficult and painful that they could not be imitated by our tumblers' (Bernier 1688: 47–52, in Singleton 2010: 37). Similarly, Tavernier, writing in 1679, asserted that there was an 'infinity' of penitents, 'some of whom assume positions altogether contrary to the natural attitude of the human body' (Tavernier 1679: vol. II, 154).

Niccoló Manucci, in India from 1656 to 1712, produced two books preciously illustrated with miniatures and watercolours. As described by Rasa Maria Cimino (2014: 131), in his *Red Book*, there is a miniature of the world of *sādhus* (fig. 172) while his *Black Book* presents several portraits of *tapasvīs*: an *ūrdhvabāhu*; a *sādhu* with his arms crossed behind his head; an ascetic living on a small hut built on top of a pole; another with his head inserted in a wooden board; one tied to a tree upside down with a fire under him; and a *khaṛeśvarī*. According to Manucci, these ascetics did penance for money and to attract women. These accounts, in fact, present

26 R.M. Cimino (2014: 129–137) provides a useful collection of the names and works of some of these travellers.

often biased comments on the ascetics/*tapasvīs*, who were often misjudged as charlatans.[27]

Especially useful is the account of Jonathan Duncan (later the Governor of Bombay, 1795–1811), who transcribed the travels of a *saṃnyāsī*, Pūrṇa Purī, whom he interviewed in Benaras in May 1792 (Duncan 1810: 262–271; 1799: 37–48). Pūrṇa Purī, an *ūrdhvabāhu*, explained why he chose this form of *tapasyā*, and while doing so also provided a (possibly unique) list of possible *tapasyās*. In his narration, Pūrṇa Purī defines *tapasyā* as a 'devotional discipline' and explains that, when he went to the Allahabad Melā—having already spent two years with his guru Lat Purī Svāmī—he heard *sādhus* talking about the peculiar benefits each *tapasyā* had, listing 18 different penances (Duncan 1810: 263–264):[28]

1. Ṭhādeśvarī ('Lord of Standing'). Standing upright during life, and never sitting down.
2. Ākāś muni ('Sky Sage'). Fixing one's regards towards heaven, and never looking down towards the earth.
3. Med'ha-muni ('Sacrificial Sage'?). Keeping both hands fixed on the chest.
4. Phersa-bahan (?). Keeping both hands extended horizontally.
5. Dhūmrapāna ('Smoking'). Tying the feet with a cord to the branch of a tree, or other high place and swinging with the head downwards with a fire underneath, the smoke of which is taken in at the mouth.
6. Pātāl-muni ('Underworld Sage'). Looking always towards the earth, the reverse of Ākāś muni.
7. Muni ('The Sage'). Observing constant silence.
8. Caurāsī Āsana ('Eighty-four Posture'). Different postures in sitting, such as continuing several hours with the feet on the neck or under the arms; after which the limbs are returned to their natural positions.

27 Although we cannot underplay the bias these travellers displayed in their descriptions of *tapasvī*, nonetheless, as Pauwels argues (2019: 50), we cannot forget that these 'Orientalists were hardly the first to misinterpret others' viewpoints since 'each generation of transmitters has added its own preconceptions'. And, as we have already seen, the undertaking of demanding austerities has always attracted criticism—and still does—in various religious contexts.

28 I use here the translations of the *tapasyās*' names as they appear in Mallinson and Singleton (2017: 119–121). Mallinson was the first, in 2013, to shed light on this important document.

9. Kapālī ('The Skull'). Placing a betel nut on the ground and standing with the head on the nut, and the feet in the air.
10. Pātālī ('Of the Underworld'). Burying oneself underground up to the chest with the head downwards, and the body from the waist down suspended in the air, and in that situation to be engaged in the ceremony termed *Yap* [*sic*], or the silent repetition of the names of God.
11. Ūrdhvabāhu ('Arm in the Air'). Having both arms forcibly raised up above the head, and extended fixed permanently in that position.
12. Baiṭheśvarī ('Lord of Sitting'). To constantly maintain a sitting posture, without ever rising or lying down.
13. Nyāsa dhyāna ('The Meditator'). To hold in the breath; this is necessary for those who become eminent in science. Such people, when they practise meditation as a devotional exercise, in doing so confine their breath, so that there doesn't appear to be any respiration in the corporeal frame, allowing them to be elevated to beatific visions of the Deity.
14. Caurangī-Āsana ('Caurangi's Pose'). To sit down on the knees for hours, bringing the right foot over the left shoulder, and the left over the right, with the arms in like manner over the back, so as to hold the toes of the feet on both sides in the hands.
15. Paramahaṃsa ('Ultimate Ascetic'). To go naked, and not to engage in conversation or connection with any person whatsoever. If any person brings you food, you are to receive and eat it, otherwise you are to remain immersed in contemplation of the divinity and not stand in awe of anyone.
16. Pañc-Agni ('Five Fires'). To be immersed in the smoke of fire from all sides, and having, fifthly, the sun above; thus to live naked, and to remain fixed in meditation on the deity.
17. Tribhangī ('With Three Bends'). Standing always on one foot.
18. Sūrya Bhāratī ('Sun Saint'). He who eats only after seeing the sun.

Pūrṇa Purī calls these the '18 mudrās' or 'ways of Brahmā', because Brahmā's sons had practised them. Since he was an *ūrdhvabāhu*, he mentioned that to begin this practice 'it is necessary to be abstemious in eating and sleeping for one year, and to keep the mind fixed, that is to be patient and resigned to the will of the Deity' (Duncan 1810: 264). According to Duncan (1810: 263), Pūrṇa Purī intended to lower his arms again. A similar comment had already been made by Colonel Samuel Turner who met him in Kolkata in 1783. Indeed, Mallinson (2013b) reports that Turner (1800: 269–271) wrote:

> The circulation of blood, seemed to have forsaken his arms; they were withered, void of sensation, and inflexible. Yet he spoke to me with confidence, of recovering the use of them, and mentioned his intention to take them down the following year, when the term of his penance would expire.

Considering that Turner met him in 1783 and Duncan in 1792, it would seem that Pūrṇa Purī, after nine years, had still not managed to lower his arms.

Duncan also refers to the *tapas* of 'Purrum Soutuntre Purkasanund Brahmacary', whom he met in 1792, lying on thorns and pebbles. According to Brahmacārī's narration, he locked himself in a cell near a village in Kashmir and vowed to remain there to do penance for 12 years:

> Vermin or worms gnawed my flesh, of which the marks still remain; and when one year had elapsed, then the Rajah opened the door of the cell, whereupon I said to him, 'either take my curse or make me a *ser-seja*, or bed of spikes'; and then that Rajah made for me the *ser-seja* I now occupy (Duncan 1799: 50).

During the four winter months, he also used to do '*jel-seja*' on his bed, i.e. stay night and day with water dripping on his head. At the time of his narration, Brahmacārī is said to have spent 35 years of *tapasyā* on that bed, even being carried on it. According to Brahmacārī, the same penance had already been endured in the *Satya yuga* by *ṛṣi* Agnivarṇa, in *Tretā yuga* by Ravana and in *Dvāpara yuga* by Bhīṣma Pitāmaha. He did this in the *Kali yuga*[29] and felt he was simply following in their footsteps (Duncan 1799: 49–51).[30]

---

29 These yugas represent four cosmological time intervals, a four-age cycle: *Satya yuga* (the accomplished age, virtue reigns supreme), *Tretā yuga* (the threefold-life age, hence three-quarters virtue and one-quarter sin), *Dvāpara yuga* (the twofold age, hence one-half virtue and one-half sin), and *Kali yuga* (the age of vice and misery, one-quarter virtue and three-quarters sin). The cycles are said to repeat like the seasons, within a greater time-cycle of the creation and destruction of the universe.

30 Oman says that once he saw 'a sadhu's wooden shoes bristling inside with a close crop of pointed nails'. He reports that the practice of lying on nails (*śara-sayyā*, 'arrow bed', in his book also called *kaṇṭaka śayyā*) comes from Bhīṣma, one of the heroes of the *Mahābhārata*: 'he was covered all over by the innumerable arrows

J.C. Oman (1903: 207–208) mentions an *ūrdhamukhī*, i.e. a *sādhu* hanging upside down, suspended from tree branches or other suitable supports, for half an hour at a time, but he had only met one. He also mentions the practice of '*samādh*', a period of burial—which can last 'from a few days to five or six weeks'—that conferred particular prestige, but had inevitably led to attempts made by fake *bābās*, with sometimes fatal outcomes (Oman 1903: 46–47).[31] Oman reports the verified case of a well-known *samādh* that lasted for 40 days and ended in success: that of Yogi Haridās in the time of Ranjit Singh of Punjab (1792–1839). Another *tapasyā* he mentions is the *aṣṭāṅga daṇḍavat*, or prostration of the body, 'involving the performance of a pilgrimage by a slow and most laborious mode of progression', repeatedly touching the ground with the eight limbs of the body (forehead, hands, chest, and feet). Since the latter two examples are not mentioned by Pūrṇa Purī, it is clear that the forms of *tapasyās* practised by ascetics was vast and probably constantly updated. It is also clear that, over the centuries, the word *tapas*/*tapasyā* has become an umbrella term used by various religious groups and lineages to refer to different sets of practices or attitudes based on endurance and discipline: practices consisting of bodily 'self-tortures' and penances; practices used to produce and conserve energy; and practices aimed at mental and behavioural self-training. Such understandings are still present among contemporary *sādhus*.

Tapasyā today

> 'These *tapasyās* have been done for a long time, they are not something new. *Śarīr ko kaṣṭh denā*! [You have to trouble your body!].'
>
> Yogī Śivanāth

In the contemporary ascetic world, words are fluid as they carry with them the history and layers of meanings accumulated over the centuries. Referring to *tapasyā*, we could say that among ascetics it can be defined as any practice or activity or attitude that develops discipline through intense physical or mental effort and willpower, in order to enable an individual to achieve his/her goal. All *sādhus*, in one way or another, practise *tap* (i.e.

discharged at him by Arjuna, and when he fell from his chariot he was upheld from the ground by the arrows and lay on a couch of darts' (Oman 1903: 45).

31 Oman refers here to two cases described by Sir Monier Monier-Williams in his *Modern India* (1878: 73–74).

tapasyā), although some do it in more complicated ways. As in the past, the typologies of *tapasyā* still vary significantly. The word may refer to practices one undertakes for a certain period, or to specific practices one performs at a certain time of the year. In some cases it may refer to austerities that last for years, many of which can damage the body or involve intense pain. In yet other cases it may refer to intensive study or practice or, as we will see in detail in Chapter 4, it may be synonymous with *haṭha* yoga. *Tapasyā* can also mean constantly doing the inner *jap* or meditating for long periods. For these reasons, it is not unusual to see the conflation of the terms *tap*, yoga and *haṭha* yoga.

This section aims to describe contemporary forms of *tapasyā* in order to compare them with the practices of the past and to introduce the reasons behind them. Before we begin the descriptions, however, because austerities are performed in religious contexts and are consecrated practices a few more words have to be introduced.

Tapasyās should be accompanied by *vrata* (vow), *saṅkalpa* (commitment; for practices that are conducted for longer periods), and *anuṣṭhāna* (spiritual retreat). I will now briefly introduce these terms because they are fundamental to understanding not only ascetic practices but also how the life of an ascetic is structured. A *vrata* relates to restrictions to be applied to daily life and can be followed by both ascetics and lay people.[32] Anyone who undergoes a formal religious observance is called a *vratī*, a 'vower', and the term indicates the effort involved 'in separating oneself from physical attachments and various objects of desire in order to attain ritual purity and spiritual ends' (Gross 1992: 336). The most common *vratas* are fasting,[33] celibacy and silence, which aim to produce detachment from food, sex and thoughts. It is believed that the results and the power produced by the *sādhanā* are superior when vows are involved, and obviously the

32 See for example the importance of *vrata* in women's lives. Pearson (1996: 10) has emphasised that vows provide women with the feeling that 'they are in control' of their own bodies and that they can control 'men's use of their bodies'. As *vratas* are religious practices performed for the benefit of male family members, 'there is little resistance to a woman's performing as many *vratas* as time, resources and her stamina allow'.

33 For example, it is common to fast during the 11th day of a fortnight in a lunar month (*ekādaśī*), or to fast during the new moon (*amāvasyā*), or the full moon (*pūrṇimā*). On Mount Abu, Bālyogī Muralī Dās gave me the example of *candra vrata*, the *vrata* one follows when one has done something wrong. He said: 'You start eating one *tulsī* leaf and go up to 15 leaves in *pūrṇimā*, then decrease again to zero in *amāvasyā*, and in the meantime you can eat only dried fruits.'

stricter the vows and the more severe the practices, the greater the power gained (Lamb 2012: 442).

An intense *vrata* or *tapasyā* begins with a *saṅkalpa*: that is, the ascetic expresses the intention and commitment to complete the practice. Ramdas Lamb (2012: 443) notes that during a *saṅkalpa* the *sādhu* recites a mantra to propitiate the deity or 'the form of the divine to whom the efforts are being directed', then

> recites his own name and, in précis, his denominational affiliation and its history, to remind him of the tradition from which he comes and the responsibility he faces in undertaking the vow. Finally, he specifies the particular forms of *sādhanā* and *tapasyā* to be done, as well as the intended goal or recipient of the fruit of the undertaking.[34]

The word *anuṣṭhāna* refers to a 'retreat', a period of isolation in which the *sādhu* channels his attention and efforts. As specified by a Rāmānandī *tyāgī* I met at Mount Abu, Bālyogī Muralī Dās, 'An *anuṣṭhāna* is a period of time during which a specific activity is carried out and followed according to specific rules', and this period can last from a few days to several months. Gross (1992: 352) lists several reasons for taking *anuṣṭhāna*: to alleviate some physical ailment, to inaugurate a new ascetic practice, to replenish physical and mental energies depleted by outward activity, or simply to withdraw from social interaction in order to access deeper inner spiritual realms.

According to *tyāgī* Rām Bālak Dās, *tapasyā* can be practised without having a complete knowledge of yoga, because those who do *tapasyā* do not have much time for other *kriyās* (actions).[35] However, he stressed that it is always important to have a guru who can explain correctly how to practise austerities and who can tell if the disciple is suited to them. The example of Hari Giri is useful in clarifying this point. He told me that he did many *tapasyās* in his life: at first he only applied *vibhūti* to his body, then he went barefoot, and eventually lived in a cave in the snow. Nonetheless, these experiences always resulted in failure: when he went barefoot, he contracted a disease in the sole of his foot, and one spot remains painful to this day; when he lived in the mountains and followed the rule of bathing early in the morning, breaking the ice to get some water, he almost froze and had to ask another *bābā* to light a *cilam* to keep him warm. According to him, it was his own fault for trying these practices without asking his

---

34 Ramdas Lamb's work offers a very useful insight into the Rāmānandīs' world as he was a Rāmānandī *sādhu* in his youth and is still involved in the *sampradāya*.

35 See Chapter 5, p. 213f.

guru. His guru would probably have discouraged him from doing them. He admitted, 'If one decides to start a practice without having knowledge, one will not get results.'

If not the guru, there are always *sādhus* within each order who can guide the younger ones in the practice of *vrata* and austerity. Often within a *sampradāya* there are specific groups specialised in a particular *tapasyā* or set of *tapasyās*, so a *sādhu* interested in engaging with them may decide to ask for a further initiation in one of these groups.

Some forms of *tapasyā* have become particularly rare to observe. Gross, for example, who did his field research in the 1970s, described some *tapasyās* that I have never seen practised: lying on a bed of thorns or nails (*kaṇṭā kā śayyā-tapas*), hanging upside down over a fire of burning cow dung (*ūrdhvamukhi-tapas*); sitting under a suspended jar of constantly dripping water (*jalandhārī-tapas*), a practice that seems more extreme than the one I describe in the next section; and doing full-body prostrations (touching eight parts of the body on the ground: *aṣṭāṅga daṇḍavat praṇām tapas*) (Gross 1992: 329). Another *tapasyā* he mentions, which I have heard of several times, is the *samādhi-tapasyā* (i.e. the *samādh tapasyā* mentioned by Oman): being completely buried or burying only the head in the ground (which Kamal Giri claimed to practise) for varying lengths of time: weeks or even months. Today, a well-known case is that of Pilot Bābā[36] and his disciple Keiko Mata, a Japanese *saṃnyāsinī* who publicly demonstrated *samādhi* on a total of 18 occasions between 1991 and 2007.[37] Only once did I see a *sādhu* doing *ākāś muni* or *sūryopāsana*—he was a Nāth *yogī* in Mangalore: just by chance, while Professor Mallinson and I were talking to other Nāths, we noticed the *sādhu* completely reclining on his back, staring at the sky (or at the sun) with bloodshot eyes.[38]

In the following sections, I classify the most common *tapasyās* in three groups: behavioural, yearly, and long-lasting/highly physically demanding. After these, under the label 'others', I describe practices that can also become *tapasyās*. Obviously, this is an 'etic', academic classification that

36 http://www.pilotbaba.org/babaji (last accessed 30 November 2020).

37 http://www.yogmata.org/siddha-master/yogmata-keiko-aikawa (last accessed 30 November 2020).

38 His posture was very much similar to that of a painting from Mandi (1725–1750) described by Debra Diamond (2013: 142): 'an ash-smeared and talon-nailed yogi engaging in austerities [. . .] With his legs crossed, back exceedingly arched, and fingers extended in a ritual gesture (mudra), the Sannyasi is immobilised, his body moulded into a form that both enables and expresses his transaction with higher worlds.'

sādhus do not use. Moreover, they often practise several *tapasyās* simultaneously. For example, the Udāsī Bhole Bābā pursued four *tapasyās* for nine years: he was *monī* (remained silent),[39] used *vibhūti* (covered his body only with ashes), did not touch money, and was *phalāhārī* (ate only fruits).

Behavioural *tapasyā*

I use the label 'behavioural *tapasyā*' to describe austerities that influence a *sādhu*'s daily routine or life and thus become part of his/her habits. Of course, the *tapasyās* of the other groups also may have similar effects. Behavioural *tapasyā* include walking barefoot, not sleeping for long periods or sleeping for only a few hours each night. Some *tapasyās* are renowned and highly respected, so the *bābās* who practise them or have practised them are known by their names, as epithets. For example, Monī Bābā is usually the name given to a *sādhu* who has practised *monī tapasyā* for a long time.

As we shall see, behavioural *tapasyās* focus on celibacy, fasting and silence because 'food, sex, and thought represent a psycho-physiological configuration that conditions human existence' (Gross 1992: 351); therefore, these forms of *tapasyā* imply overcoming these conditions to achieve ritual purity and altered states of consciousness.

Vibhūti

Covering the body only with *vibhūti* (ash) is a very visible form of *tapasyā*. *Vibhūti* (or *khāk* or *bhasm* in Hindi) can be produced by the burning of cow dung, or by the woods used for ritual or cremation fire, and it is an important element of the ascetic world, symbolising both sacrifice—the consummation of the body in the sacred fire—and austerity itself. Furthermore, the naked body of the ascetic—or almost naked body in the case of *tyāgīs*—covered with ashes, places him in stark contrast to the lay people and also emphasises his disregard for the body.

In all the *sampradāyas* considered in this book, there are sections whose ascetics follow this practice (Dasnāmī *nāgās*, Rāmānandī *tyāgīs* and *mahātyāgīs*, Nāth Yogīs from the *jamāt*, and Udāsī *nāgās*). While there are some who apply ashes in specific circumstances (such as, for example, before *pañca-dhūnī tap*; see below), others may take a vow to cover themselves with it thus remaining completely, or almost completely, naked customarily for a period of 12 years. Usually, *sādhus* apply *vibhūti* immediately

39 I use here the colloquial transliteration of the Hindi term *mouni*, which comes from the Sanskrit *mounin*, i.e. one who is in the condition of *mauna*, silence. I thank Gianni Pellegrini for the clarification about the term.

after bathing, so that the water on the body mixes with the ash and creates a layer on the skin. This layer also protects against the cold and insects.

Monī

As we saw in the previous section, the practice of silence is very ancient and is still practised by *sādhus*. Monī Bābā, a *tyāgī* whom I met during the Ardh Kumbh Melā in 2019, remained silent for 35 years and, according to his disciple Jagannāth Dās, it was through this practice that he obtained the *darśan* of God.

Through the practice of *monī*, the *sādhu* aims to achieve silence of the mind, while trying to prevent the loss of breath and energy, in order to facilitate meditation. The *monī tapasyā* is considered one of the most difficult *tapasyās* because of the isolation from human interaction that follows. Bhole Bābā, for example, remained *monī* for nine years, but then modified his practice and decided to talk for four hours a day, from 8 pm to midnight. He justified this change by saying that the inability to talk to his friends made him suffer and did not allow him to practise properly, because it made him overthink. The change he applied brought concentration back into his mind and he was able to continue for years.

There are, indeed, also ascetics who are *monīs* for a couple of hours a day or some who decide to speak only when necessary. The use of writing is often discouraged because it is seen as a form of cheating, but *monīs* who have disciples may prefer to transmit their teachings in written form.

Dietary *tapasyā*

Some forms of *tapasyā* concern the ascetic's eating and drinking habits. A *phalāhārī* is an ascetic who eats mostly fruits (from *phala*, fruit). Yogī Hīrā Nāth has eaten only fruit for the last 30 years. His disciple Maheś Nāth has done the same for the last eight or nine years. They both eat only fruits, drink *chai* and smoke *cilam*.

According to Jagannāth Dās, *phalāhārī* means 'not eating cooked food', so it is acceptable to eat only fruit, a few nuts and drink milk.[40] However, during my fieldwork I realised that the idea of what is considered a 'fruit' among *sādhus* may vary considerably. Rādhe Purī, who is *phalāhārī* only during Navarātri (see below), eats fruits and boiled potatoes. Kamal Giri said that a *phalāhārī* stops eating grain (H., *ann*), which means that he

40 When Bhole Bābā was *monī* he was also *phalāhārī*, but since he could not touch money (another form of *tapasyā*), it was difficult for him to eat since *sādhus* don't always receive food as offerings. So, once, he had to survive on sugar and *caras* (resin extracted from the new leaves of the cannabis plant), and, in Nepal, on dried fruit.

does not eat rice or bread (H., *capātī*) but can eat potatoes and *śuddha cal*, a kind of millet from a white jungle plant.[41] According to Kamal Giri, foods derived from milk, such as *panīr* and some sweets, are acceptable, as are green vegetables, tomatoes and salt, but not peas because they are difficult to digest.[42]

However, *sādhus* may impose strict dietary rules on themselves for a shorter or longer period of time. Taruṇ Bābā from Kamakhya said that he only eats once a day, in the evening, around 10 pm, and has been doing so for the last 17 years to keep his body stable (H., *sthir*). Kamal Giri ate only sweet food (like milk and fruits) and nothing salty for three months; then for another month he ate only *nīm* leaves. Śyām Dās, a Rāmānandī *mahātyāgī*, drinks only fruit juices and *chai* and smokes *cilam*.[43] *Sādhus* who drink only milk are called *payahārī*.

Clothing *tapasyā*

Another form of *tapasyā* is related to the ascetic's clothing: *sādhus* may wear different, 'painful' loincloths (*laṅgoṭīs*) to ensure their celibacy. Again, it is not unusual for a *sādhu* to be called according to the *tapasyā* he practises, or wears (in this case). For example, Kāṭhīyā Bābā is the label used for any *sādhu* who wears a belt (*aṛbandha*) made of wood (*kāṭh* in Urdu). This wooden belt is rather thick, is locked and cannot be removed, making several actions, especially sleeping, uncomfortable. Particularly rough are the *laṅgoṭīs* made from banana bark (*kelā laṅgoṭī*) (see Photo 2). Those made from *muñja* grass, a reed-like plant, can be abrasive and irritating, while *lohālaṅgaris* are *sādhus* who wear *laṅgoṭīs* made of metal (iron, steel or brass) and have a massive iron chain belt that is never removed. The *tapas* produced by these *laṅgoṭīs* transcends sexual arousal.[44] Another *tapasyā* to

---

41 One time, in his *āśram* in Jhargram, Kamal Giri prepared for me his special *phalāhārī khicṛī*. The ingredients: potatoes, cumin, ginger, tomato, green chilli (not red because it too 'tamasic' compared to the green and therefore bad for your health), *makhāna* (a kind of popcorn made with the seeds of the lotus flower) and the seeds of a plant that he called by different names (*phalāhārī cal*, *syamba cal*, etc.). He added black salt, *deśī ghī*, *dhaniyā* and then everything was boiled for a while. At the end it looked like porridge.

42 Kamal Giri was *phalāhārī* because he became *khaṛeśvarī* (standing *bābā*); see below, p. 135.

43 On the use of *caras*, see Chapter 6, p. 245.

44 See Gross 1992: 333–334.

Photo 2 Rāmānandī *tyāgī* wearing a *kelā laṅgoṭī*, Allahabad Ardh Kumbh Melā, 2019.

ensure celibacy involves piercing the penis (usually the foreskin) to insert a ring[45] through which a heavy chain is attached to weigh down the penis.

Seasonal *tapasyās*

Similarly to Pārvatī's practice described in the *Śiva Purāṇa*, ascetics may practise different austerities depending on the time of the year. During the rainy season, they may decide to remain outdoors exposing their bodies to the rain;[46] during the cold season, they may do *jal dhārā* or *jal tap*, while in the hot season they may perform *pañca-dhūnī tap*. These different forms of *tapasyā* must be performed at specific times to get the best result. Furthermore, as Rām Caraṇ Dās stressed, for these three *tapasyās* (each of which

45 H.H. Wilson (1976 [1861]: 151) identifies these *sādhus* by the label '*kara lingis*': 'they go naked and to mark their triumph over sensual desires affix an iron ring and chain on the male organ.'

46 Tripathi (1978: 112) calls this *tapasyā maidān* (field), since the *sādhu* has to remain in an open space. *Maidān tapas* begins when *pañca-dhūnī tap* ends (see below) and lasts the entire monsoon season.

lasts four months)[47] there are different foods to eat, *āsana*s to practise and behaviours to maintain. If these rules are not followed, the body can be compromised.

In this section we shall explore these three *tapasyā*s and *jau tap*, an austerity that takes place at another specific time of year, Navarātri.

Pañca-dhūnī tap

As we have seen in the textual evidence above, sitting among five fires is an ancient practice. Today this *tapasyā* is not only performed with five fires but with an increasing number of fires—a development the origin of which is unknown. It is executed especially by Rāmānandī *tyāgī*s, *mahātyāgī*s and Udāsīs, with some variations by Nāth Yogīs and only occasionally by Dasnāmī *nāgās*. During my fieldwork, I attended several *pañca-dhūnī tap*, but always held by *tyāgī*s and *mahātyāgī*s, while I only collected information on the other groups. For this reason, I describe the Vaiṣṇava *pañca-dhūnī* here,[48] hoping that future research will fill this knowledge gap.

Pañca-dhūnī tap is performed during the hot season. It begins on the day of *vasant pañcamī* (the fifth lunar day of the bright fortnight of Māgh, February–March) and ends at Gaṅgādaśaharā[49] (the tenth lunar day of the bright fortnight of Jyeṣṭh, May–June). *Tyāgī*s who received the ash initiation (*khāk dīkṣā*) can also be initiated into *pañca-dhūnī tap*. On the day of *vasant pañcamī*, the *sādhus* who are going to begin the *tapasyā* make a *saṅkalpa*.

Photo 3 shows *tyāgī*s of the *Terah bhāī tyāgī khālsā* during the Ardh Kumbh Melā of Allahabad in 2019, participating in a wide *havan* conducted by the elder *sādhus*, during which, if I understood correctly, each *sādhu* declares his family and the number of fires he will use. After that, each *sādhu* would occupy a space in the area reserved for the *pañca-dhūnī*, and begin the practice according to his stage. Each stage, which depends on the number of fires used, must be performed over three consecutive summers. In the first stage, the practice is conducted with five fires made of small piles of cow dung (*gobar*); in subsequent stages the number of fires

47 Rām Caraṇ Dās also mentioned a *tapasyā* in spring during which *sādhus* will eat fruits and red chilli, sitting in *gomukhāsana* for four hours.

48 From my conversations with *sādhus* it appears that *dhūnī tap* can also be understood as the *sādhu*'s practice of always sitting in front of his *dhūnī*, thus rarely leaving the place.

49 Gaṅgādaśaharā or Gaṅgāvataraṇa is the celebration of the descent of the Ganges from heaven to Earth.

Photo 3 Rāmānandīs' *havan* before the performing of *pañca-dhūnī tap*, Allahabad Ardh Kumbh Melā, 2019.

increases to seven, 12, 84, and then the circle is uninterrupted.[50] In the final stage, called *khappar dhūnī*, the burning cow dung is placed in a pot on the head (Photo 4).

Since each stage lasts three years, it takes 18 years to complete this *tapasyā* but, if by chance a *sādhu* misses a day of practice, he will have to add another year.

During the 2019 Melā, *sādhus* would begin the *tapasyā* at different times of the day, so the ground was busy from 11 am until 3 pm; Rām Dās from Chitrakut explained that, during the days of the Melā, *tyāgīs* were not going to do it too 'seriously' because there was a large audience: once back in their *āśram* they would do it from 11 am till 2 pm.

50 Van der Veer (1988: 116) mentions the significance of the different number of fires: *pañca-dhūnī* (5) fires symbolise the *pañca-tattva*, the five elements; *sapta-dhūnī* (7) symbolise the seven skins of the body; *dvadaśa-dhūnī* (12) symbolise the 12 suns of creation; *caurāsī-dhūnī* (84) symbolise the 84 creations; *koṭ-dhūnī* (endless); he calls the last one *śiragni* (fire put on the head) but I have heard it called *kapāl-dhūnī*. This explanation was never given by my informants.

Photo 4 *Khappar dhūnī*, Allahabad Ardh Kumbh Melā, 2019.

Basically, the *sādhu* sits in the midday sun surrounded by burning cow dung. Rām Bālak Dās said that with this *tapasyā* the body becomes stronger and does not get diseases because three fires are united: the inner fire, the outer fire of the sun and the fire of the *gobar*.[51] Before the practice, *sādhus* have to prepare their bodies: some will not eat or drink, while others will only drink water or a *lassī*; they will take baths to cleanse their external body and, once seated, they will cleanse themselves internally by means of *prāṇāyāma*.

However, before sitting, they have to prepare the *tapasyā* ground: they smear a mix of cow dung and mud on a circular area while repeating mantras. Then, the *gobar* is piled up according to the number of fires they have to light. Once the area is ready, the ascetic enters the circle with a *praṇām* (reverential bowing) and sits. There are only a few objects around him: a conch shell, his *cimṭā*, a small pot with water and a spoon, a *mālā*

51 According to Choṭīyā, a disciple of Rām Bālak Dās, it is not useful to do this *tapas* if the *sādhu* has too much anger (H., *krodh*) in him: it would cause an excess of fire. Once again, this shows how important it is to recognise the 'nature' of an ascetic, because his or her practices must be suited to it.

for the practice of *jap*, a small towel and a *kaṭorī* (bowl) with *sāmagrī*, i.e. a mixture of dried roots and leaves. This mixture is necessary for the *havan* made in the main fire in front of the *sādhu* which will light all the others.

After seating, the Rāmānandī applies the Vaiṣṇava *tilaka* on the forehead and other parts of his body (arms, chest, stomach and throat). He then blows the conch to announce the beginning of the practice. During these preparatory steps the *sādhu* does various hand *mudrās*. He may stand on one foot, looking towards the sun through his fingers, to create a connection with the sun, with the aim of controlling its energy. Once seated, he sprinkles water from the conch shells three times and repeat mantras to Mother Earth and the sun. Then he may do other *mudrās* which Rāghavendra Dās called *havan mudrās*. It seems that different *sādhus* perform different *mudrās* towards the main fire: Rāghavendra Dās spoke of 12 *mudrās*; according to Choṭīyā there are as many *mudrās* to perform as the number of *avatāras* of Viṣṇu (i.e. ten). Other *sādhus* I have recorded did *mudrās* differently from those done by Rāghavendra Dās. This differentiation depends on the different lineages they belong to and shows how varied the explanation of a practice can be, even within the same *sampradāya*: it depends on who the *sādhu* learnt it from. In any case, as Phalāhārī Bābā affirmed, the purpose of these *mudrās* is to call the *devatās* to come to the *havan*, 'so then their *śakti* is gained' (*prāpt ho jātī hai*), because 'if you do not have that *śakti* you won't last more than five minutes'. For the same reason, before starting *tapasyā*, all *sādhus* move from one *dhūnī* to another to get the blessing (H., *āśīrvād*) from the other practitioners. Once finally seated, using the *cimṭā*, the ascetic takes some coals from the main fire and lights the piles of cow dung around him, always rotating the *cimṭā* above his head (Photo 5).

Once everything is ready and the various piles are steaming, the ascetic can start his practice, which according to Phalāhārī Bābā can be summarised as:

> Only *jap*. A *vairāgī* must repeat the name of God at least 11,000 times. For each seed of the *mālā* you have to say 'Rām Rām'. It can take three hours, two hours, four hours. But every *vairāgī* should do it. So, the *saṅkalpa* of *pañca-dhūnī tap* is to do the 11,000 repetition sitting there. And you won't get up unless you have done it![52]

During my attendance, I saw *sādhus* reciting *jap*, others reading what were probably devotional pamphlets, and others simply mentally absorbed.

---

52 *Jab tak nahīṃ hogā, tab tak uṭhegā nahīṃ!*

Photo 5 *Mahātyāgī* Śyām Dās lighting piles of cow dung during *dhūnī tap*, Ujjain Siṃhasth Melā, 2016.

In this situation, where several *sādhu*s do this *tapasyā* together, it is not only the heat that can be unbearable but also the air, full of smoke as it is (Photo 4). For this reason, some ascetics completely cover themselves with a white sheet. After many years, the smoke can even affect the lungs. Jagannāth Dās told me that he cannot do another 18 years of *pañca-dhūnī tap* because of lung problems. It is indeed not unusual for *sādhu*s to continue practising this *tapasyā*. When I met, in Allahabad, Kākā jī, a tough wandering *tyāgī*, he was doing *pañca-dhūnī tap* for the third time: he had completed two cycles of 18 years (thus a total of 36) and was already halfway through his third round.

When the daily practice is concluded, the *sādhu* blows his conch to announce its end and extinguishes the embers with water. After that, he may do *āsana*s to stretch the body (see Photo 15 on p. 213). He again does the *praṇām* to his place, circumambulating it as a sign of respect, and does the same around the other practitioners before leaving the area to wash and apply *vibhūti*.

Although I have not witnessed *pañca-dhūnī tap* performed by *sādhu*s of other *sampradāya*s, I have been told that the Udāsīs follow this 'Vaiṣṇava style', and according to some Rāmānandī *tyāgī*s they do it in a very *pakkā* (sound) manner: they remain seated for even longer. Nāth Yogīs organise it differently: they use a much wider area and, at the edges, pile higher mounds of cow dung. They start with five mounds and then, gradually over the days, add another mound until they reach the number of 41.

They perform surrounded by fires, but in front of a temporary altar with a *dhūnī* under it. I was told that in rare cases Dasnāmī *nāgās* also practise *pañca-dhūnī tap*, but generally they do not follow this practice. This is obvious for the *daṇḍī* and *paramahaṃsa* section, because they are not allowed to handle any sacred fire, while it seems surprising for the *nāgās* section, given their use of the *dhūnī*.

Jal tap

With reference to the Hindu calendar, there are two types of *jal tap* every year: one during the rainy season, from Gaṅgādaśaharā to *śarad pūrṇimā* (the full moon of the month of *Aśvin*), and one in winter, from *śarad pūrṇimā* to *vasant pañcamī*, in which the body is subjected to the cold. In the first case, the ascetic exposes his body to the rain by living outdoors. In the second case, there are several possibilities: some *sādhus* sit outside in an open space, in the cold winter air, or some immerse themselves in cold water for several hours a day.

According to Rām Caraṇ Dās, who has done this *tapasyā* immersed in water many times, one usually stays in the water from 4–8 am, but he used to stay for 12 hours. He explained that to perform this *tapasyā* a special diet is adopted: the ascetic must eat only once a day—no fruit, black pepper but no chilli, only *ann* (crops) and especially boiled *laukī* (bottle gourd)[53]—otherwise the body may suffer physical complications that may even lead to death.[54] Once in the water, the ascetic must sit in a specific position (he called it '*jalāsana*') and breathe in a specific way to keep the body underwater. According to Rām Caraṇ Dās, 'Those who know *jalāsana* know how to use the five *prāṇa*', referring to the control of the five 'breaths' present in the human body according to yogic physiology.[55]

The *mahant* of the Āvāhan *akhāṛā* of Varanasi also emphasised the possibility of holding the breath during this *tapasyā*, but for more surprising ends: he told of a *tyāgī* from Govardhan who did *jal tap* sitting in a pond and was able to remain completely submerged for long periods of time thanks to his knowledge of *kumbhaka* (breath retention). The *bābā* in question was about 75 years old and was still alive in 2017.

53 Rām Caraṇ Dās said that one has to eat *laukī*, because *laukī* is cold: if one eats something hot while cold, then one will ruin one's blood. A *laukī*, on the other hand, by creating balance between blood and water, works properly.

54 Rām Caraṇ Dās told the story of an ascetic who did not know how to do this *tapasyā* correctly. He wanted to stay in the water, and he did so for 12 days and eight hours, but eventually ruined his body completely. His blood deteriorated and he had to stay in hospital for 15 days.

55 See Chapter 5, p. 184.

Photo 6 Phalāhārī Bābā performs *jal tap*, Allahabad Ardh Kumbh Melā, 2019.

The last form of *jal tap* I saw was performed by another Phalāhārī Bābā, a *tyāgī* from Indore whom I met at the 2019 Allahabad Melā. He used to do *jal tap* at 4 am, sitting in a special structure the seat of which was covered with nails and the top of which supported a clay pot with a hole in the bottom. A devotee had the task of pouring the cold water collected from 108 jars into the clay (Photo 6). While the devotee poured the water, the Bābā did his *jap*, despite sometimes shivering from the morning cold.[56] His *jal tap* lasted about 30 minutes: the time it took to empty the jars.[57] However, it is not uncommon to hear stories of *sādhus* performing this *tapasyā* in flowing mountain rivers; in this case they hold their bodies with ropes so as not to be dragged away.

Jau tapasyā or *navarātri tapasyā*

During Navarātri, a religious celebration spanning nine nights and ten days, some *sādhus* may conduct some form of austerity. There are four Navarātris in a year, but among them the *śarad navarātri*, which begins on the first day of the bright fortnight of the month Āśvin (September–October), is the most celebrated. After this, the most famous is *vasant navarātri* which falls on the first day of the bright fortnight of the month of Caitra (March–April). A *tapasyā* performed during Navarātri lasts for nine days. The one discussed here is the *jau tapasyā*, or barley austerity.

I have evidence of two ways of performing it: in one, the ascetic lies down completely covered with soil except for his/her head; in another he/she sits in a meditative posture surrounded by soil. In this soil are seeds of barley (H., *jau*), which sprout in nine days, thus at the end of this *tapasyā* the ascetic is covered or surrounded by grass. During these nine days, however, the ascetic does not move, drink, eat, defecate or urinate. Rām Priya Dās, the only female ascetic I met who practised this form of *tapasyā*, told me that, two days before it, 'You must stop drinking and eating, you must not put anything in your mouth.' She did *jau tap* nine times in different places:

---

56 As soon as the *jal tap* period ended, he began the *pañca-dhūnī tap*.

57 Oman (1903: 50) reports a similar account, but closer to that mentioned by Gross: 'a *sadhu* whom I saw at a religious festival, a big and powerful fellow, had a strong wooden framework erected to support a huge earthenware jar provided with a perforation at the bottom, from which a stream of water could flow out. Round about there were at least twenty-five large pots of water, to replenish the great jar when in use. Under the jar the *sadhu* was in the habit of sitting during the night, particularly in the small hours, from about three o'clock till daybreak, with a stream of water falling on his head and flowing down over his person to the ground. It was winter time, and very cold work no doubt [. . .] This man [. . .] would be known as a *jaladhara tapashi*.'

Photo 7 Old photo of Yogī Somnāth performing *jau tap*, Dhinodhar, 2017.

the first time in her birthplace, Gujarat, then three times in Varanasi, then in Surat, twice in Bombay (one in Malar and one in Dahisar, two suburbs of Mumbai), in Indore and in Somnath. Since she was completely covered by soil, she usually performed it in the roofed terraces of temples.

In Dhinodhar (Gujarat), Yogī Somnāth does it sitting on a throne (*gaḍḍī*).[58] I have only seen pictures of him, but Professor Mallinson, in 2018, attended his *tapasyā* and reported that during the nine days, while seated, Yogī Somnāth would smoke a lot of *cilams* (Photo 7). Someone informed him that the Yogī had stopped eating five days earlier to drink only milk; then, with just three days to go, he had switched to water, while during the *tapasyā* he only sipped opium water.[59] A *bābā* living in Loyal Guphā (Rishikesh) recounted a similar, but less strenuous, practice: he puts soil with *jau* around his sleeping place and spends the day in mantras and *pūjā*. He eats only at night, and moves only for physical needs. As with the other expressions of this *tapasyā*, he does this until the grass sprouts.

Long-lasting, highly physically demanding *tapasyā*

In this section I will present two *tapasyā*s, *khaṛeśvarī* and *ūrdhvabāhu*, which are very physically demanding and can have long-lasting consequences for the body. For these reasons, not all the *bābā*s support their practice. Jogī Bābā, for example, considers *tapasyā*s that harm the body completely useless (H., *bekār*) and done only to attract attention. According to him, practices like *ūrdhvabāhu* or *khaṛeśvarī* should be practised only for a couple of hours a day: 'You need to do *tap*, that is good! (*Tap karnā hai, vah ṭhīk hai*!)'. Try once and keep trying', but to meet God, he declared, 'Focus on *brahman* (*Brahman lagāo*!)'. According to him, if someone creates problems for themselves in their body, nothing spiritual can happen: the body has to be fit and able to do everything, like eat or sleep, following the correct rules. Jogī Bābā's opinions were similar to those of several Vaiṣṇava *sādhus* I met. Nonetheless, the majority of *sādhus* regard *khaṛeśvarī* and *ūrdhvabāhu* ascetics with great respect.

58 In a personal communication (March 2022), Véronique Bouillier pointed out the similarity between these practices and the widespread traditions of barley germination in Navarātri. She mentioned a similar practice followed in Udaipur in front of the temple of the Devī: the ascetic remains seated for nine days surrounded by sword points. She did not hear of barley at that time, but she pointed out that in some regions during Navarātri it is typical to plant barley, which grows during the festival time and the strands of which are cut on the tenth day to be distributed as *prasāda* (consecrated food).

59 James Mallinson, personal communication, 20 November 2020.

Photo 8 Kamal Giri as *khaṛeśvarī* and his swing, Kamakhya, 2018.

Khaṛeśvarī

The practice of standing is well known from Indian historical sources, and standing *bābās* were often represented in temples as decorative motifs. The *khaṛeśvarī* is the *bābā* who never sits. There are ascetics who practise this daily: when Rām Priya Dās was young, she used to stand on a piece of wood with only one leg, all day long, and did so for a year. There are ascetics who practise this *tapasyā* continuously for 12 years, and others who change the duration depending on their goals and the *saṅkalpa*.

Sometimes, the duration of the *tapasyā* depends not on the *sādhu* but on physical hurdles. In fact, several physical problems can arise during this practice, mainly related to blood circulation and ulcers in the feet and legs, which can make the *tapasyā* so painful that the *sādhu* is forced to stop. Under these conditions, body weight is important for the practice; and for this reason *khaṛeśvarī*s are often *phalāhārī*s. A light diet is also necessary as they have to bend down to sleep. To support themselves, *khaṛeśvarī*s are usually provided with a swing (or a mobile support) on which they lean to sleep or to stand when they are not moving (Photo 8).

The case of Kṛṣṇānanda Purī, a Dasnāmī *nāgā* I met in Varanasi in 2017, is interesting. At that time, he had been *khaṛeśvarī* for the previous 18 years. He chose to wear many *rudrākṣa mālā*s; the *mahant* of the Āvāhan *akhāṛā* was also making a *rudrākṣa* jacket and cap for him. The purpose was to make his *sādhanā* heavier because these accessories would add 20 kg to his weight, thus increasing the pressure on his legs, which were already quite swollen. According to Kṛṣṇānanda Purī, due to this additional strain his body would become empty (*śūnya*), reaching 'up' (H., *ūpar*, i.e. God) faster.

Yogī Oṃ Nāth told me that he had only been *khaṛeśvarī* for three years because an infection had spread in his leg. He had started his practice so that it would rain in a specific area of Gujarat, and stated that it would be necessary for other areas of Maharashtra. Kamal Giri began his practice in winter 2017 and told me he would remain *khaṛeśvarī* until a statue of Hanumān was installed outside his *āśram* in Jhargram, West Bengal.

Ūrdhvabāhu

The *ūrdhvabāhu* is the ascetic who keeps his arm (or arms) permanently raised, which makes this *tapasyā* particularly painful. Historically, we have evidence of ascetics who used to remain with both arms raised, but this form of the practice is not followed today. The reason would not be the absence of dedicated *sādhu*s, rather the lack of dedicated disciples, since a *sādhu* who holds both arms up needs someone to be constantly with him,

Photo 9 Someśvar Giri, Ujjain Siṃhasth Melā, 2016.

helping him in everything. A one-armed *ūrdhvabāhu*, however, can be completely independent.

We have already mentioned Pūrṇa Purī in the 18th century, who used to hold both arms up. With regard to the beginning of his practice, he affirmed that 'For one year great pain is endured, but during the second less, and habit reconciles the party; the pain diminishes in the third year; after which no kind of uneasiness is felt' (Duncan 1810: 264). A similar account came from *mahant* Someśvar Giri of the Jūnā *akhāṛā*, who confirmed that the practice was very painful for about a year and a half before it improved, because he 'simply' lost perception of the arm, which had atrophied.

To maintain the position, especially in the beginning, the arm is sometimes tied with a piece of cloth. Gross (1992: 331) also mentions a T-shaped wooden crutch which he calls *bragan* (the same used during meditation) to help support the arm before it becomes permanently immobilised.

As in many portraits of the past, the *ūrdhvabāhu*'s fingers lose their normal appearance, becoming immovable, with long twisted nails, while the arm becomes a kind of deadwood. This seems to be a long-life *tapasyā*, because after years of such a practice the individual is no longer able to use the arm, and for this reason it is considered one of the most difficult. However, during my fieldwork, it was pointed out to me by a friend[60] that Amar Bhārtī, a famous *ūrdhvabāhu*, had in recent years changed the position of his arm, which was no longer straight, but was moving slowly downwards (Photo 9). This alerted us to the possibility that Amar Bhārtī was trying to lower his arm, a very dangerous practice and seemingly impossible. However, we mentioned that Duncan and Turner had both written that Pūrṇa Purī believed he would recover the use of his arm, as the practice would be completed once his arm was restored. Sadly, Amar Bhārtī passed away in 2019 and we will never know whether he was doing some secret practice to restore the health of his arm.

Usually, *ūrdhvabāhu tapasyā* is traditional among *nāgā saṃnyāsīs*. Vaiṣṇava *sādhus* are actually rather disgusted by it since, as Rām Bālak Dās said, 'It is not a practice for keeping the body clean!' His implication was that everything—which means both eating and cleansing, especially cleansing after defecation—must be done with only one hand, the left, which is usually the one used for 'impure' actions. According to Mallinson (2016b: 10), *tyāgīs* 'stand out from other renunciate orders in their fastidious observance of purity rules', which is understandable since they still participate in brahmanical rituals.

60 I thank Dorothea Riecker and Pankaj J. Dutta for insightful conversations about Amar Bhārtī, his life and ideas.

Other forms of *tapasyā*

In this section, a few more examples of *tapasyā*s will be given to further demonstrate how this word can refer to very different practices and activities and, once again, how in *sādhu* society anything can be considered an austerity, depending on the intention and the way it is performed.

Āsanas

As we will see in detail in Chapter 5, the way ascetics learn *āsana*s can make their training very close to austerities. Then there are *sādhu*s who actually undertake the *caurāsī āsana tapasyā*: the learning of 84 *āsana*s as a form of austerity. This is evidenced in Duncan's aforementioned account: when Pūrṇa Purī decided to become an *ūrdhvabāhu*, he chose from among several possibilities including *caurāsī āsana*, 'difficult contortions to be held for hours on end'. *Aughaḍ* Rāj Nāth, in Dhinodhar, mentioned that to do the 84 *āsana*s as *tapasyā* each *āsana* must be perfected before moving on to another. For this reason, one can remain on the same posture for months. Dīpak Giri, a young *saṃnyāsī* of the Āvāhan *akhāṛā* whom I met in Rishikesh, told me that he had perfected 70 *āsana*s, but then had an accident: a car hit him while he was eating in New Delhi railway station. He spent three days in a coma, after which (in 2015) he stopped *āsana*s and started *vibhūti tapasyā*.[61]

This approach to postures harks back to the austerities practised by gymnosophists, described keeping postures for long periods, and further supports the idea that some present-day *āsana*s may come from a tapasic environment (see Birch and Hargreaves 2023). We have already mentioned the story of Dharamnāth and his *tapasyā* based on a 12-year-long headstand (see footnote 23, p. 111): even today, Maheś Nāth, the *mahant* of the Dhinodhar monastery (where Dharamnāth is supposed to have practised), follows the tradition and practises a tapasic headstand daily, which lasts one hour and 15 minutes (Photo 10).

Meditation

One of the most traditional forms of austerity consists, as the textual sources demonstrate, of sitting in the same posture and concentrating: deep meditation. For Garuḍ Dās, in fact, rather than comprising a specific painful practice, *tapasyā* is to sit in *samādhi*: 'Like a turtle, the four legs retracted,

---

61 It is interesting to note the attitude of this *bābā* towards this event. He said that the accident was part of his *karma*, and therefore he had to accept it: if one does not acknowledge events, he claimed, one goes on the side of the *rākṣasas* (demons), while those who learn from situations are on the path of *devatās* (deities).

Photo 10 Maheś Nāth performing headstand as *tapasyā*, Dhinodhar, 2017.
© 2024 Daniela Bevilacqua

staying within: this is *tapasyā*, an inner journey (*andar kī yātrā*)'. Similarly, the Udāsī Gopāl Dās claimed that the most important *tapasyā* is that which enables one to achieve *ekāgratā*, the focus of the mind, i.e. meditation.

Again, it is the intensity of the practice that transforms it into *tapasyā*. One can meditate every day, but if one does it daily for a long time and over the course of many years, then it becomes a form of austerity. For this reason, among *sādhus*, *tap karnā* (doing *tapas*) is also understood as *dhyāna lagānā* (applying meditation), which means meditating deeply or doing *jap*, the repetition of the name of God. Jogī Bābā, who spent three years in the jungle meditating in the hollow of a tamarind tree, described his practice as *tapasyā*, because of the condition in which he did it: completely alone, barely dressed, sustaining himself with the little food and milk brought to him by random tribal people. But, thanks to this *tapasyā*, he said he obtained *siddhis*.[62]

Hence, it is important to note that *tapasyā* should be associated not only with physical practices but also with mental ones and with discipline.

Bhajan and *sevā*

As noted by DeNapoli (2014: 275–278), the practice of *bhajan* can also represent a form of *tapasyā*. Although DeNapoli highlights this practice

62 On Jogī Bābā's *tapasyā* and his *siddhi*, see Bevilacqua 2018b.

especially among female ascetics, I find it common among men as well.[63] Jogī Bābā, for example, emphasised the importance of *bhajan* as a form of *tapasyā* and chanting as a source of *gyān* (S., *jñāna*), considering the power of sound in creating connection and resonance with reality.[64]

The use of *bhajan* as a form of *tapasyā* can be associated with a specific, devotional *sādhanā* which an ascetic follows under the advice of his/her guru. This is especially true for senior ascetics (men and women). During the time I spent at the Śrī Maṭh in Varanasi,[65] I remember an old Rāmānandī spending the entire morning chanting *bhajans*, and a similar situation occurred in the *āśram* of Rām Priya Dās, where endless devotional singing (*akhaṇḍa kīrtan*) was maintained by the locals. Such practices are examples of dedication and *bhakti*, but, as already mentioned, it is the attitude, intensity and discipline of the practice that transforms it into *tapasyā*.

This also applies to *sevā* (service), a widespread practice among *sādhus*: as Rām Bālak Dās argued, doing the *sevā* of the guru is in itself a form of *tapasyā*, given the discipline, concentration and 'tests'[66] that the disciple must undergo. This way of practising *tapasyā* can become a *sādhanā* because not all *sādhus*, by nature, are suited to intense physical or meditative practices. There are some centres, for example, whose *sādhus* take care of other people (especially other *sādhus*) and practise *sevā* as a discipline and spiritual path. This demonstrates, once again, how flexible the term *tapasyā* can be and how a situation can be interpreted and 'experienced' in different ways. Thus, an ascetic may practise *tapasyā* as *sādhanā*, but what

63 DeNapoli especially highlights the pain, sufferance and patience experienced and acknowledged by female ascetics in their practice. She points out an 'embedded gendered discourse on suffering' experienced by female ascetics whose painful experiences result not only from their religious voluntary penance and self-denial but also from 'their subordinate gender status in a patriarchal Indian society' (2014: 84). As Hara (1977: 155–157) shows, *tapas* as patience, pain and endurance is presented in textual sources as being suffered by both men and women. These qualities are also present in literary sources attributed to the poor heroine, also termed as *tapasvinī*, because by having the absolute absence of anger, and lust, being patient despite maltreatment, and demonstrating endurance, she is in full possession of *tapas* (Hara 1977: 159).

64 See Chapter 6, p. 247f.

65 See Bevilacqua 2018a.

66 Usually, a guru tests the disciples to verify their commitment to the *sādhanā*, their actions and behaviours, and it is not unusual for the guru to physically punish the disciple who has behaved wrongly or made mistakes.

is understood as *tapasyā* can vary greatly: it is the intention and the endeavour behind it that transforms it into *tapasyā*.

Tapasyās and their display

Tapasyās are often displayed at religious festivals. During these events, which are also attended by lay people, *sādhu* society and lay society officially meet, and *tapasyās* like *pañca-dhūnī tap*, *jal tap* or *jau tap* are performed openly. For example, the information on *pañca-dhūnī tap* I have presented was acquired because ascetics performed it in a highly visible area of their camp so that pilgrims, devotees and even photographers could observe them.

Tapasvīs like *khaṛeśvarī* and *ūrdhvabāhu* are also visible during religious festivals because these ascetics usually camp in highly visible places where more people can see them. Their practices are often publicised on billboards placed in front of their tents. Since *jau tap* is closely related to Navarātri, the practice of this *tapasyā* is most followed by the devotees of an ascetic residing in a specific area, or by people who are aware of the celebrations taking place in specific religious places.

It is not uncommon for a *bābā* who decides to start a *tapasyā* to announce it publicly and, if he has to make a small investment, his lay devotees are likely to support him financially to organise the *tapasyā* and celebrate its end. Rām Priya Dās and her guru have also made their practice of austerity public in the past. However, it has not always been easy for her, as the *sādhu samāj*—and, in her specific case, the *tyāgī* society—is not very open to the idea of a woman performing austerities. She lamented the fact that men often try to prevent *sādhvīs*' practices, despite the fact that past examples of *tapasvinīs* abound (cf. p. 103). As I pointed out in Chapter 2, the position of women in traditional ascetic groups is still very subordinate, and, not infrequently, *sādhus* discourage the presence of women in their ranks. Rām Priya Dās told me that another female *tyāgī* was treated badly when she tried to start *pañca-dhūnī tap*, and she herself always had to perform *jal tap* in safe places.

The display of *tapasyā* has been justified as a way of increasing the faith of devotees or people in general: seeing what a faithful individual can achieve through devotion and stubbornness is supposed to improve the audience's religious commitment. This idea is also found in textual sources. Again, I refer to the *Śiva Purāṇa*: the text claims that, in watching the difficult penances that Pārvatī was performing, 'people were struck with surprise':

> All of them came there to witness her penance. Considering themselves blessed, they proclaimed thus approvingly. (22.62)
>
> 'To follow the standard of the virtuous personages is declared to be conducive to greatness. There is no delimitation in penance. Virtue shall be honoured by the wise always. (22.63)
>
> After seeing or hearing about the penance of this lady what penance will be pursued by a man? A penance greater than this has never been before, nor will it ever be.' (22.64)
>
> Saying thus, they praised the penance of Pārvatī and joyously returned to their abodes. Even persons of sturdy countenance praised her penance. (22.65)

Today, lay people routinely visit *tapasvīs* and are eager to have their *darśan* because they believe their *tapas* results in powerful blessings for them or wise advice.

However, some *sādhus* are not in favour of this public display. Jogī Bābā stated that *tapasvīs* who display themselves in markets, towns and religious festivals do so only for money: 'He will not get God, he will not get the Lord, he will not obtain knowledge, but only money.'[67] According to him, *tapasyā* should be done in the jungle, where the only spectator is God: in such a place a *sādhu* is able to complete his practice. Although Jogī Bābā's words do not do justice to the many *sādhus* who openly practise their *tapasyā* in good faith, there are nonetheless *sādhus* who begin an austerity just before a religious festival, and some who even pretend to practise one just to gather devotees and to gain authority from their brethren.

The performativity that underlies the practice of *tapasyā* demonstrates the strong connection and interdependence between lay society and *sādhu* society: on the one hand, the ascetic seeks to cross the physical realm of the body to reach a superhuman-spiritual realm but, on the other, his practice can create or be used as a bridge to approach lay people and, thus, the worldly realm and its worldly aims.

Why *tapasyās* are performed

In the past, *tapas* was a 'psychophysical energy, the accumulation of which determined one's position in the universe. The aim, therefore, was to reach a higher position with greater power' (Klostermaier 2007: 37). It was linked

---

67 *Vah Bhagvān nahīṃ milegā, Īśvar nahṃī milegā, gyān bhī nahīṃ milegā, only paise milegā!*

to the acquisition of powers and benefits from the gods, to which spiritual goals were then added.

Even for today's practice we can consider 'spiritual' and 'secular' aims. If we look at the spiritual reasons, the practice of *tapasyā* can be associated with the notion of 'sacred pain' (Mulemi 2016). The mental and physical pain and the power resulting from *tapasyā* resounds with Glucklich's considerations about the role of pain in religious context. Pain is

> an alchemical force which magically transforms its victim from one state of existence to a higher, purer state. [. . .] in its relation to pain, the goal of religious life is not to bring anaesthesia, but to transform the pain that causes suffering into a pain that leads to insight, meaning, and even salvation. Ascetics and mystics know that they possess effective techniques, short of raw pain, for unmaking their own profane selves (Glucklich 2003: 40–43).

Tapasyās are indeed transformative practices which through body-mind efforts lead to results which, as Rām Priya Dās said, will occur if not 'today, maybe tomorrow, or if not in this life, maybe in the next one'.[68]

In general, ascetics claim that many forms of *tapasyā* are undertaken to confront and overcome the limitations of the body and to control the senses, bodily functions and needs, as well as to purify the mind and thought.[69] For example, behavioural *tapasyās* are considered tools to facilitate disengagement from the material world and sensual pleasure, tools to develop detachment from comforts (such as walking barefoot or being naked) or pleasure (food pleasure by being *phalāhārī*, sexual pleasure by being celibate). But they are also tools to enhance the development of willpower and prepare the individual for other forms of religious discipline. The pain of the body would be part of the gain, as Īśnāth says:

> *Sādhus* like pain because it is what drives them most towards God. For God they will suffer. I do that too. Because when I want to suffer, I just go and I give my body every pain, just exposing the body to pain [. . .] in the rain, without food [. . .] and this really creates a strength within, a

68 Rām Priya Dās also stressed the fact that a Vaiṣṇava should not focus attention on the result, otherwise *bhakti* cannot be detached and as a consequence results cannot be achieved. Ultimately, only God is the bestower of results.

69 Alter (2004: 266n15) also connects the practice of *tapas* with that of *kāyakalpa*, a practice used by ascetics to rejuvenate their body. He mentioned the example of a 185-year-old *tapasvī* who claimed to do both *tapas* (standing on one leg for years at a time) and going through drug-based rejuvenation therapy. See also Chapter 7, p. 287f.

> confidence [. . .] because the body is suffering but not the mind, because the mind expands. And I like that too, because in the end there is no pain.

Bhole Bābā also pointed out that through *tapasyā* one detaches oneself from the gross body, making the subtle body predominant, a comment also made by Kṛṣṇānanda Purī about his practice of *khaṛeśvarī*. Jagannāth Dās said that by doing *pañca-dhūnī tap*, one completely loses the feeling of the body due to the heat, and it is then that one can have the feeling of Bhagvān. Some *sādhus*, in fact, see the practice of *tapasyā* as a means of creating a connection with their *iṣṭa devatā* and finally attaining his/her *darśan*.

The discipline of *tapasyā* and its endurance lead to the purification not only of the body and mind but also of the individual *karma*. As we will see in Chapter 6, the role of *karma* is very important in the life of a Hindu and especially an ascetic. The life of a *sādhu* can be the result of previous ascetic lives and is seen as an opportunity to eliminate residual *karma* and liberate the soul, at least for those *sādhus* who aim for *mokṣa*.[70] Maheś Nāth said that the purpose of his *tapasyā* (headstand) was to break the *saṃsāra*, and his human birth was the opportunity to achieve this.[71] Some ascetics, therefore, consider *tapasyā* a way of burning personal *karma* and, in doing so, a means of avoiding rebirth, because if personal *karma* is not accumulated and the remains are burnt, the absence of *karma* leads directly to liberation.

There are not always, however, spiritual reasons behind the practice of strenuous or long-lasting *tapasyās*. As in the past, even today there are *sādhus* who associate them with the acquisition of powers: *sādhus* believe that the fulfilment of *tapasyā* necessarily brings with it specific powers, although these powers should only be recognised as evidence that one has gone in the right direction (see Chapter 6, p. 265). *Mahātyāgī* Śyām Dās said that, through *pañca-dhūnī tap* and use of the right mantras, one can obtain the following results: *agni stambhan*[72]—the *sādhu* can light fires; *jal stambhan*—the *sādhu* can walk on water; *vāyu stambhan*—the *sādhu* can walk in the wind; *ākāś siddhi*—he can fly; and with *pṛthvī siddhi* he can walk without touching the ground, walking through vibration. According

70 As mentioned in the previous chapter (pp. 79f.), Vaiṣṇava *sādhus* see *mokṣa* as a result that depends only on the grace of God. Therefore, the aim of their practice is *bhakti* itself.

71 According to him, if someone does *tapasyā* just for money, then in the next life they will be reborn as a worker for the person who has given them money, paying for the result of their *karma*.

72 *Stambhana* is an interesting word which is used in Sanskrit textual sources in various contexts: to mean magic tricks, or practices with which to attain specific yogic skills and *siddhis*. See Goudriaan 1979.

to Rāghavendra Dās, when *mahātmās* do *dhūnī tap*, they attract the power of *agni* (fire), because its heat enters them and they, through the power of mantras, can trap it. Śyām Dās also mentioned that by doing a thousand *jap* every day for a month he got the *siddhi* of seeing into the physical distance. Jogī Bābā claimed that, thanks to the powers obtained through his meditative *tapasyā* in the jungle, he was able to discover the place where the first Durgā *pūjā* took place.[73]

As we have already mentioned, *tapasyā* can also be performed to set an example to lay people. Some *sādhus* justify their *tapasyā* as a service (*sevā*) they do for the well-being (H., *kalyāṇ*) of society: since lay people do not follow their religion and *dharma* properly, ascetics must perform austerities to sustain the world, which would otherwise fall apart. The *ūrdhvabāhu* Rādhe Purī, in fact, claimed that his *tapasyā* was for everyone, the world being a *karma bhūmi* (a place of *karma*) in which everyone is subject to the laws of *karma*. He believed that the fruits of his *tapasyā* were not just for him, but that everyone benefited.

However, as examples from the past show us, there may be more secular and 'concrete' aims behind the practice of *tapasyā*. In this case, a *tapasyā* may be done for the collectivity, with the *sādhu* once again interacting with and for the lay society. I mentioned, for example, that Yogī Oṃ Nāth became *khaṛeśvarī* to bring rain to Gujarat. A Rāmānandī *monī* whom I met in the Allahabad Melā wrote in the sand that he decided to start his *tapasyā* in honour of the Rām temple of Ayodhya and declared that he would keep silent until the temple was built over the Babri Masjid. Kamal Giri said that a few years ago a devotee asked him to stand for the installation of a *śivaliṅgam* (aniconic representation of Śiva). He did this for 11 days and many people gathered to have his *darśan*: he collected several thousand rupees from them which allowed the *liṅgam* to be installed. Now that he was doing *khaṛeśvarī* for a longer period, with the aim of installing a Hanumān statue, he complained that not many people visited him. He said that people were simply ignorant about *bābās*' practices. He also stated that doing *tapasyā* is a way to improve not only one's individual practice but also the individual's prestige among other *sādhus*, attracting more devotees and followers. Indeed, Kamal Giri was expecting a good position in the camp of the Jūnā *akhāṛā* in upcoming religious festivals, as having a *khaṛeśvarī* is a good way to appeal to people.

---

73 See Bevilacqua 2018b.

Conclusion

This chapter has demonstrated that the practice of *tapas* is transformative and that from pain or endurance it can confer powers, purification and liberation. But it has also shown that the history of *tapas* is an example of how words, and the ideas and practices associated with them, change over the centuries. And that it is therefore also a history of transformation and adaptation.

We have seen that techniques that had previously been identified as examples of *tapasyā* (for example *prāṇāyāma*) were later understood as yoga practices; and so strong is the connection between *tapasyā* and yoga that it is not surprising that the *ūrdhvabāhu* Amar Bhārtī defined the practice of *tapasyā* as *prācīn yog*, the ancient yoga. Some of the practices used to develop *tapas* have become methods of yoga but with different attitudes and purposes, infused by the theories of *saṃsāra*, *karma*, *mokṣa*, etc. Considering the merging of *tapas* and yoga, it is possible that, in redacting the Upaniṣads, their authors wanted to appropriate the etymological importance of the word *tapas* while making it more suitable and accessible, thus stressing its meditative potential and giving it a more ethical nuance. This approach was supported by Patañjali and other authors who did not favour strenuous practices or painful bodily austerities. This becomes particularly evident in medieval *haṭha* yoga texts that eliminate extreme practices and advise against exerting the body.

Contemporary ascetics seem to maintain this two-pronged approach: on the one hand, certain practices are condemned in favour of a more meditative form of *tapasyā*; on the other, *tapasvī*s are held in high regard. In general, while the practices themselves have survived, the names and theories associated with them have undergone changes. While the theories and reasons underlying the word *tapas* evolved, the idea remained of *tapas* as the intention and necessary 'passion' to pursue a goal. Gross's (1992: 327) conclusions are quite useful: over the centuries, the word *tapas* simply came to indicate 'any practice leading to self-control, for this is closely aligned with the goals and ideal of yoga as a sadhana. To attain a desired end, endeavours are necessary and there is no greater goal than attaining god.' The examples of *tapasyā*s given in this chapter have fully vindicated Gross's statement. They also have shown that, transmitted in oral form, past practices are still attested today, performed by ascetics belonging to various traditional *sampradāya*s, which highlights not only how these practices have managed to survive in different religious contexts but also how ascetics belonging to different *sampradāyas* often practise and explain *tapasyās* in a similar way.

We have seen, however, that there are some groups that disdain certain austerities; among them the *ūrdhvabāhu*, or others who perform a *tapasyā* following their *pārampārik* tradition: that is, following the way they have learnt according to their lineage of transmission, or according to the order to which they belong. In the next chapter, the link between *tapas* and yoga will be further analysed by taking *haṭha* yoga into consideration.

4
Haṭha Yoga from a Historical and Ethnographic Perspective

This chapter draws on the textual research of the other members of the Haṭha Yoga Project and attempts to tie it in with my ethnographic findings. Hence, its purpose is to frame the development of *haṭha* yoga by considering textual sources in Sanskrit and in vernaculars (although these are still under-researched) and comparing them with the ascetics' own understanding of *haṭha* yoga in order to assess the use of the word and the presence of its techniques in different contexts.

Given the shortage of early textual sources that describe in detail physical practices among ascetics, it is not impossible to imagine that the distinctive practices of *haṭha* yoga, or at least some of them, were already in use among ascetics prior to the composition of the *haṭha* yoga corpus. Furthermore, given the lack of cogent evidence to clearly trace the development of the theories and practices, to date it is impossible to determine who originally 'invented' or practised these techniques. Recent studies have demonstrated that the earliest references to the term *haṭha* yoga and some of its practices appear in Buddhist milieux, but neither should the influence of Chinese practices be underestimated.[1]

1 Needham (1983: 282–283) asserts that between the 4th and 14th centuries there was a continual exchange between China and India, with China contributing

Hence, the history of *haṭha* yoga is a history of exchanges, adoptions and adaptations that were facilitated by the itinerancy of ascetics (and monks), who wandered in search of gurus to develop their religious paths. Competitiveness was also a variable that pushed orders to adjust to new and 'trendy' practices. In fact, *haṭha* yoga techniques became so popular that they spread to different religious and intellectual contexts.

Haṭha yoga in Sanskrit textual sources

The ground-breaking and ongoing work of James Mallinson, Jason Birch and Mark Singleton has been instrumental in gathering evidence that can help reconstruct the history of *haṭha* yoga as a yogic method in which physical practices predominate. In this section, I will summarise the most important stages of its development, highlighting in particular the different religious contexts in which *haṭha* yoga practices occurred.

The term *haṭha* yoga first appeared within Buddhist contexts,[2] specifically in the *Bodhisattvabhūmi* (a Mahāyāna Yogācara text from the 3rd century CE), which argued that one becomes a *bodhisattva* not by '*haṭhayoga*' and, according to Mallinson (2020), this would mean not 'by the application of force' nor 'with effort'. The term then reappears in tantric Buddhist works from the 8th century, reinterpreted within sexual rituals and in relation to the retention of semen. Here the practice is associated with the mastering of *bodhicitta*, i.e. semen. Likewise, in the *Vimalaprabhā* by Puṇḍarīka (c. 1030 CE) it is related to the restraint of semen during sexual rituals, but also to moving the breath in the central channel (see Birch 2011: 535–537).

Later Buddhist tantric sources associate the practice of *haṭha* yoga not with sexual rituals but with breath retention, considering *haṭha* yoga, however, as a method of last resort to be used when other methods have failed (Mallinson 2020: 182). For instance, the *Yogimanoharā* (c. 1200 CE) claims that 'holding the breath and other ascetic practices are unnecessary because success may be achieved' through repetition of the *vajra* mantra (Mallinson 2020: 182).

---

greatly, especially with regard to alchemy and physiology. Steavu (2023: 399) claims that 'between the 6th and 9th centuries, alchemy, sexual practices, but also breathing and postural techniques had enjoyed in China a level of conceptual consistency and unity that was achieved in India only appreciably later; thus a transfer hypothesis from China to India during this period, for certain elements at least, would be conceivable'. Correspondences are indeed striking, but it is impossible here to present an accurate parallelism. See Yang 2023; Steavu 2023.

2 On *haṭha* yoga in Buddhist sources, see Mallinson 2018b, 2020; Birch 2011.

The first text to describe some of the practices that would later be classified as *haṭha* yoga is also Buddhist. Composed in a Vajrayāna setting, the *Amṛtasiddhi* (c. 11th century CE) rejects sexual rituals and addresses its teachings to an ascetic, celibate audience.[3] Several of the teachings present in this work had not previously been documented. These include the idea of relocating the tantric triad of sun, moon and fire in the body, so that the moon is in the skull and drips *amṛta*, the nectar of immortality, which is consumed by the sun (conflated with the fire) in the stomach. This *amṛta* is also identified as *bindu*, which, for the first time, designates semen (labelled *rajas* in its 'female' aspect). *Bindu* is closely connected with the mind, and its preservation is essential for immortality. In the *Amṛtasiddhi*, for the first time, a connection between breath, mind and *bindu* is outlined.[4] Control over them is achieved through practices involving bodily postures and breath control: *mahāmudrā*, *mahābandha* and *mahāvedha*.[5] These three techniques will be taught in all subsequent texts on *haṭha* yoga, sometimes under different names. Their purpose is to converge the breath to the centre, so that the mind, 'having taken hold of all the elements, is everywhere' (8.20), leading to knowledge, meditation, perfection and, ultimately, immortality (8.21). Therefore, in this yoga, the control of the breath is the source of liberation (6.13), and by holding the *bindu*, and thus protecting it from being burnt by fire, one conquers immortality and supernatural powers (7.25).[6]

This theoretical paradigm can be adequately understood if it is framed in a tantric background, i.e. considering the interpretations and theories relating to the body that have developed in tantric milieux. In fact, it is necessary to point out that *haṭha* yoga practices, as presented in texts from the

3 See the critical edition by Mallinson and Szántó (2021). For details about its Vajrayāna origin, see Mallinson 2019; Schaeffer 2002.

4 The link between breath and mind, however, appears as early as the *Chāndogya Upaniṣad* (6.8.2).

5 The Great Seal (*mahāmudrā*) consists of pressing the perineum with the left heel, extending the right foot and holding it steady with the hands; raising the hips on a seat, resting the chin on the chest, filling the abdomen with air and performing breath holding. The Great Lock (*mahābandha*) consists of the techniques to properly master the Great Seal; hence it teaches the perineum lock and the throat lock. The Great Piercing (*mahāvedha*) involves lifting the buttocks and dropping them to the floor in order to let the breath flow back into the central channel. See Mallinson and Szántó 2021.

6 These are translations from the Mallinson and Szántó (2021) critical edition.

11th century onwards, work on 'tantric bodies',[7] seen as micro representations of macro forces/realities/elements, hence as a place where homologies with external cosmic energies and deities can be activated, manipulated and controlled within the body, in order to transform it into an instrument capable of providing immortality, powers or *mokṣa*.[8]

The history of *haṭha* yoga continues with the dissemination of *Amṛtasiddhi* theories and practices in various religious contexts, especially those related to the lineages that would later be associated with the Nāth *sampradāya*. Composed in Mangalore, around the 12th century in a Śaiva-Nāth framework, the *Amaraugha*[9] is the first text to use the term *haṭha* yoga to describe one of the four methods of yoga, the others being mantra, *laya* (dissolution) and *rāja* (royal) yoga.[10] The *Amaraugha* defines *haṭha* yoga as 'that which is intent upon stopping the breath' (Birch 2011: 547) by having the breath 'rise up the central channel in order to prevent the emission of semen' but, as in the case of the *Amṛtasiddhi*, not in the context of sexual rituals.

From a similar religious context, the *Vivekamārtaṇḍa* is the first text to combine tantric *kuṇḍalinī* techniques with the practices taught in the *Amṛtasiddhi*. Probably composed between the 12th and 13th centuries, it teaches a yoga with six auxiliaries but does not mention *haṭha* yoga. However, it contains one of the earliest accounts of *mudrā*s, and includes *mūlabandha*, *uḍḍīyānabandha*, *jālandharbandha*, *mahāmudrā*, *khecarī* and *viparītakaraṇa*.[11]

---

7 I use the plural form because the representation of the body in tantric texts is strictly related to the tradition from which it derives; there are therefore as many tantric bodies as there are textual traditions (Flood 2006: 4–5).

8 On the tantric/yogic body, see Chapter 5, p. 180.

9 On the *Amaraugha*, see Birch 2019, 2024. A later recension of the *Amaraugha* appears under the name of *Amaraughaprabodha* and takes some verses from another interesting work, the *Amanaska*, which, however, rejects the practices of *haṭha* yoga. On the *Amanaska*, see Birch 2013.

10 Although different hierarchies of yogas have been attested, this fourfold hierarchy became prominent. While the order of the first three varies, it is generally accepted that *rāja* yoga is the best of all.

11 *Mūlabandha* is the perineum contraction, *uḍḍīyānabandha* is the stomach contraction up toward the abdomen, while *jālandharbandha* is the lock created by holding down the chin on the chest. *Khecarī* is generally the *mudrā* in which an elongated tongue tip is turned back into the mouth until it reaches the soft palate and the nasal cavity; *viparītakaraṇa* is an inverted posture. The *haṭha* yogic *mudrā*s and *bandha*s will be described in detail in Chapter 5, pp. 219ff.

The next step occurred between the 13th and 15th centuries when *aṣṭāṅgayoga* was combined with the *haṭha* yoga 'followed by Kapila', as seen in the *Dattātreyayogaśāstra*. This 13th-century Vaiṣṇava work teaches the fourfold system of *Amaraughaprabodha* and expands on *haṭha* yoga. This method can be practised by following an *aṣṭāṅgayoga* 'known by Yājñavalkya and others' (most probably Patañjali) or by following the doctrine of '[a]depts such as Kapila',[12] which is based on nine techniques. These techniques are: *mahāmudrā*, *mahābandha* and *mahāvedha*, *khecarī* and *vajrolī mudrās* (the latter also consisting of *amarolī* and *sahajolī*), *jālandhara*, *uḍḍīyāṇa* and *mūlabandhas*, and *viparītakaraṇī*. These practices aim to manipulate vital energies, but mostly prevent the downward flow of *bindu*, allowing the practitioner to become liberated while still alive.[13]

Another text that contains some of the earliest teachings of *haṭha* yoga, but does not use the label *haṭha* yoga, is the *Gorakṣaśataka*[14] (probably 13th century CE), attributed to Gorakṣa (i.e. Gorakhnāth).[15] The *Gorakṣaśataka* teaches that liberation comes through control of the mind and that this is attainable through control of the breath. In fact, this is the first text to describe four complex methods of *prāṇāyāma*[16] and *sarasvatīcālana*, the

---

12 Bronkhorst (1998: 57–59) makes an interesting connection between Kapila and non-Vedic asceticism. Kapila is primarily known for having created the Sāṃkhya system of philosophy; however, while in some texts (such as the *Śvetāśvatara Upaniṣad* or the *Mahābhārata*) he is described as a supreme seer (*paramarṣi*), others (such as the *Baudhāyanadharmasūtra*) call Kapila an *asura*, i.e. a demon, the enemy of the Vedic gods. This could indicate that he practised a form of religion different from the orthodox one.

13 See Mallinson 2013a on the *Dattātreyayogaśāstra*. The *Śārṅgadharapaddhati*, an anthology on various subjects compiled in 1363 CE, maintains this idea of two sets of *haṭha* yoga: one practised by Gorakṣa (and others) and one practised by *ṛṣi* Mārkaṇḍeya (and others). The former is associated with the teaching of *āsana*, *prāṇāyāma*, *pratyāhāra*, *dhāraṇā*, *dhyāna* and *samādhi*, while the latter also includes *yama* and *niyama* (Mallinson 2011a: 772).

14 See Mallinson 2012a and his critical edition of the text (forthcoming).

15 According to tradition, Gorakhnāth is said to have produced several works in Sanskrit, such as the *Vivekamārtaṇḍa*, *Gorakṣaśataka* and the *Siddha Siddhanta Paddhati*, but he is said to have also produced works in vernacular languages such as the *Gorakh Bodh* and the *Gorakh Bānī* (see below), metaphorical poems that attempt to express the experience of the Absolute (Muñoz 2011: 112). Despite this attribution and considering the date attributed to Gorakhnāth, it is unlikely that Gorakhnāth produced all these works.

16 *Sūrya kumbhaka* is performed by inhaling through the right nostril and exhaling through the left; *ujjāyī* by making a rasping sound in the lower part of the throat

stimulation of Sarasvatī, a practice to awaken *kuṇḍalinī* similar to *khecarī mudrā* (Mallinson 2012a: 257).

Produced in a similar Nāth environment is the *Yogabīja*[17] (c. 14th century CE), which is the only text that includes philosophical notions to support a soteriology based on the fourfold system of yogas (Birch 2020a: 219–220). The text declares that both gnosis and yoga are necessary for liberation and emphasises that, in order to achieve *jīvanmukti* (freedom of the self while living), a perfected body must be produced through the practice of yoga (Mallinson 2012a). As Birch (2020b: 453) notes, the definition present in this work of *haṭha* as the union of the sun and the moon is a later addition made before the production of the *Haṭhapradīpikā*.

The *Haṭhapradīpikā* (mid-15th century CE) is a collection of earlier works and provides the theoretical systematisation of *haṭha* yoga that remains mostly dominant to this day. Its author, Svātmārāma, introduces a lineage of 29 great Siddhas—starting with Ādināth and followed by Matsyendra, Gorakṣa, etc. It describes 15 *āsanas* (seven of which are non-seated), but focuses mostly on *prāṇāyāmas* consisting of eight complex practices (*kumbhakas*) culminating in total breath retention (*kevala kumbhaka*) and ten *mudrās* (which also include the *bandhas*) the main aim of which is to enhance the rising of *kuṇḍalinī* up the central channel of the body, in order to unite with Śiva in the head. To note, six acts of self-cleansing (*ṣaṭkarma*) are described for the first time here. These practices aim at purifying the body and healing physical imbalances. They operate on a body constituted by a system of *nāḍīs* and *cakras*, and vitalised by energies such as *vāyus* and *kuṇḍalinī* which shall be controlled.[18] By identifying *samādhi* as *rāja* yoga and *haṭha* yoga as the path leading to it, Svātmārāma succeeded in reconciling the two traditions into an independent soteriological system.

Between the 15th and 18th centuries, *haṭha* yoga techniques, theories and praxis proliferated and were incorporated into an increasing number of texts. While the early literature consisted of short texts with few theoretical details and a simple 'outline' of practices—which may suggest an audience of practitioners—later texts were more elaborate, both linguistically and in terms of content, suggesting a more scholarly audience (Birch 2020b: 456).

---

while inhaling; *śītalī* is performed by inhaling through a rolled tongue; *bhastrī* by pumping the breath in and out as if working with a pair of bellows (Mallinson 2012a: 258).

17 See the critical edition of the text by Birch and Mallinson (forthcoming).

18 See Flood 2006 and Chapters 5 and 6.

Birch extensively described and analysed the development of *haṭha* yoga textual production in his 2020b article. He divides the texts produced between the 17th and 19th centuries into two main categories: 'extended works' and 'compendia' that borrow from *haṭha* and *rāja* yoga texts. In the extended works, the number of *āsana*s increases significantly as does the number of *ṣaṭkarmas*, thus suggesting a growing interest in physical practices. New, original techniques find space in monographic works that manifest a more 'praxis-oriented' attitude. The compendia, on the other hand, reveal the attempt of erudite brahmins to integrate *haṭha* yoga into brahmanical and Vedantic yoga, which led, in fact, to the production of the so-called Yoga Upaniṣads. This assimilation was conducted by stripping *haṭha* yoga of its tantric heritage, especially that represented by practices such as *vajrolī mudrā*, strongly associated with sexual practices. Interestingly, however, not all texts use the label *haṭha* yoga. The *Siddhasiddhāntapaddhati*, a text produced in a Nāth milieu around 1700, does not mention the word *haṭha*,[19] and neither does the *Gheraṇḍa Saṃhitā* (c. 1700 CE), an encyclopaedic Vaiṣṇava text probably from Bengal, call its yoga *haṭha* but rather *ghaṭa*: *ghaṭastha* yoga, the yoga of the pot/body.

The techniques of *haṭha* yoga presented in these Sanskrit texts aimed to lead the individual to experience union with the Absolute within the body, and to progressively control physiological and mental processes by internalising tantric concepts and esoteric rituals in the body in order to attain superhuman powers (*siddhis*). Although the role of the guru was still fundamental to the practice, the lack of exclusivity captured the attention of a wider audience, appealing to practitioners from different religious backgrounds. This means that the texts could imply different metaphysics and doctrine, refer to different contextually constructed yogic bodies, have different perceptions of ideal practitioners (ascetic or householder) or ultimate goals, while sharing the same set of practices.

Haṭha yoga practices in vernacular sources

Most likely, wandering *sādhus* transmitted their teachings orally to their disciples, imparting knowledge passed down for generations. Repetition and 'rhymes' facilitated the memorisation of concepts, while riddles and

19 Mallinson (2020) points out that 'in the few instances in which Śaiva texts give a generic name to practices that in later works were designed as *haṭhayoga*, they use the near synonym *kaṣṭayoga*, indicating that the later usage of the term *haṭhayoga* was not current in those traditions.'

enigmatic phrases helped maintain the secrecy of esoteric teachings. Sometimes, these were transcribed into vernacular languages, often centuries after the first guru had imparted them. These works retained an esoteric nuance through the use of a *sandhyā bhāṣā*, a twilight or intentional language,[20] still used today among contemporary *sādhus*.

In this section, examining songs, poems and texts probably written as manuals or notebooks for practitioners or aspiring practitioners, we will evaluate the presence of the label *haṭha* yoga and of *haṭha* yoga practices in vernacular sources. The earliest presence in vernacular sources are presented by Sarde (2023: 146–149) in an analysis of early Marathi texts (late 13th to 15th centuries). He shows how these texts are suffused with vocabulary and practices relating to *haṭha* yoga and strongly connected to the practice of Nāth Yogīs. For example, in *Līlācaritra* 195 we find the term *haṭa* along with breathing and cleansing practices performed by Salivahan, an officer of the Yādava king Mahadeva, and presented to Chakradhar, the supposed funder of the Mahānubhāva sect. Sarde also mentions that the *Tattvasara*, another Marathi work attributed to the yogi Changdev (c. 14th century, associated with the Vārakarī tradition), has a section called *haṭha* yoga, demonstrating the strong presence of Nāth Yogīs in Maharashtra and their association there with the practices of *haṭha* yoga.

If we consider the *Gorakh Bānī* (Sayings of Gorakh) and other vernacular works[21] attributed to Gorakhnāth but probably composed much later, we can recognise the practices found in Sanskrit texts on *haṭha* yoga. However, the term *haṭha* yoga is not mentioned here.[22] The practice of the *Gorakh Bānī* focuses on redirecting the flow of the *bindu* to escape or 'trick' death (Djurdjevic and Singh 2019: 10). The text mentions the importance of breath and *bindu* retention for every yogi 'who holds above what goes below' (*sabadī* 17) and also emphasises the importance of a practice such as *khecarī mudrā* ('reverse the tongue and touch the palate', *sabadī* 133). Additionally, it also highlights the act of drinking the *amṛta* produced in the skull (*sabadī* 87) and the inversion of the breath to pierce the six *cakras*

20 This language, which is also used in Tantras, is incomprehensible to uninitiated people or readers. Therefore, oral explanation by a guru is necessary. This issue has been discussed by several scholars: see Bharati 1961; Lessing and Wayman 1968; Kværne 1977; Bucknell and Stuart-Fox 1986.

21 I make use here of the translation of the *Gorakh Bānī*, and other works such as the *Sisyā Darsan*, *Narvai Bodh*, etc., as presented in Djurdjevic and Singh 2019.

22 In a personal communication (22 December 2020), Gordan Djurdjevic confirmed that the label *haṭha* yoga never appears in the *Gorakh Bānī* as such, while the word *tapas* is mentioned a couple of times.

(*sabadī* 105). *Sabadī* 141 describes the *haṭha* yoga practices of *vajrolī* and *amarolī* to obtain the retention of the semen (see Mallinson 2018a), while *sabadī* 48 mentions six postures without naming any. However, in *pad* 45.1 (*Rāg Rāmgrī*) there is mention of *biparati karaṇī*, i.e. *viparītakaraṇī* the inverted posture or *mudrā*.

Similar practices were attributed to Nāth Yogīs by those who criticised them. Considering Kabīr's oeuvre (15th century CE), further clues to Yogīs' practice are offered. In *sākhī* 43 of his *Bījak*, Kabīr states that Gorakhnāth was a 'yoga connoisseur' who 'for nothing polished his body' (Hess and Singh 1983: 94), most likely referring to *ṣaṭkarmas* and *nāḍī* purification through *prāṇāyāma* techniques. In *pad* 174 of the *Granthāvalī*, Kabīr criticises the way Yogīs hold back their seed (Hawley 2005: 275), while in a poem from the *Ādi Granth*, he states: 'Madman, give up yogic posture (āsanu), and breath control' (Lorenzen 2011: 34).

Other information can also be gleaned from these sources. The *Gorakh Bānī* seems to criticise collections on physical yogic practices when it says:

> 134. Oh scholar, why do you die struggling for knowledge?
> Know the highest place in some other way!
> You are creating commotion with *āsan* and *prāṇāyam*.[23]

These verses seem like the answer of an ascetic disturbed by the proliferation of *āsanas* and *prāṇāyāmas* in works written by *paṇḍits*. But the author does not even tolerate those who excessively display their practices:

> 82. Sitting in the posture, stopping the breath,
> All these stations of pride are just worldly business.
> Gorakhnāth says: Thinking about the self
> Is like watching the moon in water.[24]

Again, these could be the words of an ascetic criticising practices probably done only for the purpose of exhibition to attract devotees and their money ('worldly business'), which is not uncommon among ascetics even today. The author of this *bānī* draws attention to the importance of a more meditative practice to achieve, in a detached way, knowledge of the self.

As we saw in Chapter 2, medieval Nāth Jogis (Yogīs) profoundly influenced other wandering ascetics,[25] such as the tapasic *śākhā* of the

---

23 Djurdjevic and Singh 2019: 76.
24 Djurdjevic and Singh 2019: 65.
25 See for example the strong link between the Nāth order and the Dādū *panth* in Horstmann 2021.

Rāmānandī *sampradāya*. Contemporary Rāmānandī *sādhus* still acknowledge Nāths as those who invented or mastered yogic *kriyās*, while others merely copied them. For this reason, the so-called Hindi works[26] of Rāmānanda bear several similarities to the Nāth works we have mentioned and sometimes use their verses, though attributing different meanings to certain words according to their religious backgrounds and *sādhanā*.[27] It is impossible to date the works cited here because they are editions found in a private collection at the beginning of the 19th century.

Verse 19 of the *Rām Rakṣā* lists five *mudrās* that—with the exception of *khecarī*—do not appear in Sanskrit texts, but in a short vernacular composition attributed to Gorakh, the *Aṣṭamudrā*, and in the *Jogapradīpakā* (see below). They are *cācarī*, *bhūcarī*, *khecarī*, *agocarī* and *unmanī*. The author of the *Rām Rakṣā* has probably taken them from a Śaiva source as he compares himself to the king of the Siddhas. The *Rām Rakṣā* and *Aṣṭamudrā* do not explain the practices, but they are explained in a Nepali text called *Vairāgyāmvara* from the second half of the 18th century and the *Jogapradīpakā*. Śaśidhara, the author of the *Vairāgyāmvara*, says that *khecarī* consists of pushing the tongue towards the palate; *bhūcarī* consists of concentrating the gaze on the space between the eyebrows, while *cācarī* requires concentrating with closed eyes. With *agocarī* the concentration shifts to the ears, while *unmanī* is an inner gaze directed at *brahman* (Caracchi 1999: 264). In the *Jogapradīpakā*, *cācarī* is directing the gaze towards the nose while sitting in \, observing the shining image of the half-moon and meditating on *kuṇḍalinī*. *Bhūcarī* is meditating between the eyebrows in *siddhāsana*, observing 'the whole body from top to bottom as illuminated', thus generating great bliss. *Agocarī* is defined as meditating 'on the seven *cakras* and then moving the point of meditation to a thousand petalled lotus to obtain imperceptible meditation'. *Unmanī* is practised in *svastikāsana* by performing skilful *prāṇāyāma*, i.e. adopting all *bandhas*, stabilising the mind and *vāyu* and withdrawing the senses. This *mudrā*, which is the essence of all *mudrās*, would lead to hearing different *anāhata* sounds, which is the main goal of these practices (Gharote 1999: 24).

Another interesting composition attributed to Rāmānanda is the *Yogacintāmaṇi*, a name also used in Sanskrit works. It consists of 23 stanzas in a rudimentary language (*sādhukkari bhāṣā*) and recalls several haṭhayogic ideas and practices. The *sādhanā* is 'fought' in the *suṣumṇā*

26 Scholars have long debated on the authenticity of these compositions and their attribution to Rāmānanda; see a summary of the debate in Bevilacqua 2018a.

27 See the work of Caracchi 1999. I use here her remarkable translations in Italian of these works.

valley (1), its aim being to conquer the fortress of the body, which should be taken care of (8b) through an inverted practice in which the *sādhu*, after sitting for a long time in *siddhāsana*, performing a *prāṇāyāma* consisting of 12 measures,[28] reverses the flow of the *prāṇa* which, crossing the *suṣumṇā*, reaches the *sahasrāra* (Caracchi 1999: 312–314). This explanation, however, is not easily recognisable from a reading of the original:

> 8. Now turn and ascend
> Where the city is located
> Take care of your body, brother,
> Where the light of Rāma radiates.
>
> 9. Walk through the city of Surati,
> Where the palace of the *ātmā* resides.
> Where the roots of the ocean of senses meet,
> Put the left foot.
>
> 10. Put the right foot in the middle
> And prepare an *āsana* in the immortal abode.
> Drink twelve measures of air,
> Turn and ascend to the abode above your head.[29]

Another work is the *Gyān Tilak* which recalls the *Gyān Tilak* attributed to Gorakhnāth and actually uses some of its verses, although its third part is similar to the *Gorakh Bānī* in that it is organised as a *goṣṭhī* (dialogue). In the text, Kabīr, traditionally a disciple of Rāmānanda, is presented as a Siddha.[30] Here the author criticises those practices done for specific reasons or to obtain specific results, without leading to any spiritual benefit:

> 3.17. The whole world is devoted to *jap* and *tapas* in the mirage of merit and demerit,
>
> But if a *sādhu* has practised with body and mind, then he resides in the pure supreme State.

Other sections entail the practice of techniques such as those we find in *haṭha* yoga textual sources, especially if we consider verses such as:

> 34b [. . .] where the life-breath and self-stop, there, there is the house in which, by means of yoga, I can dwell. [. . .]

---

28 'Twelve measures' is an amount of air often mentioned in texts on yogic practices, such as the *Gheraṇḍa Saṃhitā*.

29 This is my translation from the Italian version provided in Caracchi 1999: 306.

30 Given the presence of Kabīr in this work, Caracchi (1999: 333) suggests that Rāmānanda could have learnt these practices from Nāths and then transmitted them to Kabīr.

> 36. I joined *iḍā* and *piṅgalā* and brought them together in the house of *suṣumṇā*. Where the mind stops, O Kabīrjī, there I saw the meeting of all eras. [. . .]
>
> 45. Follow these precepts, O Kabīrjī, and naturally detach from your body. *Siddhas* understand this ambiguity of the body [or *Siddhas* know how to take care of the body].

It is clear that even in these Vaiṣṇava texts there is an underlying idea of conquering death, although devotion still plays a fundamental role. The body is not understood as a trap but as a fortress to be conquered and an instrument through which freedom or immortality can be achieved.

These vernacular sources, therefore, present an understanding of the body typical of *haṭha* yoga Sanskrit textual sources, with its *nāḍīs* and *cakras*, and its inner flow of *bindu* manipulated through *prāṇāyāmas* to attain the *amṛta*, or to raise *kuṇḍalinī* from the root *cakra* to the *sahasrāra cakra*. Physical body practices are, however, mentioned in passing and never described. They were probably shown directly by the guru to the disciples. Vernacular sources were better suited to conveying the feeling and experience of the practices, something that was inexpressible through 'common' words because it referred to spiritual experiences, difficult to understand for non-practitioners. As the *Gyān Tilak* (3.12b) says, 'In the self the self is seen, if it is not seen it cannot be known': only those who are able to see the self—therefore those who are practising correctly—know it and can therefore talk about it.

It is worth noting that, apart from in Marathi texts,[31] the term *haṭha* yoga is rarely used in medieval vernacular sources. The *Prāṇ Samkalī* of Cauraṅgīnāth (v. 256) claims that '*haṭh jog*' is the union of the sun and moon (Mallinson 2016a: 136n116). In his *Padāvali* (135.1),[32] Sant Sundardās (1596–1689) associates *hātha* [*sic*] yoga with Gorakhnāth, and in his *Sarvāṅgayogapradīpikā* he proposes a classification of three yogas (*bhakti*, *haṭha* and *sāṃkhya*), dividing them into further subgroups.[33] In the *haṭha* yoga section he recalls the *Haṭhapradīpikā*, both in the introduction to the topic and in the way the practitioner should live and cleanse his body. He defines *haṭha* yoga as 'when the sun and the moon are made to

31 Since research on vernacular sources is still in its infancy, it is likely that further studies undertaken on a regional basis may yield interesting results and lead me to qualify this statement.

32 I would like to thank Pinuccia Caracchi for bringing this passage to my attention (personal communication, 26 September 2020).

33 On this work and the classifications proposed by Sundardās, see Burger 2014.

meet as one',[34] thus recalling the *Yogabīja* understanding but also associating it with the manipulation and unifications of *vāyus*. In the subdivisions of this *haṭha* yoga section, *rāja* yoga follows, but the author defines it very differently from Svātmārāma and closer to what is found in other vernacular sources, i.e. related to sexual practices. *Lakṣa* yoga is then introduced, which resembles techniques of visualisation, followed by *aṣṭāṅgayoga*, with its typical steps, along with *kumbhakas*, *mudrās* and *bandhas*. Maya Burger (2014: 700), who analysed the work, has highlighted that it is not necessarily addressing practitioners and that its author probably wanted to gain a certain authority among the followers of various forms of yoga by displaying his knowledge in a treatise that intends to be systematic about yoga.

Other vernacular sources in which we find mention of *haṭha* yoga are the *Prāṇ Samkalī* of Caurangīnāth (v. 256), 'in which *haṭh jog* is said to be the union of the sun and moon', and in the *Guru Granth Sāhib* (905.4 and 1305.6), in which it is associated with extreme austerities, such as hanging upside down (Mallinson 2016a: 136n116). To note, the 12th–13th-century *Tirumantiram*, in Tamil language, uses the word *tava* (the equivalent of the Sanskrit *tapas*) to refer to its new method of yoga, the practices of which, however, are the same as those classified as *haṭha* in Sanskrit works (Mallinson 2018b).

At the beginning of the *Pavanavijayasvarodayabhāṣānibandha*, probably from the second half of the 16th century CE, Alakhdās, the author, pays homage to Mohandās—possibly a yogi-disciple of Dādū (1544–1603 CE)—who combined *svarodaya* (an astrological system of prognostication based on nasal dominance) and *haṭha* yoga.[35]

Other vernacular texts that mention *haṭha* yoga are hagiographies. The *Rasik Prakāś Bhaktamāl* (1712), as we have seen in Chapter 3 (p. 111), describes the Rāmānandī Kīlhdev as so absorbed in '*haṭha* yoga' that when a royal cortège passed by and someone, seeing him so immobile, put a nail (*kīl*) in his head, he did not feel it and the nail even disappeared (Śrīvāstav 1957: 189). This mental absorption, which in older sources was described as *tapas*, is here considered to be *haṭha* yoga.

Even in the *Guru Granth Sāhib* (905.4 and 1305.6), it is associated with extreme austerities, such as hanging upside down (Mallinson 2016a: 136n116). To note, the 12th–13th-century *Tirumantiram*, in Tamil language, uses the word *tava* (the equivalent of the Sanskrit *tapas*) to refer to

34 Burger 2014: 695.

35 In a forthcoming book, Birch analyses the work and compares it to the *Yogacintāmaṇi* and the *Baḥr al-Hayāt* (see below).

its new method of yoga, the practices of which, however, are the same as those classified as *haṭha* in Sanskrit works (Mallinson 2018b).

Several of the *āsanas* described are similar to those in the *Baḥr al-Hayāt*, a Persian work attributed to Muhammad al Ghaws, whose history has been explored in depth by Carl Ernst (2003, 2016). This text is derivative of another work, the *Hawd ma' al-Hayāt*, probably written by an Arab scholar, whose introduction claims (probably falsely) to be the translation of a lost Sanskrit work known as the *Amṛtakuṇḍa*. This unknown Arab scholar is said to have travelled to India to encounter Nāth Yogīs or yogis in general, as Muhammad al Ghaws probably did, to expand his work. In the *Baḥr al-Hayāt* there are, in fact, 21 postures instead of the five in the *Hawd ma' al-Hayāt* (Ernst 2016: 152). Muhammad al Ghaws appreciated the ascetics of 'the society of Jogis and Sannyasis' as experts in 'interior practices, visualisation exercises, descriptions of holding the breath, and other types of meditation' (Ernst 2016: 153). While reinterpreting the theological context of these practices to make it closer to Islam, the author admits that the yogis' practical knowledge of the body was 'highly advanced and valuable for the pursuit of mystical knowledge':

> The Yogic group has grasped the means, and they have observed and investigated it, because by the means of the body the real gnosis is discovered [. . .] Therefore the protection of the body is a duty (*fard*), because it is the means to gnosis (Ernst 2016: 158).

Of note is the absence in the text of any attempt to translate the label *haṭha* yoga, while yoga is translated as *riyazat.* Carl Ernst agrees with me in assuming that the yogis encountered by Muhammad al Ghaws were non-elite, hence closer to a vernacular idea of yoga, i.e. without classifications.[36]

A similar absence of the label *haṭha* yoga is found in the *Jogapradīpakā*, a work in Braj Bhasha composed by Jayatrāma[37] in 1737 CE, in Vrindavan. Although based on the *Haṭhapradīpikā*, none of its 964 verses ever uses the word *haṭha* or *haṭh* (Mallinson 2016a: 136n116). Jayatrāma declares himself to be a disciple of Payahārī Bābā Kṛṣṇadās who lived in Galta. This was probably a namesake of Kṛṣṇadās Payahārī who, as we have seen in Chapter 2 (p. 77), began the tapasic *śākhā* of the Rāmānandī *sampradāya*, or it represents an attempt by the author to link himself with his *paramparā.* In its eight chapters, the text describes *yama*, *niyama*, *āsanas* and

36 Personal communication, 14 January 2020.

37 Another text attributed to this author is the *Yogāsanamālā*, which contains 70 of the 84 *āsanas* of the *Jogapradīpakā* and was written in 1768 (Bühnemann 2007: 28).

prāṇāyāmas, going so far as to distinguish between Vedic and tantric typologies of *prāṇāyāmas* based on caste issues. Elsewhere, the chapters describe *ṣaṭkarmas*, eight *kumbhakas* and their effects; it mentions 24 *mudrās* and *bandhas* and discusses *pratyāhāra* and *dhāraṇās* as based on the five elements. Jayatrāma reveals a particular interest in the calculation of time and especially of the time of death, which he claims can be determined by considering the flow of air out of the nostrils upon awakening.

Another, more recent, work to consider is the *Caurāśī Āsana* in Hindi, written by Brahmacārī Śrīnṛsiṃhaśarmā around the end of the 19th century (the preface is from 1897). The author provides an interesting definition of *haṭha* and *rāja* yoga. He says that there are two typologies of yoga, one that works on *prāṇa* and one that works on *citta*. He claims that, in his time, *haṭha* yoga is defined as the yoga that works on the *prāṇa* and *rāja* yoga on *citta*. However, he stresses, this is actually not the case: both yogas have the same aim, to stop the senses, but *haṭha* yoga is *balpūrvak* (coercive), while *rāja* yoga works with time. In his list of *haṭha* yoga practices, Brahmacārī gives examples of *tapasyās*: *pañca-dhūnī*, *jal tap*, etc., and *caurāsī āsanas* (Brahmacārī Śrīnṛsiṃhaśarmā 1911: 8–10).

The understanding of the *haṭhayogī* as *tapasvī* was well established during the British Raj,[38] demonstrating that there is a long history of the mixing of *tapas* and *haṭha* yoga. As a final example, let us recall that Monier-Monier, in the 19th century, described *haṭha* yoga as a:

> kind of forced Yoga or abstract meditation (forcing the mind to withdraw from external objects; treated in the Haṭha Pradīpikā by Svātmārāma and performed with much self-torture such as standing on one leg, holding up the arms, inhaling smoke with the head inverted &c.) (Monier-Monier 1964: 1,297).

It should be noted that the approach and ideas presented in these texts, and especially in the *Caurāśī Āsana*, are closer to the idea of *haṭha* yoga formulated by contemporary ascetics than in the Sanskrit texts.

On the meaning of *haṭha* yoga among contemporary *sādhus*

The label *haṭha* yoga never spontaneously occurred in my conversations about yoga with *sādhus*; when I mentioned that I was doing research on *haṭha* yoga or when I directly asked the question 'What is *haṭha* yoga?',

38 On this topic, see Singleton 2010.

sādhus would often look at me in surprise. This reaction is understandable considering that most *sādhus* associate *haṭha* yoga with tenacity and, therefore, they would not expect to find anyone researching the subject. This already suggests an understanding of *haṭha* yoga that departs from its textual (Sanskrit) definition.

In this section I will report on the meanings of *haṭha* yoga in the ascetic context, also showing that different meanings may co-exist at the same time. Conversations with *sādhus* revealed that *haṭha* yoga is associated with four main understandings:

1. *Haṭha* yoga is strongly related to *tapasyā*.
2. *Haṭha* yoga is strongly related to *prāṇāyāma*.
3. *Haṭha* yoga is understood as the union of the sun and the moon.
4. *Haṭha* yoga consists of *kriyās*.

However, these are not rigid definitions and other meanings may co-exist. To give a few examples, several Nāths I met in Mangalore claimed that *haṭha* yoga was the set of rules and behaviours that a Nāth must follow for life. Yogī Vijay Nāth in Kolkata, on the other hand, maintained that *haṭha* yoga can have a general meaning, a physical meaning and an inner meaning. In general, the word stresses the *dṛḍhatā* (solidity), the intention to reach a specific goal, which is why one can say, 'I have *haṭha* and I do things with *haṭha*.' However, this approach is not necessarily good, because with the same approach one can aspire to bad goals, so the intention behind the effort is very important. The physical meaning would instead refer to those practices we have seen described in Sanskrit texts. Yogī Vijay Nāth did not specify the inner meaning, probably considering it a secret topic not to be shared with an uninitiated person. His approach is interesting because it sums up some of the emic answers I have collected during my fieldwork. It is also interesting to note that these different meanings, and in particular the four I listed above and will analyse below, are scattered throughout the early textual sources from different religious backgrounds which often do not correspond to that of the *sādhu* who mentioned them. This proves that ideas and practices were flowing without sectarian barriers.

Haṭha yoga and *tapasyā*

> '*Haṭha* means power, so it is more than a *saṅkalpa* because a *saṅkalpa* can be broken, but the power of *haṭha* is what makes a *sādhu* who he is. It is the power that makes it possible to achieve the goal one had in mind.'
>
> Sanjay Giri (Koṭiliṅgam Bābā)

In this section we will continue the discussion begun in the previous chapter in which we touched on how *tapasyā* practices and certain meanings of *tapasyā* have been associated with *haṭha* yoga. In fact, according to most of the ascetics I interviewed, *haṭha* yoga is strongly related to the practice of *tapasyā*. Following this perspective, *haṭha* yoga should be explained as a method (yoga) based on 'obstinacy' (*haṭha*), and would thus represent an attitude that has been defined by Rām Priya Dās as *dṛḍh saṅkalpa*: a firm intention to realise or achieve an aim (and/or) tenacity. For this reason, according to Yogī Vilāsnāth, '*Haṭha* yoga is really simple, its meaning is "I want", then I will keep doing it, hundred per cent! *Haṭha* develops from doing. If you do *tap* you need *haṭha*, if you want to meet the *paramātman*, have his vision, you need *haṭha*'. And, again, a Rāmānujī in Varanasi said: 'The meaning of *haṭha* yoga is this: that, by force, everything that has to be done, is done completely, with full power—what has to be done, is accomplished.'

Haṭha yoga is propaedeutic to *tapasyā* and yoga: in order to accomplish any form of austerity or deep meditation, one must have or cultivate strong determination. For this reason, the practices that are often presented as examples of *haṭha* yoga coincide with those of *tapasyā* described in Chapter 3. The definition of *haṭha* yoga given by devotees of Śrī Nārāyaṇ Dās, a *sādhu* who has been sitting in *padmāsana* in Lalitā Ghāṭ, Varanasi, for the last ten years, is exemplary of this understanding of *haṭha* yoga. Referring to him, one of them said: 'He always walks barefoot, he makes his pilgrimages barefoot, he sits in that position all day long; this is *haṭha* yoga, ma'am!'

It was during the 2016 Ujjain Kumbh Melā that I understood the meaning of this definition in a straightforward manner, when I met Bholā Giri, an *ūrdhvabāhu sādhu* of the Āvāhan *akhāṛā*. While walking in the Melā ground, I saw one of the boards advertising his camp, on which he was labelled *tapasvī* and *haṭhayogī*. Seeing this, I assumed he was a *sādhu* who practiced *tapasyā* but was also involved in other physical practices. However, when I had the chance to talk to him and I asked him about his being a *haṭhayogī* and what it meant, he simply replied: 'If I decide to do something, I will do that [. . .] If I ask Viṣṇu for something he will do that.' Given this answer, I asked him if he had ever done practices such as *āsanas* or *prāṇāyāmas*, and he replied that he had never done any of those and that he was a *haṭhayogī* because he was doing *tapasyā*. Moreover, he was an '*akhaṇḍa haṭhayogī*', a perpetual *haṭhayogī*, 'with knowledge of the universe', he said.

I continue with other examples that reinforce this meaning and add further interesting nuances. According to Kamal Giri, *haṭha* yoga means that 'whatever happens, you will not stop or break your *sādhanā* [. . .] You will use your body as much as possible to get what you want, no matter what happens to it.' He also added: 'You can do yoga, but when you do not get the fruit then do *haṭha* yoga.' This last sentence was interesting, because *haṭha* yoga appeared there as a last resort, a meaning that we had encountered in early Buddhist sources.

For the Udāsī Lakṣmaṇ Dās, today not many *sādhus* practise *haṭha* yoga because

> the body gets afflicted. The second reason is that without a guru yoga is not possible. And this is especially true of *haṭha* yoga, because in *haṭha* yoga there are certain *kriyās* that one has to do only in front of the guru. This is the way a guru teaches. Because there are fewer gurus today, there are also fewer disciples [. . .] *Haṭha* yoga is not a *paddhati* (system), *haṭha* yoga is *balpūrvak* (forced), all those things that our body does not want to do, we make it do them. For the meaning of *haṭha* is *jabardastī* (force).

This definition recalls what we saw in the *Caurāśī Āsana* and reinforces the importance of the guru and the secrecy of knowledge transmission. Considering the close connection between pain and *tapasyā*, it is interesting to note that *haṭha* yoga in early textual sources was associated with pain by those who criticised it: the *Amanaska* argues that *rāja* yoga is superior to other forms of yoga because it is effortless, thus implying, without naming it, that *haṭha* yoga requires exertion (Birch 2011: 527), while the *Laghuyogavāsiṣṭha* describes *haṭha* yoga as causing suffering (Birch 2011: 531).

The association between *haṭha* yoga and *tapasyā* also concerns the powers obtained through the practice: *tapas* was necessary to obtain powers and *haṭha* yoga was necessary to obtain *siddhis*. But this idea of 'power', today, can be perceived differently. For example, Lāl Dās, a *nāgā bābā* from the Rāmānandī *sampradāya*, said:

> What is *haṭha* yoga [. . .] you do not eat for years, and it is through this that you move God to compassion towards you. So *haṭha* yoga is a power.

> You cannot do it when driven by other people, you need your whole *man* (mind).

Nāth jī in Kamakhya, on the other hand, claimed: 'Through *haṭha* you do *tapasyā*, and when a *sādhu* does *tapasyā* even *devatās* are afraid of him [. . .] that is a yogi.' But, he continued, 'this difficult path needs a guru to be started, because the guru gives *gyān*, *gyān* gives *tyāg*, *tyāg* gives *vairāgya*, *vairāgya* gives *haṭha*, *haṭha* leads to the goal'.

These two sentences, although highlighting a similar result, i.e. that *haṭha* yoga gives or is power, also show the different religious backgrounds of the two *sādhus*: for a Rāmānandī the power of *haṭha* yoga comes from God's grace, whereas for the Nāth the powers of *haṭha* yoga outdo the will of gods.

Nāths can be even more specific about the typologies of *haṭha*. Yogī Rudra Nāth claimed that in the Nāth tradition four kinds of *haṭha* are considered, meaning four forms of tenacity: *bāl haṭha*, *śrī haṭha*, *rāja haṭha* and *yogī haṭha*. *Rāja haṭha* is realised by the 'king' when he does everything in his power, even killing someone; *śrī haṭha* is the *haṭha* of a woman, which enables her to get what she wants; *bāl haṭha* refers to the child who wants something and will cry and cry until he gets what he wants. Then there is the *haṭha* of the yogi, which is the most dangerous, because, if the yogi wants something, he will do anything to make it happen (especially austerities) and get *siddhis* in return. However, the yogi uses *haṭha* for his *gyān*, for his *yogitā* (his yogi state) and also to help others: he maintains and protects the *saṃsāra* thorough his *haṭha*. This explanation further links *haṭha* yoga with *tapasyā*, since we saw in the previous chapter that *sādhus* also do *tapasyā* for the wellbeing of others.

Haṭha yoga and *prāṇāyāma*

Several *sādhus* associate the practice of *haṭha* yoga with the manipulation of the internal winds (*vāyus*), but some also identify it with the complete retention of the breath. Garuḍ Dās, for example, a guru from the Rāmānujī *sampradāya*, stressed that the purpose of *haṭha* yoga is to achieve *kevala kumbhaka* (unaccompanied breath retention) before entering *samādhi*. Therefore, according to him, a *haṭhayogī* is one who reaches a stage where he can control his breath and decide to push his body into death. The final stage of *haṭha* yoga is, therefore, the death of the yogi, who enters *samādhi*.[39] In fact, another *sādhu* defined the *haṭhayogī* as one who achieves *samādhi*

39 On the role and interpretation of *samādhi*, see Chapter 6, pp. 267ff.

by simply closing the mind and stopping the breath, so that the *ātman* leaves the body.

In his work on the Nāth *sampradāya* from the beginning of the 20th century, Briggs (1938: 273) reports a definition of *haṭha* yoga that emphasises *prāṇāyāma*: *haṭha* yoga would use physical methods to produce a voluntary suppression of breath in the body to obtain various mental states. This definition of *haṭha* yoga is interesting because there are early texts that present a similar understanding. As we have seen, the *Amaraughaprabodha* describes *haṭha* yoga as 'that which is intent upon stopping the breath' (Birch 2011: 547). However, the link with *prāṇāyāma* can also lead to less dramatic goals, and, consequently, *haṭha* yoga can simply be associated with the control of the breath.[40]

Rām Caraṇ Dās claimed: 'When you stop the breath to a certain point, when you do this, then *haṭha* happens. The exercise of *haṭha* yoga consists of stopping the flow of *prāṇa* in *iḍā* and *piṅgalā* to converge it in the *suṣumṇā*.'[41] The union of the *vāyus* is associated with controlling *iḍā* and *piṅgalā nāḍīs*, the left and right channels the flows of which should converge in the central channel. The union of these *nāḍīs* is also identified as *haṭha* yoga. This meaning was reiterated by Śyām Ānanda Nāth, a follower of the Kaulamārga, who claimed that the purpose of *haṭha* yoga is to block and hold the breath by using *bandhas*. This would then lead to *samādhi*: 'When the *vāyus* are united, the *mūlādhāra* and *sahasrāra cakras* also unify and thus yoga is achieved.' He also pointed out that the union of *iḍā* (*ha*) and *piṅgalā* (*-ṭha*) gives *haṭha* yoga its name, which is another understanding of *haṭha* yoga.

Haṭha yoga and the union of the sun and the moon

The word *haṭha* is rarely understood among *sādhus* to mean the union of the sun and the moon. Textual references for this interpretation are scattered, too. The tantric *Jayadrathayāmala*, which predates the descriptions of the early *haṭha* yoga techniques, associates the syllable *-ṭha* with the moon. The *Amṛtasiddhi* understands yoga—but not *haṭha* yoga—as the union of the sun and the moon (Birch 2011: 533). A medieval Pāñcarātra text, the

40 In general, breath control is one of the most common practices to have been used during meditation since ancient times. A source as early as the *Śvetāśvatara Upaniṣad* states that it is necessary to suppress the breath and bring the movements of the *vāyus* under control, but this is not a complete suppression, rather a diminishing of the breath (Bronkhorst 1993: 47).

41 As we will see in Chapter 6 (pp. 261ff.), the control of the breath also has the important purpose of waking/rising *kuṇḍalinī*.

Jayākhyasaṃhitā, equates the sun with the inhalation and the syllable *ha*, while Abhinavagupta's *Tantrāloka* equates the sun and moon with both the inhalation and exhalation respectively (Birch 2011: 533). Briggs (1938: 274) reports this understanding of *haṭha* as present in a commentary on the first verse of the *Gorakṣa Paddhāti*, where it is stated that *ha* means the sun and *ṭha* the moon and that their union is called yoga (not *haṭha* yoga). It is only in a later recension of the *Yogabīja* that *haṭha* is defined as the union of the sun and the moon.

It is interesting to note the relative infrequency of this understanding of *haṭha* yoga among contemporary ascetics, compared to its general prevalence in 20th- and 21st-century global yoga circles.[42] The aforementioned Śyām Ānanda Nāth, who studied *haṭha* yoga texts on his own, lamented the fact that most *sādhus* are ignorant and do not know the true meaning of the label *haṭha* yoga. In effect, out of 109 ascetics I interviewed, fewer than ten explained *haṭha* yoga as the union of *ha*-, the sun, and -*ṭha*, the moon. Furthermore, those who gave this definition were ascetics involved in publishing or who had a more modern approach to the study of yoga. For example, one of them was Yogī Śivanāth, who studied yoga at the Kaivalyadhama in Lonavala[43] and is involved in the activities of the publishing house of the Gorakhnāth temple in Gorakhpur. Therefore, he had a theoretical knowledge of *haṭha* yoga superior to that of many ascetics of his *sampradāya*. He is the only *sādhu* I met who could recite the *Haṭhapradīpikā* by heart.

Yogī Vilāsnāth, who is very active in publishing books on the Nāth *sampradāya*, also stated: 'In the *prāṇāyāma*, the *iḍā nāḍī* is the *ha nāḍī*, and *piṅgalā* is *ṭha*. Through *prāṇāyāma* one obtains their yoga (union) and *haṭha*. The encounter of *iḍā* and *piṅgalā* is *haṭha* yoga.' Omānanda Giri, a *saṃnyāsī* of the lineage of Haṇḍiyā Bābā[44] who manages the Yoga Vedānta Kuṭīr *āśram* in Allahabad, stressed the Sanskrit origin of the word *haṭha*: he said that every word in Sanskrit is composed of significant parts and, as such, *haṭha* must be understood as consisting of *ha* and *ṭha*. *Ha* is connected to the sun, *ṭha* is connected to the moon. These two sides are linked

---

42 Birch (2011: 532) suggests that the contemporary spread of this interpretation of *haṭha* yoga may be the result of Srisa Chandra Vasu's commentary in his English translation of the *Gheraṇḍa Saṃhitā* in the late 19th century.

43 See Chapter 7, p. 279.

44 Yogīrāj Haṇḍiyā Bābā was a famous *sādhu* born in 1850, in Bhagalpur, Bihar. It was because he always kept an earthen vessel (*handiyā*) that he became popularly known as Haṇḍiyā Bābā. It is said that, through yoga, he could cure almost any disease. See https://cyberdhuni.org/handiya-baba (last accessed 13 October 2020).

to *iḍā* and *piṅgalā* which represent the two energy flows within the body. Sūrya and Candra are the two *nāḍī*s that have to be balanced.

As we have already mentioned, the balance between *iḍā* and *piṅgalā* is a feature of *haṭha* yoga related to the practice of *prāṇāyāma*. In fact, Omānanda Giri said that, since through *prāṇāyāma* one achieves the ultimate goal of self-realisation, *haṭha* yoga could be understood as *prāṇāyāma*, and thus as breath control. However, he also claimed that in *haṭha* yoga there are many *kriyā*s.

Haṭha yoga and *kriyā*s

In ascetic contexts, the word *kriyā* (action) usually specifies techniques or practices within a yoga discipline intended to achieve a specific result. Although yogic *kriyā*s form a kind of general yogic knowledge that is more or less known to all ascetics in at least one form or another, there are *sādhus* who emphasise *kriyā*s as a distinctive feature of *haṭha* yoga. Therefore, even among *sādhus* there is an understanding of *haṭha* yoga closer to *haṭha* yoga textual sources.

For example, the *saṃnyāsī* Dayānanda Purī, stated: '*Haṭha* yoga has six important *kriyā*s: *neti, dhautī, kuñjal, gaṇeś, khecarī, vajrolī*. These are the six *kriyā*s of *haṭha* yoga.'[45] Omānanda Giri considers these *kriyā*s to be the *ṣaṭkarmas* that aim to purify the body, especially the 'nervous system'. He stated that these *kriyā*s are indeed necessary because, if the body and mind are not purified, then yoga is not possible. The body and the mind must be ready for meditation. To purify the body and mind, one can resort to *haṭha*

45 I provide here a quick introduction for those unfamiliar with these techniques, although some of these will be described more in detail in Chapter 5 (pp. 215ff.). Generally speaking, *neti* (for ascetics) is a technique to clean the nasal passages by inserting a cotton thread into the nostril, pulling it out of the mouth, and drawing it back and forth. *Dhautī* is a technique of cleansing the stomach by swallowing a length of cloth while holding onto one end and then slowly extracting it. The intestines are cleansed by *gaṇeś kriyā*, the activation of the bowel movement by inserting, while in a squatting position, an oily or wet finger into the anus and rotating it clockwise and anticlockwise alternatively while applying gentle pressure along the walls inside. The technique of *nauli* is a muscular cleaning of the internal organs by tensing the abdominal muscles in such a way that they form a vertical column which can also be rolled from side to side, putting variable pressure on the organs. *Kuñjal* or *gajakaraṇī* is a technique to clean the stomach by drinking water and then regurgitating it. *Vajrolī* is the technique of sucking liquid into the bladder by means of a pipe inserted into the urethra. *Khecarī* is a technique aimed at stopping *bindu*, once raised up the channels of the body, from leaving the head by turning the tongue backwards into the throat and into the nasal cavity.

yoga. Omānanda Giri defined the practice of *haṭha* yoga as compulsory for the practice of *rāja* yoga, which he identified with meditation. This understanding of *haṭha* yoga and the connection to *rāja* yoga are highly reminiscent of Svātmārāma's *Haṭhapradīpikā*. The fact that Omānanda Giri speaks of the nervous system indicates that he was likely influenced by the 'medicalisation of yoga' (see pp. 283ff.).

Another *saṃnyāsī* I met in Kamakhya, 'Digital Bābā', who gave a short speech during the International Day of Yoga in 2017, said that *nāgā sādhus* are those who practise *haṭha* yoga and *haṭha* yoga is the section of yoga in which *kriyā*s take place. He added that *nāgā*s know all the *kriyā*s of *haṭha* yoga, then he performed *nauli* in front of journalists and listed some other *kriyā*s: *neti*, *dhautī* and *vajrolī*. He emphasised that *āsana*s and *prāṇāyāma*s are easy practices and therefore suitable for everybody, whereas *haṭha* yoga is only for *sādhu*s, because only the latter have the *haṭha* (intention) to perform them, which comes directly from God. Thus, his understanding of *haṭha* yoga is that in which *haṭha* yoga is equivalent to a strict intention. He probably eliminated *āsana*s and *prāṇāyāma*s, practices widespread throughout the world, in order to create some distance and, at the same time, emphasise the uniqueness of the practice of *sādhu*s. In a private conversation, he also directly associated *haṭha* yoga with the intention necessary for *tapasyā*, because with austerities the individual keeps the senses under control.

Yogī Rudra Nāth, whom I met in Pashupatinath (Nepal), explained the potential of *haṭha* yoga with a metaphor. He said: 'See, you drink water, why do you drink water? Because you are thirsty and because your body needs it. Similarly, in the *haṭha* yoga, you do the *kriyā*s for *siddhi*s and you do them for your body.' Let us associate this definition with that of Yogī Alone Nāth who affirmed that a *haṭhayogī* is one who is in control of the body and, consequently, of the *pañca-tattva*, the five elements. This means that the *haṭhayogī* can control the elements of nature, hence other people and their energy. From their words, therefore, the practice of *kriyā*s can lead the ascetic to gain a profound knowledge of the body and especially of its components, the *tattva*s. Thanks to it, he can manipulate them thus obtaining *siddhi*s (see also Chapter 6, pp. 265ff.). At the same time, however, the knowledge of *kriyā*s (i.e. the practices and the knowledge derived from them) enables the individual to maintain the body in a condition of perfect balance and health.

Control over the physical body through *kriyā*s seems to be a fundamental skill that the practitioner must acquire. In a conversation, Viśvot Giri, a tantric *saṃnyāsī* from Birnagar (West Bengal), told me that a yogi can be recognised by his ability to perform *kriyā*s, because this proves control over the body. He gave this example: if one vomits using his fingers, that is not a *kriyā*, but if one knows how to make the vomit come up, it means he knows the *kriyā* to do it and, more importantly, has control of it. Then, I asked him how many *kriyā*s there are, and he replied that there are as many as traditions and that new ones are constantly being invented. He then explained the meaning of *haṭha* yoga: '*Haṭha* yoga, *yogāsana*s are like gymnastics, but what is different is that in *haṭha* yoga there is intention.' Again, we return to our first understanding of *haṭha* yoga, albeit with an emphasis on the 'physicality' of *haṭha* yoga.

This meaning also occurred during an interview with Svāmī Ātmānanda, an old *saṃnyāsī* whom I met in Kolkata. He argued that *haṭha* yoga is a physical yoga, the purpose of which is to prevent the body from catching diseases and becoming lazy. He expanded on this idea, noting that another purpose of this physical yoga is to reduce the breath, because, when the breath is reduced, the mind stabilises, and life lengthens. According to him, *haṭha* yoga has nothing to do with meditation: meditation is the only way to reach the Absolute, which is the 'fun' part of yoga practice, while *āsana*s are the painful part.

Likewise, talking in his *āśram* in the jungle, Jogī Bābā explained that *haṭha* yoga is for the body and consists of physical techniques (such as *āsana*s, *prāṇāyāma*s and *mudrā*s), the purpose of which is to keep the body steady (H., *sthir*). *Haṭha* yoga, therefore, while necessary at the beginning of the *sādhanā* for the health and well-being of the body, is an external practice. He also added that in *haṭha* yoga it is necessary to develop *kriyā*s and stated that he used to practise them all and still does, sometimes, to keep his body healthy.

The link between *haṭha* yoga and health was mentioned by Īśnāth in Pashupatinath, while also highlighting its modern downside:

> Today there is this idea that by doing yoga you will get physical fitness; this is true, because by doing *haṭha* yoga you can obtain physical fitness. Obviously, this is true for those who do it in the right way; those who do it wrongly will get another effect, because it has to be done in the right way, otherwise you are in trouble.

The 'rightness' of the practice is strictly dependent on its source which is identified with the teaching of the guru rather than written texts. Therefore, to return the manuscripts mentioned in the first section of this chapter, what do *sādhu*s make of them?

Sādhus on *haṭha* yoga texts

When I asked *sādhus* about *haṭha* yoga texts, or texts on yoga practices, very few claimed to have read them. Those *sādhus* who claimed to have some textual knowledge were able to recite *ślokas* (verses) or lines, but the origin of the source was unclear to them, or in other circumstances they thought that what they were reciting came from a specific text, but this was not the case. Sometimes, their knowledge on *haṭha* yoga texts was just superficial. For example, when talking about who began the *haṭha* yoga tradition, Rām Caraṇ Dās claimed that it was initiated by the god Śiva and was found in the *Gheraṇḍa Saṃhitā*, written by *muni* Gheraṇḍa according to Śiva's dictation. However, he admitted that he had never read the *Saṃhitā* itself but had heard about it. He said that he had read the *Yogasūtra* of Patañjali and the books of Nathuram Sharma, a *paṇḍit* from Gujarat who left his home to do austerities and followed a yoga *sādhanā* in the Himalayas.[46] Svāmī Ātmānanda also cited the *Gheraṇḍa Saṃhitā*, claiming this was the book that contains the real meaning of *haṭha* yoga (but, as we have already mentioned, the text does not mention the word *haṭha* at all), and he also mentioned the *Śiva Saṃhitā* as referential text.[47] Jogī Bābā admitted that he had 'seen' a few books, including the *Śiva Saṃhitā*, but he emphasised that knowledge cannot come from books because the teaching of the guru is necessary, since the practitioner has to learn step by step and it takes a lot of time to do so. When I asked him who, according to him, wrote *haṭha* yoga texts, he said that *sādhus* had the experience (*anubhava*) of things, and then they were written down. He reinforced the importance of practical experience as the main difference between *vidyā* and *gyān* (*jñāna* in Sanskrit): *vidyā* is any factual knowledge that can be reasoned about,

---

46 According to Rām Caraṇ Dās, Nathuram Sharma was living in Varanasi when some Gujarati pilgrims found him and convinced him to go back. They built an *āśram* for him and he began writing books about yoga. http://bilkhaashram.weebly.com/about-nathuram-sharma.html (last accessed 13 October 2020).

47 The *Śiva Saṃhitā* is 'an eclectic collection of Yogic lore' composed between 1300 and 1500 which borrows verses from the *Amṛtasiddhi* and *Dattātreyayogaśāstra*. It gathers different teachings not found elsewhere in the haṭhayogic canon which, sometimes, contradict each other (Mallinson 2007b: x–xiii). Its yoga, which is not defined as *haṭha*, is 'grounded in the Vedanta-inflected southern Śrīvidyā tradition' associated with the Śaṅkarācāryas of Sringeri and Kanchi. Therefore, it is probably the outcome of the appropriation of Nāth practices by a more mainstream Śaiva milieu (Mallinson 2007b: xiv). The text documents an *āsana* which is mentioned here for the first time: *paścimottānāsana*.

while *gyān* is something deeper that comes from the direct experience of knowledge.

A similar explanation came from a *bābā* in the Gorakhnāth Maṭh of Varanasi:

> This [*haṭha* yoga] is not a subject that you will find in any books; it is knowledge connected to practice. That person who does it, will feel it. There are several books that you can find, written in the past and in the present, such as those of *ṛṣis* like Patañjali and those of our Nāths, but those people had to have the experience, otherwise they could not have written about it. Moreover, we have to consider that they wrote as much as they could remember.

Yogī Rudra Nāth said that yogis do not practise by following books. He said: 'You can find yoga in books.[48] It was born there. A yogi comes from his *paramparā*, not from books. Gorakhnāth comes from Śiva. Bhagvān created the yogi. A yogi is not born from a woman's womb, he is born through his *kriyās*.' So, when I asked him who had written *haṭha* yoga texts, he replied: 'Some yogi wrote them, to explain to the yogis of the future.'

Sādhus also emphasised that books do not contain the main teachings, as these are hidden (H., *gupt*) and can only be imparted by a guru. They consider the texts as conveying knowledge that everybody can obtain, but it is a general form of knowledge. In fact, a Nāth I spoke to in Kamakhya said that those works are for *sāṃsārik log*: for those people who cannot practise yoga constantly. Similarly, the aforementioned Īśnāth told me that all the books from the past on yoga, in which attention is paid to physical practice, were for lay people, because *sādhus* did not need them. They were a way of training the laity. However, even then, it would have been difficult without a guru. Rām Bālak Dās said that his guru had never spoken to him directly about *haṭha* yoga and suggested that *haṭha* yoga was a kind of written reality for those who read the *śāstras*. He acknowledged that various philosophers and writers had written texts on *haṭha* yoga, but his own knowledge came from his guru, whose knowledge was not theoretical but practical: he knew through direct experience and *tapas*.

A different attitude towards texts was demonstrated by Yogī Śivanāth, who studied *haṭha* yoga texts in depth and possessed many of them. Several

48 Here, Yogī Rudra Nāth was referring especially to the many modern books on yoga. He pronounced 'yoga' with an open *a*, as in English (and Sanskrit), whereas in Hindi the final *a* is silent.

times I listened to his *pravacans*[49] in which he remarked on the importance of the Nāth *sampradāya* in the development of yoga practices. He pointed out that Svātmārāma, the author of the *Haṭhapradīpikā*, was a Yogī from the *paramparā* of Gorakhnāth and Matsyendranāth, that all those present in Svātmārāma's *paramparā* were Yogīs and that *haṭha* yoga texts, in fact, never mentioned a Rāmānandī name. He was quite straightforward about the Nāths' authorship of *haṭha* yoga. He said that the Mahāsiddhas were those who clarified the *haṭha* yoga path to conquer death, to remove diseases, and finally to become enlightened. None of the features of *haṭha* yoga (*neti*, *dhautī*, etc.) are present in the work of Patañjali—who, indeed, does not even have an *āsana* dedicated to him—while there are two postures under the name of Gorakhnāth and his guru Matsyendranāth (*gorakṣāsana* and *matsyendrāsana*). Although Yogī Śivanāth proclaimed Patañjali as the first sage to bring the importance of yoga to light, doing so in his talks, he nevertheless characterised Patañjali's explanations as limited: Patañjali gave a definition of *āsana*, but did not say how to do them, what their purpose was; moreover, he listed only four meditative *āsanas*.[50] Gorakhnāth, on the other hand, was credited with delving into the yoga *sādhanā*: he explained various typologies of *āsanas*, mentioning 84 postures and their use. In general, according to Yogī Śivanāth, while Patañjali did not pay attention to the body, Gorakhnāth stressed that a healthy body is necessary to do *sādhanā*: to do any *sādhanā*, any *karma* (action), even as a householder, the body must be healthy, and through *āsana* and *prāṇāyāma* one keeps diseases away. The *Haṭhapradīpikā*, the *Gorakṣaśataka*, the *Gheraṇḍa Saṃhitā*, the *Śiva Saṃhitā*, etc. were, according to him, all produced by Nāth authors. However, he also recognised that 'in the text you find only the theory, but to do all these things you need the guru, [. . .] you can only do exercises with a guru, since *haṭha* yoga is mainly practical'.

Conclusion

In this chapter I have shown that it is still difficult to ascertain the origin of *haṭha* yoga, to reconstruct the development of the label *haṭha* yoga and

49 The first time I heard a sermon (H., *pravacan*) by Yogī Śivanāth was in Mangalore in 2016, during a Nāth festival in which the *rāja yogī* of the place was elected (see Bouillier 2008); Śivanāth repeated the same concepts to me when I visited his *āśram* in April 2018.

50 In reality, Patañjali does not mention any specific posture in the *sūtras*: it is in the *Bhāṣya* (commentary) of the *Yogasūtra* in which 12 *āsanas* are mentioned.

in what contexts it was used. I have also shown that *haṭha* yoga has been perceived differently according to epochs, contexts and practitioners, and that in some cases it was not used as a label at all.

To summarise, then, we can say that the earliest texts using the label *haṭha* yoga were Buddhist and that, in these early uses, *haṭha* yoga was probably associated with physically demanding practices which, likely, focused on breath and breath retention. Considering that in early Buddhist sources the word *tapas* appears extensively to denote meditation or 'reasoned moral self-discipline' (Gombrich 2006: 62), one may wonder whether Buddhist authors coined the term *haṭha* yoga to address the other meaning of *tapas*, i.e. that of strenuous bodily austerities such as breath retention.

Haṭha yoga was subsequently associated with the retention of semen during sexual rituals. Considering the close association between breath and semen, we can say that *haṭha* yoga was related to practices for the maintenance and control of the body's life force. Later, in the context of Buddhist celibate monks, new practices for the constraint and manipulation of breath appeared but were not labelled *haṭha* yoga. As Mallinson (2020) suggests, this was probably due to the fact that *haṭha* yoga had been associated with sexual ritual and because its yoga was considered a secondary path, as also seems to be the case for the *Amaraugha*. It is important to note that the transition from a Buddhist to a 'Hindu' milieu occurred through texts linked to a Nāth background. In fact, given the connection between Vajrayāna Buddhism and Nāthism (see Mallinson 2019), it is not difficult to imagine that some of those lineages that would later converge into the Nāth *sampradāya* adopted some Buddhist practices, incorporating them into their ascetic contexts.

It is clear that a set of practices developed around the manipulation of vital essences and began to spread in different religious contexts. *Bandhas*, *mudrās* and purification to enable a proper flow of vital energies in the body were theorised accordingly. While these practices were collected in almost coherent *haṭha* yoga texts, probably still addressing ascetics, the later production of texts deals with *haṭha* yoga techniques in a more comprehensive, though not always coherent, manner. They were probably not addressed to an audience of ascetic practitioners and their authors were probably not themselves well versed in the practices.

As Mallinson (2020) pointed out, the rise of monasteries in South India and the Deccan may have been responsible for this growth and further developments in the understanding of *haṭha* yoga, in which the traditional idea of a forceful practice was basically abandoned. This abandonment meant leaving aside all those practices that were specific to ascetics. Indeed, in the *Haṭhapradīpikā*, *haṭha* is used as a category to define, in academic circles, a form of yoga based on physical activities that are not strenuous. It is also stated that exertion is one of six obstacles to *haṭha* yoga. Svātmārāma (1.61) rejects those practices that are closely associated with ascetic behaviour: 'In the same vein there is a saying by Gorakṣa: One should avoid places near bad people, frequenting fire, women and roads, and observances which harm the body such as early morning bathing and fasting.'[51] The use of fire, travelling, early morning bathing, fasting and heavy physical activities were (and still are) typical of ascetics, especially those practising austerities. *Haṭha* yoga texts do not mention the word *tapas* at all and, considering the word *tapas* was also used to refer to asceticism in general, this could demonstrate a choice to distance themselves from an exclusive ascetic world.[52] These texts probably addressed a wider audience which included lay practitioners.

It is likely that these later *haṭha* yoga texts were written by devout brahmins or followers of particular gurus, who 'worked' under specific patrons to promote yoga teachings. They wanted to present *haṭha* yoga as a practice suitable for all, disassociating it from the extreme practices that would be unfit or unattractive to householders—thus distancing it from its meaning of forcefulness—and focusing on physical practices and their benefits to the body. The *haṭha* techniques presented, if practised correctly, would have had positive effects on the body, presented in these works as a tool to attain *siddhi*s and liberation.

The absence in these texts of any exhortations to join a sect allowed them to be received as general books, to be studied under the guidance of a personal guru. And, although some were written by ascetics, this does not mean that they were written for an ascetic audience. Sanskrit works were the brahmanical means of making *haṭha* yoga's physical practices an integral part of 'brahmanical yoga', although not all authors recognised or used the label *haṭha* yoga.[53] Lubomir Ondračka (2022: 579) believes them to be

---

51 http://hathapradipika.online.

52 However, two Vaiṣṇava texts, the *Vasiṣṭhasaṃhitā* and the *Yogayajñavalkya* incorporate *tapas*.

53 There are very few Vaiṣṇava Sanskrit texts that use the label *haṭha* yoga. Jason Birch (personal communication, 5 January 2021) has mentioned the *Yogamārgaprakāśikā* composed by Yugaladāsa, who seemed partial to Rāma, Rāghava and Rāmānuja; the *Haṭhābhyāsapaddhati*, whose author seemed to be Vaiṣṇava, and the c. 17th-century *Yuktabhavadeva*, a scholarly compendium on yoga with a chapter on *haṭha* yoga, the author of which, Bhavadevamiśra (a *paṇḍit* from Mithila), was Vaiṣṇava.

'typical Sanskrit technical manuals' which, by prescribing an ideal form of practice, probably cannot be considered representative of the actual practice, especially seeing as there are important works on *haṭha* yoga in other Indian languages (Dravidian and modern North Indian languages) which remain unstudied.

In effect, the few hints about vernacular works[54] presented in this chapter show that the word *haṭha* yoga was not broadly used by ascetic practitioners and it was mostly located in a Marathi environment.[55] Ascetics continued to develop and explore their practices and to mix different practices from different contexts. They probably influenced the development of *haṭha* yoga texts, because *paṇḍits*, while referring to earlier scholarly books, may also have looked to ascetic practitioners or the practice of ascetic gurus. That is how physical practices from a tapasic/ascetic background (such as inversion or demanding postures kept for long periods of time) were probably re-assimilated into *āsanas* in later works on *haṭha* yoga.

We do not know when the association between *haṭha* yoga and *tapas* originated. As in the previous case of *tapas* and yoga, the two words accumulated layers of meanings, often similar, over the centuries. Both *tapas* and *haṭha* are linked to breath retention, the obtainment of powers, the purification of the body, and deep states of meditation. Both use the body as a tool to achieve spiritual gains, although some *haṭha* yoga practices show a form of care for the body not always present in *tapasyā*. With regard to how of *sādhus* understand it, *haṭha* yoga retains all the layers of its historical development: it is still a method to push the body to do strenuous and demanding things, be it posture, specific breathings or practices to stop the breath, methods to control the *bindu* or to move energies in the body, or techniques that include yogic *kriyās*. As Jogī Bābā told me, '*Haṭha* yoga is the control of the body!'[56] and, in fact, all the meanings associated with it (*tapasyā*, *prāṇāyāmas*, *kriyās*, etc.) unite in a determination to master and control the body.

Disciplining the body and controlling the *prāṇa* are also part of the yoga *sādhanā*. That is why *sādhus* often do not distinguish between *haṭha* yoga and yoga: these words are useful to explain to others but, in reality, they are only labels that do not change the reality of the practice.

---

54 Analysis of *paddhatis*—more technical pamphlets in vernacular languages, usually produced by *maṭhas*—might have provided further information.

55 Further investigation of Marathi texts produced after the 15th century might provide insights into the historical trajectory of the use of the term.

56 '*Haṭh yog śarir kā control hai!*'

5
The Yoga *Sādhanā* (External Practices)

'How would you translate "yoga" into English?
You can't exactly translate it into English.
You can explain it, but you can't translate it.'

Yogī Śivanāth

With this remark by Yogī Śivanāth in mind, in this chapter I will try to explain the yoga *sādhanā* as interpreted and practised by *sādhus*. This is a fundamental issue, which I have divided into two chapters; this not only acknowledges the division between external and internal practices,[1] as often emphasised by my interlocutors, but also allows space for other topics.

At the beginning of each section, I will provide a brief textual introduction on the subject before focusing on explanations from the *sādhus* themselves. From the outset, it should be understood that it is very difficult to make associations between *sādhus*' words and specific texts or textual traditions. There are two main reasons for this: firstly, the *sādhus* I spent time with do not rely on texts for their practices and their knowledge but on the

1 As stressed by Dominik Wujastyk (2009: 190), the notions of exteriority and interiority were deeply embedded in Indian thought from early on; they relate to the 'self-conscious attitude to the body as the vehicle of consciousness and as an exteriority'.

oral transmission of their gurus; secondly, each *sādhu* may have learnt from more than one guru, so their knowledge may be influenced not only by theories from their own religious order but also by what they have learnt from *sādhus* and gurus from other traditions. Thus, they often provide explanations that draw on a range of theoretical sources. For this reason, I avoid imposing an interpretation of a textual source that cannot be confirmed; instead, I will highlight similarities or differences between texts and *sādhus*' explanations, mainly in footnotes. Furthermore, as we will see in Chapter 7, New Age theories have also entered the domain of *sādhus*' knowledge, both as a result of an influx of foreigners since the 1960s and more recently through modern and social media.

In these two chapters (5 and 6), we will see that *sādhus* belonging to different *sampradāyas* might follow more or less the same practices, which goes to show how fluid is the religious context and how practical yoga is as a method: it does not matter to which deity a practice is addressed, the important thing is that a practice is followed. However, we will also see that the same practice might be interpreted or presented in different ways even by *sādhus* belonging to the same *sampradāya*. This shows how the theoretical baggage a *sādhu* carries is very personal, although influenced by guru and lineage.

Bearing in mind that yoga is an embodied practice,[2] before focusing on its *sādhanā* we should consider the body to which it relates. As already mentioned, the yogic body is mostly represented as being a male one. On the whole, this book will not represent an exception to that rule, simply because the ascetic practitioners I met were almost all men.[3] Nevertheless, a few references to the female body and practitioner will be presented here, as a result of conversations on the subject with male ascetics and with my main female interlocutors.

2 See Introduction, p. 9.

3 The female body is regarded as a distraction from the path of liberating knowledge for men. Therefore, the texts, also written by men, generally address male adepts and their male bodies (see Flood 2006: 38).

Cakras, the body and the subtle body

> 'You have to know the *pañca-tattva*: this is *aslī* [true] yoga. When you know the *pañca-tattva*, you know *paramātman*, you know what is happening inside and outside of you.'
>
> Jogī Bābā

Rather than a singular and uniform concept, early Indian sources provide a description of several bodies, some spiritually constructed, some physically, still others psychologically (Wujastyk 2009: 190).[4] However, since the end of the 1st millennium CE, yogic and tantric traditions have proposed an alternative anatomy 'which mapped the body as the locus of spiritual energies and points of graduated spiritual awakening' (Wujastyk 2009: 190).

The 'yogic body' or 'tantric body' has developed as a theoretical construct described in texts, which is why different traditions may present different yogic bodies. Thus, yogic bodies arise according to the philosophical, doctrinal and ritual needs of a tradition, and are imagined and used differently to fulfil the specific goals of a specific system. Nevertheless, as Mallinson and Singleton (2017: 172) admit, there are a number of commonalities and a consensus about some of the fundamental characteristics of this body. Physically made up of elements (*tattvas*, *dhātus*)[5] characterised by different qualities (*guṇas*), this tantric body has a psychophysical nature that manifests itself in a system of centres (*cakras*) arranged on a vertical axis that also delineates the paths of *iḍā* (on the left), *piṅgalā* (on the right) and *suṣumṇā* (in the centre). These are the three main channels (*nāḍīs*) of a network through which 'winds' (*vāyus*) and vital forces (*bindu*, *kuṇḍalinī*, etc.) are conducted. Some of these components (like the *vāyus*) were meant to be manipulated through physical techniques while others (such as *cakras* and *kuṇḍalinī*), initially imagined as visualisation tools to be employed during meditative practices,[6] have varied their ontological

4 See Wujastyk 2009 on the various bodies in pre-modern India and the tantric body.

5 According to White (1996: 32), the notion of the physical universe as an aggregate of the five elements is present in metaphysical systems of ancient and classical India. He cites the example of the *Taittirīya Upaniṣad* (2.1), which introduces a hierarchical representation of the five elements in relation to the universal and microcosmic man: 'From this ātman verily ether arose; from ether air; from air fire; from fire, water; from water, earth; from earth, herbs; from herbs, food; from food, semen; from semen, Man.'

6 As Bharati (1965: 291) points out, 'The tantric body is a model, not a fact, and the centres or lotuses, and the three ducts, are systematic fictions.'

nature over the centuries, to the extent that they have become 'increasingly corporeal and thus subject to physical manipulation' (Mallinson and Singleton 2017: 171).

Practitioners attempted to transform and manipulate the body in order to gain special powers (*siddhis*) or liberation (*mokṣa*). This was deemed possible because tantric knowledge systems considered the universe (macrocosm) and the body (microcosm) connected by an esoteric system of homologies[7] that could be activated within the body. The *Parākhyatantra* (5.2.1), for example, claims that the movements of the *prāṇa* are elaborated through the 'corporeally located realms of various deities'; the *Amṛtasiddhi* (5.2.2.) 'declares that all the elements of the three worlds are in the body, including planets, seers, sages and gods'; while the *Siddhasiddhāntapaddhati* (5.2.3) 'offers a detailed mapping of the realms of the cosmos on to the body of the yogi' (Mallinson and Singleton 2017: 174).

The body to which *sādhus* refer when describing practices is this yogic body.[8] Here I will assemble it by summarising the information and scattered references they provided.

The body is considered the starting point of spiritual practice because, as Jogī Bābā said: 'There is everything in our body, but this awareness must be awakened. [. . .] First of all, you must know your own body.' As we shall see, it is through practice that ascetics investigate their own bodies, moving from knowledge of the external and 'gross' to that of the internal and subtle. One of the main distinctions made by *sādhus* is, in fact, that between the gross (H., *sthūl*) and the subtle body (H., *sūkṣma śarīr*). The physical, gross body is often described as made of clay (H., *miṭṭī*), a container to be temporarily preserved. Awareness of this temporary nature is essential to avoid attachment to it.[9]

Āsanas, *prāṇāyāmas* and *kriyās* firstly aim to create an awareness of the gross body and its control. For this reason, a certain knowledge of them is considered propaedeutic to all practices. However, a deep knowledge of

7 This approach was already present in Vedic literature, especially Brāhmaṇas; see Witzel 2003.

8 However, as we will see in Chapter 7 (p. 284), those ascetics who have accomplished yogic studies in specific institutions or universities associate this 'yogic body' to a biomedical body.

9 This ambivalent attitude is well reflected in the dharmic literature. According to Flood (2006: 38), 'On the one hand great care is taken over the body, a guarding and control of the body's functions in accordance with highest moral duty (*parama dharma*) for a life; on the other the body is the location of the passions and is inherently impure through its desires, instincts and effluvia.'

the body and its constituents (hence of the subtle body) occurs through the practices of visualisation, concentration and meditation. Through them, advanced practitioners are said to achieve that awareness of the body whereby they perceive it as actually consisting of *tattvas* (elements) and *guṇas* (qualities). The five *tattvas* (water, earth, fire, ether and wind) have different *guṇas*, often mentioned but rarely described: *sattva*, *rajas* and *tamas*. *Sattva* is the quality of purity, balance, lightness, goodness and virtue and it is the main quality to which *sādhus* aspire and try to follow in their attitudes and practices. 'You must be *sātvik*'[10] is one of the most often repeated expressions of *sādhus* to emphasise the attitude in the life of an aspiring yogi. *Rajas* represents action, passion and fervour, while *tamas* symbolises inertia, passivity and heaviness. Essentially, all objects in the world—including bodies, minds, senses and intellect—are a combination of these elements and qualities. They are present in everyone and everything but in different proportions, thus determining different characters. In individuals, these qualities determine nature, behaviours and, from a religious point of view, the spiritual path they can follow.

According to Yogī Rudra Nāth, *sātvik*, *rājasik* and *tāmasik* can generally be used to define three typologies of ascetic *sādhanās*. A *sātvik sādhanā* focuses entirely on spiritual practice. A *rājasik sādhanā* involves taking care of places, *āśrams* and the administration of property and people: it is therefore a form of *karma yoga* because in this case ascetics do not have much time for other practices. A *tāmasik sādhanā* does not aim at *mokṣa* but at overcoming death *tout court*, so it would correspond to an '*aghor sādhanā*', which means a path involving antinomian practices.[11]

Knowledge of *tattvas* and *guṇas* is fundamental because, through an understanding of them, it is possible to control them and, as a consequence, control the senses, the body and reality. According to Jogī Bābā, one must know the activities that they manage within the body, because 'they are the body': if one element does not function properly, the body will have a problem. Furthermore, knowing how the elements manifest, Jogī Bābā continued, leads the individual to 'obtaining *śakti* from all of them', as he associated each *guṇa* with a form of the Goddess. His comment indicates the power that each *guṇa* can unleash. In fact, connections between qualities, elements of the body and deities are common, as the body is considered a

10 '*Sātvik honā chahiye*!'

11 An example of *tāmasik sādhanā* is to meditate sitting on a corpse.

temple with deities dwelling within it.[12] Nāth jī in Kamakhya declared that the body has seven protectors, seven *devatās*:[13]

> One is Brahmā who is in the water: without water we cannot exist, nothing can exist. Then there is Viṣṇu in the fire, he is *tej*. Then there is Pārvatī, *darthī*, the earth which is the mother; without her nothing can have a shape. Then there is Nīleśvar, who is the blue god because he is *ākāś*, above the earth, that is why he is the father. Without the sky, without clouds, without rain nothing can arise on earth. Then there is Vāyu, the wind that allows movement and fills all space. Without *vāyu* we would die, without breath, without air, there is no life. Then there is Sūrya, who is the one who illuminates everything; he is alone but can give light to all. Then there is Candra Mā with her shadow. These are the seven *devatās*.

These seven *devatās* are thus representations of the five *tattvas* plus Sūrya (sun) and Candra (moon). The five elements are also closely related to the *indriyas* (senses). Jogī Bābā divides them into external senses (sight, touch, smell, hearing, taste) and internal (mind, discernment, individual consciousness, intellect and knowledge),[14] and claims they produce five enemies: *krodha* (anger), *kāma* (lust), *lobha* (greed), *ahaṃkāra* (ego) and *moha* (delusion). As we shall see, *yama* (abstinence, rules of conduct) and *niyama* (observances, rules of purification) aim to control the *indriyas* so that these enemies do not arise and the yogi can detach himself from the sensory world.

Jogī Bābā suggests that, initially, one should pay attention to the senses and recognise that they are like smoke:

> Once the smoke is gone, the fire can ignite. As long as the smoke remains, the fire cannot start. That is why with *tap* you have to get rid of the smoke. Let the fire burn and you will get everything [. . .] The body may grow

12 Yogī Alone Nāth claimed that one of the purposes of *haṭha* yoga is to make the body a temple and enable the individual to do an inner *pūjā*. For this reason, he said, Nāths do not need temples, and do not follow *mūrti pūjā*, the worship of statues.

13 It is interesting to note that the presence or invocation of deities in the body is perceived by contemporary *sādhus* not only as a possible way to deify the body but also as a method of protecting it or the actions it performs. For example, calling on deities in different parts of the body ensures their presence and protection during the practice of *dhūnī tap*.

14 *Manas* is the mind, *viveka* is discernment, *citta* is the individual consciousness, *buddhi* is the intellect and *jñāna* is knowledge. This list of inner senses does not correspond to those found in textual sources. For example, in the Sāṃkhya philosophy the three inner organs are *manas*, *buddhi* and *ahaṃkāra*, which are in fact also mentioned by some *sādhus*.

> old, but the mind never does. [. . .] *Man* never dies, never grows old. Your senses and enemies may get worse with old age, but your *man* does not change. It comes from the *ātman*, and the *ātman* never dies. That is why one who is in control of *man* is a true yogi.

There are also five main *prāṇas* in the body: *samāna*, *apāna*, *vyāna*, *udāna* and *prāṇa*.[15] These *prāṇas*—also called *vāyus* by *sādhus*—represent the moving forces operating within the body. The *samāna vāyu* moves digestion; the *apāna vāyu* expels what needs to be eliminated from the body; the *vyāna vāyu* circulates blood and, in general, moves energy in the body; the *prāṇa vāyu*, referred by some *sādhus* as *sūkṣma* (light), is connected with the *ātman*, so when it leaves the body, the *ātman* follows. When the *ātman* is reborn into another body, according to *karma*, it is again inflated by the *prāṇa*.

Garuḍ Dās pointed out that the yogi aims to unify these *vāyus* into one and, when this union occurs, the individual not only has the vision of *paramātman* but also the feeling of the subtle body, its *nāḍīs* and *cakras*. Therefore, *nāḍīs* and *cakras* are characteristics of the yogic body but they belong to the *sūkṣma śarīr*. The *nāḍīs* are the bodily channels through which these vital essences flow.[16] The main *nāḍīs* unanimously recognised by *sādhus* are *iḍā*, *piṅgalā* and *suṣumṇā*: *iḍā* is the channel associated with the moon and the cold, *piṅgalā* is associated with the sun and heat, while *suṣumṇā* is the central channel, also identified as the month Meru, the mountain or centre of all the physical, metaphysical and spiritual universes. As we will see in the section on *prāṇāyāma*, the essences flowing in the side channels (which some *sādhus* identify with the *apāna* and the *prāṇa vāyus*) have to be balanced in order for them to flow into the central one. The three channels are visually imagined as the *triveṇī*: the two sacred rivers, Ganges and Yamuna, which flow into the legendary subterranean Sarasvati.

This system of channels interacts with a system of *cakras*.[17] According to Dayānanda Purī, going through the *cakra* is 'the journey of the yogi'. He

---

15 A recognition of *vāyus* circulating in the body is as ancient as the *Ṛg Veda*, and the *samāna*, *apāna*, *udāna* and *vyāna vāyus* are mentioned as early as the *Atharva Veda* (Mallinson and Singleton 2017: 173).

16 Already, by time the *Bṛhadāraṇyaka Upaniṣad* was written, the body was imagined as being crossed by a system of *nāḍīs*, the number and origin of which, however, change according to the textual source. What precisely 'moves along the channels may differ across texts and traditions' (Mallinson and Singleton 2017: 173).

17 As pointed out by Dominik Wujastyk (2009: 199–200), the idea of *cakras* is relatively recent, datable to the 10th century CE and present in texts such as the *Kubjikāmatatantra*; furthermore, he stresses that *cakras* do not appear whatsoever

stressed that each *cakra* has its own energy and vibration, and that the yogi gains specific powers by going through them.[18] *Sādhus* often speak of six or seven *cakras*.[19] Jogī Bābā said that *cakras* are also connected to the *tattvas*, and therefore each *cakra* has a specific number of *tattvas* associated with it: the *mūlādhāra*, according to him, consists of all five *tattvas*.[20]

Here are two explanations given to me about *cakras* which provide an interesting perspective on body imagery and will be useful in the next chapter in forming an understanding of the connection between *cakras* and *kuṇḍalinī*. One of these explanations was provided by Īśnāth, who described the 'development' of *cakras* in the body at birth. In this, he departs from the idea of *cakras* as visualisation tools for meditative practices, linking them instead to a subtle body wherein an 'oil' is produced in the *sahasrāra cakra* (he also suggested that this oil might be a product of the pineal gland) when the individual is born. At that stage a child draws no influence from the environment and no impressions. The oil then begins to drip down slowly,[21] due to gravity and nature, through the *suṣumṇā nāḍī*. As it descends it reaches other *cakras* and activates them, leading the child to experience new feelings, emotions and sensations. When it reaches the end of the column, it stops dripping and coils. This coincides with the full development of the individual, who at that point has all *cakras* functioning. As such, he relates *cakras* to energetic centres which work differently according to an individual's actions and dispositions as they influence the way energies in the body are distributed and 'channelled'.

---

in Ayurveda, the classical medicine of India, as they are 'implicated in the process of self-realisation and the expansion of consciousness'.

18 On powers, see Chapter 6, pp. 265ff.

19 These seven *cakras* are: *mūlādhāra*, *svādhiṣṭhāna*, *maṇipūra*, *anāhata*, *viśuddhi*, *ājñā* and *sahasrāra*. See also Chapter 6 (pp. 261ff.) on *kuṇḍalinī* and *cakras*.

20 Mallinson and Singleton (2017: 182) claim that *cakras* came to replace or appropriate the *tattvas* as objects for internal meditation. This does not always seem to be the case for ascetics continuing to meditate on *tattvas*, and not just the *tattvas* associated with *cakras*.

21 As we have seen in Chapter 4, several *haṭha* yoga textual sources contain the idea of a 'substance', *amṛta*/*bindu*, dripping from the skull. As explained by Ondračka (2022: 582), 'although the precise understanding of this substance is usually not clearly explained or differs from text to text, and the terms used to refer to it vary (*amṛta*, *bindu*, *bīja*, *soma*, etc.), its basic characteristics and importance are common to all traditions. [...] It is stored in the head and is naturally restless: either it continually drips from its source and is burnt by a digestive fire located in the lower part of the stomach, or it is ejaculated in its most visible and material form, male semen.'

According to Yogī Rudra Nāth, the six *cakras* 'do their *kriyās* within the body', while a seventh is 'for *mokṣa* and, to reach it, you have to work hard'. He said that each has specific functions and a *siddha rūpa* (perfected form) which, when realised correctly, allows the *cakra* to function properly. He links each *cakra* to specific attitudes and actions which can be improved through *yama* and *niyama* (see below). Furthermore, each *cakra* represents a stage in the spiritual evolution of an individual and each *cakra* is associated with specific *kriyās*, although Rudra Nāth did not describe them:

> The *mūlādhāra cakra* is located four fingers between the penis and the testicles, in the shape of a lotus. You can also call it the *adhāra* (root) *cakra*. From it comes the feeling of energy and joy and if you meditate on this *cakra*, or think intensely about this *cakra*, its *kriyās* are activated and through them the *cakra* becomes perfected (*siddha*). There are people who remain stuck on its *kriyā* forever. Those people who focus on sex (H., *sambhog*), luxury (H., *vilas*), pleasure (H., *bhog*), remain in this *cakra*. They turn the *kriyās* towards *bhogī* or *sambhogī*, and do not move further because they are stuck in this attitude. So they will approach death while continuing to use the same *kriyās*.
>
> Then there is the *svādhiṣṭhāna cakra*. It is located four fingers from the penis. It is a lotus with six petals. If you are in this *cakra*, entertainment (H., *manoranjan*) is here. *Manoranjan* is important in life, but you should not give it too much importance. If you get into the habit of *manoranjan* and get stuck, then you cannot proceed to further *kriyās* and you remain in this *cakra*.
>
> The third *cakra* is the *maṇipūra*, which is located near the navel. It is a lotus with ten petals. Once *siddha*, this *cakra* will put an end to thirst, envy, and so on [. . .] they are kept away. It blocks everything. Activating this *cakra*, you will accumulate a lot of energy. You will be able to stop things and dominate them. But to reach this *cakra* you will have to change yourself, your nature, you will have to understand what is inside you and bring it out, otherwise this *cakra* will not work. So, what happens with the *maṇipūra cakra* is that all negative feelings move away from you.
>
> The *anāhata cakra* is close to the heart and is a lotus with 12 petals. Through the activation of this *cakra*, violence, concern, *ahaṃkāra*, end. This *cakra* destroys the ego, so people stop doing things only for themselves. You should do the *kriyā* of this *cakra* every day, by giving respect to others, doing their *sevā* (service). The main feature of the *anāhata cakra* is to consider everyone equal. To make this *cakra siddha*, you should apply *dhyāna* during the night. Those who practise it will be individuals with many qualities and a sharp mind.
>
> The fifth is the *viśuddhi cakra*, which is located in the throat. Its lotus has a hundred petals. When this *cakra* is *siddha*, you can stop anger and

thirst by doing *dhyāna* on its petals and their colour. You will not be greedy for anything; this is the path to *bhakti* and *siddhi.*

Then the *ājñā cakra* is located between the eyes. Many things reside there. *Siddhi*s or *śakti* reside there. To manage them and keep negative energy away, you must do the *kriyā*s of the *ājñā cakra.* By moving this *cakra* you will have knowledge of the present and the future. To perform the *kriyā*s of this *cakra* you need to be *monī* (silent) which will help develop *boudhdik* (mental) *siddhis.*

The last *cakra*, the one that *sādhus*, Sants, *saṃnyāsī*s seek, is called *sahasrāra cakra.* We cannot say anything about this *cakra* except that it is the gateway to *mokṣa.* Only people who have no attachments, who are not victims of the illusion of *saṃsār* and *siddhi*s, can make this *cakra siddha.* It is very difficult, but once it is obtained, one will go straight to *mokṣa.* One will obtain the *darśan* of Bhagvān. [. . .]

The explanations of Īśnāth and Yogī Rudra Nāth connect *cakra*s, spiritual paths and behaviours in a way that echoes more contemporary explanations of the role of *cakra*s (see Foxen and Kuberry 2021: 61–67). In both explanations, it seems that, depending on the nature of the individual, one can be stuck in one *cakra* or another but, through yogic practices associated with ethical concerns, one can advance in the ascent. Yogī Rudra Nāth's words, indeed, also indicate that *cakra*s are considered part of a process made up of stages, in which obstacles, however hidden, may block the individual's progress.

In general, based on *sādhus*' understandings, two main yogic actions seem to be associated with *cakra*s: their activation and their piercing. These are consequential actions: an unactivated *cakra* cannot be pierced (by the ascent of *kuṇḍalinī*), because it indicates that the individual is not yet sufficiently developed in his practice. Activation of *cakra*s, as we will see in the next chapter, is achieved through *dhāraṇā*, *dhyāna* and *samādhi*: 'We look for subtleness through the subtle', said Rām Avadhūt Dās. A Nāth in Varanasi pointed out that it usually takes about 12 years to activate the *cakra*s. Only then can they be pierced, because only then can the *kuṇḍalinī* rise. He also added that, in the process, one should not assign too much importance to the '*cakra siddhi*s', the powers developed by the *cakra*s, because they can produce a kind of *naśā* (intoxication) for power. That is why they must be mastered and it takes a long time to do so.[22]

Most of the *sādhus*' comments emphasised the ambiguous ontological nature of the subtle body. According to Rām Avadhūt Dās, during the time

22 I will describe the role of *siddhi*s in Chapter 6 (pp. 265ff.), as one of the results of the yoga practice.

of *sādhanā*, an accomplished person is able to lift his subtle body from the gross body, so, while the physical body does something, the spiritual body does something else. But, he highlighted, only accomplished persons have the ability to see their real shape in motion. According to Rāghavendra Dās, the *sūkṣma śarīr* can be sent to other places: he gave the example of Śaṅkarācārya, who kept his gross body in one place while learning about love, and of Matsyendranāth who got stuck in Kamakhya and Gorakhnāth had to go there to save him.[23] In fact, according to Garuḍ Dās, the body of the yogi is a body of *śūnyatā* (emptiness): the yogi is present in the body but his *ātman* can go wherever he wants. For Monī Bābā, the *sūkṣma śarīr* is made of *ākāś* and *vāyu*, and therefore does not dissolve with the end of the gross body. Since the subtle body remains, one may then wonder whether it corresponds to the *ātman*. This is an important point which we will continue to discuss in the next chapters.

Hence, the ascetic yogic practice has as its ultimate goals the detachment from and overcoming of the gross body. Thus, the practices occur within the body system, but some of their results manifest outside it. While the gross body is a temporary tool with which to begin the practice, the main *sādhanā* seems to take place on other levels of reality and, for the most part, not through the physical but the subtle body. Therefore, whether gross or subtle, the 'body' in the yoga *sādhanā* is a fundamental and complex tool to reach the spiritual goal.

The yoga *sādhanā*

> 'The path of yoga is very difficult and is like walking on a sword.[24] A *fakīr* can do that, not everyone. So not everyone can become a yogi.'
>
> Nāth jī

When *sādhus* talk about the yoga *sādhanā*, they basically mean a path the main practice of which is meditation. The path is yoga and the result is yoga. However, there is no unambiguous meaning of yoga or its goals.

---

23 Both of these accounts refer to the ability of the two masters to leave their bodies or to occupy other bodies through which they could experience sexuality. In some hagiographies, in fact, Śaṅkara takes King Amaruja's body to acquire the knowledge of *kāmaśāstra* (Clark 2006: 156).

24 This may also recall the imagery of the *Kaṭha Upaniṣad* which likens the spiritual path to crossing a razor's sharp edge (see Hatley 2016).

Talking to Cetan Purī about my research, he warned me that I was going to receive many different answers because there cannot be a single meaning of yoga, as yoga is related to experience,[25] and experiences are individual and private. He also pointed out to me that those who have had the experience of *paramātman* (hence have achieved and experienced 'the' yoga) would probably not be the ones to tell me about it, because it is a difficult thing to express. He also added that a *sādhanā* is something people do for themselves, so it should not be shared.

Given the privacy of *sādhanās*, I never directly asked about it. It seemed to me that, in several *sampradāyas*, yoga can be an auxiliary practice to the ascetic's main *sādhanā*. For some *sādhus*, *bhakti* is the main *sādhanā*, despite their knowledge of physical yogic practices. For example, Rām Bālak Dās said that the main yoga of a Rāmānandī is *bhakti* yoga: they may follow different methods and practices, but the most important practices remain *bhajan* and *jap*, the repetition of God's name. Through them, the *bhakta* (devotee) is said to obtain a peaceful mind and the right concentration to calm mental flows, and that is what is necessary to attain yoga.

As testified by several *sādhus*, a devoted discipline (*sādhanā*) is the basis of the practice: 'Without *sādhanā* no yoga is possible![26] It is like a train. If you do not build the platform, it cannot move', Rājeś Cetan Brahmacārī claimed; '*sādhanā* is the basis for everything; without *sādhanā*, *dhyāna* is empty. Without a mantra, the *jap* is empty', said Kamal Giri.

Focusing on the yoga *sādhanā* (whether or not it is the main *sādhanā*), *sādhus* refer to it as an '*aṣṭāṅgayoga*'[27] to stress the fact that it generally consists of eight typologies of practices, divided into five external ones (*yama, niyama, āsana, prāṇāyāma, pratyāhāra*) and three internal (*dhāraṇā, dhyāna, samādhi*). Their externality or internality is in relation to the body.

---

25 This emphasis on experience and the individual path differs from the focus on individuality and experientiality in modern yoga (see De Michelis 2004: 181–205), as it is framed in a specific ascetic context and influenced and interpreted through the religious background of a *sādhu*.

26 '*Bīnā sādhanā koi yog nahīṃ ho saktā hai.*'

27 Mallinson and Singleton summarise the yoga-*āṅga* issue and explain that not all the systems present eight sections. Some texts present fivefold, fourfold, etc. methods, although the most common are the sixfold—present in several tantric texts and in the *Gheraṇḍa Saṃhitā*—and the eightfold methods. While the elements of eightfold systems do not vary from text to text, barring a few exceptions, there is considerable variation in the sixfold systems, which often do not include *yama* and *niyama* (Mallinson and Singleton 2017: 11–13, 475nn15, 17, 18, especially the references to Vasudeva 2004 and Goodall 2004).

Initially, the body is central to the practice because the individual has to learn how to control it, not only in the muscles and breath but also in the instincts and senses, especially by controlling sexuality. Only through the control of the body, breath and senses can one pursue the other parts of yoga: those that can actually lead to yoga. Not all *sādhus* need to follow the 'physical' path so literally, and indeed, not all yogis are also *yogīrāj*. This title is usually given to *sādhus* who have complete mastery over their body and are experts in yogic *kriyās*, as they have performed yoga practices as a *sādhanā* or a form of *tapasyā*. But not all *sādhus* can learn yogic practices: it is the guru who decides whether or not to direct a disciple to the yogic path. Below, in the section on *āsanas*, I will provide some insights into the ways in which *sādhus* learn physical practices. However, a general process of learning was explained to me by Omānanda Giri. He said that in the beginning his guru gave him some spiritual knowledge that was a great inspiration to him. Then his guru taught him how to keep his body healthy. Thereafter, he did 50 minutes of *āsanas*, *kriyās* and *mudrās* to purify his body and keep his senses under control. His guru finally taught him the *prāṇāyāma* to control the energies of the body, before teaching him all the remaining steps. Omānanda Giri said that in theory the guru had already taught him *dhyāna*. But in practice he started to meditate 'for real' only after he had accomplished all the previous steps, spending six years with his guru to learn properly.

In the next sections, following the steps mentioned by Omānanda Giri, we will delve into the external ascetic path of yoga, considering relevant topics such as *ṣaṭkarmas* and other important *kriyās*. Obviously, as mentioned in the Introduction, at the beginning of the practice the guru must be present to guide the disciple: solitary retreat can only be undertaken when the individual is ready.[28]

Yama and *niyama*

The presence of constraints (*yama*) and rules (*niyama*) in yoga systems is not compulsory and the texts that discuss them do not always agree on their number.[29] The *Haṭhapradīpikā*, for example, does not include *yama*

28 See Chapter 6, pp. 241f.

29 Lists of similar rules and observances can be found as early as the *Mahābhārata* (2.6.1) and the Jain text *Ācārānga Sūtra* (350 BCE) (see Mallinson and Singleton 2017: 51). Patañjali (2.6.2.) begins his method with five restraints (non-violence, truthfulness, not stealing, sexual continence, non-acquisitiveness) and five rules

and *niyama* among its *aṅgas*, but presents a list of things that hinder or favour the yoga practice.

In the ascetic world, the observance of restraints and rules is obligatory, since ascetic life is articulated and based on rules to be respected. Serving as an example in this regard are the words of Ravīndra Giri who said:

> from the moment one enters this [ascetic] path, one is taught how to do the daily practices (*nitya paddhati*), the daily activities (*nitya kriyā*), then with whom one can sit and how one can sit; with whom one can have certain kinds of conversations and how to behave with different people. All these rules are taught. When the person has learnt all this, then the yoga *sādhanā* begins.

Thus, contemporary *sādhus* regard *yama* and *niyama* as fundamental primary steps through which the individual begins the spiritual path, and without which any other practice is aimless. The word *niyama* is often used to stress the fact that 'one must follow the rules',[30] be they the rules of the *sampradāya* or those of the *sādhanā*.

Unless the individual changes his approach and behaviour to make it suitable for the *sādhanā*, results cannot come. Often these changes concern the attitudes towards *bhakti* and *karma*. *Bhakti* and *karma* are constantly mentioned by *sādhus* in conversations about the yoga *sādhanā*.[31] *Bhakti* is considered fundamental in reaching God, 'because if you disregard God, and only practise for a selfish reason, to have good health or a good physical body [. . .] then nothing is going to happen', said Īśnāth. *Bhakti*, according

(cleanliness, contentment, austerity, recitation of sacred texts, devotion to the Lord). The *Śāradātilaka* 2.6.4 (c. 11th century) lists among the *yamas*: non-violence, not stealing, sexual continence, compassion, honesty, patience, rectitude, moderation in food and cleanliness. For the *niyama*, it lists austerity, contentment, belief in authoritative texts, charity, worshipping the deity, listening to canonical teachings, modesty, resolve, mantra repetition and sacrificial offerings (Mallinson and Singleton 2017: 51). Similar tenfold lists are present in the *Śāṇḍilya Upaniṣad*, one of the so-called Yoga Upaniṣads the date of compilation of which is still uncertain, and which lists among the *yamas*: non-violence, truthfulness, not stealing, celibacy, compassion, rectitude, forbearance, fortitude, temperance in food and cleanliness. The ten *niyamas* in this case are: penance, continence, belief in the existence of the other worlds, munificence, worship of Īśvara, study of systems of philosophy, a sense of shame, the proper frame of mind, prayer, and observance of vows (see Srinivasa 1938: 449–450).

30 '*Niyam kā pālan karnā hī padegā!*'

31 *Bhakti* pervades all the *sampradāyas*, demonstrating the importance that *bhakti* currents had in influencing the historical development of religious groups. I will return to this topic at the conclusion of this book.

to Īśnāth, results in *karma* yoga: the individual must question the reasons for his actions and who will benefit from them. He should calm the 'animal instincts', he said, renouncing what can harm others in order to develop a proper human nature. The importance of *bhakti* in the practice is not only a feature of devotional *sampradāyas* (such as the Rāmānandī), but seems to be a constant value present in all the *sampradāyas* considered here.

Through restrictions and rules, one cleanses one's actions related to the five senses, which is fundamental to the yoga practice. I again quote the words of Īśnāth: 'Discipline is there for the senses, to control your senses and to direct you inwards, so that you begin to lose all unnecessary interest in worldly things that have no meaning.' This process also includes the aim of controlling the ego and negative emotions. As we have mentioned, these are referred to as 'enemies'.[32] According to Durgā Bhārtī:

> There are five things to give up before starting the path: *moh* (attachment), *himsā* (violence), *krodha* (anger), *lobha* (greed), *ahaṃkāra* (selfishness). Because of these five things the world is sick. Instead, there are five things to follow: *dayā* (compassion), *upkār* (kindness), *vicar* (consideration), *pavitratā* (purity), *ahiṃsā* (non-violence). This is the right path. Why give pain to others when you can give them happiness?

From the conversations I have had with *sādhus*, it appears that the ascetic's behaviour is today underpinned by an ethical-moral code dedicated to the development of an empathetic approach to other beings and the development of detachment (with a broad understanding), *viz.*: detachment from selfish behaviour; detachment from negative emotions and feelings; detachment from wrong behaviours; and detachment from sensual pleasures such as taste and sex.

On *brahmacarya*

Of all the rules, celibacy (*brahmacarya*) is the one given the most emphasis by ascetics, because the discharge of semen nullifies the entire yogic practice.

---

32 *Sādhus* were quite consistent in their descriptions of these five enemies. However, again, such descriptions do not always correspond to the obstacles (*kleśas*) described in textual sources. In general, the obstacles in textual sources are more mundane and practical, like bathing early in the morning or mixing with bad company (and therefore easy to eliminate), or else obstacles that are constituents of the human condition, such as pride or ignorance—the latter often being portrayed as the source of all others (see *Pātañjalayogaśāstra* 2.3-4; and refer to Mallinson and Singleton 2017: 46–47).

Originally the term *brahmacarya* had nothing to do with sexuality[33] but referred to the study period of an adolescent, characterised by a strict chaste and celibate life. By extension, it came to refer to celibate ascetics, although it seems 'that this term refers more specifically to the virtue of chastity' (Olivelle 2008b: 152).[34] The virtue of chastity in Hindu religious contexts depends on the importance given to semen, which is seen as the essence of life, spiritual energy and source of immortality. In texts on yoga that have *yamas* and *niyamas*, *brahmacarya* (as synonymous with celibacy) 'is a *sine qua non*' (Bharati 1965: 293). In fact, from a historical perspective, sexual abstinence has been seen as a necessary condition for the advancement of mental training and the pursuit of liberation, to the point that techniques have been developed to prevent the loss of semen.

Obviously, the celibate individual referred to in the texts is male,[35] with women being depicted as obstacles to spiritual practice—Svātmārāma (1.61) says so explicitly—and we saw in Chapter 2 that there are, in fact, different attitudes towards female ascetics. The fear is that of sexual temptation and the eventual breaking of *brahmacarya*.

Jogī Bābā explains *brahmacarya* by making a comparison between the worldly people (H., *sāṃsārik log*) who engage in sexual activities and the ascetics who have to retain their semen (*bindudhāraṇa*):

> *Sāṃsārik* people find their place in their [sexual] union. But '*bindu patan mānam, bindu dhāraṇam jīvam*': in our Sanatan Dharma one who drops semen [*bindu patan*] will get temporary *ānanda* (enjoyment), but if he

---

33 From an etymological point of view, *brahmacarya* stems from two Sanskrit roots, *brahman*, to be understood as the 'ultimate reality', and *carya*, which means 'behaviour, conduct'. As pointed out by Alter (1997: 282), the control of sexual pleasure does not lie in the idea that it is wrong, sinful or evil: it is one of the 'four aims of man' and therefore legitimate, although considered inferior to *dharma* (right action), *artha* (economic prosperity), *kāma* (love) and *mokṣa* (liberation). The main role of *brahmacarya* is therefore one of conserving the semen in pursuit of higher results.

34 On the ethical and moral role of *brahmacarya*, see Alter 1992. On celibacy and religions traditions, see Olson 2007.

35 Khandelwal (2004: 157), on the basis of her research on female ascetics in Haridwar, has proposed an alternative female model to understand celibacy which goes beyond 'the hydraulic model of semen retention'. Considering that *brahmacarya* is more than 'abstaining from sex', she points out that among female ascetics the word is understood as the control of passions, attachments and appetites and therefore based not so much on a specific physiology but rather on moral and ritual purity, self-restraint and detachment (Khandelwal 2004: 169–173). See also DeNapoli 2014: 280; Khandelwal, Hausner and Grodzins Gold 2006: 15–19.

> does *bindudhāraṇa*, he gets *satguṇa*, the vision of *paramātman*. It is with this *satguṇa* that one obtains *ānanda*. In the ocean of *bindu* the transformation takes place, slowly one goes towards the *darśan* [. . .]. This is also *tapasyā*. This is yoga.

It would seem that among ascetics the main purpose of *brahmacarya* is to control the semen, but this control not only leads to spiritual attainment but also to a form of inner pleasure.[36] According to Viśambhar Bhārtī, during an orgasm *kuṇḍalinī* rises a little and the individual has a hint of *paramātman*, but it is a very temporary sensation. *Brahmacarya*, on the other hand, takes this feeling to higher levels. *Brahmacarya* is possible through strong control of the senses and desire and when this is achieved the individual becomes *śuddha* (pure) and accumulates *pūrṇa śakti* (absolute power).[37] This depends on the nature of semen itself and its function within the body. According to Rām Caraṇ Dās:

> Breath, mind and *vīrya* (semen), these three elements have a similar *śakti*. Semen is created through the blood produced by the food we eat. At first the blood is *kaccā* (raw), and when this *kaccā* blood enters the *aṇḍkoṣ* (testicles), it becomes *pakkā* (mature). From this blood comes *śakti*. From *vīrya*, *ojas* (strength) is produced and it is through this *ojas* that *śakti* comes into being. Like milk . . . from milk you get *dahī* (curd) and from *dahī* you get *makkhan* (butter). And what happens when you heat the butter? You get *ghī* (clarified butter). That is why *vīrya* is very important, because through it *ojas* is awakened. From the *ojas* then *śakti* is produced. *Sādhus* know this, that is why they preserve their semen.
>
> [. . .] There are eight *dhātus*[38] that are produced by *vīrya*. In the bones there is marrow. When its quantity decreases, pain begins. That is why, I told you, *brahmacarya* is so important.

Rām Caraṇ Dās's explanation gives several important clues. First of all, it stresses the connection between semen, breath and mind that we find

---

36 See below on the *vajrolī mudrā* section and in Chapter 6 in the section on *kuṇḍalinī* (pp. 261ff.).

37 Jogī Bābā said that, because of its retention, the semen of a yogi is very hot. That is why yogis can create directly through their semen. He supported this idea saying that the world and all the creatures come from the semen dropped by *ṛṣis*.

38 In early literature of Ayurveda there are seven main *dhātus*, seven fundamental principles (elements) that support the basic structure (and functioning) of the body: *rasa* (lymph), *rakta* (blood), *māṃsa* (muscles), *medas* (fat), *asthan* (bone), *majjan* (marrow) and *śukra* (semen). To these seven *dhātus* sometimes an eighth, *ojas*, is added, although texts may differ with regard to their lists (see Maas 2007).

mentioned in the *Amṛtasiddhi* (7.17)[39] and, as emphasised in that text, semen has a fundamental role as the essence of the body. However, the words of Rām Caraṇ Dās also recall a form of Ayurvedic knowledge, specifically the idea of the *dhātus* (bodily tissues or elements) nourishing one another. There is a kind of digestion chain, which starts with the food eaten being transformed into nutritional juice (*rasa*), which in turn becomes blood, which becomes flesh, which becomes fat, which becomes bone, which becomes marrow, which becomes semen.[40] Sometimes, *ojas* is included as an additional *dhātu* that is produced from the semen.[41] In Ayurveda, *ojas* appears as an essential element for the preservation of life and health, a constituent of all human beings, both male and female (Meulenbeld 2008: 160). However, as Dagmar Wujastyk pointed out to me, although closely related to *bala* (force), it is worth noting that no mention of *śakti* is found in pre-modern Ayurvedic texts.[42]

Rām Caraṇ Dās emphasised the importance of *brahmacarya* for both men and women. The presence of a partner is not always rejected because celibacy can be also maintained while living as a couple.[43] Dayānanda Purī stated that it is possible to have a '*śakti*', i.e. a *sādhakī*, a female partner. He said that when a *sādhu* is a *siddha* (a perfected being) or is on the path of *siddha*, if he has a *sādhakī* he can be even more powerful because he can concentrate more on his practice due to the energy that the presence of the partner gives him.[44] Therefore, it is not actually impossible for a *saṃnyāsī*

39 Mallinson (2021: 10) points out that links between the mind and breath and the mind and semen can be found as far back as the *Chāndogya Upaniṣad* and *Mahābhārata*, but the *Amṛtasiddhi* is the first text to teach that mind, breath and semen are connected.

40 I thank Dagmar Wujastyk for this concise and clear summary (personal communication, 5 April 2021). On the connection between digestion, blood and semen, see also Alter 1997: 283; Zimmer 1948.

41 As Meulenbeld (2008: 156) says, '*ojas* represents an archaic idea, concretising and visualising an abstract vital force as a material substance [. . .] a fluid with a fixed number of qualities'. On *ojas* in Vedic literature, see Meulenbeld 2008: references to Gonda 1952 and Dumézil 1969.

42 Personal communication, 5 April 2021.

43 As Olivelle (2008b: 152) explains, 'As a social institution [. . .] celibacy can have social and ideological dimensions different from simple chastity, such as negating the religious value of the institution of marriage and of procreating children.'

44 Hamaya (2019: 8) informs us that a few female ascetics in her research stated that it would be better to live with a male partner ('if he was nice') because it is 'never safe for a single woman to live alone'. The ascetic couples she describes are based on a guru–disciple relationship: a male ascetic who has a *celī* (female disciple) and does his *sevā*. This situation is sometimes exploited (Hamaya 2019: 8–13), and it is

to have a 'spiritual partner', and if this couple is strong in their practices and celibacy, they are highly respected and equated with divine couples.[45]

Describing relationships between men and women, Ravīndra Giri recognises three paths: the path of *nāgās* who must be celibate; the path of Rajneesh (Osho) which he calls '*bhog yog*', where a man and a woman can be naked together but without penetration; and the path of the Aghorīs (or of anyone who can, he added), where a man and a woman can have sexual intercourse but there is no ejaculation by the man. Since this requires enormous control of the mind, he said, those who can do this are called *mahāyogīs*, great yogis. This latter definition recalls antinomic tantric practices in which sexual intercourse was considered part of the rituals, as well as yogic sources in which mastery of practices like *vajrolī mudrā* would allow the yogi to enjoy himself with a hundred women without losing his *bindu*.[46]

Diet

Recommendations on food and diet are often found in yoga texts to facilitate the practitioner's training.[47] For example, *Dattātreyayogaśāstra* 70 states that one should avoid salt, mustard, sour, hot, dry or sharp foods and overeating (Mallinson 2013a). By contrast, *Haṭhapradīpikā* 1.62 lists the food that a yogi *should* eat: wheat, rice, barley, milk, ghee, sugar, butter, sugar candy, honey, dry ginger, green leafy vegetables, etc. It goes on to insist (1.63) that the yogi should consume food that is 'sweet, delicious, unctuous, contains cow products, nourishes the bodily constituents (*dhātu*), is desired by the mind and is appropriate', while unsuitable for foods include 'Pungent, sour, bitter, salty and hot foods, horseradish, sour gruel, [sesame] oil, sesame and mustard seeds, fish and intoxicating drink, flesh of goats and so forth, curds, diluted buttermilk, [. . .]' (1.59).

often seen by other *sādhus* as ambiguous and merely an excuse for a guru to have a female partner.

45 Dayānanda Purī made the distinction between this kind of couple, who are not married, and those who are married but are called *gosvāmī* or *gosain*. He said that, in South India, married *saṃnyāsīs* are quite widespread, and there are actually more *gosvāmī* than ascetics. This is not perceived as a rift in the rules since these *sādhus* follow the *ṛṣis* traditions, which allow them to have wives in their hermitages.

46 See for example Mallinson 2007b on the *Śivasaṃhitā*, a work on yoga composed in the 14th or 15th centuries CE.

47 When a diet is listed, it is defined as *mitāhāra* (measured diet).

Gheraṇḍa Saṃhitā 5.16 is quite severe about the consequences of a wrong diet: 'should the yogi undertake the practice of yoga without having a measured diet, he will get various diseases and his yoga will in no way be successful'. According to this text—but note there is a general textual consensus on this—'one should fill half the stomach with food, a quarter with water and leave the fourth quarter for the movement of air' (5.22), and one 'should not eat only once a day, not eat at night nor at the end of the night' (5.29).[48]

As we saw in the chapter on *tapasyā*, *sādhus* might be following very strict dietary regimes and, in general, they maintain an attitude towards food that is close to that described in texts, recognising the value of a proper diet to sustain their *sādhanā*, the importance of being vegetarian and eating only as much as is sufficient for the body. Food control is considered fundamental to improving the *sātvik* qualities of an individual and to enhance discipline. A *sādhaka* of the Gorakhnāth temple in Varanasi called it 'tongue control'. He specified that, if one does not give up eating certain things, then 'yoga cannot be, it becomes useless (H., *bekār*)'. Therefore, he continued, one must satisfy only the *āhāra-vihāra*, the 'essential needs':

> *Āhāra* means food and it has to be *sātvik*. If the body does not eat *sātvik* food, the digestive power becomes bad (H., *kharāb*). For example, if you eat meat you cannot do yoga, because your mind won't be ready for awakening. That is why you have to be vegetarian. That means rice, *roṭī*, *capātī*, vegetables, milk, curd [. . .] If you eat these things, the body remains free from diseases. Those who do the opposite, who eat chickens, eggs, fish, goats, cannot do yoga *sādhanā*, because their mind won't focus.

According to Ravīndra Giri, non-vegetarian people can do yoga and even improve a little, but they will not be able to do it well because they will become wakeful, distressed, lazy and sleepy, and thus unable to attain true knowledge. He also listed the foods that are absolutely not good for yoga practitioners who want to maintain their state of *brahmacarya*: garlic, onions, horseradish and drumstick tree, *lasoṛā* (Indian cherry), carrots, beetroot, *masūr dāl* (orange lentils) and fish. According to him, these products would make the sperm more liquid, thus increasing the chances of losing it in unexpected situations. In general, a proper diet promotes the practice of *brahmacarya*.

Moreover, the quality and quantity of food eaten is also a concern of *sādhus*, especially during practice. For example, Rām Priya Dās once told me that, when she began her yoga practice, her diet was initially based on

48 Translation from Mallinson 2004.

eating only fruit for a few months, followed by a break in which she would eat something else, and then start again with just fruits. She said that she continued to eat this way to keep her body in balance, justifying the light diet also in view of the fact that, since the yoga *sādhanā* is mostly done while seated, too much food would hinder the posture.

Āsanas

Given the importance of *āsana*s in contemporary modern yoga practice, I will provide here a brief reconstruction of their history, referring to the work of several scholars who have visually and textually investigated their development. This will be helpful in contextualising the ascetic use of *āsana*s that will follow.[49]

A brief history of *āsanas*

The word *āsana* is derived from the root *ās*, which essentially means 'to sit'. Until the end of the 1st millennium CE, when used in a yoga context *āsana* referred to the seated postures to be adopted for meditation. As a matter of fact, in early textual and visual sources it is difficult to identify non-seated *āsanas*: ascetics and gurus have always been described and represented in meditative postures such as *padmāsana*.

The earliest evidence thus far of non-seated postures is found in sculptures in Dabhoi, a small village in Gujarat, which Professor Mallinson and I noticed while examining its northern gate, the Mahudi. Likely built in 1230 CE, the gate has several arches between its outer façades, and it is there that we found carved sculptures of ascetics performing complex *āsana*s, particularly inverted ones. Interestingly, some of these *āsana*s are not described in any contemporaneous texts (Photo 11).[50]

49 I devoted part of my fieldwork to collecting visual and material evidence that could shed light on the historical development of *āsanas*. Dr Singleton and I discussed several times how this form of investigation could be very successful if combined with a comparative study of other traditional bodily and embodied practices in India and neighbouring areas. This led us to organise a workshop that brought several specialists together and resulted in the volume *Yoga and the Traditional Physical Practices of South Asia: Influence, Entanglement and Confrontation* published by the *Journal of Yoga Studies* (Bevilacqua and Singleton 2023).

50 This gate was described by Shah (1957), who emphasised the importance of its Nāth background. It was only after our curiosity had led us there that we realised that the gate held information of particular interest us which had not previously

Photo 11 A detail of the Mahudi Gate, Dabhoi, representing a complex *āsana*.

The same can be said of the sculptures in the Hampi temple complex (c. 15th–16th centuries). As Seth Powell has shown in two fascinating papers (2018, 2023), while representations of seated ascetics abound on temple walls,[51] some more complex postures have no pre-modern textual referent (that we are aware of), and some seem to anticipate postural forms of which we have no trace until perhaps the 19th or 20th centuries (Photo 12).

The presence of these complex *āsanas*, although limited in number, raises several questions. Considering their scarcity, it could indicate their relatively low importance. However, the fact that they are depicted proves that they were indeed performed by ascetics in temples. We should then wonder why they performed them. A probable answer is to amuse pilgrims. The pillars of medieval temples suggest that the artists were inspired by a whole range of practitioners alongside yogis and *fakīrs*: that is, by acrobats, wrestlers and dancers.[52] If, as these sculptures suggest, these various figures shared temple spaces with yogis (perhaps especially during religious festivals), it is possible that the yogis learnt some postural practices from other classes of practitioners and introduced them into their own repertoires as *yogāsanas*, either for pragmatic reasons (e.g. to attract the attention of pilgrims) or spiritual ones (e.g. to push their bodies into new forms of *tapasyā*). Such an environment would also be suggested by textual sources. Saran Suebsantiwongse (2023) has noted that Chapter 107 of the *Sāmrājyalakṣmīpīṭhikā* (c. early 16th century CE), in describing the celebration of Navarātri (*patala*s 101, 102), presents the various entertainers of the king including wrestlers (women as well), dancers, acrobats, but also yogis. This would demonstrate that yogis probably displayed some of their bodily skills to entertain the king, an activity that does not seem uncommon among ascetics during religious festivals even today. Powell (2023), considering a wide range of carved images from South Indian temple sites, including Pattadakal (c. early 8th century), Hampi and Bangalore (c. 17th century), visually demonstrates that the boundaries between yoga, asceticism and gymnastics are not immediately obvious, raising an interpretive and categorical challenge. This is made even more difficult by the condition of many of these temples today: the deterioration of the statues often prevents a clear identification of the practitioners.

---

been noticed. On this gate and its sculpture, see Mallinson 2019; Sarde 2017; Powell 2018, 2023.

51 See Dallapiccola and Verghese 1998.

52 On the role of yogi as magician and entertainer, see Zubrzycki 2018.

Photo 12 Carved columns of a temple in Hampi, 2016.

How can we distinguish yogic practices from other physical practices—for instance, a dance posture from an *āsana*, or a practice of *tapasyā* from an *āsana*? And how can we distinguish a yogi from a dancer, given that dance was considered a form of yoga with similar transcendental aims (see Ganser 2023)?[53] A similar assumption might be justified when considering *sādhus* from the *akhāṛās*—their training and their involvement in the war politics of the time: were they influenced by practitioners of traditional martial arts or military training? And did some *vyāyāms* (exercises) or demanding postures originate from these martial contexts?[54] Further investigation is required to fill in the many gaps that remain in our knowledge of the development of *āsanas* practice.

From the point of view of textual sources, it is with the development of the literature on *haṭha* yoga that more complex, non-seated *āsanas* have gained space. As Birch (2020b) has shown, from the 17th century onwards there was an increase in the number, typologies and descriptions of *āsanas*

53 Dance itself could be part of the practice of ascetic groups. As pointed out by Gaenser (2023), among the Pāśupatas dancing and singing were important ascetic stages. Hence, it appears that these physical practices were also used in the *sādhanā*.

54 See for example O'Hanlon 2007; Pinch 2006; McCartney 2023; Rochard and Bast 2023.

across different intellectual contexts. Mallinson (2019) explains this production as a form of competition for patronage among monastic centres, offering potential patrons more techniques to practise to increase health and powers. Although these texts were probably not intended for ascetics, those depicted in rare illuminated manuscripts were indeed ascetics, demonstrating the role that ascetic practitioners played as a source of authority and legitimacy.[55]

To conclude, the fact that non-seated, complicated postures were only described in later texts does not mean that they were not practised earlier, but rather that they probably remained in the circle of oral transmission, because the physical and practical techniques were mostly taught through direct demonstration, from guru to disciple, or, more generally, from experienced practitioner to novice.

Āsanas for ascetics: to sit, to stretch

> 'The label *āsana* is properly used when an *āsana* is perfected and can thus be used as a meditative posture; otherwise it must be understood as a form of exercise.'
>
> Omānanda Giri

Two ideas about *āsanas* prevail in the ascetic milieu. The first is that *āsanas* can be regarded as spiritual (H., *ādhyātmik*) and be used as stable, seated postures for practising *dhyāna*; such *āsanas* are, in particular, *sukhāsana*, *siddhāsana* and *padmāsana*. Then there are *āsanas* that are 'temporary', the purpose of which is to keep the body healthy, prevent diseases and make it stable (H., *sthir*), because, when the body is stable, then the mind can be stabilised and it becomes easier to meditate. As Rām Priya Dās pointed out:

> *Āsanas* are not done for pleasure; there are benefits in doing them but the purpose is not gratification [. . .] While doing our *sādhanā* we can get tired, that is why we do *āsanas*. *Āsanas* are necessary to give balance to the body, to relieve stiffening parts of the body.

55 The earliest known treatise to systematically illustrate yoga postures is the Persian *Baḥr al-Hayāt* (c. 1602 CE). According to Carl Ernst (2016), the author was probably a Persian scholar who travelled to India and observed Nāth Yogīs—as can be deduced by their apparel, especially by the presence of the *siṅgī*—practising physical postures (seated, inverted *āsanas*, and breathings), which were then painted in the manuscript. Another illustrated manuscript is an edition of the *Jogapradīpakā* produced probably in Punjab around 1830 CE; see Bühnemann 2007.

Her guru, Rām Caraṇ Dās, further explained that, since a yogi usually practises in a limited space, his movements are limited too: 'That is why one does *āsanas*. Otherwise, one could simply walk after meditation,' he claimed.

These physical *āsana*s are taught at the beginning of the practice to help the body find its balance, so that obstacles such as fatigue and weakness are controlled and do not trouble the more advanced practices. Although *sādhu*s claimed that the *sādhanā*, if correct, will itself help the body stay healthy, many also added that practising a couple of these physical *āsana*s every day is also helpful.

Following a definition by Yogī Śivanāth, we can therefore divide *āsana*s into *dhyānātmak āsana*s (meditative postures) and *vyāyāmātmak āsana*s (cultural postures). The latter *āsana*s can be associated with *vyāyām*s (physical exercise), although *vyāyām* is usually more aerobic and, according to Rām Bālak Dās, not entirely necessary for the yogi. *Vyāyām*s are associated with the practice of wrestlers (H., *pahlvān*s). But it is interesting to note that, sometimes, *pahlvān*s become *nāgā*s and *nāgā*s are often understood or seen by other *sādhu*s as *pahlvān*s. As mentioned earlier, the link between the martial and the ascetic worlds is not surprising.[56] Nāth jī said that in his youth he was a *pahlvān* because there was an *akhāṛā* in his guru's *āśram*, so there were wrestlers exercising together with young *sādhu*s. Therefore, when he was young, he used to practise both *āsana*s and *vyāyām*s. He said that the exercises in the *akhāṛā* are quite different from *āsana*s, mainly because they have different aims: *vyāyām*s serve to increase the strength of the body and its muscles, whereas *āsana*s require less effort and do not need equipment.[57]

While the topic of *āsana*s and health will be discussed more fully in Chapter 7, I would like to briefly touch on the names and numbers of *āsanas*. Different texts may ascribe different labels to the same *āsana* (see Birch 2020b). This problem is also evident in ascetics' oral transmission: sometimes ascetics use or change the names of *āsana*s depending on the context in which they use them. The *āsana* for staying in water, for example, is called *jalāsana* (from the word *jal*, water), but it is a kind of *padmāsana* which requires practitioners to stand on their knees. Īśnāth used the label *Hanumān-āsana* to describe not the 'split', as it is generally understood in

56 On the topic of wrestling and yogic practices, see also Alter 1992.

57 He also used to do *kuśtī* (a type of wrestling tradition), as well as weightlifting, even with his mouth. However, as soon as he received the complete Nāth *dīkṣā*, he had to stop to protect his *kuṇḍal*.

modern yoga today, but the pose in which Hanumān is often depicted, i.e. with one knee on the ground and the other bent.

Sādhus were often embarrassed to be unable to label the various postures they showed me, and would justify themselves by stressing that they had learnt the practice from observing other people doing it, and that in those practical contexts labels were secondary to the satisfactory execution of the postures. Furthermore, the word *āsana* in ascetic contexts can refer to several things: the physical place where the *sādhu* sits; the object on which he sits; or the shape his body takes. For example, *mṛgāsana* is a seat made of the hide of a black deer and *baghachālā* is one made of tiger skin; and there are also *āsana*s made of *kuśa* grass. According to Yogī Rudra Nāth, there are different *āsana*s depending on the *siddhi* to be achieved and depending on where the *āsana* is to be placed.[58] The *āsana* of a *sādhu*, he explains, should not be used for resting. Phalāhārī Bābā stated that 'Those who practise yoga have different *āsanas*. To sit, to sleep, even to be in the water.' Clearly, his idea of *āsana* refers to the body itself, thus meaning that a practitioner should adopt specific postures in his activities to achieve yogic results. This also demonstrates that following the rules of yoga practice is a constant and ongoing process.

In view of the number of *āsana*s and their origin, the ascetics' answers were rather 'traditional'. Rām Avadhūt Dās claimed that there are as many *āsana*s as there are body shapes, and, since there are approximately 84 *lakh* (8,400,000) typologies of *yoni*s (vaginas), the number of body shapes a living being can have is similar. Although there are, therefore, over eight million *āsana*s, the main ones number 84 and their names are often connected to living beings. This was mentioned by several *sādhu*s, some of whom referred to the *Gheraṇḍa Saṃhitā* (2.1), the text in which we find the idea of 84 *lakh* of *āsana*s. However, Rām Caraṇ Dās also pointed out that 'there are 84 main *āsana*s, and of these only 32 are important; of these 32, 16 are important, and of these eight; of these eight, four are important, and in the end only one is important: *siddhāsana*, the posture used for meditation.'

---

58 In general, Indians use the word *āsana* for the small piece of cloth they use to cover where they sit. During the Kumbh Melā 2013 I acquired a woollen *āsana* from a temporary shop following the example of a lady who always had one in her bag.

How do *sādhus* learn *āsanas*?

> '*Āsana* means being able to sit in a position for an hour and remain there comfortably. Then, when this happens, one does another *āsana*. Yoga is not jumping from one posture to another, but being able to concentrate in one of them.'
>
> Yogī Alone Nāth

As emphasised many times, the yogic path, and the ascetic path in general, is a journey influenced by numerous individuals and trainings. Therefore, it is impossible to delineate a single way in which all *sādhus* learn techniques. About the teaching of *āsanas* Jogī Bābā said:

> Each guru teaches *āsanas* differently. Firstly, because the guru will not teach *āsanas* to everyone, but only to those who he believes are, or will be, able to accomplish that path; secondly, he will teach differently because by observing the body of the disciple he will understand what to start with. This is the difference between *vidyā* and *gyān*. *Vidyā* can also be read in books; *gyān* is a different form of knowledge. Your guru has to show you everything. Otherwise, what can you do? You cannot learn properly. He has to tell you, '*this is done this way, this is done that way*'.

The first *āsana* usually to be taught is a seated posture, because it is in the seated posture that the *sādhu* 'will do his job'. The first *āsana* learnt by Jogī Bābā was *padmāsana*, then *siddhāsana*. The first time he sat in *padmāsana* he did so for one to two hours. Rām Avadhūt Dās's initial training was similar: he started with a few hours, then, as his practice improved, partly due to some specific *prakriyā*[59] (technique) taught by his guru, he increased the practice to ten hours. The Udāsī Bhole Bābā said that the first *āsana* his guru taught him was *sūrya āsana*: that is, *añjalī mudrā* standing in front of the sun. The experience of Īśnāth was similar:

> The first posture my guru taught me was to stand. Because many people do not know how to stand. Some put most of their weight on the front of their feet, and others on their heels. Instead, the weight must be balanced. The weight must be distributed correctly on all feet. This is very important for the spine. This was the first lesson from my yoga guru. That is how my practice started, learning to stand. Then the simple *āsanas* could begin. The first sitting posture was *sukhāsana*, then *padmāsana* [. . .].

---

59 One example comes from Kamal Giri, who said that, if one cannot do a posture, or has some difficulties, then apply mustard oil to facilitate the body looseness and consequently the execution of the posture.

These examples conjure up two different scenes: on the one hand, the novice is immediately asked to adopt a seated posture in order to learn to concentrate and meditate; on the other hand, the novice is guided to acquire an awareness of his own body. In general, *sādhus* said that one can properly master *āsanas* if these are learnt during childhood. As a matter of fact, all the *yogīrāj* I met learnt physical practices in their childhood, even though they were not yet *sādhus*: in some cases, they learnt in the *āśram* of a local *sādhu* who taught them. During the 2019 Melā in Allahabad, Phalāhārī Bābā introduced me to a 'baby *sādhu*' (probably four years old) and he proudly said: 'You should see how much yoga he does. He knows a lot!' The thinking behind this attitude is that young people are supposed to have more energy to work hard on the physical practices and perfect them.[60] Furthermore, as mentioned in Chapter 3, 84 *āsanas* are also practised as a form of *tapasyā* and this is usually done by young *sādhus*.

It is important to note that an acquisition of full training in *āsanas* during childhood or youth is a limiting factor for women when it comes to being fully accomplished in these practices, as well as in *kriyās*. While little girls might visit the *āśram* of a *bābā* together with other children and learn *āsanas*, this does not necessarily imply that these girls will be initiated in the future. Rām Priya Dās was the only woman I met who had undergone actual physical yoga training. Hence, since it is more difficult for a woman to be initiated in her youth,[61] this often limits the typology of *sādhanā* she

60 This recalls the *Mokṣadharmaparvan* section of the *Mahābhārata* (289.51–52), which says: 'only a youngster could easily fly down a path dotted with robbers [. . .]' (Fitzgerald 2012: 57).

61 Rām Priya Dās was my only informant to ask about women and yoga in the ascetic context. To take an example, I asked her if a woman should continue to practise during menstruation; she replied that it is best to avoid any practice: 'Nothing, no *prāṇāyāma*, no *āsana*, no *jap*, no *pūjā*, just wait and keep the faith.' She added that with physical yoga a woman can regulate her menstruation: 'It will come according to *niyam* (H., rule) and leave soon.' When I asked her if this was the only difference between a man's and a woman's practice, she said yes. However, during our conversation, the idea emerged that *siddhāsana* is recommended more for men than for women: when a man practises *siddhāsana* he has to put his penis between his feet and assume a very tight posture, whereas a woman has to do it with her heels close together, but not on top of each other because she does not have to hold the penis. Therefore, since a woman has to perform *siddhāsana* differently, a better posture for her instead is *sukhāsana*. In the ascetic world, there seems to be no particular difference in the posture practised. When I asked Rām Priya Dās about *mayūrāsana*—which is sometimes discouraged for women—she replied that this posture might not be good for women who want to have children but, since an ascetic is supposed to maintain *brahmacarya*, that doesn't present a problem.

will be able to practise; this does not, however, exclude deep meditative practices.

Often, new *āsanas* or *kriyās* are learnt from different *sādhus* skilled in specific practices, during pilgrimages or religious gatherings. But most *sādhus* only learn a few seated postures, which are compulsory, and perhaps a few others. According to Kamal Giri, one should learn at least *sukhāsana*, *gomukhāsana* and *padmāsana*, because these are the three main *āsanas* for *dhyāna* and *jap*. Therefore, the number of postures learnt will depend on the nature and age of the *sādhu*, but the training will also depend on the *sampradāya* and the branch in which he is initiated.

Based on the interviews collected, it seems that those *sādhus* who intend to properly complete the *āsana* training learn one *āsana* at time, i.e. they devote days and hours to just one *āsana*.[62] How many days are needed to practise an *āsana* depends on the *sādhu*, although some have given specific answers: *mahant* Aśok Giri, for example, said that each *āsana* should be practised for one month and eight days, every day, especially *āsanas* for meditation; Svāmī Ātmānanda said that 'When you can keep an *āsana* for three hours and 48 minutes, then the *āsana* is perfected and can also be used as a meditative posture.' The purpose of this method of training is to master the *āsana* so that it becomes *siddha*, perfected or accomplished.[63] When an *āsana* is *siddha*, there is no need to continue practising it except when necessity arises: for example, to alleviate particular physical problems or to maintain the health of the body, thus using it as daily exercise. But, even in such a case, *sādhus* warn that one should not spend too much time on physical *āsanas*: 'If one spends time doing *āsanas*, then one has no time for the *āsana* one needs', said Rām Caraṇ Dās.

The *āsana* the ascetic needs is the perfected *āsana* to be used for inner practices, especially *dhyāna* and *jap*. The importance of this single seated

62 Even in the *Jogapradīpakā* there are indications about the timing of *āsanas*: for example, *paścimottānāsana* (70–78), which also requires a special diet, is practised for 168 days and is held continuously for the last 84 days of this period (Birch and Hargreaves 2015).

63 The *Caurāśī Āsana* (Brahmacārī Śrīnṛsiṃhaśarmā 1911: 8–10) claims that perfected *āsanas* are necessary for any form of yoga, because, without a perfect *āsana*, *prāṇāyāma* is not effective, nor are *mudrās*, and, therefore, *śakti* cannot be achieved. It is important to make *āsanas siddha*, but if one is not able to achieve this goal a mantra provided in the text can be used. The author also points out that, without a guru, who can explain how to perform the *anuṣṭhāna* of the mantra, this will not work. *Āsanas*, then, should be practised in an isolated place, not exhibited here and there, because only by practising *ekānt*, alone, can one enjoy the fruits of yoga.

posture became evident one day when I was with Rām Priya Dās and Rām Caraṇ Dās at their temple in Varanasi. A follower from Gujarat had arrived and began meditating in front of them, because he claimed he wanted his *kuṇḍalinī* to rise. Both Rām Priya Dās and Rām Caraṇ Dās scolded him, saying that he would achieve nothing until he sat correctly. The guy countered by saying that the position only had to be comfortable, which Rām Caraṇ Dās agreed with but stressed that it also had to be correct. The body, he said, must be stable otherwise the mind cannot be. He explained that, if the seated posture is not performed properly, the *prāṇa* does not flow in a linear way, compromising the ability to control the mind.

However, everyone has to find their own *āsana*. For example, Īśnāth said that it is necessary to try several *āsana*s to find the one that is good and stable for individual spiritual practice. Jogī Bābā's *āsana*, for example, is *siddhāsana*. He said: 'I have spent so much time in this position, in different conditions, that no one can pull me out of it. No one can lift me up.'

Sādhus doing *āsanas* in their everyday life

> 'Morning is the best time; everything happens in the morning!'
>
> Jogī Bābā

Jogī Bābā wakes up every morning around six o'clock, goes to the toilet, brushes his teeth and does *nauli* (see below, p. 218) to start his day. After the *ārtī*s in his various temples, he looks after the *āśram* and the animals, working hard, jumping and running around the area, before resting for a while. When he sits down, he usually does some *āsana*s to stretch the body and remove fatigue from the muscles. 'When I work here, sometimes I feel a lot of pain [. . .], then I practise *āsana*s to find relief. When I realise that something is wrong with the body and needs to be fixed, then I practise *āsanas*.' Jogī Bābā's approach is quite common among *sādhu*s who are familiar with *āsana*s (Photo 13).

Rām Avadhūt Dās has no precise rules: he practises occasionally, when he has time, and on those occasions he does '*āsana*s that are usually practised, such as *uttanpadāsana, paścimottānāsana* and *alāsana*.' According to him, 'There are two or three categories of *āsana*s that are practised sitting, lying down or standing. Thus, the practice depends on the time and the needs of the body.' This obviously refers only to the *āsana*s practice, because when I asked him about *dhyāna* he said that that practice must be done daily and for a couple of hours, because 'This is our *śakti*, this is the nourishment of our *ātman*. If you don't nourish your body, you don't live;

Photo 13 Jogī Bābā doing *āsana* in his *āśram*, Garh Jungle, 2018.

in the same way you have to nourish your subtle body and that makes it happy and fed.'

When I asked Rām Priya Dās what kind of practice she does as soon as she wakes up, she replied that first she cleans the floor! After *nitya karma* (daily morning rituals), she does some *prāṇāyāmas*: *anulom vilom* for two minutes to calm her mind, and then *kapālabhāti* for about 15 minutes. Then she repeats *anulom vilom*, and then she does ten minutes of *ujjāyī prāṇāyāma*. As such, she does about 35 minutes of *prāṇāyāma* then *āsana*s and *vyāyām*s for between 45 minutes and an hour. When I met her, she had just started this practice again, mainly to lose weight. She said that she only practises between 15 and 20 *āsana*s, repeating each *āsana* about 30 times. However, she referred several times to Bābā Rāmdev and this made me wonder whether her way of practising *āsana*s today is the result of Rāmdev's TV programme,[64] which she suggested I watch, or of the teaching of her guru.

Like Rām Priya Dās, several *sādhu*s practise *āsana*s and *vyāyām*s as a daily routine among their morning activities. Kamal Giri's *vyāyām* practice consists of rotating the feet while seated, rotating the hands and shoulders and bending to the sides when standing. He also does pull-ups. According to him, it is necessary to do *vyāyām*s before doing *āsana*s, otherwise the body gets stiff. They are necessary for the bones and muscles and to

64 See Chapter 7, p. 307.

accelerate the perfection of *āsanas*. Fundamentally, *vyāyāms* are a kind of warm-up for the body. Kamal Giri said that this practice should be done before dawn, around 4–5 am. Physical *āsanas* can then follow, but only five or six, depending on the purpose.

Jvālā Purī, the *mahant* of the Jūnā *akhāṛā* in Varanasi, practises daily. He begins with *padmāsana* while reciting the Gāyatrī mantra five times. Then he does *śīrṣāsana*, followed by *tulāsana*, *mṛgāsana* and then *murgāsana*, before sitting in *padmāsana* again and repeating the Gāyatrī mantra. He claims that he does not have much time, however, as he has to perform four *ārtīs* a day. When he was with his guru, he used to practise a couple of hours, from 8 am to 10 am. Now, however, he practises a few *āsanas* in a short time simply to maintain a healthy body. When it is hot, he practises early in the morning; when it is cold, he waits until 8 am. However, he also affirmed that 'Those who do yoga feel neither hot nor cold; they are always in between. Yoga is very good for the body.'[65] I also asked other *sādhus* whether there were *āsanas* specifically suited to the hot and cold seasons. According to Rām Caraṇ Dās, in the heat, the body is protected by doing *āsanas*. He specified that *padmāsana* is for the hot season whereas *gomukhāsana* is better for the rainy season, while Ravīndra Giri claimed that *siddhāsana* is also good in winter since this position, with a straight back, produces a lot of heat. Rām Avadhūt Dās had a completely different opinion:

> Depending on the environment, you and your body will adapt. If you stay in an environment for a long time, your body adapts to that environment. But, in particular extreme situations, it is your *śakti* that improves the conditions, not the *āsanas*. *Āsanas* cannot help in this respect, but *āsanas* have an effect whereby a yogi can remain, even in the cold, for a long time. The purpose of *āsanas* is to produce *śakti*. In extreme cold [. . .] it is not because of the *āsana* that the yogi does not feel cold, *āsanas* cannot protect him, he can die. But the yogi who has the perfection of his *śakti* [. . .] will be protected by that.

65 It is clear from this conversation how labels can be used interchangeably among *sādhus*: yoga becomes a synonym for *āsanas* as well as *haṭha* yoga.

Āsana as performance

> 'Yoga is not to be shown; you can only show *āsanas*!'
> Jogī Bābā

The Hindi verb *dikhānā* (to show), when used in a conversation about yoga, sometimes annoyed *sādhus*,[66] who often responded harshly by saying that yoga and *tapasyā* are not meant to be shown. Consequently, *āsanas* are not always openly displayed, as ascetics may see them as personal practices. According to the *tapasvī* Bhole Purī, *āsanas* are only shown by *dukān-dārī sādhus*, those who use their practice as a 'shop' (*dukān*) in order to profit from it. In fact, ascetics may occasionally perform *āsanas* during religious gatherings, and *yogīrājs* often have boards with photos of them showing some recognisable *āsanas*. Usually, the *āsanas* performed are the most spectacular ones in order to catch the attention of pilgrims or onlookers.

Kamal Giri admitted that *āsanas* can be like a theatrical act (*nāṭak*) and that they are meant for the public. Kamal Giri's board at Gaṅgā Sāgar,[67] for example, showed him standing with one leg behind his head. I asked him the purpose of that *āsana* and he simply said that it was a *kalā*, a form of art, to be compared to dancers dancing on the blades of swords. The *saṃnyāsī* Viśvot Giri, who comes from a tradition of *kriyā* performers, claimed that a display of *āsanas* or particular techniques (such as putting one's head in the sand for days) are done to impress a crowd,[68] to give them *ānanda* (delight). This performative use of *āsanas* is nothing new: as we have already seen, in the past, yogis were counted among the performers during Navarātri. This performance of *āsanas* occurs mostly during religious festivals.

It was an interesting experience to witness an exhibition of this kind during the Ambubācī Melā in Kamakhya in June 2017, as the International Day of Yoga (celebrated on the 21st of June) happened during the festival.[69] On that day, a demonstration was organised on the temple premises by local yoga teachers who tried to engage passers-by in their practice. Meanwhile,

---

66 I was once treated badly by a *bābā* who completely misunderstood my words and thought I wanted him to show me *āsanas*. He made me finish my *prasāda* and then told me to leave the camp. My apology did not have the slightest effect on him.

67 Gaṅgā Sāgar is a religious festival held in West Bengal about 100 km from Kolkata, at the southern end of the Ganges Delta (see Appendix 1, pp. 324ff.).

68 From the pictures he showed me, it was clear that Viśvot Giri embodied the role of a contemporary *fakīr*: he would lie on swords, hang himself with hooks on his back, etc. Doing these things, he said, amused the audience.

69 On the International Day of Yoga, see Chapter 7, pp. 307ff. On the Ambubācī Melā, see Appendix 1, pp. 322ff.

Photo 14 *Nāgā sādhus* performing *āsanas* in Kamakhya, 2017.
© 2024 Daniela Bevilacqua

in the *āśram* of the Jūnā *akhāṛā* located just above the temple, a group of *nāgā bābās* decided to please a crowd of journalists by demonstrating acrobatic *āsanas*, reinforced by the sounds of drums and cries of 'Har Har Mahādev'. It was almost as if they were competing for the photographers' attention, while those incapable of displaying demanding *āsanas* simply cheered the others on. This exhibition was ultimately particularly powerful due to the atmosphere created by the ash-covered *sādhus* chanting and at the same time playing (Photo 14).

A less ostentatious display of *āsanas* might occur when *sādhus* do them after performing *tapasyā* like *dhūnī tap*. At the 2019 Allahabad Kumbh Melā, I was fortunate enough to be acquainted with a group of *Terah bhāī tyāgīs* who were well versed in *āsanas* and in *tapasyās*. On attending their *dhūnī tap* practice, I noticed that many did a series of *āsanas* afterwards as a form of stretching.[70] Again, several onlookers stood to take pictures. (Photo 15).

In both these cases, it was interesting to note the ease with which postures were performed and the naturalness with which *sādhus* practised them: since *āsanas* are not a spiritual practice, they can become a form of

70 It is likely that, being aware that I was there to conduct research on yoga, many of them showed their *āsana* knowledge in order for it to be photographed. I collected several videos of these moments in a short documentary titled *Yogāsana* which can be found on YouTube (https://www.youtube.com/watch?v=k25uHiKj3Q4).

Photo 15 Rāmānandī *tyāgīs* doing *āsanas* for stretching after *dhūnī tap*, Allahabad Ardh Kumbh Melā, 2019.

entertainment as well as a form of stretching after the demanding effort of austerities.

Sādhus' understanding of *āsanas* is very much consistent and it seems that *āsanas* belong to a kind of knowledge shared by the majority of *sādhus*. It is clear that certain seated *āsanas* are fundamental to any spiritual practice. For those who engage in the yoga *sādhanā*, the other *āsanas*, despite their temporary use, are nevertheless an essential first step in meditative practice: learning to practise an *āsana* for a long time increases the practitioner's perseverance and intention, thus enabling an application of the same perseverance when following religious aims. Furthermore, these *āsanas* are necessary for the correct functioning of the body and to keep it healthy and stable. But other practices have similar functions too.

Kriyās

In a yogic ascetic context, the word *kriyā* (or sometimes *karma*) is a general term for techniques or practices aimed at achieving specific results.[71]

---

71 When associated with yoga, the word *kriyā* can have more specific meanings. In the *Bhagavadgītā*, for example, Kṛṣṇa describes *kriyāyoga* as the neutralisations of the outgoing breath and the incoming breath (offering the inhaled breath in the outgoing breath and offering the outgoing breath into the inhaled breath) in order to release the life force from the heart to bring it under control, a technique

However, unlike *āsanas*, *kriyās*, or at least some of them, represent a more concealed practice. When I asked Phalāhārī Bābā if he was teaching *kriyās* to the 'baby *sādhu*' practising *āsanas*, he specified: '*Kriyās* are for later [. . .] first *āsanas*, then, if he becomes a true *sādhu*, *kriyās*. Since *kriyās* are hidden (H., *gupt*), if you teach them to other people then they will become garbage, they will be ruined.'

This secret aspect of *kriyās* could link them to tantric practices. In fact, Govind Giri stated that 'Tantra and yoga are similar because both have secret *kriyās* and through these *kriyās* they produce a state that is yoga.' However, *sādhus* always try to distance themselves from tantric practices. Speaking of *kriyās*, Rām Priya Dās specified that she does not practise any tantric *kriyās*. I asked her whether all *kriyās* were tantric and she replied that they are not tantric *per se*, but they can be used by tantric practitioners. To emphasise her point she gave the example of a tantric master using *trāṭaka kriyā*.[72] According to her, *trāṭaka* is a practice of *haṭha* yoga but, when a tantric master uses it, he does so to impose his will on other people: 'By simply staring at someone, by simply moving his head, he will be able to control the breath of others', because a tantric master 'can impose his will on others'.[73]

As we saw in the previous chapter, some ascetics described *kriyās* as a distinctive feature of *haṭha* yoga. Dayānanda Purī identified six *kriyās* of *haṭha* yoga: *neti*, *dhautī*, *kuñjal*, *gaṇeś*, *khecarī* and *vajrolī*, and he associated these techniques with the purification of the body. In an online video,[74] Devrāhā Bābā, one of the greatest yogis of the 20th century, claims

which, as we have seen, was later associated with *haṭha* yoga. Patañjali, on the other hand, describes *kriyāyoga* as necessary for the distracted mind, also saying that *kriyāyoga* is asceticism, self-study and devotion to Īśvara, in order to cultivate *samādhi*.

72 In several haṭhayogic texts, starting from the *Haṭhapradīpikā*, *trāṭaka* is listed among the *ṣaṭkarmas*. According to Svātmārāma (2.32), the practice of *trāṭaka* consists of constantly staring at a very minute object while remaining concentrated, until tears fall.

73 According to Īśnāth, Tantra is a form of knowledge (*vidyā*), a science: anyone can study it, in the presence of an accomplished tantric guru (usually an experienced householder), practising *brahmacarya* when performing this *sādhanā*. Anyone, therefore, can become a tantric practitioner. A *sādhu* can follow a tantric practice, but he will have to get permission from the guru. Śyām Ānanda Nāth described the tantric path as a path for those who do not rely on faith in God but want to see him directly to also obtain specific powers through mantras and rituals.

74 YouTube: https://www.youtube.com/watch?v=7grzKLWgkpE (last accessed 23 March 2021). Given the importance of Devrāhā Bābā in the Hindu ascetic

that there are ten *kriyās*: *mahāmudrā*, *mahābandha*, *khecarī*, *uḍḍīyāna*, *mūlabandha* and *jālandharbandha*, *bhujakarni*, *viparītakaraṇī*, *vajrolī* and *śakticālana*. These two lists show how the term *kriyā* can be used to refer to cleansing techniques or in general to all those physical practices that are not *āsanas*—hence *ṣaṭkarmas*, *mudrās* or *bandhas*—and which, if properly mastered, lead the yogi to the full knowledge of his own body. According to Viśvot Giri, in fact, yogis are recognised by their ability to perform *kriyās*, not *āsanas*.

In the next sections I will discuss different *kriyās*, dividing them into *ṣaṭkarmas*, *mudrās* and *bandhas*. I will not describe all the techniques mentioned in textual sources because *sādhus* talked about them in a very general way: as I mentioned, some *kriyās* are considered a form of secret *yoga vidyā*.

On *ṣaṭkarmas*

> '*Ṣaṭkarmas* are very important because they give energy and enable the body to reach *ānanda*. But they must be performed correctly'.
>
> Lokeśvarānanda Giri

Ṣaṭkarmas are practices the main purpose of which is the purification of the body. The first text they are found in is the *Haṭhapradīpikā* (2.22–36), which mentions *dhautī*, *bastī*, *neti*, *trāṭaka*, *nauli* and *kapālabhāti*, in addition to *gajakaraṇī*.[75] These are described as preliminary cleansing techniques that remove impurities from the body, cure a variety of diseases and make one fit for *prāṇāyāma* practice. To note, in the *Haṭhapradīpikā* (2.21), these practices are recommended for those who do not have the three humours (*doṣas*) in equilibrium, an advice reminiscent of *sādhus*' approach to physical practices.

As with *āsanas*, later texts present a proliferation of *kriyās* but not all texts present the same techniques and in the same order. The *Haṭharatnāvali*

---

landscape and the fortunate availability of this video, I felt it important to use his words as part of this section.

75 Mallinson and Singleton (2017: 50) point out that this declaration of six (*ṣaṭ*) practices, while actually describing seven, could be evidence that the author was probably emulating other sets of six, such as brahmanical duties or, in the tantric traditions, the six 'rituals for curing diseases and controlling other people'. 'This may indicate', the two scholars continue, 'that Svātmārāma [. . .] wished to trump these established systems of six processes with a hathayogic variety'.

describes *aṣṭakarmas*, i.e. eight cleansing practices, including *cakrī karma*,[76] *gajakaraṇī* and some variations, while the *Gheraṇḍa Saṃhitā*, the yogic practices of which are said to make the practitioner's *ghaṭa* (earthen pot)[77] *śuddhi* (purified), teaches over 20 *kriyās* (see Birch 2018: 49).

In the ascetic context, *ṣaṭkarmas* are part of a shared health knowledge which gives *sādhus* knowledge of at least one or two practices to be used in case of need. Calling to mind Svātmārāma's concern, Rām Caraṇ Dās's idea of *ṣaṭkarmas* is that they can be practised only when necessary: for example, when there are problems with *kapha*, *pitta* and *vāta*.[78] He referred to these three *doṣas* as *vāyus* and explained that, when they are in balance in the body, the mind is also in balance. But, when one of them predominates, one has to resort to *kriyās* to rebalance them. Among the *kriyās*, he mentioned *vaman kriyā* (emesis) to cleanse the stomach, which is one of the *pañca-karma* of Ayurveda, but it is not usually listed among the haṭhayogic *kriyās*, except in the *Ṣaṭkarmasaṅgraha*, where these two forms of knowledge (Ayurvedic and yogic) are from time to time mixed.[79] The approaches of Rām Caraṇ Dās and the *Ṣaṭkarmasaṅgraha* raise the question of whether, as Birch noted (2018: 48–49), Ayurvedic practices actually influenced (*ṣaṭ*) *karmas*, despite the fact that the contexts in which they were practised differed completely: a yogi would have to practise them alone, while an Ayurvedic patient would need a doctor to receive treatment. However, one can imagine another context, in which, through individual experimentation, the cleansing practices would be adapted and then applied to others, achieving similar results with the help of herbs and oils.

Kriyās should usually be performed before the *āsana* practice, only if they are necessary and have been properly mastered. Cleansing techniques should be learnt from a guru who can guide the disciple through the various steps to avoid creating further problems for the body. However, there are also *sādhus*, Yogī Rudra Nāth for one, who argue that an accomplished yogi has no need of *ṣaṭkarma* since his body is always clean due to the control of the *cakras* and the use of other *kriyās*.

---

76 This is a practice for cleaning the anal canal by dilating the anal opening and rotating the finger inside until it is completely open.

77 *Ghaṭa* in the *Gheraṇḍa Saṃhitā* could be understood as the body of the practitioner who attains proper purification and accomplishment through the fire of yoga, i.e. the various yogic practices.

78 *Vāta* (wind), *pitta* (bile) and *kapha* (phlegm) are the three humours (*doṣas*).

79 According to Birch (2018: 49–56), the c. 18th-century *Ṣaṭkarmasaṅgraha* is likely the 'most ambitious' text on *ṣaṭkarma* as it incorporates Ayurvedic practices to 'build a repertoire of thirty-seven therapeutic techniques for Yoga practitioners'.

Neti, mūl-śuddhi, dhautī and *nauli*

Neti is the technique of cleaning the nasal passages, which consists of inserting a cotton thread into the nostril, pulling it out of the mouth and drawing it back and forth. However, it is also commonly done by substituting the thread with water (*jal neti*). While *jal neti* often consists of pouring water into one nostril and releasing it from the other, ascetics might also take water into both nostrils and release it from the mouth.[80] Jogī Bābā said that one can also swallow the water because the purpose of the practice is to clean the nose and throat. After that, it is necessary to practise *kapālabhāti* or *bhastrikā* (fast breathing; see below) to clean the airways and dry the water completely, otherwise it may cause problems.

Dhautī is a stomach-cleansing technique that involves swallowing a piece of cloth while holding one end, and then slowly pulling it out. Jogī Bābā uses an orange *luṅgī* as his cloth. He said that one has to start gradually by swallowing small pieces of cloth before ultimately using pieces of between five and ten metres. Again, he stressed that this practice should only be done when necessary.

I will discuss *kapālabhāti* in the *prāṇāyāma* section; here I will briefly touch on *trāṭaka*. As already mentioned, *trāṭaka* is a *kriyā* in which the individual stares at something, without blinking, bringing tears to the eyes. According to Jogī Bābā, it is a practice to develop eyesight; I wear glasses, and he suggested that I practise *trāṭaka* at least 20 minutes a day to cure my eyesight. All the same, the idea persists that, through this practice, a special power in the gaze may be developed, through which one is able to manipulate the minds of others.

Mūl-śuddhi or *gaṇeś-kriyā* is a practice of cleansing the intestines, activating the bowel movement by inserting, in a squatting position, an oily or wet finger into the anus and rotating it alternately clockwise and counter-clockwise while applying gentle pressure along the inner walls. According to him, this practice should be done in the morning after waking up, its benefit being that one will never fall prey to diseases such as piles.

80 This practice, described in the *Haṭhayogasaṃhitā* and *Gheraṇḍa Saṃhitā* as a variety of *kapālabhāti*, appears in the *Haṭhasaṅketacandrikā* (see Birch 2020b), a voluminous compendium on yoga written by Sundaradeva, a brahmin living in Varanasi in the 18th century, described there under the name *śaṅkhaprakṣālana*. As Birch (2020b) points out, this practice differs from the one that goes under the same name popularised by Svāmī Satyānanda in the Bihar School of Yoga. According to the Bihar School of Yoga's version, one drinks large quantities of hot salt water and then performs five *āsana*s that favour the excretion of water through the rectum and the cleansing of the intestine.

Photo 16 Jogī Bābā performing *naulī* in his *āśram*, Garh Jungle, 2018.

Jogī Bābā said that some people also do this with a pipe, in which case the practice is called *bastī*. Jogī Bābā said that, during *bastī*, not only water but also medicated oil or herbal decoctions are administered anally.[81] Jogī Bābā added that one can practise *bastī* alone only having mastered *nauli*.

Technically, *nauli* is a muscular cleansing of the internal organs by tensing the abdominal muscles to form a vertical column that can be rolled clockwise or counter-clockwise, exerting varying pressure on the organs. The practitioner stands with the feet about hip-width apart and the body slightly tilted forward (Photo 16).

Although this practice (like *āsanas*) can be used to attract and impress people, it is actually a fundamental *kriyā*. It is important for the abdominal muscles, as it provides a kind of massage. According to Jogī Bābā, who practises *nauli* not only in the morning but on any other possible occasion (i.e. when the stomach is completely empty), this technique 'is a way to make the engine of the body work properly [. . .] a way to stay powerful and to distribute energy in the body'. Furthermore, it is important because it is through the vacuum created by *nauli* that one performs *vajrolī mudrā*.

---

81 According to the *Haṭhapradīpikā* (2.27) during *bastī* the practitioner inserts a tube into the anus, adopts the *utkaṭāsana* pose to enable water to come up to the navel, then 'one should wash [the interior] by contracting [and relaxing after the tube is removed]'.

On *mudrās* and *bandhas*

'*Mudrās* are like *āsanas* but they are more special!'
Omānanda Giri

The word *mudrā* means 'seal' and is often associated with hand gestures.[82] The *mudrās* of *haṭha* yoga may instead refer to the seal created by the body as it assumes specific postures, and, together with *bandhas*, they block and manipulate vital energies. *Bandhas* are the locks through which the *vāyus* are blocked by the practitioner and forced into specific areas of the body. However, *mudrās* can also refer to 'face seals', with particular reference to the eyes acquiring a specific gaze.

As we saw in the previous chapter, *mudrās* and *bandhas* are the techniques that most characterise the *haṭha* method. In the *Amṛtasiddhi*, three *mudrās* appear: *mahāmudrā* (the great *mudrā*), *mahābandha* (the great lock) and *mahāvedha* (the great piercing). These three practices, with the addition of other techniques, are present in all later systems of *haṭha* yoga. In the *Dattātreyayogaśāstra* the yoga of Kapila consists of *mahāmudrā, mahābandha, mahāvedha, khecarī mudrā, jālandharbandha, uḍḍīyānabandha, mūlabandha,*[83] *viparītakaraṇī;*[84] *vajrolī, amarolī* and *sahajolī* are also mentioned. Some of these *mudrās* are present in other Śaiva works contemporary to the *Dattātreyayogaśāstra* and in texts that do not call their yoga *haṭha*,[85] namely the *Vivekamārtaṇḍa* and the *Gorakṣaśataka,* which also teaches *śakticālanīmudrā* (Birch 2020b: 454).

---

82 See Serbaeva 2013 for a general introduction on *mudrā* and the use of the word and the practice in different religious contexts.

83 *Jālandharbandha*: '[The yogi] should constrict the throat and firmly place the chin on the chest.' *Uḍḍīyānabandha*: 'With special effort [the yogi] should pull his navel upwards and push it downwards.' *Mūlabandha*: 'he should press his anus with his heel and forcefully contract his perineum over and over again, so that his breath goes upwards' (Mallinson and Singleton 2017: 241–242).

84 'On the first day the head should be down and the feet up for a short while' (Mallinson and Singleton 2017: 242). As understood from a reading of the *Vivekamārtaṇḍa*, inverting the body would stop the dripping of the nectar of immortality from the palate into the navel fire (Mallinson and Singleton 2017: 245).

85 Birch (2020b: 454) suggests that 'from the twelfth to the fifteenth century the practice of these particular *mudrās* was more widespread than the use of the term *haṭhayoga* for designating a system of praxis'. Clearly, even in the past, actual practices and their benefits were of greater value to practitioners than the use of theoretical labels to categorise them.

To these practices, Svātmārāma added *śāmbhavīmudrā*,[86] which was mentioned as long ago as the *Amanaska* (Birch 2020b: 456n16), while the *Haṭhayogasaṃhitā* mentions 25 *mudrās* (Birch 2020b: 460). Vernacular sources present lists of *mudrās* with other names and functions (such as *cācarī*, *bhūcarī*, *khecarī*, *agocarī*; see p. 157), mostly to aid concentration and meditation, but I did not find these names used among *sādhus*.

The presence of *mudrās* with the necessary *bandhas* is closely linked to the idea that there are vital 'fluids' in the body that need to be manipulated and preserved, especially the nectar of immortality. The *mudrās* of the *Amṛtasiddhi* and the *Dattātreyayogaśāstra*, for example, are practised to raise the *bindu* and prevent it from falling. In the *Gorakṣaśataka* and *Haṭhapradīpikā*, on the other hand, the *kuṇḍalinī* is raised through these *mudrās*. In the *Haṭhapradīpikā* it is also claimed that they overcome old age and eventually death, while in the *Gheraṇḍa Saṃhitā* their aim is to establish equilibrium (*sthiratā*) in the body.

With regard to the specific *mudrās* mentioned in textual sources, however, I did not hear *sādhus* talking about *mahāvedha* or *mahābandha*. The only exception was Jogī Bābā who—positioning his left heel under a testicle and grabbing his right big toe with his hands—demonstrated *mahāmudrā*. In this same position he also did *nauli*. He said that through this *mudrā* one preserves the *śakti* and directs it towards the *brahmarandhra*. He also described *śakticālinī mudrā* as producing energy. He showed me this practice a few times (Photo 17). Sitting in *siddhāsana*, he exhaled his breath completely, did *mūlabandha* and *uḍḍīyānabandha*, then completely lifted his back, supported by a rotational movement of the hips, which made him assume a kind of *bhadragorakṣāsana*.[87] With his arms straight by his side and his hands resting on his knees in *prāṇamudrā*,[88] he pulled his head upwards as he looked up.[89] According to Jogī Bābā, this practice produces

---

86 According to the *Haṭhapradīpikā* (4.36): 'Fixing the mind on an internal object and keeping the eyes open without winking, is called *śāmbhavī mudrā*.'

87 In this *āsana* the soles of the feet are together, the toes and the knees are on the ground, the anus is on the heels and the hands are on the knees.

88 In this hand *mudrā*, the thumb is on the last two fingers of the hand.

89 The *Gorakṣaśataka*, which is the first known text to mention this practice, describes another form of *śakticālinī* in which the practitioner, sitting in *padmāsana*, should 'spread out a cloth twelve fingers long and four fingers broad', wrap it around the tongue 'and hold it firmly with the thumbs and index fingers of both hands'. He 'should move it left and right over and over again, as much as he can' (Mallinson and Singleton 2017: 244).

Photo 17 Jogī Bābā performing *śakticālinī* in his *āśram*, Garh Jungle, 2018.

a prolonged feeling of *ānanda*, similar to that produced during intercourse, but without the loss of semen.[90]

However, according to Satyā Vedānanda,[91] *śakticālinī* is performed by sitting in *padmāsana*, pulling the body upwards through a kind of jump and then falling, bumping the buttocks. This form seems very similar to the practice of *mahāvedha* described in the *Dattātreyayogaśāstra* (136): 'while in the great lock, [the yogin] should gently tap his buttocks on the ground. This is the great piercing (*mahāvedha*)' (Mallinson 2013a).[92]

Clearly, there are different understandings of *mudrās* among contemporary ascetics. Yogī Rudra Nāth mentioned *mudrās* for the hands, *mudrās* for the body, five *mudrās* for the *tattvas*, and then 64 *mudrās* for each Yoginī.

We have already seen the importance of hand *mudrās* among *tapasvīs*, and in the next chapter we will mention the importance of having a mantra associated with its specific *mudrā*. Here I want to focus on bodily *mudrās*

90 I will deal with inner *ānanda* in the next chapter (p. 264). However, here it is interesting to note that the *Haṭhapradīpikā* (3.99) speaks of *śakticāla* as a practice that stimulates the *vāyus* by channelling the *rajas* and *bindu* within the practitioner's body, transforming the body of a yogi into a divine body.

91 He said that the body is a *yantra*, the mouth is a mantra and these two together are *tantra*.

92 The practice described by Satyā Vedānanda did not seem so gentle, however, but resembled more the jumps of the Buddhist *trulkhor* practice (see Baker 2019).

because they are important for our discussion. In general, it seems that among ascetics *mudrās* are used to refer to a shape assumed by the body. Rām Avadhūt Dās said that, when the body is in specific and natural conditions, it assumes a *mudrā* by itself:

> Just as when you feel sleepy (*nidrā*), the body assumes *nidrā mudrā*. [. . .] When you start to feel tired, the body assumes a posture, or if you feel sad, the body assumes another posture. When we do a *mudrā*, it represents the condition of our body. But with *mudrās* we also release the influences of the atmosphere on the body, we control the substances in the body. That is why there are also *mudrās* such as *ākāś mudrā*, *vāyu mudrā*, *jal mudrā*. It is as if you get powers and let them go outside.

Rām Avadhūt Dās also mentioned hand *mudrās* and *mudrās* associated with the *tattvas*, but above all he emphasised the close connection between the shape the body takes and the ability to control the energies in it in order to balance them or use them as a source of power. A wrong shape, therefore, would not lead to the right results. For example, Sanjay Giri said that sitting with the knees raised, with the arms crossed or with the head resting on the hand, are not good *mudrās* because, through these, nothing will happen within the body.

According to Rām Caraṇ Dās, *mudrās* and *bandhas* are important to 'fix' what cannot be fixed with food or drink: they are useful for the harmony of the body, creating the right conditions for meditation. 'When you do *dhyāna*, all organs must be under control [. . .] with *mūlabandha* the breath rises[93] and helps in meditation because, when the *vāyus* are locked within the body and are united in one channel, then the mind follows.'

Important *mudrās* in the history of *haṭha*, and renowned among *sādhus*, are *vajrolī* and *khecarī*.

Vajrolī, *amarolī* and *sahajolī mudrās*

In order to properly evaluate the importance of these three *mudrās*, some further examination is necessary of the role of semen in haṭhayogic and tantric contexts. Here, semen is seen as 'the raw material and fuel of every psychochemical transformation the yogin, alchemist, or tantric practitioner undergoes, transformations through which a new, superhuman and immortal body is 'conceived' out of the husk of the mortal, conditioned, biological body' (White 1996: 27).

---

93 As we will see in the next chapter (p. 262), the practice of *mūlabandha* is also associated with the rising of *kuṇḍalinī*.

The retention and manipulation of the seed—which has a female counterpart, the *rajas*—is a source of power and energy that can lead to spiritual attainment. The first text to use the word *bindu* to refer to semen was the *Amṛtasiddhi*. In its closing section (36.6), *bindu* is called *amṛta*, the liquid that confers immortality.[94] Following Mallinson's and Szántó's critical edition (2021), I summarise what the text has to say about the elements of the body, as it is useful for the following discussion. The central channel is seen as a microcosmic equivalent of Mount Meru. At the top of the head is the moon which pours nectar. But there are two types of nectar: 'one flows downwards through the left channel, nourishing the body, the other through the central channel, causing procreation'. Therefore, there are two kinds of *bindu*: a lunar one, actually called *bindu*, which is situated at the top of the central channel; and a solar one, called *rajas*, which is at the base of the central channel. The sun moves upwards through the right channel, pervading the body, but it consumes the lunar excretion, burning the seven bodily constituents. The fire of the sun has 'its fuel' in food and makes the *bindu* flow, thus bringing health to the body. The fall of *bindu* causes death and must be preserved. The aim of the practitioner, therefore, is to join the sun and the moon within the head. It is in this text that, for the first time, semen, breath and mind are all connected: by controlling one, the other two are controlled as well.[95]

Similar words were used by a female ascetic, Yogī Durgā Bhārtī, whom I met at the 2016 Ujjain Siṃhasth Melā. She claimed that both men and women have *amṛta* that is wasted during sexual relationships. This *amṛta*, according to her, flows upwards through meditation and then down again via the heart and stomach: 'It goes up and then down in the *agni* (fire)'. A similar explanation was also given by Īśnāth, according to whom 'one must push this fluid up to where it belongs to [the skull and over it], and make his own body nourished by it'. He also said that this fluid has to pierce the *cakras*.

One of the practices for manipulating and controlling semen is *vajrolī* and its related *mudrās*, *amarolī* and *sahajolī*. In this practice, the individual, by creating a vacuum in the stomach, is able to draw liquids up into the urethra.[96] As we saw in Chapters 1 and 2, the retention and upward

94 Mallinson (2021) therefore proposes that its title could be translated as 'The Attainment of [mastery over] Semen'/The Attainment of Immortality', etc.

95 It is in tantric contexts that the connection between mind, breath and seminal fluid is examined (see Bharati 1965: 291; White 1996: 45).

96 According to Mallinson (2018a: 194n36), it is likely that *vajrolī mudrā* originally functioned as a tool to clean the bladder.

movement of the semen were mentioned in Vedic times in the description of the *ūrdhvaretā muni*, a label we also found in medieval sources.[97] However, what is to be sucked in, and in what context, is still a matter of debate.

The historical development of *vajrolī* is not clear; it cannot always be contextualised in a celibate ascetic milieu. According to Mallinson (2018a: 193), in the earliest textual teachings the main purpose of *vajrolī* is *bindudhāraṇa* during sexual intercourse. We can therefore imagine two possibilities: the practice originated in a celibate environment and was then adopted by tantric lineages which transformed it (in texts if not in reality) into a means of absorbing the combined products of sexual intercourse within the yogi's body (Mallinson 2018a: 200); or the practice originated in a tantric milieu and was then adopted and adapted in a celibate ascetic context.[98] What seems certain is that the description of *vajrolī mudrā* indirectly testifies to the presence of female practitioners. In *Dattātreyayogaśāstra* 156 it is said that women are able to achieve *siddhi* by means of *vajrolī*, and *Haṭhapradīpikā* 3.95 claims that women who are *yoginīs* use *vajrolī* to preserve their *rajas*. Sexual intercourse is explicitly mentioned in the description of *sahajolī*, which is to be practised after it (3.90). It could be that *vajrolī mudrā* was a method for householders to remain sexually active without losing the benefits of their yoga practice (Mallinson 2018a: 201).[99]

Jogapradīpakā 7.552, nevertheless, claims that *vajrolī mudrā* (here called *bījrūpaṇī mudrā* or *vīrajmudrā*, the 'semen *mudrā*') leads to *rāja* yoga, but here *rāja* yoga does not mean meditative practices: rather the possibility of enjoying women without discharging semen.

The *Jogapradīpakā* and the *Haṭhābhyāsapaddhati* give the most detailed explanations of this practice. As demonstrated by Birch and Singleton (2019: 28–31), the *Haṭhābhyāsapaddhati* describes preparatory practices for the *mudrā*: inserting 'stalks of distinct vine plants and probes made of various substances into the urethra as deep as ten finger-breadths for up

---

97 See for the example the references present in the Āraṇyakas (Malamoud 1977: 73). Another practice is *asidhārāvrata*, described by Shaman Hatley (2016) as 'the razor's edge observance', which involves a man lying next to a woman or having sexual intercourse with her, but not ejaculating. This practice has been attested since the early part of the 1st millennium. I was invited by a *sādhu* to participate in a similar practice.

98 On the development of tantric sexual practices, see the useful summary presented by Hatley (2016: 2–4 and bibliographic notes).

99 For example, the *Śiva Saṃhitā* teaches *vajrolī mudrā* in a householder context; it involves the drawing-up of a woman's *rajas* through the penis with the purpose of obtaining *bindu siddhi* and the rise of the *kuṇḍalinī*. See Mallinson 2018a: 191–192 for *vajrolī mudrā* and non-celibate context; Darmon 2016.

to three hours', while singing the names of God to endure the pain in the bladder; to then insert a 'stalk as deep as twenty-four finger breadths into the urethra'. The yogi then learns to move air in and out of the tube by contracting the lower abdominal muscles. 'The yogin begins by stimulating the movements of sex with his hips, moving them in space until he is close to ejaculation', then he inserts the pipe and 'draws air into the bladder to prevent the loss of semen'. He develops the ability to block the flow of semen, stopping and releasing the flow of urine and faeces. The *Jogapradīpakā* (5.552–561) explains that the practitioner must acquire the correct *āsana* and mastery of breath before starting this practice (which should initially be conducted in front of the guru), and must exercise the contraction and opening of the penis. During the practice of *vajrolī*, he should also practise *khecarī*.[100]

This practice demonstrates the importance given to the retention of the semen (*bindudhāraṇa* for men, *rajodhāraṇa* for women) as a source of power but also as a tool to defeat death. *Dattātreyayogaśāstra* 158–159b says that 'Semen preserved in this way truly overcomes death. Death [arises] through the fall of semen, life from its preservation' (Mallinson 2013a: 8). This sentence recalls Jogī Bābā's claim about *brahmacarya* quoted above (pp. 193f.). However, references to sexual practices were omitted in later texts: editors and translators often chose to leave out *vajrolī mudrā* because they considered it an obscene practice.[101]

It seems that both of these ways of performing *vajrolī*, alone or in pairs, are still present in the ascetics' understanding of *vajrolī* and related *mudrās*. Among the *sādhus* I met, very few claimed to be able to perform it: some had precise ideas about what this practice was; others were more uncertain or unaware;[102] others still were completely sceptical about its use. Yogī Śivanāth, for example, associated the practice with the sucking in of semen, but he questioned the use of this practice and its safety. He stated:

> If the sperm is out, how does it get back in? [. . .] If you pull it in, where does it go? And then, when the semen comes out, it comes into contact

---

100 I would like to thank Professor Mallinson for helping me with the translation of this section of the text.

101 Birch (2020b: 458n17) points out that the *Gheraṇḍa Saṃhitā* omits the teachings on *vajrolī*, redefining this *mudrā* as a handstand.

102 For example, Rām Caraṇ Dās, a *yogīrāj* well acquainted with yogic practices and *tapasyā*, said that *vajrolī* is another name for *vajrāsana*, because it makes the body like a diamond and because in this position it is possible to push with the heel the spot close to *kuṇḍalinī*.

with the outer *vāyu*, which can contain germs. So if you pull it in, you can create problems. It is not scientific; *sādhus* do it just to show off.

The possibility of 'showing off' is indeed a concern for those few gurus who can still practise *vajrolī*.[103] Jogī Bābā said that he taught *vajrolī mudrā* to a disciple who went on to become a *bhogī*, started having *celīs* (female disciples) and wasted all his practice. Garuḍ Dās, too, mentioned that he taught some disciples to practise *vajrolī mudrā*, but one began sucking flammable liquid into his urethra and expelling it to light candles, with the purpose of attracting and astonishing devotees.

Although textual sources do not go into details about what liquid should be aspirated,[104] ascetics claimed that the practice should be done with water, milk, oil, honey, ghee and mercury. According to Omānanda Giri, when a practitioner is able to suck mercury in, then he has attained a perfected body. He claimed to have reached the honey stage. According to him, the purpose of this *mudrā* is to control sexual energy.[105] When I asked him about *amarolī* and *sahajolī* he answered that *amarolī* is sucking urine with the penis, while *sahajolī* is the same practice of *vajrolī* but for women.

Garuḍ Dās claimed to be a master of *vajrolī mudrā*. He told me that, initially—as several texts and other ascetics suggest—he used to practise by inserting rubber pipe, but now he no longer needs it.[106] He confirmed to me that the practice is used to control and preserve semen and that it can be practised by men and women, and even by householders if they start practising when they are not too old. According to him, *vajrolī* is the practice of pulling up liquids, while *sahajolī* is the practice of releasing them. *Amarolī*, on the other hand, is the practice of sucking up another person's 'juice' (H., *rās*) (in this context, sexual fluids), thus when a man sucks up a woman's *rās*. This can happen even without her knowing it: she will lose her energy, which the man will acquire instead and redistribute around his own body.

103 According to Bhole Bābā, among one *lakh* of *sādhus*, only one will know how to do it properly.

104 Mallinson (2018a: 189n23) reports that there is only one text that does so: the *Bṛhatkhecarīprakāśa* (fol. 103v6), which prescribes drawing up milk and mercury; later references are from the 20th century.

105 Omānanda Giri said that *aśvini mudrā* is also good for controlling the sexual energy, because it deals with the contraction and expansion of the anus, and these contractions affect the penis and the vagina. This *mudrā*, to be done after defecating, would solve all diseases of the anus.

106 Mallinson (2018a: 186n14) reports that one book published in Jodhpur in 1937 claims that advanced practitioners should be able to practise *vajrolī* without a pipe, but the methods it describes are only for the absorption of *vāyu* and not liquids.

He added that *amarolī* can also be understood as the internal distribution of the semen in one's own body. According to Garuḍ Dās, *vajrolī* keeps the body healthy and prevents it from ageing. However, it does not lead to any spiritual knowledge.

A more detailed explanation of the practice and its contexts was given to me by Jogī Bābā. At the beginning of his training, he too used a pipe and sucked in milk.[107] According to him, it is fundamental to know how to do *nauli*,[108] because it is the abdominal vacuum created by *nauli* that allows the liquid to be sucked in, along with the *bindu* (*ūrdhvaretā*). By doing so, the semen is not lost and the *sādhu* can have an internal *ānanda* (pleasure), which, in fact, should not come from the body, since the body is 'nothing', but should come from within. The retention of *bindu* would allow this. Dharam Giri said that, after practising *vajrolī*, his guru could stay in a state of peace and deep calm for at least three hours.

According to Jogī Bābā, *vajrolī-amarolī* are practices for householders, too: for those couples who want to do a *sādhanā* together. However, he insists, one should only have one partner with whom to practise this '*gupt yog*' (secret yoga), and both man and woman must learn to do *vajrolī* correctly. This way, when they have intercourse, they do not lose their semen and maintain the effect of the *sādhanā*. Eventually, both gain *ānanda* and the control of the semen.[109] Since Jogī Bābā was married in the past, I asked him why he did not practise with his wife. He replied that he wanted to do his *tapasyā* alone and, moreover, she was not the right partner. He explained:

> J: Yesterday I told you I was married. I am a yogi, but she was not a *yoginī*. So, this yoga with her could not take place. The *bindu sādhanā* could not take place. For the *bindu sādhanā* you have to find the right woman.
>
> D: A *yoginī* . . . ?

107 Mallinson (2018a: 185) clarifies that, traditionally, yogis have used an elongated S-shaped pipe made of copper, silver or gold, rotating 180 degrees through the urethral sphincter.

108 Mallinson (2018a: 191) points out that there are in fact textual sources that do not mention *nauli*, without which it is impossible to draw liquids up into the body. Viśambhar Bhārtī also said that *vajrolī* has to be done with the three *bandhas*, otherwise it does not work.

109 Mallinson (2018a: 202) notices that the 17th-century *Yuktabhavadeva* (7.239) says that *vajrolī* was taught by Gorakhnāth 'for those householders who practise yoga but are devoted to the pleasure of sex because through it they obtain *brahmānanda*, the bliss of *brahman*'.

J: Yes, a *yoginī*. You need a *yoginī*, otherwise the other person will just get sick. If one is a yogi but the other is not a *yoginī*, it means she has no control and her body can catch fire. The one who controls it has the *darśan*, the power increases and pours out of him. It is difficult to explain, many things happen at the same time and one has to do many things at the same time. It is very difficult. You must practise a lot; it is not for everyone.

Jogī Bābā's explanation, similar to that of Garuḍ Dās, confirms that the practice can be done in pairs or alone, and that, while *vajrolī* is the sucking part, *amarolī* is the inner spreading part. While in the couple practice, it is a mixed product that is distributed; in the individual practice *rajas* and *bindu* belong to the same individual. They would flood the body, as mentioned by several early *haṭha* yoga texts.

It should not be ignored that, in some ascetic contexts, there are still *sādhus* who practise *vajrolī-amarolī* in pairs. According to Yogī Vilāsnāth, *vajrolī mudrā* was practised by Matsyendranāth, Nāgārjuna and Mallikarjuna with their *celīs*, and he stressed that the use of sex for spiritual goals developed from the Nāth *sampradāya*. He said it is a secret knowledge known in Tarapith and Kamakhya, two famous *śakta pīṭhas* in West Bengal, and it is still practised among Nāths. When I asked him for further explanation, he was a little suspicious and said that *vajrolī* is not something theoretical but a very practical knowledge, that it is not for everyone and that not everyone can succeed. According to him, disciples who have excessive ego, and the wrong attitude towards the meaning of the practice, see it as sex and not as a spiritual technique, and therefore do not succeed in this *sādhanā*.

This was confirmed by Śyām Ānanda Nāth, a follower of the Kaulamārga. He explained that the path of Devī (goddess) laid out by the Kaulamārga includes *pañca-makāra* practices.[110] Included in the *pañca-makāra* is *maithuna* (sexual intercourse). But this should not be perceived as sex, as it is a ritual pursued by a woman and a man through the repetition of mantras and the performance of other practices, such as the contracting of specific muscles and the control of contractions without wasting semen. This control is achieved by a man through *vajrolī* and *amarolī*. The latter should be performed in *gomukhāsana* so that the pressure in the testicles moves upwards and mixes with the *prāṇa* and the two channelise. *Sahajolī*

110 On *pañca-makara*, or the five 'Ms', see footnote 37 on p. 41. According to Śyām Ānanda Nāth, these five *m* are only the counterparts of the five elements. The tantric yogi uses them in rituals, so he is not affected by them. In fact, when he ingests them, he is actually making an oblation to the *kuṇḍalinī*. Even the *maithuna* is nothing more than a way of gaining control of the semen in order to control the mind.

is actually the union of the *liṅgam* (penis) and the *yoni* (vagina), so it is not a practice for celibate ascetics. According to him, this sexual practice is nothing more than a way to work on semen control and, as a consequence, to achieve control of the mind.

It seems that there are different understandings of *vajrolī*, *amarolī* and *sahajolī*. Some *sādhus* stressed that only *vajrolī* can be practised by an ascetic, as the others involve the presence of a female partner. Others identified the three *mudrās* as three steps of the same practice, while others still recognise only *vajrolī* and *amarolī*. In any case, it is clear that, whether performed in a household or an ascetic context, the main purpose of these practices is to control semen. The results or interpretations differ with regard to what this semen control produces. It is said it can cleanse the body and keep it healthy, even prolonging lifespan; or it can help maintain the state of *brahmacarya*, even avoiding 'wet dreams'.[111] It can be used to develop energies during the ritual and to develop control of the senses and mind. Eventually, it can aim to achieve an inner state of pleasure: *ānanda*.

Some of these results, however, are also achieved through *khecarī mudrā*.

Khecarī mudrā

Khecarī mudrā can be traced back to at least the 1st century CE, as its 'technique' is found in the Pali Canon and Sanskrit epics. The Pali Canon contains passages in which the Buddha presses the tongue against the palate to control hunger and the mind. Later Sanskrit texts more or less follow this description and link the practice to meditation.[112] In tantric texts, the practice is visualised in relation to the lunar *amṛta* stored in the head which, when accessed through the breath or *kuṇḍalinī*, pours into the body, nourishing and immortalising it (Mallinson 2007a: 42). In *haṭha* yoga texts, which often provide full descriptions of the practice, the tongue is inserted into the nasopharyngeal cavity, but it can lead to quite contrasting results: in some textual sources it floods the body with *amṛta*; in others, the *mudrā* actually aims to block the falling of *bindu*. Vernacular texts also mention it. For example, in *Gorakh Bānī* 133 we read (Djurdjevic and Singh 2019: 76):

> There are nine veins and seventy-two rooms.
> All *aṣṭaṅga* is a lie.

---

111 According to Darmon (2016: 232), practising *vajrolī* repetitiously with the pipe would desensitise an erogenous region that is close to the bladder mouth and is fundamental to ejaculation. When the region becomes desensitised, the practitioner is able to control the ejaculatory impulse.

112 For a comprehensive reconstruction of the practice in textual sources, see Mallinson 2007a.

> Use the *suṣumṇā* as the key and the lock.
> Reverse the tongue and touch the palate.

Among the *sādhus* I spoke to, many were familiar with the practice and gave explanations similar to those present in textual sources, although none suggested any connection to *bindu*, and some referred to it as the 'flooding of the body'. Several mentioned the lengthening of the tongue by using a cloth and pulling or cutting the frenulum.[113] According to Garuḍ Dās, the tongue should touch at least the tip of the nose in order to start practising the *mudrā* internally.

Garuḍ Dās explained *khecarī mudrā* emphasising its role as a seal: pushing the tongue towards the nose aims to create a seal that locks everything, mouth, ears and nose. This seal allows practitioners to have a feeling of the *amṛta* located at the back of the skull. His guru, the aforementioned Devrāhā Bābā, is supposed to have nourished himself by practising *khecarī mudrā*. The main aim of the practice, therefore, is to enable the yogi to create a healthy, sane, tranquil form (H., *svasth rūp*), to remain in *dhyāna* for a long time and thus achieve a stable *samādhi*. Obviously, simply lengthening the tongue will not produce the result.

Rām Avadhūt Dās, a disciple of Garuḍ Dās, offered me a further explanation about the link between *khecarī mudrā* and meditation, which seems to be the most common association, as is also evident from the texts.[114] He said that, to practise *dhyāna* correctly, one must take control of the breath. With *khecarī mudrā*, the breath is kept inward and moves inward: it cuts the connection with the external *vāyu*, and this would help *dhyāna* and *samādhi*. In fact, when the individual can properly perform *khecarī*, he is able to sit in his *āsana* for a long time without feeling any pain in the muscles.[115]

Omānanda Giri, too, connected the practice to meditation and *samādhi*. He recalled the story of Bhagvadānanda (his guru's guru-*bhāī*, guru brother) who was an expert in this practice. When he decided to leave his body, he gathered all his disciples and announced that he was about to go. Then he sat in *padmāsana*, performed *khecarī mudrā* and died, or, better, his body died.

Śyām Ānanda Nāth claimed that the production of *amṛta* during *khecarī mudrā* has also the purpose of gaining youth, while Jogī Bābā said that

---

113 *Haṭhapradīpikā* 5.37–48 describes the practice in detail.

114 Mallinson (2007b: 51) points out, for example, that in the *Haṭhapradīpikā* the *mudrā* is explained as both a physical practice as well as *rāja* yoga practice.

115 Even in the *Yogacintāmaṇi* of Śivānanda Sarasvatī (c. 1600 CE) *khecarī mudrā* is said to be useful to hold the *prāṇa* in the head (see Bouy 1994: 119).

khecarī brings *ānanda* through the body. Again, it seems that for some *sādhus* the *amṛta* is stored, while for others it circulates in the body.

According to Bhole Bābā the best practitioners of *khecarī mudrā* are the *monī sādhus* because the daily training of this *mudrā* should be three hours, and with a mouth firmly closed. Obviously, an ascetic who does not speak is less distracted in the practice of *khecarī* and will accomplish it faster. A *sādhu* met by Professor Mallinson claimed to practise *khecarī mudrā* two to three hours a day, and the *amṛta* he obtained was a kind of *naśā* (intoxication). Another said that the taste of *amṛta* cannot be described.[116]

Rāghavendra Dās associated the practice of *khecarī mudrā* with another form of *tapasyā*, one in which the *sādhu* is buried. He gave the example of Pilot Bābā, who is well known to have practised this *samādhi tapasyā* (see p. 302), and claimed that he could survive thanks to the practice of *khecarī*.

Yogī Śivanāth demonstrated some scepticism towards this practice. He told me the story of a Rāmānandī *sādhu* whom he had met and who had been doing the exercises for *khecarī mudrā* for many years. Because of this, his tongue had become so long that he could no longer put it in his mouth. He pointed out that, although the texts state that through this practice one gets the *amṛta* to kill death, he had never met anyone who had found *khecarī* really effective. He exclaimed: 'I met this Rāmānandī: he was able to pull up his tongue but when he became old, he died anyway. So, clearly he did not achieve anything.'

Prāṇāyāma

> 'Do you think that just breathing can change anything? We have been breathing since we were born. Other *kriyās* are necessary to bring balance in the five *vāyus*.'
>
> Monī Bābā (Bārphanī Bābā's disciple)

Yogī Śivanāth explained:

> *Prāṇāyāma* comes from *prāṇa* and *ayāma*. *Ayāma* means *niyantran* (control), the *prakriyā* (process) by which one controls the *prāṇa vāyu*. Therefore, the name of this technique is *prāṇāyāma*. *Prāṇa* is everything,

116 The *Gheraṇḍa Saṃhitā* (3.28) mentions the flavours of the liquid once it touches the tongue: 'At first the fluid on the tongue is salty and brackish then bitter and sharp, then like fresh butter, ghee, milk, curd, buttermilk, honey, grape juice, and nectar' (Mallinson 2004: 69).

while we have *prāṇa* the body is alive; as soon as the *prāṇa* leaves the body, death comes.

The earliest, though obscure, references to breath control practices are found in the *Atharva Veda* and in the *Jaiminīya Upaniṣad Brāhmaṇa*. The former prescribes joining two breaths to attain immortality, the latter to hold the breath while chanting the Gāyatrī mantra (Mallinson and Singleton 2017: 128). In the *Mahāsaccakasutta* the Buddha is described performing a strenuous non-breathing meditation that caused him great pain and distress. In effect, as we saw in Chapter 3, *prāṇāyāma* was considered a form of *tapasyā* and a purificatory act. The various meanings and uses of *prāṇāyāma* conflated in yoga textual sources and especially in *haṭha* yoga texts, which recognise the importance of breath control to such an extent that in the past it was the defining practice of physical yoga.

Patañjali's definition of *prāṇāyāma* outlined the technique that will later develop in various way. He claims (2.49) that *prāṇāyāma* is 'stopping the flow of inhalation and exhalation' while sitting in a comfortable posture, which allows one to obtain a mind capable of fixations (2.53). Later texts of *haṭha* yoga follow a similar idea. The *Dattātreyayogaśāstra*, for example, explains that the yogi should assume a stable posture, inhale through the left nostril, hold the breath as long as possible, and then exhale through the right nostril; then inhale through the right nostril, hold the breath again and exhale through the left. By repeating this practice 20 times, four times a day, the individual purifies the body's channels (Mallinson and Singleton 2017: 155–156). Other methods of inhalation and exhalation have evolved from this preliminary practice, some of which have been extolled for their physical benefits. However, as stressed by Mallinson and Singleton (2017: 134–135), unlike *āsana* and *mudrā* practices, there was no proliferation of *prāṇāyāma* techniques between the 16th and 19th centuries.[117]

In the contemporary ascetic world, *prāṇāyāma* practices can be divided between those that purify the body and support the health of the body and those that enhance *dhyāna*, *samādhi* and *kuṇḍalinī* awakening.[118] In both cases, the core of the practice is based on sequences of *pūraka* (inhaling), *kumbhaka* (retaining) and *recaka* (exhaling) through which the practitioner, who has already brought the body under control through *āsanas*, brings the *prāṇa* under control. A correct *prāṇāyāma* starts from a correct

117 Their number remained mostly fixed at eight: *sūrya-bhedana*, *ujjāyī*, *sītkara*, *śītalī*, *bhastrikā*, *bhrāmarī*, *mūrcchā* and *kevala*.

118 The use of breathing practices to 'quickly' purify the body is well known in Hindu religious contexts: before religious ceremonies, rituals, etc., the specialists often practise quick rounds of *prāṇāyāma* for this purpose and to set their mind.

seated posture with a straight back. A seated, straight posture is necessary because, as Garuḍ Dās said, 'If the back is not straight and the lower part of the belly does not push inwards, then the *prāṇa* does not flow correctly. When it moves properly, it reaches the *brahmarandhra*, and if you practise *dhyāna* correctly, you reach the vision of everything.'

When the winds flow correctly through the body, the concentration of the mind is facilitated: when the *prāṇa* is under control, the mind too can be taken under control. However, before reaching the mind, it is necessary to purify the channels of the body.

Prāṇāyāmas for balancing and 'investigating' the body

Since the body is a useful tool for the spiritual path, it is taken care of in the yoga *sādhanā*. In the previous sections we saw the role of *āsanas* and *kriyās* in purifying the body and rebalancing it; here we will describe the role that *prāṇāyāma* plays in this regard. Since the body is sustained by the movement of the *vāyus*, if the *vāyus* do not move correctly, the body becomes unbalanced and diseases arise. *Sādhus* believe that working on *vāyus* through *prāṇāyāma* helps to purify the *nāḍīs* (*nāḍī śodāna*) in the body. As a result, it restores balance and helps cure diseases. Given its health benefits, it is recommended that an ascetic should know some basic practices. For example, Svāmī Ātmānanda said that one should practise *kapālabhāti* by inhaling and exhaling very fast and concentrating the attention on the part of the body that needs to be purified. Speaking of *prāṇāyāmas*, Rām Avadhūt Dās referred to the *Gheraṇḍa Saṃhitā* and mentioned that *ṛṣi* Gheraṇḍa taught eight *prāṇāyāmas*,[119] but he also said that the number of *prāṇāyāmas* is greater because each *mahāṛṣi* (great *ṛṣi*) taught a different *prāṇāyāma*.

Ascetics learn *prāṇāyāmas* after mastering seated postures. Despite the presence of different *prāṇāyāmas*, it is not that an individual has to do them or know them all: they are understood as different paths to achieve the same goal, i.e. bringing the breath under control so that it becomes *sthambhit* (brought to a stop).

As in the case of *āsanas*, it cannot taken for granted that ascetics know the names of the different *prāṇāyāmas* or list those that are described in yoga manuals. *Sādhus* in fact know some practices that are not described in texts, at least not in those that I am aware of. Bhole Bābā, for example,

119 *Gheraṇḍa Saṃhitā* 5.46 describes *sahita*, *sūryabheda*, *ujjāyī*, *śītalī*, *bhastrikā*, *bhrāmarī*, *mūrcchā* and *kevalī*; however, as with other earlier texts, it calls them *kumbhakas* (see Mallinson 2004).

showed me a *prāṇāyāma* which he said is useful for balancing the area around the navel. In *siddhāsana*, he put his right little finger into his navel and, exhaling, bent down, trying to touch the thumb with his head. Then, inhaling, he returned to the starting position, with his back straight, and exhaled again.

Svāmī Ātmānanda showed a *prāṇāyāma* in which the practitioner closes his nose, eyes and ears with his fingers, then inhales through his mouth and does *jālandharbandha* with swollen cheeks. This position, according to him, should be held as long as possible, releasing the fingers, but not from the ears. This would cause the feeling of the *nāda* sound.

Some *sādhus* pay particular attention to their breath, considering it a source of information not only about their body but also their life. Kamal Giri was a great advocate of the 'understanding of the breath'. According to him, one should check the flow of the breath daily:

> Check from which nostril it passes through. Check, according to the time of the day, how your breath changes. Sometimes it passes from the left nostril, sometimes from the right. Usually the breath comes out of the left. When you wake up, you have to check which nostril the breath flows through the most. Accordingly, you place your foot on the floor. This tells you how the day will go. The day when you get up and recognise that the breath has changed, it means that some problem (H., *nukhsān*) is about to happen. If something is about to happen, the breath will flow from the right nostril. Thus, you can tell from your own body what is about to happen to you, something good or bad.

Interestingly, this practice is also found in textual sources. For example, the *Haṭhasaṅketacandrikā* mentions *svarodaya*, the 'prognostication by means of the breath' (see Birch 2018: 125); the *Pavanavijayasvarodayabhāṣānibandha*, in Hindi (c. 16th century), pays homage to Mohandās who combined *svarodaya* and *haṭha* yoga.[120] Chapter 7 of the *Jogapradīpakā* deals with *kāla jñāna*, the knowledge of time, and it 'refers to the indication of death based on the observation of the Svara, that is free flow of air through a particular nostril' (Gharote 1999: 26). So, for example, if the right nostril is active for two days, one should assume that death is approaching, whereas if the right nostril flows uninterruptedly for five days and nights without any intervention of the left nostril, the duration of life is three years, after which death occur (Gharote 1999: 26).

---

120 See Chapter 4, p. 160.

Pūraka, *kumbhaka*, *recaka*, inducing *samādhi* and rising *kuṇḍalinī*

It seems that the main *prāṇāyāma* practice revolves around a breathing circle in which the various steps have to be increasingly protracted, especially the retention of the breath—the reasons why these practices are generally referred to as *kumbhaka*s in textual sources.

Pūraka-kumbhaka-recaka is the main and most important *prāṇāyāma* technique to perform. It consists of controlling the breath by regulating the time of inhalation (*pūraka*), retention (*kumbhaka*) and exhalation (*recaka*). The handling of this process depends on the capacity of the individual.[121] Usually, breath duration is calculated in *mātrā*s (units). *Sādhus* who indicated the duration of each step were fairly consistent with the texts: 16 seconds for *pūraka*, 64 for *kumbhaka* and 32 for *recaka*.[122] But this is only an exercise, since the main goal of the practice is to prolong *kumbhaka* as long as possible, until it becomes unintentional (*kevala*). Rām Caraṇ Dās explained the dynamics behind the practice:

> There are two types of *kumbhaka*. There is an external *kumbhaka* and an internal *kumbhaka*. During the external *kumbhaka*, the *prāṇa* is outside, and the exercise is to stop the body in a condition of no *prāṇa* inside. Then you count how long you can maintain this condition. And the counting slowly increases. By doing this, you improve. Through this *kumbhaka*, the body becomes light. That is why the body can rise from its *āsana*. Even with internal *kumbhaka* you can make the body light. It is like putting air into a balloon.[123] The same happens with the body: you can feel it, it becomes light. That is why it rises. I taught this to a girl who

---

121 Rām Caraṇ Dās pointed out that a lot depends on the age and health of the practitioner: a young person can do *kumbhaka prāṇāyāma* in the morning, and his breath will come out easily up to 16 fingers, whereas this is difficult for the elderly or sick.

122 See *Gheraṇḍa Saṃhitā* 5.49–53: 'The wise yogi should inhale through *Ida* for sixteen repetition [. . .] and hold his breath by means of *kumbhaka* for sixty-four repetitions [. . .] then exhale through the solar channel for thirty-two repetitions' (see Mallinson 2004: 101).

123 This could be associated with *plāvinī kumbhaka* of the *Haṭhapradīpikā* (2.70): 'With the stomach completely filled with a liberal quantity of air introduced (through the mouth and the oesophagus) a Yogī easily floats like a lotus leaf even on deepest of waters.' Even today, ascetics describe 'floating *bābā*s' able to cover long distances in holy rivers. Viśvot Giri said that he is able to lie on swords with his belly by completely filling the stomach with air.

was practising with Rām Priya Dās, and while doing *kumbhaka* her body levitated.[124]

Once in Jogī Bābā's *āśram*, I noticed that he was doing breath retention in *siddhāsana*, adjusting his body a lot. I waited for him to finish and asked:

D: What is this *prāṇāyāma* Bābā jī?

J: *Sūrya bhedī prāṇāyāma.*

D: So you have to exhale all the *prāṇa* . . . ?

J: Yes.

D: Then, you move the body to fill all the parts?

J: Yes, and then you breathe out.

D: How long, Bābā jī, should one hold the breath?

J: For as long as one can. One can count two *mālās*, three *mālās*.[125]

D: First from one nostril then from the other. And with this *prāṇāyāma* . . .

J: Now I have become very hot!

D: So, it's like you've increased your *tapas*?

J: Yes, it opens up completely. This is very good when it is cold. [. . .] If you keep doing it, *kevala prāṇāyāma* occurs. In the beginning it can be dangerous. One has to start very slowly. Then, once you have acquired the practice, you can even hold a one-hour *kumbhaka*! [. . .] *Kevala prāṇāyāma* is an automatic *kumbhaka*. If it remains stable, then [it unifies] *iḍā*, *piṅgalā*, *suṣumṇā*! If you do it two, three times, you can get *samādhi*.

D: But it is not that simple, is it, Bābā jī?

J: Yes, it is not simple. You have to do *tapasyā*.

Kevala prāṇāyāma or *kevala kumbhaka* is actually the last stage of the *kumbhaka* practice: then the individual is able to hold the breath as long as he wants.[126] Clearly, the process of holding the breath is neither easy nor quick. Rām Caraṇ Dās claimed that at the beginning of his practice he used to check the length of his exhalations through a *yantra* (a diagram usually associated with a particular deity, a mantra or a ritual). Although he did

124 Svāmī Ātmānanda also said that with a proper use of *prāṇa* an individual can levitate: 'It is not magic, it is practice and physics: if you try and try again, you become able to fill your belly like a balloon and this makes you levitate.'

125 Jogī Bābā refers here to the time it takes to complete one round of mantra repetition using the beads of a *mālā*.

126 See for example *Haṭhapradīpikā* 2.74, which says: 'The person who can by Kevalakumbhaka hold breath, as and when he wishes, is a capable Yogī. Verily, he (who has mastered it) attains the state of Rājayoga.'

not explain the details of how this worked, he mentioned that through the use of the *yantra* he could chart his progress, slowly decreasing his breath until it was completely internalised. According to him, when the *prāṇa* is not exhaled, it goes in the *trikuṭī* (the space between the eyebrows) and this would lead to *samādhi*, because 'When you internalise your breath, your vision also becomes an inner vision and this allows you to visualise God within you.'

Rām Caraṇ Dās told me the story of a *mahātmā* who lived many centuries retaining his breath. He was alive during the war narrated in the *Rāmāyaṇa*. In order to avoid seeing the war, he decided to sit in *samādhi* and wait for its end, and then get the *darśan* of Rām. He was discovered by accident during the British Raj. Someone found his body in *samādhi* and, thanks to the smell of sandalwood, revived him. He asked if they were still living in the reign of Rām. Receiving the answer that *Kali yuga* (the last and most corrupt of the four Indian eras) was by then under way, he realised that he had waited too long.[127] This story brings us to another aim of breath retention: to increase lifespan.

The number of breaths in a life is said to be fixed so, when someone increases the time between breaths, he prolongs his life. Prolonging life would not only be a step towards immortality but would also give the ascetic the opportunity, if necessary, to complete his spiritual journey during his lifetime, having more time to achieve results such as burning off all individual *karma* or raising *kuṇḍalinī*.

In fact, the retention and control of the breath is also associated with the raising of *kuṇḍalinī*. *Kuṇḍalinī* is often called *prāṇa-śakti*. Therefore, *kuṇḍalinī* can be understood as a personification or visualisation of *prāṇa* and, indeed, both are supposed to rise. Whether the *prāṇa* is channelised into the *suṣumṇā* or whether the *kuṇḍalinī* is channelised and pierces the *cakras*, in the end they both represent the same thing: an 'energy' that is pushed upwards.[128] For several *sādhus* the awakening of *kuṇḍalinī* through

---

127 Rām Caraṇ Dās said that this event happened in Hyderabad, but a similar story is told in Varanasi. It is said that in the Śiva temple close to Maṇikarṇikā, which had slipped into the River Ganges, engineers who were digging to determine the cause of the temple's instability found a yogi seated in an underground cavern. 'Awakened from his meditation, the yogi was shocked to discover that the golden era of King Rāma and Queen Sītā of Ayodhyā had long passed away and that the Kali Age had arrived. He leapt up from his long-held seat, plunged into the Ganges and disappeared' (Eck 1982).

128 We must add *bindu* to *kuṇḍalinī* and *prāṇa* since, as we saw in the *vajrolī* section, *bindu* is also meant to be pushed up.

prāṇāyāma is actually the main yoga practice. According to Yogī Santoś Nāth, it is only through *prāṇāyāma* that one can awake and raise *kuṇḍalinī*. This would ascend from the back to the top of the head, and then descend from the front. But how can *prāṇāyāma* stimulate *kuṇḍalinī*? According to Rām Caraṇ Dās:

> In the lower part of the *nāḍīs*, *kuṇḍalinī* lies in a spot that is named differently depending on the person's experience. *Kuṇḍalinī* lies there, unconscious. Due to the waves produced by the *prāṇāyāma*, it becomes hot in there, so *kuṇḍalinī* needs to cough and in doing so she opens her mouth and rises through the central *nāḍī* called *suṣumṇā*, *kharor* or *meru*.

As we will see in the next chapter, different practices were mentioned to increase this heat to awaken *kuṇḍalinī*: some argue that one should converge the *sūrya nāḍī* and *candra nāḍī* (*iḍā* and *piṅgalā*) breath into the *suṣumṇā*; others favour *kumbhaka* practices.

Pratyāhāra

> 'When you succeed in not falling into the desires created by the senses, then that is *pratyāhāra*.'
>
> Rām Avadhūt Dās

Pratyāhāra (withdrawal) is a crucial stage in the transition from outer to inner practices. Textual sources consistently associate *pratyāhāra* with the detachment of the senses from their objects, sometimes connected to breath retention (see *Dattātreyayogaśāstra* 93–96).[129] Interestingly, the *Vivekamārtaṇḍa*'s definition compares it to a tortoise withdrawing its limbs, a metaphor that Garuḍ Dās used to describe *samādhi* as *tapasyā*.

In the contemporary ascetic world, *pratyāhāra* is described as a practice by which the individual learns to detach himself from the sensory world. Rām Avadhūt Dās said:

> *Prati* means 'against'; *āhāra* in general means 'food'. So *pratyāhāra* means against *āhāra*. There are five senses, and each sense is related to a form of *āhāra* [. . .] you have to stop the senses in order to direct your *śakti* within, turning off the external activities of the senses [. . .].'

129 In some textual sources, *pratyāhāra* is found among *prāṇāyāmas*, which is 'hardly surprising given the close association of the control of the breath with the control of the mind' (Mallinson and Singleton 2017: 284).

The control of the senses and, as a consequence, detachment from them, is a necessary condition for achieving results from yoga practice.

Īśnāth provided a useful explanation for understanding *pratyāhāra* and its connection to the inner steps of the yoga *sādhanā*. He said that, once the individual is able, through *yama* and *niyama*, to control his actions, behaviours, diet, senses; through *āsanas* to control his body, and through *prāṇāyāma* his breath, then he can begin to train his mind with the practice of *pratyāhāra*. This consists of managing and maintaining these different forms of control until the *sādhu* is able to sit and create an inner stillness that makes him unaware of his surroundings. For this reason, *pratyāhāra* has to be practised for as long as necessary. Only when stillness and sensorial isolation is achieved does *dhāraṇā* (concentration) really begin in the empty space created by *pratyāhāra*. In the words of Īśnāth:

> When these things are stable, what happens? Then you can have only one thought! This is the moment when *dhāraṇā* comes to you! Do you see? Then you can choose. Because now you have bliss! You are in balance. Everything is in balance within you. So at this moment, from that moment onwards, the practice of concentration begins.

Then the *antaraṅga* yoga can begin.

6
The Yoga *Sādhanā* (Internal Practices)

Only once the external stages have been perfected can the yoga *sādhanā* proceed through the internal ones: *dhāraṇā*, *dhyāna* and *samādhi*. These three practices are called *antaraṅga* yoga because, as Jogī Bābā said, 'Their *kriyā*s happen within the body', meaning that their actions, as well as their effects, are 'produced' within the body, and specifically at the mental level. Before addressing these practices, however, we will consider some general issues such as where to practise the internal steps of yoga, the role of mantras, and also that of cannabis—in order to clarify its use among ascetics. This will allow us to properly introduce the discussion on *dhāraṇā* and its relationship to *dhyāna*. We will see that *dhyāna* can be achieved through different practices and can lead to different results (such as the awakening of *kuṇḍalinī*, or the attainment of powers). Finally, we will deal with the topic of *samādhi*, also recalling the concepts of *karma* and *mokṣa*, as they are fundamental to framing the goals of the yoga *sādhanā* in the religious context of Hinduism.

Where to practise

'Śiva goes to those who are *ekānt.*'
Rāghavendra Dās

An apparently quite necessary prerequisite for practising the various steps of yoga is finding the right place. As long ago as the Vedic texts, hermits have been associated with secluded places, often in the jungle, where they can practise without being disturbed or distracted by others. Isolation, therefore, seems to be an indispensable condition for spiritual enhancement, and this also seems clear with reference to yogic texts. The *Haṭhapradīpikā* is clear about the ideal place to practise: an isolated hut, built in a place 'with plenty of food and free from upheaval' (1.12); which has 'a small door and is without cracks, holes and bumps. It is neither too high nor too low in extent and is thickly smeared with cow dung in the proper way', which is 'free from all annoyances, pleasing on the outside with a verandah, altar and well, surrounded by a wall' (1.13). This description, which is echoed in other Sanskrit texts such as the *Gheraṇḍa Saṃhitā* (5.5), applies to a practitioner who remains in his place in order to focus on the practice, almost as if he were shutting himself inside a small fortress. A similar approach is reported in the *Caurāśī Āsana* in which the author says: 'Only by practising *ekānt* (alone) can one obtain the fruits of yoga.'[1]

There is also material evidence to attest to yogis retreating to quiet places for their practices, namely the several 'hidden' places, the names of which today echo the stories of those who inhabited them. With Professor Mallinson and Dr Singleton, I visited several caves and huts known to have been used as shelters for practitioners. In Panhale Kaji, on the Konkan coast between Mumbai and Goa, we visited 29 rock-cut caves, probably used from the 6th century CE onwards, first by Buddhist monks and then by Śaiva ascetics. They reveal rooms of various sizes, often with a single window and a bed and pillow also carved into the rock (see Deshpande 1986; Mallinson 2019). Similar places can be found all over India. For example, Guru Śekar on Mount Abu in Rajasthan, is the so-called 'Pitch of the guru', one of several caves on Mount Abu dedicated to isolation and asceticism[2] (Photo 18).

1 My translation from a 1911 edition (Brahmacārī Śrīnṛsiṃhaśarmā 1911: 8–9).

2 The *Gheraṇḍa Saṃhitā* (5.3–4) advises the practitioner to avoid remote areas and wilderness because 'a remote area is not secure', and in the 'wilderness there is no food' (see Mallinson and Singleton 2017: 62).

Photo 18 Siddha Śila, a cave that contains the footprint of a yogi, Taranga Hill, 2017.

At Taranga Hill, in Gujarat, a whole area is to be found filled with massive boulders and hidden paths leading to caves or ravines named after yogis: for example, a Siddha Śila, 'rock of the Siddha', and a Jogī kā Guphā, 'cave of the yogi'. Therefore, we can infer that the use of caves or isolated places is more than just a stereotypical aspect of a hermit, but actually constitutes a necessity. Several of these ancient caves are still inhabited by *sādhus*, and some places are considered *tapobhūmi*, 'soil of *tapas*', powerful places which have assimilated the spiritual power of those who practised there. Some caves have become important pilgrimage sites, preserving the memory (and often the *pādukā*, the footprint) of the famous gurus who once dwelt there. Such places are maintained by ascetics who continue the practice, keeping the tradition alive. Contemporary ascetics still value the role of the *guphā* (cave). Rām Caraṇ Dās explained:

> The cave is like the mother's womb. There you can practise *tapasyā* properly. Why? Because outside of it the air is thin: where there is wind, the mind wanders, following thoughts. In the cave, on the other hand, the air becomes heavy, it does not move. Then the mind can concentrate too, in *bhajan* and meditation.

This place must also be peaceful. As Sanjay Giri said: 'A yogi, a sage who wants to continue his [spiritual] quest needs a quiet place where he cannot be disturbed by the feelings and behaviour of others.'

An example of extreme seclusion is provided by Jogī Bābā, who decided to spend his *tapasyā* in the jungle and, having found an ancient tamarind tree with a hollow trunk, stayed in it for three years. This form of isolation is used particularly during meditative *anuṣṭhāna*.

As already mentioned, solitary retreat of this kind is undertaken only once the individual is ready for it. Moreover, not all practitioners retire to mountain caves or jungles: the cave could be a room built specifically for the practice in a monastery or *āśram*.[3]

The role of cannabis among ascetics

Contemporary *sādhus* are often associated with smoking: they are regularly photographed in a cloud of smoke emerging from a *cilam* (conical pipe). If one visits religious festivals, it is not unusual to see groups of *sādhus* gathered around a *dhūnī* concentrating on preparing or smoking a *cilam*. This has led to the misconception that smoking intoxicants, particularly cannabis, is a fundamental tool in the practice of ascetics. While this is not necessarily untrue, it is a partial truth which needs to be properly contextualised.

In India, the consumption of intoxicants for religious purposes has been attested since Vedic time. In the *Ṛg Veda* and *Atharva Veda* we find the word *bhāṅgā*, associated with a plant used to produce *soma*, a ritual drink that was supposed to confer immortality.[4] Although *bhāṅgā* recurs as an epithet for *soma*, this term is sometimes misinterpreted as cannabis (Dash 1980: 142). As demonstrated by Dominik Wujastyk (2002), synonyms for *bhāṅgā* were also used for other plants, while no reliable references to cannabis in pre-modern India are to be found before 1000 CE.[5] It is from the 10th century onwards that we see intoxicants (i.e. cannabis) exploding onto the scene: in tantric texts cannabis is prescribed as one drug (among others) for regulating the functioning of the mind, while Ayurvedic texts cite cannabis among drugs for maintaining positive health, useful for the prevention and cure of diseases. However, the bulk of the information on the plant and its properties comes from a work on alchemy, the *Ānandakanda*, written after the 13th century (Hellwig 2011: 464).

---

3 For example, in Revasā, a Rajasthani Rāmānandī centre supposedly established by Agradās (16th century), the most important sites are the tree under which Agradās used to meditate, his garden and his cave, a kind of basement where, according to tradition, Agradās had his *dhūnī*.

4 For a summary of *soma*, its alleged composition and its connection to similar traditions, see Clark 2017.

5 See Wujastyk 2002; Hellwig 2011.

In the context of yoga textual sources, *Yogasūtra* 4.1 refers to the possibility of using certain herbs (*oṣadhi*) to attain spiritual perfections (*siddhis*), although the nature of these herbs is not revealed and the author relates them to the practice of *rasāyana*.[6] Other texts, such as the fourth chapter of the *Khecarīvidyā*,[7] recognise the possibility of using drugs exclusively for *siddhis*. The *Khecarīvidyā* provides several recipes in which powders of leaves, fruits, milk, etc. are used to produce pills that are beneficial against illness and useful as a remedy for old age and death (Mallinson 2007a: 134). This seems to be the trend: when mentioned in yoga texts—albeit rarely—medicinal herbs, rather than intoxicants, are used to confer powers.[8]

Medieval vernacular texts evince a rather critical attitude towards the use of intoxicants. For example, *Gorakh Bānī* 208 proclaims (Djurdjevic and Singh 2019: 91):

> How could those who consume opium and eat *bhāṅg* achieve wisdom?
> The bile increases, the breath gets shorter:
> For these reasons, Gorakh does not eat *bhāṅg*.

And again in 213 (Djurdjevic and Singh: 92):

> Dry throat, suffering from hunger;
> One's body neglected, overcome by sleep;
> Speech without wisdom, restlessness
> For these reasons, Gorakh does not eat *bhāṅg*.[9]

It is clear from these verses that the intoxicant, *bhāṅg* (Hindi; S., *bhāṅgā*) is not smoked but eaten.

Bhāṅg nowadays is understood as a product of cannabis. The cannabis plant provides several products: from the dried leaves of a male and a pollinated female plant a powder called *bhāṅg* is obtained; from the dried buds of female plants, *gañjā*, which has a stronger narcotic effect than *bhāṅg*;

---

6 On *Yogasūtra* 4.1, see Maas 2017: 66–84. On *rasāyana*, see Chapter 7, pp. 287ff.

7 Mallinson (2007a: 13) suggests that this chapter has been likely 'appended to the *Khecarīvidyā*, perhaps on the model of the *Yogasūtra*'s fourth *pāda*, which mentions drugs.'

8 These recipes are mainly found in works that teach *rasāyana*, the medicine of elixir. On *rasāyana*, see the work of Dagmar Wujastyk (2015, 2021); Palit and Dasgupta 2009; Maas 2017.

9 Pinuccia Caracchi, who has worked extensively on Sants' songs and medieval compositions attributed to Rāmānanda, acknowledges that intoxicants are mentioned in Vaiṣṇava productions but in a metaphorical manner to refer to symbolic inebriation (personal communication, 19 May 2021).

while *caras* is the resin extracted from the flowering tops or new leaves of the cannabis plant.

The use of cannabis as a spiritual intoxicant was probably adopted following the example of Muslim ascetics, such as those of the Madāriyya known for their use of hashish (Sanderson 2003: 366n43). Given the absence of tobacco in India (which did not arrived until the early 17th century), cannabis was initially eaten or drunk in suspensions, but not smoked. As noted by Mallinson (2013c), there are no images of ascetics smoking cannabis before the 18th century.

Today, although cannabis use among ascetics is often justified as a religious means to 'meet God and receive his darśana' (Gross 1992: 367), this is not always the case. Contemporary *sādhus* admit that in *Kali yuga* no *sādhanā* can function properly, so smoking *cilam* is the only way to achieve spiritual results. Some *sādhus* have even joked that smoking should be thought of as *gañjā-yoga*. Furthermore, because *bhāṅg*, *caras* and *gañjā* are recognised as *prasāda* (consecrated food) from Śiva, smoking is also interpreted as a form of *pūjā* towards the deity.

In collective situations, such as religious festivals, or during a spiritual gathering (*satsaṅga*), the preparation and sharing of *cilam* becomes a ritual that encourages conversations on religious topics. Rām Caraṇ Dās, for example, recalled the *cilam* that his guru used to smoke: 'As big as an arm with five pipes', each one containing a different intoxicant: *gañjā*, tobacco, *caras*, opium and another plant that I could not identify.[10] It was hung above where the ascetics were sitting, so that they could take turns smoking: when one had finished his puff, he would throw the hanging *cilam* to another *sādhu* and so on.

Smoking is in fact also associated with relaxation and companionship. According to Īśnāth, the original word is not *gañjā* but '*gyān-jog*'. Since the 'Westerners' could not pronounce it, they started saying *gañjā*. *Gyān-jog* would mean to unite, bring people together (*jog*, i.e. yoga) to discuss knowledge (*gyān*). Therefore, smoking time is said to be an important

10 With regard to the most recent work of Matthew Clark (2017, 2019) on *soma* and other Indian intoxicants, I asked the author what this plant might be. It seemed, in fact, that Rām Caraṇ Dās enunciated a word similar to *saṅkhiyā*, which could imply arsenic trioxide. Clark has shown that the use of toxic metals and minerals was quite widespread in Ayurveda, alchemy and so on. They could be added in small amounts to give plants a 'boost'. Therefore, the fifth element of the five-armed *cilam* could be a small amount of arsenic added to tobacco (Clark, personal communication, 18 May 2021).

opportunity for *sādhus* to share their knowledge—but not when a *sādhu* has to do his *sādhanā*. Īśnāth was very clear in this regard, and said:

> You cannot bring drugs into yoga, because intoxication and yoga do not work at all. You cannot be stoned. If one is intoxicated and does *āsanas*, something may happen, maybe not immediately but later. When you are intoxicated you cannot control your mind, which is instead the main reason for yoga, and concentrate. How can you do that if your thoughts are somewhere and your body is somewhere else, and you cannot even control your tongue? Some people make this mistake: they take psychotropic drugs and then do yoga.

Many ascetics affirm that when a *sādhu* practises intensively and does spiritual retreat (*anuṣṭhāna*), he should avoid smoking or taking drugs because these substances spoil the practice. That is why there are *sādhus* who are completely against smoking.

Svāmī Ātmānanda emphasised that smoking *gañjā* prevents the practitioner from going beyond the physical level, because, if one needs to smoke to sustain the practice, it means that one is not independent, still has attachment and needs external substances. According to Garuḍ Dās, a real yogi does not smoke or even drink *chai* (tea).[11] For this reason, he turned away several disciples who had taken up smoking. Phalāhārī Bābā (despite being a smoker) said that not only cannabis but all forms of addiction should be avoided. Tobacco (*bīḍī*),[12] etc. ruin the *sādhanā* ('*barbād ho jaegā*!'): smoking before trying to practise *kumbhaka* cannot lead to anything good, he explained, because the smoke will enter the lungs, create pain, and the *kriyā* will be destroyed.

But, as always, a variety of attitudes are to be found, and so it is with regard to cannabis and *sādhanā*. It is very much tolerated in the case of those *tapasvīs* who use cannabis to relieve bodily pain. A few *sādhus* have also stated that smoking can help relax the mind and this can support the practice, so long as used in limited quantities. Jogī Bābā said that *gañjā* is like *prasāda* and that *ṛṣis* and *munis* used it. However, he also made it clear that only yogis and *munis* know how to smoke properly; others just become intoxicated. According to him, a yogi who smokes correctly first does *kumbhaka* and then exhales the smoke slowly. A similar idea was

---

11 However, according to those *sādhus* who smoke a lot, drinking *chai* helps clear the throat. As for *chai*, they are concerned not only about becoming addicted to it but also about the amount of sugar that is usually added to it.

12 *Bīḍī* are small hand-rolled cigarettes filled with tobacco and wrapped in *tendu* or *temburni* leaves.

articulated by Lokeśvarānanda Giri, a *nāgā* from West Bengal. He also claimed that the meaning of *gañjā* is *gyān-jog*, because it helps *gyān*:

> It is like if you want to climb a tree: obviously, if someone pushes you, you can climb faster. So, it helps. But there are specific times to smoke while doing *sādhanā*. The main purpose is to quiet the mind. If you have a restless (H., *cañcal*) mind you might have problems calming down and concentrating, so smoking might help.

When I told him that some *sādhus* were saying exactly the opposite, i.e. that it is better not to smoke while doing *sādhanā*, he replied: 'Just as there are many fingers in one hand, so there are many answers depending on who you talk to. So different ascetics will deal with it in different ways.' This again demonstrates the empirical approach used in the yoga *sādhanā*, and the fact that it is a personal path.

Unfortunately, an increasing number of *sādhus* are becoming addicted to cannabis (or other substances such as alcohol or heavy drugs, like heroin), and to intoxication in general, a fact recognised and criticised even by those *sādhus* who smoke daily.

Mantra

'Everything can happen, if the mantra is really *siddha*.'
Kamal Giri

To properly understand the value of mantras (sacred formulas) and their repetition, it is crucial to remember that sound-speech (*vāc*) and *brahman* form a unity in Indian religious and spiritual traditions. This unity is indicative of the transformative power of language and mantras, which, being associated with the cosmos, possess 'creativity, symbolic and salvific power' capable of modifying a person's consciousness (Olson 2015: 120).[13]

In Vedic and Hindu tantric traditions, sacred sounds have inspired cosmologies, theologies and soteriologies based on their phonemes. The mantras of the Vedic Saṃhitās were chanted during sacrificial fire offering, while the tantric tradition produced a new set of mantras, from *bīja* (seed) mantras to *mālāmantras*, 'garland' formulas of 20 or more syllables, often uninterpretable, which embodied tantric deities. A main distinction,

13 Feuerstein (2003) states that, likely, mantras were originally used to avert undesirable events and to attract desirable ones—a still predominant use of mantras—and they were employed in 'spiritual contexts as instruments of empowerment, where they aid the aspirant's search for identification with the transcendental Reality'.

in fact, can be made between Vedic and tantric mantras, although a number of Vedic mantras have been reincorporated into Tantras in the course of time (Padoux 1989: 299). In general, we can say that mantras were and are used for worldly and soteriological aims.[14]

As both in the past and in the present, the 'meaning' of a mantra is fully realised in the specific ritual context in which it is used. This meaning—which may not appear in a verbal or phonetic sequence and its function may not be one of those associated with languages (informative, constative, communicative)—is related to a direct action, usually ritual, psychological or mystical (Padoux 1989: 300). Mantras are uttered for a purpose, to create an effect, which is why they are deemed effective. Thus, they can be understood as religious instruments or procedures, subordinated to ritual action or a yogic practice (Padoux 1989: 296).

Considering the relationship between mantra and yoga from a historical perspective, it seems that, in its earliest formulation, yoga was not associated with the practice of mantra repetition. For example, the *Mahābhārata* makes a distinction between the yogi and the mantra reciter (*jāpaka*), despite their having identical aims, while the *Bhagavadgītā* does not mention mantra in relation to yoga (Mallinson and Singleton 2017: 259–260). Moreover, while in the tantric Mantramārga, mantras were of paramount importance, *haṭha* yoga texts ignore or dismiss the practice of mantra repetition. In fact, *mantra* yoga is presented as the lowest in a hierarchy of four yogas.[15] The detachment from mantra practices probably depended on the idea, still present, of a connection between mantra, Tantra and magic, a connection normally made with regard to medieval yogis. It is therefore likely that *haṭha* yoga texts wanted to distance themselves from the representation of yogis as magicians by limiting the importance given to mantras.[16]

In the contemporary ascetic world, mantras, whether sentences, words or syllables, are fundamental parts of specific rituals and religious contexts. If we consider their use among *sādhus*, it is clear that an ascetic may use different mantras in different situations. Therefore, it is best to clarify this

---

14 On mantras, see Alper 1989; Padoux 1990, 2011; Beck 1993; Olson 2015: 120–133.

15 There have been numerous classifications of yoga (*jñāna* yoga, *bhakti* yoga, *karma* yoga, etc.); however, in *haṭha* yoga texts, as mentioned in Chapter 4, there is a fourfold classification consisting of *mantra* yoga, *laya* yoga, *haṭha* yoga and *rāja* yoga.

16 Zubrzycki (2018: 38n41) gives several examples of magical spells and powers attributed to yogis. He also talks about 'the southern Mantravadis' who, in case of 'snake-bite wave a cock over the patient's body from the head towards the feet while reciting mantras' (Zubrzycki 2018: 190).

aspect to avoid thinking that all the mantras used by *sādhus* may be part of their yoga *sādhanā*.[17]

In the daily life of a *sādhu*, there are different mantras to be used for different purposes. Generally, it is the guru who teaches the different mantras that will accompany the disciple in his daily practices. The first mantra one receives is the *dīkṣā* mantra given by the guru on the day of the initiation. This is the one that is repeated daily, especially for the *jap* (see below). Then there are mantras associated with specific rituals and activities which take place during the day: basically every action an ascetic takes could be accompanied by its own specific mantra. So, as they drink water, eat, bathe in sacred rivers,[18] prepare a *mālā*, arrange an *āsana*,[19] etc., *sādhus* recite mantras. There are also mantras associated with specific *sādhanās*, even temporary ones, which aim to achieve specific results. For this reason, not only the role but also the goals of mantras can differ: purification; activation of deities and *cakras* within the body; development of *bhakti*; and, obviously, support of concentration and meditation.

In any case, each mantra, in order to be effective, must be made *siddha* (perfected) by the ascetic, and this is achieved through repetition: an ascetic is supposed to repeat it '*lakhs* of times', sitting for hours on end, every day or night. It is this continuous repetition that creates the power

17 During my fieldwork I was given several mantras to improve my work. Kamal Giri gave me the mantra of Sarasvatī, to improve my intellectual work. Jogī Bābā gave me a crystal *mālā* to help me write better and a Cāmuṇḍā mantra to sustain my energy. Vijay Giri gave me a mantra to concentrate better and to increase my memory. He also showed me the associated breathing to make it effective: he sat in *padmāsana*, sucked in air from the right nostril, bent his head a little so that the right nostril was up, then pulled his head up a little and bent to the left side inhaling the breath. His arms were straight, and the hands were in *śakti mudrā* or held one above the other, close to the belly, with the thumb pressing the fourth finger. He said that, when this posture and the breathing are *siddha*, then the *āsana* can lift. He told me that I had to repeat the mantra every day as soon as I woke up, as many times as possible, so as to internalise it. Then, after three months, if I practised correctly, he would give me another mantra, and then others to follow.

18 Using the examples of bathing in sacred rivers or going to the temple to ring the bell, Jvālā Purī pointed out how people often perform religious acts without knowing the associated mantras. To obtain the blessing of a sacred river, he explained, one has to recite a specific mantra about the sacred rivers of India. Likewise, mantras must also be recited when ringing a temple bell. According to him, deities consider mantras, not offerings: it is the mantra that awakens the deities and consequently prompts them to give blessings.

19 As explained by Yogī Rudra Nāth, an *āsana* (to be understood here as a place or object to sit on) must be purified by the power of the mantra before being used.

and vibration capable of reaching the object towards which the mantra is directed. As such, by repeating mantras or the names of deities, the practitioner is able to create a connection with them and make them manifest. Through vibration, a bridge is created between the repeater and the object of repetition. When this connection is stable, the repeater—though his efforts—gets what he asked for. This is partly due to the inherent powers of the mantra. However, it is important to remember that a true yogi can create his own mantra, which means that whatever he utters can become a mantra.

A perfected mantra can also be used for other people and not always for spiritual reasons. That is why, for example, Viśvot Giri drew a distinction between *nigamik* (i.e. Vedic) mantras, which will only work for certain people (e.g. a ritualist performing them for someone else), and *āgamik* (i.e. tantric) mantras, which work according to the wishes of the individual performing them and who can decide how to use them.[20] This leads us to consider the importance of the intention behind the use of a mantra: whether is it to help someone, to attack them, or on someone else's behalf. An experienced *sādhu* may recite a mantra to bless or help someone,[21] but there are also *sādhus* who can be paid for rituals involving specific mantras and *yantras* aimed against someone. Some mantras are seen as magic spells for worldly gains, some to conquer worldly powers, some to heal[22] but also to curse. This is why both Tantra and mantra are associated today with black magic.

It seems to be a fairly widespread idea among *sādhus* that mantras are not as powerful today as they were in the past. Although *sādhus* believe in the power of mantras, they also think that people today are not able to use

20 Śyām Ānanda Nāth had the same typology of two types of mantras: *rehnī* and *denī*—the first used to keep the fruits, the second to give them.

21 Once, when I was suffering a terrible headache (see pp. 286f.), Dayānanda Purī told me that perhaps someone had given me the evil eye. So, he applied a *tilaka* on my forehead, made a dot with the *vibhūti* and then, using a peacock feather and applying full concentration, he recited the Bhairava mantra against the evil eye—after which he gave me some *vibhūti* to eat. Another time, Yogī Alone Nāth did the same but in a more elaborate way: he made me sit near his *dhūnī* while he recited the Bhairava mantra and placed *vibhūti* on my forehead, earlobes and throat. With the feather stick he beat both my arms and my back. Finally, he made me eat ash and used his hand to beat me hard on my back.

22 Bhole Bābā said that he often fell ill as a child so his parents took him to a *sādhu* who, through *vibhūti* and mantras, was able to cure him. In this way he became particularly attached to mantra, *vibhūti*, Bhagvān and *sādhus* in general, which is why he decided to become a renouncer.

them as the *ṛṣis* did: once they literally made things fly with their mantras but few people today really know how to use them and understand their powers. According to Śyām Ānanda Nāth, in this *Kali yuga* not only are mantras less effective but also fewer gurus know how to unlock them. In fact, referring to tantric mantras, he explains that a mantra usually requires another mantra in order to activate it: an expedient to prevent them from being accessible to everyone. For this reason, a guru who knows how to unlock mantras is indispensable. By contrast, he concluded, a guru who is unaware of this can only offer the wrong teachings and people can only get the wrong results.

The most indispensable and powerful mantra is the *oṃ*. In the words of Kamal Giri: '*Oṃ* is a *bindu*, it is a zero, it is the Ādi Śakti, it is Brahmā, Viṣṇu, Maheś. If you want to make a mantra *siddha*, apply *oṃ*, then you will never be afraid [. . .] Some mantras become *siddha* with *jap*, others with the *oṃ*.' This sentence reveals several things to note about the '*oṃ* sound' (*oṃkāra*). On the one hand, as Gerety (2020: 506) points out, in Vedic texts *oṃ* and variants of the syllable are added to other mantras to increase their efficacy in performance, and this practice is 'so frequent that the syllable comes to characterise the acoustic environment of Vedic ritual performance'. On the other hand, this makes the *oṃ* represent the power of sound before and beyond language, a position summarised by the *Taittirīya Upaniṣad* (1.8) which proclaims that 'this whole world is OM' (Gerety 2020: 506).

Ascetics regard the *oṃ* as the '*mūl* mantra', the root mantra, the source of all sounds and words, powerful even in its silence. Yogī Śivanāth stressed the importance of the 'inner *oṃ*', when the sound is internalised into an inner vibration, as during the performance of the *bhrāmarī prāṇāyāma*.[23]

Some *sādhus* have emphasised its threefold nature of *a-u-m*.[24] Yogī Alone Nāth associated the threefold nature of *oṃ* with the purification of the body: 'a' cleanses from the tongue to the skull, 'u' cleanses the neck and

23 In *bhrāmarī prāṇāyāma* the practitioner closes the eyes and the ears with the fingers, then takes a breath and emits the *oṃ* sound but with the mouth closed, creating an inner vibration.

24 Gerety (2020: 506) shows that 'by 800 BCE, Vedic authors had analysed the sequence of constituent phonemes that make up OM's articulation, explaining the syllable as the euphonic combination of the phonemes a, u and m (Aitareya Brāhmaṇa 5.32), while the *Māṇḍūkya Upaniṣad* claims that the phonemes correspond to the three Vedas, the three worlds, the three states of consciousness, the past, present and future, and so on.' The scholar also points out that, '[t]he fame of the a-u-m analysis is such that many scholars and practitioners hold that "aum" is the original form of the sacred syllable. Yet the reverse is true: aum is derived from ancient phonemic analysis of OM.'

throat, and 'm' cleanses from the stomach to the anus. Mantras can indeed be used to purify the body. In fact, according to Yogī Rudra Nāth, the true yogi does not need practices like *ṣaṭkarmas* because he can purify his body through mantras.

The uses of mantra also include the 'activation' of *cakras*. In tantric traditions, *cakras* can be associated with *bīja* mantras and their related deities. They can be activated by meditation—focusing the practice on a specific deity and its *bīja* mantra—or through *nyāsa*. As explained by Rāghavendra Dās, within the body there are *devīs* and *devatās* who control its different parts. The practitioner must control the deities in order to acquire and activate their powers within the body, which he or she can do through the practice of *nyāsa*. We have already seen in Chapter 3 (p. 127) that, before *dhūnī tap*, Rāmānandī *tyāgīs* install deities in different parts of their bodies by uttering mantras. 'It is like a computer: you have to touch all the different buttons to feel something', said Dayānanda Purī speaking of *nyāsa*. He then recited a long mantra related to the heart:

> To awaken the heart, first you have to collect the energy of the *nyāsa* on your fingers by reciting this mantra '*Oṃ* [. . .]', so that you have a different energy, and then you put the five fingers on your heart! Or you can open the third eye by reciting another mantra '[. . .]'. This is *nyāsa*!

The practice of *nyāsa* is closely associated with the practice of hand *mudrās*. Several meditative practices include repeating mantras and placing the hands in specific *mudrās*. According to Taruṇ Bābā, *mudrās* and mantras are done together and their purpose is the same as *dhyāna*: to create in the mind a focus on the deity.

As we will see in the next sections, mantras can play a fundamental role within the inner practices of yoga, as it is believed that they can change the mental state of the person pronouncing them.

Dhāraṇā

Today, the practice of *dhāraṇā* is often forgotten: more often people speak of meditation and their attempts to meditate, rather than of the prior step that actually enables a meditative result. In the previous chapter we mentioned the role of *pratyāhāra* in preparing the individual for the inner practices of yoga. In fact, we can consider *pratyāhāra*, *dhāraṇā* and *dhyāna* as practices that represent each other's development: they concern the gradual detachment of the individual from the senses and mental faculties in order to cultivate an advanced ontological state. In the *samādhi* stage, this transcends all forms of intellectual and rational perception and leads to absolute absorption.

The word *dhāraṇā* can be translated as 'concentration' or 'fixation', therefore the activity of focusing the attention on something. Looking at textual sources, it seems that the content of *dhāraṇā*—that is, the 'point' on which one should fixate—changes according to religious contexts. A broad and general distinction can be made between the *dhāraṇā* of the *Yogasūtra*—i.e. locking the mind on a point,[25] such as a body part or an external object—and that of the tantric sources, where *dhāraṇā* includes a sequential visualisation of elements (*tattvas*), *cakras*, etc. In any case, it appears that the fixation is 'spatial': the practice aims to reduce the space of focus, so that it is eventually directed at something that occupies a single space, without considering anything around. This activity, if correctly pursued, then leads to meditation which, as we shall see, works on 'time'.

As in textual sources so in the ascetic world: *dhāraṇā* is a propaedeutic practice; since meditating is very difficult at first, one must exercise the mind to focus on one point, which is the exercise of concentration. Īśnāth described *dhāraṇā* as follows:

> Concentrate on one point, *ekāgratā*. It is like when you have to kill a bird with one shot: you have to practise shooting. Obviously, you will be able to kill the bird when you have acquired the skill of shooting correctly. Similarly, to make the mind *ekāgratā* you have to become proficient. Initially, you can concentrate on a part of your body, or on a form of Bhagvān.

So *dhāraṇā* is the training practice that enables the mind to concentrate on something specific. It is an important stage in *sādhus*' practice because, when the concentration is stable, one can enter the meditative stage, which is one of the main techniques (*upāya*) to achieve the spiritual path. Rām Avadhūt Dās gave a practical example:

> Suppose you want to meditate on the god Sun. Initially, you have to create an image of the sun, you have to constantly think of the sun. This is doing *dhāraṇā*. When you move forward, when the mind is completely focused, when your *pravṛtti* and *nivṛtti*[26] move in the same direction and only one thought appears, then you have achieved *dhyāna*.

---

25 *Yogasūtra* 3.1: 'Fixation is fastening the mind to [one] place' (Mallinson and Singleton 2017: 299).

26 As explained by Gross (1992: 221), '*Pravritti* is the tendency for physical and psychic energy to flow downward into multiplicity and form, and *pravritti-marga* (on a human level)' refers to the 'path of active involvement in mundane affairs while *nivritti* or *nivritti-marga* is the opposite: energy is withdrawn or reabsorbed from

From this very practical example, it seems clear that *dhāraṇā* is the practice not yet perfected, when the individual is learning to make the mind *ekāgratā* but can still be distracted by mental thoughts (not the senses). However, it is very difficult to draw a line or create boundaries between what is *dhāraṇā* and what is *dhyāna* because, even among *sādhus*, the term *dhyāna* can be commonly used to refer to those practices that lead to *dhyāna*, hence *dhāraṇā*.

Sādhus may undertake the practice of *dhāraṇā* by concentrating on different objects. When the individual applies a protracted concentration on one of them, then *dhyāna* is achieved. From a practical point of view, the ways of practising *dhāraṇā* and *dhyāna* are very similar, so at this point I will introduce *dhyāna*, taking it as the accomplishment of *dhāraṇā*.

Dhyāna

Dhyāna is the most important part of ascetics' yoga practice; it is one of the main religious practices of *sādhus* in general and the one that occupies most of their time. Mainly because, as explained by the *mahant* of Jūnā *akhāṛā* in Varanasi, 'It is *dhyāna* that gives way to *gyān*.' *Dhyāna* is a state in which the mind is calm and completely focused. *Gyān* refers here to those forms of knowledge that lead to the Absolute or God. The path to achieve it is a gradual one, and this means that there are different forms of meditations to train the mind until it remains in a state of prolonged concentration.

As Svāmī Ātmānanda claimed, *dhyāna* should arise on its own. According to Rām Caraṇ Dās, to practise *dhyāna* one must be in a pleasant place with a good atmosphere, because if there are people quarrelling 'one can worship, but not meditate!' As mentioned, in practising *dhyāna* the location is important because of the part it can play in facilitating the mind's entry into deep meditative states.[27] Certain places are particularly conducive—for example, the banks of the Ganges river—and, in general, places known to have been used by ascetics in the past are considered particularly propitious (*tapobhūmi*) for successful practice.

The practice of *dhyāna* must be done according to appropriate rules and timing: by complying with these, the individual becomes sattvic and his mind becomes powerful. The time taken for the practice can vary: from 30

---

the objective, illusory world and directed back to its source in God.' Therefore, *pravṛtti* is the creative process, and *nivṛtti* is the dissolution process.

27 Some Vaiṣṇava *sādhus* wear long dangling earrings which they can be inserted into their ears during the practice to improve the sense of isolation.

minutes to many hours a day. Basically, the practice lasts 'Until you have the desire to sit and concentrate on God,' as said Rāghavendra Giri. According to Omānanda Giri, sunrise and sunset are the best times to practise because there is a balance between the sun and the moon: the atmosphere is balanced and this favours practise. Several *sādhus* practise *dhyāna* both in the morning and in the evening.

As mentioned in the previous chapter, performing *dhyāna* correctly necessitates a seated posture. The *āsana* may vary: several *sādhus* have mentioned *padmāsana*, *sukhāsana* and *siddhāsana*, while Svāmī Ātmānanda found *paścimottānāsana* a good meditative posture because it automatically reduces breathing. The general rule is to use the posture the practitioner is most comfortable with, so that it can be maintained for an extended period of time.

On asking Rām Caraṇ Dās the reason behind using a seated *āsana* to practise meditation, he replied: 'When you sit on a chair the ligaments push down and the movement of the *vāyus* is restricted: they cannot be pushed upwards. This does not happen if you sit cross-legged, with the muscles supporting your back.' He said that one can indeed use the word *āsana* to apply to sitting on a chair; however, that will not work for meditation. On a chair, he added, it would be difficult to perform *mudrās* or *bandhas*. Many people today, he opined, think they are meditating when they are actually in *tandrā*—lassitude, drowsiness: they think they are in a meditative state when it is just numbness. *Dhyāna* can only arise, he said, through proper control of the body and the breath.

However, simply sitting and trying to concentrate is not the same as actually being able to meditate. According to Yogī Sumit Nāth:

> One is in *dhyāna* when there is an inner feeling of constant awareness. When one realises this level of awareness, one sees the body only as a container for the soul. One realises that the true reality is something else, not what appears to our eyes.

Eventually, he said, the individual does not meditate only when he is seated: his mind is always concentrated. When the individual is able to do this, he becomes completely detached. How, then, to achieve this condition? The answers may differ.

According to Rām Priya Dās, one reaches this condition by meditating and using the breathing associated with the *iṣṭa devatā* mantra. She claimed that it takes three years, seven months and 3 days to achieve *dhyāna*. This time should be understood as the time to perfect the practice itself. Vijay Giri told me that one should practice *dhyāna* by reciting a mantra several hours a day, morning and evening, and this would lead in three months to a vision of God. He had these visions three times, and thus considers himself quite accomplished.

Garuḍ Dās confirmed the possibility of achieving results in a short time if one practises seriously for one or two months for at least five hours a day. Initially, he said, the practitioner should meditate on the *nāḍī* or the *tattva* 'to find them'. This produces a profound knowledge of the body, one of the forms of *jñāna* that can result from practicing *dhyāna*. This form of meditation can be for anyone, and I was able to verify this during the 2016 Siṃhasth Melā in Ujjain, when Garuḍ Dās held a yoga camp (H., *śivir*) to teach his lay disciples how to practise *dhyāna*. He advocated teaching meditative techniques to lay people to help them acquire correct knowledge useful not only for the later stages of their life but also for their present existence.

I attended a few of these classes alongside them. The lesson started at 4 am with a physical warm-up, taught by Garuḍ Dās's lay disciples, which consisted of a few jumps, a couple of simple *āsana*s and a couple of sun salutations. Then we sat in *siddhāsana* and did *anulom vilom* for 30 minutes, continuing with a slow *bhastrikā prāṇāyāma*. When we were starting to concentrate, he had us repeat four words—*som, maitrī, mudita, karuṇā*—[28] from Patañjali's *Yogaśāstra* (1.33) with the aim of internalising them. Meanwhile, we were to follow the movements of the *prāṇāyāma* in the abdomen and try to visualise its *nāḍī*s. Hands were placed one on top of the other under the abdomen. We did three sessions like this. During the practice, Garuḍ Dās would look at each of us in turn and give precise guidance. After such a practice, he would routinely spend two hours answering his followers' questions. A disciple asked what to do with the flow of thoughts, to which he replied that thoughts come and go and that only with practice

---

28 These words were used as mantras in order to internalise their meanings. *Som*, for *samvitam*, was taken from Patañjali 3.34 (*hrdaye citta-samvit*), which means that by concentrating on the heart one becomes aware of the mind creating union. Garuḍ Dās explained that *kūrma-nāḍyām sthairyam* (3.31) means gathering the senses under control like a turtle retracting its limbs. These two are to be supported by *maitrī, karuṇā, mudita*, which appear in the same *śloka* (1.33, *maitrī-karuṇā-muditopeksānām sukha-dukha-puṇyāpuṇya-visayānām bhāvanātaś citta-prasādanam*): one should be a friend even with one's enemies, said Garuḍ Dās, to be a friend with the universe. *Mudita*, to relate with *prasannatā*, is the feeling of non-violence even towards those who are violent, to achieve *karuṇā*: compassion towards all beings. These words would help the individual in developing those ethical qualities and attitudes suggested in the *yamas* and *niyamas*. Through benevolence, compassion and detachment from pleasures and deeds, one attains mental serenity.

and doing preparatory exercises can they be diminished until *dhyāna* is achieved. The true state of *dhyāna*, he said, is similar to a state of sleep because the mind does not feel what surrounds the body, but is nevertheless fully aware. According to him, *dhyāna* when fully accomplished does not leave the practitioner with a fixed image in the mind, but opens the mind with an awareness that completely floods the body:[29] the individual reaches the *brahmarandhra* and attains a vision of everything. That is why, he continued, one must not concentrate on the light in between the eyebrows: everything should become light (H., *prakāś*).

The technique of concentrating on the eyebrow is ancient, going back as far as the Upaniṣads. Concentration on various points of the body is, in fact, a well-known practice for inducing meditative states: the *Bhāṣya* of the *Yogasūtra* cites different parts of the body as a means of practising *dhāraṇā*. A similar expedient is used by *sādhus*.

Rāghavendra Dās's typology of *dhyāna* divided it into five, using a terminology reminiscent of the five *mudrās* mentioned in the *Jogapradīpakā*: *cac(a)rī*, *bhūc(a)rī*, *agoc(a)rī*, *unmanī* and *sanmukhi* (see p. 157). According to him, the individual can therefore exercise different forms of concentration/meditation by focusing on specific 'facial' *mudrās* (in *cac[a]rī*, for instance, the individual does *dhyāna* by looking at the tip of the nose). *Sanmukhi dhyāna* is an exception: in this case, according to Rāghavendra Dās, the individual must focus on the top of the head, the place whereby the *prāṇa* leaves the body.

Although there are different forms of meditation in which the practitioner focuses the attention on a specific 'object', in reality, *dhyāna* is practised by *sādhus* mostly by the repetition of a mantra. Ascetics, both Vaiṣṇava and Śaiva, also seem to call this practice *bhajan*—a term that usually refers to devotional chanting—especially when it focuses on the repetition of God's name, the practice of *jap*.

Jap

> 'Because the life of a *sādhu* is such that in the end there is only *jap*. And it is because of the *jap* that anything can happen.'
>
> Phalāhārī Bābā

---

29 We have already seen the image of the 'flooded' body in several early *haṭha* yoga texts and in the words of several *sādhus* who mention it as the result of various techniques.

Jap (S., *japa*) is one of those terms so imbued with meanings and practices that it is difficult to translate. In general, we can associate *jap* with recitation and repetition, mostly in a low voice. This form of repetition is attested to in Vedic literature. In the *Śrautasūtra* the word *japa* indicates a whispered prayer and, in general, the individual recitation of Vedic texts during *svādhyāya*; thus it can be interpreted as a sacrifice to which recitation is offered (Padoux 1987: 118). This repetition is a highly ritualised mobilisation of the powers of speech—but can also be repeated mentally—which requires the practitioner's complete attention on the repeated words, their role and purpose (Padoux 1987: 140).

Rām Caraṇ Dās's typology of *jap* yields four types: *vaikharī*, *madhyamā*, *paśyantī* and *paravānī*. *Vaikhāri* is pronounced aloud, so that everyone can hear it; *madhyamā* is whispered, so that the individual murmuring it can hear it but the others cannot. In *paśyantī jap* the sound passes from the nose to the throat, while *paravānī* occurs through the *nāḍīs* and requires the performance of special exercises.[30]

The internal repetition of the *jap* seems to be a widespread practice among various orders, especially among Vaiṣṇava *sādhus*. According to the *tyāgī* Phalāhārī Bābā, the life of a *sādhu* is such that 'He only has to do *jap* and give *āśirvād* (blessing). Then everything depends on God's grace.' *Jap* is the core of the Vaiṣṇavas' *sādhanā*. For example, Rām Priya Dās practised '*jap kā anuṣṭhāna*' for years: she used to sit for 10–12 hours, five hours in the morning and then in the evening, repeating her mantra. Her guru, Rām Caraṇ Dās, did the same: he would sit for up to 18 hours, in *siddhāsana*, doing *jap*.

Garuḍ Dās considered the practice of mantra-*jap* to be one of the simplest, but no less effective, paths: by doing *jap*, he said, one can lose oneself in *ānanda* and experience God. A Rāmānujī *sādhu* of the Dvārkādīś in Varanasi, Rām Svarūp Dās, claimed that:

> Those who do not practise *jog* [i.e. yoga] sitting in an *āsana* must repeat the name of Rām. By constantly repeating the name of Rām, their mind

30 These exercises invoke four different locations: mouth, ears, heart and *nāḍī*. This classification is well known in tantric sources, both Śaiva and Vaiṣṇava, and is associated with a four-stage speech pattern which corresponds to four levels of increasing subtlety of speech, language and word. As summarised by Feuerstein (2001), tantric groups propose a supreme speech (*parā-vāc*), which is sound as pure potentiality—subtle and interior (*nāda*); a visible speech (*paśyantī-vāc*), which is sound as mental image, prior to thought; intermediate speech (*madhyamā-vāc*), i.e. sound as thought, from which distinct audible sound arise; and eventually manifest speech (*vaikharī-vāc*), i.e. audible sound (*dhvani*).

> can still become *ekāgratā*, and they will reach a stage where the articulation of Rām's name will endure. At this point, whatever they do (eat, sleep, etc.) the name of Rām will remain in their mind. They will not do *haṭha* yoga, but they will repeat the name of Rām, which will become perfected (*siddha*).

The most often cited numbers of repetitions were 108 and 1,008, but *sādhus*—also attested to in the texts—often talk in terms of hundreds of thousands of repetitions.[31] Counting the *jap* can be done by means of a *mālā*, a necklace which is often protected by a small cotton sack (*gaumukhi*), leaving only the second and third fingers on the outside, which are not used.[32]

The materials that comprise the beads and thread of a *mālā* may differ depending on the religious affiliation of the *sādhus* (e.g. *rudrākṣa* for Śaivas and *tulsī* for Vaiṣṇavas), the *sādhanā* in question and its purpose. The *mālā* must be purified and sanctified. The number of beads may vary, but one is always larger than the others being the one that closes the two ends of the *mālā*. This is called the *meru* bead and should not be counted or crossed; instead, it should be turned over to begin a new round of repetitions. The thumb of the right hand counts the beads of the *mālā*, which rest on the ring finger.

The *jap* is not just a Vaiṣṇava practice: the *saṃnyāsī* Jvālā Purī claims that it is important for a *sādhu* to do *bhajan* (devotional singing), a word he uses as a synonym for *jap*. According to him, one should repeat God's name at least 2,100 times a day. He said that, when someone does this, he acquires a different approach to life, different feelings and begins to see everything in a new light, with new thoughts, hence improving every day.

In the words of Viśambhar Bhārtī:

> When the name of God and his *smaraṇa* (remembrance) are constantly in the mind of the devotee, then he has achieved the goal. Then he has reached the point where he desires nothing else and remains detached from all that belongs to the *saṃsāra*.

---

31 A *bābā* I met in Allahabad, Rājānanda Giri, devotes his *sādhanā* to *jap*: he repeats his mantra 13,000 times every day.

32 This practice is well evidenced in the temples of Hampi. Sculptures there show ascetics sitting with a *mālā* in their hand, sometimes supported by a T-shaped rod. The latter was called an *āsanī* by Gopāl Dās because it facilitates *jap*: it is a tool that allows an individual to support his arm and continue practising *jap* for hours. Padoux (1987: 131) also mentions the use of the phalanges of the fingers to count *jap* repetitions, a method generally used by Indians. This is usually done beginning with the ring finger (of the right hand), then the little finger and ending on the index finger, so as to count ten. The left hand can be used to count the tens.

While we can frame this attitude towards *jap* as coming from a *bhakti* context, there are other forms of inner repetition that may have more *sampradāyik* nuances. This is the case, for example, for the practice of *ajapājap*, as explained by Yogī Śivanāth.

> *Ajapājap* is related to the breath. When you exhale you say the word *ham* and when you inhale you say another word, *sa*. So, if you consider this, there is no need to do the *jap* because it happens automatically. Even in deep sleep, even in dreams, *ajapājap* continues to take place, even without your knowledge. Even in the waking state. So it means that from birth to death *ajapājap* goes on. This is why Gorakhnāth said: '*ajapā nām gāyatrī jogī nām mokṣa rahegī*'. For the *jogī*, this is a kind of silent *gāyatrī*; it is an important mantra that gives *mokṣa*, so one who follows this *sādhanā* gets *mokṣa* and does not accumulate sins.
>
> This *ajapājap* goes on for 24 hours. During this time, 21,600 breathing *kriyā*s occur, every day. This means that the *ajapā* is repeated 21,600 times.
>
> Gorakh said that there is no better *jap* than this, no better *tap* [*tapasyā*] than this. And there is no better knowledge than this, neither in the past nor in the future.
>
> This is the *jap* of the *jogī*; no one else follows this. In the Rāmānandī *sampradāya* they chant '*Jay Rām Jay Rām, Jay Jay Rām, Sītā Rām, Sītā Rām*'. Different *sampradāya*s use different mantras, but the *ajapājap* is part of the *sādhanā* of the Nāth *sampradāya*. This mantra is unnamed. What is the meaning of this mantra? *Ajapā* means 'one who does not *jap* from the mouth'. It goes with the breath, this *ham-sa, ham-sa*. If you consider it in reverse, it is *sa-ham, so-ham*, which means 'I am that'.[33] And it means I am that *paramātman*, I am not this body, I am not this mind, I am that *paramātman*. This is its meaning. Advaita, *jīva* and *paramātman* are the same thing, there is no difference. It is only because of ignorance that the *jīvātman* forgets its true nature and thinks to be the body, the mind. To be a householder, a *saṃnyāsī*, or to be fat, or white . . . This is just ignorance. But when knowledge happens and the *jīva* recognises that *aham brahmāsmi*, I am that *brahman*, that is *ātman gyān* (the knowledge of the *ātman*). This is the meaning of the *ajapājap*.

Yogī Śivanāth also added that, according to a saying of Gorakhnāth, one who controls the mind and performs the *ajapājap*, controls the five senses and 'To him Bhagvān Śiva will do the *sevā*.' This highlights a difference in the goal of the practice. While Vaiṣṇava ascetics perform their *sādhanā* in search of God's grace while feeling 'inferior' to their God, Nāth Yogīs,

---

33 This is the Sanskrit '*so ham*' mantra, which means 'I am that', that is present in Upaniṣads, for instance the *Īśa Upaniṣad* (verse 16), and later texts.

although considering *bhakti* an essential part of their lives, approach God with a different attitude: they seek to become godlike themselves.

A practice that leads to a similar result is *nādānusandhāna*, a concentration on the (inner) sound, which leads to the spontaneous arising of different internal sounds marking the yogi's progress through the four stages of yoga practice. This is found in the *Haṭhapradīpikā* (4.65–4.102), but among *sādhus* it was mentioned and aptly described only by Yogī Śivanāth who, in fact, knows that text almost entirely by heart. Therefore we may wonder whether his knowledge denotes an actual and current practice among Nāths or rather demonstrates his scholarly preparation.

The awakening of *kuṇḍalinī*

Presented as a goddess or as a sleeping serpent, *kuṇḍalinī* can be imagined as a form of energy that resides in the body and which, in order to be properly 'harnessed', must be awakened. As we have seen, different sources propose different ways to produce such an awakening: visualisation, breath control, *mudrās*, etc. This awakening is often portrayed as the rising of *kuṇḍalinī* which, in its vertical ascent, pierces the *cakras* and causes a range of effects in practitioners.[34] However, we have seen that in the history of *haṭha* yoga, and yoga in general, this idea of rising energies has been associated not only with *kuṇḍalinī*, but also with *bindu* and *vāyus*, three elements that are supposed to ascend from a lower place. When I asked *sādhus* what actually rises, the answer was that the different concepts all simply symbolise the emergence of a power: that is, the *śakti*.[35] As Īśnāth said:

> Like Śiva, who has many names, you can use different names but it is the same thing. And it is all there, and it is situated in the body itself, in the *cakras* and their functioning. But you should understand how it is in its true form, then you will be able to realise the *kuṇḍalinī*, the *cakras* and their energy and how each *cakra* is connected to something else and

34 White (2003: 230) claims that the *Tantrasadbhāva Tantra* is the first text to mention the presence of an 'indwelling female serpent' called *kuṇḍalī* (ring-shaped), possibly dating as early as the 8th century CE. The earliest text documenting *kuṇḍalinī* and five *cakras* is the *Kubjikāmatatantra*. Here, *kuṇḍalinī* identifies Kubjikā, the crooked goddess who is perhaps a precursor of *kuṇḍalinī* (see Goudriaan and Schoterman 1988).

35 An early text, the *Netra Tantra*, presents six *cakras* but does not mention *kuṇḍalinī*. Other texts explicitly link *kuṇḍalinī* to *prāṇa*. According to Flood (2006: 161–162), in several situations *kuṇḍalinī* is understood as a force inseparable from consciousness, who animates creation and who, in her particularised form in the body, 'causes liberation through her upward, illusion-shattering movement'.

affects us. You have to understand what it really is. You can call it anything, but what matters is something else.

In the ascetic world, the arising of *kuṇḍalinī* is described in two ways: as '*kuṇḍalinī jāganā*' (waking up) and as '*kuṇḍalinī prāpt karnā*' (to realise). When the process is in progress, they talk about the ascent (H., *jāgaraṇ*) of *kuṇḍalinī*; but only if this ascent is completely successful do they talk of a realised (*prāpti*) *kuṇḍalinī*. The ascending process of *kuṇḍalinī* does not coincide with the perfection of the practice, mainly because the practitioner must learn to control the power of *kuṇḍalinī*, a practice that seems more important than its visualisation.[36]

Jogī Bābā said that *kuṇḍalinī-yoga* is the stretching of *kuṇḍalinī* from the *mūlādhāra* to the *sahasrāra*, passing through the other *cakras*. But to achieve this, he claimed, 'The nine doors of the body must be closed and the tenth must be opened, but this can only be done through the grace of God!' These nine doors are the two eyes, the two ears, the two nostrils, the mouth, and the anal and genital openings. The tenth is the subtle cranial opening, the *brahmarandhra*, which must be opened to enable the individual to achieve his final goal.

This idea of the body as having nine openings, or doors, is present in the *Atharva Veda Samhitā* 10.2.18ff. and 10.8.43, where the 'mystic stronghold of *brahman*' (*brahmapura*) is described as a lotus of nine doors (Goudriaan 2002: 180). The cranial opening is mentioned in *Kaṭha Upaniṣad* (2.3.16): 'One hundred and one, the veins of the heart. One of them runs up to the crown of the head. Going up by it, he reaches the immortal. The rest, in their ascent, spread out in all directions' (Olivelle 1992: 246). The nine doors simile is also adopted in tantric contexts such as that of the *Amṛtasiddhi* which, in describing *mahāmudrā* (Chapter 11.4), emphasises the need to close the nine openings and fill the abdomen with air. This association between *prāṇa* as means to close the doors of the body represented as a fortress to be conquered, persists in later texts, especially Nāth vernacular sources. This *bānī*, translated by Djurdjevic and Singh (2019: 76) is meaningful in this regard:

---

36 According to Śyām Ānanda Nāth, there are two paths: one is the path of Tantra with rituals and mantra; the other the path of *prāṇāyāma*, i.e. the path of *haṭha* yoga since the main aim of *haṭha* yoga is to block the breath through the *bandhas*. In both the cases, however, the arising will happen while doing a meditative-like practice. This would also lead to *samādhi*.

135. The *unman*[37] yogi is in the tenth opening.
[He hears] the roaring sound of the union of the *nād* and *bindu.*
Closing the door of the tenth opening,
Gorakh has investigated [it] by other means.

However, the paths in pursuit of this result can differ. Jogī Bābā told me of three different possibilities: through five *mudrās* in *siddhāsana;*[38] through *kumbhaka,*[39] and through a guru. Taking into account the statements of other *sādhus*, we must add to these practices the use of mantra and *jap*. In essence, then, *kuṇḍalinī* can arise through physical and meditative processes.

Having mentioned most of the methods, it is important to say a few more words about the role of the guru in the process of *kuṇḍalinī* rising. Several *sādhus* asserted that only a righteous guru can make the *kuṇḍalinī* rise. Garuḍ Dās, in fact, stated that one should meditate to obtain a vision of a righteous guru, because there is nothing an individual can do alone to awaken the *kuṇḍalinī.* He said this in reference to his own experience: he tried various *sādhanās* and austerities, but only when he met a Nāth guru was he able to experience the awakening of *kuṇḍalinī.*

A guru also plays a crucial role in properly scrutinising disciples and understanding their 'spiritual' level. According to Īśnāth, it should not be taken for granted that the *kuṇḍalinī* is in the *mūlādhāra*, because it will depend on the nature of the individual and also on *karma* (see below). As a first step, the guru will teach the disciple to recognise the body, because this knowledge is essential in awakening the *kuṇḍalinī* and beginning a *śaktipāta.* But because a powerful energy that has been stored for a long time is to be moved, it is all the more necessary to have a guru to control the consequences. As several *sādhus* claimed, some people can lose control of their mind. Therefore, before working on the *kuṇḍalinī*, one has to purify the body, be able to control it, and be in control of the mind; otherwise, according to Rāghavendra Dās, 'one can have migraines, hysteria, and can become completely insane'.

The awakening of *kuṇḍalinī* must be accompanied by the knowledge of how to 'return' safely, a teaching that, as Garuḍ Dās pointed out to me,

37 *Unman* indicates the yogi who is 'beyond the mind', who has literally 'no mind' (Djurdjevic and Singh 2019: 25).

38 Kamal Giri mentioned that *gomukhāsana* (which he calls Loknāth *āsana* in memory of a famous 19th-century Bengali guru) also favours the rising of *kuṇḍalinī* because of the pressure it exerts on the *mūlādhāra.*

39 See Chapter 5, pp. 235ff.

is not described in any text because it can only be transmitted by a guru. Another precaution to be taken is to not reveal to others the stage attained, lest the accumulated power be diminished. According to Yogī Maṅgal Nāth, when *kuṇḍalinī* begins 'to react', *naśā* (intoxication) for power can occur because the individual gains powers which can be used for good or evil. There are gurus, he claimed, who can use their practice to perform miracles and manipulate others, doing much harm. That is why the practice must be undertaken under the right guru and directed towards the right intention.

As always, there are different topics that blend, and different concepts that can have multiple meanings and values. *Kuṇḍalinī* can rise via physical practices, mantras, as well as through a guru.

But where does the awakening of *kuṇḍalinī* lead? Again, the answers may differ, but basically they can be divided between *ānanda* and *mokṣa*, although the two are not necessarily in opposition but can be seen as different stages of the same path.

How to define *ānanda*? In Allahabad, a *saṃnyāsī* explained the difference between *sukh* (happiness in Hindi) and *ānanda* (joy). He said that *sukh* comes from temporary things that are outside of us, while *ānanda* comes from an interiorised search, and creates a condition in which the feeling of good or bad is overcome, in which there are no differences, and which lasts forever. But the path to *ānanda* is a long one and requires complete abandonment of worldly life. The concept of *ānanda* in relation to *kuṇḍalinī* is interesting because it recalls past meanings and probably past references to sexual rituals or, rather, the substitution of sexual rituals. Viśambhar Bhārtī said that in fact only *brahmacārī*s (celibates) can have their *kuṇḍalinī jāgrit* forever. According to him, during sexual intercourse *kuṇḍalinī* rises for a very short time, but it is for this bliss that men seek sex. However, when the *brahmacārī* does some *kriyā*s (he said that it is sufficient to do *jap* and *dhyāna* for a long time) and succeeds in awakening *kuṇḍalinī*, he gets a long-lasting *ānanda*. So it is like recreating the pleasure of sex, but without sex. As already mentioned, Dharam Giri claimed that his guru used to remain in a state of bliss for several hours after practising *vajrolī mudrā*. We can therefore associate the 'arising' of *bindu* with a pleasure similar to that of the arising of *kuṇḍalinī*, which can be described as a state of bliss.

I shall now elaborate on the connection between *kuṇḍalinī* and *mokṣa*, but first a few more words on the subject of *siddhi*s are necessary.

Siddhis

> 'It is not that the yogi looks for *siddhis*: *siddhis* go to the yogi, they appear. When everything becomes *siddha*, then *siddhis* automatically appear.'
>
> Yogī Rudra Nāth

One result of intense meditative practices is the acquisition of *siddhis*. We have already seen in Chapter 3 that strenuous or prolonged practice leads to *siddhis*.

Described in earlier texts and still attributed to contemporary gurus, powers can be divided between worldly (H., *sāṃsārik*)—such as the so-called *aṣṭa* (eight) *siddhis*—and spiritual (H., *ādhyātmik*), those with effects relating to *paramātman* and the subtle world. Eight unspecified powers are mentioned in the *Mahābhārata* and eight powers are described in the 'Vibhūti Pada' of the *Pātañjalayogaśāstra*, becoming a widespread topos in yoga texts of all traditions.[40] These eight 'traditional' powers are: *aṇimā*, to reduce one's body to the size of an atom; *mahimā*, to expand one's body to an infinitely large dimension; *garimā*, to become infinitely heavy; *laghimā*, to become almost weightless; *prāpti*, to be everywhere at will; *prākāmya*, to realise anything one desires; *īṣṭva*, to achieve supremacy over nature; and *vāśtva*, to control natural forces.

But the lists, and the powers they describe, can differ. To give a few examples, *Bhāgavata Purāṇa* 11.15.6 claims that there are 18 supernatural powers, such as moving as fast as thought, assuming whatever form one wants, entering another's body, dying at will,[41] accomplishing whatever one wishes, knowing the past, the present and the future, etc. In *Dattātreyayogaśāstra* 82, the yogi attains the 'animal power' (*bhūcarasiddhi*), i.e. the power to overcome animals; in the *Vāyavīyasaṃhitā* (which lists 64 powers), there are powers like 'finding water', or 'seeing hidden objects', while the *Pravacanasāroddhāra* mentions *akṣīṇa-mahānasi*: the power to feed hundreds of thousands from a small amount of food placed in the bowl (Wiley 2012: 157, 165).

But are *siddhis* still achieved by *sādhus*? Are they still a goal? The answer is yes, albeit with a caveat: the idea persists that through the practice of yoga one might obtain incredible powers, but to reach such a level requires

40 For detailed examples of texts dealing with yogic powers, see Mallinson and Singleton 2017: 359–394; for examples of yogic powers in various South Asian religious traditions, see Jacobsen 2011.

41 *Sādhus* mention the power of 'dying at will' mostly when talking about the yogi who decides to enter into a final *samādhi* (see below).

not only much practice but the presence of a suitable guru who can teach and who has, himself, acquired *siddhis*. According to the Udāsī Lakṣmaṇ Dās, there is a diminishing number of *sādhus* who can claim to have *siddhis*, because in this *Kali yuga* it is very difficult to realise the spiritual path through *tapasyā* or yoga *sādhanā*. According to him, *siddhis* should only be used for people's well-being, to help others find their balance, their happiness.

In general, *siddhis* are seen as an obstacle when they become a 'source of intoxication' that distracts the practitioner from his true religious and spiritual goal. However, since they are also the result of an effective *sādhanā*, they can be used to convince people of the ascetic's genuineness. People today are more sceptical, said a *sādhaka* of the Nāth temple in Varanasi, so gurus have to convince them by showing 'miracles'.

According to Yogī Rudra Nāth, the types of *siddhis* the practitioner can acquire also depend on the *āsana* used. In this case, however, the word *āsana* does not indicate the posture, rather the material that makes up the seat and where this is placed: '*jesī siddhi vaise āsana*' (as the seat so the *siddhi*), he said.[42] Somewhat reluctant to talk about *siddhis* was Jogī Bābā who, according to his followers, had manifested several forms of powers thanks to the *tapasyā* he did in the jungle (see Chapter 3, p. 139). Devotees acclaimed him for being able to feed all the people who visit his *āśram*, despite their numbers, and some swore they had seen him change size and walk on tree leaves in the jungle.[43] However, Jogī Bābā pointed out that, 'You only get *siddhi* through the Mother's *kripā* (grace). Without the grace of Mā, without *śakti*, yoga cannot produce *siddhis*.' Similarly, Rām Avadhūt Dās stated:

> *Siddhi* is a *śakti*, a form of the God we worship. All *siddhis*, all the perfections one would like to attain, cannot be achieved without the *kripā* of our God. You can maintain your *āsana* and do *sādhanā* as much as you want, but you may not necessarily achieve anything. Even the opening of the *cakra*, without the *kripā* of *śakti* is not possible.

As in vernacular sources with a strong devotional background,[44] *siddhis* are not the exclusive result of the tenacity and practice of the *sādhus*, since

42 It should be noted that in some *aghorī sādhanā* performed in crematories, a possible *āsana* might be the body of a corpse or seven skulls: the practitioner practises sitting on them to obtain *siddhis* or to have a vision of a deity.

43 On Jogī Bābā and his *siddhi*, see Bevilacqua 2018b.

44 On vernacular devotional sources versus the 'powers' of the Yogīs, see Burchett 2019: 250–270. It should be noted, however, that there are Nāth lineages that follow devotional paths, and we should not forget the role that *bhakti* has played in

the grace of God or the Goddess remains a prerogative for their attainment, an idea shared by *sādhus* belonging to all the *sampradāyas* considered here, often even by Nāths.

How, then, is it possible to obtain the *śakti* or grace of God? Through 'Worship, meditation and reflection, if we repeat the name of *śakti* a reaction is triggered,' said Rām Avadhūt Dās. The repetition of God's name or of a mantra can actually lead to the attainment of the relevant *siddhis*. For example, Śyām Dās claimed that he did 1,000 repetitions a day for one month. After that, he got the *siddhi* related to the mantra he was using, i.e. the knowledge of what happens at a distance.

Siddhis show us the interconnection between yoga, *jap*, *tapasyā*, *bhakti* and *upāsanā* (worship), further demonstrating that the life of *sādhus* is shaped by various practices and 'customs' which taken together form their spiritual, religious life.

Samādhi

> 'After *samādhi* there is nothing more, no further improvement. There is no more work to be done. With *samādhi* the *man* is free.'
>
> Jogī Bābā

Defining *samādhi* is a complicated task because different ideas merge in both textual sources and oral statements. But it should now be clear that this is just another example of different theories developing in different contexts (perhaps in different areas and times) and becoming systematised or supplemented by authors and practitioners from time to time. It is to be expected that a concept as important as *samādhi* would follow the same fate as concepts such as yoga and *tapas*, acquiring a variety of meanings, often related but not necessarily compatible. Mallinson and Singleton (2017: xxxi) summarise descriptions of *samādhi*:

> Some texts consider *samādhi* as an extension of the meditation state, sometimes itself conceived as a temporal extension of breath-control. In tantric texts, *samādhi* is usually (though not always) the last of the (six) auxiliaries (*angas*) of yoga, but is still preliminary to the goal, union with or proximity to the deity. In haṭha texts *samādhi* may also convey

---

everyday religiosity in India since the 16th century. On the issue of Nāths' adaptation, see Bouillier 2008.

> a death-like trance, and some of our selections describe the burial and revival of the yoga in *samādhi* as a kind of ritual display of yogic prowess.

It should be noted that the interpretations we find in textual sources belonging to different traditions are also mentioned by ascetics. In the ascetic world, *samādhi* takes on different meanings depending on the context: it can be a stage in the meditative process; the last practice performed by the ascetic who wants to leave the body; or a celebrative place of a past holy man: that is, a tomb.

Rām Avadhūt Dās gave a very clear definition of a meditative *samādhi*:

> What is *samādhi* . . . you are in *dhyāna* and your mind is looking at the sun. When this knowledge is fully realised, instead of looking at the sun you start feeling that you are the sun, you feel no difference. When you correctly apply *dhyāna* on God and you reach the state where you recognise yourself in God. It is like a river: a river is a river until it reaches the sea . . . *Samādhi* is when, by doing continuous meditation on God, you do not have the feeling of being different from God, you won't think about who you are. This is *samādhi.* When you are in the sea, you have the feeling that you are the sea, you cannot distinguish the sea from the river.

From a certain point of view, the development of this practice is similar to the awakening of *kuṇḍalinī*: for those ascetics who understand *samādhi* as a further step in meditation, it must be guided, especially in its 'return' aspect. Here again, the words of Rām Avadhūt Dās help to clarify:

> But you must also know the way out of the sea, which is a hidden knowledge. The person who, after knowing how to enter *samādhi,* is able to descend is a true yogi. When you are able to come out of the sea, you can realise what the sea is like, and then you can teach about it, because you now know both sides. [. . .]
>
> A guru has to teach you and show you the path. Obviously not in his gross body: here we are talking about subtle bodies. So he will accompany you on the path and show you the way back.

Īśnāth provided further explanations of this stage:

> Training is to understand what it feels when you reach *samādhi.* Training is necessary because it is sometimes frightening. So, people try it at the beginning, and then they are scared and they come back. But then you remember the feeling and you want to go back. You want to go back, up. [. . .] It frees the soul, so the soul no longer has limits and boundaries.

But he also stressed the importance of the guru because:

> You can become insane, because you don't realise reality and where you are. And that is why people become insane. *Samādhi* is actually a union.

> *Sam* means that you are a half until you are united with the divine, then you are full. When you are united with Ādi, that is Ādināth. [. . .] We are just half until we reach God. Then we are one when we connect with the source. And then, that is absolute union.

It is widely believed that there were *ṛṣis* and Sants who mastered the *samādhi* stage but deliberately preferred to remain in that state, thus 'mentally' out of society. Because of their behaviour, they were considered insane, but in fact 'normal' social conduct made no sense for them: having met the *brahman*, they thought remained in *brahman*. However, in this regard Rām Avadhūt Dās said that he considered the *siddha* yogi who behaves according to social rules while maintaining knowledge of the Absolute to be more valuable. He made a simile between a lotus flower and a yogi: just as the leaves of the lotus are in the water but are not wet, similarly the yogi lives in the *saṃsāra*, acts like a person in the *saṃsāra* but, in reality, is not affected by society. The yogi is part of society but when he wants to reach the *brahman* he acts accordingly and behaves accordingly. He is able to manage the two states.

This brings us back to the attitudes of ascetics towards the body. There is a clear idea that the subtle body can leave the gross body, and it is this subtle body that experiences detachment from the gross body during *samādhi*. However, while *samādhi* is a practice that leads to the annihilation of the yogi's identity, there are similar stages or practices that instead require the ascetic to be aware of what his subtle body is about to do.[45]

Kamal Giri recognised *samādhi* as the condition in which a *sādhu* blocks the breath and his *ātman* is able to leave the body.[46] He said that he knew a *bābā* who was able to remain in *samādhi* for 30 days. In this case, he said, the *ātman* 'wanders' in the *brahmarandhra* while the body remains motionless.

In fact, Yogī Sumit Nāth said that, when *samādhi* is attained, 'Then the body is only a container for the soul, so it is no longer necessary for the body to eat or sleep. It is not necessary to awaken anything, because that reality is always present.' Similarly, Garuḍ Dās said: 'The yogi's body becomes a body of emptiness.[47] He is present in the body but his *ātman* can go far away. After completely feeling and understanding his body, he is no

---

45 See the next chapter, p. 264.

46 As mentioned in Chapter 4 (p. 166), according to some *sādhus*, *haṭha* yoga techniques actually have the aim of manipulating the breath to force a state of *samādhi*.

47 This deep absorption state is also described in textual sources. For example, *Amanaska* 1.27 describes *laya* as the state of absorption in which the yogi 'remains lifeless like a piece of wood and [thus] is said to be abiding in absorption': here

longer sensitive to what happens to it.' When the *ātman* wants to return, the body comes back to life.

However, not all the *sādhus* recognise *samādhi* as a form of deep, supra-corporeal meditation. Jogī Bābā, for example, does not accept the possibility of returning from *samādhi*: his conception is closely connected to death and, eventually, to *mokṣa*. Therefore, he links the possibility of 'leaving the body' with some *dhyāna* practices, which according to him are simply 'different forms of yoga' and with some types of *samādhi* (he said there are seven techniques but did not mention them). However, for him the main meaning of *samādhi* is to lead life to its end. This was called by a Rāmānujī *akhaṇḍa samādhi*, the perpetual *samādhi*. Therefore, a *sādhu* who is in full control of his *prāṇa* and, consequently, of his *ātman*, is said to decide when to leave the body, a decision that is made not only on the basis of his wish but also on the right time to leave (see below).

Since the word *samādhi* is also associated with the practice of consciously leading the ascetic's physical body to death, it is not surprising that the ascetic's funeral monument or shrine is called *samādhi*. Indeed, most ascetics are not burnt as is customary among Hindus because they are said to have been purified by the inner fire of their asceticism. However, this is not always the case for Vaiṣṇava *sādhus* who may choose to undergo the *agni saṃskāra*, the sacrament of cremation.

Usually in old *āśrams* it is possible to see the *samādhis* of the different ascetics who lived there, although those of the *mahants* are the ones most commemorated, maintaining a visual presence of the *paramparā*. The word *samādhi* here does not indicate that the *sādhu* left the body through *samādhi*, but nevertheless the body is usually buried seated in a meditative posture. These *samādhis* are considered powerful places by devotees who believe past *bābās* are still able to bestow blessings despite their bodily departure (Photo 19).

Samādhi and *rāja* yoga

Following the *Haṭhapradīpikā*, Yogī Śivanāth emphasised that *haṭha* yoga is propaedeutic to *rāja* yoga. According to him, several *sādhanās* that can go under the label of *haṭha* yoga—such as the *kuṇḍalinī jāgaraṇ*, the *ṣaṭ cakra* (seven *cakras*) *sādhanā*, the *ajapājap* and *nādānusandhāna*, etc.—are intended to achieve *rāja* yoga, and *rāja* yoga is *samādhi*. Omānanda Giri supported a similar idea, pointing out that *rāja* yoga can also be practised

---

laya corresponds to the state of *amanaska* (without mind) which ultimately corresponds to *samādhi* (Birch 2013: 38).

Photo 19 *Samādhi*s in the *āśram* of Yogī Śivanāth, an old Nāth centre close to Bhubaneswar (Orissa), 2018.

without *haṭha* yoga, but it is more difficult because it requires more time to balance the mind. If one balances the body through *kriyā*s and breath, then the mind can be easily balanced and *rāja* yoga follows.

When I asked Svāmī Ātmānanda if the practice of *samādhi* should be considered *rāja* yoga, he replied that the name might be that, but it is just a label, and labels are useless to describe a result that is only available through experience. In fact, although an association between *samādhi* and *rāja* yoga did emerge, this was not the only understanding of *rāja* yoga. For example, in Delhi, Viśambhar Bhārtī said that *rāja* yoga is not for *bābā*s, because it is related to being a *bhogī*, a seeker of pleasure. Dayānanda Purī said that *rāja* yoga is power: one who feels like a *rāja*, a king, will do whatever he feels is right. It is a physical approach, he said: *haṭha* yoga and *rāja* yoga are much related, they do not have a spiritual part, but focus on the physical body.

These meanings are reminiscent of an understanding of *rāja* yoga also attested to in textual sources. It is not unlikely that the label *rāja* yoga was used to refer to the practice of those who did not have time to fully engage in yogic practices: that is, those who were involved in 'royal' and political matters (for example, *mahant*s or kings), or those who did not want to enter the path of renunciation but still wanted to undertake the practice and live like a king: indulging in sensory pleasures, and at the same time being a master yogi (Mallinson 2018a: 195). Therefore, *rāja* yoga was likely associated with a state in which the yogi could live without adhering to the strict rules of the yoga practice (Mallinson 2018b), meaning that he could misbehave without being tainted by it (as the *Śiva Saṃhitā* mentions)[48] or do whatever he wanted. Furthermore, it would be associated with the yogi's freedom to indulge in sexual intercourse without breaking the vow of continence thanks to the practice of *vajrolī mudrā*. Indeed, Chapter 5 of the *Jogapradīpakā* says that *vīrajmudrā* takes place in the house of the *rāj-jog* (5.550), associating *rāj-jog* with the practice of sexual intercourse without wasting semen, thanks to the control of the *bindu* achieved through the *mudrā*. Mallinson (2018b) suggests that this practice was proposed to justify the lifestyles of the monastic leaders who sometimes lived just like *rājas*, even having concubines. This is an interesting understanding of *rāja* yoga, which likely textual sources try to conceal by connecting the term *rāja* yoga to *samādhi*. Certainly, as we have seen, there is an aspect related to *ānanda*, pleasure, in finalising certain practices, but this result is not always certain. Some other variables need to be taken into consideration.

On *karma*, death, *mokṣa* and yoga

According to the law of *karma*, the life of an individual is the result of the *karma* (good or bad) accumulated in this and previous lives. An ascetic life is considered to be the result of positive events from previous lives[49] or the continuation of other ascetic lives aimed at ending *saṃsāra*.[50] Given the

48 The *Śiva Saṃhitā* give instructions to *bubhukṣu* practitioners (i.e. those desirous of *siddhis*) and *mumukṣus* (those aspiring to liberation); in its last verses, as emphasised by Mallinson (2007b: xiii), 'the householder is said to be able to obtain *siddhis* and become liberated by means of the techniques of Yoga—and still have fun!'

49 As Yogī Rudra Nāth said: 'The tree of sins produces fruit very quickly, while the tree of *puṇya* (merit) takes time before it bears fruit. That is why more people turn to sins, but they do not know that because of their *pāp* (sin) they are giving troubles to their future heirs. No one realises that their ancestors are probably in hell; everyone thinks they are in *vaikunṭh* (highest realm), but hell exists as well. When we die, we will see what hell is and what heaven is.'

50 Omānanda Giri gave me a useful example. He compared life to a balloon in a river: the balloon in the river moves and flows, and one day it will reach the sea. There is no telling how long it will take, because no one knows what kinds of problems and obstacles it will encounter in the river, nor is its speed guaranteed. So it could take ten hours, years, maybe the next lifetime, but what is certain is that it will reach the sea. Until then, it will keep moving and flowing, it will not be stable. The only way to make it stable is to reach the sea. It is then that the *ātman* meets *paramātman*, the infinite. Once reached, there will be no more problems in life because life becomes stable. Those who have reached this goal but decide to 'stay',

importance of *karma* in defining a person's birth, the possibility of becoming a yogi also depends on previous lives. Yoga as a method can be used by the ascetics as a tool to support and improve their main *sādhanā*. This means that one can use some of its practices (*āsanas*, or *prāṇāyāmas*, or *dhāraṇās*, etc.) without necessarily seeking 'yogic' results. Similarly, *sādhus* recognise that *samādhi* will not necessarily lead to *mokṣa*: it depends on the accumulated *karma*. If *karma* is not exhausted, *samādhi* will be a deep meditative experience that has not yet reached the last stage.

Therefore, being affected by temporality, the ascetic who realises that his physical body is decaying while his *karma* is not yet 'finished' may decide to prolong his life in order to burn off all the residual *karma*.[51] The focus on health that we find in yoga textual sources and their claim to conquer death by eliminating disease could refer to this: the possibility of maintaining the body as long as possible in order to have enough time to burn off residual *karma*. In Kamakhya, Nāth jī spoke of the need to eliminate *karma* before one can reach the ultimate goal, but he also mentioned the importance of devotion while doing the *sādhanā*. His statement reiterates the importance of *bhakti* in fulfilling the spiritual path, an approach that seems quite widespread among *sādhus*, despite their *sampradāyik* affiliation.

In the Nāth *sampradāya*, there is a well-known saying according to which the yogi should die when he is 'still alive'. As explained by Yogī Śivanāth:

> *Māro, māro, māro,*[52] what is the meaning of *māro*? Two explanations: the death of the body and the death of *man*. When does the death of the body occur? When the *prāṇa* flows away, then the body dies. But before the body dies, the yogi has already killed the mind, which is why Gorakhnāth jī said that before the death of the body there must be the death of *man*. How can the death of *man* be achieved? Through *dhyāna*. [...] That is why Gorakhnāth said that death is sweet. That is why, when death comes for the yogi, it is sweet, but not for the *bhogī*. When your *man* is dead, then you get *jīvanmukta* (freedom while alive). When you get the peace of your *man* then you get *jīvanmukta*.
>
> Some people say that one gets *mokṣa* after death, but that is not so. One must obtain *mokṣa* while one is still alive. *Jīvanmukta*. *Siddha* yogis who are able to use *kriyās* know their life; they have control and vision of their past, present and future. The *siddha* yogis will attain *mokṣa* before

---

will have a different attitude, they will consider everything the same, because in the end everything goes to the same place.

51 Yogī Śivanāth made it clear that this is only the residual, past *karma* since, theoretically, the yogi who has reached the *samādhi* stage produces no further *karma*.

52 This is the imperative form of the Hindi verb *mārnā*, to die.

> the death of the body; they will clearly say when and at what time they will enter *samādhi.*

Yogī Śivanāth's words emphasise the importance of a meditative practice to kill the mind, because only when the mind is completely under control (i.e. killed) can other levels of reality be obtained as well as freedom, *mokṣa*. Obtaining *mokṣa* during life transforms the perfected yogi (who does not accumulate *karma*) into a *jīvanmukta*, liberated while living. This corresponds to the 'first' death of the yogi and the attainment of Yoga itself.[53] As mentioned, beyond the experience of *dhyāna*—that is, when *dhyāna* becomes so profound that it transforms into *samādhi*—the union or the awareness or the vision of *ātman* and *paramātman* (the self and the supreme) can occur. This encounter may manifest in different ways depending on the theoretical beliefs of the *sampradāya.* It is indeed in the interpretation of this encounter that differences among *sādhus* appear.

According to the *saṃnyāsī* Omānanda Giri, the meaning of yoga is to unite, to end duality, to recognise, according to his Advaita approach, that *ātmānubhava* (the experience of the *ātman*) and *paramātmānubhava* (the experience of *paramātman*) are actually the same thing because in yoga there is no duality. The *saṃnyāsī* Rādhe Purī described this union with these words:

> Sitting in *padmāsana* with the mind fixed and eyes open, you visualise *paramātman* in front of you. Slowly this visualisation becomes internalised. *Paramātman* enters from the eyes, then all the visions are in front of you, then you do not have to go to the jungle; God is there wherever you are. When this union happens, the eyes close and the *sādhu* enters *samādhi.*

Nāths show a similar Advaita approach, although the goal of their *sādhanā* is the 'realisation of Śiva *nirākāra*', said Yogī Śivanāth: that is, the realisation of Śiva's 'qualities' despite his formlessness. The Udāsī Lakṣmaṇ Dās also identified the goal of yoga as ending the fluctuations of the mind through various exercises and the development of detachment to finally achieve union with God. The *tyāgī* Rām Caraṇ Dās, on the other hand, manifesting his Viśiṣṭādvaita approach, stated that the purpose of yoga is '*ātman śa-śakt kare, Bhagvān prapt kare*': to realise God through the *śakti* of the *ātman*. Therefore, yoga is the tool that clarifies the relationship with God, which enables one to have an inner vision of God. He compared it to using a torch to see in the darkness: once the ability to see in the dark is

---

53 The second death, which is 'just' that of the body, is then under the control of the yogi.

acquired, then a torch is no longer necessary. Even his disciple, Rām Priya Dās emphasised that the goal of yoga is to be able to 'abide' in God.

But what happens once the individual has achieved his or her spiritual goals?

Two results seem to be identifiable. From an 'individualistic' point of view, those who have effectively become yogi achieve a state in which they simply no longer accumulate *karma*: they are thus beyond the law of *karma* because actions are no longer driven by desires or intended to achieve a particular result. This also means that they are beyond dichotomies, beyond the idea of *sukh* (happiness) and *dukh* (sadness), beyond good and evil. For this reason, Garuḍ Dās said that a true, realised yogi can also eat meat because he is no longer conditioned by the diet, and likewise he can have sexual intercourse because he is not attacked by desire.[54]

From the point of view of human interactions, it seems that accomplished individuals decide to remain in the *saṃsāra*, taking care of other human beings: the focus is on *sevā*.

When I asked Yogī Rudra Nāth how a *sādhu* knows that he has obtained *mokṣa*, he replied:

> When the *kriyās* of the seven *cakras* are completely realised and there is this complete detachment, and you only think about the needs of others because they are still there suffering, then it means that you have attained *mokṣa*. Because it means that you have completely removed the *ahaṃkāra* within you.

It is interesting to note that I received similar answers from *sādhus* belonging to the different *sampradāyas* considered in this book. While it was almost to be expected that *tyāgī* Jagannāth Dās would tell me that, ultimately, the accomplished *sādhu* cares for the community of both lay people and ascetics, considering that *sevā* and *premā* (love) are two fundamental elements of the Rāmānandīs' *bhakti sādhanā*, I was surprised to hear similar remarks made by *nāgās* and Nāths. Yogī Sumit Nāth emphasised that the accomplished individual realises that the only purpose of the body is eventually to give love. He offered this simile: while a tree gives shade and fruit with its body, the body of a human being is useless unless it gives love. The *nāgā* Jvālā Purī said that the reason one practices yoga is to attain unconditional love, because every mind should be at peace. It would seem that the accomplished yogi engages in a form of compassion, based on unconditional, detached love towards those still suffering in the *saṃsāra*.

How to interpret this position?

---

54 On the identity of the yogi, see pp. 315ff.

On the one hand, we can see it as the result of an historical trajectory that has made *bhakti* and *premā* fundamental to both achieving religious goals and dealing with *saṃsāra* in modern and contemporary times. Indeed, it is said that the main *mārga* in *Kali yuga*, despite the use of various more or less esoteric *sādhanās*, is eventually *bhakti* and *premā*. *Bhakti* is central to contemporary Indian religiosity and has influenced the attitudes of several religious orders.

However, it could also be the influx of new ideas associated with yoga that come from a countercultural approach. It should be kept in mind that yoga practices have been further developed in the last century, and *sādhus* have not been spared from these new transformations; rather, they have often provided fertile ground for their dissemination.

7
Modern Yoga and Traditional *Sādhus*

This final chapter will assess the influence of modern yoga on *sādhus*. It begins by briefly introducing the topic of modern yoga and the role of transnational Indian gurus in order to provide a general framework within which to examine the various attitudes observable among *sādhus*. It then analyses the different ways in which *sādhus* relate to modern yoga and identifies which aspects they tend to take issue with; a particular focus is on economic and medical aspects—which enables us to address the topic of Ayurveda and related issues—and the importance given to *āsanas*. This section is followed by examples of *sādhus* who teach yoga on a random basis to those who ask, as well as examples of those who see the dissemination of yoga as a mission and, by simplifying its theories, actively participate in promoting a more globalised idea of yoga. The last section deals with the International Day of Yoga and one of the main figures behind it: Bābā Rāmdev, a well-known yoga guru whose role as *bābā* is nevertheless questioned by *sādhus*.

This chapter might correctly be considered a work in progress, because a proper evaluation of the effect of modern yoga on the ascetic world will necessitate waiting for the next generation to come through, when the old *sādhus* who acquired their knowledge in a traditional way—i.e. not influenced by social media—have left the scene.

Modern yoga and modern guru

Here I use the label 'modern yoga' following De Michelis (2004: 2): that is, as 'a technical term to refer to certain types of yoga that evolved mainly through the interaction of Western individuals interested in Indian religions and a number of more or less Westernised Indians over the last 150 years'.

It was with Swami Vivekananda (1863–1902) and his book *Raja Yoga* (1896), an innovative translation and commentary of Patañjali's *Yogasūtra*, that yoga began to be promoted globally as an example of Indian religiosity, a respectable interest for the middle classes of Europe and America (Newcombe 2017: 7). From Vivekananda onward, Indian ascetics have always been part of the transnational spread of yoga: Indian gurus, with their ideals of spirituality and detachment, have captured the Western imagination since the late 19th century, when some of them started travelling internationally to spread their teachings. These gurus can be considered part of Neo-Hinduism because, in order to communicate with their Western audiences unfamiliar with Hindu deities and practices, they embraced Western values, which were then assimilated into their vision of Hinduism (Altglas 2011: 234). Jaffrelot (1999: 195–196) calls them 'modern gurus', because they adapted their messages (often delivered in English) to the needs of the urban middle class, imparting teachings suitable for leading successful lives.

The success of these gurus was made possible by the 'Western' interest in Eastern spiritualism, used to assert the superiority of Hindu traditions over Christianity and materialism in the West. At the same time, as several authors have shown,[1] there was also a particular emphasis on presenting Hindu traditions in a scientific framework. Yoga underwent a similar process and was highlighted as a scientific practice with medical health benefits, thus participating in the attempt to create indigenous bodily disciplines underpinned by high morals and ethics that could present India as sufficiently masculine to compete with Western culture (see Alter 2004; Singleton 2010).

What emerges from those times—that is, the late 19th century and the first half of the 20th century—is the development of various modern aspects in the yoga tradition. De Michelis (2004: 187–188) has created useful heuristic categories to classify these developments. She argues that, after Vivekananda's *Raja Yoga*, a number of schools arose dedicated to training the body, mind and spirit, which she collects under the category of Modern

1 See for example Singleton 2010; De Michelis 2004; Foxen 2020.

Psychosomatic Yoga (MPsY). Within a couple of decades, further specialisation emerged: Modern Postural Yoga (MPY) focused on *āsana* and *prāṇāyāma* practices, while Modern Meditational Yoga (MMY) focused on techniques of concentration and meditation. The MPY and the MMY, De Michelis continues, offered rudimentary doctrinal aspects of the teachings limiting themselves to basic suggestions on the religious-philosophical aspects of their practices, assuming that understanding could come through experience.

Beginning in the early 1920s, a 'Yoga Renaissance' began in India, pioneered by such personalities as Shri Yogendra of the Yoga Institute of Santa Cruz in Bombay, Swami Kuvalyananda of the Kaivalyadhama Ashram in Lonavala, and Swami Sivananda of the Divine Life Society in Rishikesh (Alter 1997: 280). They sponsored yoga, and particularly *āsanas*, as a scientific practice useful for health and physical fitness.[2] The practice of *āsanas* was also developed by Krishnamacharya and his students (e.g. B.K.S. Iyengar and Pattabhi Jois), who created popular forms of yoga teachings which have continued to develop to the present day.[3]

Around the 1960s, several modern gurus provided a generation of foreigners with various spiritual teachings and practices. Young people driven by a desire for rebellion and the search for unconventional forms of awareness became key social agents, open to cultural innovation and ready to reject a preconceived cultural-historical inheritance (Palmisano and Pannofino 2017: 128–129). It was during this period that Modern Denominational Yoga (MDY) developed, with gurus more ideologically committed to Neo-Hinduism and manifesting more sectarian tendencies: making demands on members and establishing more exclusivist organisational systems (De Michelis 2004: 189).[4] In an attempt to be universal or

2 According to Peter van der Veer (2007: 319), this medical-scientific approach to yoga, which aimed at creating healthy and strongly masculine Hindus, was also part of the propaganda of nationalist groups, such as the Rashtriya Swayamsevak Sangh (RSS) and the Vishwa Hindu Parishad (VHP), providing these organisations with a bodily discipline to gain political relevance.

3 This was a very complex historical period, in which several social, cultural and political variables were at play in shaping ideas about yoga. Since a detailed explanation would be beyond the scope of this chapter, it is suggested that the interested reader delve into three fundamental works: *Yoga in Modern India* by J. Alter (2004), *A History of Modern Yoga* by E. De Michelis (2004), and *Yoga Body* by M. Singleton (2010).

4 We can cite as examples 'Transcendental Meditation', founded by Maharishi Mahesh Yogi, and Swami Muktananda's 'Siddha Yoga' (Khandelwal 2012; Altglas 2007). On international and Modern Yoga-related *sādhus*, see for example the

global, many of these gurus and their movements were affected by transnational processes, often advocating and promoting ideas that were those of the countercultural milieu (Altglas 2011: 237). This transnationalism was also the result of the rapid technological progress that facilitated travel and information sharing. This means that Indian gurus were (and are) influenced by transnationalism, but they were also agents in this process, strong participants in this sharing and reorganisation of traditions.[5]

Nowadays, smartphones and social media have made it easier for people to create global connections and move in a 'super-territorial space' not tied to a specific physical territory, with the potential to carry out all kinds of activities (Nanda 2009: 16). Thanks to such new technologies, even traditional *sādhus* are able to reach all corners of the world, to become globally famous and attract followers while remaining within their small religious setting. Gurus and ascetics have new approaches available to them to better satisfy the religious quests of a much wider society which now extends far beyond the geographical boundaries of India. An increasing number of *sādhus* today are therefore seeking foreign disciples, in the knowledge that some might pay handsomely in order to be initiated, or to skip certain steps of training, although not all initiations are based on such utilitarian motives.[6] Thanks to modern gurus, modernised *sādhus*, foreigners and new technologies, 'traditional' *sādhus*—that is, conventional *sādhus* belonging to old *sampradāyas*—have in many cases been affected by new trends, and this includes the field of yoga itself.

As we shall see in this chapter, the development of media and communication has revolutionised the lives of *sādhus*: the devices that have found their way into the hands of ascetics have become a new source of information and 'knowledge'.

---

work of Strauss (2005) on Swami Sivananda; of Pankhania (2008) on Svāmī Satyānanda; of Aveling (1994) on Svāmī Satyānanda and Osho; of Caldwell (2001) on Muktananda; and of Russell (1978) on Maharishi Mahesh Yogi.

5 In 2007, Colin Campbell proposed the Easternisation theory: the profound process of change in the West produced since the 1960s by new interpretations in theology, political thought and science arriving from Eastern cultures and widely adopted by new generations.

6 While in the past it was almost impossible for a foreigner to join a traditional ascetic *sampradāya*, the situation changed in the second half of the 20th century. Today not only can foreigners be initiated but some of them are even able to obtain important religious titles, sometimes after paying considerable sums of money (see Bevilacqua 2020).

Traditional *sādhus* on modern yoga

Previous chapters have shown us that *sādhus*' understanding of yoga refers to the practice of *dhyāna* rather than postures, and *their* use of *dhyāna* is for specific soteriological and devotional goals. As such, most *sādhus* with whom I have spent time do not recognise modern yoga as bearing any resemblance to their yoga practice: that is, as a *sādhanā*.[7] Essentially, there were three aspects of modern yoga that drew *sādhus*' criticism: the focus on physical practices; the emphasis on the medical effect of yoga; and its exploitation for financial gain. Although *sādhus* evidently recognise the importance of yoga's physical practices and the attendant health benefits, they dislike the undue importance attributed to them. When it comes to the commercial aspect, despite the opprobrium it receives from many *sādhus*, there are nonetheless some who seek to participate in the exploitation. Traditional *sādhus*, in fact, are beginning to adapt to new trends to allow their orders to enjoy some of the profit accruing from yoga's global popularity. The following sections will examine these three aspects and how *sādhus* react to them.

On the (excessive) attention to postures

I will begin this section with two extracts from conversations with *sādhus*:

> You see, what is called modern yoga is not yoga. They may be masters of *āsanas*, but they have no knowledge of the spiritual part of what yoga is.
>
> Rām Avadhūt Dās

> Dr Sanjay: Actually, this is totally *vyāyām*! It is not yoga; it is physical training. Iyengar also uses ropes, and benches . . . but Patañjali's yoga system is *sthiram sukham āsanas*: you go slowly and gently and when flexibility comes from within, then you are in a position without forcing the body. In many yoga schools, instead, you force the body and people are very happy because in ten days they are able to do this or that position, but it is very artificial, because you use tools. [. . .] You do a posture and you give your name to that *āsana*, but in the ancient books you will not find that name. In the ancient texts there is no mention of *vyāyām*. For example, in *Haṭhapradīpikā* you find 24 *āsanas*, in *Gheraṇḍa Saṃhitā* 33, and these are classical postures. But if you consult Iyengar's book, you will find more than 300 *āsanas* there.

7 This does not mean that modern yoga cannot be experienced as a *sādhanā per se*. While considering *sādhus*' perspectives we must always bear in mind that they are religious people and have based their life on achieving religious goals.

> D: So, do you think those *āsanas* were invented by them?
>
> Dr Sanjay: Yes, yes, by modern men with modern minds, for modern people.

These extracts exemplify a common attitude of *sādhus* towards modern yoga, which is to associate it with physical exercises rather than a *sādhanā*. As Rājeś Cetan Brahmacārī clarified: 'It is true that a healthy body is necessary for *sādhanā*, but these people do not have a *sādhanā*. That is why there is no meaning in what they call yoga. It is only an external display.'

According to Yogī Bhakti Nāth, a true *sādhaka* seeks spiritual results and these cannot be achieved through postures: 'A *sādhaka* thinks about the *sādhanā*; he has no time for mere physical practice.' Svāmī Ātmānanda echoed these words by stressing that today everyone is keen to call themselves a 'yogi', but no one is justified in doing so because to be a yogi is not to 'jump' but to have achieved union with the *paramātman*. Īśnāth sees in this emphasis on physical practices the desire of the 'West' to make simple something that it is not. To name oneself *yogī* without really being one means, in his view, that 'People do not want to understand what yoga is, which means that they do not want to change. That's the problem.' Īśnāth also pointed out that some yoga instructors can pose a danger to others because they can 'really hurt others, as they do not have the philosophy and ideas, and they do not have the right to teach yoga.' He was very clear about how he saw the process involved in the modern way of practising yoga. He said:

> What is happening in the world is only physical, many practices are missing a proper programme: *yam* and *niyam* are necessary to give discipline to the person, then *āsanas* are necessary for the body to make it strong and disease-free; then *prāṇāyāma* is necessary. *Prāṇāyāma* must be performed after *āsanas* because it is necessary for *dhāraṇā* and *dhyāna*, not for *āsanas*. Of course, during *āsanas* it is necessary to perform a correct breathing. But not all *āsanas* are even necessary.
>
> Holding the breath is very important. But no one in modern schools teaches this, just as few teach meditation correctly. Very few teach purifications, which are also essential for the body.

The greatest danger, according to him, is that yoga teachers who pretend to be or convince themselves that they are yogi are often unable to recognise their own mistakes. This constitutes a major problem as identified and reported by ascetics: whereas in the *sādhu samāj* one has to find a guru and be accepted by a guru, in modern yoga anyone is accepted, and anyone is allowed to teach yoga even after short teaching courses. This leads to standardised practices that can be dangerous.

However, if we consider yoga a general term for exercise (H., *abhyās*), then, according to Rām Priya Dās, everyone can do yoga, but still one should do yogic exercise according to the limits of one's own body. Therefore, not everyone should be practising the same *āsana* and each practice should be customised, just as each physical yoga practice should fit the body and health of the person performing it. This is why the role of the guru is so important. The wrong teaching would lead to someone becoming not a yogi but a *rogī*, a sick person. With the right teacher, Rām Priya Dās continued, householders can do yoga as exercise, unless they decide to do yoga as *sādhanā*. Then they should start following *yamas* and *niyamas*, especially celibacy. In fact, even for those who have families but want to follow yoga as a *sādhanā*, celibacy is necessary to obtain the fruits of yoga. Rām Caraṇ Dās was adamant about this point. He said:

> If you do not respect *brahmacarya* you won't get results. It is like if you go to school but don't study: you won't achieve anything. If you are married and have a family, you have to work and you have many thoughts. If you have sex while practising yoga, you can get physical results but not spiritual results, because spiritual results are washed away with ejaculation. That is why it is difficult to have a clear mind. When you have no attachment, the mind is quickly perfected.[8]

But we have to keep in mind that not everyone, according to *sādhus*, has a mind that can be brought under control through yoga practices, which is why there are different *sādhanās* in the ascetic field.

In general, it is fairly well accepted among *sādhus* that *āsanas* and other physical yogic practices taught by a good master are generally popular, especially for their health benefits (see below on Bābā Rāmdev). But householders who use physical yoga to address physical problems in their bodies should be aware that they cannot go beyond this stage. A more sympathetic attitude is that of Garuḍ Dās, who also teaches his devotees and followers meditative practices with the aim that, once they are able to leave domestic life and retire to spiritual life, they will have all the practices and knowledge they need to cope with it properly.

On modern yoga and its medical aspects

It was only recently that yoga has become a form of alternative medicine and a source of physical training. In his works, Alter analysed the early 20th-century attempts made by Shri Yogendra—a wrestler and gymnastics

8 Rām Caraṇ Dās's words recall the wrestlers' approach described by Alter (1992: 108–113).

enthusiast before becoming a yoga practitioner—and Swami Kuvalayananda to develop the scientific-therapeutic aspect of yoga. According to Alter (2005: 134), the two 'tried to reconcile magic, alchemy and secret, esoteric knowledge with the modern priorities of health, the treatment of disease, and the dissemination of knowledge about these issues to the public at large' through their centres, the Yoga Institute (1918) and Kaivalyadhama (1924), respectively.[9] After Shri Yogendra and Swami Kuvalayananda had redefined and revolutionised the field, other key institutions and teachers followed to continue the emphasis on the medical aspect of yoga, which remains one of the features attributable to yoga's global popularity.[10]

The approach of *sādhus* to this issue depends essentially on whether they have studied yoga in yoga centres. There are in fact *sādhus* who have taken courses in modern centres or universities and gained a more scientific understanding. Rām Avadhūt Dās, for example, holds a BA in Yoga from the Banaras Hindu University. In our discussions on the body and yoga practice, he talked about hormones. He related the yogic body, with its *nāḍīs* and *cakras*, to the physical medical body: the *nāḍīs* to the nerves and the *granthis* to the glands that produce hormones to create balance in the body but also to activate, develop and protect it. He also made a connection between physical and mental problems, pointing out that while physical yoga balances hormones, meditation and breathing exercises influence and balance the mind with positive effects on the *granthis*. According to him, when the *nāḍīs* prevent the circulation of hormones due to disease, yogic *kriyās* can be used to purify the body and rebalance them. When the sympathetic and parasympathetic systems are functioning correctly, there are no problems. Therefore, in his view, *āsanas* and *kriyās* can cure any illness because they balance the body by making it produce the correct quantities of hormones.

A similar mindset was apparent in Yogī Śivanāth, who went to Lonavala and studied at the Kaivalyadhama, where he did a one-year diploma course in yoga education. In his *pravacan*,[11] he assembled explanations of yoga and

9 Swami Kuvalayananda built a fully equipped laboratory and clinic, 'imported X-ray machines and electrocardiographs' and 'engaged with science as a way of knowing, as a philosophy of knowledge. In this regard he set about testing specific aspects of Yoga practice. But in this project, Yoga as a theory of psychic function came to hold a status very similar to that of evolutionary theory in biology' (Alter 2004: 30).

10 On the links between yoga, modern yoga, health and fitness, see also De Michelis 2004; Alter 2004; Singleton 2010.

11 On Yogī Śivanāth and his *pravacan*, see Bevilacqua 2022a.

health as found in textual sources and favoured a more scientific approach. He describes yoga as *cikitsā* (medicine) for all, to remove disease (H., *rog*): through yoga, mind (H., *man*) and *ātman* (self) can be at peace, because when the body is balanced then *man* follows. Yoga is therefore a knowledge that works on the *ātman*, body and mind. He called *āsanas* and *mudrās* '*śarīr vigyān*', 'knowledge of the body',[12] and *dhāraṇā*, *dhyāna* and *samādhi* '*man vigyān*', 'knowledge of the mind', which he connected to psychology.

It should be noted that when Yogī Śivanāth and Rām Avadhūt Dās explained the connection between physical glands and the yogic body, they mostly used specialist English medical terms, implying that this form of knowledge comes from a contemporary and more recent understanding of yoga.

Dr Svāmī Sanjay, who also studied at the Banaras Hindu University in Varanasi, said that although the medical aspect of yoga was being studied in India from the beginning of the 20th century, it was not until the 1960s that Western doctors and scientists began coming to India to learn how yoga practices could help fight diseases. According to him, it was when Western scholars took an interest in the therapeutic aspect of yoga that it became more popular in Western countries. When I teased him about the fact that many modern yoga schools have sprung up in India, he pointed out that they have become successful only because they attract Western students: Indian people still know little about many of these institutes, despite some of them achieving fame in the West.

It should be noted that even those *sādhus* who acknowledge the medical benefits of yoga still regard its main goal as being spiritual; conversely, those who dislike an undue emphasis on the medical aspect also recognise the importance of yoga physical practice in maintaining a healthy body. As we have mentioned, maintaining good health is functional to the *sādhus*' spiritual *sādhanā*: a healthy individual does not worry about the body and can concentrate on God.

Since not all *sādhus* are masters of yoga *kriyās*, they find other ways to keep themselves healthy. There are indeed *sādhus* who have some traditional medical knowledge and prepare medicines based on *jaṛī būṭī* (i.e. plants),[13] which they may combine with physical yogic practices to cure

12 Yogī Śivanāth gave examples of how *āsanas* can be used to make the glands in the body function properly. For example, *āsanas* such as *sarvāṅgāsana* and *śīrṣāsana* are useful for increasing the work of the pineal gland, he averred, while *sarvāṅgāsana* also increases the power of the thyroid gland.

13 Kamal Giri claimed to possess a 500-year-old medicine book containing recipes that he would use to cure poor people.

diseases. While some *sādhus* reject allopathic medicines, claiming that their chemical ingredients could ruin the *sādhanā*, others admit a role for allopathy and prefer to treat themselves with it, especially in case of diseases such as diabetes, typhus, etc.[14] As such, how a *sādhu* deals with disease can vary widely depending on his background and the knowledge he has gathered in his life. A simple example of this can be given by describing how my headache was treated by different *sādhus*.

Curing my headache

During my fieldwork in Rishikesh in 2017, I suffered from severe headaches, so I turned to *bābās* for solutions.

When Bhole Bābā heard about my pain, he suggested I might get some relief by pressing the bottom of my toes, because fingers and toes, he said, connect the whole body. Then, taking an Ayurvedic balm called *zandu*, which contains mint, eucalyptus and a few other herbs, he started massaging my neck. He applied particular pressure to the T-spot where the spine and shoulders meet, claiming it to be a crucial point where the *nāḍīs* pass through. He also claimed that the ears and eyes converge at that point, and that there are several possible causes of head pain, including the stomach. He pressed my head and massaged my temples for at least 15–20 minutes. I asked him if it was a kind of Ayurvedic massage, to which he insisted that it was Ayurvedic science, and that Ayurveda comes from the *sādhus*' world, as *sādhus* have had much experience with the body and the environment. He said he learnt it from his guru, who was quite old: he used to do his *sevā* by massaging his guru's body, too. His guru had taught him how and why to do certain things. Now, he said, he does it to other people hoping that they can learn the practice and give relief to someone else. It was, therefore, knowledge imparted while doing *sevā* and passed on in order to do *sevā* to others. I asked Bhole Bābā what the procedure was for a *sādhu* experiencing pain. He replied that he would first try some *āsanas* and then, if these did not work, massage and medicine. I asked him which *āsana* was most suitable for headaches to which he replied *śīrṣāsana*—to be done in the morning on an empty stomach—because the head gets a lot of pressure, which is helpful, and the back also gets stronger.

The same evening, I went to meet Dayānanda Purī and, despite his incredible knowledge of plants, he chose to address my headache by trying to remove a possible evil eye: he applied a *tilaka* on my forehead, with a

---

14 For example, since falling ill with typhus, Jagannāth Dās practises only certain specific *kriyās* to concentrate the energy in his stomach; lately, because of a liver problem, he only practises *vajrāsana* and follows what the doctor prescribes.

dot made of *vibhūti* and then with a peacock feather he performed a ritual against the evil eye. A woman who was present told me that he was in a state of high concentration while reciting the mantras. He then gave me some *vibhūti* to eat.

I talked about my headache to the *bābā* in the Loyal Guphā (cave)—who also was very knowledgeable about plants and had created a medicinal herb garden around his cave-*āśram*—and he pondered, touching his neck, mouth and head. He judged that my pain was due to overwork and lack of proper rest, which increased tension. He fetched some aloe vera, declaring that its juice was very good because when the head 'is too hot, the aloe sucks up some heat'. Having applied the aloe vera to my forehead, he said the juice was drying quickly because of the heat in my head.

This brief anecdote attests to how differentiated *sādhus*' approaches to physical problems can be, and how they might apply different remedies depending on what they believe to be the cause. Again, we see how multifaceted *sādhus*' knowledge can be and how further research is needed to address our lack of information. This is especially evident with a topic as complex as the relationship between *sādhu*s and Ayurveda and the use of *rasāyana* and *kāyakalpa* among *sādhus*.

Ayurveda, *rasāyana* and *kāyakalpa*

Ayurveda, the Veda (knowledge) of *āyus*, 'life' or 'longevity', is a system of general medical practice that includes both preventative and prescriptive aspects and teaches a broad range of therapies 'including diet, enemas, massage, bloodletting, leeching, ointments, douches, sweating, and surgery' (Wujastyk 2003: 3–4). This system probably originated around the time of the Buddha, but what has survived to present are some codified and reworked Sanskrit treatises from the 6th century CE and their commentaries.

Although the description of Ayurveda is beyond the scope of this book, it is useful to mention Kenneth G. Zysk's assumption that Ayurveda as a medical tradition emerged from the ascetic milieu that existed in North India in the 5th century BCE. According to him, medical practitioners were denigrated by brahmins because of their contact with sick, hence impure, peoples. However, they were accepted by ascetic renunciants and mendicants, with whom they shared a lifestyle as they wandered the countryside administering treatments and acquiring new medicines, cures and medical information (Zysk 1991: 5–6). These wandering physicians were not ascetics, but many ascetics could be physicians, therefore forms of magico-religious healing preserved by ascetic groups were transmitted and added into this medical tradition. From these healers developed a vast medical knowledge that was systematised in Ayurveda and, probably in the first centuries CE, was assimilated into brahmanical lore (Zysk 1991: 4, 37).

Zysk's assumptions echo those of *sādhus*. As already mentioned, the idea is quite widespread among *sādhus* that the knowledge behind Ayurveda came from ascetics who wandered in the jungle and learnt the powers and properties of plants and herbs by experimenting on themselves and then passed on their knowledge to others to cure their illnesses. However, although *sādhus* mention Ayurveda and use its terminology, to cure themselves they mainly use techniques such as *ṣaṭkarmas* and *prāṇāyāmas*—which are not used in Ayurveda—or herbs. It is therefore difficult to relate the medical knowledge of contemporary *sādhus* directly to textual Ayurveda. Ascetics share remedies with each other, often associating them with specific mantras, and those who are particularly skilled may become renowned among lay people as well. It should be noted that, when lay people turn to *sādhus* for healing, they are looking for something more than the skill of a physician: i.e. the ritual and magic aspect that Zysk discusses.

The link between codified Ayurveda and yoga is also quite complicated. There is some evidence that the authors of early yoga sources, such as Patañjali, had some knowledge of Ayurveda.[15] However, with regard to later yogic texts, Birch (2018: 7) argues that yogins likely drew from a common healing knowledge also present in the earlier Tantras, Purāṇas and Dharmaśāstras, while also developing specific yogic techniques for curing diseases. I believe that we cannot exclude the possibility that yogis selected and adapted Ayurvedic knowledge that could be useful for their purposes, but without necessarily being directly involved in Ayurveda. It is not possible to reconstruct what the reality was on the ground among ascetic practitioners and especially among the different lineages of transmission to which they were attached. It is not unreasonable to assume that there were, indeed, lineages associated with a medical tradition, although this is difficult to trace today. In any case, as the work of several scholars has shown,[16] prior to the 20th century Ayurvedic texts did not refer to yoga practices and meditation in their therapeutic framework (Newcombe 2017: 87), hence yoga was not used as a healing practice. The strong connection we find

15 Birch (2018: 4) points out the link between Ayurveda and Patañjali: Patañjali's 'commentarial definition and discussion of disease (*vyādhi*), which is mentioned in *sūtra* 1.30, is similar to one given by Caraka'; and there is a similarity between the respective lists of bodily constituents (*dhātu*) and their relation to the humours (*doṣa*) (see also Maas 2007: 153).

16 See for example Alter 2004, 2005; Berger 2013; Newcombe 2017; Birch 2018.

today between yoga and Ayurveda is a recent phenomenon which depends on the medicalisation of yoga discussed earlier.

There is, however, a practice that bridges the ascetic world and Ayurveda: the practice of *rasāyana* (lit., 'path of essence', practically a path of 'rejuvenation') which has its equivalent in the practice of *kāyakalpa* (renewal of the body) among ascetics. As a recent volume edited by Wujastyk, Newcombe and Barois (2017: i) has shown, longevity and vitalisation practices were common interests for yoga, alchemy and Ayurveda. I will briefly clarify this sentence and then address the contemporary use of *kāyakalpa* among ascetics, although the information I have is rather limited.

In Sanskrit medical literature (such as the *Carakasaṃhitā* and the *Suśrutasaṃhitā*), the term *rasāyana*[17] refers to a type of substance or medicine and the treatment associated with it. In most cases, this therapy is part of a more complex treatment supervised by a physician and administered to a patient. However, in the earliest medical treatises, *rasāyana* may also be a practice undertaken proactively by individuals who wish to achieve certain results (Barois 2017: iii). Sanskrit alchemical literature associates *rasāyana* with raw substances and compound formulations in which mercurial elixirs play a particularly important role. In alchemical literature, in fact, mercury is the main ingredient in the *rasāyana* process, the alchemical products for which are obtained through complex metallurgical procedures. In this context, the practitioner is the creator and the recipient of the elixir (Barois 2017: iii). The *rasāyana* literature, both medical and alchemical, speaks to the use of herbal preparations to cleanse the patient's body, a preliminary treatment aimed at creating optimal conditions for the application of the *rasāyana* tonic or elixir (Barois 2017: iv). In medical treatises, among the results of *rasāyana* treatments we find: anti-ageing effects, prolongation of life, curing of certain diseases, extension of mental and physical abilities, and the development of extraordinary powers. Alchemical *rasāyana*, on the other hand, aims to attain immortality, or a godlike state.

So why was longevity (or immortality) sought after? This is an important question, touched on in the previous chapter. A long life enables householders to fulfil brahmanical goals—*dharma*, *artha* and *kāma*—and enables the practitioner of alchemical *rasāyana* to achieve *mokṣa* and *jīvanmukti*. These are also the reasons behind the practice of *kāyakalpa* among ascetics.

The term *kāyakalpa* is not found in Sanskrit medical or yogic literature, but it appears in medical traditions associated with the Tamil Siddha under

17 The term *rasāyana* is difficult to translate because the two elements of the compound, *rasa* and *ayana* (or *āyana*) can each have a range of possible meanings (see Wujastyk 2015).

the name *kāyakaṟpam*.[18] As suggested by Ilona Kędzia (2017), *kāyakaṟpam* is likely the link between yoga, medicine and alchemy, as it combines elements of these three disciplines. The practice of *kāyakaṟpam/kāyakalpa* is associated with the *kāyasiddhars*, yogis who mastered the ability to control the body, keeping it eternally young. They are revered in Tamil texts as Siddhars/Siddhas/Cittars and are considered the founders of medicine in Tamil traditions (Newcombe 2017: 102).

As Robert Svoboda (2008: 126) summarises, *kāyakalpa* involves a prolonged retreat from the world, in a dark, quiet hut, during which the patient, after proper preparation, undergoes a cathartic purification—the skin, hair, nails, and teeth fall off and grow back again—intended to reorganise the organism into a superior state.

Newcombe (2017: 101) suggests that these treatments were preserved within ascetic communities outside the lineage traditions of Ayurvedic families. She describes a famous example of such a practice performed by Madan Mohan Malaviya (1861–1946), an Indian education reformer and politician, who in 1938 underwent a much-publicised intensive *kāyakalpa* treatment under the supervision of a wandering ascetic, a *sādhu* named Tapasvījī Bābā, who claimed to have undergone multiple *kāyakalpa* treatments himself. The one he recommended to Malaviya was in fact the *kuṭīpraveśa/kuṭīpraveśika*, the treatment conducted inside the hut.

The *kuṭīpraveśika* is described in classic medical manuals such as the *Carakasaṃhitā* and the *Suśrutasaṃhitā*, although later Ayurvedic works have foregone detailed explanations of this method, probably because it was an expensive and time-consuming treatment (Newcombe 2017). According to these texts, before entering the hut (*kuṭī*), the patient must undergo internal purification by anointing and cleansing the stomach and intestines. He then must live in the small hut for about 40 days, on a specific diet in order to achieve results such as those mentioned by Svoboda. Dagmar Wujastyk (2015: 74) suggests that *kuṭīpraveśika* was not part of standard Ayurvedic practice, which is probably why it was preserved in ascetic communities. Should we therefore be associating ascetic medical knowledge with Tamil Siddha medicine rather than Ayurveda? This is a difficult question to answer considering the current lack of extensive research on the subject.

The well-known Swami Sivananda conflated *kāyakalpa* with all the various methods that yogis or ascetics might use to prolong their lives in order to achieve liberation during their lifetime (Newcombe 2017: 102).

18 On *kaṟpam*, see Kędzia 2017: 121–142.

As reported by Newcombe, Sivananda wrote in his *Health and Long Life* (1945):

> The process of rejuvenation through 'Kaya Kalpa' is the keeping of the great Tapasvins. Kaya-kalpa is the real elixir of life by which the Rasayanas make the body immortal. [. . .] They teach to immortalise the body first by means of Kaya-Kalpa made out of herbs, or mercury, or sulphur, Neem or Amlaka fruits, in order to achieve the goal of Yoga in this very life.

Sivananda's words are confirmed by current-day *sādhus*. In fact, the word *kāyakalpa* is used by *sādhus* to refer to various practices aimed at prolonging life, and it seems that such practices are still in use. Jagannāth Dās told me that he once went to meet his guru and the latter was very thin—'As if he were made of nothing but bones!'—and everyone was very worried because they thought he was going to die. Jagannāth Dās asked him to go to the hospital, but the guru replied not to worry and to come back in a couple of months. When Jagannāth Dās returned, he found his guru full of strength: 'Cheeks like apples, the body *ekdam pakkā* (perfectly fit).' The guru (Monī Bābā) revealed to him that he had done *kāyakalpa*. He did not stay in a *kuṭī*, but took some specific *jaṛī būṭī* (herbs), especially *arhar* (the leaves of lentils). He survived for months on this alone. According to Jagannāth Dās, these herbs ate all the fat in the guru's body, rejuvenating it.

The practice of *kāyakalpa* seems to be well known among *sādhus* and to be a practice that *yogīrāj* have often used in the past. Ramdas Lamb (2012: 447) reports the story of Devrāhā Bābā, whose longevity was famous and apparently resulted from the practice of *kāyakalpa*. Lamb spoke with his main disciple, who revealed that Devrāhā Bābā began doing *kāyakalpa* in the early 20th century and did it every 20 years. His practice of *kāyakalpa* consisted of an *anuṣṭhāna* of one to three months' duration, during which 'he would not sleep, speak, or eat (except for certain herbs), and would remain in a state of great yogic meditation' (Lamb (2012: 447). However, in the present, it seems that not many gurus know how to perform it correctly.

All the references to *kāyakalpa* that I heard referred to adherence to a strict dietary and behavioural regimen rather than to performing the practice in the hut. No mercury-based alchemical remedies were mentioned, although I did meet a Nāth Yogī who claimed to wear a mercury ball on his necklace. He claimed that mercury was a symbol of its *panth*, traditionally associated with alchemy: the Kapal *panth*.[19] According to Yogī Śivanāth,

19 Briggs reports of a *panth* called 'Kaplanī' which draws its origin from Kapal Muni, which is why it is also called Kapil *panth*. According to Briggs (1938: 68), the headquarters of the *panth* is located in Gaṅgā Sāgar. Although there are no traditional

it was Siddha Yogī Nāgārjunāth[20] who 'discovered' mercury and used it to cure diseases. He later stated that among Nāth Yogīs there are several who know Ayurveda, thus linking Ayurvedic and alchemical practices. However, considering Yogī Śivanāth's involvement with Bābā Rāmdev and his desire to regain a Nāth space in the yoga scene,[21] we shall question whether his claim reflects a still ongoing tradition. In fact, the use of mercury among Nāths was very rarely mentioned—more often as one of the 'liquids' to be used for *vajrolī mudrā*—and basically its use was recognised as part of an almost lost and highly dangerous practice.[22]

Modern yoga and business

One of the features of modern yoga that distresses many *sādhus* is its transformation into a huge global business. Nonetheless, some *sādhus* and religious centres are attempting to participate in this new market. Yoga is a key area of investment for several religious centres and represents a propitious strategy for achieving long-term returns, in light of an annual turnover in India of INR120 billion (US$1.8 billion) for yoga and other traditional practices related to health and spirituality (see Gautam and Droogan 2018: 24). Aware of this recent economic boom, some Hindu ascetics are also trying to carve out a niche for themselves in this industry, targeting the educated and professional classes through the promotion of a practice that aims at empowerment and control of the body and health (Chakraborty 2006: 387).

This section will introduce *sādhus* who are opposed to the commercialisation of yoga as well as those who have embraced it. This leads to a further distinction between those *sādhus* who teach yoga on a random basis, especially to foreigners, and those who have embarked on a more 'professional' and international career, not unlike the modern gurus mentioned earlier.

---

connections between mercury, alchemy and Kapila Muni, further research would be useful to investigate this claim and verify whether there is an alchemical tradition in this subsection and, if so, what kind of practices are followed.

20 Here Yogī Śivanāth probably refers to Nāgārjuna 'whom a number of later traditions identify as a Siddha alchemist hailing from Śrīparvata' (White 1996: 60). White (1996: 66–77) demonstrated the difficulty of identifying all the 'Nāgārjunas' in Indian traditions. In the 11th century, Al-Bīrūnī mentions a Nāgārjuna who lived in Ujjain in the 10th century and to whom numerous manuscripts on the subject of alchemy and *rasāyana* are attributed (see Wujastyk 1984).

21 See Bevilacqua 2022a.

22 According to Rāghavendra Dās, *mahātmās* used to take *pārā*, i.e. mercury, but *śodhit* (refined) to avoid damaging the body as it produces too much heat.

As a result, I will address what effect modern yoga is having on 'traditional' *sādhus*.

One consequence of the commercialisation of yoga is that fewer elder gurus are now inclined to share their practices and knowledge with their disciples, fearing that the latter might exploit it for business purposes. What they find unacceptable is for a *sādhanā*, a spiritual discipline, to be turned into a business, losing its core value. A *sādhanā* cannot be sold and a guru should not sell his knowledge because his actions should not have commercial motives. A guru, according to Garuḍ Dās, should be 'someone who helps another who is searching'. According to Jogī Bābā, if one teaches others only for money, not only does he not help them to improve but he also destroys his own practice because money leads to *māyā*, delusion and attachment, which is the opposite of what yoga practitioners should aim for. If it were to become something completely physical, and for sale, then it is no longer yoga: it is just a job.

This is abundantly clear to the *sādhus* who live in Rishikesh, a well-known destination for yoga practitioners which in recent decades has been completely transformed by yoga centres, cafés, restaurants and shops selling yoga products for practitioners. Dayānanda Purī's *āśram* is there, in an area called Tapobhūmi. I witnessed him giving a video interview there to a man who was asking questions about yoga and Patañjali. The man began the conversation by mentioning the many places in Rishikesh where yoga was taught; immediately, Dayānanda Purī interjected, saying there were in fact 'Many yoga stores, but there were no yogis', since nowadays, according to him, yogis were to be found in the Himalayas, Tibet and Bhutan, while in Rishikesh were only stores of all sizes selling yoga: 'Commercial yoga, exercise yoga, similar to gymnastics'. He continued: 'You go, you pay and you take meditation classes: how much you pay is how much you get. If you pay 100 rupees, you get a 100 rupees meditation.' This is not to say, Dayānanda Purī further explained, that Rishikesh is not a special place; quite the contrary: thanks to the presence of the Ganges and the Himalayas, over the centuries it has been the place where gurus and yogis have chosen to dwell to carry out their practices. 'You just live in these places and you become yoga . . . Any stone, you sit and concentrate immediately, because of the energy of this place,' he said. No, the criticism was directed at the fast-paced yoga courses often held there. Hari Giri complained that people go to Rishikesh and in a couple of weeks acquire teaching certificates, simply because they can pay for them, and he found this very dangerous. Teaching, in his opinion, needs much more than a standardised number of certified hours.

Traditional *sādhus* teaching *yog* and yoga

Traditional *sādhus* teaching lay people is nothing new, and therefore should not be associated only with the transnational expansion of yoga. In the past and continuing today, *sādhus* have taught yogic physical practices to householders (including foreigners).[23] We have seen that the proliferation of *haṭha* yoga texts probably stemmed from the (albeit limited) need to target an audience of householders, especially potential patrons. Even today, there are local *sādhus* who teach practices such as *āsanas*, *prāṇāyāmas* and other simple *kriyās* to devotees or children in their *āśrams*.[24] This explains *sādhus* who are initiated later in life yet know *āsanas*: they learnt them as children.[25] It demonstrates the strong connection between lay people and *sādhus* and how these teachings can be considered one of the ways in which *sādhus* still contribute to the life of the lay community.

However, today, when it comes to teaching foreigners, things may be slightly different. A *saṃnyāsī* told me that he had no issue with teaching foreigners, even if meant travelling abroad. He reported having been in Italy with an Italian woman who suggested that he start teaching yoga to earn some money. At first, he said, he felt uncomfortable at the thought of making money from a practice that he considered a *sādhanā*. Eventually, he was able to come to terms with this feeling because he had to survive abroad. He also realised that he had to learn how to teach yoga to Westerners. This was a rather interesting statement shared by another *sādhu*, who made a similar distinction: he said he learnt '*yog*' (Hindi pronunciation) from his guru, but then he decided to learn yog**a** (the bold here is to emphasise the *a*, as per the 'global' pronunciation) from Westerners in order to travel to Europe because, he said, with him being a *sādhu*, people would pay him and offer him accommodation. So he learnt modern postural yoga in Rishikesh from a foreigner. This is in fact quite common. Yogī Alone Nāth said his yoga (postural) guru was a German woman and suggested that I learn *āsanas* and *prāṇāyāmas* from a Brazilian woman he knew.

---

23 See for example the experience—although called into question—of Theos Bernard (1968).

24 This is a complex issue which, unfortunately, lack of time prevented me from investigating.

25 It would be interesting to investigate the role of lay people who are familiar with yoga practices and who participate in certain traditions (e.g. the Siddha tradition). In fact, it is not impossible that the direction of exchange flows the other way: an example is given by Svāmī Satcidānanda, a *monī sādhu* from Madras, whose guru, or at least one of his gurus, was Rāghavendra: a Vaiṣṇava naturopathic doctor who taught him *yogāsanas* and purifications.

It would seem that the way in which the physical modern practices of yoga are taught is affecting the approach of those *sādhus* who are eager to learn that kind of yoga for different, often pragmatic, reasons. Moreover, *sādhus* may be attracted not only to foreigners and modern physical yoga practices but also to the theories and ideas circulating in the transnational yoga world. As mentioned earlier, new means of communication allow those *sādhus* who own a mobile phone to be in contact with people all over the world—and also be influenced by ideas from all over the word. It is not uncommon for ascetics to receive simplified information about yoga theories or a combination of yoga theories with New Age approaches via WhatsApp groups or Facebook. A *tyāgī* I met, who is also a *yogīrāj*, often associated yoga practices with reiki during our conversations and sometimes shared with me images that associated each *cakra* with specific psychological and astrological attributes, functions and qualities that have nothing to do with the explanations found in textual sources but rather with counterculture. He also suggested several times that I read Robert Greene's book *The 48 Laws of Power*, and drew on it to explain how to react to negative situations and negative people.

Mallinson (2012b: 8) made similar remarks about a *sādhu* he met, Yogī Anūp Nāth (see below), who showed *āsanas* that he had probably seen online on YouTube practised by Western practitioners; yet he claimed to have had a 'vision' of them.

It is very difficult to discern the extent to which modernity, or the pizza effect of modern yoga, is influencing *sādhus* affiliated to traditional *sampradāyas*: while young *sādhus* today may be influenced by their smartphone, we must remember that *sādhus* have been in contact with the counterculture since the 1970s, especially those who can read English or who have been in contact with foreigners at pilgrimage centres or during religious festivals. Even then, the exchanges would often have been reciprocal: it is likely that foreigners taught their gurus rudimentary English and in doing so provided them with the vocabulary (often of New Age and spiritualist extraction) that became their vehicle of transmission, indirectly modifying the explanations (and, slightly, the meaning) through the language itself. This manifests in the way traditional *sādhus* may teach yoga to foreigners (or to Indians seeking modern yoga). The aforementioned Hari Giri, for example, who lives in Manali, teaches yoga to foreigners in Goa and Gokarna. His classes usually last two hours, or longer, depending on the people and the class itself, because, he said, he needs time to teach everything correctly: the postures, the *prāṇāyāmas*, as well as meditation.

The planning of the class, however, resembles the structure of an average yoga class conducted in a studio.

Another example is provided by a video I found on Facebook,[26] uploaded by Yogī Anūp Nāth in which he teaches yoga to a foreign woman. From the beginning of the video, it is clear that the class is entirely modelled on modern yoga classes: it starts with the woman relaxing, he then has her recite some mantras, in particular the *oṃ*; Yogī Anūp Nāth then asks her to practise several *prāṇāyāmas* and then relax again. The way of getting up after relaxation (rolling to one side and sitting down slowly) is also reminiscent of a modern teaching style. Next, he has her warm up her ankles, knees, elbow and wrist with exercises, after which she begins with *sūryanamaskār,* a uncommon practice among *sādhus.*[27] *Sūryanamaskār* is repeated for some time, only to be followed again by some relaxation. From this position, he has her do leg exercises, shoulder-stand and its variations, *navāsana* and its variations, balancing postures, etc. The class does not end well, however, because, having been teased by Yogī Anūp Nāth with standing and balancing postures, she interrupts the class and declares she is out. The Nāth replies by calling her crazy and ascribing her reaction most likely to the level of difficulty of the yoga he was teaching—which did not in fact comprise particularly challenging postures. When he appears in front of the camera, unable to perform the balancing posture he had asked the woman to do, he does other balancing postures, concluding with *yogadaṇḍāsana.* Finally, he relaxes and repeats some mantras. On watching the video, one would simply assume that the instructor was a yoga teacher: even the instructions he gives echoes those one might hear walking past yoga studios in Rishikesh. Perhaps one distinction was that the Nāth only ever touches the woman's body with his feet, pushing and tapping her, which is probably why she chose to leave.

The foregoing briefly shows how ascetics may adapt or change their practice for pragmatic reasons, i.e. finding people to teach or teaching those who request it. Often, as I was told by a yoga teacher in Varanasi, the (Indian) teacher has to adapt to what the (foreign) students want in order to retain them and make a living. In the case of *sādhus*—certainly the ones

26 The video is no longer publicly available, possibly as a privacy concern for the student involved.

27 The *sūryanamaskār* as understood today is a codification of *daṇḍ*s (for leg training) and *baiṭhak*s (leg warm-up exercises), introduced by the Rāja of Aundh, Bhawanrao Pant Pratinidhi, at the turn of the 20th century (see Armstrong 2023). Given its very recent origin, it is not traditionally performed by *sādhus*. On the complexity of the history of *sūryanamaskār*, see Sarbacker 2023.

I am describing—money is often not the main goal, but rather recognition or even fame.

My yoga classes with traditional ascetics

During my fieldwork I had the opportunity, albeit rare, to practise yoga as exercise with a few *sādhus*: Rām Priya Dās, the only female ascetic I met during my research; Svāmī Ātmānanda, an elderly *saṃnyāsī*, and Viśvot Giri, another *saṃnyāsī* who sometimes visits Europe in the guise of *fakīr* (and yoga teacher) among a company of performers.[28]

As I mentioned in the Introduction to this book, traditional *sādhus* usually teach their disciples; in these cases, since they taught mostly *āsanas*, they had no particular problem sharing their knowledge with me. Moreover, at least two of them had previous experience teaching foreigners, while Rām Priya Dās simply felt comfortable practising in my presence.[29]

Yoga class with Rām Priya Dās

Before we had *āsana* class together, Rām Priya Dās suggested several times that I watch Bābā Rāmdev's video to 'learn some yoga' (see below). I can therefore assume that her way of teaching me yoga was influenced by him, albeit with knowledge derived from her guru and an approach derived from her understanding of *āsanas*, i.e. as exercises that have no particular spiritual purpose in themselves.

We would meet in her temple in Varanasi at 5.30 am. My companions were a few other *sādhus* who lived there and, on a couple of occasions, Dr Singleton. Rām Priya Dās was very clear about the goal of our classes: with *āsanas* we were going to work on muscles and bones and her specific goal was to lose weight.

The classes began with different types of *prāṇāyāmas*, a sign that she was probably copying Rāmdev, since, as mentioned in previous chapters, *prāṇāyāma* is usually performed after *āsanas*. It is likely that she followed that sequence to meet my own expectations. However, the explanations she gave, and her mastery of the practices, testified to a profound knowledge. I reproduce some of her explanatory words here:

---

28 He used also to go to Italy performing as part of the Milon Mela, a troupe comprising a variety of performers assembled in Shantiniketan (West Bengal).

29 Jogī Bābā told me several times that he would teach me, but he never did. He seemed rather torn between how to teach me and whether he could teach me. Eventually he showed me several practices and gave me very useful information, postponing the teaching step until the future.

The first *prāṇāyāma* to do is the calm (H., *viśrām*) *prāṇāyāma*: take the breath into the lungs and then exhale it slowly. Slowly fill the lungs and then slowly release the breath. The back should be straight. When the breath is collected, it expands and goes here and there, so its flow must be controlled. You have to do this *prāṇāyāma* for two minutes.

The next *prāṇāyāma* is the *anulom vilom.*[30] Push the right nostril with your right thumb and inhale through the left nostril. Then do the opposite. Inhale as much as possible into your lungs. You can stop this breathing or you can do it continuously.

Now *bāhya prāṇāyāma*. You take in the breath and then you release it, as if coughing with the mouth closed. When the breath is out, you do *jālandharbandha*, *mūlabandha* and *uḍḍīyānabandha*. You do it five, six times.

Kapālabhāti. If you want to remove water from your nose, you have to do it normally. You should not make any noise from the throat; you should not move the shoulder. The lungs do not work; you do it with the stomach: by emptying it, the air will automatically fill it. Breathing should be neither too fast nor too slow; it should be normal. If you feel tired after a while, do this three or four times, then rest and continue for a few more minutes.[31]

Bhrāmarī prāṇāyāma.[32] Place three fingers on the eyes, one on the eyebrows and the thumbs on the ears. Inhale and emit the sound *oṃ* but with your mouth closed. Perform this three, four times, but if you have time you can increase the number.

---

30 *Anulom vilom*, which is another name for *nāḍī śodān*, 'alternate breathing technique', is also mentioned in the *Dattātreyayogaśāstra* and in the *Gorakṣaśataka* under the name *sūrya kumbhaka*. Hari Giri claimed that the basic *anulom vilom* comprises inhaling for 20 seconds, retaining and then releasing for ten seconds, slowly increasing the time of the steps.

31 Presented in some textual sources in the *ṣaṭkarma* section, *kapālabhāti* also finds its place among *prāṇāyāma*s and it is associated (often assimilated) with the practice of *bhastrī* or *bhastrikā*. The latter is described as such in *Gorakṣaśataka* 44: the yogi should 'hold his neck and stomach straight, close his mouth and forcefully exhale through his nostrils in such a way that his breath makes contact with his throat, producing the sound in his skull [. . .] the wise man should pump the air that is in his body in the same way that one might quickly pump blacksmiths' bellows' (translation from Mallinson and Singleton 2017: 159).

32 *Haṭhapradīpikā* 2.69 describes the practice of *bhrāmarī prāṇāyāma* like this: 'Now bhrāmarī: Forcibly loud inhalation with the sound of a male bee; very slow exhalation with the sound of a female bee: as a result of practising thus, there arises in the minds of the best yogis an extraordinary blissful playfulness' (http://hathapradipika.online).

> *Ugdīth prāṇāyāma.* In this *prāṇāyāma* the *oṃ* is done with the mouth open. You fill your lungs with the breath, close your eyes and release the breath with your mouth while saying *oṃ.*
>
> If you have a throat problem, if you snore when you sleep, then do *ujjāyī prāṇāyāma.* You have to produce the sound of a lion. At first do it briefly, then increase the time. At first, you may cough. When you get better at it, you can block the breath and do *jālandharbandha.* Then push the right nostril and release the breath with the left.[33]
>
> If you feel too hot or sweat too much, do *śītlī prāṇāyāma.*[34] Breathe in through the tongue. You fill your lungs, then stop breathing for a while and slowly release. Do this, three to six times, and you will no longer feel hot.[35]
>
> *Śītkarī* makes the mind relaxed.[36] Put your tongue behind your teeth and inhale through your closed mouth, filling your lungs. Then stop for a bit and then release the breath slowly. If you are weak, if you have heart problems, put your fingers in *śakti mudrā.* Otherwise, if you are well, it is not necessary [. . .] Do this *prāṇāyāma* ten, 12 times [. . .]; it is very good for the mind.

After the *prāṇāyāma*, we did several warm-up exercises, which she simply called *vyāyām*, and then we started with *āsana*s, each of which was held for a couple of minutes and repeated several times. Never in the duration of the class was there any kind of mantra chanting and we never meditated. But the thing that struck me most during her classes, especially in comparison to the yoga classes I attended in yoga studios, was the complete absence of relaxation time between one *āsana* and the next, something I have also noticed with the other *sādhus* who have taught me.

---

33 *Gorakṣaśataka* 37–39 describes the practice: 'The yogi should close the mouth and gently draw in air through the two channels so that it comes into contact with [the region] from the throat to the heart, making a sound. [. . .] he should hold his breath and then expel it through the left channel [. . .] it destroys the fire which arises in the head, removes phlegm from the throat increase the fire of the body' (Mallinson and Singleton 2017: 158).

34 In *Gorakṣaśataka* 40–41, 'after holding the breath [. . .] the sage should draw in air with his tongue before gently exhaling it through his nostrils [. . .] inflammation of the spleen and other diseases are destroyed' (Mallinson and Singleton 2017: 158).

35 Svāmī Ātmānanda said that this *prāṇāyāma* is also good in purifying the vocal cords, especially when associated with *jālandharbandha.*

36 According to *Haṭhapradīpikā* 2.54–55: '[The yogi] should continuously make sīt sound in the mouth and flare his nostrils. By practising in this way he becomes a second god of love. [. . .] Neither hunger nor thirst [nor] sleep nor indolence arise [for him]' (http://hathapradipika.online).

Yoga class with Svāmī Ātmānanda

Svāmī Ātmānanda claimed to have been the yoga teacher of Jawaharlal Nehru, the first Prime Minister of India. Although it was not possible to verify this information, considering his age, some photos he showed me, and the fact that he used to do yoga competitions, it can be assumed that he did actually participate in the process that invested yoga practices at the beginning of the 20th century. However, he did not disclose to me who taught him physical yoga practice and when he got initiated.

We met late in the morning at the art gallery of a friend, Pravash, who put me in touch with Svāmī Ātmānanda in Kolkata. There were others who worked there who wanted to attend the class as well.

His way of practising *āsana*s was very strenuous; in fact, he associated *yogāsana*s with *vyāyāms*. Before starting the practice, he gave each of us (there were three in the class) a physical check-up. First, he located the pulse of the abdominal aorta in the stomach: if it was just below the navel, the stomach was healthy. Then he measured us using a thread: the men from the pubis to the tip of the toes, the women from the navel to the tip of the toes—checking 'symmetry' was another way in which to ascertain physical health. He then tested our endurance and flexibility with *navāsana*, which he said was also a way to warm up, along with other exercises for the ankles, arms, chest, feet, etc. Then we did: *paścimottānāsana*; *uttānāsana* with variations; *pavanmuktāsana*; *bhujangāsana* but without hands ('Since snakes do not have them!' Svāmī Ātmānanda said); *dhanurāsana*; *uṣṭrāsana* ('This is good for ladies,' he claimed); *pavanmuktāsana*, with the aim of sitting and, from the sitting position, getting up; *halāsana* with knees on the ground; *sarvāṅgāsana*; *padmāsana* (also done with the hands on the floor to pull the body up while the head bent towards the knee); *matsyāsana* with legs in the lotus position; *gomukhāsana* ('A great posture to meditate!' he exclaimed); *badhakonāsana* ('As it is useful for *padmāsana*'); *vajrāsana* (done in the same way as Rām Priya Dās, with the hands pressing the belly and bending over). We repeated each position at least three times, several times during the same class. He gave different exercises to each of the three of us, or the same ones but to be performed at different times, as needed. The pause (which he never called 'relaxation') was done by lying on the stomach, arms along the sides.

He emphasised several times that these exercises were for stretching and strengthening the body. As already mentioned, according to him, when one can maintain an *āsana* for three hours and 48 minutes, then the *āsana* is perfected and can also be used as a meditative posture. When a lady asked about *prāṇāyāma*, Svāmī Ātmānanda replied that everything has its own time: so first one should learn *āsana*s and then *prāṇāyāmas*. Only after a few days did he introduce breath control exercises. For him, however, *prāṇāyāma* consisted primarily of the practice of *kapālabhāti* and *bhastrikā*. *Kapālabhāti* was performed very quickly. Svāmī Ātmānanda said that, by focusing the attention on a part of the body while doing this *prāṇāyāma*, that part was purified. We also did *śītlī prāṇāyāma*, associated with *jālandharbandha*, ending it by exhaling through the nose. At the end of each lesson, we did five minutes of *oṃ* repetition.

Yoga class with Viśvot Giri

Viśvot Giri is an *adhikārī yogī*: a yogi 'by right', who is part of a yoga knowledge transmission he received from his grandfather and which he exhibits at religious fairs in India and abroad. I went to his *āśram* in Birnagar (West Bengal) in 2017. After a couple of days, another Italian woman, Anita, arrived and the two of us started learning *āsana*s with him.

These classes were very strenuous and physically demanding because there was no initial warm-up. Everything was based on physical endurance and balance. The *prāṇāyāmas* we did were aimed at levitating the body: we had to breathe so that the air coming out was less than the air going in, enabling the filled body to rise. Every day we did many postures, one after the other.[37] Viśvot Giri showed us each posture and we had to imitate him. He told us that each difficult *āsana* has its own preparation and counter-position, but he did not associate the *āsana*s with any particular breathing. Sometimes he would help us to achieve the correct position to demonstrate how it was to be done and assure us that our bodies would eventually achieve that result.

As I have summarised elsewhere (Bevilacqua 2017a: 203), based on these few classes some generalisations can be made. First of all, in each of these classes there was almost no time to relax between positions or groups

---

37 For example, one day, in one-hour-and-a-half we did: *supta pavanmuktāsana*; *uṣṭrāsana*; *supta vajrāsana*; *gupta padmāsana*; *padmāsana*; *lolāsana*; *kukkutāsana*; *garbhāsana*; *ardhaśalabhāsana*; *śalabāsana*; *dhanurāsana*; *gomukhāsana*; *paścimottānāsana* (but with open legs); *ardhamatsyendrāsana*; *parivṛtti janu śīrṣāsana*; *sarvāṅgāsana*; *śīrṣāsana*; *salamba śīrṣāsana*; *urdhvapadmāsana*; *saral natarajāsana*; *eka padmāsana*; *merudandāsana*; *niralamba paścimottānāsana*; *ardhabaddhapadmottānasana*; *pūrṇabhujangāsana*; *cakrāsana*; *brahmacaryāsana*; *padmamaryurāsana*; *mūlabandhāsana*; *padma sarvāṅgāsana*; *ekapadmaśīrṣāsana*; *padmaparvatāsana*; *titlīāsana*; *supta padangusthāsana*; *kamapidāsana*; *prasarita padottāsana*; etc. These names were obviously not used by Viśvot Giri, but I noted the positions and found the names using an encyclopedia of *āsanas*.

of positions. *Āsana*s were performed one after another. The postures were taken up naturally, according to the student's physical capability: there were no rigid rules or precise positions for the arms or legs. Often, complicated *āsana*s were chosen, to test our ability to do them and assess our possibilities. There was an almost complete absence of 'spiritual' explanations during the practice. Some explanations were proffered about the benefits of an *āsana*, but they were mostly concerned with getting us to concentrate on the posture and its perfection. There was no notion of mental relaxation while the *āsana*s were being done: it was the body and its muscles that were being stretched, while the *prāṇāyāma* was the means to make the mind 'refreshed and cleaned'. The main goal was to have full control of the body and, with the help of *prāṇāyāma*, control of the mind. In sum, they bear little resemblance to the 'ritualised' structure of a typical modern yoga practice session as described by De Michelis (2004: 251–259).

'Traditional' *sādhu*s teaching yoga internationally

Since yoga became a globalised practice, practitioners seeking spiritual and religious answers have been taking an interest in gurus and *sampradāya*s traditionally associated with the yoga *sādhanā*, such as the Nāth *sampradāya*.[38] Some *sādhu*s are responsive to this quest and are active in spreading their knowledge around the world. Some have built successful organisations thanks to their international disciples. The economic power they have acquired is easily witnessed at religious festivals by the size of their camps and the people who stay there.

Here, I will give three examples which present different types of *sādhu*s who have become 'international': one is Pilot Bābā a well-known *saṃnyāsī* and yoga guru who is especially famous in Japan thanks to his female disciple Keiko Mata; the second is Ānanda Giri, a young *saṃnyāsī* who was on the verge of becoming another international yoga guru until scandals broke out about him; the third is Yogī Vilāsnāth, an interesting ascetic who is slowly creating his own yogic niche, especially through foreign Nāths.

Pilot Bābā

Mahāyogī Pilot Bābā is an international guru associated with meditative yoga practices. According to his biography, he was a pilot in the Indian Air Force who, during an airborne incident, was miraculously saved by the vision of a *sādhu*, Hari Giri. This led him to turn his life around by embarking on the path of *saṃnyāsa*. He was initiated into the Jūnā *akhāṛā* and

38 See Bevilacqua 2022a.

dedicated himself to a path of solitude in the caves of the Himalayas under the guidance of his guru, who led him on the path to self-realisation.[39]

Pilot Bābā claims to have learnt *samādhi* techniques from various masters in the Himalayas and, over the past decades, he has repeatedly organised *samādhi* demonstrations as a form of *tapasyā*: he has had himself buried and then 'returned to life' after a couple of days.[40] He claims to know a meditative practice that allows him to leave his body at will and he declares that he wants to make his knowledge available because his mission is to raise 'the consciousness of all people'.[41] He shares this path with his main disciple, a Japanese woman whom Pilot Bābā introduced to his guru: Keiko Aikama, known today as Keiko Mata or Yogmata. She too performed the burying *samādhi* practice, several times. Together they would 'inspire and teach people the virtues of peace and love'.[42] The message of their practice and the purpose of their teachings would be to 'live as a perfect human being in this world', to 'bring success in the society', while being a 'great businessman, industrialist, professional in any stream', and 'fulfilled what ever [*sic*] you want'. As such, they advocate a yogic path that in order to succeed requires neither withdrawal from society nor separation from one's family; in fact, it takes only 40 days. They advertise their deep meditation practice as being a 5,000-year-old secret Himalayan teaching which functions as a healing journey for life-changing detoxification and transformation.

The two masters have international disciples, mainly in Japan, Latvia and the United States, and hold workshops all over the world as well as a World Peace Campaign (2000–2021): 'a non-profit organisation promoting **world peace** through individuals spiritual awakening and also charity', whereby they 'teach methods of letting go wrongs, anxieties, self doubts and fears that hinder the mind from becoming still and clear'.[43]

39 I did not actually meet Pilot Bābā because I preferred to focus my attention on *sādhus* who are less international and not too entangled with foreigners. Therefore, the information presented here is taken from Pilot Bābā's website: http://www.pilotbaba.org/babaji (last accessed 2 September 2021).

40 See references at https://barthsnotes.com/2005/10/22/going-underground-with-pilot-baba (last accessed 2 September 2021).

41 http://www.pilotbaba.org/babaji (last accessed 2 September 2021).

42 Ibid.

43 http://www.yogmata.org/world-peace-campaign (last accessed 2 September 2021); emphasis in original.

Ānanda Giri

Ānanda Giri is a *sādhu* from the Dasnāmī *sampradāya*, specifically the Nirañjanī *akhāṛā*.[44] He told me that he studied in Rishikesh and, having travelled alone to various pilgrimage sites, enrolled at the Banaras Hindu University and Sampurnanand University (also in Varanasi) where he earned two master's degrees, one in yoga and the other in *jyotiṣ*—astrology. At the time of our conversation (2019), he was also applying for a PhD on the subject of yoga and Tantra. He told me that he travelled worldwide to teach yoga and to support his devotees, whom he saw as a family. His website[45] declared that he is

> Well versed in Sanskrit Grammar, Ayurveda & Vedic Philosophies' and that he has taught: 'Mantrayoga (Attaining realisation through mantras; Hathayoga (Attaining realisation through practice—Physical & Mental process & Meditation); Rajyoga (Attaining realisation through meditation); Bhaktiyog (Attaining realisation through devotion); Jnanayoga (Attaining realisation through knowledge); Karmayoga (Attaining realisation through actions).

His approach to teaching yoga is interesting because by him yoga is defined as 'the only power through which a man can understand himself and feel the union with the divine. Yoga is not for a section of the people, but is for all.' So, depending on people's needs, he said he can teach yoga workshops (or 'pod') for 20, 35 or 65 minutes. Like Yogī Vilāsnāth (see below), his approach presents a mix of traditional and modern concepts, in which religious activities and Hindu traditional values serve to 'create a bond with the community with the dual purpose to provide life solutions to the people' so that they can be 'a change agent in society' through thought, word and deed. There are also several videos on his YouTube page[46] in which he teaches basic *āsana*s and *vyāyām*s, often reading and explaining

---

44 In 2021, Ānanda Giri had problems with the *mahant* of the Baṛā Hanumān Temple, Narendra Giri, who was also his guru and head of the Akhāṛā Pariṣad. The two had strong words to say about each other and their quarrels occupied the news for a couple of weeks. Eventually, Ānanda Giri retracted his earlier statements and publicly apologised to his guru. However, after the alleged suicide of Narendra Giri, Ānanda Giri was accused of being one of the culprits in the *mahant*'s death, as Narendra Giri wrote a suicide note saying he had taken his own life because of blackmail by Ānanda Giri and another man.

45 The website is down at the time of writing. This may be a result of the allegations directed at him.

46 https://www.youtube.com/user/AnandGiri1000/videos (last accessed 2 September 2021).

religious texts or epics. These exercises are presented as a means of losing weight and helping in daily life. His audience was mainly Hindi-speaking Indians, and in fact his followers abroad were mostly NRIs (non-resident Indians).[47]

As Indian gurus typically do, he gives lectures related to religious texts, religious events and festivals. However, he has also organised a series of lectures ('What can I do after Class 12?'; 'How can I live my life?'; 'What I can do after 60?'; 'My life, my wife'), which are presented on his website as 'Self Realisation Programmes'.

He told me that yoga can solve many problems because it is 'good for the health of people, helps eliminate stress, improves relationships and family', and that through yoga one can become a fully responsible citizen. Clearly, he was referring to a modern understanding of yoga or a modern use of some yoga practices, rather than the yoga *sādhanā* followed by his brethren.

He was a very convivial *sādhu* and was more than happy to devote 30 minutes of his time to our conversation, despite the fact that it was the busiest time of the Kumbh Melā. However, his conviviality was not entirely disinterested, because as soon as we finished with my questions, he asked me to make a live video for his Facebook page[48] where he began asking me questions about my interest in India and similar topics. In fact, he was very active on social media, which he used to update his followers and devotees about his religious activities in India and abroad.[49]

Yogī Vilāsnāth

Yogī Vilāsnāth is a Nāth Yogī with a busy publishing schedule: he has published at least 15 books,[50] with topics ranging from secret teachings to the practice of fasting and worship, while the latest, *Śrī Nāth Sampradāya ke Tīrth Sthāl*, deals with religious places, Nāths' secret traditions, stories of the Nāths and their history, their practice of yoga and *haṭha* yoga, their festivals and related rituals, and their addresses with contact numbers, photos and locations on a map.

---

47 He was alleged to have sexually assaulted two women in Sydney but was acquitted by the Australian court. https://www.hindustantimes.com/cities/yoga-guru-anand-Giri-acquitted-by-australian-court/story-5oX9wPBKVIErW5jK3hrnBP.html (last accessed 2 September 2021).

48 https://www.facebook.com/swamianandGiriji.

49 This situation changed after he was investigated for the suicide of his guru. I am keen to retain his example here, not only because of his approach to yoga but also to offer a hint of the 'dark side' of the *sādhu samāj* (see for example Jha 2019).

50 See https://www.astromantra.com/product-tag/dr-yogi-vilasnath-ji (last accessed 13 March 2024).

His activity and the fact that he can speak a little English have made him a useful bridge to those communities of yoga practitioners who have developed an interest in the Nāth *sampradāya* (see Bevilacqua 2022a). In fact, Yogī Vilāsnāth has travelled extensively in Europe and has many students in Poland, Ukraine, German and Italy, some of whom he has also made *darśanīs*: that is, they have received the highest level of initiation in the Nāth *sampradāya*.[51] On a visit to Germany, he was appointed a member of the 'European Academy of Tibetan Medicine and Yoga as a Honourable Doctor of Yoga Philosophy'.[52] As noted by Stuparich (2022), he recognises the practices of *mantra* yoga, *tantra* yoga, *haṭha* yoga, *laya* yoga, *nāda* yoga, *jñāna* yoga, etc. as being specifically Nāth paths, emphasising in his works the importance of performing mantra and tantric rituals to reach the supreme goal (*paramārtha*), as well as *siddhi* and *mokṣa*. As such, his approach falls within the mainstream parameters of a pan-Indian soteriological discourse.

When we met at the 2019 Allahabad Kumbh Melā, he said of *haṭha* yoga: '*Haṭha* yoga's masters were from our *sampradāya*. The original *haṭha* yoga is ours. Others have just taken it from us.' When I asked about the many books he had published, neatly displayed in front of his tent in the Kumbh Melā camp, he justified his output as being the result of his spiritual practice: he had visions of the most of his books, so they were the direct result of his meditative experience. He also acknowledged that thanks to these books he had became famous. He said: 'That book I wrote, *Nāth Rahasya*, I do not know how many people after its publication took *dīkṣā* and became *sādhus*!'

However, Yogī Vilāsnāth's activity is not fully supported by the *sampradāya*, and other Nāths have directed criticism at him. For example, a Nāth Yogī in Kolkata lamented the end of the secrecy of practice attributable to Yogī Vilāsnāth. He said that, in the past, some yogic *kriyā*s were out of the hands even of many *sādhus*, while today many secret teachings have been written in books that everyone can read. But he also recognised that these teachings are not effective until they are fully explained and experienced by the disciple through the teaching of the guru, the only one who can provide the true meaning of a text. Another Yogī told me in 2018: 'This

51 This facilitated approach towards foreigners could be compared to that of gurus towards *rājā*s or noblemen in medieval times: special individuals who were given mantras and taught practices, even skipping some steps, because their 'status'—and patronage—justified such an approach.

52 https://yogivilasnath.blogspot.com/p/biography.html (last accessed 13 March 2024).

activity of yoga spreading is not correct because even a thief can do yoga today; this decreases the importance itself of yoga.'

Yogī Vilāsnāth presents himself as a charismatic guru, capable of receiving the gift of knowledge through his meditative practice, knowledge that he is ready to share with a wide audience. While manifesting a quite traditional and esoteric approach to the practices, he is also willing to divulge secret teachings, seeking to gather a community, especially of foreigners, carving out a specific and international niche for himself.

However, there is a *sādhu* who in recent times has been able to create an empire using modern yoga practice, and he is Bābā Rāmdev.

Bābā Rāmdev and the International Day of Yoga

> 'Bābā Rāmdev really has no meaning. He is another empty show.'

Physical yoga, and in particular the practice of *āsanas*, is today associated in India with the image of Bābā Rāmdev, who over the past two decades has managed to create a prosperous empire using yoga and Ayurvedic medicine, thanks in part to his strong ties to the central government. Interestingly, unlike other Indian gurus, his main goal is to disseminate yoga in India, mixing political and nationalist messages with the practice, blending together public health and mass yoga performances in order to build the health of the individual and at the same time the health of the nation (Sarbacker 2014: 352). In fact, Bābā Rāmdev has brought yoga into the homes of India's middle class, including the so-called NRIs, through his videos on TV channels and YouTube.[53] As Venera Khalikova (2017) emphasises: 'If you ask any common man about Maharishi [Mahesh Yogi] they don't know, but everybody knows Ramdev. A real revolution of yoga has begun with Ramdev.'

But who is Bābā Rāmdev? It is said that he suffered from various physical ailments and found relief through the practice of yoga. He took *saṃnyāsa* at the Kripalu Bagh Āśram in Haridwar under the guidance of Svāmī Śaṅkardevjī Mahārāj. It is said that, after several years of meditative practice in the Himalayas, he returned to Haridwar and became more involved in teaching yoga, an activity he carried out in Haryana by offering free yoga classes to villagers (Raj 2010: 82). In 1995, together with Balkṛṣṇa

53 https://www.youtube.com/c/SwamiRamdevOfficial and http://www.pypt.org/63-Online-Classes.html.

(another fellow disciple), Ācārya Karamvīr and Guru Śaṅkardev, he founded the Divya Yog Mandir Trust, which became Rāmdev's platform for reaching the general public. This was also facilitated by the organisation of yoga *śivir*s (camps).[54] The word *śivir* is most often translated as 'camp' and refers to events in which different activities (lectures and demonstrations involving group participation) are used to promote cultural traditions, often under the appeal of 'Hindu ideals' and 'Vedic heritage' (Alter 2008: 36). These *śivir*s allowed Rāmdev to expose himself and his teachings to an ever-widening community interested in the practices of *āsana*, *prāṇāyāma* and yoga philosophy (Sarbacker 2014: 355). In 2002, one of the owners of a major TV network, Sadhana TV, attended Rāmdev's yoga *śivir* and shortly thereafter began broadcasting him. This additional step brought Rāmdev's teachings into the houses of millions of Indians around the world. His success led to a further move: the establishment of the Patanjali Yogpeeth Trust in Haridwar in 2005, through which Ayurveda medicines and products are sold, and yoga is promoted.

It is interesting to note the use of the name 'Patañjali' for the brand. As Singleton (2008: 77) points out, 'Patañjali is routinely invoked as source-authority and figurehead of a diverse range of techniques and belief systems commonly termed yoga' because he 'symbolises' an idea of ancient authenticity despite the fact that there are often radical divergences between the text and modern yoga practices. In this case, Patañjali is used to sell yoga and Ayurveda together, although, as we saw, the link between the two is by no means obvious.

Rāmdev claims that his products can cure everything, even if they are not confirmed by science, because they are 'science in its purest form' (Nanda 2009: 99), an attitude that seems reminiscent of the scientific approach of the early-20th-century yoga reformers, without retaining their method. Indeed, Rāmdev's products and teachings, rather than resembling traditional paths of yoga(s), recall modern yoga traditions that seek to place the (physical) practice of yoga within a modern socio-political framework, as a practice that can help keep the body—and consequently the mind and the self—healthy. According to Rāmdev, yoga is the answer to the many problems of contemporary global civilisation, and not simply or solely a philosophy or personal practice. His rhetoric, however, poorly conceals, behind the 'language of universalism, tolerance, good health, and peace'

54 As Alter (2008: 36) argues, 'The practice of organising yoga camps (shivir) for the general public and for specific institutions [. . .] most likely dates back to the early twentieth century when the yoga teachings of Swami Vivekananda and Sri Aurobindo were being integrated into the practice of postural, embodied yoga.'

(Nanda 2009: 99), a soft Hindutva propaganda in which India and Hinduism are portrayed as a superior nation and religion, with the aim of making India (indeed the whole world) more Hindu.

Rāmdev was one among those who suggested and supported Prime Minister Narendra Modi in calling for an international yoga day at the United Nations General Assembly (UNGA). The International Day of Yoga was first proposed by Modi in his address to the UNGA on 27 September 2014. He justified his proposal by stating that yoga is an invaluable gift of India's ancient tradition, which embodies the unity of mind and body and provides a holistic approach to health and well-being. He further stated that it is not about exercise but about discovering a sense of unity with the self, the world and nature.

Politicians' interest in yoga has become evident since the 2014 election, when the Bharatiya Janata Party (BJP) began using yoga as a symbol of the nationalist narrative at home and as soft power abroad through a form of cultural diplomacy (Gautam and Droogan 2018: 18). The establishment of an International Day of Yoga would be one of the outcomes of such a policy.[55] Gautam and Droogan (2018: 20) explain that Modi's approach is innovative in that it blends Hindutva with the state-centred democratic cultural nationalism embraced by Nehru and the Congress party for decades, before and after independence, thus shaping a new religious cultural nationalism that can be mobilised—domestically and internationally—by promoting popular and 'friendly' cultural symbols such as yoga. This approach has been interpreted as a way of self-appointing India, the home of yoga, as a 'world guru' that can save the world from consumerism (Singh 2014).

The establishment of the Ayush Ministry, granted independent status in 2014, aims to rebrand and promote yoga in order to reclaim it as something distinctively Indian, thus participating in building India's cultural pride and 'the multi-billion dollar spiritual-health tourism market' (McCartney 2017: 6). This also led to the establishment of the International Yoga Committee (IYC), a committee that advocates the recognition of yoga as a sport[56]

55 Established in 1995, the Department of Indian Systems of Medicine and Homoeopathy was elevated to a federal ministry in 2014 as the Department of Ayurveda, Yoga and Naturopathy, Unani, Siddha, and Homoeopathy (Ayush).

56 The Yoga Federation of India's request was accepted by the prime minister. This recognition will allow the practitioners and winners of competitions to benefit from their medals by conferring a preferential track to government jobs. The performance of *yogāsana* in competition is nothing new, as they have long been held in India (see Singleton 2010), while in the US the United States Yoga Federation has been holding regional and national championships for 12 years; in these

for increasing strength and flexibility. The committee is said to be the sole 'Yoga Sport controlling body' for international organisations,[57] but it has not yet received the attention and participation it expected.

In general, *sādhus* do not appreciate the government's role in turning yoga teachers into officers and yoga into a sport. As Yogī Śivanāth lamented, 'This is not yoga; yoga is a *gupt vidyā* (hidden knowledge), only for devotees with *dīkṣā*.' However, Yogī Śivanāth does not have an issue with being photographed with Bābā Rāmdev and has himself organised yoga *śivir*s in Gorakhpur the main purpose of which was the teaching of physical practices. As I describe in detail elsewhere (Bevilacqua 2022a), those who attended the 2018 yoga *śivir* in Gorakhpur were interested in losing weight or getting fit, not listening to *pravacan* or practising more meditative techniques.

The trend that Bābā Rāmdev has so masterfully cultivated in India is prompting *sādhus* who have a deep knowledge of yoga and who consider themselves more genuine and knowledgeable than Rāmdev to attempt to participate in this 'business'. But those *sādhus* who, as we have seen, do not approve of this excessive focus on physical practice are rather sceptical of Bābā Rāmdev, his empire and the new trend that yoga is acquiring in India. In fact, Rām Avadhūt Dās declared

> It is something based on *āsana*s, to spread it among people. That's fine: it's good if they know something [. . .] But it's a yoga that has nothing to do with that of our *ṛṣi*s; it is something that looks outward, but for the inner part you will always need the right guru.

Similar words came from Jogī Bābā:

> See, the yoga that Rāmdev does is OK for your body; your body will be OK, you will work correctly, act correctly . . . OK . . . But you cannot get God with it! You cannot have the *darśan* of God! Without the grace of God, without *śakti*, yoga cannot become *siddha*!

---

competitions, participants must hold postures for a certain period of time and are judged on the execution of the posture and the degree of difficulty.

57 '. . . for the Yoga and Yoga Sport Community, and is open to all Yoga Club-Yoga Training Centre, Individual/Faculty-Yoga Guru-Yoga Practitioner-Yoga Teacher-Yoga Therapist, Yoga-Institute-College-School-University Accreditation, Yoga NGOs and National Yoga Sport Federations, and yoga authorities.' http://www.iyc-yoga.org/aboutiyc.html (last accessed May 2022).

Conclusion

The history of embodied practices in South Asia is strongly related to the development of the religious and ascetic world. This history is often explored through the study of Sanskrit textual sources, which are crucial in acquiring a general, though probably partial, picture. In this book I have used ethnography, combined with some vernacular sources and archaeological evidence, as a tool to investigate the present and, through it, expand our understanding of the past. The simple question 'What is *haṭha* yoga?' that I put to *sādhus* has broadened the answers and stimulated an inquiry into the relationship between *tapasyā*, yoga and *haṭha* yoga, examining the history and practices that characterised these methods. This book has sought to present ascetics' understanding of these terms and practices, without suggesting particular interpretations: drawing on the words of *sādhus*, it has offered their contributions, their experiences and sometimes their confusions, to frame contexts that are indeed extremely multifaceted and not easily tamed, providing insights into ascetic society itself.

It has not been possible to divide the ideas of *sādhus* according to their affiliation with a specific *sampradāya*, as *sādhanās* can inform and influence ascetics in very similar ways, and the fluidity of the ascetic world allows *sādhus* to tread their spiritual journey in very personal ways, according to their background, natural aptitudes and goals.

In this Conclusion, I would like to further emphasise some important issues: the fluidity of the ascetic society and its interaction with lay society; the fluidity of ideas and practices associated with the words *tapas*, yoga and *haṭha* yoga, and different yogic (ascetic) 'identities'.

On the ascetic society

We have seen that the ascetic world should be understood as an alternative society in which individuals have different goals from those of the laity. In theory, they pursue a spiritual path in one of the many orders, or their subgroups, that make up this society, also chosen on the basis of caste or gender, since there are often limitations in initiation. We have seen, in fact, that in the ascetic society there are hierarchies[1] and gender issues, rivalries and competition.

Sādhus are aware that, likely, several ascetic lives are necessary to achieve results and that not all individuals will achieve the same result via the same path. *Karma* is strongly personal, although the practices explored to burn it and to end the *saṃsāra* are the result of common, historically developed efforts. Ascetic traditions, in fact, have gone through centuries of adjustment and identity formation, adapting to changing historical and political situations, but also creating, developing and adopting new religious theories and practices. Thanks to their internal differentiations—due to the presence of multiple *paramparās*—these groups have been home to innovations that spread when deemed useful or suitable. These innovations were possible because there were different roles within an ascetic order. Asceticism can be considered from the point of view of the individual but also from the point of view of its structured centres, which maintain relations with lay society and patrons. There were ascetics who addressed their teachings to the laity and those who focused on their own practice and taught ascetic disciples. These paths co-existed and collaborated to enable the survival of a tradition and its subgroups. Both of these types of ascetic individual could fulfil their religious goals by following the *karma* expected of them.

We have seen that ascetic orders have always been present and active in society, and this is also still evident in the present day. In the past, ascetics collaborated with *rājas* and emperors, managed people in the territories they administered, and sometimes offered shelters, schools and hospitals to the needy. Ascetic armies could compete with royal armies, and warrior ascetics created a specific space for themselves, also recruiting certain sectors of societies which were thus integrated into the ascetic world. In the present, ascetics receive support from a broader upper-middle class which

1 Some ascetics consider *saṃnyāsī* to be the last ascetic stage because it involves the celebration of one's own funeral. Therefore, while a Vaiṣṇava *sādhu* may decide to become a *saṃnyāsī*, the opposite is not possible. This would place the *saṃnyāsī* at a higher ascetic level than the Vaiṣṇava.

appears more involved in the religious world, while the collaboration of ascetics with politicians has led to a greater politicisation of the ascetic scene itself.

Ascetic and lay societies have always enjoyed a strong interrelationship based on constant, reciprocal exchanges. Ascetics provided, and still provide, several 'services' to lay society, among which this book has presented the possibility of teaching psychophysical—sometimes medical—techniques useful for the body and to prepare the individual for the eventuality of a spiritual path. It is difficult to know whether there were times in the past when physical yogic practices were accessible to ordinary people, taught by random *sādhus* or by village *sādhus*. However, considering that even today there are village ascetics teaching children and giving advice on postures or treatments to followers or devotees, we can assume that this was one of the ways in which ascetics recompensed householders for the economic support they received. As such, embodied yogic practices could provide a useful bank of data to assist an understanding not only of the development of theories and techniques in ascetic society but also how they were renegotiated and used to create a link with lay society. As mentioned in Chapter 4 (p. 176), it is likely that the dissemination of *haṭha* yoga texts that emphasised physical practices and the attainment of powers was a way of capturing the attention of patrons who may have been more interested in *siddhi*s and a 'diamond body' than in *mokṣa* (especially those who were not Hindu).

As the field of yoga has now expanded in directions that do not necessarily require the support of ascetics, those ascetics who wish to participate in the yoga 'business', in order to remain 'competitive', have to adapt their knowledge and practice to a form of yoga that is closer to the needs of lay people. We may suppose that the approach of many *sādhus* towards modern yoga represents a contemporary transformation of patronage research, as well as a modern evolution of the role of *sādhu*s in teaching physical practices to lay people. Thanks to new transnational movements, today the audience a *sādhu* can reach is wider, as is the competition. This has led to a simplification of contents and theories.

It is likely that, just as in the past there were different transmissions of knowledge, one for ascetics and one for lay people, so this differentiation in teachings is being maintained, although it is difficult to know to what extent old practices will be transmitted. With regard to the current situation, it seems that ascetics recognise a certain decadence and less commitment among the young generations of ascetics to undertake strenuous and more demanding practices. This has been rationalised as a direct consequence of the historical period in which we live, the terrible *Kali yuga*, which makes any effort almost useless. The possibility of knowledge being lost does not seem to worry *sādhus*.

Such an environment fostered the spread of devotional approaches, and the constant presence of certain deities—such as Rām or Kṛṣṇa—testifies to an adaptation to the needs of householders that further underscores the strong interrelation between ascetic and lay societies.

On fluid labels and practices in the *sādhu samāj*

When it comes to embodied practices, there seems to be a certain consistency among *sādhus*: for all the orders considered in this book we found practitioners. As already mentioned, it was the result that was achieved that made a practice, a technique or an austerity become valuable and, consequently, shared. This is why in this book we see *tyāgīs*, *saṃnyāsīs*, Nāths and Udāsīs practising mostly the same things—sometimes with some differences—and sharing similar understandings, at least in terms of their practical or general explanations. The differences are in fact found in the goals of the practice, which highlights the different ontological understanding of the relationship between the practitioner and God.

We have seen that *tapas*, yoga and *haṭha* yoga are, however, fluid terms that have acquired layers of meanings over the centuries and have been variously used to denote even the same technique but in different contexts. As embodied forms of knowledge based on experiential methods, they have always been evolving, changing as the people who have practised, lived and taught them have changed. Some *tapas* techniques were later identified as yoga practices, and the powers associated with *tapasyā* also became results of a yoga practice. It seems that there have often been attempts to tame some techniques to make them more accessible to 'ordinary' people: austerities were criticised and then reinterpreted with a more meditative and ethical nuance; the challenging practices of *haṭha* yoga were restricted to practices suitable for and accessible to lay people, and some forms of *tapasyās* were reinterpreted as *āsanas*.

Clearly, then, different traditions have co-existed: some more 'ascetic', others more 'academic'. The available textual sources probably represent only a limited section of the practices and interpretations that were actually present on the ground. Vernacular sources must be properly investigated if we are to fully understand the history of the various methods (yogas). Reconstructing emic definitions of the meaning of *haṭha* yoga has helped to question our understanding of the development of this term, showing how it had (and still has) different meanings in different contexts. Considering emic definitions, therefore, *haṭha* yoga becomes a fluid concept which includes various physical practices such as austerities, breath retention, *ṣaṭkarmas*, *āsanas* and *kriyās*.

Yoga, however, among *sādhus* is still associated with a meditative practice; as such, the yoga practice of ascetics cannot be assessed by considering the presence or absence of *āsanas*. As I have shown elsewhere (Bevilacqua 2022a), this means that our interpretation of *sādhus* as practitioners of yoga or *haṭha* yoga should be inferred according to their understanding of these words rather than ours. As Burchett (2019: 187) puts it, 'while it might seem that a yogī is quite simply one who practises yoga, what is considered to constitute "yoga", and to what degree that yoga is central in the religiosity of any given Yogī, varies greatly'.

What seems clear is that, despite the various classifications evident in the written history of yoga, *sādhus* do not make much use of these labels and distinctions, maintaining broad definitions and, as is always the case, porous boundaries. In general, *sādhus* speak of 'yog(a)', and only when pushed will they offer to make distinctions, which are not always clear. For this reason, '*tap karnā*' (doing *tapas*) can be synonymous with '*dhyāna lagānā*' (applying meditation) when the practice is done through *haṭha* (strong determination), and can aim at *yoga* as the result. This demonstrates the strong connection not only between these three terms but also between ways of practising.

Turning our attention to yoga, we see that new meanings have been added to the traditional layers. Their common root is the meaning of yoga as 'method', which can be interpreted differently, and can thereby be signified by a qualifying word: *haṭha* yoga, *laya* yoga, *mantra* yoga, *modern* yoga. Yoga can be a useful method for ascetics to improve or sustain their *sādhanā*—or it can *be* their *sādhanā*. But today it can also mean a predominantly physical practice to be taught in a professional (or amateur) way to uninitiated people.

In the past, as in the present, several forms of yoga co-existed and continue to co-exist: we must recognise modern practices and meanings as contemporary developments that satisfy the needs of a wider contemporary audience.

On yogic identities

In this book we have seen that a *sādhu*'s body can have a dual purpose: it can be 'mortified' through some forms of *tapasyā*, or it can be maintained in a healthy state through the practice of physical yoga. The different uses of the body may correspond to different ascetic identities, which in some cases may overlap. In Chapter 3 we met the practitioner of austerities, the *tapasvī*, who can subdue the body through pain or exertion; in Chapter 4 we met the *haṭhayogī*, who basically corresponds to the *tapasvī* or to the 'manipulator' of *vāyus*; in Chapter 5 we encountered the *yogīrāj*, the one who has complete control over the body and is skilled in *kriyās*; and in Chapter 6 we introduced the *yogī*, the practitioner and master of *dhyāna* who is able to attain and control the stage of *samādhi*.

As already mentioned in regard to other labels (*monī*, *phalāhārī*, etc.), these are titles that ascetics use to define themselves or each other and are often written on display boards at religious festivals to highlight their accomplishment. It is therefore not unusual for an ascetic to be adopt the title *yogīrāj* or *haṭhayogī*. The title *yogī*, however, is compulsory for Nāths who have received the second initiation, but it can also be attributed to *sādhus* who have had incredible meditative experiences such as Jogī (Yogī) Bābā and Yogī Durgā Bhārtī.

Here I will briefly elaborate on these different yogic identities.

A textual source such as Svātmārāma's *Haṭhapradīpikā* uses the word *yogī* to address the practitioner of its practices, and the word *haṭhayogī* only once (1.12). Other texts that use the label *haṭhayogī* mostly follow the *Haṭhapradīpikā*'s verse. As not all Sanskrit textual sources describe their yoga as *haṭha* yoga, the label *haṭhayogī* most likely was rarely associated with the practitioner of physical practices and *kriyās*. In fact, as we have seen, in ascetic society there is another label for such a practitioner: *yogīrāj*, the 'king of yoga'; Lokeśvarānanda Giri calls himself a *yogīrāj* because he knows many *kriyās*. When I asked Omānanda Giri's perspective of who a *yogīrāj* was, he replied that a *yogīrāj* is the master of yoga, one who has yoga under his control. He said that *rāj* in this case does not mean king but *śreṣṭh*, hence 'superior, supreme, special'. According to Rāghavendra Dās, on the other hand, the title of *yogīrāj* was created 'just to fill the stomach', to gain devotees and financial support.

Although the purpose of numerous *haṭha* yoga textual sources is ultimately *rāja* yoga, the label *rājayogī* is not generally used in such sources; however, it is a title used among Nāths to indicate a specific Yogī, the one who sits on the *gaḍḍī* (throne) of Mangalore.

While the labels *haṭhayogī* and *yogīrāj* indicate certain specific features and practices,[2] the word 'yogi' can refer to different identities. Just as the

2 To these two titles should also be added that of *yogācārya*, 'mentor of yoga', a title that emphasises a profound, theoretical knowledge of yoga. Of the *sādhus* I met, only Yogī Śivanāth used this title.

word 'yoga' can signify both the method and its result, so the word 'yogi' can be used to designate both those who are practising the method as well as those who have completed the practice. Let us focus, then, on the ascetics' understanding of the meaning of 'yogi' as one who has accomplished the *sādhanā*.

Monī Bābā claimed that 'the yogi is the one who has the *ātman gyān*, the knowledge of the soul'. The yogi, therefore, is superior to the *haṭhayogī* (i.e. *tapasvī*), because the latter may fall from his practice: Monī Bābā gave the example of Viśvāmitra who was disturbed several times by nymphs while doing his *tapasyā*. In contrast, the individual who has become a yogi does not return to his previous state and can never be disturbed.

Garuḍ Dās made an interesting comparison between a *tyāgī* (who, as we have seen, is often a practitioner of austerities) and a yogi: a *tyāgī* detaches himself from things with efforts (*haṭha* yoga), hence he chooses not to eat and so does not eat—but the yogi feels no hunger at all. Having attained his goal (yoga), he is no longer affected by *saṃsāra*: pleasure and attachment. Having reached this level, according to Dayānanda Purī, the yogi has an inner awareness (and powers) that enable him to change and modify reality. He defined this type of yogi as *mahāyogī*, 'great yogi', which is synonymous with Siddha. According to him, one can become a yogi in three ways: by birth, thanks to his previous lives; by place, if one lives in a sacred place and thus grasps the *śakti* of a specific site; or by doing *tapasyā* and *sādhanā*.

Jogī Bābā's definition unifies several ideas: according to him, the yogi is the one who overcomes *man* and attains and activates his inner power. This occurs because the individual has attained *ekāgratā niṣṭhā* (a firm stand, faith, reverence), and received the *darśan* and thus the *śakti* of God. Being a yogi, then, is a quality that identifies the individual from within, turning whatever he utters into a powerful mantra.

Hence, the word 'yogi' can generally be used for someone who has done several years of meditative practice, but a true yogi is someone who, through meditative practice, achieves a perfection that does not enhance daily life or exalt the ego—rather the opposite. His attention to the body has been aimed at overcoming the limitation that the body itself imposes. His focus on the self is directed towards knowing the nature of the self, overcoming the limit of the individual self. In doing so he reaches another level of reality and, through this, acquires soteriological knowledge and powers, in order to attain, eventually, unity with God or the grace of God.

Appendix 1
Religious Festivals

This appendix provides general information about the main religious festivals I attended: key places to find *sādhus* and witness contemporary dynamics in the Indian religious field. Here I will describe the Kumbh Melās, the Ambubācī Melā, Gaṅgā Sāgar and the celebration of Mahāśivarātri in Junagadh.

The Kumbh Melās

The Kumbh Melās (Festivals of the Pot) are the largest religious gatherings in the world. The name derives from the pot (*kumbha*; H., *kumbh*) of the nectar of immortality (*amṛta*) that *devatā*s (gods and demigods) and *asura*s (demons) contended for, as described in the Purāṇas. According to the legends, the *devatā*s wanted to produce *amṛta* but, being too weak, had to ask the *asura*s for help, agreeing to share the nectar once produced. To produce it, the two groups gathered on the shore of the Ocean of Milk and began churning the ocean, using the mount Mandāra as dasher and Vāsukī, the king of snakes, as a rope: the *devatā*s pulled at the tail of the snake while the *asura*s its mouth. The first product was poison which was drunk by Śiva, who became blue; when a few drops fell on earth, venomous creatures were born. After 1,000 years, Dhanvantari, the god of medicine, appeared with the *amṛta*. The *devatā*s snatched the *amṛta* pot, angering the *asura*s, who pursued them for 12 days and 12 nights.

The tradition that arose around the Kumbh Melās (probably around the 19th century) has it that the story ends with the falling of four drops of *amṛta* on the ground of four cities—Prayag/Allahabad, Haridwar, Ujjain, and Nashik—which would henceforth have special spiritual powers. Since 12 divine days are said to be equivalent to 12 human years, the festival of *amṛta* is celebrated every 12 years on the banks of the Godavari river in Nashik, the Kshipra river in Ujjain, the Ganges river in Haridwar, and at the *saṅgam* (confluence) of the rivers Ganges, Yamuna and Sarasvati (which would be underground) in Prayagraj (Allahabad). Bathing in these rivers at specific times would enable individuals to partake in the power of the *amṛta* and purify themselves of their sins.

However, there is no early evidence of four related festivals called Kumbh Melā in these cities. It seems that the original Kumbh is the one in Haridwar, which takes place every 12 years, when Jupiter is in Aquarius (H., *kumbha*). The earliest evidence of the use of the label 'Kumbh Melā' for the Haridwar festival is the *Khulasat-ut-Tawarikh* (1695 CE), a Persian chronicle of the Mughal Empire written by Sujan Ran. This text mentions similar fairs taking place in Prayag and Nashik, but they are not called Kumbh. The author says that a festival is celebrated in Nashik when Jupiter enters Leo: that is, again, every 12 years (see Maclean 2008).

A religious bathing festival held in Prayagraj is attested since at least the middle of the 1st millennium CE. Several textual sources (such as the 16th-century *Rāmcaritmānas* of Tulsidas and the *Ain-i-Akbari* of Abu'l-Fazl) mention the annual *melā* happening during the month of Māgh (January–February), a month in the Hindu calendar that begins when the Sun enters Capricorn, which is why the festival is known as Māgh Melā rather than Kumbh Melā. The association with a 12-year cycle appears only in the 19th century, probably because brahmins of Prayagraj co-opted and readapted the Kumbh legend to build up the importance of the annual Prayag Māgh Melā (see Maclean 2003).

In Ujjain, the festival was originally called Siṃhasth Melā because it falls when Jupiter enters Leo (*siṃha*) and the Sun in Aries. However, this Melā did not begin until the late 18th century, when the Maratha ruler Ranoji Shinde invited ascetics from the *akhāṛā*s of Nashik to come to Ujjain for a local religious festival in order to reinforce his image as a pious Hindu king (see Lochtefeld 2008). It is not fanciful to surmise that the *paṇḍit*s of Prayag, Nashik and Ujjain adopted the Kumbh tradition by reinterpreting and exploiting the importance of pre-existing festivals.

The control of these festivals was in the hands of ascetics belonging to the *akhāṛā*s: *nāgā sādhus* who constituted the armies of several religious orders (see pp. 49ff.). Even in the past, such festivals would attract a conspicuous number of pilgrims, and as such were important events for ascetics to

Photo 20 One of the main temporary roads of the Allahabad Ardh Kumbh Melā, 2019.

display their status, seek patronage or conduct their trade. Violent clashes used to occur between Śaiva *gosain*s and Vaiṣṇava *bairāgī*s over who controlled the festival, until the British Raj took over and organised more peaceful events (see Maclean 2003, 2008). In the last century-and-a-half, the Ardh Kumbh, the 'Half Festival', has been celebrated every six years in Haridwar and Prayag. A festival held every 12 years is called the Pūrṇa (complete) Kumbh. The Mahā Kumbh Melā is the festival that occurs after 12 Pūrṇa Melās, or 144 years.

Today, Melā sites are highly organised, transforming often vacant land into temporary cities housing millions of pilgrims and providing them with electricity, food, water and toilets, as well as hospitals and other essential infrastructure (see Photo 20).

A Melā site is divided into sectors, which in turn are divided into plots, carefully delineated by a system of temporary roads. Śaiva and Vaiṣṇava groups are often located in different sectors. The *akhāṛā*s are those closer to the main bathing place, thus determining a geographic hierarchy, with other groups camping at various levels of proximity. Each *akhāṛā* has its own internal hierarchy, with the most important subgroups in the centre of the *akhāṛā* encampment and the most important *sādhu*s close to the temporary temple and flag of the *akhāṛā*; others are positioned accordingly.

Photo 21 Procession of *nāgā sādhus* during the Ujjain Siṃhasth Melā, 2016.

Although an increasing number of religious leaders and groups now have access to the festival, the protagonists of the Kumbh Melās are still the *nāgā sādhus* who, after setting up their camps, enter the Melā site in triumphal processions, often riding elephants, horses or camels, having been awaited for hours by curious crowds of people seeking their blessings or just to catch sight of them (Photo 21).

Once settled, the *sādhus* spend their days sitting in their camps, talking to people, sometimes displaying their practices as a means of attracting devotees and supporters. But Melā time is also an important occasion on which to meet other *sādhus* and handle organisational matters related to their order, as well as participating in *bhaṇḍārās* (feasts). *Bhaṇḍārās* are an important part of the Melā for both *sādhus* and pilgrims; here, thousands of people are fed free of charge every day, an ostensible way in which *sādhus* perform their *sevā*. *Bhaṇḍārās* can also be organised to mark specific events (such as the conferring of a title on a *sādhu*); in such cases *dakṣiṇās* (donations) are given to each *sādhu* in attendance.[1]

1 On one occasion, with *tyāgī* Rām Bālak Dās, we attended three *bhaṇḍārās* in a single day. In the first camp we had only *chai* and *gulāb jāmun*—partaking of a snack

Time spent around the *dhūnī* is important: here, *sādhus* tell stories, share their knowledge and, together, wait for the main religious events of the festival: the holy baths. During each Kumbh, there are three main holy baths—called the *śāhī* (royal) *snān* (bath)—during which people are said to benefit from the *amṛta*. They take place at a specific time and the *akhāṛās* follow a specific order: first the Śaiva *nāgās* bathe, followed by the Vaiṣṇava *tyāgīs* and their *nāgās*. After the *sādhus* of the first *akhāṛās* have bathed, lay people may follow.

The bath is the climax of the journey for pilgrims who often arrive on foot from all over India. People of all social backgrounds participate: the poor often carry everything they need to make rudimentary camp in the Melā site when they cannot find shelter, while the wealthier often pay in advance to have a room reserved, or built, in a specific camp. Indeed, the touristic aspect of religious festivals is increasingly becoming bigger business. True, Melās have historically always represented opportunities for selling (goods, food, speeches, etc.) or networking, but things have changed because of the increased number of tourists (often coming for a spiritual experience or photo opportunities), which has inflated the price of nearby accommodation. For every Melā, this rise in number of participants has invited interference by politicians, much to the concern of older *sādhus* who remember Melās which may have always been crowded but used to be manageable, and at which religious aims were still the focus, rather than providing an exotic experience for the curious. The increased importance of money is strongly felt, and it has a bearing on religious titles: in the past, many *sādhus* told me, it was the spiritual path of a *sādhu*, his practices and achievements, that drew others to bestow a position on him and accord him authority. In contemporary times, however, each title (*mahant*, *mahāmaṇḍaleśvara*, etc.) has a precise cost associated with it; so, if a *sādhu* has no money, he cannot improve his status. Conversely, someone with enough money can acquire high titles without the requisite ascetic training. As a result, it has become increasingly necessary to attract followers and devotees and to be financially supported by them.

Ambubācī Melā

The Ambubācī Melā is held in Kamakhya, Assam. The village itself deserves a few words, being one of the most renowned centres of tantric practice in

---

was enough to show our respect—as we had other *bhaṇḍārās* to attend. On each occasion, despite not being initiated, I received 100 rupees.

India. Located on the Nilachal Hill, the village is named after the goddess Kāmākhyā, who has her temple here. Kāmākhyā is described in the *Kālikā Purāṇa* (c. post-10th century CE) as the 'yielder of all desires' and as the young bride of Śiva. The *mūrti* of the temple, however, does not represent a goddess, but rather a 'split' in the rock from which a natural spring flows, considered to be Satī's fallen *yoni* (vagina), from when her corpse was torn apart by Viṣṇu.[2] The temple is one of the *śakta pīṭhas*, the 'seats' of the goddess associated with the feminine power (*śakti*) emanating from Satī's dismembered body parts which landed in these places. In time, these places became renowned pilgrimage centres.

Kāmākhyā, however, is not the only important goddess in the village: the ten Mahāvidyās also dwell here: Tripurasundarī, Mātangī and Kamalā reside inside the main temple, while Bhuvaneśvarī, Bhairavī, Chinnamastā, Dhūmāvatī, Bagalāmukhī, Kālī and Tārā have individual temples located on the hill. Being such a powerful place, the hill of Kamakhya is held in high esteem by those *sādhus* who have a particular inclination toward the worship of the Devī; many practise their *sādhanā* in the jungle and caves hidden in the hill.

The Ambubācī Melā is a week-long festival held annually around mid-June (Ahār month in the Assamese calendar) to celebrate the menstruation of the goddess Kāmākhyā. In practice, the village becomes animated several weeks in advance, with people arriving from all over India to attend the festival, along with numerous *sādhus*, especially eastern India, as well as Aghorīs and *hijṛās*/*kinnars* who usually camp in the crematory area (see Bevilacqua 2022b). The narrow lanes of the village are filled with temporary stores stocking a range of the most 'esoteric' and peculiar items, especially those related to tantric practices. During the festival, animals, mostly goats, are sacrificed in the temple compound to appease the Goddess. Some *sādhus* sit in this area giving mantras, *yantras* or other tools to pilgrims and devotees. They will also remove the evil eye, if requested.

During the menstruation days—the three actual days of the festival—the temple remains closed, 'due to the perceived impurity induced by menstruation' (Borkataky-Varma 2018). During this time, restrictions are observed—all agricultural activities cease—and a strong sense of expectation may be felt in the temple. The evening *ārtī*, for example, done with the doors of the temple closed, becomes particularly powerful.

After three days, the goddess is bathed and other rituals are performed to ensure her return to purity. When the doors of the temple are reopened,

2 See Chapter 1, footnote 35 (p. 40).

Photo 22 Kāmākhyā temple: the reopening of the gate doors, Ambubācī Melā, Kamakhya, 2018.

prasāda is distributed: pieces of cloth, blessed and soaked in what is supposedly the goddess's menstrual blood, are distributed and used as protective amulets (see Urban 2010) (Photo 22).

It is interesting to note how menstruation, perceived in Hindu society as something highly polluting, here becomes a tool for spiritual attainment in this left-hand tantric tradition. As explained by Sangeeta Das (2018: 293), what is in fact being worshipped during the Ambubācī Mela is a process, 'a formal process of menstruation', which allows access to the creative and nurturing powers of the Goddess.

Gaṅgā Sāgar Melā

Gaṅgā Sāgar is the main religious fair in West Bengal and is usually set up in two locations: in Kolkata, where *sādhus* and pilgrims gather before the official festival, and on Sāgar Island—an island in the Ganges Delta, located on the continental shelf of the Bay of Bengal about 100 km south of Kolkata. Most people visit the island on the day of Makar Sankrānti (14 January) to take a holy bath at the confluence of the Ganges river and the Bay of Bengal. The main centre of worship is the Kapal Muni temple. This festival is indeed closely linked to the figure of Kapal Muni and the descent of Gaṅgā to Earth. The following summarises the story as told on the Gaṅgā Sāgar website.[3]

> According to the Bhagavat Purana, Maharishi Kapil Muni (or Sage Kapila) was born to Sage Kardama and Devahuti, daughter of Svayambhuva Manu, ruler of the earth. Kardama Muni, while adhering to the words of his father, Lord Brahma, dedicatedly performed severe austerities. Pleased with his dedication, Lord Vishnu, the supreme soul, appeared in his divine form. In ecstasy, Kardama Muni praised the Lord's magnificence. Pleased, the Lord asked him to marry Devahuti and prophesied that they would have nine daughters and, in time, fill the entire creation with living entities. And he would take birth as an avatar and teach Samkhya philosophy to the world. Kapil Muni, in his early years, attained an unfathomable knowledge of the Vedas and immortalized Samkhya philosophy.
>
> Now, on to the legend of Gangasagar. 'Raja Sagar', or 'Sagar Raja', the ancestor of Lord Ram and ruler of the Ikshvaku dynasty, decided to perform the Ashwamedha Yagya as directed by Sage Aurva. It was believed that performing 100 Ashwamedha Yagyas would help one gain dominion over the entire earth. Lord Indra (the King of God according to Hindu mythology), the only one to complete the 100 Ashwamedha Yagya, feared that he would lose his ascendancy to a mortal, and hid the sacrificial horse near Kapil Muni's hermitage.
>
> Seething with anger, Sagar Raja sent his 60,000 sons (Sagar Putras) to locate the missing horse. The Sagar Putras decimated everything in their path and reached Sage's ashram. Upon discovering the horse, the Sagar Putras mistook the sage for the thief and started hurling abuse at the meditating sage. The ensuing commotion hindered Sage's tapasya. Enraged, Kapi Muni opened his eyes and blazed the 60,000 Sagar Putras into ashes, condemning their souls to hell.
>
> Years later, Angshuman, Sagar Raja's descendant, discovered the horse still standing at Kapil Muni's ashram. He performed austerities to please the Sage. Content with Angshuman's effort, the sage gave his permission to retrieve the horse and learned that the souls of his ancestors could only be freed after performing Shraddhas with the holy water of the Ganges. Although Raja Angshuman and his son Dilip were unable to complete the Shraddhas because Agastya Muni had drunk all the water from the ocean due to a severe drought.

3 https://www.gangasagar.in/en/about/mythologicalsignificance (last accessed 18 March 2024).

Photo 23 Display of *sādhus* during the Gaṅgā Sāgar Melā, 2017.

> A generation later, King Bhagirath, undertook the task of freeing the condemned souls and prayed to Lord Brahma, the creator, to free his ancestors' souls. He asked him to pray to Lord Vishnu to allow the holy Ganga to ascend on earth. Upon agreeing, he cautioned that the sheer force of the Ganges would wipe out the entire creation if it went unchecked and asked him to pray to Lord Shiva. Shiva agreed to bear the entire force of Ganga on his matted hair. In the meandering labyrinth of Shiva's hair, Ganga lost her brute force and descended to the earth, gently caressing all existence. Bhagirath was finally able to perform the last rites of his ancestors, liberating the souls from the fires of Patal Lok.
>
> With passing years, the myths turned into legends, legends into stories, and stories into beliefs. The Ganges was also given the name Bhagirathi, after Raja Bhagirath, and the sea got its name 'Sagar,' after Sagar Raja. And the island, Sagardwip.

The descent of Gaṅgā occurred on the day of Makar Sankrānti when the Sun enters Capricorn; devotees believe that immersing themselves in the holy water of Gaṅgā Sāgar will help them to attain *mokṣa*.

On the festival's website is a slogan about the *melā*: '*har melā bār bār gaṅgā sāgar ek bār*', which means 'all the festivals several times, Gaṅgā

Sāgar only once'—in other words, one single dip in the holy water is enough to wash away all sorrows and sins. However, not all *sādhu*s agree with this interpretation, suggesting that the sentence instead implies that, because it can be attended only once, the festival is of secondary importance.

From Kolkata I reached Harwood Point by taxi on the morning of the 14 January 2017. There I took a boat and reached the island at Kachuberia. From Kachuberia, I caught a bus to Gaṅgā Sāgar, which was about 30 km away. Once there, I was rather shocked by the number of food and 'souvenir' stalls relative to the number of *sādhu*s and their tents. The latter were separated from the footpaths by a wooden fence which did not allow access. Furthermore, many *sādhu*s were to be found on a kind of raised platform, each housed within a small room, with the effect that they looked like they were on display. In such an arrangement—one after another with no space between them, and upon platforms—it was impossible to simply sit with them. It seemed that the purpose was not to encourage exchange and interaction with the *sādhu*s but rather to acquire a quick blessing and move on to the next one (Photo 23).

Mahāśivarātri in Junagadh

Junagadh is a city located in the foothills of Girnar, southwest of Ahmedabad (Gujarat). The Girnar hills are home to several important temples belonging to Jains, Nāths and other Śaiva groups. It is said that the Navanāths and the Mahāsiddhas live in Girnar and on the day of Mahāśivarātri they come to bathe in the Mrigi *kuṇḍa* (pool). According to the *Skanda Purāṇa*, when Śiva and Pārvatī were travelling through the sky on their chariot, their divine ornaments fell into this *kuṇḍa*, which is now considered auspicious and a source of salvation. The *kuṇḍa* is located near the ancient temple of Lord Bhavnāth in Junagadh, on the banks of the Suvarnarekha river. The temple contains a *svayambū śivaliṅgam*, a *liṅgam* that is said to have emerged by its own divine intention.

On the occasion of Mahāśivarātri, the 'Great Night of Śiva'—which occurs one day before the new moon of the month of Māgh (February/March)—the god is said to perform his Taṇḍava dance. In Junagadh this is celebrated with a five-day fair, which attracts thousands of devotees and of course even more *sādhu*s from the Śaiva *akhāṛā*s.

During the night of Mahāśivarātri, a procession of *nāgā sādhu*s starts around 9 pm: this is the festival's main attraction. In 2017, attending the festival with Professor Mallinson, Dr Singleton and some other friends, I noticed that pilgrims had been gathering on the sides of the main streets since the afternoon just to get a good position to see the procession. VIP seats had also been arranged for important people and foreign tourists.

The majority of the *sādhus* camping in the city were *saṃnyāsīs*, some Udāsīs and a very few *tyāgīs*. The *saṃnyāsīs* were all excited and ready for the celebration and the procession. They were also intoxicated with *bhāṅg*, which is a prerequisite for this celebration. Over the course of the procession they displayed their skill with swords, their fighting practice, as well as their frenzied dancing and their playing of the *ḍhamrū* (drums). The procession ended at the Mrigi *kuṇḍa* where they finally bathed.

Appendix 2
Notes on *Sādhus*

Here you will find short descriptions of the *sādhu*s with whom I conversed during my fieldwork. I will provide brief information about their lives (for those who shared that with me), but I will chiefly explain when and where I met them. Within these short biographies, readers will apprehend the various locations I visited and the people who sometimes accompanied me on my travels, such as the other members of the Haṭha Yoga Project and Professor James Mallinson and Dr Mark Singleton. Professor Mallinson proved an important key to unlock the world of the *Terah bhāī tyāgī*s, but others were also fundamental in building connections with *sādhu*s.

Over the years I met with some *sādhu*s on more than one occasion because they had become key interlocutors in my research. Others I met only once, but I believe each exchange was significant in that they all contributed to an understanding—or confirmation—of the general approach among *sādhu*s to the embodied practices presented in this book. In a few rare circumstances, I was unable to find a suitable interlocutor: for example in the Nāth centre of Asthal Bohar, Rohtak (Haryana), the few yogis present had rather biased ideas about a single working woman; likewise in Tarapith I was unable to find trustworthy people to sit with. In a small number of cases I was unable to write down the names of my interlocutors, or else could not understand them properly, so in such cases the *sādhu* will be identified by his role, religious title, position or with reference to the group to which he belongs.

They are listed in alphabetical order, with page references to where they may be found in the book. There are 109 *sādhu*s here in all: 32 are Nāths,

26 Vaiṣṇavas, four Udāsīs and 47 Dasnāmīs. As written here, many lack the honorary titles that should be attributed to them and appended to their names, i.e. those describing their spiritual accomplishments. Unfortunately, I was not able to write them down. I apologise for this: this omission should not be taken as a lack of respect; it was simply due to lack of time and the impossibility of finding them retrospectively.

This list does not capture the extent of all my time spent, including all my failed attempts to meet *sādhus*, the false leads, and the days spent simply building relationships, which have become those I hold most dear. Considering the thousands of hours I spent with such a wide range of *sādhus*, this section could have been much longer, but that would take it beyond the scope of the book.

The majority of *sādhus* in this list did not ultimately get a mention in the main pages of this book, but it is important that they are included here in acknowledgement of and gratitude for their time.

1. **Amar Bhārtī** was a famous *ūrdhvabāhu nāgā sādhu* of the Jūnā *akhāṛā*. I met him at the Allahabad Ardh Kumbh Melā thanks to a friend of mine, Dorothea, who knew him well. She was with him on 16 January 2019 which is when I joined them. She introduced me and in a few words explained my research to him. We started talking and he immediately gave me an interesting definition of his practice—not *haṭha* yoga but *prācīn yog*, the yoga that the ancient sages practised. During the *melā* I visited him several times more to pay homage.

   Speaking of his past, he explained that he had been married, with children and a steady job, when he suddenly decided to give it all up and became a devotee of Śiva. He became an *ūrdhvabāhu* in 1973. Well known in *sādhu* society, he sadly passed away on 18 December 2019.

   See pp. 99, 137, 146.

2. **Ānanda Giri** is a *sādhu* from the Nirañjanī *akhāṛā* whom I met at the 2019 Ardh Kumbh Melā on 11 January that year. He had a huge camp with several boards depicting him practising *āsanas*; after checking his blog, website and Facebook page, I went to meet him.

   Although busy organising an event with children for the afternoon, he was very kind in answering my questions. He told me that he took initiation at the age of 12 and sees his life as his *sādhanā*. He studied yoga in Rishikesh, but the main teachings were given to him in the Himalayas, where he stayed for six years, moving to different places, often alone. He then enrolled at the Banaras Hindu University and later at Sampurnanand University. He received two master's degrees, one in Yoga and one in Astrology.

After our conversation, he wanted me to make a small intervention on his Facebook page. As explained on p. 304, he has recently been involved in several scandals and implicated in the death of his guru, so his future in *sādhu* society remains uncertain.

See pp. 302, 304.

3. **Animā Debnāth (Yogācārya Dr)** is a Nāth woman by birth; she is not an *aughaḍ* since she belongs to the Rudra family and, according to her, this is the highest level of birth because she is a *gṛhastha* Nāth. She also had a guru, a woman called Yogī Shiddeśvar Nāth. I met Animā Debnāth in Kamakhya on 24 June 2018 while wandering among the various temporary camps built for a festival. She had erected a proper tent in which she provided Ayurvedic consultation. I asked her what her knowledge was: she told me that she had learnt yoga and 'aerobic exercises' at school. She was also a member of the International Nath Yogi Sevashram Sangha, an international research institute on Yoga and Naturopathy.

4. **Aśvinī Giri** is the *mahant* of a temple close to Ambikā Mātā, Rajasthan. I met him in Kamakhya on 25 June 2018. He said that he had been a *sādhu* since childhood. On enquiring whether he had left his family, he said yes, because he had five sisters and four brothers. He did not want to be there, so he quickly left. He always covers himself with *vibhūti*, which is his *tapasyā*, although he also has knowledge of yoga practices.

5. **Bālyogī Rām Śaraṇ Dās** is a *Terah bhāī tyāgī*, a disciple of Bārphanī Bābā, the renowned *bābā* who is said to have lived over 200 years thanks to the practice of *kāyakalpa*, but who left his body in December 2020. Bālyogī lives in Rajasthan.

   I met him in Kamakhya on 24 June 2018 at the Ambubācī Melā. He told me about his guru and his own practice of *haṭha* yoga: he has done *dhūnī tap* and completed the 18 years of the practice. That is his degree, he said, which he was only able to achieve thanks to Bārphanī Bābā's grace.

6. **Baldevānanda Purī** is a disciple of Kṛṣṇānanda Purī (no. 36); I met him in Varanasi on 13 March 2018 when he was 36 years old. He recounted that he had become *bābā* some time ago, and said that he

used to do *yogāsanas*, especially *śīrṣāsana*, but stopped after a motorcycle accident.

7. **Bālyogī Muralī Dās** is a Rāmānandī *sādhu* whom I met on 15 February 2017 with Professor Mallinson and Dr Singleton as we travelled in search of yogis' caves. We stopped at Mount Abu (Rajasthan), a place renowned for meditation and *tapasyā* which consists of several *āśrams* and caves still lived in by *sādhus*. There we met Bālyogī Muralī Dās, who lived where Bhagavadācārya, the most important Rāmānandī reformer of the early 20th century, had lived and written. Bālyogī Muralī Dās became a *sādhu* at the age of ten. We talked about yoga, *haṭha* yoga and *tapasyā*.

   See pp. 117, 118.

8. **Banglā Bābā** is an old *nāgā bābā* whom I met in Kamakhya on 9 June 2017 at the Ambubācī Melā. Initially, the conversation did not go well: the *bābā*'s mood fluctuated. He told me that he lives close to Kamakhya and has taught a number of foreigners on various issues. To be a *nāgā bābā*, he declared, there are specific *kriyās*, and there are *kriyās* for every path. Chiefly, he said, there are two paths: one is the path of *puruṣa* (man), for which *sādhus* go to the mountain and do years of *tapasyā* in order to obtain something; the other is the path of *nārī* (woman), the one found in the Kamakhya area, which is based on the female *śakti* and through which one can obtain anything immediately.

9. **Bindu Mahārāj** had an interesting board outside his door in a building that was part of the Udāsī camp at the 2016 Ujjain Siṃhasth Melā. It was 3 May 2016 when I walked by it; since it said that he was a *yogīrāj*, I knocked on his door. He is not an Udāsī—in fact, his affiliation is unclear—but the board claimed he was part of the Akhāṛā Pariṣad.

   Covered all over with necklaces, *rudrākṣa* and rings on almost every finger, Bindu Mahārāj was very kind to spend time with me, considering how busy he was. He said he received a MD in Ayurveda and explained the meaning of yoga to me. After that he left.

10. **'Bindu Vālā'** is a Rāmānandī *tyāgī* whose name I did not understand, but I am calling him 'the one with the *bindu*' because he belongs to a Rāmānandī section that uses a white *bindu* in the *tilaka*. He became a *sādhu* about seven or eight years ago, before which he used to cook in a temple. He then took *dīkṣā* and began the *monī tapasyā*. He had

begun speaking again a couple of months before I met him, on 5 April 2016, during that year's Ujjain Siṃhasth Melā. He was staying at the *mahātyāgīs*' camp. On 16 April he explained the *dhūnī tap* to me while Śyām Dās (no. 78) performed it.

11. **Bholā Giri** is an *ūrdhvabāhu* from the Āvāhan *akhāṛā*. At the 2016 Ujjain Siṃhasth Melā, he had a board declaring himself a *tapasvī* and a *haṭhayogī*, and for this reason I went to his camp, which was exceptionally large with an incredible *paṇḍāl* (temporary pavilion) to accommodate devotees and *bhaṇḍārās*. I met him on 14 April, but he told me to come back the next day. A devotee there said that this was a good sign, since Bholā Giri usually keeps people at a distance. On returning the next day, I had about 20 minutes of his time, during which we talked mainly about his *tapasyā*, which is done for the cow and for the *kalyāṇ* of society. He had harsh words to say about people who came for his blessing because, he said, they were ignorant about the *sādhu samāj* and only wanted to take from *sādhus* without making any religious efforts.

    See p. 164.

12. **Bhole Bābā** is an Udāsī who lives in Rishikesh. I found him thanks a suggestion by Andrés, a practitioner from Chile who has known him for a long time. His *dhūnī* was near the Ganges river, on the path from Lakshman Jhula to Ram Jhula. There are, in fact, on that bank several small huts inhabited by *sādhus*. Bhole Bābā has a permanent home there apart from when the Ganges is high, which forces him to move out. His *kuṭī* is like a *guphā*, small and smoky because of the *dhūnī*, but it is also full of *mūrtis* and images of deities. It is a *guphā* and a temple at the same time.

    I met Bhole Bābā for the first time on 9 March 2017. He told me that he had been *sādhu* since childhood, although he could not remember how old he was, but probably around 60. He is originally from Uttar Pradesh. He told me that as a child he often fell ill and his mother would ask *sādhus* for remedies. Eventually, an Udāsī cured him with *vibhūti*; he considered that moment his first initiation. In fact, he loved spending time with *sādhus* and decided to join them. He travelled a lot in the *jamāt* of the Udāsī *akhāṛā*.

    I met him again from 10–21 March, during which time he told me stories from the *Mahābhārata* and the *Rāmāyaṇa* about *ṛṣis* and *mahātmās*. He told me that he used to live in the Sivananda *āśram* but bathed in the place where his *kuṭī* is today. One day a man suggested that he build his *dhūnī* there and, while he was making the *havan* for the installation, an elephant appeared in the river. Initially, the *bābā* thought it was a piece of wood before seeing it for what it was. The elephant came out of the water and circled around the *dhūnī* three times. At that time the place was quite wild.

During Holi we celebrated by cleaning his *kuṭī*, which had become too smoky. On 14 March we shot some videos of *āsana*s and *prāṇāyāma*s and on the 15th we went to meet the Loyal Guphā Bābā (no. 41) with a devotee of Bhole Bābā. On the 17th he tried to cure my headache and also showed me several photos of himself.

Bhole Bābā was a very helpful *sādhu*, although unfortunately not always surrounded by the best people.

See pp. 66, 84, 87, 120, 121, 144, 205, 226, 231, 233, 250, 286.

13. **Cetan Purī** is a *bābā* of the Jūnā *akhāṛā*. His *āśram* is in Chandigarh but during the hot season he moves to the Himalayas. Many *bābā*s and yogis move there during the hot season, he said. He had some sort of medical knowledge: he had learnt from a doctor the theory of the *nāḍī*s and how to stimulate and relax them. I met him in the *āśram* of Dayānanda Purī (no. 15) on 16 March 2017.

See p. 189.

14. **Choṭīyā (Brij Mohan Dās)** is a *tyāgī*, a disciple of Rām Bālak Dās (no. 60). He was initiated when he was a child. He was somewhat outspoken about the life and society of *sādhu*s: he was quick to denounce the all-too-frequent inappropriate behaviour of *sādhu*s today, who are increasingly attached to *māyā*—a word often used in general to refer to material things. According to him, the condition of the *sādhu samāj* has worsened in recent decades because of money and politics. I met him together with Professor Mallinson on 23 March 2016 in Omkareshwar, where he has his *āśram*, and then again in April 2016 in Ujjain. Because he accompanied his guru on religious festivals, Choṭīyā was also present for the majority of the time I spent with Rām Bālak Dās. We met again in Allahabad in 2019, when the title of *mahant* was conferred upon him. He is not a *yogīrāj* because his main *sādhanā* is based on *bhakti*, *bhajan* and *pūjā*.

See pp. 126, 127.

15. **Dayānanda Purī** is a *nāgā sādhu* of the Jūnā *akhāṛā*. He lives in Rishikesh, in the Tapovan area, a beautiful and peaceful place where he has a three-storey *āśram* with a pleasant Ayurvedic garden, a downstairs kitchen, and the *dhūnī* on top.

I met Dayānanda Purī for the first time on 11 March 2017, when he was 44. He is a very straightforward person: he does not feel the need to hide anything, nor does he leave things unsaid. When we met, he told me how he became a *bābā*, an account that bears a close resemblance to the stories of several saints as told in hagiographies.

He took *dīkṣā* when he was seven years old. He left his family to go to the Himalayas, because someone had told him that was where you needed to go to meet the god Śiva. He said that in his village he used to walk naked, which made people think there was something different about him. He also said that, when he was a child, miracles happened because of him: he was able to change the weather, he said. Before going to the Himalayas, however, he went to Vrindavan (being originally from Madhya Pradesh) after his elder brother one day broke his *mālā* and slapped him, telling him he should to go to school instead of wasting his time in temples. Angered, the little Dayānanda went to the Vrindavan bus station and boarded a bus to the Govardhan *parikramā*. Some people took care of him while he did the *parikramā* with pilgrims. He lived in Vrindavan for a few months then he left for Ajmer, then Mathura, Delhi, and eventually Haridwar. In 1986, having spent several years with *bābā*s but without becoming a disciple, he attended the Kumbh Melā in Haridwar. There he met his future guru, Macchendra Purī, who had an *āśram* in Haryana. He stayed in Haryana for about 20 years doing *pūjā* and *sevā*, studying Sanskrit and Ayurveda—his parents were both Ayurvedic doctors, he said, and his father had a good knowledge of yoga. Some time later, during another Kumbh Melā, he met an Italian girl and followed her to Italy. After that, he extended his travels to, among other places, Austria, Spain, Mexico, California and Australia, thanks to the foreign disciples and devotees he has acquired.

We continued our conversations, during which he was consistently friendly and honest, and sometimes a little embarrassed to talk about money, people he had met, and the different circumstances he encountered abroad. We also met on 11, 12, 14 and 16 March. On the 17th, he too attempted to cure my headache and on that day was also accosted by a man who wished to make a short video about Rishikesh and yoga. I found myself in his *āśram* again on 19, 20 and 21 March. I also met Dayānanda Purī at the 2019 Ardh Kumbh Melā in Allahabad.

See pp. 97, 169, 184, 195, 196, 214, 250, 252, 271, 286, 293, 317.

16. **Dharam Giri** is a *saṃnyāsī* whom I met at Bhole Bābā's *kuṭī* in Rishikesh in March 2017. He was often to be seen there, and he had a good knowledge of *tapasyā* and yoga thanks to his guru jī. He also came with us to visit the Loyal Guphā Bābā (no. 41).
    See pp. 227, 264.

17. **Digital Bābā (Triambak Giri)** is a *nāgā sādhu* of the Jūnā *akhāṛā* whom I met in Kamakhya in June 2017. I first noticed him on 21 June when several *sādhus* did the *āsana* performance in front of journalists on the International Day of Yoga. I listened to him speak to a journalist and then approached him. He said that where he lives, in Omkareshwar, his guru-*bhāī* had been practising *khaṛeśvarī* for 12 years. He began this same practice himself, but after four years was experiencing problems with both legs. He claimed that he has a Spanish Mā, who supports him by sending him money with which he buys electronic items, such as an iPad, which is why he is called Digital Bābā.
    See p. 170.

18. **Dīpak Giri** is a young *nāgā sādhu* of the Āvāhan *akhāṛā* whom I met at Bhole Bābā's *kuṭī* (no. 12) in Rishikesh on 19 March 2017. He used to practise *āsanas* as a form of *tapasyā* but after an accident in Delhi he changed *tapasyā*.
    See p. 138.

19. **Doctor Svāmī Sanjay** is an interesting *brahmacārī* follower of Satuwa Bābā. He is from Gujarat and said that while studying at the university he became interested in several disciplines but eventually focused on yoga. He spent almost 30 years with Satuwa Bābā and learnt yoga from him, but also attended modern centres in order to study yoga from a more scientific perspective.
    He was about 55 when we met in Varanasi in 2015 at the temple of Rām Priya Dās (no. 64). Our first conversation about yoga was on 7 November 2015. We then met at the *āsana* classes held by Rām Priya Dās, and also had private conversations on 4, 5 and 8 December 2015.
    See pp. 281-282, 285.

20. **Durgā Bhārtī (Yogī)** is an elderly *saṃnyāsinī* of the Jūnā *akhāṛā*. She was staying in the camp of Manimaheś Bhārtī (no. 45)—who is apparently her guru or guru-*bhāī*—so I met her at the 2016 Ujjain

Siṃhasth Melā. We had our most in-depth conversation on 16 April 2016.

She is originally from Nepal, but married very young and moved to Kolkata to follow her husband. She had children and when her husband died she became a *sādhvī*. With her husband being much older, she took *dīkṣā* when still young. She met her guru in Kolkata, a *nāgā* of the Jūnā *akhāṛā*. She spent five years in the jungle practising *tapasyā* and yoga—'the spiritual yoga', she clarified, i.e. meditation. As a result, her guru gave her the title of Yogī. She still does some physical practice. On her side of the tent, with her *celī* Līlā Bhārtī (also from Nepal, having taken initiation after the death of her daughter), Durgā Bhārtī showed me some exercises for the knee—which made me realise how flexible and strong she was.

Later, she shared her concern about Rāmeśvarī, an eight-year-old girl who had been entrusted to the *akhāṛā* by her parents, but who did not have a very religious attitude. A young boy came to talk to Durgā Bhārtī for further explanation about a story she told him the day before, and I was fascinated to observe the respect she inspires in the *akhāṛā*.

See pp. 90, 95, 192, 223, 316.

21. **Garuḍ Dās** is a guru of the Rāmānujī *sampradāya* and has his *āśram* in Ujjain. He belongs to the Rāmānujī *Terah bhāī tyāgī khālsā* which is linked to the Rāmānujī Dvārkādīś centre in Varanasi.

Garuḍ Dās began his yoga practice at the age of seven and was a disciple of Devrāhā Bābā, the famous Vaiṣṇava *sādhu*. However, despite his practice, he was unable to find inner peace, he said. He therefore began to wander in various parts of India, in the Himalayas and in the jungle. Eventually, he met a *siddha* Yogī in 2000.

Being an accomplished *yogīrāj*, he was an important interlocutor for this research. When I first met him, on 9 April 2016 at the Siṃhasth Melā in Ujjain, he was sceptical about my research because I do not practise and do not have a guru. Nevertheless, we had a long general conversation and he allowed me to return over the next few days. His attitude did not change as the days went by, although he continued to answer my questions. He said that he usually does not give *pravacan* because people are not able to listen properly: what they hear they subsequently forget. He therefore delegates general teaching to others. Nonetheless, during the festival, we would talk in his tent, and I was able to observe his interactions with devotees, who were always full of practical questions. He always answered them carefully, often using mythological stories from the Purāṇas. The atmosphere in his camp and tent was, both literally and figuratively, quite different from that of other *bābā*s due to the absence of smoke and the fact that the majority there were lay people.

We met again on 10, 14 and 20 April and, having read in a pamphlet about a '*dhyāna śivir*' at his camp, I attended it from 24–27 April. We spoke for a last time on 5 May 2016.

See pp. 90, 94, 96, 138, 166, 184, 188, 226-227, 230, 233, 238, 246, 256, 258, 263, 269, 275, 283, 293, 317.

22. **Gopāl Dās** is an Udāsī whom I met on 3 May 2016 at the Ujjain Siṃhasth Melā in the Udāsī camp. He belongs to the *jamāt* of the Udāsī *akhāṛā* which, he said consists of about 40 people. We talked at length about the *sampradāya, tapasyā, haṭha* yoga and *jap*. However, he seemed somewhat confused and sometimes contradicted himself.
   See pp. 139, 259.
23. **Gopāl Giri** is a *nāgā saṃnyāsī* from Pushkar, where he lives in a hut outside the city. He is from the Āvāhan *akhāṛā* and was a friend of Vijay Giri (no. 84). I met him in Kamakhya on 18 June 2017. It was his first time in Kamakhya: he had come because one of his devotees wanted to learn some tantric *kriyā*s and he was hoping to find a good guru for him. With regard to himself, he said that he received *dīkṣā* when he was a child, but he could not perform too many *āsana*s because of a leg problem. Over dinner, we had a long conversation about yoga *sādhanā*.
24. **Govind Giri** was the young *thānāpati* and *mahant* of the Jūnā *akhāṛā āśram* in Kamakhya when I visited it on 6 June 2017. That day, I asked his permission to visit the *sādhus* and talk to them. I was allowed to sit in his room where he used to greet the *sādhus*, so by doing nothing more than sitting there for hours on end I could witness the daily routine of the *akhāṛā* preparing for the Ambubācī Melā.

   He was usually in a congenial and joyful mood, although at times stressed by festival responsibilities. In the more relaxed moments, he talked about himself. He had been a *sādhu* since childhood: he was initiated when he was only five. He did not run away from home—he said he had no one—so it is likely that a *sādhu* found him and took care of him. After the *dīkṣā* he started travelling with his guru jī. He said there was not a single place in India where they did not go. He did not learn from books but from all the *sādhu*s he met.

He said that he used to stay in Koṭiliṅgam because, before, there was nothing behind the Kamakhya temple, only the jungle, so he actually saw the *akhāṛā* rising in front of him. He said that he used to practise *āsana*s in Rishikesh when he was young. He used to know them all, but today no longer practises for lack of time. He was more on the path of *karma* yoga on account of being the head of the place. Sometimes he felt a lack of freedom because of his many duties and financial responsibilities, which made him wonder whether this situation was right for him. He mentioned being a *monī* and doing so on a daily basis, in specific circumstances.

I also met him in June 2018, again in Kamakhya for the Ambubācī Melā, and then in Allahabad at the 2019 Ardh Kumbh Melā.

See p. 214.

25. **Hari Dās** has been a *monī* for 44 years. He is a disciple of Monī Bābā (no. 47) although he did not learn all the *āsana*s he knows from him, but from different *sādhu*s. I was able to exchange some information with him at the 2019 Ardh Kumbh Melā in Allahabad, with the help of other *tyāgī*s, as he belongs to the *Terah bhāī tyāgī khālsā.* I also shot several videos after his *dhūnī tap* practice because he performed some interesting *āsana*s.

26. **Hari Giri** is a *saṃnyāsī* of the Jūnā *akhāṛā* whom I met in Rishikesh at the *āśram* of Dayānanda Purī (no. 15) on 14 March 2017. He has not been a *bābā* since childhood: he only he took *dīkṣā* later, he said. He lives in Manali and sometimes teaches yoga in Goa and Gokarna, where his classes usually last two hours or maybe longer, depending on the students and how the class is going. He was critical of *sādhu* society. We met a few more times (16 and 20 March 2017), and continued to discuss yoga and *tapasyā*.

    See pp. 118, 293, 295, 298, 302.

27. **Hari Oṃ Giri** is a fairly young *saṃnyāsī* who took *dīkṣā* in 2010, in Varanasi. However, his training took place in Kurukshetra (Punjab), where his other gurus taught him everything and where he was also trained in *āsana* and *vyāyām.* I met him in Pashupatinath, Nepal, on 9 and 19 May 2018. He said that every morning he does some *āsana*s and exercises, after which he bathes, does *sevā*, has breakfast and comes to Pashupatinath to do his *sādhanā*: he had been sitting in the same spot every day for two years doing *jap* the entire day. Even as we talked, he would constantly use his *mālā*.

28. **Indra Bhārtī** is the *mahant* of the Nirañjanī *akhāṛā* in Junagadh (Gujarat). I met him with Professor Mallinson and Dr Singleton when we went to Junagadh for the Mahāśivarātri celebration. On 22 February 2017, we chatted about *vajrolī* and *khecarī mudrā*.

29. **Īśnāth** is an *aughaḍ pīr* who lives in Pashupatinath, Nepal. He is originally from Sikkim. His family was probably well off since he studied in a Scottish school and was the only *sādhu* I could talk to in English. He took *dīkṣā* some time in the 1970s, at the age of 18, from Rām Nāth Aghorī, a famous Nāth guru. However, before embarking on the ascetic path, he followed his mother's wish for him to complete his studies in astrophysics.

Having reached Pashupatinath in the 1970s, he stayed there for 12 years and then Haridwar for another 12, thereby performing 12-year *anuṣṭhānas*, changing location each time. He had returned to Pashupatinath five years before I met him.

I went looking for him when I arrived in Kathmandu because he is the guru of a friend of mine, Heather, who suggested I talk to him. By the time I made it to Pashupatinath he had already left for a few days, but he eventually returned and we met on 12 May 2018.

Our meetings (which took place almost daily until 28 May) occurred in his small but comfortable *kuṭī*, installed in the precincts of Pashupatinath, not far from the crematory ground.

Īśnāth wears only black and also applies the *kājal* on his left eye, being part of the Natheśvar *panth*. As the days went by, we covered many different topics, always in a very relaxed atmosphere. I was accompanied at times by my friends: first Nicole and then Anya, both of whom were well received by Īśnāth. With the addition of Heather's presence, our days together became even more agreeable. When Yogī Rudra Nāth (no. 100) arrived, it was interesting to note their interactions and exchanges of information about different members of the Nāth *sampradāya*.

See pp. 67, 71, 75, 96, 143, 171, 173, 185, 187, 191-192, 203, 205, 208, 214, 223, 239, 245, 246, 253, 261, 263, 268, 282.

30. **Jagannāth Dās** is a *tyāgī* of the Rāmānandī *sampradāya*, specifically of the *Terah bhāī tyāgī khālsā*, and probably now approaching 40 years of age. He was initiated as a child because he ran away from home when he was about six or seven. Even as a child, he used to recite the *Hanumān Cālīsā* and loved to listen to the Rām *kathā*. When he left his home, he went to Vrindavan where he met his guru jī, Monī Bābā

(no. 47). He said that his guru was strict with him because he was a very active child, but he also took care of him. Afterwards, he spent seven years studying in the Rām Janakī temple in Varanasi, although moving between the various Rāmānandī *āśrams* in the city and then in India more broadly, both on his own and as part of the *jamāt*.

In 2005, he became *mahant* of the Śrī Dīgheśvarnāth Mandir Majoulīrāj in Salempur (Deoria district, Uttar Pradesh), where he lives. According to tradition, this is a very powerful place because sages have been performing *tapasyā* there since the time of the *Mahābhārata*. This responsibility limits the amount of travelling he can undertake.

Jagannāth Dās is a *yogīrāj* who has practised several *tapasyās* in his lifetime, notably *dhūnī tap*, which he did for 18 years, until he fell ill with typhoid. Because of this, he cut off his *jaṭā* and realised how heavy they were, feeling some relief in removing them and now being better able to wash his head. In fact, he never grew them back.

Yoga is part of his *sādhanā* together with *pūjā* and *bhajan*.

I met him for the first time in Varanasi on 26 October 2015 when he was staying at the Rām Janakī temple in Belopur, and we spent a couple of hours together. I met him again from 20–22 November at his temple in Deoria, together with Dr Singleton.

I have met Jagannāth Dās several times over the years at religious festivals, notably the 2019 Ardh Kumbh in Allahabad. He has always been focused and honest in sharing aspects of his life, to the extent of admitting how far he still had to go to be comparable with his guru.

See pp. 121, 128, 144, 275, 286, 291.

31. **Jogī Bābā (Brahmānanda Giri)** is a *nāgā bābā* of the Aṭal *akhāṛā* whom I met for the first time on 28 January 2017. I was in Shantiniketan, following a suggestion by Pravash, a friend from Kolkata, who said I should visit the 'yogi in the tree'. Jogī Bābā, in fact, lives just outside Shantiniketan in the Garh Jungle. The first time we met, he showed me the tamarind tree where he did *tapasyā* and we had an hour-long conversation. I also went to see him the next day, although finding the place alone was difficult given the poor state of the road. For that reason, I decided to remain in contact with him and plan a longer visit.

I visited his *āśram* in the jungle from 6–18 February 2018. I have described this place more fully elsewhere (Bevilacqua 2018b), so here I will be brief. Jogī Bābā had built his *āśram* based on visions he had during his *tapasyā*: he claimed to have found the spot where the first Durgā *pūjā* was celebrated, and he had built several temples in the jungle to honour the Devī. Every day we did the *parikramā* of the place together by doing *pūjā*, and sometimes he would give me the task of doing it in the company of a young girl who lived there. Bābā jī, in fact, looks after several tribal people and some disabled ones.

Our days were spent peacefully, cleaning the *āśram*, breakfasting together, and with some morning chats. Then he would do his work in the temple; I would study and help people if needed, talking again with Jogī Bābā in the evening.

Jogī Bābā was not *bāl brahmacārī*: he had had to marry—obliged to do so by his father, he said, because his brother died. However, according to him, he was born under the support of a guru and the grace of Bolenāth, which is why he considers himself a *sādhu* from the womb. He studied yoga with a *sādhu* from his village. He married and had a daughter, but left the family at the age of 23. His wife is in Kalyanpur and his daughter is married; sometimes they visit him, but he does not care, as he has left the *saṃsāra*. After leaving his family, he travelled a little before settling here; he did *tapasyā* practices, and his yoga *sādhanā*, in the jungle. He survived in this location thanks to the support of tribal people living in the surrounding area. People of the neighbouring towns began to become aware of him, and helped him build his place. Today, people go for a *darśan* of the various temples built by Jogī Bābā that are dedicated to the goddesses. Twice a year he organises celebrations for the festivals of Rām Navāmī and Durgā Pūjā; on those occasions, thousands of people come to celebrate.

In Kolkata, a few weeks after my return from his *āśram*, we met again to go to the hospital because he wanted me to meet his guru. I also met Jogī Bābā at the 2019 Allahabad Kumbh Melā.

Jogī Bābā was an inestimable source of information, kindness and help.

See pp. 10, 14, 91, 133, 139-140, 142, 145, 171, 172, 177, 180-183, 185, 193-194, 205, 208-209, 209(photo), 211, 217-218, 218(photo), 220-221, 221(photo), 225-231, 236, 240, 243, 246, 249, 262, 263, 266, 267, 270, 293, 297, 310, 317.

32. **Jvālā Purī** belongs to the Jūnā *akhāṛā*; I met him in Varanasi in November 2015. I do not know this *bābā*'s life story—other than that he told me he had been initiated 25 years earlier—but he was easy to talk to. He tried to persuade me to become initiated and to get a *mālā* to repeat the mantra he wanted to give me. In fact, for him *bhajan*

was the most important *sādhanā*. We met only once because he failed to turn up to our second appointment; since he was so insistent about my initiation, I decided to look elsewhere.

See pp. 210, 249, 259, 275.

33. **Kākā jī (Uncle jī)** is a Rāmānandī *sādhu* and part of the *Terah bhāī tyāgī khālsā*. His name derives from the fact that he is the guru-*bhāī* of Monī Bābā (no. 47) and therefore the 'uncle' of those *sādhus* who are disciples or closely related to Monī Bābā. I met him at the 2019 Ardh Kumbh Melā in Allahabad, but we never spoke directly because Kākā jī was not very talkative, being a solitary, wandering *sādhu*—somewhat untamed in both appearance and behaviour. I didn't attempt to trouble him, but I did observe him preparing a thread with *muñja* grass, and doing *dhūnī tap*, which he continues to perform even though he has finished the entire practice three times. He is also a *yogīrāj* and allowed me to take photos and videos of his practice. Even without words, he was a source of excellent information. As I left the Melā, when I went to say goodbye to the *tyāgīs*, he gave me plenty of *prasāda* for my journey.

See p. 128.

34. **Kamal Giri** is a *saṃnyāsī* of the Jūnā *akhāṛā* whom I met through an Italian *saṃnyāsī*, Dhruv Giri. I first met Kamal Giri on 4 May 2016, but he was not pleased to see me accompanying Dhruv Giri. Kamal Giri said that women drive *sādhus* crazy so it was not good for *sādhus* to be in their company. So I got Dhruv Giri to ask him questions on my behalf, which he did on 6 May 2016.

35. **Kamal Giri** was a *saṃnyāsī* of the Jūnā *akhāṛā* whom I found while I was wandering around the Gaṅgā Sāgar Melā. On his board he could be seen in *kukkutāsana*, which prompted me to stop and ask him about that posture. He invited me to sit down and we started talking (7 January 2017). He did not appear very healthy at the time, perhaps because of the weather. We talked a lot and he showed me photos of him doing *āsanas* and pulling a track with his penis. We continued talking over the next few days, on 8 and 12 January. On the 12th, I found out that Kamal Giri was the *sādhu* who had been suggested to me by Śyām Ānanda Nāth (no. 71); in fact I met with the latter at Kamal Giri's place on that very day. It was an agreeable and interesting encounter which opened up several topics for discussion. Kamal Giri told me that his guru had taught him yoga when he was a child—and at that time a Vaiṣṇava and later a householder. A brahmin from

Kanpur, he was married and had children. He was still in contact with his family in Kanpur, but 15 years previously he chose to undertake the *saṃnyāsī* path and found a Śaiva guru. His *āśram* at the time was in Jhargram, West Bengal.

After our last meeting in Gaṅgā Sāgar (15 January 2017), he invited me to join him at his place to talk further. He reiterated the invitation when we met in June 2017 in Kamakhya, where he displayed his skills in *āsana* in a performance he and other *sādhus* did on the International day of Yoga.

I met him again in January 2018, initially on the 12th at the Gaṅgā Sāgar Melā, so that I could acquire information about his *āśram* in Jhargram. He had moved there from Kanpur five or six years previously because he had a few followers and thus a better chance of making a living for himself. At that time, in 2018, Kamal Giri was on his swing, because he had become *khaṛeśvarī* five months before. He was therefore unable to teach me any yogic practices, but I went to his *āśram* to continue our conversations about yoga and *tapasyā*. I stayed there from 18–23 January 2017. His *āśram* was in quite a jungle-like environment, located in a village which apparently has a severe drinking problem. Many alcoholics used to visit Kamal Giri. They would do his *sevā*, but actually he was a convenient excuse to avoid work or escape from their families. However, most people who came to him were there for health remedies. Since Kamal Giri was not very fluent in Bangla, he had devotees who translated for him. He had no disciples because his guru forbade him to make any: first he was expected to finish the 12 years of *nāgā bābā* training, he said.

We also met in Kamakhya in June 2018 at the Ambubācī Melā. I have been told that he left his body in 2023.

See pp. 95, 119, 121-122, 134(photo), 135, 145, 165, 189, 205, 207, 209-211, 234, 247, 249, 251, 263, 269, 285.

36. **Kṛṣṇānanda Purī** is a *khaṛeśvarī* of the Jūnā *akhāṛā*, although when I met him in Varanasi on 11 and 13 March 2018, he was staying in the *āśram* of the Āvāhan *akhāṛā*.

He is originally from Bihar and was initiated when he was a child. Apparently—if I understood properly—he initially took *vairāgī dīkṣā* in Nepal, probably in Janakpur. Later he also took a *saṃnyāsī dīkṣā* because, according to him, this is a slow path to a more detached level of asceticism.

He was 48 years old when I met him and his disciple said that he was also a *yogīrāj*, although when I asked him directly he did not reply. Interestingly, he often answered my question in *ulṭī bhāṣā*, the *gupt* (hidden) language of *sādhus*, made up of riddles and puns, which often made his sentences difficult to understand.

Kṛṣṇānanda Purī had been *khareśvarī* for 18 years. His *āśram* is in Indore.

See pp. 135, 144.

37. **Kumbh Giri** is a *saṃnyāsī*, having taken *dīkṣā* from an *akhāṛā* in the 1970s. However, he no longer appreciates Śaiva *akhāṛās*. In fact, I met him in the *mahātyāgīs* camp at the Siṃhasth Melā in Ujjain in April 2016, where, we talked a lot about the role of the *akhāṛās* and contemporary developments in *sādhu* society.

38. **Lokeśvarānanda Giri** is the *mahant* of a temple in West Bardwam and in the Nadia district, both in West Bengal. I first noticed him on 21 June 2017 in Kamakhya, during the International Day of Yoga, performing various practices in front of journalists. However, I was unable to talk to him on that occasion. The following year, in 2018, I attended the Ambubācī Melā again and spoke to him on 23 June. He was interested in seeing the photos, which I told him I had taken of him the year before. He assumed I would have prints of them on my person.

    He told me that he was from West Bengal and received *saṃnyāsī dīkṣā* in 1979. He had started work in 1971, but soon realised that daily life was just *māyā*, a way to spend time before death. So, to give his life meaning, he decided to become initiated and practise *sādhanā* properly.

    See pp. 215, 247, 316.

39. **Lakṣmaṇ Dās** is the *mahant* of an Udāsī centre in Varanasi. The building, which probably was an old *haveli*, is pinkish in colour. I met him for the first time on 12 December 2015, and then on 2 January 2016. Although he is quite young, he is very serious and concerned about the *sādhus* under his control. He was still studying at the Banaras Hindu University and wanted to do a PhD on Vedānta *darśana*. I met him again at the Ujjain Siṃhasth Melā when I was visiting the Udāsī camp—which was impressive because the Udāsīs also have a *maṭha* there and are quite powerful in the city. We also spoke on 3 May 2016 but only briefly because, given his position, he was always busy.

    See pp. 86, 165, 266, 274.

40. **Lāl Dās** was camping with Rāghavendra Dās (no. 56) at the 2019 Ardh Kumbh Melā in Allahabad. He participated in several of our conversations and sometimes offered his point of view. He revealed to us that, before being initiated by Monī Bābā (no. 47), he was a *nāgā* of the Vaiṣṇava Digambar *akhāṛā*. For this reason, he always had a weapon with him, which he said he kept because he had made it *siddha*: that is, he had mastered its use. On account of this, other *sādhus* were prompted to question his position: usually, the initiation process is the other way round—first as *tyāgī* and then as *nāgā*.

    See pp. 165-166.

41. **Loyal Guphā Bābā** is a *saṃnyāsī* of the Mahā Nirvāṇī *akhāṛā*. I visited him with Bhole Bābā (no. 12) and Daniela, a Chilean practitioner, on 15 March 2017. We stayed for around three hours, during which time he talked on several topics, jumping from one to another. He was very energetic. He showed us documents concerning the history of the cave in which he was living, which was discovered by chance thanks to a porcupine; according to him, the porcupine was Śiva himself. He moved there in 2001 from Delhi where he had been working. Over the years he built a temple on top of the *guphā*, a gate at its entrance, a little *āśram* and a garden for medicinal plants. He was happy to be part of the Mahā Nirvāṇī *akhāṛā* because, he said, *sādhus* of the Jūnā *akhāṛā* were just smokers and attached to money and property.

    I could not record our conversation because the Loyal Bābā said that otherwise his mouth would be automatically shut: journalists and local TV crews descended on him when he moved there, but he refused to be filmed or have his words recorded. 'This is the will of Bolenāth', he said.

    We also met him on 18 March: at the time a small feast was being held and there were a few participants.

    See pp. 133, 287.

42. A ***mahant*** of the Āvāhan *akhāṛā* in Varanasi, whom I met in Varanasi on 11 and 13 March 2018 because he was playing host to Kṛṣṇānanda Purī (no. 36). He had no particular knowledge to share about yoga: he said he had no time for that because he had to run the place. The *mahant* was preparing a jacket for Kṛṣṇānanda Purī made of *rudrākṣa* and was very kind to us (I went there with Edoardo, a friend of mine), inviting us to eat our breakfast in the *akhāṛā*.

    See pp. 19, 129, 135.

43. A ***mahant*** of the Nirañjanī *akhāṛā* in Varanasi. I talked to him only once (10 November 2015), in his *āśram* near to the *ghāṭ*s. He made it clear that he was very busy and had no time. Moreover, he emphasised that his yoga practice was for himself and not for display. In our encounter, he told me that he was only practising a few *āsana*s as he was not in good health. He gave me a *mālā* to do mantra repetition.

44. **Maheś Nāth** was an *aughaḍ pīr* when I met him on 21 February 2017 with Professor Mallinson and Dr Singleton in Dhinodhar (Gujarat), not in the hilltop temple but in the *āśram* built on the hillside. He is a disciple of Yogī Hīrā Nāth (no. 91). He was remarkably thin because, like his guru, he only eats fruit, drinks *chai* and smokes *cilam*. He had been doing *tapasyā* for the last eight or nine years by staying in *śīrṣāsana* for at least an hour, daily. He did not yet have *kuṇḍal* and he considered himself a small person compared to his guru and other *sādhus*.

See pp. 121, 138, 139(photo), 144.

45. **Manimaheś Bhārtī** is a *nāgā sādhu* of the Jūnā *akhāṛā*. He was a brahmin from Ujjain who left his family and moved to Madhya Pradesh, to a remote place where he does the *pūjā* to Hanumān—the only thing he cares about, he said. He told me that he wants neither *āśram* nor temple so as to avoid developing attachment; besides, a *sādhu* does not need that kind of thing.

I met him at the Ujjain Siṃhasth Melā and I spent some time in his camp, starting on 15 April 2016, as several other *nāgā*s were staying there and they were very kind to me, going as far as to make a show of defending me with their swords when visitors to the *melā* were pestering me for photos. His camp was a safe space in which to hang around and watch the events, especially during the baths.

I met him again at the 2019 Ardh Kumbh Melā in Allahabad, whereupon I was surprised to find he remembered my name. We conversed on 1, 4, 15 and 16 January.

He seems a very genuine, 'old-style' *bābā* who is troubled by modernity, especially because of its new contraptions.

46. **Manohar Dās** is an Udāsī whom I met at the Udāsī centre in southern Varanasi on 2 January 2016. At that time, he was still studying at the Banaras Hindu University—where he also studied the *Yogasūtra*—and was about to start a PhD. We spoke again on 3 March 2016 at the Ujjain Siṃhasth Melā. Years later, I recognised him in a documentary I was watching, which contained footage of him as a child. I shared a

screenshot of the video with him and he confirmed that he had been just a child when he was initiated. He was delighted to receive the image, which he shared on his Facebook page.

47. **Monī Bābā (*mahant* Prem Dās)** is the guru of Jagannāth Dās (no. 30) and the guru/leader of the *Terah bhāī tyāgī khālsā*. I met Monī Bābā in 2019 at the Ardh Kumbh Melā in Allahabad. When I arrived at his camp on 7 February, he was doing a kind of *havan* at his *dhūnī*. He is not very talkative, having been a *monī* for 35 years. Unlike other *tyāgī*s, he said that he had never smoked, not even once in his whole life. Being part of the *jamāt*, he moves here and there, although he is building an *āśram* in Ayodhya, in Khakh Chowk. According to Jagannath Dās he obtained the *darśan* of God when he was doing his *monī* practice. I used to attend Monī Bābā's evening *ārtī* on a daily basis and sometimes, if he had time, we would talk. He was very curious about practices in Western countries in general, so there were more questions from him than from me. More specifically, on 10 February we talked about *tapasyā* and yoga.
    See pp. 80, 121, 188, 291, 317.

48. **Monī Bābā** is a *saṃnyāsī* disciple of Bārphanī Bābā, and from Badrinath. He got *dīkṣā* when he was five years old. In Badrinath, he and his guru have an *āśram* together, which hosts people from all over the world. They cure everything with yoga, he said. Their board at the Ujjain Siṃhasth Melā declares that they practise *kriyā* yoga; when I visited him on 26 April 2016, he explained to me their position and status as teachers.
    See p. 231.

49. **Nāth jī** is a mysterious wandering yogi from Haryana whom I met in Kamakhya in 2017. He spends his time travelling from one pilgrimage site to another. He did not reveal his name, not even to the other *bābā*s in Koṭiliṅgam, the temple in which I met him. Everyone called him Nāth jī, so I will refer to him as such. We first met on 7 June 2017, and thereafter on each of my visits to the Koṭiliṅgam. Between 7 and 17 June we had our most interesting conversations, but after that time the place became very crowded on account of the Ambubācī Melā.

    He told me that a true *sādhu* is he who takes *dīkṣā* during childhood, so that the uncontaminated mind can follow the words of the guru completely. Nāth jī simply took up and left his family when he was about six years old. He was quite rebellious and did not want to study. He moved here and there looking for a guru; he met great *mahants* but felt nothing for them until he encountered a poor *bābā* in Haryana who was doing his *karam* properly and would become his guru. He said that his guru used to kick him a lot, more than his guru-*bhāī*: if he did not study, if he smoked, he would be kicked. He did his guru's *sevā* for 12 years and then, at the age of 18, got *kuṇḍal.*

Nāth jī said that thanks to his *sādhanā* he was at peace. Previously, he had always been ready for a fight or a confrontation. After an unhappy encounter with some people in Nepal, however, he decided to do *tapasyā*, at which his mind became peaceful. When the mind is *śanti*, he said, it can go anywhere without having to move.

He shared some interesting information with me, which could be difficult to decode because he often spoke using *ulṭī bānī Nāth kī bāt*, the upside-down sentences typical of Nāths.

See pp. 70, 91, 166, 183, 188, 203, 273.

50. **Oṃ Nāth** is an *aughaḍ pīr* whom I met in Ujjain on 28 April 2016. He arrived with other *aughaḍ pīrs*, and they immediately captured my attention because they were all wearing black. He later told me that they follow a more tantric *sādhanā* than the other Nāths, as they were devoted to Mahākālī and have more connections with the Aghorīs—his guru, he said, used to eat parts of brains—and for the most part they live in the crematorium. They follow the left-hand path and remain *aughaḍ*, which is why they only wear black. We talked about *sampradāya*, yoga and *haṭha* yoga in general.

See p. 75.

51. **Omānanda Giri** is a *saṃnyāsī* of the Yoga Vedānta Kuṭīr, a place very close to the *saṃgam* area of Allahabad. He is a disciple of Svāmī Viśvānanda, who in turn was a disciple of the renowned Haṇḍiyā Bābā. Hence, he is part of the Haṇḍiyā Bābā lineage and theoretically related to the Jūnā *akhāṛā*, although today there is no connection between the centre and the *akhāṛā*. This demonstrates how a *sādhu*, having being initiated into a certain *sampradāya*, may start something new, thereby cutting the link with his own roots. This explains why there are a lot of foreigners in this particular lineage: it does not have strict rules for initiation. In fact, a foreigner was initiated by Haṇḍiyā Bābā as early as the 1970s: Svāmī Paramānanda, a guru-*bhāī* of Omānanda Giri.

I met Omānanda Giri on 14 and 15 March 2018, after a friend in Varanasi gave me a book on Haṇḍiyā Bābā. When I saw him, he looked a little unkempt, but his behaviour was friendly. He made some *chai* and we had an interesting and pleasant conversation about various forms of yoga.

Omānanda Giri was initiated in 1992; before that, he was a *brahmacārī*, first in Rishikesh, then in Haridwar, then Allahabad. He had been looking for a proper guru. When he first met Svāmī Viśvānanda, before three days had passed he realised that he had found his guru. Until then, he had not received any real training in yoga; he had read a few books (those written by Sivananda) but it was with his guru that he began in earnest. His guru was from Bengal, whereas Haṇḍiyā Bābā was from Bihar.

He is passing on knowledge about physical yoga practices to the numerous children who populate the *āśram*: when I was there, he quickly turned to one of them and asked for a demonstration of *nauli* for my benefit.

See pp. 168-170, 190, 202, 219, 226, 230, 255, 270, 272, 274, 316.

52. **Oṃkarānanda Sarasvatī** is a *saṃnyāsī* of the Āvāhan *akhāṛā* whom I saw on 24 February 2015 in Junagadh during the celebration of Mahāśivarātri. As I stood on the roadside, watching the procession of *sādhus* heading towards the temple, there was one in the middle who stood out, doing balancing *āsanas* accompanied by hand *mudrās*. I stopped him and asked if I might speak to him on another occasion. He gave me an appointment and on the next day, with Dr Singleton and Professor Mallinson, I visited him in his room, where some of his devotees had also gathered. He was kind and helpful; he enjoyed talking and was happy for us to take photos and videos of him. He told us he learnt yoga from his brother and from an Italian man with whom he was in touch.

53. **Phalāhārī Bābā**, from Chitrakut, is a Rāmānandī *sādhu* and a member of the *Terah bhāī tyāgī khālsā*. His name derives from the fact that he has been *phalāhārī* for the last 25 years. I met him at the 2019 Ardh Kumbh Melā in Allahabad, at which time he was about 60 years old. He was a close friend of Rām Bālak Dās (no. 60) and so I met him several times during the festival; I had opportunities to talk to him properly about yoga and *tapasyā* on 16 and 17 February 2019.

See pp. 87, 127, 131, 204, 206, 214, 246, 257-258.

54. **Phalāhārī Bābā** from Indore is a member of the *Terah bhāī tyāgī khālsā*. I met him, like his namesake (no. 53), at the 2019 Ardh Kumbh Melā in Allahabad. He is a *jaldharī* (a practitioner of *jal tapasyā*), a performer of *dhūnī tap* and, as his name implies, he has

been *phalāhārī* for 25 years. I met him several times and observed him practising his *tapasyā*s. He was at the *khappar* stage in *dhūnī tap*, after which he practised *āsanas*. After lunch, he would always be seen reading something. We discussed various yogic topics on 10 February 2019.

See p. 130(photo).

55. **Rādhe Purī** is an *ūrdhvabāhu sādhu* of the Jūnā *akhāṛā*. I met him at the Ujjain Siṃhasth Melā on 11 April 2016. He was very helpful, despite having a sore arm and suffering from the heat. He was generous with his time, despite having several others around him after his attention.

He started his *tapasyā* four years ago, before which he did *khaṛeśvarī* for 12 years and even *dhūnī tap*. 'This is the life of a *mahātmā*', he declared, informing me that he had begun doing yoga *sādhanā* before doing *haṭha* yoga, i.e, *tapasyā*.

See pp. 121, 145, 274.

56. **Rāghavendra Dās** is a *tyāgī*, probably one of the last disciples of Devrāhā Bābā, who, he said, taught him a lot. He had his tent in the camp of the *Terah bhāī tyāgī khālsā*, and would often pay a visit to Rām Bālak Dās (no. 60), so that is where I met him. We met several times (12, 13 and 16 February 2019) in the early morning to record our interviews. He recounted how he had become a *sādhu* as a child and, like many others, travelled a lot in his life. He explained the use of *mudrā*s and various yogic practices. I also made videos and took photos of him performing *dhūnī tap*, which he had almost completed. He claimed to have a number of foreign disciples.

See pp. 96, 127, 145, 188, 231, 241, 252, 257, 263, 292, 294, 316.

57. **Rāj Nāth** is an *aughaḍ pīr* whom I met, along with Professor Mallinson and Dr Singleton, at the Dharamnāth Sthān, in Dhinodhar, on 20 February 2017. After a walk, we reached a place where, according to tradition, Dharamnāth is said to have done *tapasyā* on his head. That is where we found this young *aughaḍ pīr*, who explained the history of the place and the Nāth tradition that was adhered to there. He lived there with a man who although not initiated had decided 20 years ago to leave his family and do *sevā* to *sādhus*. The reason he was not initiated was because the guru of this place is not interested in having disciples. Moreover, according to Rāj Nāth, a Nāth cannot have ever been married, lest he might not be *brahmacārī*. Rāj Nāth's

parents took him to a guru in Jharkhand to see if he could become a *sādhu*. The guru said yes and, as it turned out, he did.

See p. 138.

58. **Rājānanda Giri** is a *saṃnyāsī* who lives in the Yoga Vedānta Kuṭīr, Allahabad. I spoke to him on 14 March 2018 after Omānanda Giri (no. 51) introduced him to me. He had had an interesting life. He told me that he decided to become a *saṃnyāsī* when he was nine but his family opposed his decision, especially his mother who told him to wait until she died. So he studied and worked, but never married. As soon as his mother died, in 1988, he became a *bābā*, since which time he never returned to his family village.

His life is completely devoted to his *sādhanā*: reading sacred texts, and doing meditation and *jap* (13,000 every day).

See p. 259.

59. **Rājeś Cetan Brahmacārī** is a *saṃnyāsī* of the Purī Maṭh branch in Varanasi and a disciple of Niśalānanda Sarasvatī who, according to him, was a great yogi. Although not a physical yoga practitioner himself, he spoke highly of his guru and his practice, and we had a pleasant chat in the *āśram* garden on 24 January 2016.

See pp. 189, 282.

60. **Rām Bālak Dās** was a *tyāgī* of the *Terah bhāī tyāgī khālsā* and the beloved guru of Professor Mallinson. As the name *bālak* implies, he became a *sādhu* as a child, his guru teaching yoga to him and no other disciples because only he was suitable. At that time, he also spent time studying in Varanasi.

Together with Professor Mallinson, I visited him at his *āśram* in Barouch (Gujarat) on 18–19 March 2016, an *āśram* which, I was told, had grown rapidly thanks to the support of devotees in Gujarat. Rām Bālak Dās was highly respected in Barouch, being a highly charismatic and renowned *yogīrāj*. Our visit coincided with a ceremony which took place during the daytime; in the evenings, Rām Bālak Dās was lauded by the organisers, demonstrating the importance that a village guru still has in society.

We met and talked several times over the years. The second meeting after Gujarat was on 3 April 2016 at the Ujjain Siṃhasth Melā: he was camping with the *mahātyāgī*s, which gave me an opportunity to attend some of their practices and meet new *sādhus*. I met him almost every day from 3–24 April, when he left the *melā*.

We met again in Gujarat on 27 February 2017 and then at the 2019 Ardh Kumbh Melā in Allahabad. As before, I visited him most days from January until his departure from the festival.

Sadly, Rām Bālak Dās left his body on 23 July 2019.

See pp. 118, 126, 137, 140, 173, 189, 203, 321.

61. **Rām Caraṇ Dās**, guru of Rām Priya Dās (no. 64), is a *tyāgī* of the Rāmānandī *sampradāya*, and about 75 years old in 2015.

He told me that he was a disciple of a *tapasvī* who lived in the jungles of Junagadh, Gujarat. Only when he moved to Ayodhya in 1960, to the Rang Mahal, did he learn yoga from the *pujārī* of the temple. Although his guru smoked *cilam*, he does not. He has his *āśram* in Gujarat, near a school, which is why several children go there. He has 17 female disciples, he said, including Rām Priya Dās.

The first time we met (30 November 2015) he had just arrived from Gujarat and was very tired. When we met again, on 3 December 2015, he seemed irascible and displeased to see me, possibly because he had other things to do or on account of a health problem. However, by simply sitting in the temple I was able to appreciate the relationship between guru and disciple: Rām Priya Dās acted like a daughter and I was curious to hear her use *tum* (informal 'you') rather than *āp* (respectful form) with her guru. On 4 and 5 December, Rām Caraṇ Dās was in a better mood and we talked at greater length about yoga and *tapasyā*. He suggested I take initiation as a *gṛhastha* purely to attain respect, but did not insist. We also met on 7 and 8 December 2015.

See pp. 96, 123, 124, 129, 167, 172, 194-195, 203, 204, 207-208, 210, 216, 222, 225, 235-238, 242, 245, 254, 255, 258, 274, 283.

62. **Rām Avadhūt Dās** is a Rāmānujī *tyāgī* whom I met at the Dvārkādīś Sthān in Varanasi, a Rāmānujī centre. He was 22 when we met, on 27 January 2016. He became a *sādhu* when he was only a child. By then he had already started reading religious texts, especially the *Gītā*; through these, and on account of the many ascetics who came to his village, his desire to become an ascetic was kindled. He is a disciple of Garuḍ Dās (no. 21). However, he also studied yoga as part of a diploma course at the Banaras Hindu University.

I was introduced to him by other *sādhus* of the *āśram* in Varanasi on account of his knowledge of yoga—and indeed he was willing to expound on that topic. He also wanted to show me some *āsanas*, but was worried about being seen with me. As it happened, the *mahant* of the temple did indeed take a dim view about him showing me *āsanas* in the *āśram*. On 1 February 2016 we went to Tulsī *ghāṭ* and, on the platform of an old, secluded temple we started talking. Then he showed me *āsanas* and I was able to photograph him. For some strange unknown reason, I was never able to find those photos.

See pp. 95, 187, 204, 205, 208, 210, 222, 230, 233, 238, 253, 266-269, 284, 285, 310.

63. **Rām Dās** is a *mahant* and member of the *Terah bhāī tyāgī khālsā*. I met him in 2019 at the Ardh Kumbh Melā in Allahabad. Most often I would encounter him when visiting their camp, especially in February when many including Rām Dās had begun practising *dhūnī tap*. On our 14 February 2019 encounter, Rām Dās was a source of valuable information. He is also a *yogīrāj* and has his centre in Chitrakut (Uttar Pradesh), an important town for the worship of Rāmānandīs, being related to Sītā.

See p. 125.

64. **Rām Priya Dās** is a *tyāgī* of the Rāmānandī *sampradāya*—she dislikes the use of the feminine form *tyaginī*. She lives in Varanasi in a Rām temple/*āśram*, near the Maṇikarṇikā *ghāṭ*, which she runs, and which is also supported by her guru from Gujarat. She is also from Gujarat; in 2015, the second time I met her, she was about 46 years old.

She is the only woman I met who was initiated as a child. At the age of just six, she used to attend the religious practice that a *tyāgī* (Rām Caraṇ Dās [no. 61], who would become her guru) was performing in a cave. For six years she would continually go and see him, crying desperately when her parents would not allow her to go. Usually, they went to fetch her when the sun was high over the cave in which the *tyāgī* was performing his austerities, because by that time they could be sure that he had left to eat his meal (only milk), some of which he would have given to the girl as *prasāda*. When Rām Priya Dās was 12, she spent a year doing *sevā* in Rām Caraṇ Dās's *āśram*; she was initiated at 13 and began practising yoga *kriyās*. Her guru took photos of her performing different practices which she has kept in an album.

Her family did not appreciate her involvement in this *sādhanā*: they tried to get her to change her mind but eventually had to acknowledge her serious commitment and desire to continue the ascetic life. When Rām Priya Dās was initiated, her family cut all contact with her and she joined the *sādhu samāj*.

Yoga is part of her *sādhanā*, as well as *tapasyā*, which she used to perform especially when she was young.

I was already acquainted with Rām Priya Dās through my doctoral research on the Rāmānandī *sampradāya*. For the Haṭha Yoga Project I spent time with her in Varanasi from 27–30 October 2015; and then returned to meet her in November and December, more or less on a daily basis. On 15 November 2015, we began practising *āsanas* together.

See pp. 92, 131, 135, 140, 141, 143, 164, 197, 202, 206, 208, 209, 214, 236, 255, 258, 275, 283, 297, 300.

65. **Rām Svarūp Dās** is the *mahant* of the Dvārkādīś (Rāmānujī Piṭh) in Varanasi. I met him on 27 January 2016 and he actively participated in the conversation I was having with Śrī Rām Bālak Dās.

See p. 258.

66. **Rām Vicar Dās** is the *mahant* of the Kabīr *panth* centre in Maghar (Gorakhpur district), although I met him in Gorakhpur on 11 January 2016 while I was talking to Yogī Īśnāth. He claimed that, even in the Kabīr *panth*, *sādhus* practise yoga and *haṭha* yoga. He was wearing a light pink robe and, in contradiction to those from the Kabīr *sthān* in Varanasi, he claimed that the ascetics in the *panth* also do *tapasyās* and not just *sahaj* yoga.

He and Yogī Īśnāth said that yoga is an important part of the *sādhanā* practised in the Gorakhnāth temple.

67. **Rāmānuja Purī** is a *saṃnyāsī* of the Jūnā *akhāṛā* whom I met in Kamakhya in June 2017 and June 2018. He said he was not a *nāgā bābā* because his *liṅgam* 'had not been pulled in three directions'. He is from Kanpur and told of a troubled youth: he went to fight against Pakistan where he killed three people. Then he met his guru and decided to leave all these tribulations behind. He came to Kamakhya in 1986 and never left, becoming *koṭvāl* of the Dasnāmī *sampradāya*, which is why he always carries a sword. He revealed an ambition to go to Italy, France and the USA on foot and declared that he was prepared to fight all the states on India's borders to defend Indian supremacy.

68. **Rāmāy Nāth** is an *aughaḍ pīr* from Gujarat. I met him with Professor Mallinson and Dr Singleton at the Kantan Nāth *sthān* in Gujarat, an

ancient Nāth site, on 19 February 2017. He had no *kuṇḍal*s because, he said, he has been doing the *aughaḍ* stage properly, i.e. for 12 years. Every day, he told us, he would go to the crematory ground to take *vibhūti*, and morning and evening he would do Bhairava *sādhanā* using tantric mantras. He stressed that he only does those *kriyā*s that are useful for the yogi's body; when I asked him if he also did *āsana*s he seemed rather offended.

69. **Ravīndra Giri**, who was about 65 in 2015, is the *mahant* of the Pañcāyatī Mahā Nirvāṇī *akhāṛā* in Varanasi. I met him on 10 and 12 December 2015. He was very helpful, although he only allowed me to record 15 minutes of our conversation, whereas the first day we met we talked for hours.

He studied economics and commerce until the age of 25, when he started spending time with *sādhu*s, which he enjoyed and his desire to follow their example only grew. Embarking on such a life at that age was rather difficult, however, because a man is full of power, whereas it is easier for a child or an elderly person.

He was very kind and agreed to talk to me the same day that I entered the *akhāṛā*. He enquired as to what I was going to ask him, so I summarised my research and my questions about yoga.

He had a close relationship with the nuns of the Mother Theresa's *āśram* near the *akhāṛā*.

We met only twice because our conversations eventually took a strange turn.

See pp. 59, 191, 196, 197, 210.

70. **Sanjay Giri (Koṭiliṅgam Bābā)** is a *saṃnyāsī* of the Jūnā *akhāṛā* who lives in between Kamakhya and the Himachal Pradesh mountains. When in Kamakhya, he stays not in the Jūnā *akhāṛā āśram* but in a simple room built in the proximity of the Koṭiliṅgam, a Śaiva shrine nestling between massive rocks.

He wears nothing to indicate his affiliation, neither *rudrākṣa* nor *tilaka*: his *tilaka* was just a black *bindu* with *candan*.

When I arrived on 7 June 2017, he was playing with his phone and paid me no attention; it was only after around 30 minutes that he started talking to me. On 10 June he was less talkative and we—there were always several people sitting around the *dhūnī*: householders, other *sādhus*, *pujārī* and Nāth jī—spent an hour in silence until, all of a sudden, a kind of *satsaṅga* began. Bābā jī was always ready to give me his interpretations of teachings and practices. We had proper conversations on 11, 15, 16 and 18 June, before the place became too crowded.

See pp. 164, 222, 242.

71. **Śyām Ānanda Nāth** and I met for the first time on 27 April 2016 in Ujjain during the Siṃhasth Melā. An Aghorī ceremony had been advertised in a local newspaper and I wanted to see what was going on. When I arrived at the crematory, I found a man nearby and we struck up a conversation. A while later, Śyām Ānanda Nāth turned up accompanied by a foreign man, Richard, both followers of a tantric path. We discussed practices and yoga in general. Śyām Ānanda Nāth told me he was from Himachal Pradesh and had taken *dīkṣā* five years earlier. I met him again on 28 April and we went to the Āvāhan *akhāṛā* camp together. That day he told me that he was part of the Kaulamārga, a secret esoteric path in which mantras and *yantra*s are the core of the practice to awaken *kuṇḍalinī.* On 1 May, he told me that, initially, he did not know his guru was part of the Kaulamārga: they had been talking for years before he discovered his affiliation. At this point he took his initiation. He told me that *sādhaka*s do not usually reveal their affiliation because they do not have to beg for food: they can still work and support themselves. In fact, he said, he works ten months every year and practises for two.

I met him again in Gaṅgā Sāgar in January 2017, where we spent time together with Kamal Giri (no. 35); we also met in June 2017 and June 2018 in Kamakhya for the Ambubācī Melā.

See pp. 74, 167, 168, 214, 228, 230, 250, 251, 262.

72. **Siddha Bhārtī Bābā** is a *thānāpati* of the Jūnā *akhāṛā* whom I met in Kamakhya on 24 June 2018. We had a very interesting conversation. He told me that he was initially a *lama*, because his guru was a *lama* who later decided to join the Jūnā *akhāṛā*, as did Siddha Bhārtī Bābā. However, he still travels to all the Buddhist countries to which he travelled with his guru, but of course wearing different clothes. He went to Tibet on foot from Uttarakhand; he crossed the Himalayas and met yogis who have been there for centuries; and he saw a Tibetan yogi levitate—this being one of the goals of yoga: a very light body. According to him, yoga and Tantra have the same purpose: to create a body that one can easily control. His religious path is therefore made up of mantras and *yantra*s: sound as a tool to make the power of Tantra effective.

73. **Someśvar Giri** is an *ūrdhvabāhu* of the Jūnā *akhāṛā* whom I met in Kamakhya thanks to my friend Partha. We spoke on 21 June 2017 about his *tapasyā* which he has been carrying out since 2010. He usually lives in Himachal Pradesh.

See pp. 136(photo), 137.

74. **Śrī Kanth** is an *aughaḍ pīr* who always sits in the grounds of the Kamakhya temple. By mentioning Richard, the man in the company of Śyām Ānanda Nāth and who knew Śrī Kanth, I was able to break the ice and exchange a few words (10 June 2017). Śrī Kanth asked me some general questions but mostly he wanted to know about my dreams. He told me that he took *aughaḍ dīkṣā* in 1990 in his hometown in Uttar Pradesh, in a Nāth place. He reached Kamakhya in 1993. I asked him if he came because his guru told him to do so or of his own accord. He didn't answer me directly; he just said there had been problems in the family so he had simply left.

Every day, during festival time, all sorts of questions and advice were asked of him. As an example, one day, someone came to him with a problem, namely that he was a good man but despite all his best efforts, things were not working out for him. Śrī Kanth advised to him to be pure and to avoid eating garlic and onions. The advice didn't go down well because this man really liked onions.

I met Śrī Kanth on 10, 14, 15, 17, 18 and 19 June 2017.

75. **Śrī Nārāyaṇ Dās** is a self-made ascetic whom I met at the Lalitā *ghāṭ* in Varanasi. In fact, I had been walking close by his spot for years while I was doing my PhD, and later when I went to meet Rām Priya Dās in 2015. I always greeted him, but I never stopped because there was often a group of people sitting next to him and smoking. One day (1 December 2015), as there were only a few devotees present, I finally sat down and started talking to him.

He told me that he had run away from home when he was about 20, since which 40 years had passed. He travelled all over India both alone and with other *sādhus*. By 2015, he had been living in Varanasi for ten years, on that same *ghāṭ*, although some of his devotees were building an *āśram* for him. He goes there sometimes, but he prefers to stay close to Gaṅgā (i.e. the Ganges river) and have her *darśan*. He recites the Rām mantra, the only useful one, he said: all others, including Tantra and *yantra*, only serve to deceive people.

We had productive conversations on 1 and 3 December 2015.

See p. 164.

76. **Śrī Rām Bālak Dās** was an old Rāmānujī *sādhu* whom I met on 27 January 2016 in the Dvārkādīś, the Rāmānujī place in Varanasi run by a disciple of the famous Devrāhā Bābā. The *āśram* is closely connected to this famous guru, which is why the traditions of yoga and *tapasyā* have been transmitted in the centre ever since. Śrī Rām Bālak Dās was also a disciple of Devrāhā Bābā. He was not very talkative but he gave me some interesting definitions, and his presence in the room was incredibly powerful. Moreover, he was sitting on two pieces of wood: his brethren said he was a true yogi, a master of *khecarī mudrā*, capable even of levitation. He spoke to me for only seven minutes, at which point other *sādhus* arrived and I continued my conversation with them under the gaze of Śrī Rām Bālak Dās jī.

77. **Svāmī Ātmānanda** is a very old *saṃnyāsī* whom I met for the first time on 12 January 2017 in Kolkata at an art gallery run by a friend of mine, Pravash, who wanted me to meet him. This *sādhu* was his father's guru. He claimed to have met various yogis, such as Yogi Nityānanda (1887–1961) and Yukteshwar Giri (1855–1936). Yogananda, he said, was only a magician. He spoke of himself as one of India's last yogis. He showed me photos from 1953 in which he performs postures which, according to him, were fully realised. He also claimed to have taught Nehru (the first Indian Prime Minister) and President Kennedy. He was strict and grumpy by disposition, and saddened by the state of the yoga industry. He usually goes from one disciple's house to another, even though he has a place to stay in Kolkata. With others from the art gallery, we did *āsana* lessons with Svāmī jī from 22 January 2017 to 5 February 2017.

    See pp. 171, 172, 207, 233, 234, 236, 246, 254, 255, 271, 282, 297, 299, 300-301.

78. **Śyām Dās** is a *mahātyāgī* whom I met at the 2016 Ujjain Siṃhasth Melā. He lives at the Satyā Nārāyaṇ Mandir in Hamirpur, Himachal Pradesh. He was born in 1969 into a brahmanical family and at the age of 12 went to the *gurukul*, although he decided to become a *bābā* because he thought *sādhus* could do magic.

    He is a *tapasvī*, and in fact I observed him doing *dhūnī tap* several times. He told me that he also does yoga *sādhanā*, but only when he is in his temple, close to the mountains. He drinks only juice and *chai* and smokes *cilam*, although he claimed that he only smokes because other *bābās* do. I first met him on 5 April 2016 and subsequently spent a lot of time with him during the festival, gathering fragments of information as we talked. There were always a lot of people around him and he was very kind, especially to children.

See pp. 78, 122, 128(photo), 144, 145, 267.

79. **Surendrā Purī** is a *nāgā* of the Jūnā *akhāṛā*. I met him at the camp of Dayānanda Purī (no. 15) during the 2019 Ardh Kumbh Melā. On 16 January 2019 we talked about yoga and it became evident that he had been a *sādhu* since childhood and learnt yoga, i.e. meditation from his guru, and *āsanas* from various modern yoga classes. He had travelled extensively in Europe teaching yoga.

80. **Taruṇ Bābā** was described by Rāmānuja Purī (no. 67) as *ek nārī brahmacārī*, a man who has been with only one woman in his life. He is probably a *sādhaka* living in Kamakhya and attached to the Koṭiliṅgam temple. Taruṇ jī is a lover of the jungle, which is why he also gets the name 'Tarzan Bābā'. He makes the *parikramā* of the hill in only two hours to visit all its main temples. He follows a strict dietary regime and a specific tantric *sādhanā*. We spoke several times albeit briefly on 6, 7 and 10 June 2017.

See pp. 122, 252.

81. **Tūphān Nāth** is an *aughaḍ pīr* of the Nateśvarī *panth*, whom I met in Kamakhya in June 2018. We spoke properly on 25 June 2018.

He said that he had a famous guru who was 108 years old at the time. Tūphān Nāth had taken *dīkṣā* 35 years previously; when we met he was about 60 years old.

We talked for a while before he did the *pūjā* to the *dhūnī*: first he recited mantras and made specific hand *mudrās*, then poured *jaṛī bhūṭī* into it, then ghee and camphor.

He showed me the temple, the platform of which housed his tent. He said that the temple—which is directly in front the Jūnā *akhāṛā āśram*—is thousands of years old. Old *mūrtis* decorate its sides, some of which look like acrobats or dancers. He said that in the temple there is a cave that goes directly to the Brahmaputra river, which is where 'Maccendranāth' kept his body in Kāmarūpa before Gorakhnāth rescued him: this is when the disciple became the guru of the guru because he had had to save him.

82. **Umeś Kabīr** is a *brahmacārī* whom I met at the Kabīr Maṭh in Kabir Choura, Varanasi, on 31 January 2016. The Kabīr Maṭh is an incredible place where past and present come together: a *samādhi* in memory of Kabīr, a well and some objects used by the Sant co-exist with

contemporary statues that are worshipped, despite Kabīr having preached against this practice. Umeś Kabīr has been in the *maṭha* since he was a child, and studied there. According to him, Kabīr proposed not a *haṭha* yoga but a *sahaj* yoga, a yoga without difficulties through which one could achieve religious goals. As such, *āsanas* do not play a particular role in their *sādhanā*. According to him, physical forms of yoga are examples of the modernisation of the practice.

83. **Vidhān Bābā** was a middle-aged *sādhu* of the Rāmānandī *sampradāya*, residing at the Śrī Maṭh, an important Rāmānandī centre in Varanasi. I first met him in 2012 during my doctoral research. When I was in Varanasi in 2015, I met him again on 28 October to talk about yoga. He told me that, when he was young, he lived in Bihar and practised Bihari yoga in the *āśram* of a famous *bābā* (Sivananda?). 'Before Bābā Rāmdev was on TV explaining yoga!' he clarified.

When I met him, he had stopped doing *āsanas* in favour of some form of stretching. He was against the commercialisation of yoga and *sādhus*' exploitation of it for this purpose.

His past life was something of a mystery—even to the people of the Śrī Maṭh—but he cared for the many *brahmacārī*s who studied there. He was also very considerate to his mother and his sisters, with whom he was still in touch. Sadly, Bābā jī left his body in 2021.

84. **Vijay Giri** is a middle-aged *saṃnyāsī* of the Āvāhan *akhāṛā* who was initiated after getting married. I met him in Kamakhya on 18 June 2017. He was in the company of another *sādhu* (Gopāl Giri; no. 23) and they invited me to eat with them the next day: Vijay Giri's *celī* would prepare dinner. So at their place we had a pleasant chat about their lives, yoga and *tapasyā* while eating an amazing *panīr*.

Vijay Giri said he was from Kolkata and had started doing *sādhanā* 20–25 years previously. He also did *sādhanā* when he was married, but in secret. He also had children. One day, he simply left home, without telling anyone. He has not seen them since. He met his *dīkṣā* guru in Haridwar and took *saṃnyāsa* ten years before we met. As his guru lives in Mumbai, they mostly talk to each other by phone. He went to do *sādhanā* in the jungle, in locations close to the Ganges, repeating the mantra his guru gave him.

He does not care for the *nāgā* society: in his opinion they are just smokers, alcoholics and fake people.

I met Vijay Giri at his *āśram* as well, which is in Chuchra (West Bengal), on 2 February 2018. I rented a car to reach the *āśram*, which is 60 km from Kolkata, not knowing what to expect. It turned out the *bābā* lived in a small room, with nothing other than an anteroom in which there was a small temple and where a disciple was cooking. The toilet was in the garden of the family who had given this small room to the *bābā*. He told that day me that his plan was to buy a piece of land and build an *āśram* where he could do *sevā* to *bābā*s and children. Vijay Giri took his *celī* with him five years ago: she needed protection so he told her to stay with him and do his *sevā*.

See pp. 249, 255.

85. **Vināyak Dās** is a Rāmānandī *sādhu* and a member of the *Terah bhāī tyāgī khālsā*. I met him at the 2019 Ardh Kumbh Melā in Allahabad. He was quite young (probably in his thirties) and part of the *jamāt*. He told me that he had completed a master's degree in engineering but, after meeting Monī Bābā (no. 47), decided to give it all up and become his disciple. If I understood correctly, he had joined the *jamāt* six years earlier. Like most of the *sādhus* of the *jamāt*, he practised *dhūnī tap*, but did not know *āsanas* and did not have adequate knowledge of the yoga *sādhanā*. We talked for a long time at the *melā*, but mostly about general issues, as he was interested in the Western world and was keen to have someone to discuss things with. He is very active on social media.

86. **Viśambhar Bhārtī** is a *nāgā* of the Jūnā *akhāṛā* who left home when he was eight years old. He stayed with his guru, apparently in Kolkata, for several years until he began to wander alone. He travelled extensively on foot, covered only with *vibhūti*, to all the pilgrimage sites of India. His guru jī took *samādhi* when he was 84 years old. He then went to stay in the mountains near Nandā Devī, living on top of a village, all the locals going there for *satsaṅga*, each bringing something to eat, milk to drink and so on. In Pashupatinath he met some foreigners and learnt English from them. Wishing to continue learning English, he moved to tourist locations. Later, he fought to allow foreigners admission into the *akhāṛās*, which he now seems to regret. When his guru-*bhāī* in Delhi died, he was forced to move to the Jūnā *akhāṛā āśram* that he ran, where he became the *mahant*. It is somewhat hidden in the old part of the city, attached to a small temple just opposite Gate 5 of the Chandi Chowk metro station, and very close to the Navagraha temple. I first met Viśambhar Bhārtī in the tent of Manimaheś Bhārtī (no. 45) on 17 and 18 April 2016. He was very modern in his outlook and could speak a little English and

Italian. He acknowledged the presence of only three *sampradāyas*: man, woman and *hijṛā*.

I met Viśambhar Bhārtī again on 23 and 24 March 2018: with Professor Alex Watson and Professor Mallinson I visited him at his temple in Delhi. It was a small place, in which there was only one *mahā puruṣa* helping him: a *bābā*, Rāmānanda Bhārtī, the only permanent *sādhu* living there. From our conversation it became clear that Viśambhar Bhārtī is not very keen on giving *dīkṣā*: he probably has no more than two disciples. At that time he was *śrī mahant*, which meant he had to work hard, together with the other *śrī mahants*, until the next Kumbh Melā to collect money from all the *āśrams* of the *akhāṛā*. But he said he wanted to retire as soon as possible and build an *āśram* in the mountain where he could perform his *sādhanā* in peace.

See pp. 194, 227, 259, 264, 271.

87. **Viśvot Giri** (also known as Konkhan Adhikārī) is a *saṃnyāsī* of the Jūnā *akhāṛā* who lives in Birnagar (West Bengal). On 16 January 2016, immediately after Gaṅgā Sāgar, I followed the suggestions of a number of people and took a train to Birnagar to meet him. I phoned him and he agreed to host me at his house. I stayed there until 21 January and did *āsana* classes with him, along with another Italian woman, Anita, who already knew him.

He is an *adhikārī yogī*: that is, a yogi by right—his grandfather taught him yogic *kriyās* and he will pass this knowledge on to a chosen family member who has the aptitude to learn them. He had three brothers, but he was the only one who learnt the practices from his father. He married, but his son did not want to learn yogic *kriyās* so he will transmit the teachings to his grandson. He took *saṃnyāsa* with his wife, although he cannot remember when. He follows a tantric *sādhanā*, being originally from Assam.

He is also part of the Milon Mela, a travelling company established by Abani Bishwas at the Theatre House in Shantiniketan, which has taken him to Europe to display his practices. This is what he does in India, too: attends religious festivals showing his skills and his control over his body. This is all part of the *adhikārī yogī* tradition.

See pp. 170, 211, 215, 235, 250, 297, 301-302.

88. **Yogī Alone Nāth** is a yogi whom I met for the first time in Pashupatinath, Nepal, on 10 May 2018, while sitting at the *dhūnī* of Chand Giri.

He said that his name was not derived from the English 'alone' but from a Nepali plant. He was initially a tour guide in Pashupatinath but decided to become initiated once he started attending the *satsaṅga*s of *sādhus*: it was talking to *bābā*s that made him decide to give it all up. While I was there with my friend Nicole from the United States, he was called to by Chand Giri, because he is known for doing *āsana*s and other yoga practices. Yogī Alone Nāth showed us a tattoo on his left arm with symbols of different religions; this is the arm, he said, with which he washes his backside. He asserted that Jesus was a Nāth yogi. We realised eventually that he was drunk. He confessed that he had a problem with alcohol and had stopped drinking; however, 15 days earlier a policeman had given him a glass of whisky and he had started again.

On the 12th we met again at Chand Giri's *dhūnī* while this quiet *sādhu* was doing his morning *ārtī*. Yogī Alone Nāth told us to drink *chai* and wait. He took my notebook and disappeared with it. We began to chant the *puṣpāñjali*, very quickly, with Chand Giri and several other people present. After the chanting, Yogī Alone Nāth returned with my notebook in which various *āsana* mantras from Gorakhnāth were written. I met him on other occasions, notably at the *kuṭī* of Īśnāth.

See pp. 170, 183, 205, 250, 251, 294.

89. **Yogī Bhakti Nāth** was a 44-year-old disciple of Yogī Śivanāth (no. 104) whom I met at his *āśram* in Orissa from 23–28 April 2018. He comes from that area. He had taken *dīkṣā* 20 years earlier, although he studied until the age of 20. He studied yoga with Yogī Śivanāth after which he went to Rishikesh to continue his studies, and where he also taught, eventually returning to Orissa. He claimed to be highly educated, having learnt from various textual sources and being a follower of Vedānta. Both Yogī Bhakti Nāth and Yogī Śivanāth sometimes forwent the wearing the *siṅgī*. Yogī Bhakti Nāth explained that a learned *sādhu* knows that external manifestations of faith are not necessary. Moreover, his *siṅgī* was broken and he had yet to find someone to repair it. He would make a point of acquiring a new one at the next festival he was going to attend, because on those occasions a *siṅgī* is fundamental. Yogī Bhakti Nāth was previously a Vaiṣṇava from the Caitanya tradition.

See p. 282.

90. **Yogī Brahm Nāth** is from West Bengal and now a disciple of Yogī Śivanāth (no. 104). I spoke with him on 12 April 2018 while he was in the company of his guru. He took *dīkṣā* when he was a child and stayed with Yogī Śivanāth in Orissa, after which he spent 12 years in Gorakhpur, eventually arriving in Kolkata in the 1990s. When I met him he was trying to resolve the fate of a Nāth place in the Hooghly district: it was in the hands of a Nāth who was not from West Bengal and, according to him, was not doing a good job.

91. **Yogī Hīrā Nāth** is the *mahant* of the Dhinodhar temple and *āśram* in Gujarat. He was a somewhat bad-tempered when I met him, with Professor Mallinson and Dr Singleton, on 21 February 2017, probably because he was busy organising the Śivarātri ceremony during which he was going to eat again after 30 years of restricting himself to fruit. We were told that, after the ceremony, the *mahant* of the *jamāt* would offer him food from his own hands.

    See p. 121.

92. **Yogī Īśnāth**. I met Yogī Īśnāth when I went to Gorakhpur on 8 January 2016. The Gorakhnāth temple is always very busy, with several Nāths situated close to statues and the most important religious loci. When I went to see the *dhūnā* of Gorakhnāth, there I found Yogī Īśnāth. He was very talkative and we struck up productive conversations with *sādhus* of other *sampradāyas* who were staying in the temple *āśram* and were curious about us. The next day, I tried for an interview with Yogī Adityanāth, who is the *mahant* of the temple and the Chief Minister of Uttar Pradesh, but it was well-nigh impossible. So I found Yogī Īśnāth again, who told me he had taken *dīkṣā* in 1985. We met again on 11 January 2016 when we were joined by Yogī Santoś Nāth (no. 101) and Rām Vicar Dās (no. 66) from the Kabīr *panth*.

93. **Yogī Karaṇ Nāth** is a Yogī practitioner of *āsana*—'Even 12 hours a day!' he said. I met him in Mangalore during the 'coronation' of the new *rāja yogī*, while I was with Professor Mallinson (7 March 2016). Talking about his relationship with the order, he said that he had obtained a diploma and had been a member of the *sampradāya* for six years. Regarding his practice, he said that he had not been able to do any since he came to Mangalore. However, he usually practises in January near McLeod Ganj, on direct contact with ice, and is able to perform the cobra pose standing on the tips of his toes. He had once studied martial arts in China, and was able to hold people at

a distance with only the power of his hands. He was an interesting interlocutor and an example of how a practitioner/*sādhu* can develop his practice by travelling and delving into different disciplines.

94. **Yogī Maṅgal Nāth** was one of the Yogīs I met at the Gorakhnāth *āśram* in Varanasi on 26 January 2016 (see also no. 99). During our conversation, it emerged that he could not remember when he had taken *dīkṣā*. He said he had wandered around for a while before deciding to get *dīkṣā* from someone. His guru then transmitted him a yoga teaching called *nitya* yoga (*nitya* means daily). He said he could not share what it was because it was only for initiated people. He had some interesting theories: for example, he criticised the Buddha for not having actually been able to realise his *haṭha* yoga practice (*tapasyā*) like Gorakhnāth did.
 See p. 264.

95. **Yogī Oṃ Nāth** is a Nāth whom I met in Ujjain during the Siṃhasth Melā, more specifically at the Bhartṛhari *guphā*, the main Nāth centre in town—located very close to the Shipra river—which contains, among its various buildings, the ancient cave in which, according to tradition, King Bhartṛhari did his *sādhanā*. I spoke to Yogī Oṃ Nāth on 27 March 2016. He told me that he has many foreign disciples, around 50, including a French woman. I introduce him here purely as a representative of the many Nāths who were at the Bhartṛhari *guphā* but were too busy to talk to properly because the place attracted such a huge number of devotees every day.
 See pp. 135, 145.

96. **Yogī Phūl Nāth** caught our attention in Mangalore during the 'coronation' of the new *rāja yogī*, because of the interesting turban he was wearing: it was shaped like a hat with a slightly wide brim, which Professor Mallinson described as very traditional. On 7 March 2016, Professor Mallinson, Yogī Phūl Nāth and I had a conversation about the rules of the *sampradāya* and those Nāths who try to sell yoga or who give *dīkṣā* to people heedlessly.
 I also met him by chance at the 2019 Kumbh Melā in Allahabad, but he was not staying in the main Nāth camp so it was impossible to find him again.

97. **Yogī Rājendra Nāth** is a *khaṛeśvarī* Yogī from Haryana with whom I spoke, along with Professor Mallinson, in Mangalore on 5 and 6 March 2016 while we there to attend the 'coronation' of the new *rāja*

yogī. Yogī Rājendra Nāth was standing next to his metal stand, his body covered with *vibhūti*. At first, he was critical about our being there, one reason being that Professor Mallinson had *jaṭā*, which according to Yogī Rājendra Nāth, only *sādhus* may have. The second reason was that I was a woman. Although he eventually accepted Professor Mallinson's presence, he always directed his responses to my questions to my male friend and not to me. Women, he said, should stay at home, as Indian *sanskṛti* dictates. Sending a woman to work was a sign of disrespect, he continued. On the 7th, he made me sit so far away from him that I could not hear him.

98. **Yogī Rām Nāth** is a *pujārī* of the Gorakhnāth temple in Gorakhpur. I met him on 11 January 2016 next to the *mūrti* he was in charge of. The temple is organised so that each statue has a *sādhu* who applies *tilaka* and *vibhūti* to devotees or those who go to make donations or have the *darśan*. I disturbed him while he was on duty. He had a very complex idea of yoga, broader than that of the other *sādhus* I met in the temple. However, the most interesting point of our conversation was his suggestion that I learn from him the use of *talvār*—sword—which led me to assume that he must have some sort of martial training. Today, however, his main *sādhanā* is based on *sevā*.

99. **Yogī Rām Nāth** is the *mahant* of the Gorakhnāth *āśram*/temple in Varanasi. I went there on 26 January 2016 with a couple of friends who were interested in talking to some Nāths in Varanasi. When we arrived it was immediately clear that it contained a rather ancient temple—900 years old, according to the *mahant*, and previously dedicated to a form of the Goddess.

    Yogī Rām Nāth is originally from Nepal, but apparently took initiation in Gorakhpur. He mentioned that his guru was very busy at the Gorakhnāth temple, so had no time to teach him properly.

    Since he was in the company of a highly knowledgeable *ācārya*, he suggested that we talk to him and other *sādhus*, claiming that he had no theoretical information of his own to offer. I therefore did not push him and we addressed our questions to the *sādhus* and *sādhakas* present. I was allowed to record our conversation, which lasted a couple of hours.

100. **Yogī Rudra Nāth** is a yogi from Haryana with an *āśram* in Himachal Pradesh and more recently an *āśram* in Varanasi as well. Edoardo, an Italian friend of mine, had met him in Varanasi and suggested I meet him too. When Yogī Rudra Nāth learnt I was going to Nepal, he

told me to come and see him as he would also be there, performing a ceremony for one of his devotees.

Talking about his life, he said that he had been given by his family to a Nāth place when he was four years old. When we met, he was about 42 years old and he said that he had attended his first Kumbh Melā in 1991.

He told me he used to do practices in the crematorium when he was an *aughaḍ*: he did the *aughaḍ/aghorī sādhanā* for about six or seven years, then in 2000 became *darśanī*. He belongs to the Āī *panth*. When I met him he was wearing black on account of being a worshipper of Kālī; more recently (2021–2022) I saw a photo of him on WhatsApp wearing saffron-coloured clothes.

He has a broad knowledge of *sādhu* society, and we had interesting conversations in Kathmandu, both in his hotel room in the company of his devotee, a Nepali businessman who lives in Hong Kong, as well as in the company of Heather and Īśnāth (no. 29). We met each day from 14–17 May 2018 and then from 19–24 May.

See pp. 74, 75, 166, 170, 173, 182, 186, 187, 204, 216, 221, 249, 252, 265, 266, 272, 275.

101. **Yogī Santoś Nāth** is a Nāth from Rajasthan whom I met in Gorakhpur on 11 January 2016. He now resides in Chauri Chaura (Gorakhpur district). He told me he left his family after failing a year at school. He practises yoga and gave interesting explanations about *kuṇḍalinī* and *prāṇāyāma* while talking to me and Yogī Īśnāth (no. 92) and Rām Vicar Dās (no. 66).

See p. 238.

102. **Yogī Sarasvatī Nāth** is the guru of Yogī Lakṣmī Nāth. I met these two Nāth yogi women in Mangalore during the 'coronation' of the new *rāja yogī* in March 2016. They were both uneducated and both claimed to have been part of the *sampradāya* since childhood. Yogī Sarasvatī Nāth's guru is from Madhya Pradesh, but they are both from Gujarat. They were friendly and happy to meet a Western woman who could speak Hindi. They had no problems with Professor Mallinson's presence and were very happy to play host and talk to us in their room in the *āśram*. They were helpful in explaining the status of women in the *sampradāya* and also provided general information about yoga.

103. **Yogī Seś Nāth** is an old yogi, a disciple of Yogī Narharināth, a famous yogi from Nepal. Yogī Seś Nāth lived in Mṛgasthalī, a Nāth place in Pashupatinath, Kathmandu, where I met him on 9 May 2018.

He is Nepali and took *dīkṣā* maybe 20 or 30 years ago—he did not recall exactly when. In our discussions, he repeatedly emphasised the teachings and books of his guru jī, and in fact I went away with several pamphlets published by him.

104. **Yogī Śivanāth** is a yogi whom I heard speak in Mangalore in 2016. However, I finally met him for the first time on 12 April 2018, after contacting him through Facebook, where he is very active. We met in Kolkata, at the home of one of his devotees, who is a *gṛhastha* Nāth.

Yogī Śivanāth is completely clean-shaven and dresses in orange. On that occasion he was accompanied by other yogis. That day we also went to a Gorakhnāth Mandir in Tagheria, not far from Dum Dum, to meet the *mahant*, Yogī Vijay Nāth (no. 107). After this first meeting, Yogī Śivanāth told me he would return on the 16th and asked me to follow him to Bhubaneswar on 23 June. We then met at the Kolkata airport on 23 April to go to his *āśram*, which is near Bhubaneswar (Orissa), an ancient and beautiful Nāth *āśram* and temple, surrounded by fields.

During my stay (until 28 April 2018), the *mahant* was very kind in taking his time to answer my questions about him and especially about yoga and *haṭha* yoga.

Yogī Śivanāth was 73 years old when we met. His had been a fascinating life: he had graduated in English in 1970, but after a couple of years of teaching decided to take *saṃnyāsa dīkṣā* from Yogī Viṣṇucaraṇ Nāth. Later, he obtained a diploma in Yoga Education from the Kaivalyadhama in Lonavala. In Mumbai he stayed at the Chinmaya Mission where for three years he studied Vedānta and the most important Hindu textual sources. He left for Haridwar and Rishikesh, where he lived in various *āśrams* for seven or eight years. The death of his guru in 1989 brought him back to Orissa to become *mahant*. But he still travels regularly because his main activity is giving *pravacan*, lectures on the Nāth *sampradāya*, yoga and the different *sādhanās* related to it, mainly with the purpose of 'reconverting' householder Yogīs who have become Vaiṣṇavas.

I met Yogī Śivanāth again in June 2018 when he invited me to attend the yoga *śivir* held in Gorakhpur for the International Day of Yoga (15–21 June). There we would usually meet in the morning;

after the *āsana* class, I would attend the theoretical part of the *śivir* where he taught on a range of topics.

See pp. 13, 68, 70, 71, 74, 75, 116, 168, 173, 174, 178, 203, 225, 231, 251, 260-261, 270, 271(photo), 273-274, 284, 285, 291, 292, 310, 316.

105. **Yogī Sumit Nāth** has been a member of the Nāth *sampradāya* since the age of 12. He is a young yogi from Haryana whom Professor Mallinson and I met in Mangalore during the 'coronation' of the new *rāja yogī*. He was sitting next to Yogī Rājendra Nāth (no. 97), his body likewise covered with *vibhūti*. Unlike Yogī Rājendra Nāth, he had no problem talking to me (on 5 and 6 March 2016). He said that his guru gave him the first teachings after which knowledge came 'automatically'. When we met, he was sitting in *padmāsana* with his eyes closed; he suddenly lifted the position, holding on to his fist and, as he landed, changed it to *siddhāsana*, breathing very slowly. At first he would not tell me his name—he said to call him Cor Nāth (Thief Nāth)—names, he said, were meaningless, as were private questions. On 7 March 2016, he revealed that his name was Sumit Nāth. He claimed he had received several esoteric teachings which he interpreted through his own experiences. He said that he had spent 12 years as *monī* while also pretending to be blind, which led him to accumulate a lot of energy.

See pp. 255, 269, 275.

106. **Yogī Sūrya Nāth** is the *mahant* of a Nāth centre in Vittal, near Mangalore. The temple was magnificent and certainly ancient, very crowded at that time because of the coronation of the *rāja yogī* but probably quite isolated during the rest of the year. Professor Mallinson and I visited it on 8 March 2018. Yogī Sūrya Nāth offered some interesting insights into the role of the guru in general, and specifically on Gorakhnāth and Dattātreya.

107. **Yogī Vijay Nāth** is a yogi from Punjab who looks after two places: one in Punjab and more recently one in Kolkata, the ancient Gorakhnāth Mandir in Tagheria, not far from Dum Dum. The temple must be quite ancient, as there were several *samādhis*. Unfortunately, I could not explore the area because a festival was taking place.

I met the *mahant* together with Yogī Śivanāth on 12 April 2018. He revealed to us that he writes poetry in Punjabi. He also gave interesting definitions of *haṭha* yoga not all of which were shared by Yogī Śivanāth.

See p. 163.

108. **Yogī Vilāsnāth** is quite a well-known yogi, whom I met at the 2019 Ardh Kumbh Melā. On that occasion the Nāth camp boasted luxurious tents with small porches. Yogī Vilāsnāth's tent was close to the entrance: although small, it included an exterior space from which the yogi could sell his books. On 20 and 21 January 2019 I talked to him about his books and practices. His tent was packed full, mostly with medicines and books but also a bed and a couple of chairs. Born in 1957 in Nashik (Maharashtra), Yogī Vilāsnāth studied physics and was employed until 1991. However, at the 1991 Kumbh Melā he decided to be initiated into the Nāth *sampradāya* by Yogī Ānandnāth, and moved to the Guru Gorakhnāth Mandir in Haridwar.

See pp. 164, 168, 228, 302, 304-307.

109. **Yogī 'Uri' Nāth** was at the Bhartṛhari *guphā* when I met him at the Ujjain Siṃhasth Melā on 19 April 2016. We talked about the *sampradāya* and the practice of *tapasyā* as he had been *khaṛeśvarī* in the past. He told me that he also teaches yoga to foreigners.

References

Acharya, Diwakar. 2011. 'Pāśupatas'. In *Brill's Encyclopedia of Hinduism*, edited by Knut A. Jacobsen, Helene Basu, Angelika Malinar and Vasudha Narayanan, 458–466. Leiden: Brill.

Acri, Andrea. 2018. 'Performance as Religious Observance in Some Śaiva Ascetic Traditions from South and Southeast Asia'. *Cracow Indological Studies* 20(1) (Special Issue: 'Theatrical and Ritual Boundaries in South Asia: Part II'): 1–30.

Akira, Hirakawa. 1993. *History of Indian Buddhism*. Delhi: Motilal Banarsidass.

Alper, Harvey P. 1989. *Understanding Mantras*. Albany, NY: State University of New York Press.

Alston, A.J.A. 1980. *Śankara Source-Book*. Vols. 1–6. London: Shanti Sadan.

Altekar, Anant Sadashiv. 1962. *The Position of Women in Hindu Civilization: From Prehistoric Times to the Present Day*. Delhi: Motilal Banarsidass.

Alter, Joseph S. 1992. *The Wrestler's Body: Identity and Ideology in North India*. Berkeley: University of California Press.

———. 1997. 'Seminal Truth: A Modern Science of Male Celibacy in North India.' *Medical Anthropology Quarterly* 11 (3): 275–298.

———. 2004. *Yoga in Modern India: The Body between Science and Philosophy*. Princeton, NJ: Princeton University Press.

———. 2005. 'Modern Medical Yoga: Struggling with a History of Magic, Alchemy and Sex'. *Asian Medicine* 1(1): 119–146.

———. 2006. 'Yoga and Fetishism: Reflections on Marxist Social Theory'. *Journal of the Royal Anthropological Institute* 12(4): 763–783.

———. 2008. 'Yoga Shivir: Performativity and the Study of Modern Yoga'. In *Yoga in the Modern World: Contemporary Perspectives*, edited by M. Singleton and J. Byrne, 36–48. London/New York: Routledge Hindu Studies Series.

———. 2012. 'Sacrifice, the Body, and Yoga: Theoretical Entailments of Embodiment in Hathayoga'. *South Asia: Journal of South Asian Studies* 35(2): 408–433.

Altglas, Veronique. 2007. 'The Global Diffusion and Westernization of Neo-Hindu Movements: Siddha Yoga and Sivananda Centres'. *Religions of South Asia* 1(2): 217–237. https://doi.org/10.1558/rosa.v1i2.217

———. 2011. 'Yoga and Kabbalah as World Religions? A Comparative Perspective on Globalization of Religious Resources'. In *Kabbalah and Contemporary Spiritual Revival*, edited by Boaz Huss, 233–250. Ben Gurion University of the Negev Press.

Alvi, Sajida Sultana. 2012. *Perspectives on Mughal India: Rulers, Historians, Ulama, and Sufis*. Karachi: Oxford University Press.

Armstrong, Jerome. 2023. 'Uncovering Vyāyāma in Yoga'. *Yoga and the Traditional Physical Practices of South Asia: Influence, Entanglement and Confrontation*, edited by Daniela Bevilacqua and Mark Singleton, 271–302. *Journal of Yoga Studies* 4 (Special Issue).

Asher, Catherine, and Talbot, Cynthia. 2006. *India Before Europe*. Cambridge: Cambridge University Press.

Aveling, Harry. 1994. *The Laughing Swamis: Australian Sannyasin Disciples of Swami Satyananda Saraswati and Osho Rajneesh*. 1st edn. Delhi: Motilal Banarsidass Publishers.

Baker, Ian. 2019. *Tibetan Yoga: Principles and Practices*. London: Thames & Hudson.

Barrier, N. Gerald, Singh, Nazer, and Singh, Harbans (eds.). 2002. *Singh Sabha Movement in Encyclopedia of Sikhism*. Vol. IV. 4th edn. Patiala, Punjab, India: Punjab University, Patiala.

Beck, Guy L. 1993. *Sonic Theology: Hinduism and Sacred Sound*. Studies in Comparative Religion. Columbia: University of South Carolina Press.

Ben-Herut, Gil. 2019. 'Religious Equality, Social Conservatism'. In *Bhakti and Power*, edited by John Stratton Hawley, Christian Lee Novetzke and Swapna Sharma, 38–48. Debating India's Religion of the Heart. Seattle: University of Washington Press.

Berger, Rachel. 2013. *Ayurveda Made Modern*. London: Palgrave Macmillan. https://doi.org/10.1057/9781137315908

Bernard, Theos. 1968. *Hatha Yoga*. Red Wheel/Weiser.

Bernier, François. 1709. *Voyages de François Bernier, docteur en Médecine de la Faculté de Montpellier, contenant la description des États du Grand Mogol, de l'Hindoustan, du Royaume de Kachemire*. 2 vols. Amsterdam.

Berreman, Gerald. 1962. *Behind Many Masks: Ethnography and Impression Management in a Himalayan Village*. Ithaca, NY: Society for Applied Anthropology.

Bevilacqua, Daniela. 2017a. 'Let the Sādhus Talk: Ascetic Understanding of Haṭha Yoga and Yogāsanas'. *Religions of South Asia* 11(2–3): 182–206.

———. 2017b. 'Are Women Entitled to Become Ascetics? An Historical and Ethnographic Glimpse on Female Asceticism in Hindu Religions'. *Kervan: International Journal of Afro-Asiatic Studies*, 21: 51–79.

———. 2018a. *Modern Hindu Traditionalism in Contemporary India: The Śrī Maṭh and the Jagadguru Rāmānandācārya in the Evolution of the Rāmānandī Sampradāya*. Routledge Hindu Studies Series. London/New York: Routledge.

———. 2018b. 'Old Tool for New Times'. *Journal of the British Association for the Study of Religion* 20: 45–66. https://doi.org/10.18792/jbasr.v20i0.27

———. 2020. 'Globalization and Asceticism: Foreign Ascetics on the Threshold of Hindu Religious Orders'. In *Routledge International Handbook of Religion in Global Society*, edited by J.S. Cornelio, F. Gautier, T. Martikainen and L. Woodhead, 199–211. Abingdon, UK: Routledge.

———. 2022a. 'Towards a Nath Re-appropriation of Hatha-Yoga'. In *The Power of the Nath Yogis: Yogic Charisma, Political Influence and Social Authority*, edited by Daniela Bevilacqua and Eloisa Stuparich, 281–306. Amsterdam: Amsterdam University Press.

———. 2022b. 'From the Margins to Demigod: The Establishment of the Kinnar Akhara in India'. *Asian Ethnology* 81(1–2): 53–82.

Bevilacqua, Daniela, and Singleton, Mark (eds.). 2023. *Yoga and the Traditional Physical Practices of South Asia: Influence, Entanglement and Confrontation*. *Journal of Yoga Studies* 4 (Special Issue).

Bevilacqua, Daniela, and Stuparich, Eloisa (eds.). 2022. *The Power of the Nath Yogis: Yogic Charisma, Political Influence and Social Authority*. Amsterdam: Amsterdam University Press.

Bhagat, M.G. 1976. *Ancient Indian Asceticism*. New Delhi: Munshiram Manoharlal Publishers.

Bharati, Agehananda. 1961. 'Intentional Language in the Tantras'. *Journal of the American Oriental Society*, 18(3) (August–September): 261–270.

———. 1965. *The Tantric Tradition*. London: Rider.

———. 1970. 'The Hindu Renaissance and Its Apologetic Patterns'. *Journal of Asian Studies* 29(2): 267–287.

Birch, Jason. 2011. 'The Meaning of Haṭha in Early Haṭhayoga'. *Journal of the American Oriental Society* 131(4): 527–554.

———. 2013. *The Amanaska: King of All Yogas. A Critical Edition and Annotated Translation with a Monographic Introduction.* Doctorate dissertation, Balliol College, University of Oxford.

———. 2017. 'The Āsana That Produces Tapas (and Misunderstandings!)'. *The Luminescent* (October). Retrieved from: https://www.theluminescent.org/2017/10/the-asana-that-produces-tapas-and.html

———. 2018. 'Premodern Yoga Traditions and Ayurveda'. *History of Science in South Asia* 6 (April): 1–83. https://doi.org/10.18732/hssa.v6i0.25

———. 2019. 'The Amaraughaprabodha: New Evidence on the Manuscript Transmission of an Early Work on Haṭha- and Rājayoga'. *Journal of Indian Philosophy* 47(5): 947–977.

———. 2020a. 'The Quest for Liberation-in-Life: A Survey of Early Works on Hatha- and Rājayoga'. In *The Oxford History of Hinduism: Hindu Practice*, edited by Gavin Flood, 200–243. Oxford: Oxford University Press.

———. 2020b. 'Haṭhayoga's Floruit on the Eve of Colonialism'. In *Śaivism and the Tantric Traditions: Essays in Honour of Alexis G.J.S Sanderson*, edited by Dominic Goodall, Shaman Hatley, Harunaga Isaacson and Srilata Raman, 451–479. Leiden: Brill.

———. 2024. *The Amaraugha and Amaraughaprabodha of Goraksanatha: The Genesis of Hatha and Rāja Yoga.* Pondicherry: École Française D'Èxtrême-Orient.

Birch, Jason, and Hargreaves, Jacqueline. 2015. 'Aiming to see Miracles: Paścimatānāsana from the Jogapradīpyakā (18th Century)'. *The Luminescent.* Retrieved from: https://www.theluminescent.org/2015/09/aiming-to-see-miracles.html

Birch, Jason, and Mallinson, James. Forthcoming. *Yogabīja.* Pondicherry: École Française D'Èxtrême-Orient.

Birch, Jason, and Hargreaves, Jacqueline. 2023. 'The Confluence of Hathayoga, Tapas and Modern Postural Practice: Distinct Regional Collections of Āsanas on the Eve of Colonialism'. *Yoga and the Traditional Physical Practices of South Asia: Influence, Entanglement and Confrontation*, edited by Daniela Bevilacqua and Mark Singleton, 31–82. *Journal of Yoga Studies* 4 (Special Issue).

Birch, Jason, and Singleton, Mark. 2019. 'The Yoga of the *Haṭhābhyāsapaddhati*: Hathayoga on the Cusp of Modernity'. *Journal of Yoga Studies* 2: 3–70.

Bisschop, Peter. 2010. 'Śaivism in the Gupta-Vākāṭaka Age'. *Journal of the Royal Asiatic Society* (Third Series) 20(4): 477–488.

———. 2020. *From Mantramārga Back to Atimārga: Atimārga as a Self-referential Term.* Śaivism and the Tantric Traditions. Leiden: Brill.

Bodewitz, H.W. 2007. 'The Special Meanings of "Śrama" and Other Derivations of the Root "Śram" in the Veda'. *Indo-Iranian Journal* 50(2): 145–160.

Borkataky-Varma, Sravana. 2018. 'Menstruation: Pollutant to Potent'. In *Encyclopedia of Indian Religions: Hinduism and Tribal Religions*, edited by Arvind Sharma. Dordrecht: Springer.

Bouillier, Véronique. 1992. 'The King and His Yogi: Prithvi Narayan Shah, Bhagavantanath and the Unification of Nepal in the 18th Century'. In *Gender, Caste and Power in South Asia: Social Status and Mobility in Transitional Society*, edited by J.P. Neelsen, 3–21. Delhi: Manohar.

———. 1997. *Ascètes et rois. Un monastère de Kanphata Yogis au Népal.* Paris: CNRS Éditions.

———. 1993. 'La violence des non-violents ou les ascètes au combat'. *Puruṣārtha* 16: 213–243.

———. 2003. 'Ratannath's Travels'. In *Pilgrims, Patrons, and Place: Localizing Sanctity in Asian Religions*, edited by Phyllis Granoff and Koichi Shinohara, 264–278. Vancouver: UBC Press.

———. 2008. *Itinérance et vie monastique: Les ascètes Nāth Yogīs en Inde contemporaine.* Paris: Éditions de la Maison des sciences de l'homme.

———. 2013. 'Religion Compass: A Survey of Current Researches on India's Nāth Yogīs: Survey on India's Nāth Yogīs'. *Religion Compass* 7(5): 157–168.
———. 2015. 'Nāth Yogīs' Encounters with Islam'. *South Asian Multidisciplinary Academic Journal*, freestanding article. https://journals.openedition.org/samaj/3878
Bouillier, Véronique, and Khan, Dominique-Sila. 2009. 'Ḥājji Ratan or Bābā Ratan's Multiple Identities'. *Journal of Indian Philosophy* 37(6): 559–597.
Bouy, Christian. 1994. *Les Nātha-yogin et les Upaniṣads: Étude d'histoire de la littérature hindoue.* Paris: Collège de France, Institut de civilisation indienne—Diffusion de Boccard.
Brahmacārī Śrīnṛsiṃhaśarmā. 1911. *Caurāśī Āsana.* Mumbai: Kahānjī Dharmsimha.
Briggs, George Weston. 1938. *Gorakhnāth and the Kānphaṭa Yogīs.* Calcutta: YMCA Publishing House.
Brockington, John. 2020. 'Religious Practices in the Sanskrit Epics'. In *The Oxford History of Hinduism: Hindu Practice*, edited by Gavin Flood, 79–98. Oxford: Oxford University Press.
Bronkhorst, Johannes. 1993. *The Two Traditions of Meditation in Ancient India.* Repr. Delhi: Motilal Banarsidass Publishers.
———. 1998. *The Two Sources of Indian Asceticism.* Delhi: Motilal Banarsidass.
———. 2007. *Greater Magadha: Studies in the Culture of Early India.* Leiden: Brill.
Broo, M. 2003. *As Good as God: The Guru in Gaudiya Vaisnavism.* Åbo: Åbo Academy University Press.
Brunner Hélène. 1994. 'Un Tantra du nord: Le Netra Tantra'. *Bulletin of the School of Oriental and African Studies* 37: 125–197.
Bryant, Edwin F. 2017. *Bhakti Yoga: Tales and Teachings from the Bhāgavata Purāṇa.* New York: North Point Press.
Bucknell, Roderick S., and Stuart-Fox, Martin. 1986. *The Twilight Language: Explorations in Buddhist Meditation and Symbolism.* Richmond, UK: Curzon Press.
Bühnemann, Gudrun. 2007. *Eighty-four Āsanas in Yoga: A Survey of Traditions. With Illustrations.* New Delhi: D.K. Printworld.
Burchett, Patton E. 2019. *A Genealogy of Devotion: Bhakti, Tantra, Yoga, and Sufism in North India.* New York: Columbia University Press.
Burger, Maya. 2014. 'La Sarvāṅgayogapradīpikā de Sundardās: Une classification des chemins de yoga au 17e siècle'. *Asia* 68(3): 683–708.
Burghart, Richard. 1978. *The History of Janakpurdham: A Study of Asceticism and the Hindu Polity.* London: SOAS.
Caldwell, Sarah. 2001. 'The Heart of the Secret: A Personal and Scholarly Encounter with Shakta Tantrism in Siddha Yoga'. *Nova Religio: The Journal of Alternative and Emergent Religions* 5(1): 9–51.
Campbell, Colin. 2007. *Easternization of the West: A Thematic Account of Cultural Change in the Modern Era.* Boulder, CO: Paradigm Publishers.
Caracchi, Pinuccia. 1999. *Ramananda e lo yoga dei sant.* Alessandria: Edizioni dell'Orso.
Carpenter, David, and Whicher, Ian (eds.). 2003. *Yoga: The Indian Tradition.* London: Routledge.
Chakraborty, Chandrima. 2006. 'Ramdev and Somatic Nationalism: Embodying the Nation, Desiring the Global'. *Economic and Political Weekly* 41(5): 387–390.
Chakravarty, D.K. 1970. 'On the Sculptural Representation of Ambika-Gauri-Parvati from West Bengal'. *Proceedings of the Indian History Congress* 32: 200–210.
Champakalakshmi, R. 2004. 'From Devotion and Dissent to Dominance: The Bhakti of the Tamil Ālvārs and Nāyanārs'. In *Religious Movements in South Asia 600–1800*, edited by Lorenzen David, 47–80. New Delhi: Oxford India.
Chandra, Satish. 2003. *Essays on Medieval Indian History.* Delhi: Oxford University Press.
Chiseri-Strater, E. 1996. 'Turning in upon Ourselves: Positionality, Subjectivity, and Reflexivity in Case Study and Ethnographic Research'. In *Ethics and Representation in Qualitative Studies*

of Literacy, edited by P. Mortensen and G. Kirsch, 115–132. Urbana, IL: National Council of Teachers in English.

Cimino, Rosa Maria. 2014. 'I Sādhu dell'India e le loro estreme tapasyā nei dipinti indiani e nelle stampe e disegni occidentali'. In *"My Life is like the Summer Rose": Maurizio Tosi e l'Archeologia come modo di vivere*, edited by B. Cerasetti, B. Genito and C.C. Lamberg-Karlovsky, 123–142. British Archaeological Reports. Oxford: Archaeopress

Clark, Matthew. 2006. *The Daśanāmī-Saṃnyāsīs: The Integration of Ascetic Lineages into an Order*. Leiden: Brill.

———. 2017. *The Tawny One: Soma, Haoma, and Ayahuasca*. London: Muswell Hill Press.

———. 2019. 'Soma'. Online resource. https://www.academia.edu/41346564/Soma [last accessed 24 November 2022]

Clémentin-Ojha, Catherine. 1985. 'The Tradition of Female Gurus'. *Manushi* 31 (November–December): 2–8.

———. 1998. 'Outside the Norms: Women Ascetics in Hindu Society'. *Economic and Political Weekly* 18.

Cohn, Bernard. 1964. 'The Role of the Gosains in the Economy of Eighteenth and Nineteenth Century Upper India'. *Indian Economic and Social History Review* 1(4): 175–183.

Colas, Gérard. 2003. 'History of Vaiṣṇava Traditions: An Esquisse'. In *The Blackwell Companion to Hinduism*, edited by Gavin Flood, 229–270. Blackwell Companions to Religion. Malden, MA: Blackwell Publishers.

———. 2012. 'Vaikhānasa'. In *Brill's Encyclopedia of Hinduism*, edited by Knut A. Jacobsen, Helene Basu, Angelika Malinar and Vasudha Narayanan. Leiden: Brill.

———. 2018. 'Bhāgavatas'. In *Brill's Encyclopedia of Hinduism*, edited by Knut A. Jacobsen, Helene Basu, Angelika Malinar and Vasudha Narayanan. Leiden: Brill

Conze, Edward. 1962. *Buddhist Thought in India: Three Phases of Buddhist Philosophy*. Repr. Ann Arbor: University of Michigan Press.

Cook, Johanna. 2010. *Meditation in Modern Buddhism: Renunciation and Change in Thai Monastic Life*. Cambridge: Cambridge University Press.

Copeman, Jacob, and Ikegame, Aya (eds.). 2012. *The Guru in South Asia: New Interdisciplinary Perspectives*. London/New York: Routledge.

Crangle, Edward Fitzpatrick. 1994. *The Origin and Development of Early Indian Contemplative Practices*. Wiesbaden: Otto Harrassowitz Verlag.

Dallapiccola, Anna Libera, and Verghese, Anila. 1998. *Sculpture at Vijayanagara: Iconography and Style*. New Delhi: Manohar Publishers & Distributors for American Institute of Indian Studies.

Darmon, Richard A. 2016. 'Vajrolī Mudrā: La rétention séminale chez les yogis Vāmācāri'. In *Images du corps dans le monde hindou*, edited by Véronique Bouillier and Gilles Tarabout, 213–240. Anthropologie. Paris: CNRS Éditions.

Das, Sangeeta. 2018. 'Ambubachi Mela in Assam's Kamakhya Temple: A Critical Analysis'. *International Journal of Research and Analytical Reviews* 5(1): 293–295.

Dasgupta, S.B. 1976. *Obscure Religious Cults*. Calcutta: Firma KLM Private Ltd (1st edn 1946).

Dash, Bhagwan. 1980. *Fundamentals of Ayurvedic Medicine*. London: Bansal & Co.

Dazey, Wade Hampton. 1990. 'Tradition and Modernization in the Organization of the Daśanamī Samsyāsīn'. In *Monastic Life in the Christian and Hindu Traditions: A Comparative Study*, edited by Austin B. Creel and Vasudha Narayanam, 281–321. Lewiston/Queenston/Lampeter: Edwin Mellen Press.

De Michelis, Elizabeth. 2004. *A History of Modern Yoga: Patañjali and Western Esotericism*. London: Continuum.

DeNapoli, Antoinette E. 2014. *Real Sadhus Sing to God: Gender, Asceticism, and Vernacular Religion in Rajasthan*. AAR Religion, Culture, and History. Oxford: Oxford University Press.

——. 2019. 'A Female Shankaracharya? The Alternative Authority of a Feminist Hindu Guru in India'. *Religion and Gender* 9(1): 27–49.

Denton, L. Teskey. 2004. *Female Asceticism in Hinduism*. Albany: State University of New York Press.

Derrida, Jacques. 1978. 'Structure, Sign, and Play in the Discourse of the Human Science'. In *Writing and Difference*, trans. Alan Bass, 278–293. Evanston, IL: Northwestern University Press.

Deshpande, M.N. 1986. *The Caves of Panhāle-Kājī, Ancient Pranālaka: An Art Historical Study of Transition from Hinayana, Tantric Vajrayana to Nath Sampradāya (Third to Fourteenth Century A.D.)*. New Delhi: Archaeological Survey of India, Govt of India.

Diamond, Debra. 2013. *Yoga: The Art of Transformation*. Washington, DC: Arthur M. Sackler Gallery, Smithsonian Institution.

Djurdjevic, Gordan, and Singh, Śukadeva. 2019. *Sayings of Gorakhnāth: Annotated Translation of the Gorakh Bānī*. New York: Oxford University Press

Doniger, Wendy. 1981. *Siva the Erotic Ascetic*. Oxford: Oxford University Press.

Dumézil, Georges. 1969. *Idées romaines*. Paris: Gallimard.

Duncan, Jonathan. 1799. 'Account of Two Fakeers with Their Portraits'. *Asiatic Researches, or, Transactions of the Society Instituted in Bengal for Inquiring into the History and Antiquities, the Arts, Sciences and Literature of Asia*. Vol. 5, 36–52. London.

——. 1810. *The European Magazine and London Review, Containing Portraits, Views, Biography, Anecdotes, Literature, History, Politics, Arts, Manners, and Amusements of the Age*. Vol. 57 (January–June). London for James Asperne.

Eaton, Richard M. 1978. *The Sufis of Bijapur, 1300–1700: Social Roles of Sufis in Medieval India*. Princeton, NJ: Princeton University Press.

——. 1993. *The Rise of Islam and the Bengal Frontier, 1204–1760*. Berkeley: University of California Press.

Eck, Diana. 1982. *Banaras: City of Light*. New York: Alfred A. Knopf.

Eck, Diana, Tarun, Khanna, Macomber, John *et al.* 2015. *Kumbh Mela: Mapping the Ephemeral Megacity*. Harvard University, South Asia Institute. Berlin: Hatje Cantz.

Entwistle, A.W. 2003. *Vaiṣṇava Tilakas: Sectarian Marks Worn by Worshippers of Viṣṇu*. Vrindaban, India: Vrindaban Research Institute.

Ernst, Carl. 2003. 'The Islamization of Yoga in the *Amrtakunda* Translations'. *Journal of the Royal Asiatic Society* (Series 3) 13(2): 1–23.

——. 2016. *Refractions of Islam in India: Situating Sufism and Yoga*. New Delhi: Sage Publications. http://pi.lib.uchicago.edu/1001/cat/bib/11955387

Farquhar, John N. 1925. 'The Fighting Ascetics of India'. *Bulletin of John Rylands Library* 9(2): 431–452.

Feuerstein, Georg. 2001. *The Yoga Tradition: Its History, Literature, Philosophy and Practice*. Prescott, AZ: Hohm Press.

——. 2003. *The Deeper Dimension of Yoga: Theory and Practice*. Boulder, CO: Shambhala Publications.

Fitzgerald, James L. 2012. 'A Prescription for Yoga and Power in the Mahābhārata'. In *Yoga in Practice*, edited by David Gordon White, 43–57. Princeton, NJ: Princeton University Press.

Flood, Gavin (ed.). 2003. *The Blackwell Companion to Hinduism*. Blackwell Companions to Religion. Malden, MA: Blackwell Publishers.

——. 2006. *The Tantric Body: The Secret Tradition of Hindu Religion*. London/New York: I.B. Taurus.

Foxen, Anya P. 2020. *Inhaling Spirit: Harmonialism, Orientalism, and the Western Roots of Modern Yoga*. New York: Oxford University Press.

Foxen, Anya, and Christa, Kuberry. 2021. *Is This Yoga? Concepts, Histories, and the Complexities of Modern Practice*. London/New York: Routledge.

Freeman, John R. 2006. 'Shifting Forms of the Wandering Yogi'. In *Masked Ritual and Performance in South India: Dance, Healing, and Possession,* edited by David Shulman and Deborah Thiagarajan, 147–187. Ann Arbor: University of Michigan.

Galewicz, Cezary. 2020. 'Ritual, Ascetic, and Meditative Practice in the Veda and Upaniṣads'. In *The Oxford History of Hinduism: Hindu Practice,* edited by Gavin Flood, 35–61. Oxford: Oxford University Press.

Ganser, Elisa. 2023. 'Dance as Yoga: Ritual Offering and Imitation Dei in the Physical Practices of Classical Indian Theatre'. *Yoga and the Traditional Physical Practices of South Asia: Influence, Entanglement and Confrontation,* edited by Daniela Bevilacqua and Mark Singleton, 137–171. *Journal of Yoga Studies* 4 (Special Issue).

Gautam, Aavriti, and Droogan, Julian. 2018. 'Yoga Soft Power: How Flexible Is the Posture?' *Journal of International Communication* 24(1): 18–36.

General Department North, Western Provinces and Oudh. 1882 Proceedings Volume 1882. U.P. State Archives, Lucknow.

Gerety, Finnian M.M. 2020. 'Sound and Yoga'. In *Routledge Handbook of Yoga and Meditation Studies,* edited by Karen O'Brien-Kop and Suzanne Newcombe, 502–521. Abingdon, UK: Routledge.

Gharote M.L. 1999. *Jogapradīpakā.* Jodhapura, India: Rājasthāna Prācyavidyā Pratishṭhāna.

Ghurye, Govind S. 1953. *Indian Sadhus.* The Popular Book Depot.

Glucklich, Ariel. 2003. *Sacred Pain: Hurting the Body for the Sake of the Soul.* Oxford/New York: Oxford University Press.

Gold, Daniel. 1999. 'Nath Yogis as Established Alternatives: Householders and Ascetics Today'. *Journal of Asian and African Studies,* 34(1): 68–88

———. 2002. 'Kabīr's Secrets for Householders: Truths and Rumours among Rajasthani Nāths'. In *Images of Kabir,* edited by Monika Horstmann, 143–156. Delhi: Manohar.

Gold, Daniel, and Gold, Ann Grodzins. 1984. 'The Fate of the Nath Householder'. *History of Religions* 24(2): 113–132.

Gombrich, Richard F. 2006. *Theravada Buddhism: A Social History from Ancient Benares to Modern Colombo.* Abingdon, UK: Routledge.

Gonda, J. 1952. *Ancient-Indian Ojas, Latin *augos and the Indo-European Nouns in -Es-/-Os.* Utrecht: A. Oosthoek. http://pi.lib.uchicago.edu/1001/cat/bib/2101808

Goodall, Dominic. 2004. *Parākhyatantram: The Parākhyatantra—A Scripture of the Śaiva Siddhānta.* Pondicherry: Institut Français de Pondichéry.

Goodall, Dominic, and Harunaga, Isaacson. 2014. 'Tantric Hinduism'. In *The Bloomsbury Companion to Hindu Studies,* edited by Jessica Frazier, 122–137. London/New Delhi: Bloomsbury.

Goudriaan, Teun. 1979. 'Introduction, History and Philosophy'. In *Hindu Tantrism,* edited by Gupta Sanjukta, Hoens Dirk Jan and Goudriaan Teun, 1–67. Handbuch der Orientalistik 2.4.2. Leiden/Köln: Brill.

———. 2002. 'Imagery of the Self from Veda to Tantra'. In *The Roots of Tantra,* edited by Katherine Anne Harper and Robert L. Brown, 171–192. Albany: State University of New York Press.

Goudriaan, Teun, and Schoterman, Jan A. 1988. *The Kubjikāmatatantra: Kulālikāmnāya Version.* Leiden: Brill.

Gray, B. David. 2016. 'Tantra and the Tantric Traditions of Hinduism and Buddhism'. Oxford Research Encyclopedia: Religion. https://oxfordre.com/religion/display/10.1093/acrefore/9780199340378.001.0001/acrefore-9780199340378-e-59

Grey, Edward. 1892. *The Travels of Pietro Della Valle in India: From the Old English Translation of 1664.* Vol. II. London. https://archive.org/details/travelsofpietrod00dell/page/n7/mode/2up

Grierson, George A. 1918. 'Rākhaṛs, Sākhaṛs, —khaṛs'. *In Encyclopaedia of Religion and Ethics.* Vol. X, edited by James Hastings, 866–867. Edinburgh: T. & T. Clark.

Gross, Robert Lewis. 1992. *The Sādhus of India: A Study of Hindu Asceticism.* Jaipur: Rawat Publications.

Gupta, Ravi M., and Valpey, Kenneth Russell (eds.). 2013. *The Bhāgavata Purāṇa: Sacred Text and Living Tradition.* New York: Columbia University Press.

Hacker, Paul. 1995. *Philology and Confrontation: Paul Hacker on Traditional and Modern Vedanta.* Albany: State University of New York Press.

Halbfass, Wilhelm. 1990. *India and Europe: An Essay in Philosophical Understanding.* Delhi: Motilal Banarsidass.

Hamaya, Mariko. 2019. 'Feminisation of Ascetic Celibacy in Haridwar'. *South Asia Research* 39 (3suppl): 26–41. https://doi.org/10.1177/0262728019872051

Hara, Minoru. 1977. 'Tapasvinī'. *Annals of the Bhandarkar Oriental Research Institute* 58/59: 151–159.

———. 1979. *Koten Indo no kugyō* [tapas in MBh.]. Tokyo: Shunjūsha.

———. 1999. 'Pāśupata and Yoga. *Pāśupata-Sūtra* 2.12 and *Yoga-Sūtra* 3.37'. *Asiatische Studien Études Asiatiques LIII*, 3: 593–608. Bern: Peter Lang.

Hatley, Shaman. 2012. 'From Mātṛs to Yoginīs: Continuity and Transformation in the South Asian Cults of the Mother Goddesses'. In *Transformations and Transfer of Tantra in Asia and Beyond*, edited by István Keul, 99–129. Berlin: Walter de Gruyter.

———. 2016. 'Erotic Asceticism: The Razor's Edge Observance (Asidhārāvrata) and the Early History of Tantric Coital Ritual 1'. *Bulletin of the School of Oriental and African Studies* 79(2): 329–345.

Hausner, Sondra L. 2007. *Wandering with Sadhus: Ascetics in the Hindu Himalayas.* Contemporary Indian Studies. Bloomington: Indiana University Press

Hawley, John Stratton. 1995. 'The Nirguṇ/Saguṇ Distinction in Early Manuscript Anthologies of Hindu Devotion'. In *Bhakti Religion in North India*, edited by Lorenzen David, 160–180. Albany: State University of New York Press.

———. 2005. *Three Bhakti Voices: Mirabai, Surdas, and Kabir in Their Time and Ours.* New Delhi: Oxford University Press.

Hawley, John Stratton, Novetzke, Christian Lee, and Sharma, Swapna. 2019. *Bhakti and Power: Debating India's Religion of the Heart.* Global South Asia. Seattle: University of Washington Press.

Heesterman, Jan C. 1964. 'Brahmin, Ritual and Renouncer'. *Wiener Zeitschrift für die Kunde Südasiens* 8: 1–31.

Hellwig, Oliver. 2011. 'Intoxication'. In *Brill's Encyclopedia of Hinduism*, edited by Knut A. Jacobsen, Helene Basu, Angelika Malinar and Vasudha Narayanan, 459–471. Leiden: Brill.

Hess, Linda, and Singh, Shukdev (trans.). 1983. *The Bijak of Kabir.* San Francisco: North Point Press.

Horstmann, Monika. 2014. 'The Emergence of the Nāthyogī Order in the Light of Vernacular Sources'. *International Journal of Tantric Studies* 10(1).

———. 2021. *Bhakti and Yoga: A Discourse in Seventeenth-century Codices.* Delhi: Primus Books.

———. (forthcoming). 'Power and Status: Ramanandi Warrior Ascetics in 18th- Century Jaipur'. In *Asceticism and Power in South and Southeast Asia*, edited by P. Flügel and G. Houtman. London: Routledge

Houtman, Gustaaf. 1990. *Traditions of Buddhist Practice in Burma.* Tokyo: ILCAA.

Jacobsen, Knut A. (ed.). 2005. *Theory and Practice of Yoga: Essays in Honour of Gerald James Larson.* Numen Book Series, Studies in the History of Religions, 110. Leiden: Brill.

———. 2011. *Yoga Powers: Extraordinary Capacities Attained through Meditation and Concentration.* Leiden: Brill.

Jaffrelot, Christophe. 1999. *The Hindu Nationalist Movements and Indian Politics.* New Delhi: Penguin Books India.

Jha, Dhirendra K. 2019. *Ascetic Games: Sadhus, Akharas and the Making of the Hindu Vote*. Chennai: Westland Publications Limited.

Jordt, Ingrid. 2007. *Burma's Mass Lay Meditation Movement: Buddhism and the Cultural Construction of Power*. Athens: Ohio University Press.

Kaelber, O. Walter. 1989. *Tapta Marga: Asceticism and Initiation in Vedic India*. Albany: State University of New York Press.

Kasturi, Malavika. 2010. 'All Gifting is Sacred: The Sanatana Dharma Sabha Movement, the Reform of *Dana* and Civil Society in Late Colonial India'. *Indian Economic & Social History Review* 47(1): 107–139.

Katsuyuki, Ida. 2011. 'The Concept of Bhakti In the Tantric Tradition'. In *Historical Development of Bhakti Movement in India: Theory and Practice*, edited by I. Shima, T. Sakata and I. Katsuyuki, 113–130. New Delhi: Manohar Publishers & Distributors.

Kędzia, Ilona Barbara. 2017. 'Mastering Deathlessness: Some Remarks on Karpam Preparations in the Medico-Alchemical Literature of the Tamil Siddhas'. In *Transmutations: Rejuvenation, Longevity, and Immortality Practices in South and Inner Asia*, edited by Dagmar Wujastyk, Suzanne Newcombe and Christèle Barois. 121–142. History of Science in South Asia.

Khalikova, Venera. 2017. 'The Ayurveda of Baba Ramdev: Biomoral Consumerism, National Duty and the Biopolitics of "Homegrown" Medicine in India'. *South Asia: Journal of South Asian Studies* 40(1): 105–122.

Khandelwal, Meena. 2004. *Women in Ochre Robes: Gendering Hindu Renunciation*. Albany: State University of New York Press.

———. 2012. 'The Cosmopolitan Guru: Spiritual Tourism and Ashrams in Rishikesh'. In *The Guru in South Asia*, edited by Jacob Copeman and Aya Ikegame, 202–221. London: Routledge.

Khandelwal, Meena, Hausner, Sondra L., and Grodzins Gold, Ann. 2006. *Women's Renunciation in South Asia: Nuns, Yoginis, Saints, and Singers*. New York: Palgrave Macmillan.

Kiss, Csaba. 2021 *The Yoga of the Matsyendrasaṃhitā: A Critical Edition and Annotated Translation of Chapters 1–13 and 55*. Pondicherry: Institut Français de Pondichéry/École Française D'Èxtrême-Orient.

Klostermaier Klaus K. 2007. *A Survey of Hinduism*. 3rd edn. Albany, NY: State University of New York Press.

Kværne, Per. 1977. *An Anthology of Buddhist Tantric Songs: A Study of the Caryāgīti*. Skrifter det Norske videnskaps-akademi 14. Oslo/Bergen/Tromsø: Universitetsforlaget.

Lamb, Ramdas. 1994. 'Asceticism and Devotion: The Many Faces of Rām Bhakti in the Rāmānanda Sampradāy'. *Journal of Vaishnava Studies* 2(4): 129–143.

———. 2005. 'Raja Yoga, Asceticism, and the Ramananda Sampraday'. In *Theory and Practice of Yoga: Essays in Honour of Gerald James Larson*, edited by Knut A. Jacobsen, 317–331. Leiden: Brill.

———. 2011. 'Rāmānandīs'. In *Brill's Encyclopedia of Hinduism*, edited by Knut A. Jacobsen, Helene Basu, Angelika Malinar and Vasudha Narayanan, 478–488. Leiden: Brill.

———. 2012. 'Yogic Powers and the Rāmānanda Sampradāy'. *Yoga Powers: Extraordinary Capacities Attained through Meditation and Concentration*, edited by Knut A. Jacobsen, 427–457. Leiden: Brill.

Larios, Borayin M. 2017. *Embodying the Vedas: Traditional Vedic Schools of Contemporary Maharashtra*. Open Access Hinduism. Warsaw: De Gruyter Open.

Larson, Gerald James, and Bhattacharya, Ram Shankar (eds.). 2008. *Yoga: India's Philosophy of Meditation*. Encyclopedia of Indian Philosophies, 12; series ed. Karl H. Potter. Delhi: Motilal Banarsidass.

Leslie, Julia. 1992. *Roles and Rituals for Hindu Women*. Delhi: Motilal Banarsidass.

Lessing, F.D. and Wayman, Alex. 1968. *Introduction to the Buddhist Tantric Systems*. Delhi: Motilal Banarsidass.

Little, Layne. 2018. 'Nāyaṉārs'. In *Brill's Encyclopedia of Hinduism Online*, edited by Knut A. Jacobsen, Helene Basu, Angelika Malinar and Vasudha Narayanan. http://dx.doi.org/10.1163/2212-5019_BEH_COM_9000000119 [last accessed 22 March 2022].

Llewelyn, J.E. 2005. *Defining Hinduism: A Reader.* New York: Routledge.

Lochtefeld, G. James. 2008. 'Getting in Line: The Kumbh Mela Festival Processions'. In *South Asian Religions on Display: Religious Processions in South Asia and in the Diaspora*, edited by Knut A. Jacobsen, 29–44. Abingdon, UK: Routledge

Lorea, Carola Erika. 2018. '"I am Afraid of Telling you This, Lest You'd Be Scared Shitless!": The Myth of Secrecy and the Study of the Esoteric Traditions of Bengal'. *Religions* 9(6), 172: 1–24.

Lorenzen, David N. 1972. *The Kāpālikas and Kālāmukhas: Two Lost Śaivite Sects.* Vol. v. 12. Australian National University Centre of Oriental Studies, Oriental Monograph Series. New Delhi: Thomson Press.

———. 1978. 'Warrior Ascetics in Indian History'. *Journal of the American Oriental Society*, 98(1): 61–75.

———. 2004. *Religious Movements in South Asia 600–1800.* Delhi: Oxford University Press.

———. 2010. *The Scourge of the Mission: Marco della Tomba in Hindustan.* New Delhi: Yoda Press.

———. 2011. 'Religious Identity in Gorakhnath and Kabir: Hindus, Muslims, Yogis and Sants'. In *Yogi Heroes and Poets: Histories and Legends of the Naths*, edited by David Lorenzen and Adrian Muñoz, 19–49. Albany: State University of New York Press.

Losty, J.P. 2016. 'Ascetics and Yogis in Indian Painting: The Mughal and Deccani Tradition'. Online paper. https://blogs.bl.uk/asian-and-african/2016/08/ascetics-and-yogis-in-indian-painting.html [last accessed 26 February 2023]

Lutgendorf, Philip. 1994. 'The Quest for Legendary Tulsīdās'. In *According to Tradition: Hagiographical Writing in India*, edited by W. Callawaert and R. Snell, 65–85. Wiesbaden: Harrassowitz Verlag.

Maas, Philipp A. 2007. 'The Concepts of the Human Body and Disease in Classical Yoga and Āyurveda'. *Wiener Zeitschrift für die Kunde Südasiens/Vienna Journal of South Asian Studies* 51: 125–62.

———. 2013. 'A Concise Historiography of Classical Yoga Philosophy'. In *Periodization and Historiography of Indian Philosophy*, edited by Eli Franco, 53–90. Vienna: Sammlung De Nobili.

———. 2017. 'On the Meaning of Rasāyana in Classical Yoga and Āyurveda'. *History of Science in South Asia* 5 (December): 66–84.

Maclean, Kama. 2003. 'Making the Colonial State Work for You: The Modern Beginnings of the Ancient Kumbh Mela in Allahabad'. *Journal of Asian Studies* 62(3): 873–905.

———. 2008. *Pilgrimage and Power: The Kumbh Mela in Allahabad, 1765–1954.* Oxford: Oxford University Press.

Maitra, Keya. 2018. *Philosophy of the Bhagavad Gita: A Contemporary Introduction.* London/New York: Bloomsbury Academic.

Malamoud, Charles. 1977. *Svādhyāya: Récitation personelle du Veda Taittirīya-Āranyaka livre II: Texte; traduit et commenté par Charles Malamoud.* Paris: Institut de civilisation indienne.

Malinar, Angelika. 2009. *The Bhagavadgita.* Cambridge: Cambridge University Press.

Mallik, K. 1960. 'Gorakhnath'. In *A Seminar on Saints*, edited by T.M.P. Mahadevan, 74–82. Madras: G.S. Press.

Mallinson, James. 2004. *The Gheranda Samhita.* YogaVidya.com

———. 2005. 'Rāmānandī Tyāgīs and Haṭhayoga'. *Journal of Vaishnava Studies* 14(1): 107–121.

———. 2007a. *The Khecarīvidyā of Ādinātha: A Critical Edition and Annotated Translation of an Early Text of Haṭhayoga.* London: Routledge.

———. 2007b. *The Shiva Samhita.* YogaVidya.com

———. 2011a. 'Haṭha Yoga'. In *Brill Encyclopedia of Hinduism*. Vol. 3, edited by Knut A. Jacobsen, Helen Basu, Angelika Malinar and Vasudha Narayanan, 770–781. Leiden: Brill. https://eprints.soas.ac.uk/17971

———. 2011b. 'Nāth Saṃpradāya'. In *Brill Encyclopedia of Hinduism*. Vol. 3, edited by Knut A. Jacobsen, Helen Basu, Angelika Malinar and Vasudha Narayanan, 407–428. Leiden: Brill.

———. 2012a. 'The Original Gorakṣaśataka'. In *Yoga in Practice*, edited by David G. White, 257–272. Princeton, NJ: Princeton University Press.

———. 2012b. 'Yoga & Yogi'. *Nāmarūpa* 3(15): 1–27.

———. 2013a. *Dattātreya's Discourse on Yoga*. Translation based on a 2012 critical edition. https://terebess.hu/keletkultinfo/lexikon/Datta-Mallinson.pdf

———. 2013b. 'Purn Puri and Jonathan Duncan'. Conference presentation. https://www.academia.edu/3492951/Purn_Puri_and_Jonathan_Duncan

———. 2013c. 'Yogic Identities: Tradition and Transformation'. In *Yoga in Transformation*, edited by Debra Diamond, 69–83. *Smithsonian Institute Research Online.*

———. 2016a. 'Śāktism and Haṭhayoga'. In *Goddess Traditions in Tantric Hinduism*, edited by Bjarne Wernicke Olese, 109–140. London: Routledge.

———. 2016b. 'Rāmānandī Tyāgīs Haṭha Yoga'. Unpublished paper.

———. 2016c. 'Yogi Insignia in Mughal Painting and Avadhi Romances'. In *Objects, Images, Stories: Simon Digby's Historical Method*, edited by Orsini Francesca and David Lunn. Oxford: Oxford University Press.

———. 2018a. 'Yoga and Sex: What Is the Purpose of Vajrolīmudrā?' In *Yoga in Transformation*, edited by Karl Baier, Philipp André Maas and Karin Preisendanz, 181–222. Vienna: V&R Unipress.

———. 2018b. 'Early Haṭha'. Unpublished paper.

———. 2019. 'Kālavañcana in the Konkan: How a Vajrayāna Haṭhayoga Tradition Cheated Buddhism's Death in India'. *Religions* 10(4): 273.

———. 2020. 'Haṭhayoga's Early History: From Vajrayāna Sexual Restraint to Universal Somatic Soteriology'. In *The Oxford History of Hinduism*, by James Mallinson, 177–199. Oxford: Oxford University Press.

———. 2021. 'Yoga: Haṭha'. In *The Encyclopedia of Philosophy of Religion*, edited by Stewart Goetz and Charles Taliaferro, 1–3. Hoboken, NJ: Wiley-Blackwell.

Mallinson, James, and Singleton, Mark. 2017. *Roots of Yoga*. 1st edn. London: Penguin Classics.

Mallinson, James, and Szántó, Peter. 2021. *The Amṛtasiddhi and Amṛtasiddhimūla*. École française d'Extrême-Orient.

Marcus, George E. 1995. 'Ethnography in/of the World System: The Emergence of Multi-Sited Ethnography'. *Annual Review of Anthropology* 24: 95–117.

McCartney, Patrick. 2017. 'Politics beyond the Yoga Mat: Yoga Fundamentalism and the "Vedic Way of Life"'. *Global Ethnographic* 4: 1–18.

———. 2023. 'Poles Apart? From Wrestling and Mallkhamb to Pole Yoga'. *Yoga and the Traditional Physical Practices of South Asia: Influence, Entanglement and Confrontation*, edited by Daniela Bevilacqua and Mark Singleton, 215–270. *Journal of Yoga Studies* 4 (Special Issue).

McGuire, Meredith B. 2008. *Lived Religion: Faith and Practice in Everyday Life*. New York: Oxford University Press.

McLeod, W.H. 1980. *Early Sikh Tradition: A Study of the Janam-Sākhīs*. Oxford: New York: Clarendon Press/Oxford University Press.

———. 2004. *Sikhs and Sikhism* (Comprising *Guru Nanak and the Sikh Religion*, *Early Sikh Tradition*, *The Evolution of the Sikh Community* and *Who is a Sikh?*) Delhi: Oxford University Press India.

———. 2007. *Essays in Sikh History, Tradition and Society*. Oxford: Oxford University Press.

Meulenbeld, Gerrit Jan. 2008. 'The Woes of Ojas in the Modern World'. In *Modern and Global Ayurveda: Pluralism and Paradigms*, edited by Dagmar Wujastyk and Frederick M. Smith, 157–175. Albany: State University of New York Press.

Monier-Williams, Monier. 1878. *Modern India and the Indians*. Trübner & Company.

———. 1964 [1899]. *A Sanskrit English Dictionary*. Oxford: Clarendon Press.

Moran, Arik. 2013. 'Toward a History of Devotional Vaishnavism in the West Himalayas: Kullu and the Ramanandis, c. 1500–1800'. *Indian Economic Social History Review* 50(1): 1–25.

Mulemi, Benson A. 2016. 'Sacred Pain'. In *Encyclopedia of Psychology and Religion*, edited by David A. Leeming, 1–6. Berlin/Heidelberg: Springer.

Muñoz, Adrián. 2010. *La piel de tigre y la serpiente: La identidad de los Nāth-yoguis a través de sus leyendas*. Mexico City: El Colegio de México.

———. 2011. 'Matsyendra's "Golden Legend": Yogi Tales and Nāth Ideology'. In *Yogi Heroes and Poets: Histories and Legends of the Nāths*, edited by David Lorenzen and Adrian Muñoz, 109–127. Albany: State University of New York Press.

———. 2022. 'Powerful Yogīs: The Successful Quest for Siddhis and Power'. In *The Power of the Nāth Yogīs*, edited by Daniela Bevilacqua and Elisa Stuparich, 55–80. Amsterdam: Amsterdam University Press.

Nanda, Mira. 2009. *The God Market. How Globalization Is Making India More Hindu*. Noida/London: Random House Publishers.

Needham, J. 1983. *Science and Civilisation in China*. Vol. 5. *Chemistry and Chemical Technology*. Part 5. *Spagyrical Discovery and Invention: Physiological Alchemy*. Cambridge: Cambridge University Press.

Neevel, Walter G. 1977. *Yāmuna's Vedānta and Pāñcarātra: Integrating the Classical and the Popular*. Harvard Dissertations in Religion, 10. Missoula, MT: Scholars Press for *Harvard Theological Review*.

Newcombe, Suzanne. 2017. 'The Revival of Yoga in Contemporary India'. In *Oxford Research Encyclopaedias: Religion*. Oxford: Oxford University Press.

———. 2019. *Yoga in Britain: Stretching Spirituality and Educating Yogis*. Sheffield, UK: Equinox Publishing.

Novetzke, Christian Lee. 2019. 'The Political Theology of Bhakti, or When Devotionalism Meets Vernacularization'. In *Bhakti and Power*, edited by John Stratton Hawley, Christian Lee Novetzke and Swapna Sharma, 85–94. Debating India's Religion of the Heart. Seattle: University of Washington Press.

O'Hanlon, R. 2007. 'Military Sports and the History of the Martial Body in India'. *Journal of the Economic and Social History of the Orient* 50(4): 490–523.

Olivelle, Patrick. 1992. *The Saṃnyāsa Upaniṣadas: Scriptures on Asceticism and Renunciation*. Oxford: Oxford University Press.

———. 1993. *The Asrama System: The History and Hermeneutics of a Religious Institution*. New York/Oxford: Oxford University Press.

———. 2008a. 'The Ascetic and the Domestic in Brahmanical Religiosity'. In *Collected Essays*. ii. *Ascetics and Brahmins: Studies in Ideologies and Institutions*, edited by Federico Squarcini, 27–41. Firenze: Firenze University Press. [Originally published in *Critics of Asceticism: Historical Accounts and Comparative Perspectives*, edited by Oliver Freiberger. New York: Oxford University Press, 2006.]

———. 2008b. 'The Semantic History of *Āśrama*'. In *Collected Essays*. ii. *Ascetics and Brahmins Studies in Ideologies and Institutions*, edited by Federico Squarcini, 145–163. Firenze: Firenze University Press.

———. 2008c. 'Introduction to Renunciation in the Hindu Traditions'. In *Collected Essays*. ii. *Ascetics and Brahmins: Studies in Ideologies and Institutions*, edited by Federico Squarcini, 11–26.

Firenze: Firenze University Press. [Originally published as 'The Renouncer Tradition' in *The Companion to Hinduism*, edited by Gavin Flood, 271–287. Oxford: Blackwell.]

———. 2008d. 'Contributions to the Semantic History of Samnyāsa.' In *Collected Essays. ii. Ascetics and Brahmins: Studies in Ideologies and Institutions*, edited by Federico Squarcini, 127–143. Firenze: Firenze University Press. [Originally published in *Journal of the American Oriental Society* 101 (1981): 265–274.]

———. 2008e. 'Renunciation in the Saṃnyāsa Upaniṣads.' In *Collected Essays. ii. Ascetics and Brahmins: Studies in Ideologies and Institutions*, edited by Federico Squarcini, 165–196. Firenze: Firenze University Press.

Olson, Carl. 2007. *Celibacy and Religious Traditions.* New York: Oxford University Press.

———. 2015. *Indian Asceticism: Power, Violence, and Play.* Oxford: Oxford University Press.

Oman, John Campbell. 1903. *The Mystics, Ascetics, and Saints of India: A Study of Sadhuism, with an Account of the Yogis, Sanyasis, Bairagis, and Other Strange Hindu Sectarians.* London: T.F. Unwin.

Ondračka, Lubomir. 2022. 'Hathayoga.' In *Hinduism and Tribal Religions: Encyclopedia of Indian Religions*, edited by J.D. Long, R.D. Sherma, P. Jain and M. Khanna, 577–588. Dordrecht: Springer.

Orr, W.G. 1940. *Armed Religious Ascetics in North India.* Manchester.

Padoux, André. 1987. 'Contributions à l'étude du Mantraśāstra. III. Le Japa.' *Bulletin de l'École Française d'Extrême-Orient* 76(1): 117–164.

———. 1989. 'Conclusion: Mantras What Are They?' In *Mantra*, edited by Harvey Alper. Albany: State University of New York Press.

———. 1990. *Vāc: The Concept of the Word in Selected Hindu Tantras.* Albany: State University of New York Press.

———. 2002. 'What do we mean by Tantrism?' In *The Roots of Tantra*, edited by Katherine Anne Harper and Robert L. Brown, 17–24. New York: State University of New York Press.

———. 2011. *Tantric Mantras: Studies on Mantrasastra.* Routledge Studies in Tantric Traditions. Abingdon, UK: Routledge.

Palit, Chittabrata, and Dasgupta, Nupur. 2009. *An Ancient Indian System of Rasayana: Suvarnatantra a Treatise of Alchemy.* Delhi: Kalpaz Publications.

Palmisano, Stefania, and Pannofino, Nicola (eds.). 2017. *Invention of Tradition and Syncretism in Contemporary Religions: Sacred Creativity.* Palgrave Studies in New Religions and Alternative Spiritualities. Cham: Springer International Publishing/Palgrave Macmillan.

———. 2018. 'Spiritualità: Note su Una Categoria Controversa.' *Quaderni di Sociologia* 77: 35–54.

Pande, Govind Chandra. 1974. *Studies in the Origins of Buddhism.* 2nd rev. edn (1st edn 1957). Delhi: Motilal Banarsidass.

Pankhania, Josna. 2008. *Encountering Satyananda Yoga in Australia and India: Reflections of a Complex, Postcolonial, Gendered Subject.* Penrith: University of Western Sydney.

Parveen, Babli. 2014. 'The Eclectic Spirit of Sufism in India: An Appraisal.' *Social Scientist* 42(11–12): 39–46.

Pauwels, Heidi R.M. 2019. 'Caste and Women in Early Modern India.' In *Bhakti and Power*, edited by John Stratton Hawley, Christian Lee Novetzke and Swapna Sharma, 49–62. Debating India's Religion of the Heart. Seattle: University of Washington Press.

Pearson, Anne Mackenzie. 1996. *Because It Gives Me Peace of Mind: Ritual Fasts in the Religious Lives of Hindu Women.* McGill Studies in the History of Religions. Albany: State University of New York Press.

Pechilis, Karen. 2019. 'Affect and Identity in Early Bhakti: Kāraikkāl Ammaiyār as Poet, Servant and *Pēy*.' In *The Power of Bhakti: Social Location and Public Affect in India's Religion of the Heart*, edited by John Stratton Hawley, Christian Novetzke and Swapna Sharma, 25–37. Seattle: Washington University Press.

Pederson, Morten Axel. 2012. 'Common Nonsense: A Review of Certain Recent Reviews of the Ontological Turn'. *Anthropology of this Century* 5 (October). http://aotcpress.com/articles/common_nonsense

Pinch, William. 1996. *Peasants and Monks in British India*. Berkeley: University of California Press.

———. 2006. *Warriors Ascetics and Indian Empires*. Cambridge: Cambridge University Press.

———. 2018. 'War and Succession: Padmakar, Man Kavi, and the Gosains of Bundelkhand, 1792–1806'. In *Text and Tradition in Early Modern North India*, edited by Tyler Williams, Anshu Malhotra and J.S. Hawley, 235–259. Delhi: Oxford University Press.

———. 2020. 'Yogis' Way of War'. In *The Cambridge World History of Violence*. Vol. III. *1500–1800 CE*, edited by R. Antony, S. Carroll and C.D. Pennock, 156–173. Cambridge: Cambridge University Press.

Powell, Seth. 2018. 'Etched in Stone: Sixteenth-Century Visual and Material Evidence of Śaiva Ascetics and Yogis in Complex Non-seated Āsanas at Vijayanagara'. *Journal of Yoga Studies* 1 (May): 45–106.

———. 2023. 'Yogi Sculptures: Complex Āsanas across the Deccan'. *Yoga and the Traditional Physical Practices of South Asia: Influence, Entanglement and Confrontation*, edited by Daniela Bevilacqua and Mark Singleton, 85–111. *Journal of Yoga Studies* 4 (Special Issue).

Pragya, Samani Pratibha. 2020. 'Yoga and Meditation in the Jain Tradition'. In *Routledge Handbook of Yoga and Meditation Studies*, edited by Karen O'Brien and Suzanne Newcombe, 171–188. Abingdon, UK: Routledge.

Raj, A. 2010. *The Life and Times of Baba Ramdev*. New Delhi: Hay House Publishers.

Rastelli, Marion. 2011. 'Pāñcarātra'. In *Brill's Encyclopedia of Hinduism*. Vol. 3, edited by Knut A. Jacobsen, Helene Basu, Angelika Malinar and Vasudha Narayanan, 444–457. Handbook of Oriental Studies, 22.3. Leiden/Boston, MA: Brill.

Rigopoulos, Antonio. 1998. *Dattātreya: The Immortal Guru, Yogin, and Avatāra: A Study of the Transformative and Inclusive Character of a Multi-faceted Hindo Deity*. SUNY Series in Religious Studies. Albany: State University of New York Press.

———. 2009. *Guru: Il fondamento della civiltà dell'India*. Rome: Carocci Editore.

Rochard, Philippe, and Bast, Oliver. 2023. 'Zurkhāneh, Akhārā, Pahlavān, and Jyestī-mallas: Cross Cultural Interaction and Social Legitimisation at the Turn of the 17th Century'. *Yoga and the Traditional Physical Practices of South Asia: Influence, Entanglement and Confrontation*, edited by Daniela Bevilacqua and Mark Singleton, 175–214. *Journal of Yoga Studies* 4 (Special Issue).

Russell, Peter. 1978. *The TM Technique: An Introduction to Transcendental Meditation and the Teachings of Maharishi Mahesh Yogi*. 3rd edn. London/Boston, MA: Routledge & Kegan Paul.

Samuel, Geoffrey. 2008. *The Origins of Yoga and Tantra: Indic Religions to the Thirteenth Century*. Cambridge: Cambridge University Press.

Sanderson, Alexis. 1988. 'Śaivism and the Tantric Traditions'. In *The World's Religions*, edited by S. Sutherland, L. Houlden, P. Clarke and F. Hardy, 660–704. London: Routledge & Kegan Paul.

———. 1995. 'Meaning in Tantric Ritual'. In *Essais sur le Rituel*. III. *Colloque du Centenaire de la Section des Sciences religieuses de l'École Pratique des Hautes Études*, edited by A.-M. Blondeau and K. Schipper, 15–95. Bibliothèque de l'École des Hautes Études, Sciences religieuses CII. Louvain/Paris: Peeters.

———. 2003. 'The Śaiva Religion among the Khmers (Part I)'. *Bulletin de l'École française d'Extrême-Orient* 90(1): 349–462.

———. 2006. 'The Lākulas: New Evidence of a System Intermediate between Pāñcārthika Pāśupatism and Āgamic Śaivism'. *Indian Philosophical Annual* 24: 143–217.

———. 2009. 'The Śaiva Age: The Rise and Dominance of Śaivism during the Early Medieval Period'. In *Genesis and Development of Tantrism*, edited by Shingo Einoo, 41–349. Tokyo: University of Tokyo, Institute of Oriental Culture.

———. 2014. 'The Śaiva Literature'. *Journal of Indological Studies* (Kyoto) 24–25: 1–113.

Sandhu, Kiranjeet. 2011. *The Udādīs in the Colonial Punjab 1849 A.D.–1947 A.D.* PhD thesis, Faculty of Arts and Social Sciences, Department of History, Guru Nanak Dev University.

Sarbacker, Stuart Ray. 2014. 'Swami Ramdev: Modern Yoga Revolutionary'. In *Gurus of Modern Yoga*, edited by Mark Singleton and Ellen Goldberg, 351–371. Oxford: Oxford University Press.

———. 2023. 'Prostration or Potentiation? Hindu Ritual, Physical Culture, and the "Sun Salutation" (Sūryanamaskār)'. *Yoga and the Traditional Physical Practices of South Asia: Influence, Entanglement and Confrontation*, edited by Daniela Bevilacqua and Mark Singleton, 303–329. *Journal of Yoga Studies* 4 (Special Issue).

Sarde, Vijay. 2017. '"Yoga on Stone": Sculptural Representation of Yoga on Mahudī Gate at Dabhoī in Gujarāt'. *Heritage: Journal of Multidisciplinary Studies in Archaeology* 5: 656–675.

———. 2023. *The Archaeology of the Nātha Sampradāya in Western India, 12th to 15th Century.* Abingdon, UK: Routledge.

Sardella, Ferdinando. 2013. *Modern Hindu Personalism: The History, Life, and Thought of Bhaktisiddhanta Sarasvati.* New York: Oxford University Press.

Sargeant, Winthrop. 2009 [1984]. *The Bhagavadgītā.* Albany: State University of New York.

Sarkar, Jadunath. 1930. *A History of Dasnami Naga Sanyasis.* Sri Panchayati Akhara Mahanirvani, Daraganj, Allahabad.

Schaeffer, Kurtis R. 2002. 'The Attainment of Immortality: From Nathas in India to Buddhists in Tibet'. *Journal of Indian Philosophy* 30(6): 515–533.

Sears, Tamara I. 2013. 'From Guru to God: Yogic Prowess and Places of Practice in Early-Medieval India', In *Yoga: The Art of Transformation*, edited by Debra Diamond, 47–57. Washington, DC: Arthur M. Sackler Gallery.

———. 2014. 'Encountering Ascetics on and beyond the Indian Temple Wall'. In *Material Culture and Asian Religions: Text, Image, Object*, edited by Benjamin J. Fleming and Richard D. Mann, 172–194. Abingdon, UK: Routledge.

Ser, S.N. (ed.). 1949. *Indian Travels of Thevenot and Careri: Being the Third Part of the Travels of M. de Thevenot into the Levant and the Third Part of a Voyage round the World by Dr. John Francis Gemelli Careri.* Delhi: National Archives of India.

Serbaeva Saraogi, Olga. 2013. 'Mudrās'. In *Brill's Encyclopedia of Hinduism*, edited by Knut A. Jacobsen, Helene Basu, Angelika Malinar and Vasudha Narayanan. Handbook of Oriental Studies, 22.3. Leiden/Boston, MA: Brill

Shackle, Christopher, and Mandair, Arvind (eds.). 2013. *Teachings of the Sikh Gurus: Selections from the Sikh Scriptures.* Abingdon, UK: Routledge.

Shah, Umakant Premanand. 1957. 'Nāth Siddhoṁ kī Pracīn Śilpamūrtiyāṁ'. *Nāgarīpracārinī Patrikā varsa* 62: 174–207.

Sharma, Mahesh. 2009. *Western Himalayan Temple Records: State, Pilgrimage, Ritual and Legality in Chambā.* Leiden: Brill.

Shastri, J.L. 1970. *The Siva-Purana.* Delhi: Motilal Banarsidass Publishers.

Shea, David, and Anthony Troyer (trans.). 1843. *Dabistān (or School of Manners).* Vols. 1–3. Composed in 1645, attributed to Mośul Fānī; trans. from Persian. London: Allen & Co.

Singh, R.K. 2014. 'India Can be a Vishwa Guru'. *The Pioneer.* http://www.dailypioneer.com/todays-newspaper/india-can-be-vishwa-guru.html [last accessed June 2021]

Singh, Sulakhan. 1982. 'Heterodoxi in Sikhism: The Case of the Udasis'. *Proceedings of the Indian History Congress.* Vol. 43: 383–387.

———. 1983. 'Literary Evidence on the Udasis: Sant Rein's *Udasi Bodh*'. *Proceedings of the Indian History Congress.* Vol. 44: 292–297.

Singleton, Mark. 2008. 'The Classical Reveries of Modern Yoga: Patanjali and Constructive Orientalism'. In *Yoga in the Modern World: Contemporary Perspectives*, edited by Mark Singleton and Jean Byrne, 77–99. London: Routledge.

———. 2010. *The Yoga Body: The Origin of Modern Posture Practice.* Oxford: Oxford University Press.

Singleton, Mark, and Byrne, Jean (eds.). 2008. *Yoga in the Modern World: Contemporary Perspectives.* Routledge Hindu Studies Series. London: Routledge.

Singleton, Mark, and Goldberg, Ellen (eds.). 2014. *Gurus of Modern Yoga.* Oxford: Oxford University Press.

Smith, John D. 1990. 'Worlds Apart: Orality, Literacy, and the Rajasthani Folk-Mahābhārata.' *Oral Tradition* 5(1): 3–19.

Squarcini, Federico. 2008. *Tradens, traditum, recipiens: Studi storici e sociali sull'istituto della tradizione nell'antichità sudasiatica.* Florence: Società Editrice Fiorentina.

Srinivasa Ayyangar, G. 1938. *The Yoga Upanishads.* http://archive.org/details/TheYogaUpanishads

Srinivasa, Chari. 1994. *Vaishnavism, Its Philosophy, Theology and Religious Discipline.* Delhi: Motilal Banarsidas Publishers.

Śrīvāstav, B. 1957. *Rāmānanda Sampradāya tatha Hindī Sahitya Pe Uskā Prabhāv.* Allahabad, India: Lokbhārtī Prakāśan.

Steavu, Dominic. 2023. 'Is There Such a Thing as Chinese Yoga? Indian Postural Therapies in Mediaeval China.' *Yoga and the Traditional Physical Practices of South Asia: Influence, Entanglement and Confrontation,* edited by Daniela Bevilacqua and Mark Singleton, 375–412. *Journal of Yoga Studies* 4 (Special Issue).

Stoker, Valerie. 2016. *Polemics and Patronage in the City of Victory.* Berkeley, CA: University of California Press.

Strauss, Sarah. 2005. *Positioning Yoga: Balancing Acts across Cultures.* Oxford/New York: Berg.

Stuparich, Eloisa. 2022. 'Self-orientalism at Europe's Margins: Historical Imaginary, Ritual Practice, and Interfaith Dialogue in an Indo-Baltic Nath Network.' *Religions of South Asia* 16(1): 66–89.

Suebsantiwongse, Saran. 2023. 'Royal Amusement, Sports, Acrobats and Yogic Practices according to the Sāmrājyalaksmīpīthikā.' *Yoga and the Traditional Physical Practices of South Asia: Influence, Entanglement and Confrontation,* edited by Daniela Bevilacqua and Mark Singleton, 113–135. *Journal of Yoga Studies* 4 (Special Issue).

Svoboda, Robert. 2008. 'The Ayurvedic Diaspora: A Personal Account.' In *Modern and Global Ayurveda: Pluralism and Paradigms,* 117–128. Albany, NY: State University of New York Press.

Tavernier, Jean-Baptiste. 1679. *Les six voyages de Jean-Baptise Tavernier, écuyer Baron d'Aubonne, qu'il a fait en Turquie, en Perse, et aux Indes.* 2 vols. Paris.

Timalsina, Sthaneshwar. 2011. 'Songs of Transformation: Vernacular Josmanī Literature and the Yoga of Cosmic Awareness.' *International Journal of Hindu Studies* 14(2–3): 201–228.

Torcinovich, G. 2007. 'The Custodians of Truth.' In *Guru: The Spiritual Master in Eastern and Western Traditions,* edited by Rigopoulos Antonio, 137–156. Venetian Academy of Indian Studies. Delhi: Printworld Ltd.

Törzsök, Judit. 2011. 'Kāpālikas.' In *Brill's Encyclopedia of Hinduism,* edited by Knut A. Jacobsen, Helene Basu, Angelika Malinar and Vasudha Narayanan, 355–361. Leiden: Brill.

———. 2020. 'Why Are the Skull-Bearers (Kāpālikas) Called Soma?' In *Saivism and the Tantric Traditions,* edited by S. Hatley, D. Goodall, H. Isaacson and S. Raman, 33–46. Leiden: Brill.

Tripathi, Bansi Dhar. 1978. *Sadhus of India: The Sociological View.* Mumbai: Popular Prakashan.

Turner, Samuel. 1800. *An Account of an Embassy to the Court of the Teshoo Lama in Tibet.* London: Bulmer & Co.

Urban, Hugh B. 1998. 'The Torment of Secrecy: Ethical and Epistemological Problems in the Study of Esoteric Traditions.' *History of Religions* 37: 209–248.

———. 2003. *Tantra: Sex, Secrecy, Politics, and Power in the Study of Religion.* Berkeley: University of California Press.

——. 2010. *The Power of Tantra: Religion, Sexuality, and the Politics of South Asian Studies.* London: I.B. Tauris.

Van der Veer, Peter. 1988. *Gods on Earth: The Management of Religious Experience and Identity in a North Indian Pilgrimage Centre.* London: Athlone Press.

——. 2007. 'Global Breathing: Religious Utopias in India and China'. *Anthropological Theory* 7(3): 315–328.

Vasudeva, Somadeva (ed.). 2004. *The Yoga of Mālinīvijayottaratantra: Chapters 1–4, 7–11, 11–17.* Collection Indologie 97. Pondicherry: Institut Français de Pondichéry/École Française D'Èxtrême-Orient.

Voix, Raphael. 2008. 'Denied Violence, Glorified Fighting: Spiritual Discipline and Controversy in Ananda Marga'. *Nova Religio: The Journal of Alternative and Emergent Religions* 12(1): 3–25.

Waaijman, Kees. 2002. *Spirituality: Forms, Foundations, Methods.* Leuven: Peeters.

Werner, Karel. 1989 [repr. 1994]. 'The Longhaired Sage of RV 10,136: A Shaman, a Mystic or a Yogi?' In *The Yogi and the Mystic. Studies in Indian and Comparative Mysticism*, edited by Karel Werner, 33–53. London: Curzon Press.

White, David Gordon. 1996. *The Alchemical Body: Siddha Traditions in Medieval India.* Chicago: University of Chicago Press.

——. 2003. *Kiss of the Yoginī: 'Tantric Sex' in its South Asian Contexts.* Chicago: University of Chicago Press.

——. 2009. *Sinister Yogis.* Chicago: University of Chicago Press.

——. (ed.). 2012. *Yoga in Practice.* Princeton Readings in Religions. Princeton, NJ: Princeton University Press.

Wiley, Kristy. 2012. 'Supernatural Powers and their Attainment in Jainism'. In *Yoga Powers*, edited by Knut A. Jacobsen, 145–194. Leiden: Brill.

Wilson, H.H. 1976 [1861]. *Religions of the Hindus.* Vol. 1. *Essays and Lectures on Religious Sects of the Hindus.* Delhi: Asian Publication Services.

Witzel, Michael. 2003. 'Vedas and Upanisads'. In *The Blackwell Companion to Hinduism*, edited by Gavin Flood, 66–101. Oxford: Blackwell Publishing.

Wujastyk, Dagmar. 2015. 'On Perfecting the Body: Rasāyana in Sanskrit Medical Literature'. *AION: Sezione Filologico-Letteraria* 37: 55–77.

——. 2021. 'On Attaining Special Powers through Rasāyana Therapies in Sanskrit Medical Literature'. *Body and Cosmos*, September: 140–165.

Wujastyk, Dagmar, Newcombe, Suzanne and Barois, Christèle. 2017. 'Transmutations: Rejuvenation, Longevity, and Immortality Practices in South and Inner Asia'. *History of Science in South Asia* 5(2): i–xvii.

Wujastyk, Dominik. 1984. 'An Alchemical Ghost: The Rasaratnākara by Nāgārjuna'. *Ambix* 31(2): 70–83. https://doi.org/10.1179/amb.1984.31.2.70

——. 2002. 'Cannabis in Traditional Indian Herbal Medicine'. In *Ayudveda at the Crossroad of Care and Cure*, edited by A. Salema, 45–73. Delhi: Manohar Publishers & Distribut.

——. (ed.). 2003. *The Roots of Ayurveda: Selections from Sankskrit Medical Writings.* Rev. edn. Penguin Classics. London/New York: Penguin Books.

——. 2009. 'Interpreting the Image of the Human Body in Premodern India'. *International Journal of Hindu Studies* 13(2): 189–228.

Yang, Dolly. 2023. 'Knowledge Transfer of Bodily Practices between China and India in the Medieval World'. *Yoga and the Traditional Physical Practices of South Asia: Influence, Entanglement and Confrontation*, edited by Daniela Bevilacqua and Mark Singleton, 413–440. *Journal of Yoga Studies* 4 (Special Issue).

Zimmer, Henry R. 1948. *Hindu Medicine.* Baltimore: The Johns Hopkins University Press.

Zotter, Christof. 2018. 'Ascetics in Administrative Affairs: Documents on the Central Overseers of Jogīs and Saṃnyāsīs in Nepal'. In *Studies in Historical Documents from Nepal and India,* edited by Simon Cubelic, Axel Michaels and Astrid Zotter, 445–491. Heidelberg: Heidelberg University Publishing.

———. 2022. 'Shades of Power: The Nāth Yogīs in Nepal.' In *The Power of the Nāth Yogīs*, edited by Daniela Bevilacqua and Elisa Stuparich, 197–226. Amsterdam: Amsterdam University Press.

Zubrzycki, John. 2018. *Empire of Enchantment: The Story of Indian Magic*. Oxford: Oxford University Press.

Zysk, Kenneth G. 1991. *Asceticism and Healing in Ancient India: Medicine in the Buddhist Monastery*. Delhi: Motilal Banarsidass.

Index

I

J

K

R

www.ingramcontent.com/pod-product-compliance
Lightning Source LLC
Chambersburg PA
CBHW060132280326
41932CB00012B/1493